A History
of the Problems
of Education

FOUNDATIONS IN EDUCATION
Harold Benjamin, *Consulting Editor*

A History
of the Problems
# of Education

JOHN S. BRUBACHER

Professor of Education
University of Michigan

2D EDITION

McGraw-Hill Book Company

New York   Toronto
St. Louis   London
San Francisco Sydney

A History of the Problems of Education

To W. W. B.

The occasion for this revision is not so much that new researches require the rewriting of the past as that new events demand its extension and reappraisal. In updating this book by nearly two decades, however, I must say that I see no reason to alter the form of its organization. If anything, my teaching experience in the intervening years has confirmed my original conviction. Since my point of view is somewhat different from the conventional one, I feel that I should repeat here much of my earlier preface so that those who read this book for the first time will better understand its structure and perspective.

Presumably, people are chiefly interested in the history of education as well as history in general because it gives them an account of how the present came to be what it is. Of course there will be some who have an antiquarian interest in the past as the past, but they are not likely to be many among professional students of education. Such students will have an interest in the history of their profession, if at all, because it illuminates the contemporary problems with which they have to deal. They will have little time for a purely antiquarian study of the subject.

No doubt most conventional histories of education are written with the best of intent to serve the professional student in coming to grips with the practical problems of his day. Unfortunately, though undertaken with this intent, the ultimate effect of these histories seems to be to make the student feel that the history of education is of antiquarian interest only. Why this outcome? The author believes the cause is that conventional educational historians have organized their materials principally in chronological order. They commence with the education of some early civilization such as the Oriental, Babylonian, or Greek and then come on down toward the present, taking each civilization in turn. In each period they try to give a well-rounded account of education in all its major phases. Educational aims, methods, and curriculum are sketched at the elementary, secondary, and higher levels in the light of conditioning political and economic trends as well as of psychological and philosophical theory. To give a well-integrated account of these factors in each period takes many pages and much instructional time. It takes up so much space and time, indeed, that the student has to postpone reaching the present so long that he loses contact between the past and the present. He easily lapses into the habit of thinking that it is a knowledge of the past as the past that he is after rather than a knowledge of the past as the genesis of the present. Only at the very end of the book or at the end of the course is he likely to get a fleeting glimpse of the vital relation between the past and the present, but by then he has perhaps forgotten much of the early material which would make the present significant. Equally unfortunate, little time may remain, with the result that the developments of the recent past are slighted with the excuse that the student will not lack for other opportunities to learn about the background of contemporary events.

The present volume seeks to avoid these difficulties by making the basis of its organization not the great epochs of the past but the problems or problem areas of contemporary education. Thus, instead of having chapters on Greek, Roman, and medieval education, and the like, it has chapters on aim, method, and curriculum; on elementary, secondary, and higher education; on political, psychological, and philosophical bases of education; and the like. The merit of this organization is that each chapter begins and ends with contemporary interests. Historical materials are selected and introduced because they are relevant to an understanding of current education. Instead of having to wade through a long book or a long course to reach the present, the reader or student reaches it at the end of each chapter. Thus he is constantly ferrying back and forth between the past and the present. The line between the two never sags and breaks of its accumulated weight because it has been spun out too long, as is usual in conventional accounts.

Because historical materials are organized according to contemporary problems or areas of problems, it is obvious that the conventional epochs of educational history such as the ancient, medieval, and modern are traversed again and again. Of course, each time a period is traversed, it is examined with a new and different thread of interest. The same is true of great educational leaders. One aspect of their work will appear in one chapter and another aspect in another chapter. It is necessary to point this out, for nowhere in this volume will one find a complete account of any epoch or the work of any single man. For such accounts the student will still have to consult conventional treatises on the history of education. Indeed, advantageous as the author believes the organization of this volume is to motivate the historical study of education and to set it off in its most useful relationships, he is far from denying any merit at all to the conventional arrangement of the history of education. The conventional arrangement is still the best organization for the student with a purely academic or esoteric interest in the past. For that reason the present and the conventional organizations of educational history should not be viewed as excluding but rather as supplementing and complementing each other.

In organizing the history of education so as to shed light on the present, there is, of course, risk that the present will change and thus put the proposed organization of materials out of date. To avoid this risk, an endeavor has been made to organize materials about the perennial problems of education, the problems that recur again and again throughout history. When it is remarked that history never repeats itself, the statement should probably be understood to mean that history repeats itself but never *exactly*. This is particularly true of the way in which educational problems are solved. Solutions differ according to time and place, but the problems themselves tend to recur. Since educators can be pretty well assured of this, it behooves the historian to equip practitioners with the clinical record of these problems and their accumulated solutions.

What the perennial problem areas of education are, may be gathered from the table of contents. That there may be more or fewer areas than those listed can be conceded at once. It is only fair to remark, however, that the areas have been chosen with the problems of American rather than foreign educators in mind. This does not mean that this account is limited to American sources. On the contrary, many American educational problems have a record that can be traced beyond our shores and beyond our time span as a distinct people.

The order of chapters in this volume is not the only necessary one, as it might have been if the conventional sequence of temporal epochs had been followed. One can read the book in almost any sequence which happens to suit his purpose. Nevertheless, there is an order in case one wishes to commence at the beginning and read through to the end. The volume moves from an historical account of the broad underlying factors conditioning education to their specific embodiment in educational practices and institutions. Thus it opens with a development of the aims that have governed education. Then follow several chapters dealing with major social forces that have determined education, such as politics, nationalism, and economics. Perhaps even more influential in their effect on the quality of the educative process have been the philosophy and psychology of education, which occupy the next two chapters. The way in which aims, social forces, and philosophical and psychological theory affect method and curriculum is the subject of the following four chapters. Religious and moral education as a phase of the curriculum is treated in a chapter by itself. From educational practices the volume proceeds to the evolution of educational institutions. After a chapter on the evolution of informal and formal educational agencies, a chapter is devoted to each of the various rungs of the educational ladder. Then ensues a chapter on public and private schools, which in turn opens the way to a chapter on the more general phases of administration and supervision of the schools. The volume comes to a close with a final chapter that endeavors to assay what progress has been made in twenty-five centuries of education.

The fact that this history is organized about the perennial or persistent problems of education need not commit one to an instrumentalistic philosophy of education. Without being accused of an exclusively pragmatic viewpoint some authors have made whole books out of what appear as mere chapters in the above résumé, as, for instance, histories of elementary and secondary education, histories of manual and industrial education, and histories of nationalism and education. In a sense, the current book compresses whole volumes into chapters and therefore resembles a series of essays in the history of education. But even if the present volume still seems highly instrumentalistic, the reader can take comfort in the fact that while probably only one philosophy of education, the pragmatic, is exclusively instrumentalistic, all the remaining ones have at least a subordinate place in their systems for some degree of instrumentalism.

John S. Brubacher

18. *Educational Administration and Supervision*   *540*

19. *The School and Progress*   *581*

1 *Educational Aims*

Some educational aims are very general; that is, they apply to many people, hold for a long time span, and are controlling considerations when more specific aims are vague or conflicting. Other educational aims are limited and specific. They apply to particular individuals, hold for a particular level of schooling, or are controlling in preparation for a specific vocation or profession. On the whole, the present volume deals with educational aims in their more general phases.

There have been many statements of the general aims of education. This variability raises a number of persistent problems. How are educational aims determined? Must they vary according to time and place? Are there any educational aims that transcend time and place by their invariability? How is the statement of educational aims conditioned by differing economic and political factors, by differing philosophical and religious conceptions of man, and by differing notions of the psychology of learning?

CONSERVATION AS AIM

In the informal education of primitive times there was probably little if any separate awareness of educational aims. Such aims, if they existed, were most probably identical with the aims of life itself. The young aimed to learn what they expected to do as adults. Furthermore, what they expected to do as adults was exactly the same as what the current generation of adults was doing. The aim of education, therefore, was definitely conservative: it was to conserve

1

and perpetuate the funded capital of social experience. In fact, social survival depended upon conservation. Group survival was not only the group aim of education but the individual aim as well. Indeed, the individual had no aims of education distinct from those of the group. Individual variation in educational aims was not tolerated. How could it be tolerated in the precarious environment of primitive times? Any untoward outcome of a new departure in educational aims was likely to be far more disastrous for primitive man than for his modern descendents. His margin of security to cushion disaster was so slender he could not afford to risk an education that aimed at anything but the rigid reproduction of the folkways, or mores, of his group.

Even those early civilizations which had advanced far beyond the primitive level were distinctly conservative in their educational aims. Thus ancient Chinese culture has become almost a byword for an education that aimed at the perpetuation of a static social order. In fact, it remained nonprogressive so long that the Chinese examination system, which is an indirect measure of the country's educational aims, was still requiring a test of archery from public officials when wars were being fought with firearms. China's pursuit of educational aims regardless of their congruity with the circumstances of life led in the long run to considering education not as a preparation for participation in adult activities but as an end in itself. Indeed, for centuries the ideally educated man in China was the scholar. To be sure, the scholar was also the civil servant, but in later centuries much if not most of what he had to learn was quite unrelated to civil affairs. His aims as represented by the study of the Chinese literary classics were quite esoteric since no one but scholars ever used the language in which the classics were couched.

The conservative educational aims to which China clung by the sheer weight of inertia of the folkways, ancient India followed for philosophical reasons as well. In the main the Hindu sought nirvana, a state of selflessness in which one's individuality is absorbed in the universal world spirit. Since this was the ideal of life, education aimed to cultivate patience, resignation, and docility. India, an Oriental country, had no regard for such Occidental social aims of education as patriotism, economic prosperity, and social progress or for the individual aims of ambition, personal responsibility and self-reliance.

Ancient Hebrew civilization also had built-in conservative tendencies. Thus writings of the Old Testament enjoined Hebrews—and subsequently long generations of Christians as well—to "train up a child in the way he should go," with the assurance that "when he is old he will not depart from it."[1] Not only that but the fifth

---

[1] Proverbs 22:6.

of the Ten Commandments, "Honor thy father and thy mother,"[2] enforced and identified conformity to the older generation's point of view as the way to social well-being.

Even the early Occidental civilization of Greece reflected some of the conservative influence of the Orient. The aim of Spartan education, for example, was almost as strictly conservative of the folkways as primitive and Oriental aims had been. In Sparta social survival depended principally on the military ability of the Spartans to keep themselves constantly atop the subject populations that surrounded them. Consequently, the chief aims of her educational system were identical with the military virtues of courage, endurance, respect for and obedience to superiors, patriotism, and loyalty to the state. Not only were the finer sentiments of mercy, sympathy, and generosity neglected as educational aims, but their extirpation was deliberately sought.

EDUCATION FOR CITIZENSHIP

The difference between Oriental and Occidental educational aims is most clearly revealed in the Greek city-state of Athens. Here for the first time clearly emerged educational aims that were not merely conservative but progressive as well. The Athenians were able to make this advance because after their successful wars with Persia they had the economic and political security to suffer the individual to pursue educational aims of his own. The result of this policy was a controversy that involved a comparison of the new private and individual aims of education with the old public and social ones. The outcome was a reconstruction and restatement of educational objectives that aimed not only at survival of the group but at individual development as well. This recognition of the importance of individual variation from the norm was not only a step forward in educational aims; it was itself the very seed principle from which Western educational progress was to issue.

Athenian educational aims were also distinguished by a certain aesthetic proportion. More than any people up to their time and more than many peoples since, the Athenians aimed at a balance among all the parts of an education. While on the one hand they sought a well-rounded individual, one whose physical, moral, intellectual, and aesthetic sensibilities were developed, on the other they were careful to guard against overdevelopment or narrow specialization. Important as physical fitness was as an educational aim, the tendency toward athleticism among competitors in the Olympic games

[2] Exodus 20:12.

caused genuine anxiety. Furthermore, Aristotle criticized the Spartans severely for brutalizing their youth by an overemphasis on physical education for military purposes and for degrading them to the level of artisans by neglecting their intellectual education. Again, suitable as it was to aim at learning to play a musical instrument like the flute, Aristotle held it debasing to become an expert player.

The concrete embodiment of the Greek educational ideal was the citizen. This was attested not only by practice but by the theories of such philosophers as Plato and Aristotle. The good citizen was the one who had had a harmonious development of all his capacities. Moreover, he aimed to learn the virtues of good citizenship, to be temperate and brave, magnanimous and just. True to the Greek meaning of μηδὲν ἄγαν, nothing too much, he aimed to cultivate self-control.

In *The Republic,* Greece's great educational philosopher Plato (427–347 B.C.) differentiated three grades of citizens, the artisans, the warriors, and the philosophers, or guardians. Since each had a particular contribution to make to the city-state, the educational aims of each were different. The educational aims of the philosophers were naturally the highest since theirs was the duty of guiding the state in the light of their unremitting search for the metaphysically true and good. On this account, some have thought that the philosopher was the Greek educational ideal.

Aristotle (384–322 B.C.), no less distinguished a philosopher than his master, Plato, conceived of the educational ideal of the citizen in more general terms. To him the citizen was primarily a freeman. To be a freeman had two dimensions, one political, the other economic. On the political side a freeman bore arms, voted, and held public office. On the economic side he did not have to do the menial work of a slave. The educational aim befitting a freeman was that of liberal education.[3] The distinguishing aim of liberal education was the cultivation of the intellect since intelligence or reason was the peculiar excellence of man that marked him off from the brute. By following the ideal of liberal education man not only achieved the best citizenship but also most nearly attained self-realization and the highest aim of life, namely, happiness.

The rhetorician's educational ideal of the citizen differed somewhat from the philosopher's. The rhetorician was more interested in preparing for such active public careers as the political and military as well as in forming the gentleman of culture and polish. "This is my definition of the educated man," said Isocrates (436–338 B.C.), one of Athen's most popular teachers of rhetoric. "First he is capable of dealing with the ordinary affairs of life, by possessing a happy

---

[3] For a more complete account of liberal education, see *infra,* pp. 445–455.

sense of fitness and a faculty of usually hitting upon the right course of action. Secondly, his behavior in any society is always correct and proper. If he is thrown with offensive or disagreeable company, he can meet it with easy good temper; and he treats everyone with the utmost fairness and gentleness. Thirdly, he always has the mastery over his pleasure and does not give way unduly under misfortune and pain but behaves in such cases with manliness and worthily of the nature which has been given to us. Fourthly (the most important point), he is not spoilt or puffed up nor is his head turned by success, but he continues throughout to behave like a wise man, taking less pleasure in the good things which chance has given him than in the products of his own talents and intelligence."[4]

In early Roman culture, educational aims were largely conditioned by the ideal of citizenship, just as they were in Athens. Breaking citizenship down into its component parts, the Romans aimed to inculcate in their youth the virtues of *constantia,* firmness; *virtus* or *fortitudo,* bravery; *pietas,* reverence of the gods; *modestas,* self-restraint; *gravitas,* dignity; *prudentia,* prudence; and *justitia,* justice. It is notable that the motivating force behind these aims or virtues was different from that in the case of the Greeks. While the Greeks were moved by a sense of aesthetic balance between the various aspects of education, the Romans were moved by a much more practical sense of what political realities demanded for the successful administration of civil affairs.

Perhaps it was on this account as well that the Romans were not much given to theorizing about the aims of education. Even when Quintilian (35–100) in his *Institutes of Oratory* came to describe the orator as the educational ideal, he did not approach his task from the viewpoint of principle. Rather did he describe an idealized type of man of affairs of his day. "My aim, then," he wrote, "is the education of the perfect orator. The first essential for such an one is that he should be a good man, and consequently we demand of him not merely the possession of exceptional gifts of speech but of all the excellencies of character as well . . . . The man who can really play his part as a citizen and is capable of meeting the demands both of public and private business, the man who can guide a state by his counsels, give it a firm basis by his legislation, and purge its vices by his decisions as a judge is assuredly no other than the orator of our quest."[5]

[4] Quoted in K. Freeman, *Schools of Hellas* (Macmillan & Co., Ltd., London, 1922), pp. 192–193.

[5] H. E. Butler, *Quintilian, Institutes of Oratory* (G. P. Putnam's Sons, New York, 1921–1922), vol. 1, pp. 9–11.

CHRISTIAN SALVATION

On the whole, the aims of Greek and Roman education were quite secular. This conclusion stands in spite of the general moral tone of these aims, for their moral character, such as it was, was civic rather than religious, naturalistic rather than supernaturalistic. It remained for the Judaeo-Christian tradition to introduce the religious and supernatural as prominent educational aims. This trend was evident at least as early as the compiling of the Book of Proverbs, which seems to have had a more or less educational purpose.[6] The aim of the book as stated in the preface was "To know wisdom and instruction; to perceive the words of understanding; . . . to give subtilty to the simple, to the young man knowledge and discretion."[7] This educational aim took two directions. On the one hand, the aim was to learn the secular wisdom of temperance in eating and drinking, of avoidance of sloth, of respect for property, and of such virtues as courage, self-sacrifice, and truthfulness. On the other hand, the aim was to learn the wisdom inherent in nature, especially as nature provided evidence of supernatural design. Thus, the compiler of Proverbs called attention to the fact that "The Lord by wisdom founded the earth; by understanding hath he established the heavens."[8]

This metaphysical or theological objective of education received further impetus and elaboration in the New Testament. There divine wisdom and understanding were found incarnate in the person and character of Jesus.[9] Consequently it became a chief end of Christian education to make oneself more Christlike. The Biblical account of the teachings and crucifixion of Jesus profoundly affected educational aims not only in Roman times but in all centuries following. From the Greco-Roman preparation for the secular life of this world, the Christian shifted his educational aim to preparation for immortal life in the world to come. Christians, because they regarded the end of the world as imminent, largely neglected education for the here and now. To the extent they paid attention to it, education was governed preponderantly by moral ends sanctioned by the Maker of the world Himself.

The otherworldly ideal of education reached one of its fullest embodiments in the monastic life of the Middle Ages. The men who first repaired to such monasteries as the Benedictine were primarily

---

[6] J. B. Shouse, "Proverbs: A Treatise on Education," *Educational Forum,* 19: 389–398, May, 1955.

[7] Proverbs 1:2, 4.

[8] *Ibid.,* 3:19.

[9] For a further consideration of this doctrine, see *infra,* pp. 111–112.

interested in saving their souls. Since the pattern for salvation was supposed to lie in a denial of material and worldly desires, the aim of education turned ascetic. Much ingenuity was shown in devising ways to discipline physical nature in the interests of growth in moral and spiritual stature.

Toward the end of the Middle Ages social as well as individual regeneration became an object of the monastic orders. Scholars in these orders turned from copying manuscripts to studying them. Greek philosophy was brought to the support of Christian doctrine. The aims of education were considerably expanded to train men for these enlarged activities. Discipline of the mind as well as of the body became a chief objective. Contact with the philosophy of Aristotle led the Dominican St. Thomas Aquinas (1225–1274), greatest of the Catholic theologians, to prescribe that the end of education, as of life itself, is the attainment of happiness through the cultivation of the moral and intellectual virtues.

More immediately practical than the otherworldly ideal of monasticism was the contemporary education of chivalry. As the cleric was the ideal of medieval religious education, so the knight was the medieval secular ideal. The aim of the knight's training was not only to form a man of great physical courage and military prowess but also to bring his rough fighting spirit under the discipline of the gentlemanly code of chivalry. This code or ideal obviously showed the imprint of Christian ethics. The knightly aims set before the young page or squire required that he consecrate his life to the service of others and that he have a high sense of personal honor. Reverence for superiors, consideration for the weak and lowly, and courtesy toward women were added chief objectives.

THE GENTLEMAN

From the tenth century onward the revival of commerce forecast a decline in the hegemony of the rural castle and monastery. The subsequent rise to prominence of urban life during the Renaissance saw the emergence of a new and much more secular aim of education. Satiated with preparing for eternal life with God, men eagerly turned to embrace the rediscovered joys of the world about them. The education that freed these new energies passed as "Humanism." Its aim was well epitomized by Desiderius Erasmus (1466–1536), perhaps the greatest Humanist of them all. "The first and principal function" he assigned to education "is that the tender spirit may drink in the seeds of piety, the next that he may love and learn thoroughly the liberal studies, the third is that he may be informed concerning the duties of life, the fourth is that from the earliest childhood he may be habituated in courteous manners."[10] Thus, the new aim of education was, in part, a revival of the Greco-Roman ideal of liberal education, in part a retention of the Christian aim of immortal salvation, and in part a continuation of the knightly code of chivalry.

The concrete embodiment of the Humanistic ideal of Renaissance education was the courtier. The courtier, it has been well said, was a product of the fusion of the old feudal aristocracy with the new class of merchant princes. The details of his training were set forth in a number of treatises of the period, such as Conte Baldassane Castiglione's *Courtier* and Sir Thomas Elyot's *Book Named the Governor*. Seeing that political power was lodged in courtiers and governors, a number of authors proceeded to discuss the aims that should be controlling in the education of such rulers. Charged with the conduct of public affairs, the courtier obviously needed training in law and rhetoric, the latter for use on the many occasions he had for making public addresses. But, equally important, he was also possessed of greater leisure and energy for emotional enjoyment than could be satisfied by the aesthetic heritage of the Middle Ages. He therefore needed linguistic training to bring within reach the richer forms of enjoyment to be found in the literatures of Greece and Rome. If, in addition, he himself aspired to turn a neat phrase, compose poetry, and play a musical instrument, his achievement would be a source of gratification to himself and would enhance his charm for others. While aiming at these accomplishments, the courtier's education did not neglect physical development, as had that of the medieval monks. On the contrary, since the courtier was always called upon for leadership in time of war, physical fitness demanded instruction in such manly arts as swimming, wrestling, fencing, and riding. Finally, in social affairs at court he was expected to display manners of dignity and grace.

It should be pointed out that although the courtier was to have a well-filled head, there was no thought of aiming to make him learned. "We must distinguish between a man of polite learning and a meer scholar," wrote the English man of letters Daniel Defoe, "The first is a gentleman and what a gentleman should be; the last is a meer bookcase, a bundle of letters, a head stufft with the jargon of languages, a man . . . full of tongues but no language, all sence but no wit, in a word, all learning and no manner."[11] Indeed, polite manners might excuse some intellectual shortcomings of the future courtier. As a more obscure author put it, "The sweet and orderly

---

[10] From the Latin quoted in W. H. Woodward, *Erasmus concerning Education* (Cambridge University Press, London, 1904), p. 73.

[11] D. Defoe, *The Compleat English Gentleman* (D. Nutt, London, 1890), p. 203.

behavior of children addeth more credit to a Schoole than due and constant teaching, because this speaketh to every one that the childe is well taught though perhaps he learn little, and good manners are indeed a main part of good education."[12]

While south of the Alps the Renaissance had taken an aesthetic turn, north of them its tone was distinctly moral. The free personality released by Humanistic education, which reached almost libertine proportions in Italy, was directed to the attack of ecclesiastical abuses in Germany. Johann Sturm (1507–1589), the great Humanistic schoolmaster of Strassburg, summed up this moral temper neatly when in the Latin idiom he declared the aim of education to be *sapiens atque eloquens pietas*, a wise and eloquent piety. Martin Luther (1483–1546), the leader of the Protestant Reformation in Germany, urged Humanistic studies, that is, the study of the Latin and Greek tongues, for the same end. But he added, "Even if there were no soul and men did not need schools and the languages for the sake of Christianity and the Scriptures, still for the establishment of the best schools everywhere, both for boys and girls, this consideration is of itself sufficient, namely, that society, for the maintenance of civil order and the proper regulation of the household, needs accomplished and well-trained men and women."[13] And the Puritan poet and Humanist John Milton (1608–1674), after stating in his *Tractate of Education* that "The end then of Learning is to repair the ruins of our first parents by regaining to know God aright," concluded by saying, "I call therefore a complete and generous Education that which fits a man to perform justly, skillfully and magnanimously all the offices both private and public of peace and war."[14]

These Protestant statements of the aim of education greatly influenced the early colonists who settled America in search of religious and political liberty. The principles so set forth not only became the foundation of colonial school policy, but they also were incorporated into the Ordinance of 1787 when that early national document was drawn. There it was reiterated, "Religion, morality, and knowledge being necessary to good government and the happiness of mankind, schools and the means of education shall forever be encouraged."

The Humanistic aim of education, whether in its aesthetic or its moral phase, was subject to one recurrent criticism. Since its fulfillment was found chiefly in the literatures of Greece and Rome, Humanism

[12] C. A. Hoole, *A New Discovery of the Old Art of Teaching* (C. W. Bardeen, Syracuse, N.Y., 1912), p. 63.

[13] F. Eby, *Early Protestant Educators* (McGraw-Hill Book Company, New York, 1931), p. 68.

[14] E. E. Morris, *Milton's Tractate of Education* (Macmillan & Co., Ltd., London, 1911), pp. 4, 9. See also G. N. Vose, "Milton's Tractate: An Attempt at Reassessment," *History of Education Quarterly*, 1:27–36, December, 1961.

was frequently attacked for its excessive verbalism. Most biting perhaps was the criticism of Erasmus, who accused Humanists not only of aiming at a narrow literary proficiency but of attempting to pattern their own expression after the words and style of just one writer, the Roman orator, statesman, and author Cicero. Various antidotes were prescribed. Men like the Spaniard Juan Luis Vives (1492–1540), the Frenchman François Rabelais (1490–1553), and the Englishman John Milton in the sixteenth and seventeenth centuries accepted Humanistic educational aims but sought to reinforce them by making them realistic. They aimed to enrich the life of their times through the study of appropriate classics instead of studying the classics regardless of their relevancy. Other men, like the French aristocrat and essayist Michel de Montaigne (1533–1592), sought to make the aim of education more realistic not only by avoiding hollow verbalism but by adding travel and social contacts as educational objectives. Still others, like the Englishman Francis Bacon (1561–1626) and the Moravian Johann Amos Comenius (1592–1670), sought to infuse vitality and realism into educational aims by stressing the study of science as a sound and practical guide to life.

KNOWLEDGE AS AIM

Bacon and Comenius especially pressed a pansophic aim of education. As the etymology of the word suggests, the aim of pansophism was to take the whole of knowledge as the domain or province of the educator. This was an ambitious program; yet it had just about been achieved by Aristotle. From his day onward there had been recurrent attempts to organize the whole field of learning for educational purposes. The attempts at this ideal in the Middle Ages had amounted to little more than compendia and digests, such as Martianus Capella's *Marriage of Philology and Mercury,* Boethius's *Consolations of Philosophy,* and Cassiodorus's *On the Liberal Arts and Sciences.* What gave renewed hope of encompassing the pansophic or encyclopedic aim of education in the day of Bacon and Comenius was the rise of modern science. Science, it was expected, would not only offer a simplified and accurate diagram of knowledge but would also be the key to unlock a psychology which would make the learning of all knowledge easy for all people.

But science did much more. It vastly expanded the domain of human knowledge. In fact, it extended it far beyond the possibility of any one man's ever being able to master its whole again, as had Aristotle. Despairing of reaching the pansophic aim, John Locke (1632–1704), the English philosopher, concluded that the business of education is not to make the young perfect in any one of the sciences but to open and dispose their minds for learning any of them, should occasion demand it.[15] Or, as Jean Jacques Rousseau (1712–1778), the adopted Frenchman, put it later, "My object is not to furnish his mind with knowledge, but to teach him [Émile] the method of acquiring it when necessary."[16] Louis René de La Chalotais (1701–1785), another Frenchman, thought this an invaluable art, perhaps superior to knowledge itself.

MENTAL DISCIPLINE AS AIM

Making the method of acquiring knowledge rather than the content of knowledge itself the aim of education led to the formulation of the aim of education as mental discipline. This has been a most persistent aim, especially in periods of cultural lag. Perennial as were many of the truths embedded in the Latin and Greek classics, numerous authors of antiquity no longer spoke with authority to the people of the seventeenth and eighteenth centuries. Nonetheless they remained in the curriculum of the schools by the sheer weight of inertia of social prestige, to say nothing of the formalism and obscurantism of the schools and universities. Hence, a new reason or purpose had to be found for their continued study. This new purpose or aim was the discipline of the mind. Education was to aim not so much at storing the memory with information as at exercising and improving the analytical and organizational faculties of the mind. Brought to a fine edge, these faculties could later cut into any field of human knowledge with equal incisiveness. Discipline of the mind, furthermore, was to be matched by discipline of the body. The two disciplines together were popularly epitomized as educational aims in that immortal Latin phrase, *mens sana in corpore sano,* a sound mind in a sound body.

Another corrective of pansophism's overemphasis on mere quantity of knowledge was John Locke's stress on the importance of building character. In *Some Thoughts concerning Education* Locke remarked, " 'Tis virtue, then, direct virtue, which is the hard and valuable part to be aimed at in education, and not a forward pertness, or any little arts of shifting. All other considerations and accomplishments should give way and be postponed to this."[17] What is character?

---

[15] J. Locke, *Conduct of the Understanding* (Clarendon Press, Oxford, 1890), p. 35.

[16] R. L. Archer, *Rousseau on Education* [Edward Arnold (Publishers) Ltd., London, 1912], p. 176.

[17] J. Locke, *Some Thoughts concerning Education* (Cambridge University Press, London, 1889), p. 50.

For Locke it rested in this, "That a man is able to deny himself his own desires, cross his own inclinations, and purely follow what reason directs as best, 'tho the appetite lean the other way."[18] Few educational aims have been more persistent than this.

ARISTOCRATIC AND DEMOCRATIC AIMS

The French aristocracy of the eighteenth century yielded yet another version of the educational ideal. This was the *galant homme,* a revised version of the earlier courtier. Not so ready to dash off Latin verse, the gentleman of this period nonetheless aimed to be at home in the vernacular literature of his day and to express himself with fluency and polish in the same medium. Further removed in time from the heyday of Scholastic philosophy, he was perhaps unable to discuss its subtleties. Yet, trained to be familiar with natural science and modern political history, he had, as a rationalist and freethinker, a tendency to be impatient with the narrow orthodoxies of theology and the political tyrannies of the state. Unlike the courtier in these respects, the *galant homme,* or cavalier, was quite like him in others. Thus his education aimed to enable him to deport himself with elegance in the drawing room and with bravery and distinction in the military or civil service of his country.

So far, in recounting the best at which education has endeavored to aim, the result has pretty generally been a portrait of the education of the upper classes. This result should occasion no surprise, for these were the only classes which had either the political power or the economic means that required or could make available a formal education largely based on literacy. This situation, however, should not obscure the fact that informal and nonliterate types of education in the lower strata of society had aims, too. Much time and effort, for instance, were spent on the formation of the brave and hardy warrior, the wise and daring mariner, the skillful artisan, the hardworking peasant, and the obedient slave. Yet no pretense was made that these educational stereotypes constituted an ideal superior to the aristocratic one. It was pretty generally accepted on all sides that an education predicated on literacy—on the cultivation of intelligence, Aristotle would have said—was to be preferred because of the richer store of social experience and human potentialities it unlocked.

Toward the end of the eighteenth century profound sociological changes were afoot which made it necessary that a far broader base of the population share the aims of education hitherto the privilege of the favored classes. Such a move had already been foreshadowed

[18] *Ibid.,* p. 21.

by the Protestant Reformation in the sixteenth century. Two centuries later shadow became substance in the democratic political revolutions in America and France, which assigned new dignity to the common man, and in the Industrial Revolution in England, which promised a standard of living commensurate with the ambitions of democracy for the education of all its future citizens. Aiding and abetting these revolutions was a contemporary romantic nationalism, which linked the strength and destiny of the nation with the vigor and enlightenment of each of its nationals.

It was the writers of the French Revolutionary period who most brilliantly translated these grand-scale social movements into terms of educational aims. And among these none was a more able spokesman than the Marquis de Condorcet (1743–1794), author of a famous essay on the progress of the human spirit. First, in his mind, education was "to offer to all individuals of the human race the means of providing for their needs, of assuring their welfare, of knowing and exercising their rights, of understanding and fulfilling their obligations." His second aim of education was individualistic, "To assure each one of the facility of perfecting his skill, of rendering himself capable of the social functions to which he has the right to be called, of developing to the fullest extent those talents with which nature has endowed him; and thereby to establish among all citizens an equality, thus rendering the political equality recognized by the law." The social end of education, his third aim, he stated thus: "To direct the teaching in such a manner that the perfecting of the industries shall increase the pleasures of the generality of the citizens and the welfare of those who devote themselves to them, that a greater number of men shall be capable of exercising the functions necessary to society, and that the ever-increasing progress of enlightenment shall provide an inexhaustible source of help in our needs, of remedies for our ills, of means of individual happiness and of general prosperity." And "in short," Condorcet concluded, the object of education as of every other social institution is "to cultivate in each generation the physical, intellectual, and moral faculties and thereby contribute to the general and gradual improvement of the human race."[19]

HARMONIOUS SELF-DEVELOPMENT

So stirring and inspiring are the objectives of education just stated that it almost seems as if no improvement could be made upon them. Yet amendment was attempted. As Condorcet stated these revolutionary aims, they were recommended as proper aims of a national

[19] F. La Fontainerie, *French Liberalism and Education in the Eighteenth Century* (McGraw-Hill Book Company, New York, 1932), pp. 323–324.

state. But Rousseau, while he subscribed to ends like those of Condorcet, had no confidence that the governments of his day, corrupted with age-old injustices, could be depended upon to institute means to achieve the ends set forth. Consequently, he thought that social reform as the aim of education should be stated in individual rather than in social terms. Instead of trying to make the individual over from without by an alteration of social institutions, Rousseau proposed that institutions be made consistent with giving free play to the native instincts and impulses of the individual. On the assumption that nature was fundamentally good, the proper aim of education was to follow its lead and to develop free, spontaneous expression.

Furthermore, education should aim to cultivate enjoyment of the present moment. The child should be treated as a child, not as a miniature adult. In other words, education should have a regard for children's own aims. "What are we to think of that barbarous education which sacrifices the present to the future," cried Rousseau, "and begins by rendering it miserable, in order to prepare it for some distant, pretended happiness, which it will probably never enjoy."[20] Yet, permitting himself a glance into the future, Rousseau also optimistically remarked, "I know of no philosopher who has been rash enough to prescribe a limit which a man cannot pass. We do not know what nature allows us to become. . . . Why should my equal go farther than myself?"[21]

Immanuel Kant (1724–1804) wrote in a no less utopian vein. "Children," he urged, "should be educated, *not* with reference to their present condition but rather with regard to a possibly improved future state of the human race." There is no hope of realizing so grand a design if parents or princes are left to set the ends of education. "Parents exercise forethought for the home, princes for the state. Neither have for their ultimate aim the good of the world and the perfection for which man is intended, and for which he also has the capacity."[22]

The influence that Rousseau exerted on subsequent statements of educational aims was tremendous. The Swiss reformer Johann Heinrich Pestalozzi (1746–1827) and the German mystic Friedrich Wilhelm August Froebel (1782–1852) both oriented their educational aims in large part at least from the point of view of the child's interests and capacities. The philosophical reasons they assigned for doing so and the methods they employed to effect their ends differed

[20] Archer, *op. cit.*, p. 88.

[21] *Ibid.*, p. 79.

[22] Quoted in E. F. Buchner, *The Educational Theory of Immanuel Kant* (J. B. Lippincott Company, Philadelphia, 1904), pp. 116–117.

considerably, but on the aim of education as social reform through the development of the child's unique potentialities they were in essential agreement.

Pestalozzi was a social reformer of long standing, having devoted his life to education as the most promising instrument of social regeneration. It is not surprising, therefore, that he should state that "the ultimate end of education is not perfection in the accomplishments of the school, but fitness for life; not the acquirement of habits of blind obedience and of prescribed diligence, but a preparation for independent action."[23] Regardless of their social origin, Pestalozzi thought all children had pretty much the same set of faculties. To achieve independence the further aim of education should be a harmonious development of all these faculties. In fact, Pestalozzi claimed that "We have no right to withhold from anyone the opportunities of developing all his faculties."[24] It does not require much imagination to see that if such an educational aim of individual development from within were pursued, it would not be long before the restricting bands of social privilege would be burst.

In America, where a Declaration of Independence had already been made and where democracy was already well on its way to fulfillment, one of its literary leaders was reaching a wide audience with the same doctrine of individual development. "Education," said Ralph Waldo Emerson (1803–1882), "should be as broad as man. Whatever elements are in him it should foster and demonstrate. If he be dexterous, his tuition should make it appear; if he be capable of dividing men by the trenchant sword of his thought, education should unsheathe and sharpen it; if he is one to cement society by his all-reconciling affinities, oh! hasten their action! If he is jovial, if he is mercurial, if he is greathearted, a cunning artificer, a strong commander, a potent ally, ingenious, useful, elegant, witty, prophet, diviner—society has need of all of these."[25]

Froebel, too, in spite of the governmental repression he suffered, had ambitions to rear up free, thinking, and independent men. Like Rousseau he aimed to arrive at this result by developing the inner nature of the child. This inner nature, like the divine nature of which it was a part and with which it sought unity, Froebel thought was self-active. The proper aim of education, therefore, was to afford opportunity for the self-expression of this inner principle of activity.

[23] L. F. Anderson, *Pestalozzi* (McGraw-Hill Book Company, New York, 1931), p. 166.

[24] *Ibid.*

[25] W. W. Emerson, *Education* (Houghton Mifflin Company, Boston, 1909), pp. 9–10.

What was the end of this activity? It had no other end than its unfoldment according to the inner unitary laws of its nature.

While Pestalozzi and Froebel followed Rousseau literally in their aim to draw out the child's inner capacities, others looked askance at such an objective for education. The German philosopher Georg Wilhelm Friedrich Hegel (1770–1831) and more notably the German philosopher-educator Johann Friedrich Herbart (1776–1841) rejected the ideal of the unhampered development of inner nature. Hegel thought education should strive not for individuality but for universality. Herbart contended that the aim of self-development was based on a false analysis of human nature. To him human nature was a colorless datum whose only initial positive characteristic was a tendency to maintain itself against encroachments of the environment. Hence educational aims were derived from contact with the environment, not imposed upon it. In spite of their differences, Hegel and Herbart joined forces long enough to employ the neohumanism of the early nineteenth century to aid in defining the educational ideal. But, in application again, the two men diverged. The ideal man was best formed, in Hegel's view, by seeking to capture what is universal in the free intellectual spirit of the Greco-Roman world. He was best formed, in Herbart's view, by gaining and elevating moral ends to predominance through a many-sided interest.

COMPLETE LIVING

In mid-nineteenth-century England a somewhat different approach was being made to educational aims by Herbert Spencer (1820–1903), the social philosopher. Perturbed by the confusion in educational aims in his day, Spencer looked about for a standard by which to determine their relative value. This he found in the contemporary emphasis on utilitarianism and on science, especially evolutionary thought, to which he was quite sympathetic. Answering his own question of how to live completely, he arranged the aims of education in the order of their survival value to the individual and to society. First of all, education should aim to teach the art of self-preservation; second, it should teach one how to earn a living; next, it should ensure survival by teaching knowledge about bearing and rearing children; fourth, education should aim to fit one for social and especially political duties; and, last, though most of Spencer's predecessors put this aim among the first, education should equip one for enjoyment of the refinements of culture—of art, literature, and the like.

Before the Civil War America had very few leaders who endeavored to state the theory underlying American educational aims. As already noted, the colonial aim of education had been primarily religious, with a secondary political emphasis. In the early national period the political aim of education caught up with and perhaps passed the religious. In the nineteenth and early twentieth centuries the utilitarian economic aim, always in the race from the first settlement of the country, came up from last place and even overtook the political in importance. Because America had such vast natural resources to be developed, it should occasion no surprise that people looked to the schools to prepare them and their children to win a portion of the national wealth and to mount the social-economic ladder as high as possible while the unprecedented opportunity lasted.

In the last decades of the nineteenth century American educational aims were complicated by the importation from Europe of the more theoretical statements of Herbart, Froebel, and Spencer. From the clash of theory and practice a considerable ferment of thought arose. In fact, when this situation is taken in conjunction with other factors at the turn of the century, it is evident that the times were ripe for America to do some thinking of its own in the field of educational aims. For one thing, the decades immediately preceding the First World War were decades of unusual activity in political and economic reform. For another, the enormous increase in school and college enrollments forced a reassessment of the aims of all three levels of education. Even more important were the intellectual changes, which resulted in a scientific and pragmatic attack on educational problems, including educational aims.

One of the earliest and certainly one of the most widely cited results of this ferment was the formulation in 1918 of the *Seven Cardinal Principles of Secondary Education* by the National Education Association. Originally conceived for secondary schools alone, these principles or aims were so well chosen that they recommended themselves to all levels of schooling. Eschewing the traditional aims of education, such as knowledge for its own sake, mental discipline, and harmonious self-development, this commission sought to state the aims of education in terms of the sociological realities of the America of its day. American life is divided into seven areas. According to this division, education should aim at preparation for health, command of the fundamental processes, home membership, vocation, citizenship, leisure, and ethical character. Though these areas were of cardinal importance, the order of their inclusion was not significant. In spite of the fact that these aims were arranged in no ordinal hierarchy, they obviously followed Spencer's in attempting to formulate the aim of "complete living."

THE SCIENTIFIC DETERMINATION OF AIMS

Yet, more relevant and realistic though this statement of aims was as compared with most earlier ones, there were those who thought that it still was too haphazardly empirical. These educators turned to science for greater reliability and objectivity in the determination of educational aims. From science they borrowed several techniques. One was to get a consensus, usually of those expert or qualified to judge, of what the aims of education ought to be. Another was to make a statistical count of the items that occurred or recurred most frequently in life and then to erect them into educational aims. Still another popular technique was to make a job analysis of current life activities and then erect the component parts into educational aims.

Most prominent in job or activity analysis were Franklin Bobbitt[26] (1876–1956) and Werrett W. Charters[27] (1875–1952). The former expanded to ten the number of areas necessary to complete living, including one on religion. Both men agreed that educational aims at this level were far too general to be effectively translated into teaching directives. Consequently, by careful analysis they broke the broad aims down into their constituent parts. Good citizenship, for example, yielded such further aims as being a good neighbor, a conscientious voter, a watchful parent. These categories were still further subdivided till Bobbitt in particular succeeded in analyzing his ten major areas into literally hundreds of specific aims. In fact, spread out in this detail they amounted practically to a statement of the curriculum itself. In this welter of aims it is interesting to note that Charters held to the view that there was no ultimate aim which could serve as a yardstick by which to measure the importance of all others.

Other educators, seeking a psychological basis for greater objectivity and reliability, tried to predicate educational aims on the "needs" of children. Inherited psychological or biological drives and dispositions were formulated into objectives. Especially was this true among educators influenced by Freudian psychoanalysis and by the theories of the therapeutic value of free expression for native impulses. Others considered needs to be as much a function of the environment as of the organism. Borrowing from biology, they stated the aim of education in terms of "adaptation" or "adjustment" to environment.

[26] F. Bobbitt, *How to Make a Curriculum* (Houghton Mifflin Company, Boston, 1924), chap. 2.

[27] W. W. Charters, *Curriculum Construction* (The Macmillan Company, New York, 1929), chaps. 4–6.

The scientific determination of educational objectives met opposition from educational philosophers, especially Boyd H. Bode[28] (1873–1953). Science, Bode claimed, was not equipped to determine educational aims. It could determine as a matter of fact what children and adults in society desired, but it could not, he stoutly maintained, determine what they "ought" to desire. Science could determine desire but not desirability. Through activity analysis, science could bring together data that would be useful to the philosopher in his determination of educational objectives, but scientific analysis alone was not enough.

PROGRESSIVE-EDUCATION AIMS

The philosopher who made the most influential and positive contribution to the philosophic determination of educational aims in the twentieth century was John Dewey (1859–1952), the American pragmatist. He did not take his point of departure from Spencer and the aim of complete living, the architects of the seven cardinal principles, or the job analysts. To him the various categories of complete living were not aims at all but merely a useful device to check whether education was achieving balance and proportion. From Dewey's viewpoint genuine educational aims were the outgrowth of problematic situations arising in "ongoing" activities. Aims, in other words, were projected ends or anticipated outcomes of these activities. They were determined internally within the process, not externally to it. For this reason it might be said that aims had an instrumental quality for Dewey. They gave direction to present action, provided its motivation, and at the conclusion of action were the standards by which consequences were evaluated.

Since Dewey made educational aims depend on each situation, to him they were as numerous and varied as the situations of life. Hence he offered no list of the aims of education. Indeed, he did not even suggest a hierarchical principle by which the multiplicity of aims could be ranked. Rank depended on the immediate task in hand. The only generalization that he permitted himself with regard to the over-all end of education can be stated in the form of a syllogism. Since all education involves growth and since "there is nothing to which growth is relative save more growth, there is nothing to which education is subordinate save more education."[29] Or, as

[28] B. H. Bode, *Modern Educational Theories* (The Macmillan Company, New York, 1927), chaps. 4–6.

[29] J. Dewey, *Democracy and Education* (The Macmillan Company, New York, 1916), p. 60.

Dewey has said in other words, "The educational process has no end beyond itself; it is its own end."[30]

This philosophy of Dewey's had great weight in determining the child-centered aim of progressive education in the 1920s. Progressives patterned the form of their aims after both the uniqueness of the individual and the uniqueness of the educational circumstances of time and place in which he found himself. But the individualistic aims of progressive education were compounded of historical factors other than Dewey's pragmatic philosophy of education. From more remote origins they brought to a focus forces that had long been conditioning American life. Protestantism in colonial religion, democracy in early national politics, and *laissez faire* in the exploitation of our economic resources all stressed individuality and freedom as educational aims.

A strong reaction against the aims of progressive education set in about the time of the Great Depression at the end of the 1920s. Progressive education was severely rebuked by one of its own leaders, George S. Counts (1889–   ), for failure to elaborate a theory of social welfare.[31] About the time the New Deal was taking shape, Counts summoned progressives from their child-centered aim of education and invited them to embrace the educational ideal of building a new social order, one dedicated to collectivism rather than laissez-faire individualism. Although many progressives did not share Counts's collectivism, they were persuaded that the times did demand a predominance of social aims in education.

On the philosophical front, too, there was a reaction against the relativistic and individualistic aims of progressive education. Herman Harrell Horne (1874–1946) and others criticized "growth" as the aim of education. Growth was a good aim as far as it went, these men agreed, but it did not go far enough. Growth might be good or bad. Hence, before fully accepting this aim, they wanted to know what direction growth was to take. Nor were they satisfied to be told that educational aims should take the direction promising continued growth.

In the meantime, a reassertion of Aristotelian and Thomistic educational philosophy offered the certainty of direction in educational aims that many had found wanting in progressive education. Taking the Aristotelian point of view, Mortimer J. Adler (1902–   ) asserted that the pursuit of happiness through the practice of the moral and intellectual virtues is the chief end of education. Not only that, but he also contended that "the aim of education should be the

[30] *Ibid.*, p. 59.

[31] G. S. Counts, *Dare the School Build a New Social Order?* (The John Day Company, Inc., New York, 1932), p. 7.

same for all men (*i.e.,* everywhere and always, in every mode of society, every condition of life, etc.).")[32] At the same time Roman Catholics turned to the papal encyclical *The Christian Education of Youth,* which reiterated in 1929 that "the proper and immediate end of Christian education is to cooperate with divine grace in forming the true and perfect Christian, that is, to form Christ Himself in those regenerated by Baptism."[33] In "this ultimate aim of Catholic education," Father William J. McGucken commented, "there never has been, there can be no change."[34]

The criticism of the aims of progressive education grew so strong by the end of the third decade of the twentieth century that Dewey felt called upon to reprimand his more extreme followers by distinguishing himself from them.[35] He expressly rejected the progressives' aim of unguided and even unhibited self-expression, just as he always had rejected Rousseau's romantic reverence for the inner development of the child. Instead, he pointed out unmistakably the need for the mature adult to assist in giving direction to the budding capacities of children. A consideration of his earlier writings further sustains the conclusion that Dewey had a strong social orientation. His early volume *School and Society* and his classic *Democracy and Education*[36] were eloquent proof of the fact that he expected the individual's aims to be basically conditioned by the need for social efficiency in industry and politics.

The return to a social emphasis in educational aims was none too soon. The entrance of the United States into the Second World War required the nation to stand to the defense of democratic ideals. To do this it had to mobilize the moral ends of the school as well as to strengthen morale in the fighting forces and among the nation's workers. This could be done most powerfully by making group survival the focus of both formal and informal educational aims.

In the postwar world there was some confusion of educational aims. There was, to be sure, a reaffirmation of education for the ideals of democracy for which the war had been fought. Yet, the sense of security which might have been expected to result from victory over the fascist powers yielded to a sense of insecurity and frustration growing out of the "cold war" among the victors. Hence

[32] National Society for the Study of Education, *Philosophies of Education,* Forty-first Yearbook (Public School Publishing Company, Bloomington, Ill., 1942), Part I, p. 238, also p. 221.

[33] *Catholic Educational Review,* 28:160, March, 1930.

[34] National Society for the Study of Education, *op. cit.,* p. 264.

[35] J. Dewey, *Art and Education* (The Barnes Foundation Press, Merion, Pa., 1929), pp. 175–183. See also Dewey's *Experience and Education* (The Macmillan Company, New York, 1938).

[36] See especially pp. 138–144.

the "progressive" aims of the prewar years slipped into eclipse, to be succeeded by more conservative ones of long standing. Indeed, as recently as 1961 the Educational Policies Commission of the National Education Association reached back into past centuries to come up with the announcement that the central purpose of American education is the cultivation of one's rational powers. If they plucked this statement from the past, happily they hoped to deck it out in modern dress by new research on just how rationality operates.[37]

[37] *The Central Purpose of American Education* (National Education Association, Educational Policies Commission, Washington, D.C., 1961).

2 Politics and Education

The word "politics" has both a savory and an unsavory meaning. Etymologically, it stems from the Greek word πόλις, meaning "city." At first the word simply denoted the city as a physical fact. In the course of time, however, it came to connote the various transactions of city life as well, particularly the management of public affairs. Now, one need not have lived long in a city to realize that one may take a narrow and petty view of such affairs or a broad and statesmanlike view of them. It was from the latter view that the great Greek philosopher Aristotle took his point of departure when he wrote his *Politics,* and it is at this level that the course of the relation between politics and education is now to be traced through the history of education.

A chief problem in the management of public affairs, as Aristotle stated in his *Politics,* centers in the holding of political power. Is political power to be held by one man, divided among a few, or shared with the many? The corresponding political forms of the state are monarchy (despotism, dictatorship), oligarchy (aristocracy), and democracy. Historically, of course, there has been some overlapping of these forms. The problem here is to see how the kind and amount of education has persistently varied throughout history with the waxing and waning of these political forms. More specifically, these forms raise such persistent questions as the following: Who is to be selected for the sort of education that fits one to hold power? What sort of curriculum is it that best fits one to manage public affairs? How long does it take to get such a formal education? What sort of education shall be provided for the rest of the people?

THE SCHOLAR AS PUBLIC SERVANT

Perhaps no people of antiquity had an educational system more highly coordinated with their political life than had the ancient Chinese. In the many centuries of advanced culture that the Chinese enjoyed prior to the Christian era of Western Europe, China was ruled by several dynasties of emperors through a social structure that bore many evidences of feudalism. In these respects, however, China was not very different from other civilizations at a similar level of culture. But it was distinctive in the manner in which it recruited its civil servants. Posts in civil administration were not all hereditary. Rather were large numbers of them open to any and all who could prove they had the talent that fitted them for the management of public affairs.

Since from earliest times a large number of major as well as minor officials were required, China evolved an elaborate examination system, which it used both as a pedagogical device and as a means of screening out the most promising civil servants. Although there were several rungs of examinations, it was success in the provincial examination that first qualified a man for public office. But even then it only qualified him; it did not guarantee him an appointment. Besides, he received no pay while thus an "expectant." If he received no pay, he did gain greatly in social prestige. It was his privilege now to wear the yellow coat and coveted colored button of rank on his headdress. This was a great distinction; for where thousands presented themselves for examination, only hundreds passed. It is little wonder that out of this ancient custom has grown the centuries-old tradition of Chinese reverence for the scholar.

It is noteworthy not only that the Chinese reverenced success in their examination system but also that the system had from time immemorial been open to all who wished to enter it. Moreover, failure did not preclude as many renewed attempts as one had courage to put forth. This being the case, there were no age limits either. Hence, in spite of the fact that the examinations admitted men to the service of a hereditary emperor, there was a large measure of democracy or equality of opportunity inherent in the plan. So much was this the fact that it was proverbial in China for the poorest to attribute their lowly lot to the "will of Heaven" rather than to disqualifications of birth and social rank. Unlike the ancient Hindus, who recognized formal education as the privilege of a particular caste, the Chinese kept the competence of their rulers, their bureaucracy, constantly recruited from the widest possible base of the population.

Advanced as this relation between politics and education seems to be, nevertheless there were evidences that talent and training were not the exclusive avenue to public office and political power. Economic circumstance was also a factor. The examinations, for instance, required preparation, in fact, very thorough preparation. Public teachers were provided, but in addition there was an abundance of private tutors. Candidates with extensive means could afford the best in the way of private instruction. In addition, preparation required a considerable expense in time deflected from other, gainful pursuits. The wealthier the candidate, the more time he could afford to devote to study.

The civil servants who were the product of the examination system were almost literally enthralled to the past, for the main feature of the examination was a searching inquiry into the candidate's knowledge of the Chinese classics. The degree of familiarity demanded here could be achieved solely through extensive memorization of not only the content but the literary style of the classic texts. Consequently, when men so educated came to hold political power, they administered it so as not to vary from the past. Yet, even in ancient China times changed, and as changes accumulated over the centuries, the educational system, still enthralled to the past, gradually lost touch with many of the current aspects of living.

GREEK INDIVIDUALISM

It is to the eternal credit of the Greeks that they gave the Occidental world a conception of education free from the rigidities of the Oriental pattern. But it took them centuries to evolve the concept. In the early, or heroic, period of Greek history, Greek politics and education displayed much of the same inflexibility that most cultures of antiquity have shown. The chief virtue or worth ($\dot{\alpha}\rho\epsilon\tau\dot{\eta}$) of the individual was civic or political. The individual so identified himself with the group of which he was a part that it probably never occurred to him that he had interests separate from or antagonistic to those of the state. This was particularly true at Sparta. Education consisted of rigid reproduction and imitation of the mores or folkways and culminated in the ephebic oath of citizenship. The norm of civic character and morality derived from aristocratic or noble example. Not only was the norm set by the nobility, but it was transmitted from generation to generation through noble blood. It was never acquired through instruction.

In the half-millennium preceding the constitution of Cleisthenes in 509 B.C., Greek political life underwent a profound change, especially at Athens. From a hereditary nobility it passed into a pure democracy. This transformation did not occur easily. It was contested at every turn, and in no field were the issues more clearly drawn than in education.[1] The encroachments of the middle classes on the political power of the hereditary nobility had their educational counterpart in a growing insistence that character and morality were qualities not restricted to noble blood but capable of being acquired through education. Hence, the Greeks evolved a new norm of conduct to take the place of noble example, the laws of the city-state. These laws they set for the children to learn and by them to model their lives.

It was the Greek teachers known as "Sophists" who led in advancing the claims of this new education. They conceded that education had to build on hereditary qualities, that is, on human nature. But they made the further optimistic assumptions that human nature is pliable or educable, that it is capable of good, and that men of evil disposition are the exception rather than the rule. Carrying the argument a step further, the Sophists contended that the norm of conduct should be not the example of the nobility, nor even the laws of the city-state, but the standard afforded by the individual himself. Hence, their famous cliché, "man the measure of things." This individualism was the high-water mark of Greek democracy. Through it and the freedom that followed in its wake, the Greeks escaped from the tyranny of enslavement to the folkways. Making man the measure of things enabled them to distinguish the individual from the group. Hence, individuality took on a new civic significance. It furnished a point of view from which to criticize the conventional culture of both the folkways and the laws of the city-state and to restate them in improved form.

The Athenians took great pride in this democratic individualism of their education. Much of the success that Athens enjoyed in the first year of its Peloponnesian War with Sparta Pericles, its great statesman and orator, ascribed to the uniqueness of Athenian education. In his famous funeral oration honoring those who had died in the first year of that war, he declared, "While in education, where our rivals from the very cradle by a painful discipline seek after manliness, at Athens we live exactly as we please and yet are just as ready to encounter every legitimate danger. . . . I doubt if the world can produce a man who, where he has only himself to depend

---

[1] "The classical city-state," says Werner Jaeger, "is held in constant tension between two poles, power and education." [*Paideia* (Oxford University Press, Fair Lawn, N.J., 1939), vol. 1, pp. 318–319.]

upon, is equal to so many emergencies and graced by so happy a versatility as the Athenian."[2]

Individualism as the high-water mark of Greek democracy was not only a notable achievement; it was also a subtle threat. True, it laid the basis for a dynamic culture and a progressive education, but by the same token it threatened the stability of the state. Accustomed for centuries to the static stability produced by an education that led unwaveringly to acceptance of the folkways, the Greeks did not adjust themselves quickly or easily to a more dynamic stability in which education encouraged free criticism. As public anxieties mounted, notable proposals were made to reconcile the conflict between the old and the new patterns of political thought. Of these, Plato's *Republic* and Aristotle's *Politics* give the best accounts of the proper relation of politics and education.

Plato (427–347 B.C.) realized how difficult it was to achieve consistency of mind or stability of social order when partial, individual, and conflicting ideals were contending for the citizen's allegiance. Only when everything is seen in relation to the whole, he claimed, is consistency or stability to be had. Knowledge of such a complete whole would, however, if attainable, afford a clue to the way in which a harmonious or stable society might be organized. But, as hinted, such a complete and perfected knowledge could not possibly be learned in a society that itself was distorted by factional strife, as the Greek democracy was. At this point, Plato seems in danger of becoming involved in a vicious circle. To state the idea in educational terms, a proper education depends on a proper state, but a proper state cannot be set up till a proper education makes it possible to know the outlines of the proper state. The only avenue of escape from this hopeless circle, so far as Plato could see, was to await the happy time when a philosopher happened to be king. When this time should come, the political ruler, guided by his philosophical insight into the ultimate harmony of what seem to us competing and conflicting facts and interests, could set up the just and stable state. Of course, even a philosopher-king could do no more than approximate this coincidence of fact and ideal. But, once approximated, it would be the function of education to prevent changes that would mark a defection from the ideal.

In his *Republic* Plato went on to indicate what seemed to him some of the outlines of this ideal state. These he pointed out in his discussion of justice. A just state, he wrote, is one in which each individual is doing that thing for which he has a natural aptitude

[2] Quoted in J. K. Hart, *Creative Moments in Education* (Henry Holt and Company, Inc., New York, 1931), pp. 31–32.

and doing it in such a way as to be of use to others. Two thousand years have done little to improve on this statement. But of chief import here is the fact that Plato looked to education both to sort individuals out according to their talents and to train them for the best use of their special gifts. In classifying individuals, he paid no attention to birth or social origin. To do so would have distorted his notion of justice.

Perhaps because of the limited social differentiation of his times, Plato recognized only three classes of citizens. These were the artisans, the warriors, and the philosophers, or rulers. The way in which even these three classes were sifted out is further illuminating. Those children in whom the passions and appetites were preponderant were assigned to become artisans and tradesmen. Those whose education revealed that over and above animal appetites they had an assertively generous and courageous disposition and yet insufficient reason to be included in the next class were designated to be trained as warriors, guardians of internal and external peace. Finally, those with sufficient reason to be able to grasp universals were given the most advanced education within the power of the state. They were educated particularly in mathematics and dialectic as the disciplines most useful in searching out and defining the outlines of the ideal state in which all were to live.

Aristotle (384–322 B.C.) made an analysis of politics and education less extensive and thorough than Plato's, but he had the same interest in stability that Plato had. Cautious about social change, he also tended to be cautious about the claims of individuality in education. "Again," he wrote in the *Politics,* "since the state as a whole has a single end, it is plain that the education of all must be one and the same. . . . Besides, it is wrong for any citizen to think that he belongs to himself. All must be regarded as belonging to the state: for each man is a part of the state, and the treatment of the part is naturally determined by that of the whole."[3]

IMPORTANCE OF POLITICAL INDEPENDENCE

Nothing that Plato or Aristotle could write, however, succeeded in staying the ultimate disintegration of Greek civic life patterned after Athens. Because of their individualism, the Greek city-states were powerless to unite in the face of the common danger offered by Philip of Macedon. After the Battle of Chaeronea in 338 B.C., they lost their political independence. It is notable that from this time on there was a marked decline in the quality of the educational process. The vitality of Greek education down to this time had been

[3] Aristotle, *Politics,* book VIII, chap. 1.

born of the fact that education was one of the chief arenas in which political differences were examined and reasoned out. Conflicting political theories were discussed at least in part in terms of their educational consequences. Furthermore, there was a directly felt need for education on the part of everyone who wished to participate effectively in the political contest. But after Chaeronea the nourishment of these invigorating conditions was lacking.

The state, to be sure, continued its interest in education; but since civic responsibility no longer rested on the shoulders of the citizen, the state was no longer able to infuse education with its former originality and creativity. The study of rhetoric, grammar, and logic became purely formal because there was no longer need of them as a means of persuading others as to what was politically expedient to do in the public interest. Men came to find motives for education in their private lives rather than in public life. The appearance and popularity of the Epicurean and Stoic philosophies about this time are some evidence of this trend. Though these philosophies took opposite directions, both sought to help the individual find within himself some standard by which to judge his life, since the sadly disjointed times provided none.

The Romans went through much the same cycle of political and educational experience as did the Greeks. In the early days of the Republic, Roman education, too, had been characterized by strict adherence to the folkways. Later, when these folkways became codified in the form of the Twelve Tables, every Roman youth was expected to learn them and pattern his life after them. As Roman civilization became more mature, it, too, came to discover the worth of the individual. While the Greeks debated the political and educational significance of individuality, the Romans embodied their contribution in a system of law that defined the rights and duties of individuals more adequately than at any previous time. Consequently, while Greek education drew its inspiration from the strife of political systems, Roman education was valued for the preparation it gave for participation not only in legislation but also in public administration and in the adjudication of the laws.

Roman education enjoyed its greatest vitality while Rome yet remained a republic. During this period the Senate was still a top-ranking political body. It was still a forum where cogent and persuasive speech determined public policy. As long as this was the case, rhetorical education and the educational ideal of the orator prospered. With the coming of the Empire and the concentration of political power in the hands of the Emperor, however, the significance of the Senate declined. And with the decline of the political vitality of this body came an ebb in the vigor of the schools despite their later subsidy by the state. Forced to renounce serious political topics for declamation, oratory in the schools became less genuine and more servile. While the Republic had produced orators, the Empire produced mere rhetoricians. As able and ambitious men were deprived of significant political careers, they took refuge in erudition and speculation or in the formal display of the learning that frustration in political life had rendered otherwise useless. At a loss for a way to anchor their lives, the Romans, like the Greeks, turned to Stoicism and Epicureanism.

CHRISTIAN CONCEPTION OF THE INDIVIDUAL

Meanwhile, another force, Judaeo-Christianity, was making itself felt in the Mediterranean world. It had within it a new conception of individuality. Although this concept had little political and even less educational significance at first, it must be mentioned here because of its mounting importance as the centuries rolled by. This concept maintained the worth of all mankind. Advanced as were the Greek and Roman concepts of individuality, Greek democracy had been only for the Greeks and Roman law had still recognized the distinction between freeman and slave. It was therefore a bold step forward to proclaim the equal worth of all men regardless of nationality, race, economic status, or sex. Even the Jews, who had early insisted on the education of the whole people, made the demand only for their own people. Since they were children of God, ran their claims, all should be trained in the law, and the law should not become the secret of a particular class among them like the scribes. What the Jews claimed for themselves as a chosen people, Jesus proclaimed the birthright of all men.

But there were other subtle and far-reaching differences. The Greco-Roman tradition of justice for man was reached on secular grounds. The Judaeo-Christian tradition of equality was reached on religious grounds. It was partly on account of this difference that the Judaeo-Christian tradition failed to influence the politics of the ancient world and, through politics, education. The worth of the individual it had in mind was not of this world. Furthermore, Jesus enjoined men to keep the kingdoms of God and Caesar—religion and politics—distinguished from each other. Equality before God was thus many centuries in becoming equality before the law, equality at the polls, and equality of educational opportunity as well.

Moreover, the Judaeo-Christian conception of individuality was slow in realizing itself politically, for confusion arose in the minds of men between justice and equality. The political life of the Middle Ages and the Renaissance seemed to be dominated by the Greco-

Roman notion of justice. It will be remembered that Plato defined a just society as one in which all were occupied according to their different aptitudes. Nothing was politically more obvious to the Middle Ages and the Renaissance than the differences among men. Feudal social organization in both state and church was predicated on a hierarchy of differences. The system of vassal and overlord seemed so much a part of the order of things that it came to be justified as the apparent will of God. Consequently, whatever a man's status in the world to come, it was generally conceded that inequality characterized his status in the world of here and now.

ECLIPSE AND REVIVAL OF THE POLITICAL IDEAL IN EDUCATION

In a world organized into a hierarchy of vassal and overlord, significant and effective political power clearly rested with the overlord, and only he, therefore, needed an education worth the name. But formal education even for the overlord was meager enough, for after the disintegration of the Roman Empire an overlord had much greater need of training in the use of arms than in the use of letters. In the small-scale social organization of the medieval castle into which the large-scale organization of the Empire disintegrated, the maintenance of some semblance of order by force of arms made the chief political demand on education. It is not surprising, then, that the training of the knight, the discipline of chivalry, became the dominant mode of education during the medieval period.

Of course, the overlord had other political duties in addition to the maintenance of law and order by force of arms. But these duties made relatively slight demands on education, especially while the domain of the castle was still limited in scope. Ordinarily, they did not even presuppose or require literacy on the part of the lord of the castle. As great an overlord and ruler as Charlemagne, although he encouraged literacy in his officials, did not himself learn to write till late in life. Even when literacy became a requisite of public administration toward the end of the feudal era, it was an educational qualification of clerks and subordinates. Fighting as a form of public service long enjoyed a social prestige superior to that of learning. As late as the sixteenth century Martin Luther found it advisable to try to contradict this popular conception. In trying to enhance schooling as a preparation for political careers, he claimed it taxed the same qualities of courage and stamina that fighting did.

With the coming of the Renaissance there occurred a dwindling of the political significance of the medieval castle and a revival of city life. As gunpowder threatened and later destroyed the physical security formerly found in the thick walls of the medieval castle, so, too, new intellectual forces cradled in the rising cities made untenable the security that the medieval mind had found by locking itself up in bastions of authoritarian dogma. City life revived with the great boom in trade. The *nouveaux riches* appeared in the new middle class, and out of their profits life became more urbane. As the political center of gravity shifted from the country to the city, the old feudal nobility was gradually transformed. The nobles began to move to town, where, together with the merchant princes of the middle class, they took on new political significance. Many from these well-to-do classes became courtiers, that is, men in attendance at court, where they had useful as well as ornamental, public as well as private, functions.

The effective fulfillment of these functions laid new demands on education. In large part these demands were met by a revival of the civic and liberal ideal of education of the Greeks and Romans. Vittorino da Feltre (1378–1446), popular Renaissance educator, was among the first and most successful founders of a school to train *l'uomo universale*. Later, this social stereotype prompted the writing of such books as Conte Baldassare Castiglione's *Courtier* and Sir Thomas Elyot's *Book of the Governor,* in which the education of the man of affairs was described in some detail. Naturally, the studies of youth preparing for such a career included not only the literary classics of Greece and Rome but also practical studies like law and the arts of war. Knightly exercises were carried over in the form of such manly sports as horsemanship and fencing.

Political power being vested in the prince and courtiers, it was only the few who gained an education that fitted them for making important decisions. Beyond the education necessary for their trades, the great mass of people were relatively neglected. Even though the Protestant side of the Renaissance reasserted the early Christian notion of the equality of all men, this affected the political distribution of power and therefore the educational offering little if at all. In the long run Martin Luther's early position of "the priesthood of all believers" was to have momentous import for a democratic education. But in the short run Luther (1483–1546), the leader of the Reformation in Germany, soon saw, as had Plato, that abilities were not equally distributed and that it was better that those with more extensive training, like himself, should judge the meaning of the Scriptures. So, in the end, his acquiescence in the leadership of the capable few turned out to be little different from the aristocratic notions of his time. The Treaty of Augsburg, with its principle that the religion of a principality should depend on the choice of religion of the prince, confirmed the fact that political power was still very narrowly held. Only the prince and, perhaps, his courtiers were to have an education that fitted them to make such important public decisions. Under these circumstances schools like the *Fürstenschulen* (schools for princes) and *Ritterakademien* (academies for knights) held front rank from the sixteenth to the eighteenth centuries in Germany.

The schools of the Jesuits readily conformed to the political structures of these centuries. For one thing, the Jesuits were primarily interested in secondary and higher education, levels ordinarily patronized only by the well-to-do classes. For another, their famous *Ratio studiorum* made small concessions to the sons of the nobility. To them were assigned the "more convenient" benches, and severe disciplining of students, "especially if they are of higher rank," was to be called to the attention of the prefect.[4] Yet it is notable that the Jesuits opened their schools to all without charge, progress through the schools being dependent only on native talent. For the fact that this must have been an educational innovation we have the word of the great French philosopher René Descartes (1596–1650). Educated by the Jesuits, he later recorded that he was much impressed by the impartiality with which they treated their students of both high and low estate. In fact, he called this an "extremely good invention."

By the eighteenth century, then, little educational progress had been made with the Christian doctrine of the equality of man. On the contrary, not only had the social and political structure been organized on a theory of inequalities, but these inequalities had become entrenched in a hereditary class structure. During the eighteenth century, however, there was a rising tide of discontent with this traditional scheme of things. Indeed, not since the time of the Greeks had social and political fermentation had such educational repercussions.

CONSERVATIVE DESIGNS

Eighteenth-century educational conditions under the old aristocratic order out of which reform arose are best revealed by English thought. Worth-while education in England was open to the capable poor but more often than not was the privilege of the wellborn. As for the rest, it was the opinion of the day that there was no need for learning among the meanest ranks of mankind, for their business was to labor, not to think; their duty, to fill the most servile posts

[4] E. A. Fitzpatrick, *St. Ignatius and the Ratio Studiorum* (McGraw-Hill Book Company, New York, 1933), pp. 185, 206.

and to do as commanded; their function, to perform the lowest offices and drudgeries of life for the convenience of their superiors, for which common nature gave them knowledge enough.

Earlier, even the Englishman John Locke (1632–1704), to whom the forefathers of the American Constitution owed much of their political wisdom, had shown himself far less democratic in his educational than in his political outlook. He revealed his conservatism by favoring no more than work schools for the laboring classes. Not only were these schools to inure children to hard work from infancy onward, but they were to be supported in niggardly fashion out of what the product of the children's labor would bring on the open market.

Many members of the upper classes preferred to alleviate the lot of the poor through charity rather than to cure it through education. But Thomas Robert Malthus, the noted student of population, decried this choice. "We have lavished immense sums on the poor," he said, "which we have every reason to think have constantly tended to aggravate their misery. But in their education and in the circulation of these important political truths that most nearly concern them, which are perhaps the only means in our power of really raising their condition, and of making them happier men and more peaceful subjects, we have been miserably deficient. It is surely a great national disgrace, that the education of the lower classes of people in England should be left entirely to a few Sunday schools, supported by a subscription from individuals, who can give to the course of instruction in them any kind of bias which they please."[5]

Yet even those in the upper classes who did have qualms about the education of the underprivileged and who did wish to see an improvement in their educational opportunities often had definite limits to their enlightenment. For the most part they went no further than to advocate schools as a matter of charity. The heavy emphasis on religion in these charity schools tended not to exalt the Christian dignity of the common man but to habituate him to moral obedience to his social betters and his political masters. Hardly any of the backers of these schools expected or wished them to make poor children dissatisfied with their servile lot, for, in their opinion, menial tasks were inescapable in any society and a wise Providence seemed to intend the poor to undertake them.

Surprisingly enough, the poor themselves in many cases accepted the shackles of their social inferiority. They seemed as fearful as the upper classes lest they become unhappy and discontented with their lot when educated beyond it. If having their children learn to read would make them proud and idle, they wanted none of it.

[5] T. R. Malthus, *An Essay on Population* (J. M. Dent & Sons, Ltd., Publishers, London, 1914), book IV, chap. 9, p. 212.

Often, if they overcame these anxieties, they were suspicious that the philanthropically minded were selfishly motivated. Nor were their suspicions unfounded in view of the fact that much of this philanthropy was indulged as a sort of social prophylaxis against the ugly specter of social unrest.

PRELUDE TO LIBERALISM

If education under the old aristocratic order was typified by England, education under the new democratic order was formulated in eighteenth-century France, especially revolutionary France. The French Revolution was preceded by several decades of discussion of new philosophical principles. These principles found much of their inspiration in the rising science of the times, which in turn revived confidence in human reason and experience. The new rationalism of science led to a critical examination of the social and political inequalities sanctioned in the old order as part of the divine plan. Under this scrutiny, social and political institutions were seen to be merely human conventions instead of divine ordinances. Hence, the miserable and unequal lot of the masses was ascribed to unjust social arrangements that deprived them of educational and political opportunities, injustices that human reason could and should correct.

Proceeding further with this analysis, liberals of the French Revolution advanced the proposition of the universal equality of man. This equality might have found its support in a revival of the early Christian tradition, but unhappily the church was too greatly compromised by its sanction of the *ancien régime*. The new doctrine of equality, therefore, instead of being grounded in the fatherhood of God, was grounded rationally in the state of nature. If inequalities existed, and they did, they were the result of unequal education.

It is perhaps noteworthy that this approach to education had been advanced almost with the birth of modern science, but the seed had been sown too soon on social soil unprepared to nourish it. The Englishman Francis Bacon (1561–1626), for instance, was bold enough to think that in its full flower science would give such an exact, even mechanical, explanation of phenomena that even mediocre men would be able to control their lives by it. "For our method of discovering the sciences," he declared, "merely levels men's wits and leaves but little to their superiority, since it achieves everything by the most certain rules and demonstrations."[6] Again, but also prematurely, the great French rationalist Descartes in the century preceding the French Revolution expressed the optimistic opinion that of all men's gifts the one of good sense is most evenly distributed.

[6] Quoted in J. W. Adamson, *Pioneers of Modern Education* (Cambridge University Press, London, 1905), p. 8.

Of course, the heyday of such educational doctrines was the period of the revolution itself. Such doctrines were not only good theory; they seemed to be substantiated by facts as well. Convincing evidence of equalitarianism was found in the fact that the French Revolution, like nearly every other revolution, revealed a wide capacity for leadership among men hitherto altogether unknown. The idea reached high tide with an educational bill presented to the National Convention by Louis Michel Lepeletier de Saint-Fargeau and backed by Maximilien de Robespierre. This bill proposed that all children of both sexes be compelled to attend the same schools at public expense. Not only were they to attend the same schools, but there they were to receive the same food, the same clothing, and the same instruction. The bill, however, failed of enactment. Equalitarianism apparently was a better weapon to attack old abuses than a tool to construct a new social order.

As a matter of fact, most of the advocates of equalitarianism did not claim that individuals were qualitatively alike. French liberals like Jean Jacques Rousseau (1712–1778) and the Marquis de Condorcet (1743–1794) were well aware of physical and psychological differences. The equality of which they were in search was rather an equality of economic and legal circumstances so that each might have a fair chance to develop his unique capacities. Therefore, provision for the conditions under which each might have an education in proportion to his talents and needs was to be made a first charge on a just government. Another Frenchman Louis René de La Chalotais (1701–1785), thought, as Plato had before him, that provision should also be made to develop the variety of talents of which a whole society might be in need. Thus, he showed equal solicitude that there be instructed competent men in the fine and useful arts and in the arts and sciences, competent generals, magistrates, and ecclesiastics, "all in fit proportion."

The idea in the new democratic theory of education that the state owed some duties to the individual is deserving of further consideration. Unlike Aristotle, who had said that the individual belonged to the state, Rousseau conceived of humanity apart from the state; he distinguished man from the citizen. As a citizen, man was the numerator of a fraction whose denominator was the state. Therefore, his education would depend on the kind of state to which he belonged. But the states that Rousseau knew in the eighteenth century were corrupted with injustices. Hence, the education of citizens could produce only distorted individuals. It could never bring about a new and better social and political order. Confronted by the same dilemma, Plato had decided to await the time when a philosopher-king should happen to be the ruler of the state. Unlike Plato, Rousseau did not wait for such a happenstance but sought social reform through the education of the unspoiled man of nature as contrasted with the corrupted man, the citizen. This relative emphasis has misled many to think that Rousseau's scheme of education was antisocial. But this was not so. Really Rousseau hoped that, by emancipating the individual from the artificial conventions of existing states and by educating him according to nature, the individual would become a purifying agent for the reconstruction of a wider, freer, more progressive society—cosmopolitan society.

Encouraging as was the prospectus of the new democratic theory of education, its nineteenth-century development into fact was slow and halting. The prospectus was ushered in with such an accompaniment of physical violence that many lost their initial enthusiasm for the emancipation of the common man from his age-old disabilities. Consequently, the move to provide by law for the enlargement of educational opportunity was delayed. Besides, the aristocratic habits and prejudices of centuries were not easily laid aside. When the commotion of revolution had subsided in France, it was evident that the more stable *bourgeoisie* had been the chief beneficiary of the upheaval. Because the *bourgeoisie* patronized the secondary schools— which in Europe have long been distinguished from elementary schools by social class as well as by curricular distinctions[7]—these schools developed most steadily in the nineteenth century. Indeed, the *lycée* and the *collège* came to pride themselves on their education of the elite. Universal public elementary education was also enacted in the Ferry laws (1881–1886), but this was to fit the masses to the demands of nationalism[8] and industrialization[9] as much as to the democratic enlargement of the suffrage. Between the First and the Second World War, fees for secondary schools were reduced or abolished, but the schools were still so few that competition for entrance eliminated large numbers of children. On the eve of the Second World War the masses still awaited a government and an education predicated primarily on their interests. Upper and lower classes were still at war with each other. The French Revolution was not yet completely won.

PRUSSIAN CONSERVATIVE LIBERALISM

Reverberations and repercussions of the revolution were felt in countries outside France. When Prussia was struggling to rise after being overthrown by Napoleon, its great advocate of nationalism,

[7] For a fuller account of this aspect of school organization, see *infra*, pp. 365, 399.

[8] For a fuller account of nationalism and education, see *infra*, chap. 3.

[9] For a fuller account of industrialism and education, see *infra*, pp. 87–92.

Johann Gottlieb Fichte (1762–1814), drew in part on French liberalism of the preceding century for his educational ideas. The rehabilitation of Prussia, he thought, depended on the education of its whole citizenry, not just that of a particular class. Human beings, he held, should be educated because they were human beings. Their development was the chief end of the state. Through this agency all were to have equal access to the sources of culture so that each might order his life in accord with the laws of reason. Fichte received reinforcement in this democratic conception of education from his friend and acquaintance Johann Heinrich Pestalozzi (1746–1827), the great educational reformer. But neither of these men followed the chimera that all men were to have equal opportunities in the sense of uniform opportunities. Yet, after making due allowance for variety of talents, Pestalozzi insisted that none should be deprived of "acquiring that portion of intellectual independence without which the true dignity of the human character cannot be maintained nor its duties adequately fulfilled."[10]

The Prussian schools of the first half of the nineteenth century were ordered on the notions of these two men. As long as the schools continued to be inspired by these men's humanity, they were the envy of both Europe and America. Unhappily these democratic notions of education did not have their origin among the masses of the people themselves. They were a concession from the aristocratic *Junker* class. When the democratic leaven of Fichte and Pestalozzi expanded so as to encroach upon their prerogatives, the *Junkers* withdrew what they had conceded. After the abortive democratic revolution of 1848, the political aspirations of the common people were curtailed. In place of the independence that Pestalozzi had urged, the repressive school regulations of 1854 sought to develop a readiness of obedience to command. Extensive memory work, especially in the authoritarian field of religion, was recommended as the best way to achieve this obedience. Moreover, from being the means for the liberation of man, the state came more and more in the latter half of the nineteenth century to be the aim of his development.

The political setting of Prussian education remained largely aristocratic as late as the end of the nineteenth century and the opening of the twentieth.[11] Although perhaps of little actual effect on the education of his times, the German philosopher Friedrich Wilhelm Nietzsche (1844–1900) showed the drift of thought. Impelled by

[10] L. F. Anderson, *Pestalozzi* (McGraw-Hill Book Company, New York, 1931), pp. 183–184.

[11] For the character of the elementary schools during this regime, see T. Alexander, *The Prussian Elementary Schools* (The Macmillan Company, New York, 1918).

the theory of Darwinian evolution to contemplate the development of supermen, Nietzsche deprecated the "education of the people," who, he said, were born to serve and obey. "The education of the masses cannot, therefore," he declared, "be our aim; but rather the education of a few picked men for great and lasting works."[12] The idea of the evolution and education of a *Herrenvolk* thus considerably antedated the Third Reich of the Nazis, who extended the notion to all Germans.

Not much later than the statement of Nietzsche was a declaration by Kaiser Wilhelm II himself, which further revealed the persistence of the feudal tradition in German education. Alarmed by the growth of social democracy, he called upon the schools to teach that social democracy contradicted both divine commands and Christian morals. To counteract this bad influence he furthermore called upon the schools to teach the German masses to look to the Prussian monarchy as the ancient and future protector of their welfare.[13] Instead of education's cultivating a sturdy independence and self-reliance, it was to inculcate dependence on the *noblesse oblige* of a royal house.

Under the democratic constitution of the Weimar Republic a brief attempt was made to equalize the educational opportunities of the upper and lower classes. In the first place, every child, regardless of his social origin, was required to attend a common elementary school, the *Grundschule*. Such a regulation, it was hoped, might dull the sharp edges of class distinction and at the same time make for greater social solidarity. In the second place, the weakening of the class difference between elementary and secondary education was undertaken. Through a new school, the *Aufbauschule,* provision was begun for aiding promising children in the elementary school to continue their education at the secondary level.

TOTALITARIANISM

But these democratic beginnings were short-lived. With the accession to power of the Nazis there was a revival of the narrow holding of political power by a *Führer* and a closely knit group of political-party leaders. Consequently, educational opportunities, especially in the universities, were severely curtailed. Schools for leaders, notably the *Adolf Hitler Schulen,* were set up. While these claimed to sift out leadership where it might be found, their curricula put qualities of physical vitality ahead of intellectual vigor. Moreover, the intellec-

[12] F. Nietzsche, *The Future of Our Educational Institutions* (T. N. Foulis, Edinburgh, 1909), p. 75.

[13] F. Clarke, *Essays in the Politics of Education* (Oxford University Press, London, 1923), p. 34.

tual life of the schools was vitiated by asserting that there could be no such thing as the free pursuit of truth without political-party bias.

Perhaps the most significant point of incidence of Nazi politics on education was its totalitarian theory of the state. Although the Nazis tried to demonstrate that the political conceptions of the Third Reich were revolutionary and in no way indebted to preceding culture patterns,[14] nevertheless totalitarianism did seem to have an affinity to the conception of the state held by the German philosopher Georg Wilhelm Friedrich Hegel (1770–1831) in the nineteenth century. This is best evidenced by the educational writings of an Italian Fascist, Giovanni Gentile (1875–1945), who was an avowed Hegelian.[15] The totalitarian took exception, as did Hegel, to Rousseau's differentiation between the education of the man and the citizen. Since there are no rights for the individual outside his citizenship in a good state, Hegel was confident that to educate the man rather than the citizen must fail because such a man would be a stranger to the laws.[16] Both he and the Nazis were inclined to agree with Aristotle that the individual belonged to the state.

Gentile represented the totalitarian state in quite Hegelian terms when he described it as the concrete embodiment of universal will or reason. On this account the state had an existence over and beyond that of the individual. Because the state represented the universal, the good of the individual must be identical with it. Therefore the aim of education was to evoke the will of the state in the individual will. The curriculum most likely to evoke this common will was one based on the national language, history, and culture. The education of the individual therefore became an instrument for realizing the ends of the state. Obviously, these ends were less selfish than those of the individual, for the state was the link between generations of individuals.

The most startling and enduring embodiment of Hegelianism in a modern totalitarian state has been Communist Russia. Unlike Germany and Italy, Russia built on Hegel's unique dialectic. Central in this dialectic was the triad of thesis, antithesis, and synthesis. Following Karl Marx, Russia gave this dialectic a revolutionary social turn. Thesis and antithesis, instead of being merely logical terms,

[14] G. F. Kneller, *The Educational Philosophy of National Socialism* (Yale University Press, New Haven, Conn., 1941), chap. 4.

[15] G. Gentile, *The Reform of Education* (Harcourt, Brace and Company, Inc., New York, 1922), *passim*. See also M. M. Thompson, *The Educational Philosophy of Giovanni Gentile* (University of Southern California Press, Los Angeles, 1934).

[16] F. L. Luqueer, *Hegel as Educator* (The Macmillan Company, New York, 1896), p. 148.

represented the economic struggle between workers and capitalists, a struggle which could only be resolved by the forceful overthrow of the latter. Such an overthrow did occur in the Russian Revolution of 1917. Presumably this overturn resulted in the dictatorship of the proletariat. As a matter of fact, the revolution has become a dictatorship of the Communist party, in which there is a hierarchy of power leading up through the Central Committee and the Presidium to the personal dictator himself.

At first this dictatorship was devoted to a "progressive" education of the proletariat. Yet, as communism entrenched its power and matched its strength against non-Communist powers, it renounced such liberal tendencies. Instead, Communists talked more and more about the education of the "new Soviet man." While the education of this "new" man was supposed to prepare him for the freedom of a "people's" rather than a bourgeois democracy, it became increasingly evident that this meant fitting him to realize not so much his individual ends as those of the Soviet state.

INDUSTRIAL DEMOCRACY IN ENGLAND

While repercussions of eighteenth-century French liberalism were felt in England, too, the immediate effect was an attempt to hold steady against their initial impact. Thus it was not till the second quarter of the nineteenth century that England commenced the democratization of her educational system, and even then educational expansion came as the result of a series of reform acts enlarging the base of suffrage. These acts were the product of different revolutionary forces from those in France. In England it was the more gradual process of the Industrial Revolution that brought about political reform. Through the wealth produced by the Industrial Revolution large numbers of people were being added to the middle class. In England, where suffrage was based on property, it was but natural that Englishmen should demand political and educational opportunities commensurate with their property holdings.

The Reform Act of 1832 enfranchised only the more well to do of the *nouveaux riches*. As a result, the educational activity in the interim before the Reform Act of 1867 largely concerned the extension of secondary educational opportunities. The Clarendon and Taunton commissions were appointed to report on the provision for education at this level and for this class of society. Some interest was shown, however, in the education of the masses by a series of acts commencing in 1833 that subsidized philanthropic enterprises already set up for the education of this class.

The Reform Act of 1867 went much further than the Reform

Act of 1832 in expanding the electorate. With the supplementary act of 1884 England achieved all but universal manhood suffrage. The need for a corresponding extension of educational opportunities was recognized almost at once. In 1870, Parliament passed the basic legislation by which the English hoped, as they put it, to educate their new masters. When women were enfranchised in 1918, Parliament again kept pace with another notable extension of educational facilities.

In spite of this activity on behalf of universal education to match universal suffrage, up to the eve of the Second World War the English continued to manifest most pride in their great public schools like Eton, Harrow, and Rugby.[17] The upshot of the nation's system of schools has been, as a number of Englishmen have pointed out, the education of two nations. Be that as it may, perhaps nowhere and at no time has the relation between the base of political power and the base of educational opportunities, described by Aristotle, been so neatly documented as by this period of English history.

THE AMERICAN REPUBLIC

Prior to the American Revolution and to the impact of eighteenth-century French liberalism on colonial America, the status of education in relation to political structure in the American colonies more or less closely reflected contemporary European conditions. Frontier conditions had softened some of the acerbities of the European class structure but had not obliterated them. Nowhere was this state of affairs more evident than in the plantation-holding South. But even in the New England states of the time, to be a gentleman implied social distinctions definitely beyond having refined manners. And nearly everywhere in politics property qualifications were a prerequisite to voting. Circumstances such as these definitely conditioned colonial education. They account for the preeminence of the Latin grammar school and the college in colonial education, for these were the schools patronized by the more well to do.

The accomplishment of the American Revolution had no immediate effect on the schools. Their colonial character was carried over into the early national period with little or no alteration. It was not long, however, before Noah Webster (1758–1843), the great American lexicographer, took exception to this situation. "This appears to me a most glaring solecism in government," he declared. "The constitutions are *republican,* and the laws of education are *monarchical.* The *former* extend the civil rights to every honest and industrious man; the *latter* deprive a large portion of the citizens of a most valuable

---

[17] English "public" schools are private, not tax-supported like American ones.

heritage."[18] While despotic governments may well restrict education for fear enlightenment will corrode their own power, in a republican government corrosion will set in unless public enlightenment is as widely suffused as possible, Webster further opined.[19]

The fathers of the Federal Constitution made similar remarks. While Thomas Jefferson stated that the safest repository for political power was with the people, he recognized they were an unsafe repository without knowledge and information. Education is the counterpoise of liberty. Freedom as defined by law, which in a republic is the will of the people, must not be at the mercy of the tumultuous opinions of an ignorant multitude. To practice freedom in a state of ignorance was so paradoxical to James Madison that he was uncertain whether to call the paradox a comedy or a tragedy. Both John Hancock and John Adams shared similar beliefs and begged their contemporaries to provide liberally for the education of all classes. And in his Farewell Address George Washington called for the promotion of education "in proportion" to the extent the government gave force to public opinion.

Probably Washington was closer to the temper of his times than were the others mentioned. In this connection it will be well to remember that the Federal Constitution had left the specific qualifications for suffrage to the determination of the several states. On this point the states varied widely in their liberality. For the same reasons educational provisions in the states varied widely, too. Moreover, it is on this account that in the early national period our government was known as a republic rather than a democracy. It gave force to only a limited instead of an inclusive public opinion.

POLITICAL EQUALITARIANISM

The foregoing facts should be borne in mind in considering the equalitarian tradition in American education. As in France at the time of the revolution, so in America there was an almost fierce insistence on the equality of man. The most notable enunciation of this belief was in the American Declaration of Independence. There it was stated as a self-evident truth that all men are created equal.

---

[18] Quoted in A. O. Hansen, *Liberalism and American Education in the Eighteenth Century* (The Macmillan Company, New York, 1926), p. 235.

[19] In the first half of the nineteenth century Daniel Webster was the great political exponent of the idea that the ills of free institutions were to be cured by popular education: "On the diffusion of education among the people rests the preservation and perpetuation of our free institutions. . . . Make them intelligent, and they will be vigilant—give them the means of detecting wrong, and they will apply the remedy." [*The Works of Daniel Webster* (Little, Brown and Company, Boston, 1885), vol. 1, pp. 403–404.]

One school of educational opinion has held to the literal truth of this statement.

Since so much of the composition of the Declaration of Independence was the work of Thomas Jefferson, it might be well to try to ascertain the educational significance of this part of the declaration by examining the educational conceptions that Jefferson held. These were most clearly set forth in the scheme of education that he proposed for the state of Virginia. It was his proposal there to provide elementary education for all children. At the completion of elementary schooling, the more promising boys were to be sent on to secondary school, and in turn the more promising products of this school were to be sent on to college.[20] Obviously, Jefferson had no illusions about the equality of native endowment in children. Otherwise he would not have provided a school system to screen the school population according to their abilities. Hence, it is much more likely that the sort of equality in which he was interested was the legal and economic arrangements which would make it possible for talent to assert itself wherever found.

Equalitarianism reached its height on the Western frontier. There the public domain was free and open to all on the same terms. This resulted in an equality of economic opportunity that ultimately led to equalization of political rights as well. Free land made it absurd for the new states of this region to raise property qualifications for voting. It also had an effect in persuading the older states of the Atlantic seaboard one by one to reduce and finally abolish theirs. The equalization of the economic and political conditions of men became so marked in the Western states that it was easy for many to believe in the equality of psychological talents as well. No doubt the assumption that one man was as good as another lay at the bottom of the spoils system of distributing public offices, which was introduced by Andrew Jackson, the first president from a frontier state. Indeed, no educational qualifications whatever were thought necessary for the office of state superintendent of public instruction, whose popular election at the polls generally dates from this period.

In view of this rise of the common man, it was no mere coincidence that the period of Jacksonian democracy also coincided with what is generally referred to as the great American revival in education. The times were ripe for educational advance on a wide front. State educational administration was established under the leadership of

---

[20] C. F. Arrowood, *Thomas Jefferson and Education in a Republic* (McGraw-Hill Book Company, New York, 1930), chap. 7. See also J. C. Henderson, *Thomas Jefferson's Views on Public Education* (G. P. Putnam's Sons, New York, 1890); R. J. Honeywell, *The Educational Work of Thomas Jefferson* (Harvard University Press, Cambridge, Mass., 1931).

such men as Horace Mann (1796–1859) in Massachusetts, Henry Barnard (1811–1900) in Connecticut, Calvin Stowe (1802–1860) in Ohio, and Calvin Wiley (1819–1887) in North Carolina. The public school system was born in this period, and compulsory attendance followed soon after. High schools had their inception. Here for the first time was a secondary school distinguished from the elementary only by the level of instruction rather than by the social class to which it appealed. Normal schools were started. This period was also the heyday of the academy, largely because this institution extended its curriculum to give instruction in many activities of the common man that were neglected in the old Latin grammar school.

Perhaps the Welsh *émigré* Robert Owen (1771–1858) exemplifies the drive for equalitarianism on the American frontier at its farthest reach. His strictures echoed those of the French Revolution, demanding that all children in the schools "receive the same food; should be dressed in the same simple clothing; should experience the same kind treatment; should be taught . . . the same branches; in a word that nothing savoring of inequality, nothing reminding them of the pride of riches or the contempt of poverty, should be suffered to enter these republican safeguards of a young nation of equals."[21]

To his equalitarian demands Owen added Socialistic ones. The state schools of a republic, he thought, should take responsibility for children, "not just six hours a day, but altogether; must feed them, clothe them, lodge them, must direct not their studies only but their occupations and amusements."[22] In spite of these Utopian sentiments and the wide discussion they provoked, American workers wanted nothing so radical. It satisfied them if their children would have access to the same ladder of educational opportunity open to the children of the "haves."

CAPITAL, LABOR, AND POLITICAL REFORM

Democracy in American education was thus largely the product of frontier conditions. But there were other forces, notably labor. Enterprising artisans and mechanics were fast becoming class-conscious in this period. They joined with others in employing the ballot to demand that the state provide the education whereby all might have an equal start in this land of opportunity. Nevertheless, the advancing interests of the laboring classes were not nearly so influential in procuring democracy in American education as they were in English education. Democracy in nineteenth-century English education was the result of a slow and extended political struggle between economic

[21] Robert Owen, *The Workingman's Advocate,* 1:4, April, 1830.
[22] *Ibid.*

interests sharpened by the Industrial Revolution. In America, democracy in education came more quickly and with less effort. Indeed, one might almost say that it was the gift of a bountiful mother nature.

Yet, the trend was not all downhill. Great as were the benefits conferred by mass production, nevertheless deep anxieties were felt about the way in which industrial capitalism often ruthlessly exploited the working classes for its selfish ends. Capitalism in economics, like aristocracy in politics, tended to treat the individual as a means rather than as an end. Moreover, it exploited the commonwealth by corrupting politics to gain special favors. Even before the Civil War, Horace Mann had noticed the dangers of industrial capitalism threatening a diminution of educational opportunities. For the most part, however, educators of the latter part of the nineteenth century arrayed themselves with the forces of conservatism and urged the schools to aid in resisting radical movements for reform.[23]

The tide of protest, however, did not subside. The demand for political reform became a major national issue in the campaign of 1912. Two parties carried the banner of reform, the Democrats and the new Progressive party. It is probably no mere chance that these years were also the incubatory period of the Progressive Education Association. It was during this time that a number of men and women, dissatisfied with the inflexibilities that had settled on education in the latter part of the nineteenth century, launched new schools. These schools experimented with procedures that later came to be known as the "new education," and it was they who came together in 1918 to form the Progressive Education Association. The Progressives in politics and the progressives in education were imbued with a common spirit. Both showed a renewed solicitude for the interests of the individual and a renewed confidence in human intelligence as an instrument for political and educational reconstruction.

Respect for individuality marked a new stress on an old ingredient in the democratic conception of education. But gone now was the conviction that individuals were equal in native endowment. Psychology's scientific study of individual differences had given the *coup de grâce* to any such lingering notion. Individuality now took on an ethical worth. The oft-repeated democratic cliché of "respect for personality" took its meaning from the Kantian imperative to treat the individual always as an end and never as a means merely.[24] Yet there was no agreement as to whether this democratic worth of personality stemmed from the fatherhood of God, from the Platonic

[23] M. Curti, *The Social Ideas of American Educators* (Charles Scribner's Sons, New York, 1935), pp. 563–564.
[24] For a further consideration of this theme, see *infra,* p. 124.

conception of justice, or from the naturalism of Rousseau and the eighteenth century. In any event, while formerly people were insistent in demanding equal opportunities for education, now they demanded freedom for the expression of their individualities. To many the essence of democracy was freedom. In not a few quarters, freedom for the child became a cult.

RACIAL EQUALITY

In the second half of the nineteenth century there was some recession from the optimistic prospects for democracy in education during the first half. The advancing interests of democracy, for instance, had to pause so that the political base for suffrage could be extended to include the Negroes as well as the white men. Yet, in spite of the war fought on his behalf, the Negro of the Southern states continued to suffer under such political disabilities as the poll tax. Although his educational opportunities improved greatly compared with those offered before the Civil War, his inferior political stature was long reflected in educational opportunities that were meager judged by those offered the white population.[25]

Two events toward the end of the century tended to entrench the Negro in this position. The first was the Atlanta Compromise, announced at an international exposition of the cotton states in 1895. In Atlanta Booker T. Washington, one of the great representatives of the Negro race, sanctioned a platform on which both whites and blacks could agree. This platform called for educating the Negro to be a skilled hand in shop and field and for nurturing in him habits of thrift and industry.[26] The Pestalozzian[27] overtones of this kind of education, which Washington had learned at Hampton Institute, no doubt sugar-coated the inferior political status to which it consigned the Negro.

The second event which blocked the Negro's further political advance was the adjudication in 1896 of the famous case of *Plessy*

[25] For an account of the education of slaves prior to the Civil War, see C. F. Arrowood, "The Education of American Plantation Slaves," *School and Society,* 54:174–184, September, 1941; C. G. Woodson, *The Education of the Negro Prior to 1861* (G. P. Putnam's Sons, New York, 1915). For a more extended history of Negro education, see H. M. Bond, *Education of the Negro in the American Social Order* (Prentice-Hall, Inc., Englewood Cliffs, N.J., 1934), chaps. 2–9; G. S. Dickerman, *Negro Education,* U.S. Bureau of Education Bulletin 38, 1916, vol. 1, chap. 12; E. W. Knight, "Southern Opposition to Northern Education," *Educational Forum,* 14:47–58, November, 1949.

[26] John Dewey Society, *Negro Education in America,* Sixteenth Yearbook (Harper & Row, Publishers, Incorporated, New York, 1962), p. 48.

[27] *Infra,* p. 270.

v. Ferguson.[28] This decision was the origin of the oft-cited doctrine of "separate but equal." According to this doctrine, the segregation of the races was sanctioned as long as the facilities provided for Negroes were substantially equal to those provided for whites. Although this doctrine was both honored and dishonored in practice, it was accepted well into the twentieth century as giving Negroes the equal protection of the laws guaranteed by the Federal Constitution.

Of course the vulnerable point in this interracial compromise was the question of whether equality genuinely obtains under conditions of separation and segregation. Indeed a number of cases arose in which the very fact of separateness of educational opportunities or facilities created conditions of inequality. Consequently a line of decisions evolved which whittled away at the doctrine of "separate but equal."[29] This line of attack eventuated in the famous case of *Brown v. Board of Education,*[30] in which the United States Supreme Court finally decided to overrule *Plessy v. Ferguson.* Although school accommodations were substantially equal in the Brown case, the social and psychological damage of separation was held to be so severe as to deprive Negroes of the equal protection of the laws.

Of course the Supreme Court realized that the long-standing social arrangements predicated on *Plessy v. Ferguson* could not be readjusted overnight. Nevertheless, it directed that states bring themselves in line with *Brown v. Board of Education* as rapidly as possible. In spite of this directive there was considerable dragging of social feet. Negroes, however, did not stand by inactive. In 1963, the centennial year of the Emancipation Proclamation, they made an energetic drive for civil rights. Adopting Gandhian methods of nonviolent resistance, they demonstrated across the land with parades, boycotts, and picket lines for both *de jure* and *de facto* desegregation of the schools.

DEMOCRACY AND EDUCATION

Probably the most significant educational event of this era was the appearance in 1916 of John Dewey's epoch-making volume *Democracy and Education.* This was undoubtedly the most important treatise on education and political or social theory since Plato's *Republic.* Here for the first time was a thorough and systematic presentation of the educational implications of democracy. The appearance of this book at the end rather than at the beginning of a century

[28] *Plessy v. Ferguson,* 163 U.S. 537 (1896).
[29] For example, *Missouri ex rel. Gaines v. Canada,* 305 U.S. 337 (1938); *McLaurin v. Oklahoma State Regents,* 339 U.S. 637 (1950).
[30] *Brown v. Board of Education of Topeka,* 347 U.S. 483 (1954).

of evolution along democratic lines is significant. Up to this time no one had been able to grasp the broad and enduring meaning of nineteenth-century educational trends in their entirety. Dewey (1859–1952), however, reviewed and criticized the miscellany of educational conceptions of this period and then went on to present a constructive synthesis to direct educational activity in the future.

Dewey commenced with the familiar fact that democracies have been devoted to education, but he held it is a relatively superficial explanation of this fact to say that the success of popular government rests on the education of the populace. A deeper explanation he assigned to the view that democracy is more than a form of politics, that it is primarily a way of associated living, of communicating experience.[31] Starting with the notion that society or community exists in and by communication, that is, through consciously shared interests, Dewey proceeded directly to formulate an ethical criterion of the good society. This he located in two traits: the number and variety of interests that individuals consciously and mutually share in society and the extent and freedom of interplay between one society and another. Both these traits point to democracy.

From these premises it is not difficult to restate the relation of democracy and education. As Dewey himself epitomized it, democracy "is but a name for the fact that human nature is developed only when its elements take part in directing things which are common, things for the sake of which men and women form groups—families, industrial companies, governments, churches, scientific associations, and so on. The principle holds as much for one form of association" as for another.[32]

The educational merits of this view were several. In the first place, increasing the interpenetration of interests inescapably breaks down the barriers of race, nationality, and social or economic class. Removing such impediments from the channels of communication and education enables all individuals to plan their activities in the light of the fullest information available. Moreover, a stratified society where the sharing of leading ideas is limited to the education of a select ruling class must depend in time of crisis on the intellectual and moral resources of a very restricted few. On the other hand, a society with many channels of communication between all its elements can mobilize resources of initiative and inventiveness limited only by the numbers and native talent of the whole body politic.

In the second place, as these barriers are lowered, there is an

[31] J. Dewey, *Democracy and Education* (The Macmillan Company, New York, 1916), pp. 96–102.

[32] J. Dewey, *Reconstruction in Philosophy* (Henry Holt and Company, Inc., New York, 1920), p. 209.

increase in the number and variety of points at which individual interests touch and interpenetrate each other. This greater diversity of stimuli puts a premium on an education that cultivates individual ingenuity and adaptability. Here Dewey was at one with Plato in the idea of justice as obtaining where individuality is cultivated in a setting of social usefulness. But he criticized Plato for recognizing only three kinds of individual differences in *The Republic*. In his *Democracy and Education* Dewey proposed that each individual is unique to the extent of being thought of as a class by himself. Yet, while the educational psychology of his day enabled him to see a greater variety of individual differences than Plato did, Dewey still insisted that the only way to develop individual differences was in a social matrix.

In writing *Democracy and Education,* Dewey was not delineating a Utopia, as probably Plato was. He realized that democratic education such as he had in mind is not initiated by deliberate effort and planning. It is rather the secondary outgrowth of a society already made interdependent by pathways that manufacture, commerce, transportation, and communication in an age of science have already worn down. The practical bearing of this insight was attested and illustrated by twentieth-century legislation to equalize educational opportunity. To mention one instance, the physical plants of industry have tended to become concentrated in urban areas while commerce in its products has extended far beyond urban political boundaries. Hence many states have recognized the need for legislation that taxes industry where it is located and distributes revenues in more remote and usually poorer areas that support it but cannot tax it.

The wider sharing of educational opportunities in America in the twentieth century was also evident at other points. Compulsory attendance was extended to include two or more years beyond the elementary school. That this became possible was due in part to the phenomenal growth of public secondary education. The unprecedented popularity of the secondary school was due partly to its being the upward extension of the elementary school, that is, to its being a democratic rather than an aristocratic secondary school. But it was also due to the fact that modern industry and agriculture made extensive use of science in the production and distribution of their goods. The new and intricate pathways blazed both inside and outside these economic processes required a more extensive, a more democratic sharing of cultural resources than ever before. These same forces were felt, too, at the level of higher education, where the college also enjoyed unprecedented enrollments in the twentieth century. With the increase in the numbers attending schools came an inevitable increase in the variety of interests represented there. These led to a still further democratization of the curricula at all levels by greatly increasing the variety of offerings.

REAFFIRMATION AND REDIRECTION
OF DEMOCRACY IN EDUCATION

The Depression of 1929 brought a rude shock to the easy optimism of expanding opportunities that had characterized the twentieth century and that had only temporarily been interrupted by the First World War. School programs were pared to bare essentials and in many cases discontinued altogether. The school careers of hosts of children were cut short or permanently stunted. The Depression was so severe and prolonged that a number of people began to wonder whether there might be something wrong with the fundamental structure of American society.

As a matter of fact, before both the Depression and the war, signs of changing circumstances had been warning those alert enough to see. The easy educational opportunities conditioned by free land had culminated with the formal closing of the frontier in the last decade of the nineteenth century. A long period of dispersal of wealth was followed by one of concentration of wealth. As industrial capitalism moved toward larger and larger combines, class lines sharpened. The public school system expanded, but so did the number and clientele of private schools for the upper and the upper middle classes. While perhaps the frontier was shifting from the land to industry, commerce, and science, nevertheless opportunities for the display of energy and ingenuity were slowly becoming more difficult of access.

The Depression was a sharp aggravation of these symptoms. There were a number in educational circles who became convinced that the social system required overhauling. The vigorous manner in which the totalitarian systems of communism and fascism were combating adverse economic conditions made them the object of considerable study. The conviction gripped many in this country that our democracy could not succeed unless it adopted some form of collectivism. This was the theme of the *Report of the Commission on the Social Studies* and the new educational magazine *The Social Frontier*. Although books appeared setting forth the educational implications of communism and fascism,[33] they gained only the most precarious hold on American educational thought.

By the outbreak of the Second World War, the upshot of a welter

---

[33] For example, A. Pinkevitch, *The New Education in the Soviet Republic* (The John Day Company, Inc., New York, 1929); G. Gentile, *op. cit.;* L. Dennis, *The Coming American Fascism* (Harper & Row, Publishers, Incorporated, New York, 1936), chap. 17.

of opinion and discussion was a reaffirmation of confidence in democratic education. But it was a different democracy from that of the progressive era in politics and education. At that time and down to the Depression, democracy and education had been preoccupied with freedom for the individual, as had Woodrow Wilson in his *New Freedom*. From the Depression onward, there was a new social emphasis in democratic and progressive education. Doubtless the New Deal, with its inherent collectivism and nationalism, had much to do with this change. At the conclusion of the Second World War two major political systems emerged as dominant, the Communist and the democratic. The uneasy balance of power existing between them resulted in what came to be known as the "cold war." As rivalry stiffened. both systems, especially the Russian and the American, tightened their educational policies to improve their competitive positions. Neither abandoned proletarian and equalitarian educational policies, respectively, but there was an unmistakable emphasis on high standards in student and curriculum selection for advanced training.

3

Nationalism and Education

It is perhaps too easy to think of nationalism as a persistent problem of education because of the recurrent international wars to which it seems to lead. As a matter of fact, nationalism is no less persistent a problem of education if one confines himself simply to a nation's internal affairs. In every country where a sense of nationalism has been cultivated, it has released enormous human energies for the solution of purely domestic problems. It is only occasionally that these expanding energies have collided externally with each other and led to international rivalry and conflict.

But whether nationalism be viewed internally or externally, its incidence on education is the same. It persistently creates problems for the schoolman with reference to the curriculum and educational administration. The curriculum problem is probably the more familiar. Should conventional curriculum materials like history, geography, and literature be taught to cultivate a sense of loyalty to national institutions? Should special patriotic materials like the hand salute to the flag also be included? If so, how can one guard against a chauvinistic or jingoistic nationalism? Furthermore, should the national government promote this patriotic type of education? Perhaps most important of all, should the national government extend its administration and supervision to general and vocational phases of education as well as patriotic ones?

PATRIOTIC EDUCATION

In proceeding to study the historical record of these problems, it may be well to note a distinction between nationalism and patriotism. Patriotism is much the older concept and probably has existed almost from time immemorial. Originally referring to ties of blood through a common ancestor, it has come to refer to love for the land of one's fathers and hence the land where one was born. The geographical area thus referred to has customarily been quite specific and circumscribed. Nationalism is a term that has come into prominence since the Renaissance and particularly since the French Revolution. It ordinarily indicates a wider scope of loyalty than patriotism. In addition to ties of place, nationalism is evidenced by such other ties as race, language, history, culture, and tradition.

In classical times education was definitely patriotic. Greek boys were taught loyalty to the city-state, but the loyalty so cultivated was to Athens or Sparta rather than to Greece as a whole. No doubt the fact that Greek education was patriotic rather than nationalistic was a contributory factor in the inability of the city-states to unite in opposition to the successful aggressions of Philip of Macedon. Roman education, too, was patriotic rather than nationalistic. It taught loyalty to the City of the Seven Hills, not to the Empire nor to the Latin-speaking peoples. Although among the subject provincials of the Empire there was a common respect for Roman law and the Pax Romana, this loyalty was, nevertheless, always supplementary to provincial patriotism.

Patriotic education was carried on in various forms. Naturally much was made in both Greek and Roman cities of local heroes and divinities. Both the oral and the written records of their deeds were employed to develop pride in one's locality. Perhaps even more effective was the patriotic education incidental to military training in the camps and in the line of duty. At the completion of his training the young man usually took a solemn oath to support the state. Even religious sanctions were attached to patriotic education, for youth were generally taught that cowardice in the service of the state was not only dishonorable but impious.

The Jews, too, during Biblical times trained their youth in habits of patriotism. But it is also among the Jews that one sees an early example of transition from patriotic to nationalistic education. Enjoying political independence for only brief periods and being a subject people throughout most of their history, the Jews were constantly in danger of losing their identity as a separate people. They escaped this fate by employing education to bind them together even when, as in periods of captivity away from the homeland, they had no place to call their own. When the ties of patriotism might have failed, they still inculcated the ties of a common race, a common language, and above all a common religion.

Incipient forces of nationalism were afoot during the Middle Ages and the Renaissance. This can be seen both politically and economically. Politically, kings were gaining an ascendancy over local barons and dukes and thus directing the loyalty of the latter to a central and ultimately national authority. Economically, mercantilism as the dominant policy of the day was only viable with strong support from the central government.

Part of the educational atmosphere in which these movements culminated can be seen in the Italian scholar Petrarch (1304–1374). His revival of the study of classical tongues was owing to his desire to restore the magnificence of Roman culture. It was glowing pride in the achievements of the Romans of the Augustan age that spurred this great Italian Humanist on to try to recapture through education the thoughts and deeds of that golden age. But Petrarch was not content that education should reclaim those past glories. He also preached their renewal and idealization.

It should be observed that the patriotism, possibly nationalism, which Petrarch had in mind could not be the inspiration of very many in the population. Depending, as it did, on a study of Greek and Latin, it was a distinctly upper-class affair, for only the upper classes had the opportunity for such an education. There was nothing extraordinary in this situation. The virus of nationalism was generally felt in the upper classes of European society before it spread to the masses at the end of the eighteenth century. Thus the great English public schools like Eton, Harrow, and Westminister for long previously had instilled pride of country and a sense of national destiny in the sons of English gentlemen in spite of the fact that their curricula were too much encumbered with Latin and Greek to teach these loyalties specifically. What the curriculum lacked, traditional class rule supplied.

COSMOPOLITAN EDUCATION

It was in these same upper classes, too, that nationalism fell to its lowest ebb in the eighteenth century. It was they who, by virtue of their superior education, cultivated the rationalism of the day. Under the scrutiny of reason nationalism and patriotism were seen to be undesirable social conventions. "Love of country is at best but an heroic vice," the German dramatist Gotthold Ephraim Lessing wrote. At worst, according to Samuel Johnson, it is "the last refuge of the coward." Replacing patriotism, Thomas Paine, the Englishman,

proclaimed, "The world is my country." Giving educational expression
to this spirit of cosmopolitanism was Jean Jacques Rousseau, who
proposed mankind as the proper yardstick of instruction in place
of citizenship as exemplified in the national states of the day.

This cosmopolitan ideal of education also had its advocates in
America. There the American Philosophical Society offered a prize
for the best essay on a proposed system of education adapted to
the newly born Federal republic. Samuel Smith, the runner-up in
this contest, recommended an educational system predicted on virtues
so enduring as to be "unconnected with any particular time, person,
or place" and hence one "superior to the ardent feelings of
patriotism."[1]

ROMANTIC NATIONALISM IN EDUCATION

Surprisingly enough, these cosmopolitan fulminations were only the
overture to a deluge of nationalism. In 1789 the French Revolution
rudely broke in on the urbane upper-class world of cosmopolitanism.
The deposing and beheading of the King of France frightened the
other monarchs of Europe. A coalition of national armies was sent
against the revolutionaries to prevent the spread of their disturbing
and unorthodox notions about the rights of man. The masses of
the French people, however, having once looked down the vista of
human rights, raised a people's army to keep it unobstructed. This
was the first instance in European history of a whole people going
to war. Up to this time armies had been relatively small professional
organizations. This was also the first time a whole people had been
inspired with patriotic fervor. For the first time class nationalism
gave way to a nationalism of the masses. This new nationalism
was symbolized by yet other new precedents, a national flag and
a national anthem.

The great wave of patriotic and national feeling that surged through
the masses was only one important instance of a much wider movement, romanticism, that was beginning to sweep over Europe at this
time. Romanticism was almost the opposite of rationalism. Rationalism
emphasized reason; romanticism emphasized feeling. Reason may have
been a sharp-edged tool to point up the inadequacy of the *ancien
régime,* but feelings had to be aroused to carry out the needed reforms.
Indeed, the great German philosopher and patriot Johann Gottlieb
Fichte was ready to say that will rather than reason was the basic

[1] Quoted in A. O. Hansen, *Liberalism and American Education in the
Eighteenth Century* (The Macmillan Company, New York, 1926), p. 145.

reality. As emphasis shifted from reason to emotion and will, there was a corresponding shift from the interests of the upper classes to those of the common people. If rationalism cultivated the interests of the elite, romanticism extolled those of the common man, his folkways, legends, music, and language.

In order to attach the people more securely to their newly won liberties, it was necessary to incorporate this new romantic nationalism into the curriculum. Since the best expression of the national will was to be found in the legends and folkways of the common people, literature and history were raised to a new position of prominence in the curriculum of the nineteenth century. The patriotic possibilities of geography were also recognized, but language was perhaps most important. Nothing reveals this better than the revolutionary demand that all French children be required to learn the same mother tongue. Not only did this requirement bind Frenchmen together by a new tie, but it also removed provincial impediments from the channels of communication that were so necessary for the free expression of political opinion in a republic.

As if this were not enough, the French of the revolutionary period made the teaching of "republican ethics" a required subject along with the three R's. Having promulgated the dogmas of popular sovereignty and self-determination, the revolutionaries saw that these dogmas would be ineffective unless the people were educated to take advantage of them. In spite of the free expression of national will, which flowed from the reservoirs of national folk tunes and folklore, the revolutionaries were taking no chances. They indoctrinated the next generation with what a century later would have been called republican propaganda.

In the United States, which contributed the only other revolutionary democratic government contemporaneous with the French Revolution, the introduction of nationalism into the schools was a bit delayed. At first, in spite of their forcible separation from Britain, the former colonists continued to use English texts in their schools. Not till the nineteenth century did Noah Webster (1758–1843) succeed in arousing Americans to the need for nationalizing their education. To this end he contributed no little himself by introducing selections into his readers that were American in theme and authorship. Probably his single most powerful nationalistic influence was his dictionary of the American language. This he described as a "method of education designed for the use of English schools in America." Evidently he expected to put his lexicon to the same nationalistic uses as the French in respect to their national tongue. "Our national honor," he declared, "requires us to have a system of our own, in language as well as government. . . . Besides this, a *national language* is a bond of *national union.*"[2]

Education as a bond of national union was prominent in the thoughts of other American patriots of the day. Samuel Knox, the winner of the prize contest of the American Philosophical Society already mentioned, thought that national education was the only way to unify a population sprung from as diverse European origins as the American. Benjamin Rush urged national education not only to achieve social homogeneity but also to produce political homogeneity along republican lines, as the French had attempted. Again, Noah Webster went so far as to decry the American practice of educating boys abroad. He would have their political dispositions well settled along republican lines in adequate American institutions before sending them traveling.

The romantic quality of nationalism called not only for new content in the curriculum but also for new methods of instruction. This was more clearly perceived in Prussia than anywhere else. Prussian nationalism was the aftermath not of revolution but of a military disaster at the Battle of Jena. In casting about for an explanation, Prussian leaders pointed to the helpless subordination of the people to authority and their consequent indifference toward the national state. The remedy was to make the national state as much a concern of the people as of the dynasty. But this could be done only by raising people from the passive lethargy of subjection to the great landowners up to the level of independent citizens of the state acting of their own free will.[3]

Happily, the method of instruction that would develop such free individuals already lay at hand. Its unique feature, which its author, Johann Heinrich Pestalozzi (1746–1827), had already been advocating for some time, was to give children an opportunity for the spontaneous expression of their natural powers. Instead of forcing knowledge upon children from without and under compulsion, the new method sought to awaken dormant capacities and stimulate their exercise.[4] This was to be the method in judgment and reasoning as well

[2] *Ibid.*, p. 243. But note that in an aftermath of the First World War the Supreme Court held unconstitutional a state statute which made English obligatory as the language of instruction in all schools [*Meyer v. State of Nebraska*, 262 U.S. 390 (1923)]. See, however, the dissenting opinion of Justice Oliver Wendell Holmes in *Bartels v. Iowa*, 262 U.S. 404, in which the facts were essentially the same. For a more general consideration of Webster's educational activities, see H. R. Warfel, *Noah Webster: Schoolmaster to America* (The Macmillan Company, New York, 1936).

[3] F. Paulsen, *German Education Past and Present* (Charles Scribner's Sons, New York, 1908), pp. 238–239.

[4] For a fuller account of this method, see *infra,* pp. 207–211.

as in sense and perception. The nationalistic potentialities of this method were particularly appreciated by Fichte (1762–1814), who more than any other single man stirred up the sentiment of nationalism not just in Prussia but in the whole of Germany. His philosophy of will and Pestalozzi's emphasis on self-expression went hand in hand. Both fitted the romantic pattern. Both were ready tools for conveying national feeling.

NATIONALISM, DEMOCRACY, AND EDUCATION

From the foregoing it becomes increasingly evident that nationalistic education not only aimed at the cultivation of patriotic feelings but also embodied a particular conception of the common man. Nationalism was invoked to release his feelings, to be sure, but the release also resulted in his enlargement as a person. Identifying him with a tradition and ideals whose historical and geographical scope were so much more inclusive—and hence less selfish—than his previous provincial outlook was bound to enlarge and enrich his personality. So, too, encouragement to express his undeveloped powers could hardly escape developing the common man's independence, initiative, and self-reliance. Moreover, he was learning what could be done with these newly released powers when coordinated and organized on a national scale.

What the heady wine of nationalism was doing in America is well described by no less a person than the Englishman Adam Smith. "The persons who now govern the resolutions of what they call their continental congress, feel in themselves at this moment a degree of importance which, perhaps, the greatest subjects in Europe scarce feel. From shopkeepers, tradesmen, and attornies, they are become statesmen and legislators, and are employed in contriving a new form of government for an extensive empire, which, they flatter themselves, will become, and which, indeed, seems very like to become one of the greatest and most formidable that ever was in the world."[5] Such stirrings as these could only be the prelude to the demand for educational opportunities commensurate with the opportunities and responsibilities indicated.

Obviously, a nationalism so greatly concerned with the education of the common variety of people could hardly escape having definite democratic implications. Certainly Fichte did not miss this point. In fact, he went further and showed annoyance at Pestalozzi's phrase the "education of the common people." Truly national education, Fichte declared, should liberate the moral, intellectual, and physical potentialities of all men just because they are human beings. It is

[5] A. Smith, *The Wealth of Nations* (W. Strahan, London, 1778), vol. 2, p. 234.

well to remember this early affinity of nationalism and democracy, for a later day was to cloud their relation.

Indeed, reduced to democratic terms, nationalism had some resemblance to cosmopolitan education. Both sought the liberation of human capacities, but the two diverged on where to place the responsibility for carrying out the program. The great shortcoming of the cosmopolitan ideal lay right here. Outside the private efforts of people of enlightened inclinations, there was no agency to give it effect. It was this lack which nationalism fulfilled. Cosmopolitanism feared that contemporary princes would educate their subjects for selfish princely ends. Yet, gain that it might be for freedom, to leave education to nature or to private initiative under the policies of *laissez faire* would not extensively promote the cosmopolitan ideal either. Even the reputedly antisocial Rousseau seemed to realize this. Confronted with a concrete problem when asked to recommend a system of education for Poland, he flatly urged a national one.[6]

RELATION OF THE INDIVIDUAL TO THE NATIONAL STATE

The practical problem historically was not so much whether the national state should provide education as what should be the relation between the individual and the state. Initially, the major concern was with the individual. The individual was the end, and the nation-state the means. The point was eloquently stated by a French philosopher, the Marquis de Condorcet (1743–1794), at the end of the eighteenth century. "To offer to all individuals of the human race," he wrote in a famous essay, "the means of providing for their needs, of assuring their welfare, of knowing and exercising their rights, of understanding and fulfilling their obligations.

"To assure each one the facility of perfecting his skill, of rendering himself capable of the social functions to which he has the right to be called, of developing to the fullest extent those talents with which nature has endowed him; and thereby to establish among all citizens an actual equality, thus rendering real the political equality recognized by the law.

"This should be the first aim of any national education; and from such a point of view, this education is for the government an obligation of justice."[7]

[6] W. Boyd, *The Minor Educational Writings of Jean Jacques Rousseau* (Blackie & Son, Ltd., Glasgow, 1911), pp. 141–149.

[7] F. La Fontainerie, *French Liberalism and Education in the Eighteenth Century* (McGraw-Hill Book Company, New York, 1932), p. 323.

This subordination of the nation to the individual underwent a subtle transformation at the beginning of the nineteenth century in Prussia. In urging a nationalistic education in his famous addresses to the German people, it is noteworthy that the patriot-philosopher Fichte did not break completely with his earlier commitments to cosmopolitanism. The ideal of an education that liberated human capacities seemed as valid to him after the Napoleonic defeat of Prussia as before. What it needed, in addition, was implementation by the national state.

But when Fichte, and Georg Wilhelm Friedrich Hegel (1770–1831) after him, stated that the main function of the national state was educational, they meant something more than Condorcet probably had. They meant that the individual could liberate his potentialities only by enlisting them in the service of the nation. In the nationalistic rivalries of the day, both military defense and international competition in trade demanded that the individual subordinate himself to the superior interests of the nation-state. Yet disciplinary as this aim was, the aim of forming man as man still persisted very strongly. Thus side by side were advocated an education that subordinated the individual to the nation and an education that claimed to employ the nation-state to liberate the potentialities of the individual.

If this seemed a contradiction in terms, the contradiction was apparent only. The terms were reconciled in the organic theory of the nation-state. The state, according to Hegelian philosophy, was a manifestation of objective reason. The private individual by himself was irrational, an egotistic creature of appetite. The individual's best hope for optimum development, therefore, lay in his voluntarily submitting himself to the educative discipline of the institutions and laws of the national state. Only thus could he hope to become truly rational.

Clever balance that Hegel struck between the education of man as man and man as citizen of a national state, it was an unstable one. As long as romanticism, liberalism, and humanitarianism continued to hold sway in the first half of the nineteenth century, nationalism was held in reasonable subjection to the ideal of education as personal development. But when the liberal democratic revolutions of the mid-century in Prussia, France, and elsewhere proved abortive, conservative governments repressed liberal nationalism in continental Europe. Especially were teacher-training institutions singled out as centers where the movement should be repressed. Sharpened military rivalries for European hegemony soon distorted nationalism to narrower ends. Consequently, a more chauvinistic nationalism arose. Its chief end was to maintain national integrity, especially military, territorial, and racial integrity. To achieve this end both aggressive nations like Prussia in the 1860s and defeated ones like France after 1870 found it advantageous to cultivate a collective egotism among their citizens.

The educational result was that the nation-state began to gain a definite ascendancy over the individual. It became the predominant end of education, and the individual was relegated more and more to the role of means. Thus the nationalism that began at the time of the French Revolution as a democratic movement to liberate individual potentialities ended in the last half of the nineteenth century as a movement to aid and abet nationalistic rivalries that could be arbitrated only by war. Between the First and the Second World War in the twentieth century it got out of hand in Germany and Italy. National Socialism in Germany and fascism in Italy produced a totalitarian form of nationalistic education in which echoed overtones of Hegel's organic philosophy of the state.[8] Through totalitarian nationalism the state swelled to such monistic proportions as to be identical with society itself. As there was no society but the national state, so there was no education but that of the citizen. The education of the individual was so much occupied with service to the nation-state that he no longer had any individuality to be cultivated on its own account.

The effect that chauvinistic nationalism had on the curriculum in the nineteenth and twentieth centuries can easily be imagined. The curriculum was a Procrustean bed where the individual was proportioned to national requirements. The romantic feelings formerly stirred by reading literature in order to awaken the dormant abilities of the common man were diverted to promote nationalistic ambitions. The historical record was distorted so as to put a highly favorable aspect on the victories and defeats of the child's own country. Even geography had its jingoistic uses, as witness the German schoolboy who described his homeland as bounded by enemies. In the totalitarian period, when the Second World War was already a foregone conclusion in Germany, the Nazis put education in health, physical vigor, and race purity definitely ahead of intellectual studies.

NATIONAL EDUCATIONAL ORGANIZATION IN EUROPE

Nationalism, both liberal and chauvinistic, also definitely left its mark on educational organization.[9] Following the French Revolution, when Europe became ripe for the nationalistic education of the masses, educational administration naturally followed national lines in a coun-

[8] G. Gentile, *The Reform of Education* (Harcourt, Brace and Company, Inc., New York, 1922).

[9] For a fuller account of this topic, see pp. 39–41, 125.

try like France. Napoleon thus gave a permanent national turn to French education when he organized all levels of instruction from the primary to the university into the Université de France. While this national organization was subdivided into academies for local administration, control was closely held at the top or center of the system. The finger-tip control that this system afforded over the curriculum and methods of instruction was preferred, surprisingly enough, by both chauvinistic *and* more liberal nationalist regimes. It was acceptable to both Napoleon III, who used it to restrict academic freedom and promote a dubiously risky foreign policy, and to the Third Republic, which was more deeply interested in realizing the ideals of the revolution.

While France may be taken as typical of continental Europe, where legal forms tend to follow the old Roman law, a somewhat different pattern of national educational administration evolved in England. Yet no early need was felt for schools to join in a release of romantic nationalism, such as had occurred on the Continent either in France or in Prussia. The national state stood aloof from educational enterprises. For the first quarter of the nineteenth century it adopted a laissez-faire attitude. Between 1832 and 1884, however, the accumulating pressure of the Industrial Revolution forced a series of reform acts that virtually enfranchised the common man in England. Even so the nation was brought but slowly to serve his educational needs. At first the national state merely subsidized existing private agencies. Later it exercised a centralized supervision of this bounty through a "payment-by-results" policy. This policy produced national uniformity but was found correspondingly narrow and inflexible. It failed to serve individual and local needs. In 1870, therefore, the English passed a national education act that recognized the important place of local education authorities in a national system of education. Since then the suppport and control of education have been slowly worked out into a delicate balance between these two authorities. The check each has exerted on the other has gone a long way toward keeping the nation subordinated to the educational needs of its citizens and toward saving Englishmen from sacrifice on the altar of a narrow chauvinistic nationalism.

The Industrial Revolution was a contributor to the nationalistic trend in education in other ways than the political just noted in England. As revolutionary France perceived the educational importance of a common language as a vehicle of nationalism, so the Industrial Revolution in England enormously increased the area reached by it. Railroads, steamships, power-driven presses, and the telegraph in the nineteenth century and radio in the twentieth brought people together in a sense of proximity and unity never known before.

But improvement in transportation and communication also led to imperialism and sharpened competition between industrial nations for world markets. Countries like Germany and the United States, which were handicapped by becoming industrialized later than England, turned to national subsidies for trade education as one means of closing the competitive gap. England resorted to national trade education, too, when she began to feel that her competitors were catching up with her.

THE FEDERAL GOVERNMENT AND EDUCATION IN THE UNITED STATES

In the United States the growth of national educational organization has been very halting. The first national gesture toward education was made in the Ordinance of 1787, establishing the government of the Northwest Territory. This act, opening up the national domain for settlers, provided that "Religion, morality, and knowledge being necessary to good government and the happiness of mankind, schools and the means of education shall be forever encouraged." Favorable as this statement is, it was not an unambiguous declaration of national interest in education. Rather it seems that this clause was inserted into the ordinance as a means of attracting settlers from New England, where there was an already strong school tradition. It was a kind of sales promotion rather than a commitment on national policy.

The adoption of the Federal Constitution two years later revealed that the nation was still unprepared to make a positive commitment on education. In fact, the Constitution was most eloquent by its silence on the subject. This omission, which has so profoundly influenced the subsequent course of American education, can be accounted for in several ways. For one thing, precedents were wanting. In 1789 there was practically no European state with a national system of schools. To be sure, Prussia had a national school system, but this was still largely a collaboration of the Prussian state with the Lutheran Church. Furthermore, among the fourteen new American state constitutions adopted between 1776 and 1800 and the two colonial charters carried over into the national period, only five mentioned education. In most of these states education was and had long been undertaken privately or by the churches. Indeed, most of the founding fathers had been educated under such auspices, and perhaps this experience limited their vision.

Whatever the cause for the omission of specific mention of education in the Constitution, certain it is that it was not omitted from the deliberations of the Constitutional Convention. The delegates who raised the matter there apparently pressed it no further because they were satisfied that the Constitution, as finally drafted, contained an implied grant of power sufficient to cover educational purposes. Yet after the Constitution was adopted, there was still much doubt on this point in some quarters. For most people these doubts were dispersed by the addition of the Tenth Amendment, which reserved to the states such powers as were not delegated to the Federal government. It was generally agreed that education was included in this reservation to the states.

As a result, the first half-century and more of our national existence showed little or no inclination of the national government to participate in education. First George Washington's legacy for a national university lapsed. Some of his early successors in the presidency, including Thomas Jefferson, tried unsuccessfully to revive it. But it was the National Education Association after the Civil War which endeavored most persistently to carry through Washington's idea of a national university. At one point emphasis was laid on the need for a research if not a teaching university. Nevertheless the long-standing project was laid to rest when a notable committee of college presidents, including Charles W. Eliot of Harvard, its inveterate enemy, reported against it. Second, the educational policy of the Ordinance of 1787 was continued. As each new territory was admitted to statehood, it was required to set aside a certain amount of its domain as an endowment for education. But, as already seen, this was not a positive declaration of national policy on education. Third, the Surplus Revenue Act of 1837 returned Federal moneys to the states with a recommendation that they be devoted to educational ends. But the recommendation was not binding; many states spent the funds for other purposes. The country still lacked a national educational policy. School readers, following Webster's lead, had become nationwide; the people were patriotic; yet the national government held aloof from education.

Abraham Lincoln's presidency inaugurated a brief interlude in this policy of aloofness. Early in his administration, Lincoln signed the first Morrill Act, which set aside public lands for the support of colleges of agriculture and mechanical arts, the so-called "land-grant colleges." A second Morrill Act in 1890 strengthened the financial sinews of these institutions, while the Smith-Hughes Act in 1917 inaugurated a similar national subsidy for trade education at the secondary level. Interestingly enough, Lincoln did not entertain the constitutional scruples that had prevented his predecessor in office from signing the first Morrill Act.

The interlude from aloofness was extended by the Civil War. As a war to test the unity of nationhood, it had at least two nationalistic educational repercussions. In 1867 provision was made by Congress for the first and only national Secretary of Education the country has ever had. Although the nation's preeminent authority on public education, Henry Barnard, was appointed to the post, this national venture in education did not prove very successful. Its scope was too limited for a man of Barnard's large capacities. In a few years the secretaryship was demoted to a subordinate bureau in the Department of the Interior, where it operated as a research and statistical agency. The United States Commissioner of Education at the head of this bureau had no authority to exercise leadership in the formation of large-scale national educational policies. This situation was improved in 1953 with the creation of a Secretary of Health, Education, and Welfare in the President's Cabinet.

While the national government was lending but a limited and restrained direction to the education of its youth, subtle forces in this period were inevitably nationalizing education. Literature, history, and geography were being turned to national ends under state if not national leadership. Teachers gained a national orientation through the National Education Association, which was formed and matured in this period. Graduate schools of education like Teachers College, Columbia University, exercised a national leadership by virtue of their national clientele. Supplementing these forces were educational periodicals, which reached a wide professional audience and provided a national clearinghouse for educational opinion and research.

Shifting the emphasis slightly, Carlton Hayes, student of nationalism, has gone so far as to claim, "To assure national unity between West and East and to guard national customs and ideals against foreign contamination, these, rather than mere a priori reasoning about political democracy, were the effective, if somewhat unconscious, motives for the building of the American system of national education. The system was definitely fashioned by the generation which participated in the nationalist War for the Union and its later minor amendment has been conditioned less by the New Freedom than by the New Nationalism."[10]

The army draft statistics of the First World War momentarily shocked the American public. The percentage of illiteracy and physical unfitness made Americans seriously question how far education could be the object of limited national endeavor and the result of the drift of chance. As soon as the war was over, proposals originated in Congress for a Secretary of Education in the President's Cabinet and a large subsidy to wipe out the national menace of illiteracy and physical unfitness. Of several bills none ever reached a vote. The national crisis of war had passed successfully—almost with one

[10] C. J. H. Hayes, *Essays on Nationalism* (The Macmillan Company, New York, 1937), p. 86.

arm of the nation tied behind its back.[11] The people could no longer be aroused to the gravity of the situation.

Besides, there were not a few who opposed the bills on historical grounds. The bills were drawn so that the nation with its greater resources and vision might be put at the service of the youth of the nation. The nation was to be the means of equalizing educational opportunity; the individual was to be the end. However much this might be the worthy intent, the opposition feared that the centralization, the nationalization, of educational administration offered too tempting an opportunity to subvert the whole process. In unscrupulous hands the individual's education could be subordinated to national ends, as had occurred in Prussia and to a large extent in France. In spite of revisions to guard against this possibility, the fear lingered.

Another national educational crisis occurred with the Depression of 1929. Many states could not raise sufficient taxes to keep a large number of their schools open, let alone extend their facilities. With schools closed or their offerings curtailed and with industry unprepared to receive them, youth had nowhere to go. In this crisis the national government chose to aid youth directly insofar as taking up the slack of unemployment through further education was concerned. Instead of trying to reach youth through the existing public school facilities, the Federal government itself set up two important agencies with educational functions, the Civilian Conservation Corps and the National Youth Administration, or the CCC and the NYA, as they were more familiarly known. Aided by ample Federal subsidies, the activities of these two agencies rapidly expanded till in some respects they presented almost a parallel system of education to the regularly constituted public school system. This situation, naturally, was not long in generating alarm among public school men, which finally was voiced by the National Education Association through its Educational Policies Commission.[12] During the Second World War Congress gave heed to this growing opposition and withdrew its subsidies from these organizations, thus causing them to wind up their affairs. Although the idea of a separate system of national schools—whatever its name might be—had been subject to severe criticism, it had at least demonstrated the need for exploring new opportunities in secondary education, especially in the field of the educational value of work experience, and had revealed how the nation's educational facilities could be

---

[11] For a complete account of the nationalistic uses to which American schools were put during the First World War, see L. P. Todd, *Wartime Relations of the Federal Government and the Public Schools* (Bureau of Publications, Teachers College, Columbia University, New York, 1945).

[12] *The CCC, the NYA, and the Public Schools* (National Education Association, Educational Policies Commission, Washington, D.C., 1941).

expanded if only help from the Federal government were properly safeguarded.

While the national government was hestitating to come to the direct financial aid of the public schools, a committee of nationally eminent persons was appointed to advise the President as to a proper policy on Federal relations to public education.[13] This committee recommended a national subsidy for education, but it came to nought. A provision for subsidizing parochial schools was the chief stumbling block. Inclusion of this provision would have alienated the support of many advocates of public schools. In 1943 yet another bill for a national subsidy to education reached the floor of the Senate, where it failed of a majority. This time the stumbling block was a provision for equal subsidies to both Negro and white schools in the South. Southern congressmen refused to vote for the bill is this form, and Northern congressmen refused to vote for it without the provision. After the Second World War there was a renewed demand for Federal subsidies, this time to keep abreast of technological change in world competition. On this occasion the national emergency was great enough to secure enactment of the educational provisions in the National Defense Act.

It is notable that, in the intensified agitation for an increased nationalization of education in the twentieth century, the constitutional objection of the nineteenth century was heard less and less. This specter seems to have been laid to rest by decisions of the United States Supreme Court on New Deal legislation, legislation that probably accelerated the pace of nationalism in this country more rapidly than at any previous time in its history. Coincident with this nationalization has come a new and more nationalistic interpretation of the Federal Constitution.

The most probable defense of the constitutionality of education always lay in Article I, section 8, of the Federal Constitution. The first paragraph there provided that Congress shall have power to lay and collect taxes, pay debts, and provide for the common defense "and general welfare." Did this last phrase include education? Down to the nationalizing era of the New Deal, the Madisonian interpretation of this clause prevailed. James Madison took a narrow view of the power granted here. This paragraph, he claimed, was primarily a grant of financial power. Therefore, the phrase "general welfare" was no added grant of power to Congress. On this reasoning a national child-labor act had been declared unconstitutional. Presumably a general education act by Congress would have received the same disposition. But since the national crisis created by the Depression of

[13] *Federal Relations to Education* (United States National Advisory Committee on Education, Washington, D.C., 1931).

1929 the Hamiltonian interpretation of this paragraph has come to prevail in the Supreme Court. Alexander Hamilton took the broader, more nationalistic view that the general-welfare clause was an additional grant of power. Yet, even with the constitutional hurdle overcome, the Supreme Court has still left open the question of whether or not any particular legislation does in fact concern the general or national welfare. This question of fact has yet to be settled for education.[14]

THE CHURCH AND NATIONALISM IN EDUCATION

As the secular state was first servant and later more or less master of the nationalistic education called forth by the French Revolution, so nationalistic education was from the first largely secular in quality. Louis René de La Chalotais (1701–1785), writing on national education at the end of the eighteenth century, was one of the first to insist that national education be secular. "I do not presume," he set down, "to exclude ecclesiastics but I protest against the exclusion of laymen. I dare claim for the nation an education which depends only on the state, because it belongs essentially to the state; because every state has an inalienable and indefeasible right to instruct its members; because, finally, the children of the state ought to be educated by the members of the state."[15] It was not because La Chalotais was irreligious that he was anxious to make this point. It was rather because he had grave doubts that a cleric, who had renounced the world, could conduct civic education with the same vital interest a lay citizen could bring to the task.

The chief opponent of this secular nationalism in education was the Catholic Church. As Catholicism had opposed rationalism for its too exclusive reliance on reason, so it opposed the romanticism of nationalism for going to the other extreme in its emphasis on emotionalism. Nationalism, furthermore, was fractional; it stressed man's accidental loyalties to a particular place, a particular language, particular folkways and legends. The danger was that these partial truths might become such an absorbing loyalty that they would compete with loyalty to the universal truths of religion. All this, of course, is to say nothing of the advantage secular schools might have over those in the church in being able to dip into the national exchequer for their support.

In Catholic France, the secular and anticlerical party was the re-

[14] J. S. Brubacher, "The Constitutionality of a National System of Education in the United States," *School and Society*, 46:417–423, October, 1937.

[15] Quoted in G. Compayré, *History of Pedagogy* (D. C. Heath and Company, Boston, 1885), p. 345.

publican middle class. The royalists, though no less nationalistic, were the party kindly disposed toward an important role for ecclesiastics in the new national education. These opposing attitudes seesawed in control in the nineteenth century. As the Third Republic became consolidated, however, events moved to a climax in the law of 1904. This law went a step further than La Chalotais had recommended and banned members of Catholic teaching orders from instructing in the public schools. Meanwhile, the state managed to teach nationalism and secular morals in a course designated as "moral and civic instruction"—the lineal descendant of the revolutionary course in "republican ethics and morals."

In Protestant countries like Germany and England the church was even less successful in resisting the secular pretensions of nationalism. This is not surprising. Protestantism, like nationalism, was itself fractional. But, more important, Martin Luther (1483–1546), the leader of Protestantism in Germany, had already set a fatal precedent. After his successful appeal to the secular princes in the sixteenth century to support education in Protestant countries, the Protestant churches could only with ill grace fail to collaborate with the state in the national phase of its development. Indeed, almost everywhere in the nineteenth century most Protestant churches backed the public school systems of national secular states as if they were their own. Germany even went further and organized its public elementary schools on a confessional basis. Thus, whether the elementary school was Lutheran, Catholic, or Jewish, nationalism and religion could be taught side by side. In fact, the teaching was often done in such a subtle way that religion was invoked to bless the righteousness of nationalistic aspirations.

It is significant, however, that the Lutherans did resist the extreme educational pretensions of National Socialism in Germany from 1933 onward. The Catholics, as might be expected, joined the Lutherans. For the Catholics this was their second bout with an extreme nationalistic control of education in Germany. When Pius IX announced his opposition to nationalism in his *Syllabus of Errors* in 1864, the great German chancellor Otto von Bismarck, for one, took up the challenge. One of his chief nationalistic objectives was to insist that such of the clergy as might be school inspectors not only should be German nationals but also should have received a thorough education in German educational institutions. The policy was not administered strictly, however, and the Catholic Church was at least successful in outlasting Bismarck in his famous Kulturkampf.

In America a different situation obtained. Since the days of Noah Webster, nationalism had been intensively cultivated as curriculum content but only slightly as a form of educational administration. What was even more significant, the sentiment of nationalism had been cultivated almost altogether independently of Federal educational administration, limited as that had been. Rather had private and state school systems voluntarily introduced national and patriotic materials into their curricula. Hence nationalism, though ardent and at times even jingoistic, never seemed an ominous ingredient of American education. On the one hand, the growth in stature of a central administrative structure had been checked in part by church opposition, as noted previously. On the other hand, control of the curriculum had been left in the hands of the state governments.

Yet this decentralization was not always a protection of religious interests. State laws occasionally tried to compel uniformity in nationalistic observances in school. The hand salute to the flag was a case in point. Some religious sects claimed that this physical posture was an offense to their religious beliefs against bowing to a graven image and appealed to the Federal Constitution for relief. The Supreme Court of the United States thus had to face the question of whether national or religious interests were paramount in the schools. In 1943 it decided that national security did not require the uniform observance of such laws.[16]

INTERNATIONALISM AND EDUCATION

As two devastating world wars attest, the church has not been appreciably successful in the abatement of chauvinistic nationalism in education. When communism was in its international phase in Soviet Russia, it appeared for a while as if a new counterweight to nationalistic education had been found. Soviet youth were educated for loyalty to an economic class, the working class of all countries. Such a loyalty was designed to transcend nationalism, with its loyalty to a locality having a particular sovereignty and cultural tradition. In fact, nationalistic education was condemned as one of the barriers that prevented the working classes everywhere from uniting to enforce a recognition of their rights. Excepting the economic bias of this view, one might almost detect here a new cosmopolitanism in education. But valiantly as the Russians tried to arouse this new loyalty of economic class, the Second World War brought about a change of policy. Their very existence threatened by German military might,

[16] First the Court decided that national interests were paramount; see *Minersville School District v. Gobitis,* 310 U.S. 586 (1940). Subsequently, in *West Virginia State Board of Education v. Barnette,* 319 U.S. 624 (1943), it reconsidered its earlier decision and overruled it.

the Soviets found it necessary to draw on every resource possible to save their institutions. Consequently, Russian education became more and more nationalistic in tone in order to profit by the dynamic energies nationalism could release.

A different maneuver to overcome the disadvantages of nationalistic education and yet preserve its advantages was the effort to form some sort of international organization of education. Though nothing effective was accomplished in this direction till after the first World War, the idea was not without precedent. The eighteenth-century cosmopolitan ideal of education has already been mentioned. But Johann Amos Comenius (1592–1670), the great Moravian pansophist, had already conceived the idea in the century preceding. His self-dedication to pansophy and to a pansophic college, which would take all knowledge[17] as its province, was not just in the interests of accumulating knowledge for its own sake. He also sought the coordination and unification of knowledge as a means of advancing human welfare and universal peace.

Writing with great modernity exactly three centuries before the Second World War, Comenius declared in 1643, "There is needed in this century an immediate remedy for the frenzy which has seized many men and is driving them in their madness to their mutual destruction. For we witness throughout the world disastrous and destructive flames of discords and wars devastating kingdoms and peoples with such persistence that all men seem to have conspired for their mutual ruin which will end only with the destruction of themselves and the universe. Nothing is, therefore, more necessary for the stability of the world, if it is not to perish completely, than some universal rededication of minds. Universal harmony and peace must be secured for the whole human race. By peace and harmony, however, I mean not that external peace between rules and peoples among themselves, but an internal peace of minds inspired by a system of ideas and feelings. If this could be attained, the human race has a possession of great promise."[18]

Comenius's ideal of undergirding world stability through education far outran the imagination of his day. Indeed, the idea of an international commission to compile and disseminate information on national systems of education was still far in advance of the day of its realization when it was put forward by Marc Antoine Jullien in the second decade of the nineteenth century just after the cessation

[17] "All knowledge" is the literal translation of "pansophy," which is taken from the Greek roots for "all" ($\pi\hat{\alpha}\nu$) and "wisdom" ($\sigma o\phi\acute{\iota}\alpha$).

[18] Quoted in I. L. Kandel, "John Amos Comenius, Citizen of the World," *School and Society*, 55:404, April, 1942.

of the Napoleonic Wars.[19] A hundred years later there was agitation for a world educational union; in fact, the Netherlands, the seat of international peace efforts at the time, was prevailed upon to issue a call for an international conference on education. The date set for the conference to convene unfortunately happened to coincide with the outbreak of the First World War in 1914. Plans for an international educational agency, therefore, had to stand in abeyance till the conclusion of hostilities.

At the Paris Peace Conference the committee that worked on the draft of a League of Nations received an urgent plea that an International Bureau of Education be stipulated in the Covenant of the League. Nothing immediate, however, came of this plea. Apparently the nineteenth-century idea of education as an instrument of national policy was so deeply entrenched that the framers of the Covenant were afraid meddling with it might be taken as an unwarranted interference in a member nation's cultural autonomy. Nothing daunted, advocates of this Bureau managed to survive their disappointment by establishing an International Bureau of Education on a private basis at Geneva. Financial difficulties beset the Bureau from the outset. As late as 1938 only seventeen nations belonged to it, the United States being laggard in joining till 1958! The great demand that soon manifested itself for information from its files on national systems of education quickly justified the undertaking. In fact, the governments patronizing it soon took it over and made its support and control an intergovernmental project. Since the Second World War the annual meetings of the Bureau have been sponsored by UNESCO.

Although the Covenant of the League of Nations made no mention of education, the Assembly of the League at an early meeting made some amends for this omission by setting up a Committee on Intellectual Cooperation. The purpose of this Committee was to parallel League organs for international political and economic cooperation with one for spiritual cooperation in the arts and sciences. As the Committee was composed of savants from the member nations in the different fields of cultural endeavor, intellectual cooperation was limited for the most part to the university level of education.

Just as a propitious start was being made in this direction, the world was submerged by the worst deluge of chauvinistic nationalism it had ever experienced. Fascism in Italy and National Socialism in Germany in the 1920s and 1930s taught a virulent nationalism that made the democracies appear decadent. The democracies apparently were already succeeding in teaching internationalism only too well.

[19] I. L. Kandel, "International Cooperation in Education: An Early Nineteenth Century Aspiration," *Educational Forum*, 7:22–29, November, 1942.

No better proof of this achievement exists than the fact that Marshal Henri Philippe Pétain charged French teachers in 1934, five years before the outbreak of the Second World War, with having failed to provide France with a generation of young men physically fit and mentally disposed to fight.

In spite of international machinery for the maintenance of peace, including the Committee on Intellectual Cooperation and the International Bureau of Education, the Second World War broke out. Yet, discouraging as this was, it did not prevent meetings and plans for more effective international cooperation in education at the war's end. While the war was yet going on, the first meeting was held. This was a meeting of the ministers of education of the countries overrun by the Nazis to consider mutual problems of educational reconstruction after the war. It soon became evident, however, that the problem of remedying the physical and spiritual impairments resulting from the holocaust of war were not limited to the conquered territories but were world-wide in scope. Subsequent meetings were therefore attended by observers from such countries as Russia and the United States. The upshot of these meetings at the end of the war was a provision in the San Francisco Charter that stated that in order to promote international stability "the United Nations shall promote . . . international cultural and educational cooperation."[20] Pursuant to this declaration a meeting was called at London to consider a proposal for an educational organization of the United Nations. This resulted in the formation of the United Nations Educational, Scientific and Cultural Organization.

The purpose of UNESCO was primarily to act as a clearinghouse for educational ideas in the various member nations. By making information about national educational aims, curricula, methods, and texts easily available, it was hoped to get an early check on countries that might commence to use education for purposes of national aggression. In addition, in much the same way as minimum working conditions had been so successfully prescribed by the International Labor Office of the League of Nations, it was hoped that minimum standards of education might be laid down, for unfavorable educational opportunities, like bad working conditions, are breeders of international unrest. In any event, the role of UNESCO was not to be coercive but merely to make suggestions. All this, though belated, was earnest that the world was coming to realize that the disarmament of nations must be accompanied by the disarmament of the mind.

UNESCO spent its early days in formulating a program. In one direction it tried to make headway in liquidating illiteracy. In a more important direction it launched "fundamental" education, which spread

[20] United Nations Charter, Chap. IX, Art. 55.

beyond the liquidation of illiteracy into community development. Yet another program was student exchange to improve international understanding. Textbook revision to erase misunderstanding stems from the nineteenth century. The Committee on Intellectual Cooperation lent its aid to the idea, but the results have been only partial. Undergirding all these projects has been a need for a philosophy of UNESCO. The Organization's first Secretary-General, Julian Huxley, undertook to formulate one, but it failed of general acceptance and consequently was published privately.[21] Agreement in practice seems easier than agreement in theory at this stage of world affairs.

[21] Julian Huxley, *UNESCO: Its Purpose and Philosophy* (Public Affairs Press, Washington, D.C., 1947).

Economic
4 Influences on
Education

Of all the sociological factors that have conditioned the
course of educational history, perhaps none has so
persistently posed problems as has the economic. And,
oddly enough, perhaps none has been so overlooked,
neglected, or thrust to one side. Education owes its
support to the basic economy but has been reluctant
to accord it a prominent place in the curriculum. Why
is this? Why are practical and vocational subjects held
in lower esteem than cultural ones? The problem thus
raised is one that has persisted through periods of
economic prosperity and periods of economic decline.
And therein lies another persistent problem of education. Why is it that education seems to have cycles of
rise and decline that not only correspond to but also
coincide with economic cycles? The fact that these
cycles seem more pronounced in industrial than in
commercial and agrarian economies poses yet another
persistent problem. Must education make different
adjustments for the various ways in which man earns
his bread?

EDUCATION IN SUBSISTENCE AND SURPLUS ECONOMIES

A subsistence economy is one in which people are just
able to make ends meet. That is, by devoting their
whole effort to hunting, fishing, or farming they are
just able to get enough food to survive. If they relax

their efforts ever so slightly, they endanger their livelihood and render precarious the livelihood of all those dependent on them. This has been the economic status of nearly all early cultures, especially primitive ones. Under such circumstances cultural advance is either impossible or at best accidental. Education is necessarily informal.[1] It occurs on the job; it is incidental to hunting, fashioning implements, propitiating the spirits, and the like. There is no time available for formal education, no time for exclusive and deliberate attention to training.

Formal education or schooling is the product of a surplus economy, in which production exceeds consumption. The surplus may be due to well-stocked hunting grounds, to fertility of the soil, to exceptional industry on the part of man, or to chance improvements in his art or skill. But whatever the cause, the continuance of life is assured for a time even when productive efforts are relaxed. Herein lies the beginning of civilization or at least the promise of civilization if the eased conditions of life are put to good effect. Such was the case with the great river-valley civilizations of ancient times. Nearly everyone is familiar with how from time immemorial the flooding of the Nile has annually enriched the soil of this Egyptian valley. The crops of this valley not only sustained life but yielded a handsome surplus as well. At least the surplus was sufficient to sustain a small number of the population in leisure. In this small number were the priests. Happily they employed their leisure to study the more subtle forces that affected human living, such as the motion of the heavenly bodies and the rotation of the seasons.

None put their leisure to better use than did the Greeks. Their economic prosperity was built on a surplus derived from commerce with their neighbors. Yet so persistently did they devote their leisure to schooling that they formed the metaphor where σχολή (schole), their word for leisure, came to mean, not leisure, but the use to which it was put. In fact, the word for school in most Western tongues stems from this old Greek word σχολή.[2] The relation of leisure to education, however, was widely understood. Ancient Jewish culture had an excellent appreciation of this relationship, for the apocryphal writer of Ecclesiasticus set it down that "The wisdom of a learned man cometh by opportunity of leisure; and he that hath little business shall become wise. How can he get wisdom that holdeth the plough, and that glorieth in the goad, that driveth oxen, and is occupied in their labors, and whose talk is of bullocks?"[3] Moreover, what is true of a whole society

---

[1] For a further account of formal and informal education, see *infra*, pp. 340–354.

[2] Greek σχολή; Latin *schola;* English schole, later school; French *école;* German *Schule*; Spanish *escuela*.

[3] Ecclesiasticus 38:24–25.

is just as true of that smaller unit the family. Thus Plato (427–347 B.C.) noted that the children of the rich are the earliest to begin their attendance at school and the last to leave off.

For another thing, the identification of school with leisure marked the achievement of the basic economic conditions that later permitted the pursuit of education as an end in itself, as something more than just the means of entering the adult group and maintaining its continuity. At first, leisure was the indispensable prop for any education whatever. The quantity of leisure and education at this stage was just enough to cover the minimum necessary to ensure the continuance of society. Later, notably in the commercial culture of the Greeks, when peace and the arts and sciences produced a superabundance of leisure, education could be pursued not merely as a means but as an end as well.

This point was a very critical one for the subsequent relation of education and life. When reached by various civilizations, it was, all too often, the last step in the separation of education and life. While education was pursued as a means of entering the adult group and preserving its social continuity, there was a constant check on the effectiveness with which one was achieving this end of life. But once a leisure class made education its own end, education constantly ran the risk of becoming esoteric and out of touch with life. This, however, was a late development. Yet, in spite of this risk, the pursuit of education as an end in itself also paradoxically led to a new identity of education and life. Reaching the stage of indulging in education for its own sake implied that leisure pursuits had become regularly accepted as adult activities. In other words, education took its place with politics, religion, and the like in its demands on adult time and attention.

Indeed, one might go further and assert that the periodic advance and decline of education throughout its history can almost always be associated, respectively, with periods of economic prosperity and depression. The best and most interesting early instance of this parallelism is to be found in Greece. The golden age of Greek education, the age of such teachers as Socrates (469–399 B.C.), Plato, and Aristotle (384–322 B.C.), to mention only the greatest, was also an age of great economic prosperity. The period coincided with Athens's headship of a great commercial combine, the Delian League. As head of the League, she became the great center and crossroads of trade. It is small wonder, therefore, that her citizens had the wealth and consequent leisure to afford her young men more extensive education than any previous civilization had been able to afford. Not only was literacy more widespread in the population, but education continued longer. Furthermore, prosperous conditions raised up a whole class of professional teachers, the Sophists, who were attracted to

Athens not only by the prospect of good fees but also by the commerce in ideas. The market place where strange goods are exchanged is bound to be the place where novel ideas rub elbows as well. But equally important for the high level of culture in the schools of this time was the spirit of tolerance shown to new ideas. In part, this was due to economic prosperity. A people with a comfortable surplus can afford to take risks with new ideas that a people living in a subsistence economy cannot think of taking.

This relatively high level of economic well-being continued for many centuries in the ancient world. In fact, it reached a new height during the Roman Empire. The wealth of Rome at its peak of power so far exceeded that of Athens that one might easily imagine its education to have been superior, but this was not the case. The Romans went to school to the Greeks. In the language of the poet Horace, "Greece took captive her rude conqueror." Rome may have become the political and economic center of the Roman Empire, but the eastern Mediterranean still remained the educational capital of the ancient world. Good schools spread through this area. Among the best were those located on the island of Rhodes and at Alexandria in Egypt. If these schools failed to equal the originality and creativeness of the schools in the golden age of Athens, the cause is probably to be sought elsewhere than in the general economic situation.[4]

The converse of these conditions, that is, a period of economic decline paralleled by a period of educational decay, is nowhere better seen on a grand scale than in the gradual disintegration of the Roman Empire. No doubt this disintegration was due to a multiplicity of causes, but there can be no doubt either that a declining economy was one of the important ones. The fact that the later emperors commenced to subsidize education from the imperial treasury is valuable evidence that economic surpluses among private citizens were diminishing. The standard of living was falling below the point at which private initiative could be depended upon to provide schooling.

Of course, these conditions were aggravated during the medieval period. A profound depression settled down on the western half of Europe. As the small-scale agrarian economy of the medieval castle succeeded the large-scale agrarian and commercial economy of the Empire, Europe was reduced almost to a subsistence economy. There were pitifully little surplus wealth and leisure for the pursuit of learning. What schooling survived was only a distorted epitome of the earlier extensive schooling. It is an interesting commentary on these conditions that in the contemporary eastern half of the old Roman Empire, where commerce still thrived under a regime of law and order, education flourished with undiminished vigor and industry.

[4] *Supra,* pp. 28–30.

No precise date marks the conclusion of the medieval period. The transition to the Renaissance was gradual. Of chief significance here is the fact that the transition was marked by the gradual revival of a commercial economy. For the first time in several centuries there began to appear an economic surplus sufficient to support an interest in formal education. This interest was first manifested toward the end of the medieval period in the rise of the medieval university. It is noteworthy that the instruction there was primarily professional in character. Probably this was to be expected from an institution predicated on the reinvestment of the first profits of reviving trade. As these profits pyramided, the margin of leisure of the *nouveaux riches* greatly expanded. With this greater margin of economic security the focus in education shifted from professional study to an interest in culture for its own sake. In the course of the next several centuries the boom in commerce reached such proportions that the revival of education it promoted marked one of the outstanding periods in educational history.

From the Renaissance onward the standard of living stayed generally high enough in Western civilization to maintain a relatively high standard of education for at least a small proportion of the population at all times. Only on the frontier and during prolonged and widespread wars was society reduced to the subsistence or near-subsistence level of medieval Europe, where educational enterprise had all but come to a halt. The Thirty Years' War of the post-Renaissance period was an outstanding instance of the effect of war. It was so ruinous economically that it retarded education in the devastated area for several generations. So, too, the Civil War in nineteenth-century America was so destructive of the economic capacity of the Southern states that the educational handicaps it imposed were still evident in the second quarter of the twentieth century.[5]

The colonization of America illustrates the effect of frontier conditions on education. Fighting Indians and pushing back the forest to make the land arable consumed practically all the physical and material resources of the early settlers. So close were they to a subsistence economy that education was in grave danger of neglect. The "old deluder Satan" law of Massachusetts clearly indicates the apprehension of the settlers that learning might die with the first generation of colonists, who had had their education in Europe. As they became economically established on the Atlantic seaboard in the eighteenth century, however, wealth began to accumulate to permit an increasing interest in education. Yet the difficult circumstances of the seaboard

[5] Yet see H. G. Richey, "The Persistence of Educational Progress during the Decade of the Civil War," *Elementary School Journal*, 42:358–366, 456–463, January, February, 1942.

in the preceding seventeenth century recurred again and again on the Western frontier as each wave of migration moved farther and farther westward in the eighteenth and nineteenth centuries.

Down to the nineteenth century even under the most prosperous economic conditions there was only enough surplus wealth to maintain a relatively small percentage of the population in the leisure necessary to go to school. Neither the agrarian economy nor the agrarian supplemented by the commercial economy had in its most productive and profitable days been able to support more than the upper and upper middle classes at school. But at the end of the eighteenth century occurred a revolution in economy, the Industrial Revolution, which in the nineteenth and twentieth centuries was to pile up such gigantic surpluses that for the first time in educational history it became possible to realize the dream of enough leisure to put the children of the whole population to school.

The universal education of all children has often been thought to be the logical outgrowth of Christian principles. The idea of the equal dignity and worth of all mankind regardless of race, sex, or political and economic status, it would seem, should result in educational opportunities for all. No doubt such principles did animate humanitarian and philanthropically minded persons in the first half of the nineteenth century, but they were already centuries old. The question arises: Why did they take so long to come to fruition? The answer is: Fruition was delayed 1,900 years till the economic conditions that could implement the educational implications of the ideal evolved.

Beneficial as the Industrial Revolution has been in creating the wealth that could be taxed for school purposes, it has also subjected school revenues to abrupt ups and downs of the economic cycle. Periods of industrial expansion seem to have been followed by periods of economic contraction. In America periods of prosperity were followed by major depressions in 1837, 1857, 1873, 1893, and 1929.[6] Each left its mark upon the schools. Ordinarily, the adverse effect of depression is not felt on the schools till a year or two after it has been in full swing. School revenues, teachers' salaries, and per capita costs seem to stand up pretty well during the first year or two, but then they decline rapidly and are at their worst in the fourth and fifth years. Thereafter, they slowly rise again. So far, school expenditures have risen to new highs in the periods following depressions. Perhaps that has been due to the fact that the country still has such vast unexploited resources that these depressions have been only temporary setbacks in a still-expanding economy.

[6] R. S. Pitkin, *Public School Support in the United States during Periods of Economic Depression* (Stephen Daye Press, Inc., New York, 1933).

But it is also to be noted that the shock of depression has become increasingly severe with each succeeding depression. The latest depression, in 1929, was by far the worst. In the poorer areas thousands of schools closed for the whole or part of the school term. In these places there was virtually a return to a subsistence economy. Schools could be kept open only by aid from some larger area of tax administration, by transferring economic surpluses from larger to smaller geographical areas.

Much as past centuries seem to support the notion that advances in education wait on advances in the standard of living, there have been recent instances which may show an opposite trend. Thus there have been a few cases, notably Denmark in the late nineteenth century and Mexico between the two world wars of the twentieth, in which people have resorted to education as a means of reversing a period of economic decline. In both these countries educational innovations enabled them to increase their human resources to such an extent that they were virtually able to lift themselves by their educational bootstraps out of their economic doldrums. Perhaps an economist epitomized the situation neatly when he said, "There are two kinds of poverty—one a lack of goods for the higher wants, the other a lack of wants for the higher goods."[7] If so, education, instead of continuing to be the mere resultant of economic forces, may be standing on the threshold of itself taking the initiative in stimulating economic circumstances for its own and the national advantage.

ORIGIN OF THE DUALISM OF WORK
AND LEISURE IN EDUCATION

So far the chief emphasis has been on the way education has been dependent on the amount of leisure made possible by economic surplus. Only minor attention has been given to the distribution of leisure and the effects different conceptions of work and leisure have had on education. To commence, it will be well to note that in ancient societies leisure was not something each man earned as a result of labor. Rather was it the possession, the badge of distinction, of a particular class in society. This class, the aristocracy or nobility, had leisure because it was supported by the economic toil of another class—slaves in the ancient world, serfs in the medieval one. In addition, the upper class had continuous leisure while the lower class lived a life of unremitting toil.[8]

[7] R. T. Ely, *Outline of Economics* (The Macmillan Company, New York, 1926), p. 3.

[8] The Hebrews even viewed work—earning one's bread in the sweat of his brow—as a curse visited upon men because of the disobedience to God of their original ancestor, Adam.

There was no middle ground in this dichotomous class structure of ancient times. True, there were artisans and tradesmen who worked as freemen rather than as slaves and who accepted pay for their services. Yet these men were degraded by the fact that there were many skilled slaves with whom they were in competition. But, above all, they were rendered servile by the fact that they worked with their hands. Thus, Spartans were forbidden to learn a trade, and Aristotle advised giving one up as soon as possible if one were intent upon virtue. To accept pay for one's services did not distinguish one from being a slave. It was only further proof of not being "well-born" and of being incapacitated to pursue virtue because of being motivated by gain. Thus social class was a matter of status. One was born to a life of leisure or to a life of toil. There was practically no social mobility by which one might improve his social status.

From this social-economic structure, profound educational consequences developed. The kind of education which fitted one for the profitable use of leisure obviously pointed in a widely different direction from that which fitted one for labor with one's hands. No formal education whatever was necessary for those who labored with their hands. For centuries all that they needed to know could be learned informally in the course of their daily tasks. On the whole, this was as true of artisans and tradesmen as of those who labored on the land. For the upper class formal education was both a necessity and a luxury. Training in the symbols of written language was necessary to give them access to the recorded culture. While this training was indispensable to the priestly caste, it was only varyingly useful to those engaged in civil administration. Over and above those who performed these functions of an upper class were a few who indulged in the luxury of learning verbal and mathematical symbols for their own sake.

The kinds of education befitting these two social classes also had a deeper rationale. Thus Aristotle found justification for existing social stratification in man's psychological nature. In this nature he noted two characteristics, the appetitive and the reasonable. To the higher, or reasonable, of course, was given direction and control over the lower, or appetitive. To these two characteristics of the individual corresponded the two classes of society. Since the upper class held the offices in society that were directive and controlling, their proper education was the education of the mind. Since the lower class corresponded to the appetitive, their proper education was that of the body. The one was an education in thinking, the other an education in doing: the one literary, the other manual. The one demanded leisure for the development of ideas, and the other opportunity for work. Herein lay an early criterion for evaluating education. The more purely mental an educational activity, the more valuable. Indeed, the most profitable use of leisure was regarded as the pursuit of knowledge for its own sake, anciently the discipline of liberal education.[9]

Aristotle's analysis of the nature of the individual and of society seemed so reasonable that the educational corollaries based thereon dominated the history of education down to modern times. An interesting outcropping of this early stratum of educational history occurred in the late medieval period. The medieval agrarian economy was also socially dichotomous. The feudal system was a hierarchy of various levels; the fundamental distinction was that between the landed nobility and the serfs. It is not surprising, therefore, to find the perpetuation in feudal society of the distinction between work and leisure or at least between using one's hands to work and using them to fight.

Thus, among late medieval studies philosophy, theology, and logic ranked first in prestige because of their purely mental character. Law and medicine were included within the sphere of respectability only because the element of manual service to others was less evident than in handicraft industry. But medical education was on a lower plane than legal education because it was more deeply concerned with the body than with the mind. Thus, too, the fine arts stood below the liberal ones because of the element of manual dexterity involved in their mastery. And even in the liberal arts there existed a hierarchy predicated on the dualism of mind and body as allied to that of work and leisure and arising from social stratification. The trivium of logic, grammar, and rhetoric outranked the quadrivium of music, arithmetic, geometry, and astronomy.

RISE OF COMMERCIAL CAPITALISM AND MIDDLE-CLASS EDUCATION

The revival of trade and commerce that underlay the Renaissance initiated a fundamental change in the social-economic class structure. It marked the rise of a third class, a middle class between the upper and the lower classes of feudalism. The character of the feudal classes depended on their relation to the land since theirs was almost exclusively an agrarian economy. The character of the new middle class, however, was defined by the more fluid wealth of commerce. Its members were the forerunners of capitalism. Their wealth lay in currency, credits, and stock in trade. To undertake risk for profit they had to be free from the rigid feudal restrictions of an agrarian economy. This gave them an independence that engendered for them considerable social prestige. Here was a hard-working class of people who

[9] For a further account of liberal education, see *infra*, pp. 445–455.

lacked the status of the landowning nobility but who at the same time were not degraded by their work to the level of serfs.

The educational effects were notable. The more practical sort of education befitting such a class enjoyed a rise in public esteem. Artisans formed themselves into guilds that required long periods of apprenticeship education to gain the high degree of skill demanded by the trade of the times. The "overhead" organization of business expanded rapidly. There was a greatly increased need for formal education in the symbols of language and mathematics so that one could keep the accounts of trade. The need was met by schools maintained for the purpose either by municipalities or by the guilds themselves. There was also a modest demand for new studies in these schools. As the boom in commerce expanded into a search for new trade routes and into the age of exploration, such practical studies as geography and navigation gained some popularity.

While the middle class was on the rise and while it was struggling for recognition, its economic surpluses were never great enough to relieve it of continued hard work. In the course of time, however, its enterprise and industriousness yielded profits so great that a leisure class began to emerge from its ranks. The altered economic outlook of this group led to a revival of the classical conception of liberal education. Their formerly practical education gave way to one more aesthetic. The instrumental value of knowledge was superseded by a revival of the Aristotelian ideal of knowledge for its own sake. Though the rise of the middle class had given new dignity to the education of the artisan and tradesman, the dignity of this education was still no match in an open choice between it and the traditional liberal education. Witness how little headway one so respected in England as John Locke (1632–1704) made by recommending in his *Thoughts concerning Education* that a gentleman's son should learn a trade as part of his education. The stereotype of the leisured class, whether this class was entered by the avenue of land or trade, was unwilling to compromise the social prestige it held over the middle class.

The school that was the most characteristic expression of this upper stratum of the middle class was the Humanistic school. Its curriculum was composed of the humanities, that is, the literary classics of Greece and Rome. It was this school, under the name of the Latin grammar school, that was imported from England into the American colonies. It did not, however, long satisfy Americans once their economy turned commercial as well as agrarian. Halfway through the eighteenth century, commercial interests inaugurated a new school, the academy, whose curriculum was more amenable to their demands. This curriculum included instruction in such middle-class activities as bookkeeping, surveying, and navigation. Indeed the original academy proposed by Benjamin Franklin, the personification of middle-class achievement, contained no studies whatever that were not utilitarian in character.

The full importance of the academy will not be appreciated unless it is realized that its middle-class sponsors were in a sense a revolutionary class. They were creating not only a new capitalistic economic structure but also correspondingly new cultural values, which were competing with traditional feudal ones. As it was Aristotle who had rationalized the educational privileges of the leisured class of his own and medieval feudal society, so it was Protestant religious reformers who undertook the rationalization of the economic position of the middle class. Vocation they interpreted in the literal etymological meaning of the word as a "calling."[10] The diversity of calling among men they ascribed to the fact that God had called men to different duties. Vocation therefore being the will of God, it behooved men to be content in their callings. Such contentment, especially where one was born to work rather than to the enjoyment of leisure, was to be gained by treating one's vocation as an ascetic discipline. If profits were an incidental outcome of this discipline, then a blessing accrued to this incipient middle-class capitalism. All this gave a dignity to the vocation of work of which it was sorely in need.

This middle-class viewpoint not only sponsored the academy in the American colonies but also penetrated American education generally in the nineteenth century. One of the great vehicles for spreading middle-class ideology was Noah Webster's famous speller. The selections of this book inculcated middle-class virtues at every opportunity. On the one hand, they taught calm acquiescence in one's calling, accompanying this with praise for the virtues of the middle-class worker. The virtues of patience, fortitude, and prudence would not be called into action, it was thought, without a measure of misfortune and insecurity. On the other hand, these selections also taught the more positive middle-class virtues that were so successful in launching bourgeois capitalism. Thus Webster's speller and readers encouraged the young in habits of hard, industrious work. Nor was much less emphasis laid on the habit of thrift. In addition, of course, the rewarding qualities of independence, enterprise, and self-reliance were not neglected.[11]

As for the class below the middle class, their humble economic

[10] Note the injunction of a catechism of the Anglican churches "to submit myself to all my governors, teachers, spiritual pastors and masters; to order myself lowly and reverently to all my betters . . . and to do my duty in that state of life to which it shall please God to call me."

[11] For a similar effect of the McGuffy readers, see R. D. Mosier, *Making the American Mind* (King's Crown Press, New York, 1947).

activities handicapped their educational ambitions for some time yet to come. Nor did they benefit from the rationalization of the middle-class position just mentioned. If anything, that rationalization immobilized them in their callings without much chance of escape. How little their economic condition justified educational pretensions is revealed by Bernard Mandeville. Writing in 1724, he declared, "In a free nation where slaves are not allowed of, the surest wealth consists in a Multitude of laborious poor; for besides that they are the never-failing nursery of fleets and armies, without them there could be no enjoyment and no product of any country could be valuable. To make the society happy and people easy under the meanest circumstances, it is requisite that great numbers of them should be ignorant as well as poor. Knowledge both enlarges and multiplies our desires, and the fewer things a man wishes for, the more easily his necessities may be supplied. . . . Reading, writing, and arithmetic are very necessary to those whose business requires such qualifications; but where people's livelihood has no dependence on these arts, they are very pernicious to the poor, who are forced to get their daily bread by their daily labor."[12]

Even some of the more liberal-minded looked with disfavor and alarm on any attempt by the lower classes to advance a rung up the social-economic ladder by using the school to escape from the occupation of their fathers and the stratum of society to which that committed them. The great French editor of the *Encyclopaedia*, Denis Diderot (1713–1784), for instance, favored the rigorous application of high scholastic standards "to temper the ambition of parents who are desirous of withdrawing their children from the subordinate occupations which they themselves follow, and of having them educated for the priesthood, medicine, or law. Nothing is more fatal to society than this disdain of parents for their own calling and these senseless migrations from one state in life to another."[13]

CHANGES IN EDUCATION DUE TO THE INDUSTRIAL REVOLUTION

The inroads that the middle class made in upper-class domination of formal education were increased by another revolution in the economy, the Industrial Revolution. In addition to confirming certain forces

[12] B. Mandeville, *An Essay on Charity and Charity Schools* (J. Johnson, London, 1724), p. 328.

[13] F. La Fontainerie, *French Liberalism and Education in the Eighteenth Century* (McGraw-Hill Book Company, New York, 1932), p. 300. To the same effect see a remark of Louis René de La Chalotais recorded in G. Compayré, *History of Pedagogy* (D. C. Heath and Company, Boston, 1885), p. 353.

released by the commercial revolution, the Industrial Revolution introduced innovations of its own. On the one hand, it accelerated the development of capitalism and the nineteenth-century ascendancy of middle-class ideals. On the other hand, it set in motion slow forces that attempted to shift the center of gravity from middle- to lower-class culture. But in both cases the shift from hand- to power-driven machine production so vastly multiplied economic surpluses that a redistribution of leisure and a reassessment of the significance of work as underlying conditions of education were demanded.

The immediate effect on education produced by the impact of industrialization gave no indication of the benefits that were later to accrue. In fact, at the outset industrialization worked genuine harm. Most directly, it upset the long-standing apprenticeship system of education. In the commercial economy an apprentice learned his trade under the personal supervision of his master, often in the master's own household. This supervision extended to habits of work and morals as well as to skills of production and trade. When these skills were mechanized and embodied in machines, the need for long periods of training was rendered unnecessary. Moreover, the relation between employer and employee became much more impersonal and limited in extent.

The instability caused by the disintegration of this long-standing educational pattern was increased by other effects of industrialization more or less directly related to education. Perhaps most notable here was child labor. Of course, there was nothing new about children working. What was disturbing, however, was having them work at such tender ages and for such extremely long hours as the new factories permitted or demanded. Such conditions endangered their health as well as deprived them of the broader training in moral habits that the apprenticeship characteristic of the commercial economy provided. This lack of moral training became a particularly distressing feature in the cities where the factories were located and where, of course, population became congested.

The deterioration produced by these conditions was slow at the end of the eighteenth century, but it quickly gained momentum in the early part of the nineteenth. Happily, positive and constructive forces soon began to counteract the worst results of the transition from a commercial to an industrial economy. The first of these was philanthropic. Humanitarian-minded people raised funds to sponsor charity schools for the neglected children whom the Industrial Revolution had disinherited of their meager educational patrimony. Prominent among such charitable agencies were the National Society and the Society for Promoting Christian Knowledge.[14] Notable among the schools these agencies promoted were the infant[15] and Sunday[16] schools.

Especially deserving of note here was the school that the enlightened Welsh industrialist Robert Owen (1771–1858) instituted in connection with his model mills at New Lanark. There Owen made ten the minimum age for employing children and provided a free school for those below that age. Being firmly convinced that children were the products of their environment, he furnished a school that had a playground as well as a light and airy schoolroom. In the school, pictures and objects of nature held places of importance along with the three R's. The great German critic of capitalism, Karl Marx, referred to this school in *Das Kapital* as providing the education of the future, "an education that will, in the case of every child over a given age, combine productive labor with instruction and gymnastics, not only as one of the methods of adding to the efficiency of production, but as the only method of producing fully developed human beings."[17]

Charity, however, was only a stopgap. By the second quarter of the nineteenth century the Industrial Revolution had released economic forces that demanded a fundamental reconstruction of the educational outlook. It raised up voices in the lower middle and lower classes that began to insist on education, not as a charity, but as a right. Philanthropically minded as were the humanitarians, there were many of them who never intended that the education proffered by their charity should break down economic class barriers. The philanthropy of the upper class was still as firmly rooted in a feudal *noblesse oblige* as that of the upper middle class was embedded in the paternalistic relation between master and apprentice.

The demand for education as a matter of right rather than as a matter of charity took the form of an appeal to the state to employ its power to tax to provide the enlarged educational opportunities

[14] W. O. B. Allen and E. McClure, *The History of the Society for Promoting Christian Knowledge, 1698–1898* (E. and S. B. Young & Company, New York, 1898). For similar efforts in America, see W. W. Kemp, *The Support of Schools in Colonial New York for the Propagation of the Gospel in Foreign Parts* (Bureau of Publications, Teachers College, Columbia University, New York, 1913); S. E. Weber, *The Charity School Movement in Colonial Pennsylvania* (George F. Lasher, Philadelphia, n.d.).

[15] For an account of the educational character of this school, see *infra*, pp. 368–369.

[16] For an account of the educational character of this school, see *infra*, p. 320.

[17] K. Marx, *Das Kapital* (George Allen & Unwin, Ltd., London, 1938), p. 489.

that were needed. The appeal was made at a time when in England and America state activity was dominated by the theory of *laissez faire*. Naturally, such a "do-nothing" policy favored the *nouveaux riches* of the Industrial Revolution, upon whom the proposed taxes would weigh quite heavily. The struggle for educational opportunities proportionate to conditions as altered by the Industrial Revolution thus settled down into a contest between the propertied and under-privileged but aspiring classes. Before the latter could win this contest, however, they had to win the preliminary contest of extending the franchise so that they could by the weight of their numbers command the state as their servant. As one can see, the problem was very complicated. It was a broad battle on many fronts.

The economic alignment of interests in America is informing. Urban interests, on which the impact of the Industrial Revolution had been felt most keenly, were very largely in favor of public schools. Rural areas, where the economy was still overwhelmingly agrarian, were not yet sensitive to changes produced by the factory system and opposed a change in governmental policy. Besides, the rural areas were largely propertied and thus stood to bear a substantial portion of the property tax to educate the children of factory workers, who were largely tenants. While for the most part the industrial upper middle class opposed the liberal educational legislation, some of the best leadership favoring the movement came from the old commercial upper middle class. Thus it is noteworthy that men like James G. Carter (1795–1849), Horace Mann (1796–1859), and Henry Barnard (1811–1900) came from families of this economic status.[18] In the end it was the fact that this group of men joined hands with the oncoming laboring classes that signally won the day for public education.[19]

In trying to win friends for the public school idea, Mann, in particular, addressed his argument in part to the economic advantage of such an institution. Although he considered economic value the faintest praise that could be bestowed upon education, he was not one to fail to mention it for what it was worth. After soliciting opinions from businessmen he declared in one of his later reports

[18] F. T. Carlton, *Economic Influences on Educational Progress in the United States, 1820–1850* (The University of Wisconsin Press, Madison, Wis., 1908), pp. 39–42. Apropos of the fact that it was members of this class who were leading in literary and philosophical as well as educational activities of the period, the author quotes the statement that "The commercial classes of New England robbed of their functions as a ruling class, while still retaining a sufficient wealth to maintain them, were dying out in a blaze of intellectual fireworks."

[19] For a fuller account of the democratization of education, see *supra*, pp. 42–52. For a fuller account of the development of public schools, see chap. 17.

that the returns "seemed to prove incontestably that education is not only a moral renovator, and a multiplier of intellectual power, but that it is also the most prolific parent of material riches. It has a right, therefore, not only to be included in the grand inventory of a nation's resources, but to be placed at the very head of that inventory."[20] In fact, Mann did so place it in accounting for New England's industrial supremacy at this time.

When the group friendly to public schools was able to make its voice heard, it pressed for the social legislation necessary to protect its interests. In addition to providing for free schools, it moved within the second half of the nineteenth century for compulsory-attendance and especially for child-labor laws. The apprenticeship system of the commercial economy having completely broken down, agitation was started for the introduction of commercial courses and vocational training in the schools. Besides state provision for vocational training, ultimately national support was obtained for the program in the Smith-Hughes Act of 1917. Beyond this a few states enacted legislation setting up continuation schools for those who wished to continue their schooling after they had embarked on regular employment.

In addition to these more obvious results, there were other educational evidences of a new economic group having been brought into prominence by the Industrial Revolution. A new middle-class school came into prominence in early-nineteenth-century America, the high school, which gradually displaced the academy. This upward extension of the elementary school was an excellent symbol of the upward reach of energetic and ambitious economic classes on the march. Often known as the "poor man's college," it was intended to have a terminal curriculum; that is, its curriculum was intended to cater to the life anticipations of its middle-class clientele without preparation for higher education.

This curriculum began also about the same time to reflect the Industrial Revolution by its increasing inclusion of science. Hitherto science had often been viewed as interesting knowledge. As such only, it waged an unequal and losing war with Humanistic literary studies for preference in the secondary school curriculum. But now that the revolution from *manu*-facture to *machino*-facture had so convincingly demonstrated the social significance of science, its inclusion and recognized status in the curriculum were definitely assured.

Science was catapulted into curriculum prominence not only by the Industrial Revolution but also by the old agrarian economy. The

[20] M. Mann, *Life and Works of Horace Mann* (Horace B. Fuller, Boston, 1868), vol. 3, p. 109. At the opening of the next century this economic argument was developed at considerable length in a government bulletin, *The Money Value of Education,* U.S. Bureau of Education Bulletin 22, 1917.

agrarian economy, oldest and always basic, was profoundly modified both by the introduction of machines into nearly all phases of farming and also by the light shed by science on soil chemistry and kindred technical subjects. Consequently, agricultural courses, even agricultural colleges and high schools, elevated the significance and dignity of the education of a class of workers who for centuries had held the humblest of positions.

DECLINE OF THE LEISURE-CLASS IDEAL OF EDUCATION

Great and genuine as the success of the middle class had been with the aid of the Industrial Revolution, its success in projecting its culture patterns into American education was not complete. The traditional aristocratic leisure-class ideal of education still held key points of the educational front. Most notably, it was entrenched in the liberal arts college. There a sturdy attempt was still being made in the nineteenth and twentieth centuries to maintain the superiority of cultural education, the education of the intellect for its own sake, over vocational education. The badge of this education, the bachelor of arts degree, had a definite prestige value over all other bachelor's degrees. Higher education in such fields as technology and teaching consequently suffered in comparison because of their more practical character. Moreover, from the citadel of the college, the cultural ideal of education tended to exercise a tyranny over the curricula of secondary schools. There the college preparatory course topped a hierarchy that tapered down to technical and commercial courses.

Yet even this citadel was being slowly besieged by middle-class forces. The clientele of the colleges was drawn almost exclusively from middle-class families. The middle class in America, however, was undergoing a transformation. The only landed gentry America ever had in significant numbers, the plantation owners of the South, had been ruined by the Civil War. Hence the middle class, whether of commercial or industrial origin, gained social domination more quickly and more firmly in this country than anywhere else. This domination once achieved, it tended to divide into upper and lower strata. The upper stratum, composed of the large capitalists, became whatever leisured upper class existed in the United States. But it is educationally significant that its class status rested on wealth rather than on blood or primogeniture.

Other forces favorable to middle-class interests were also undermining the leisure-class conception of liberal education. They were revealed chiefly in the curriculum. The Humanistic studies long thought to be of chief significance in the intellectual education of a directing and controlling upper class were beginning to lose their grip. Latin,

Greek, and mathematics instead of being pursued for their own sake were studied for purposes of formal mental discipline. The rise of an extracurriculum was a further eloquent protest that the traditional curriculum did not satisfy middle-class aspirations. Charles W. Eliot (1834–1926), president of Harvard University, endeavored to vitalize the curriculum by making it elective, but from an economic angle the elective principle will be seen to be an instance of the operation of the laissez-faire liberalism of middle-class capitalism. Under these circumstances it is not surprising that subjects tinged with vocationalism made ever-increasing inroads in liberal arts colleges from the Civil War onward.[21]

DOMINATION OF CAPITALISTIC
MIDDLE-CLASS EDUCATION

While the middle class was stabilizing its victory in superseding the landed aristocracy's dominance of education, it was beginning to be aware of a challenge to its domination by the newly aggressive lower class. As already noted, members of this neglected and long-suffering class were not noticeably benefited by the commercial revolution. The benefits of the Industrial Revolution, however, gave them the same advantages originally sought by the middle class. Thus along with the middle class they had gained universal suffrage and through it the public school, compulsory attendance, child-labor laws, and access to vocational education. Naturally, advantages such as these operated as a tonic on their long-dormant or suppressed ambitions.

Yet these advantages, great as they were, had the impress of the middle class upon them. They did not adequately express the longings of the lower class. Several pieces of evidence point to this conclusion. The high school, which started out to be a terminal institution for the ambitious in the working classes, was captured in the latter half of the nineteenth century by the families anxious to prepare their children for college. Sociological studies of the high school population in the twentieth century showed very clearly that it was the children of the middle classes who attended high school in the largest numbers and who remained there longest.[22] A similar study of what elements of the population predominated on boards of education of public schools as well as boards of trustees of colleges and universities indicated just as clearly that it was this same middle class which was

[21] Earl J. McGrath and Charles H. Russell, *Are Liberal Arts Colleges Becoming Professional Schools?* (Bureau of Publications, Teachers College, Columbia University, New York, 1958).

[22] G. S. Counts, *The Selective Character of American Secondary Education* (The University of Chicago Press, Chicago, 1922).

in control there.[23] Furthermore, the schools were middle class in spirit as well as in personnel. The aim of nearly every American schoolboy and schoolgirl to "get ahead" was the living embodiment of the free competitive principle of middle-class capitalism. The teachers of these children, as convoked in the National Education Association, repeatedly aligned themselves with the property interests and the profit motive of the middle class in an effort to combat the spread of socialism in the lower class of this country.[24]

Even vocational education, which had been introduced into the schools as a result of the Industrial Revolution, carried a class stamp. For the most part it was narrowly conceived. Frequently, trade education was given in a separate building and under a separate administration from cultural education. Also, employers often wished the vocational curriculum to consist of training for routine and automatic skills. Insufficient time was provided for the social and scientific studies that would have enabled children to understand the larger significance of their labor. In view of such a conception vocational guidance was little more than job placement. To summarize the situation in a sentence, vocational education aimed to fit children into the existing middle-class capitalistic system rather than to improve this system as but the current phase of the age-long struggle for human liberties.

ATTITUDES OF ORGANIZED LABOR TOWARD EDUCATION

These being the facts, it should occasion no surprise that the laboring classes sooner or later became aware that, advantageous as the public school had been to them, it still was not designed primarily to liberate and fulfill the potentialities resident in their workaday culture. At first these classes did not perceive that their educational interests were notably different from those of the middle class. Throughout practically the whole of the nineteenth century organized labor confined itself to sitting in judgment on the course of the rapidly growing public school system.

Prior to the Civil War labor was an ally, although not a very well-organized one, in support of the middle-class effort to gain free compulsory education. Between that war and the formation of the American Federation of Labor, the most notable workers' organization was the Knights of Labor. On the whole, this group represented

[23] G. S. Counts, *The Social Composition of Boards of Education* (The University of Chicago Press, Chicago, 1927); H. P. Beck, *Men Who Control Our Universities* (King's Crown Press, New York, 1947).

[24] M. Curti, *The Social Ideas of American Educators* (Charles Scribner's Sons, New York, 1935), p. 218.

largely the interests of the unskilled or semiskilled workers. From this it is easy to understand its major interest in the elementary school and its opposition to the high school "craze" of the period. This position stood in sharp contrast to the later one of the American Federation of Labor, which, with its skilled clientele, endorsed the high school and was also kindly disposed toward college education. The cardinal point of its educational policy was to insist on the unitary administration of cultural and vocational studies. The education of the worker and the citizen, the federation maintained, must go hand in hand under the same roof and under the same professional supervision.

This broad outline of policy shows how little labor had been able to differentiate its educational interests from the predominant middle-class interests till as late as the First World War. Perhaps there were reasons for this. For one thing, American labor did not suffer the unmitigated misery that European laboring classes did. All during the nineteenth century, free land on the frontier afforded an escape, a sort of safety valve, that eased the pressure of class consciousness. Besides, the social mobility provided by the frontier kept drawing off labor's most promising leaders. Moreover, not only did the leaders of labor move up the social ladder, but also the mass of labor tended to regard itself as middle class. Perhaps, too, labor failed to differentiate its peculiar educational requirements because it had too much confidence in what undifferentiated education could do.

On this point it is notable that the great publicist Horace Greeley warned the people of his day against thinking of education as a panacea for the laboring classes. His personal opinion was that economic reform would have to precede educational reform. A few labor leaders in the early nineteenth century also understood this point. In fact, they feared those who preached that there must be a period of education and preparation prior to the reform of franchise and property rights. They were afraid that this was but a ruse for diverting people from their major economic objective. How, they inquired, could a family ground down by poverty be in a position to take proper advantage of the benefits of education? Besides, in putting educational reform ahead of economic, there was danger that the laboring classes would be accepting the appearance of power for the real thing.

In the twentieth century labor began to have more significant misgivings on the extent to which the cultural interests of the laboring classes could be genuinely furthered without indigenous workers' education. Much as middle-class schools gave lip service to the dignity of labor, it was largely the administrative, supervisory, professional, and clerical types of work whose values were advanced in the schools. The manual occupations of factory and farm did not yet form the axiological core of the curriculum. While some wished to reconstruct the public school curriculum, the chief effort was expended in starting a variety of workers' schools to supplement the public school program, particularly at the levels of college and adult education.

PROLETARIAN REVOLUTION AND EDUCATION

Of course, workers' education was nothing novel, having already been considerably developed in England. But the English and American movements added together were only a straw in the wind. They were only a minor variation in school systems still dominated by the upper and middle classes. The first instance in the history of education of a national system of education dominated by the cultural interests of the lower classes or proletariat came with the Russian Revolution of 1917. Here for the first time was a government controlled by and in the interests of those who wielded the hammer and the sickle. The dignity of work was established by establishing the dignity of the working class. This the revolution achieved by abolishing the institution of private property, thus making impossible the exploitation of the working class by the *bourgeoisie* and upper classes, the customary owners of capital. Instead of the acquisitive society in which each competes for as much economic goods as he can acquire, the Communist society called on each to give according to his ability and receive according to his need. Obviously this meant a revolution in the motivation of human nature. Russians realized this and set about making, that is, educating, a "new Soviet man," a man who loved work and put social interests ahead of individual, personal ones.

Once the political and economic aspects of the revolution were stabilized, the schools were brought in line by a curriculum that centered in the interests of the working proletariat. This did not mean that all education was made vocational. Far from it. It rather meant that work, the main activity of the proletariat, was made the core of the curriculum. School, factory, and farm were always close together. Social, scientific, and aesthetic studies were not neglected but rather were taught so as to enlarge the significance of the life of the worker. Yet it was surprising how the actual labor demands of the various Five-Year Plans aborted early Communist idealism and how intellectual demands returned the schools to the conventional European standards, as seen in even Joseph Stalin's advice that students "study, study, study."[25]

While the most novel achievement of working-class education oc-

[25] William R. Frazer, "The Traditional and the Distinctive in Soviet Education," in Edmund J. King (ed.), *Communist Education* (The Bobbs-Merrill Company, Inc., Indianapolis, 1963), chap. 4.

curred in Russia, perhaps one must turn to America for the best rationalization of this point of view. Among educational philosophers none attacked more persistently the dualism between work and leisure than John Dewey (1859–1952), America's great philosopher of democracy. For him the dualism was false on two counts. In the first place, appropriate though the dualism might have been in a society composed of freemen and slaves, it was altogether an anachronism in one where all men were free. Our democratic industrial society necessitated a reconstruction of the notion of leisure, once the possession of a single class. Machine production increased economic surpluses to a point at which leisure could be brought within reach of all. Instead of one class having leisure in which to do the thinking and the other having only time to do the working, now everyone had significant work to do; everyone had leisure in which to recreate his energies for work or pursue an avocation. Indeed, the worthy use of leisure was one of the seven cardinal principles of education stated in 1918 by the National Education Association.

In the second place, Dewey rejected the dualism between work and leisure because it was based on a further outworn dualism, that between mind and body. Aristotle, it will be remembered, justified the dualism between the education of the leisured upper class and that of the working lower class because it corresponded to a psychological dualism he noted between reason and appetite, mind and body. Dewey rejected this dualism as contrary to the biological and psychological sciences of his day, which viewed mind and body as parts of a single continuum. Once this ancient dualism was refuted, the dualisms between leisure and work, thinking and doing, collapsed too. Thinking and doing went hand in hand; they were parts of a single educational process. Thinking was to direct doing, and the consequences of doing things in the physical and social environment operated as a check on the validity of the thinking. Thus education for doing work should enjoy an indivisible prestige and dignity with education for thinking.

Although his pragmatic philosophy of education had a definite labor orientation, Dewey did not accept the further Marxian conclusion that the viewpoint of labor could gain ascendancy only through seizure of power. To him the Marxian conception of class struggle would be just another instance of the unfortunate dualism between upper and lower classes. Moreover, to hold the conclusion that class struggle was inevitable indicated to him a want of faith in educative processes as a means of social amelioration. Instead of intensifying class antagonisms, Dewey, true to his conception of democracy, preferred to keep open the channels of communication between classes.[26]

[26] J. Dewey, "Class Struggle and the Democratic Way," *Social Frontier,* 2: 241–242, May, 1936.

5 Philosophy of Education

The problems of philosophy and the problems of education have long been closely interrelated. Sometimes educational innovations have been instituted without awareness of the philosophical problems involved. At other times new departures have been made in education under the deliberate guidance of philosophy. In either event, educational practice down the centuries has been persistently dogged by philosophical implications. Perhaps no century has been so aware of these implications as the twentieth. In the current century, in fact, philosophy, that mother of so many disciplines, has given birth to yet a new form of herself, the philosophy of education.

Since education is by nature a process of change, it has peculiar need of guideposts by which to direct its activities. For these guideposts it must go to philosophy. Because education is concerned with what man may become, it is particularly under obligation to inquire about its aims. What are good aims? More basic, what is the good? These problems belong to the subdivision of philosophy known as ethics. But how does man come to know the good, and when can man be sure that he knows? Moreover, what is knowledge, and how can the educator be sure that it is true? And what is truth? These are questions that must be asked of epistemology, another subdivision of philosophy. Coincident with these are problems of another sort. What is the nature of the world in which education takes place? Is it one of flux, or are there some stable elements by which education can take its bearings? Should man be educated only for this world or for a world to come as well?

What is the nature of the human nature to be educated? These questions as to the generic traits of existence or reality belong to that branch of philosophy known as metaphysics. No age has failed to raise one or more of the foregoing questions about the education of its day. In fact, it is these questions and others like them which constitute the perennial problems of the philosophy of education.

SOPHISM

In the folkway culture of people of remote antiquity there was probably little or no conscious philosophy of their educational processes. The main function of education was to conserve the past, to ensure against the loss of the race experience that gave what measure of security these people enjoyed against a precarious environment. If there was any implied assumption in this education, it probably was that whatever is, is right. Since the folkways, or mores, changed very slowly if at all in early times, it was very easy to conclude that whatever is, has always been. And, of course, if it has always been, it must be of the very nature of reality itself. In such a culture, the function of education is so clear and undeviating that there is little or no need for a conscious philosophy to direct the process.

Early Greek education was no exception to the foregoing, but commencing about the fifth century B.C. the Greeks began to devote more conscious attention to their educational problems. The underlying sociological conditions, which had earlier led to great rigidity in their folkways and customs, became subjected to stresses and strains that rendered the old ways of living unsatisfactory. The successful conclusion of the wars with Persia and the unprecedented economic prosperity of the time were perhaps the chief factors that led to social unrest and demanded new social adaptations. The more clearly people became aware that the old customs no longer fitted the new circumstances, the more acute the educational problem became. How should the young be taught when the old customs were no longer adequate and the new were too untried to receive general acceptance? Here indeed was a situation calling for the earnest and conscious attention of philosophy.

The Greek Sophists were perhaps the first to address themselves to the problems of educational theory created by the social unrest of their times. They particularly employed reason to criticize the traditional pattern of education, which was largely transmissive in character and sought to preserve the accepted social forms. Over against the uncritical transmission and perpetuation of custom, they early selected their curricula on rational grounds and in terms of the needs of the individuals they instructed. Instead of using social custom as a yardstick of their offerings, they made "man the measure of things." Having committed themselves to this famous cliché of Protagoras, many Sophists taught what they were paid to teach. Not only that, but in controversial matters they willingly taught either the affirmative or the negative side, depending upon who happened to engage them as teachers. As the individual was the measure of things, everything was relative to him.

The individualism and relativism of the Sophists were heartily disliked and condemned by the protagonists of the old order. Individualism and relativism, it was objected, ultimately led to skepticism. Willingness to teach either side of an issue for a fee not only cast doubt on the possibility of teaching stable moral principles but also opened the Sophists to the indictment of insincerity. Coming closer to educational theory, the protagonists of the old order tried to parry the cutting edge of Sophistic reasoning by seriously doubting that a man could be taught to have virtue or worth (Greek ἀρετή) through the rational methods of linguistics and dialectics employed by the Sophists. According to conservative tradition, the norm of virtue was set by the example of the aristocracy or nobility. Virtue was thus something inherited, not something taught. It was learned through an apprenticeship to action, to doing noble deeds, rather than through the exercise of reason or intelligence. Therefore the democratic endeavor of the Sophists to teach virtue to those not wellborn must fail.

The issue so drawn between the Sophists and the conservatives obviously was the educational overtone to a more basic political struggle occurring contemporaneously between aristocratic and democratic factions.[1] This close connection is important because it gave the educational problem a top-ranking priority in the minds of the best thinkers of the day. No less a one than Socrates (469–399 B.C.) paid considerable attention to its theoretic implications. This great philosopher and teacher, sprung from modest social origins, took the democratic view and sided with the Sophists in claiming that virtue was teachable. He arrived at this conclusion by first pointing out that no act deserved to be called good unless the action was undertaken with knowledge of the good aimed at. In other words, in order to do a good act, one must initially have knowledge or a theory of what the good is. But theoretical knowledge, it was generally admitted, could be taught. Therefore, to the extent that action depended on this sort of knowledge, virtue certainly could be taught. But would mere knowledge of virtue ensure virtuous conduct? Since Socrates held that no

[1] For a further account of this political phase, see *supra*, pp. 25–28.

one would wittingly do the wrong, it necessarily followed, in the language of the Socratic epigrams, "To know the right is to do it," and therefore "Knowledge is virtue."

PLATONISM

Plato (427–347 B.C.), pupil of Socrates, was not so confident of the possibility of teaching virtue. While early in his career he had defended the Socratic position, later, when he wrote the *Meno,* he seems to have rejected it. In that dialogue he found support for his rejection in the instances of boys growing into licentious young men in spite of the fact that they were reared under fathers of great probity or under teachers of known integrity. Similarly Plato rejected the notion that virtue was a function of nature, for he could point to too many fathers of great ability and rectitude whose sons turned out to be worthless or even scoundrels.[2] Having come to this impasse, the *Meno* ends unsatisfactorily, Plato suggesting that perhaps we shall have to think of virtue as a mysterious gift of the gods, at least till the nature of virtue is known more precisely.

Here, then, is the setting for Plato's greatest contribution to the philosophy of education, *The Republic.* In this book he undertook a synthesis of the opposing considerations for which he had no adequate answer in the *Meno.* To achieve this synthesis he gave his problem a much wider setting than formerly. Into it he drew the nature of man, the nature of society, and the nature of knowledge. If knowledge was virtue, as Socrates claimed, then Plato saw that he must inquire into the nature of knowledge as well as the nature of virtue. But even the nature of knowledge was larger than just the matter of how to balance learning as the acquisition of theoretic knowledge and learning as the habituation of instinct in any one individual. Knowledge had a social dimension as well. To what extent, for instance, should education be a matter of habituation to social tradition and to what extent a critical analysis of tradition by individual intelligence? To restate this question in terms of the controversy current in Plato's day, to what extent should the individual be the measure of things, as the Sophists contended, and to what extent the social group, as the conservatives maintained? Should education cultivate the expression of individual opinion, or should it aim to inculcate knowledge that is universal for all individuals? Should the curriculum

[2] For a discussion of teachers who had spectacular failures among their pupils, see G. Highet, *The Art of Teaching* (Alfred A. Knopf, Inc., New York, 1950), pp. 199–212.

be composed of a description of current conventions or of the abiding nature of reality?

To see how in his philosophy of education Plato reduced these diverse factors to a systematic, harmonious whole, it will be well to commence with his analysis of the nature of the individual, the educand. Under the heading of human nature Plato distinguished three components. The first was that of appetite. Here he referred to man's senses and his various bodily drives to action. The second component was spirit. Spirit referred to the human tendency toward self-assertiveness. It was the human function, or faculty, of will. Finally, the three components of human nature were completed by reason, or intelligence. It was the function of reason, of course, to comprehend and to direct. While appetite and spirit were classed as functions of the body, it is important to note that reason had no such affinity. Reason belonged to an entirely different category, for it traced its lineage to some state of preexistence in another world.

In addition to this description of the fundamental nature of the educand, Plato found it necessary to evaluate or attach a moral worth to each of the functions of human nature. The peculiar good, or virtue, of the appetites he set down as temperance, or self-control. Of spirit the unique good, or virtue, was courage, fortitude, or bravery. And of reason, it is almost superfluous to say, wisdom, or prudence, was the special virtue. Of course, this complexity of human nature required some principle of harmony, or integration. Otherwise, these functions, or virtues, might conflict with each other. Here Plato introduced the virtue of justice, the chief objective and quest of *The Republic*. To Plato—and to many generations that followed him—the components of human nature and their corresponding virtues were arranged in a just hierarchy when reason with the aid of spirit or will governed appetite.

Plato's analysis of society, the second dimension of his educational philosophy, was very similar to that of his analysis of the individual. As there were three facets to the nature of the individual or learner, so he recognized three classes of society—the artisan, warrior, and philosopher classes. The artisan, or lowest, class was composed of those who were largely governed by their appetites; the warrior, or intermediate, class, by those in whom spirit was dominant; and the philosopher, or highest, class, by those who showed unusual intellectual capacity. The peculiar virtue of each class was the same as the virtue associated with the kind of human nature characteristic of each class. Thus the virtue of the artisan class was temperance, of the warrior class bravery, and of the philosopher class wisdom. Furthermore, just as the virtue of justice was necessary to regulate and integrate the various functions of human nature, so, too, justice was the hierarchical principle that regulated and harmonized the three classes of society. In other words, a just society was one in which each individual was performing that function in that social class for which he was equipped by nature and doing it in such a way as to benefit the whole group. Naturally, such a society was one in which the philosopher class with the aid of the warrior class ruled the artisan class.

Now, how does the nature of the individual and society condition the nature of education? By the time he wrote his *Republic* Plato had resolved the problem of knowledge left by the *Meno* by stating that knowledge was a joint product of nature and education. Indeed, in his later *Laws* he made this conclusion quite specific by stating, "Now I mean by education that training which is given by suitable habits to the first instincts of virtue in children."[3] From this it follows that the proper education of each individual and each class in society was to train or exercise their peculiar instincts or functions in their appropriate virtues. Moreover, a just education was one by which each individual was educated in and for the class for which his native talents, *not* his family status, fitted him and by which within his class he learned to live a life in which appetite was controlled by reason.

It is of importance to note here the order in which children's instincts develop. According to Plato, the virtues associated with appetite and spirit were due at first to habit and not to the control of intelligence. This was because, while appetite and spirit were active in a child at birth, the rational component of his nature or soul was comparatively late in manifesting itself. Consequently, in the early stages of childhood pleasure and pain were the forms through which virtue and vice were presented to children. Only later on, when the child was more mature, did it become the chief object of education to awaken his rational capacity and to habituate it in its sovereign control over appetite and spirit.

A question of cardinal importance next arises: How is reason to obtain reliable and dependable knowledge by which to rule its subjects, spirit and appetite? Or where is the philosopher class to find the precise knowledge by which to govern justly the other two classes? Delving into this problem, Plato distinguished three levels of knowledge. At the lowest level was the knowledge derived from sense. The next level was that of opinion. Neither of these levels was very dependable. On the one hand, it was notorious among the ancient Greeks how easily a man could be betrayed by his senses. On the other, opinion had become so closely identified with the Sophistic

[3] Plato, *Laws,* sec. 653.

doctrine of "man the measure of things" that Socrates called opinion but a "half thought." It was on this account that Socrates initiated the use of dialectic (literally, talking things through) with as many as would engage in discourse with him. By seizing upon whatever germ of truth he found resident in individual opinions, he tried to arrive at the whole thoughts of which these opinions were but parts. This gave Plato the clue to his third level of knowledge—knowledge that did not vary with the passing phases of sense or opinion but that, on the contrary, was invariant and universal.

Knowledge such as this was the result of a further distinction made by Plato. The world of true reality, he asserted, is not the world presented to us through our senses. Our senses report only what is constantly undergoing change and therefore what only appears to be real. Behind the shadow world of appearance, according to Plato, lies the true world of unchanging reality. The element in our experience that never changes or alters is the ideal. By ideal Plato meant the idea or concept of a thing, whether that thing is a physical object like a child's toy or the quality of an action like goodness. In conceptualized form the ideal is not only unchanging but perfect.

Yet how are mere human beings with the limitations of their physical senses and their finite intellects to learn knowledge so ideally perfect and eternal? Meno, in the dialogue named after him, asked Socrates much this same question. How can knowledge be possible, he inquired, seeing that it is futile to learn what one already knows and equally futile to try to learn what one does not yet know since in that case one would not even know where to commence learning? To this question Plato put a famous answer in Socrates's mouth. Reason, or intellect, obtains such knowledge from a prior life of perfect existence. Yet though this is the source of a child's knowledge of ideas, his reason does not possess such ideas at birth. It seems that at birth, according to the Platonic fiction, the nature of the child is overtaken by a strange forgetfulness. Hence, after birth, learning at the rational level is a process of reminiscence, or recall.[4] Here, then, is the origin of Plato's famous doctrine of innate ideas.

The most outstanding instance of this sort of ideal knowledge is to be found in mathematics. Geometry may be taken as a case in point. There it appears as if one may have knowledge that does not originate in the senses. No one, for example, has ever seen or drawn a perfect circle. Yet everyone capable of mathematical thinking has a clear idea in his mind of what a perfect circle is. In fact, without that ideal in mind it seems doubtful that one could draw a circle or design a wheel in this imperfect shadow world of appearance. It is small wonder, therefore, that Plato thought of mathematics

---

[4] For the role of this theory in educational psychology, see *infra*, p. 138.

as being the single most important ingredient of the curriculum. It was the discipline par excellence and set the pattern for the study of such other ideals as truth, goodness, and beauty—justice being no exception.

Thus Plato rounded out his philosophy of education in an integrated whole or synthesis so harmonious that it leaves a definite aesthetic impression. Nature is harmonized with nurture, intellect with habit, opinion with knowledge, individual with society, the changing with the eternal, and appearance with reality. Yet, guide though his educational philosophy was to be to future centuries, it was incapable of reducing the volatile forces of his day to a stable equilibrium. It remained a utopia rather than a practical program of action.

ARISTOTELIANISM

It was Aristotle (384–322 B.C.), pupil of Plato, who carried Greek philosophy of education to the form in which it was best known during the Middle Ages and Renaissance. Although his writings that bore directly on the subject of education were not so extensive as his master's, Aristotle did make some notable advances beyond Plato. In many respects, however, his indebtedness to his teacher is quite obvious.

Like Socrates and Plato before him, Aristotle addressed himself to that persistent problem of Greek educational philosophy, the problem of how virtue is to be acquired. At the very outset it appears that Aristotle was not satisfied with the simple theory that knowledge is virtue. He conceded that arguments and theories might possibly be strong enough to inspire goodness in a character that is naturally noble, but for the mass of men he feared they were ineffective. Something more was needed. Instead of just one thing, knowledge, "There are," said Aristotle in the *Politics,* "three things which make men good and virtuous; these are nature, habit, and reason."[5]

First, as to nature, it is necessary to be a man. The implication is strong that there is no use in talking about educating the nonhuman in goodness and virtue. If it is the education of man with which we have to deal, then it is necessary to distinguish further characteristics of his nature or soul. To Aristotle the fundamental characteristic of the soul is activity, of which he distinguishes three levels. At the lowest and simplest level is the vegetative, where action is manifested in growth, reproduction, and decay. At the next or intermediate level is the animal, where, in addition to the vegetative, activity is further represented by sensation, appetite, and locomotion. Both these levels of activity are found in the soul of man just as definitely

[5] Aristotle, *Politics,* book VII, chap. 13.

as they are found at the vegetative and animal levels. But at the next level of activity, the level of reason, man has capacity for a kind of activity that differs not only in degree but in kind from the preceding two levels.

Second, as to habit, it was Aristotle's notion, like Plato's, that young children were akin to animals in the way in which their activity was motivated by appetite. In their early behavior he found no evidence of moral virtue arising out of their native endowment. On the contrary, virtue appeared to be a habit that had to be learned. Habit Aristotle described in definitely activistic terms. "For," said he, "the things we have to learn before we can do them, we learn by doing them."[6] Hence, the virtue to be learned through combining appetite and reason must wait till the maturing of the child's rational powers.

Third, as to reason, Aristotle found it necessary to distinguish two aspects, the practical and the theoretical. The former of these, the practical reason, functioned with the two lower levels of the activity of the soul. It helped to curb and give direction to the proper expression of the soul's appetitive activity. Morals and politics were the fields of its special endeavor. The latter, the theoretical reason, functioned as a pure activity on its own account. In this role reason was purely cognitive and engrossed in speculating on the nature of universal truth.

So far no mention has been made of the norm that the educator should have in mind for the various levels of activity, nor of the particular habits or virtues in which the activity of the soul should be disciplined. The norm on which Aristotle thought everyone agreed was happiness. This was to be gained by the practice of virtue, the norm of which Aristotle approached by first inquiring as to the unique function or excellence of the activity under consideration. In the case of man this has already been seen to be his activity of reason. He is not distinguished by such activities as growth or sentiency, for, as already noted, in such activities he is in no wise different from the vegetative and animal levels of life. But reason is something that he alone possesses. Hence man's unique excellence is his capacity for rational thought. Therefore the cultivation of the intellect is the chief virtue by which he achieves happiness.

At this point it is important to remember that Aristotle differentiated between practical and theoretical reason. The difference is important because the virtues of practical reason that the teacher should aim at are not the same as those of theoretical reason. The virtue of practical reason is moral and political, while that of theoretical reason is intellectual. In practical reason, the activity of reason operates

[6] Aristotle, *Nicomachean Ethics,* book II, chap. 1.

in conjunction with the activity of the appetites in such a way as to maintain a mean between the extremes of excessive and deficient activity. The virtue of courage affords a good illustration. An excess of courage would amount to foolhardiness, while a deficiency would constitute cowardice. And so it is with such other moral virtues as temperance, magnanimity, modesty, and righteousness.

In the case of theoretical reason, it will be remembered, the activity of reason functions purely on its own account. The aim of the activity of practical reason is in some moral or political product beyond itself, but the activity of theoretical reason has no end beyond itself. It is purely speculative. Indeed, Aristotle bestowed upon it the highest possible praise when he wrote, "The activity of God, which surpasses all others in blessedness, must be contemplative; and of human activities, therefore, that which is most akin to this must be most of the nature of happiness. . . . Happiness extends, then, just as far as contemplation does, and those to whom contemplation more fully belongs are more truly happy, not as a mere concomitant but in virtue of the contemplation; for this is in itself precious. Happiness, therefore, must be some form of contemplation."[7] The educational corollary of this conclusion, the cultivation of intellect and knowledge for their own sakes, has exerted a powerful influence on the philosophy of education in practically every century since Aristotle's death, the twentieth not excepted.

It would be a mistake to think that the norm of happiness, which was to be achieved through training and practice in the moral and intellectual virtues, was purely individual in Aristotle's mind. On the contrary, he held that happiness was the aim of education and the aim of the state as well. The good state, therefore, depended on being composed of good citizens. Good citizenship, however, was not a matter to be left to chance. Referring to a passage from Plato's *Laws,* Aristotle says, "We ought to have been brought up in a particular way from our very youth, as Plato says, so as both to delight in and to be pained by the things that we ought; for this is the right education."[8] Hence the state should take a positive interest in the education of its citizens. Education should be a branch of politics, and indeed it is in his *Politics* that Aristotle gives his most systematic presentation of educational theory. It is most regrettable that he did not finish this section of his book or that only fragments of it remain extant.

It will be remembered that the oughtness of "right education" in Plato's philosophy stemmed from his theory that perfect and unchanging archetypal ideas lay behind the phenomena of the everyday world.

[7] *Ibid.,* book X, chap. 8.
[8] *Ibid.,* book II, chap. 3.

Aristotle did not accept this sharp contrast between the apparent and the real and between the changing and the unchanging. In reconstructing this metaphysical conception, however, he did not disturb the idea that there was a right education; in fact, he accepted it and put it on so sound a basis that it was not seriously challenged till the nineteenth century.

Instead of assigning to abstract universal ideas an existence independent of the world of flux and appearance, Aristotle contended that the universal is always to be found in and connected with some particular instance of its manifestation. The abstract concept of man, for instance, is always to be associated with some particular man, and each particular man in some measure manifests the abstract universal. This seems to afford the basis for a common-sense synthesis of the individualistic conception of knowledge put forth by the Sophists and the idealistic conception of knowledge propounded by Plato.

In addition to laying this base for the resolution of the problem of the one and the many as it affected education, Aristotle offered a remarkably ingenious metaphysical theory to account for stability in the midst of change. The nucleus of this theory was the distinction between matter and form. To Aristotle, matter was formless and inert while form exhibited the principle of order, creativeness, or intelligence. The world, as we learn it, is the result of form operating on matter. Matter is constantly undergoing change as it takes on the various forms that are imposed upon it. To state this differently, there is a continuous process from potentiality (matter) to actuality (form). But while matter is always changing, form is constant. Take any growing species such as an oak tree for illustration. Its active nature gets under way with its germination in the acorn. It puts forth a shoot above the ground, grows into a sapling, and later matures into a full-grown oak. At this stage it reproduces itself in the form of other acorns, which, under the proper conditions of soil, temperature, and moisture, reenact the same cycle of growth. The matter, or substance, of the tree undergoes a number of changes, but the cycle, or pattern, of these changes remains the same from season to season. What is true of the oak species is true of other species as well, including the human. While Aristotle thus came to terms with the reality of change and becoming in a way that Plato never could, nevertheless he conceived of change as always occurring within immutably prescribed limits. The ultimate effect of his theory on education was much the same as the effect of Plato's theory. It caused educators to emphasize the formal aspects of learning and to set great store by those elements of the curriculum which were permanent and enduring.

THOMISM

The advent of Christianity was the next great force to require a restatement of educational philosophy. Although Christianity became a powerful moral and religious force during the Roman Empire, it was not till the end of the Middle Ages that a Christian philosopher turned his attention to its underlying theory of education. Fortunately for education the philosopher who did so at this time was none other than St. Thomas Aquinas (1225–1274), the Angelic Doctor. His educational philosophy, presented in *De magistro,* takes on all the more significance since he was also the author of the *Summa theologica,* the standard authoritative work on Catholic theology to the present day. Rather neglected in his day, St. Thomas Aquinas's *De magistro* became the accepted pattern of the Catholic or Scholastic philosophy of education in succeeding centuries, especially the twentieth.[9]

To begin again with the conception of the human nature to be educated, it is noteworthy that St. Thomas Aquinas held with Aristotle to the conception of the soul as an active principle. Hence education involved self-activity on the part of the learner.[10] St. Thomas Aquinas illustrated his meaning here by comparing the art of the teacher to the art of the doctor of medicine. The doctor cannot heal the sick in body, he pointed out; with his therapy he can merely aid the body to heal itself. The body has natural potentialities for maintaining an equilibrium of health, and it is these which the doctor stimulates. So too with teaching; to put it ungrammatically, the teacher cannot "learn" the child. The teacher can only help the child to exercise his own natural potentialities for learning. Education, far from being an imposition on the child from without, is rather a solicitation of the child to exert the potentialities that lie within himself.

[9] For example, see J. Maritain, *Education at the Crossroads* (Yale University Press, New Haven, Conn., 1943).

[10] In his editorial introduction to M. H. Mayer's *Philosophy of Teaching of St. Thomas Aquinas* (The Bruce Publishing Company, Milwaukee, 1929), pp. 4–24, E. A. Fitzpatrick calls this activity concept "progressive, evolutionary, and developmental." Furthermore, he thinks it anticipates John Dewey's emphasis on growth, self-activity, and experience. These remarks are probably overstatements. St. Thomas Aquinas's views are progressive, evolutionary, and developmental only in an Aristotelian sense, not in a Darwinian sense, as is the case with most progressive educators of the twentieth century. Similarly, St. Thomas Aquinas deals with growth, self-activity, and experience in an Aristotelian sense, too, and not the experimental sense employed by Dewey. For further exposition of these points see *supra,* pp. 19–20, and *infra,* pp. 130–134, 228–233.

While St. Thomas Aquinas clearly recognized that the child brings positive qualities to the educative process, he rejected the Platonic notion that these positive qualities consisted of innate ideas. He adopted neither the theory that learning was a recollection of these innate ideas nor the theory implied in medieval nominalism that ideas are but names for particular things, knowledge of which is primarily learned through the senses. Instead, he preferred to explain learning through the key distinction Aristotle made between matter and form, potentiality and actuality. If ideas were innate at birth, they would exist in actuality and would be merely awaiting the removal of an impediment to their seizure. St. Thomas Aquinas took the view that ideas, instead of existing in actuality, existed merely in potentiality and that therefore learning was an actualization of this potentiality.

The chief potentiality that the learner has is a capacity to form universal concepts. This potentiality, however, is effective only as it is developed in conjunction with some actual or particular object or species that is an instance or embodiment of the universal. When the senses report the object, its essence is stripped of accidental qualities and presented to the intellect. The intellect, then, by virtue of its inherent potentiality to conceptualize, makes the sensible concept over into an intelligible one. Thus learning as an actualization of the potential turns out to be a connecting of the universal and the particular, of relating form and matter.[11] As a matter of logic, learning is identifying objects and assigning them their proper classifications.

The process of conceptualization, St. Thomas Aquinas pointed out, is the same whether the pupil's senses were stimulated by physical objects in the environment or by the written or spoken word of the teacher. In both cases the intellect seizes upon the intelligible essence or meaning of what is presented through the senses. "Yet," St. Thomas Aquinas significantly added, "the words of the teacher have a closer relation to causing knowledge than have the mere perceivable things outside the mind, inasmuch as words are symbols of intelligible content."[12] No doubt he was on strong ground in asserting that conceptualization occurs more readily through the employ-

---

[11] St. Thomas Aquinas explained this further in *De magistro:* "Likewise, we must say about the acquisition of knowledge that there preexists in us certain potentialities of knowledge; namely, the first concepts of the intellect which are recognized immediately by the light of the active intellect through the species abstracted from sense impressions, whether the concepts be complex as axioms or simple as an idea of being, or unity, or something of this nature which the intellect grasps immediately. From these universal principles all principles follow as from germinal capacities. When, therefore, from these universal cognitions, the mind is led to know particular things in actuality which before were known potentially and, as it were, under the aspect of the universal, then one is said to acquire knowledge." (Quoted in Mayer, *op. cit.*, p. 51.)

[12] *Ibid.*, p. 15.

ment of words or symbols, themselves a sort of concept. But the perversion from which this doctrine suffered for many centuries of educational history was the almost exclusive emphasis placed upon verbalistic education through books.

So far only the influence of Aristotle is clearly discernible in the Scholastic philosophy of education. The Christian contribution has not been made apparent. This latter contribution is not so much found in *De magistro* as it is gathered from Scholastic or Catholic philosophy in general. The distinguishing feature of Christian teaching is its supernaturalism. For the most part Aristotle's conclusions were sound as far as unaided human reason was concerned. With the further aid of supernatural revelation, as entrusted to the Christian tradition, St. Thomas was able to recast philosophy in a form which has been so enduring that Scholastics often refer to it as the *philosophia perennis*.

With the aid of reason alone Aristotle had arrived at his famous distinction between matter and form. In his theory of causation he had reasoned even further to the conclusion that at the beginning of the world there must have been some pure form which determined the shape or order of all things to come. This pure form, or pure act as contrasted with potentiality, was identified with reason. We come upon the same thought in the Bible, when we read that "In the beginning was the Word, and the Word was with God, and the Word was God."[13] This statement is known as the doctrine of the *logos* (Greek λόγος; English "logic"). While "word" is undoubtedly the primary meaning of the Greek word *logos,* a freer and probably more appropriate translation in this text would have been "reason." Be that as it may, we probably have here in the first sentence of the Gospel according to St. John a most interesting early endeavor to make Christianity and Greek philosophy acceptable to each other. By this interpenetration of culture it becomes the revealed God of Christianity who is the Aristotelian pure form, pure act, the first cause uncaused, the creator and sustainer of all truth and goodness.

Placing God at the center of Christian philosophy had very definite educational consequences. For one thing, it made the Scholastic philosophy of education strictly authoritarian. Since Jesus "taught . . . as one having authority,"[14] in the same spirit the early and medieval church executed its Master's mandate, "Go ye therefore, and teach all nations . . . : Teaching them to observe all things whatsoever I have commanded you."[15] Not only was Scholastic teachings authoritative; it was often dogmatic as well. But it could well

---

[13] John 1:1.
[14] Matthew 7:29.
[15] Matthew 28:19–20.

afford to be so if the doctrine taught was predicated not only on right reason but on the unimpeachable authority of divine revelation.

For another thing, this supernatural philosophy of education was theocentric in its aims. These were of two sorts, ultimate and proximate. The ultimate aim of Christian education turned on man's ultimate end, or destiny. To find that out, one had to go back to his origin to inquire of man's Maker, God, for what purpose he had made him. According to the Christian tradition, God made man after his own image, to serve and love him and after death to enjoy eternal happiness with him. The proximate aims of education were more immediate in character, having to do with such matters as citizenship and vocation and, at a later day, health and nationalism. Although the proximate aims of Christian education were more generally taken up with the here and now, it should not be forgotten that they were always measured in the perspective of the ultimate theocentric objective.

In order to serve God one had to know and obey his moral law; one had to habituate himself in Christian virtues. Here again the influence of theocentricism is evident. The Scholastic philosophy of education noted two kinds of virtues, the natural and the supernatural. In respect to the natural virtues they took over the Aristotelian distinction between moral and intellectual virtues. In Aristotle's mind there was no doubt that education in the intellectual virtues was superior to education in the moral ones. Among the Scholastics, however, there was some difference of opinion on this point, a difference that has persisted into succeeding centuries. The Franciscans seem to have stressed the moral virtues, and the Dominicans the intellectual ones, while the great teaching order of the Jesuits took a middle position.

More distinctive of the Scholastic Christian philosophy of education was the addition of supernatural virtues as habits to be cultivated. The supernatural virtues are three in number—faith, hope, and charity. Faith is knowledge of God, hope a desire for God, and charity a love of God. The supernatural virtues, however, are not learned like the natural ones. Since there is no knowledge of God in the senses, learning cannot proceed as a coordinate effort of intellect and senses, as described earlier by Aquinas. Instead, the supernatural virtues are "infused" by sanctifying grace. Yet, though they are free gifts of God, their origin does not relieve the individual of the duty of constant effort at self-improvement.

Another thing to note as a distinctively new contribution made to the philosophy of education by Christianity is its conception of original sin. In the Sophist philosophy, which made the individual man the measure of what is educationally good, there was an essential hopefulness about the fundamental goodness of man's nature. In Christianity there was a sharp warning against any such optimism. The Judaeo-Christian tradition noted that at some time in the past—in the Garden of Eden, according to the Book of Genesis—man's nature, both human and supernatural, had been in complete order. Owing to the sin of his first ancestor, man fell from his former exalted condition and in doing so suffered a loss of his supernatural nature, his human nature, however, remaining intact. Consequently, instead of all his inclinations being orderly and praiseworthy, some of them are now disorderly and not to be depended on. This was felt to be particularly true of bodily inclinations as compared with those of the soul, a contrast that incorporated into the Christian philosophy of education the old Platonic dualism between appetitive and rational functions. Christian educational philosophy, therefore, tended to distrust educational procedures that were predicated on unreconstructed human nature alone.

Happily there was a brighter side to this picture. Man's nature, though fallen, was not wholly devoid of regenerative powers. It was redeemed through the grace of God and the example of the God-man Jesus. In educational terms this meant that by self-activity, as St. Thomas Aquinas described it, and by the aid of a divinely appointed teaching church, man could hope to repair the deficiencies in his original nature.

Moreover, this hope was held out to *all* mankind. This final fact is of stupendous significance for all future philosophy of education. While Greek educational philosophy had had a high regard for the worth of the individual, this regard was circumscribed in application. It included only Greeks and at that only Greek males who were freemen. The worth and dignity that the Greeks attached to only a few Christianity extended to all. In Christianity all persons, whether Greek or barbarian, slave or free, black or white, male or female, were children of God and, because children of God, of infinite worth.

The Aristotelian-Thomistic synthesis was so inclusive and so closely reasoned that it stood for many centuries. Indeed, it still stands as the *philosophia perennis* of the Catholic Church. During the Renaissance it was the underlying philosophy of Humanistic education. The Renaissance, it will be remembered, was a rebirth of secular interests after the long preoccupation with religious matters during the Middle Ages. From an absorbing concern in God and angels, full attention was turned on man and human interests. "By the *nature* of man we mean, as a rule," said the great Humanist Desiderius Erasmus (1466–1536), in his treatise on education, *De pueris instituendis,* "that which is common to Man as such: the characteristic, namely, of being guided by Reason."[16] What could be more Aristotelian than this emphasis on intellectual education? And, to remember St. Thomas Aquinas's preference for education through the symbols of written and oral speech, what better authority than St. Thomas Aquinas for a Humanistic education that concentrated so heavily and almost exclusively on literary classics as did that of the Renaissance.

PROTESTANTISM

Yet, in spite of its prestige, the Aristotelian-Thomistic synthesis did not go unchallenged. It was consistently pursued by the irrepressible nominalism of the Middle Ages. Doubts were continually raised as to whether or not Aristotelian-Thomistic philosophy emphasized the supernatural at the expense of the natural, the universal, or whole, at the expense of the individual, or accidental, and intellect and verbalization at the expense of sense experience. The philosophies of education that arose to compete with those of St. Thomas Aquinas and Aristotle during the Protestant Reformation and after tended to give nominalistic answers to these doubts, that is, to give greater emphasis to the natural, to the individual, and to the sensory in their educational viewpoints.

The first shift away from the Aristotelian-Thomistic synthesis as a basis for Christian educational theory was made by Protestantism. The nominalistic feature of Protestantism was the importance it attached to the individual. Whereas in the Greek and medieval systems of philosophy the individual had been but the channel through which the universal or reason expressed itself, under Protestantism the individual became an independent agent free to acquire knowledge for himself. Formerly, also, it was thought conceit and unseemly pride—at worst, of course, heresy—for the individual to depend upon his own judgment as against the collective authority of the ecclesiastical hierarchy. During the Protestant Reformation, however, independent thinking on the part of the individual was encouraged as the cutting edge of ecclesiastical reform.

It is surprising, however, how little this spirit of Protestantism affected educational theory in Protestant schools during the Reformation and for a long time thereafter. Instead of looking to education to release individuality as the instrument for renewing the spirit of continuous reform in each succeeding generation, Protestantism apparently became frightened by the uncertainties that might be released.

[16] W. H. Woodward, *Erasmus concerning Education* (Cambridge University Press, London, 1904), p. 195.

Even Martin Luther (1483–1546), who had successfully broken with the authority of the Catholic Church, found it necessary to appeal to some authority to settle disputes with those who would break with him. Instead of a divinely appointed teaching church he set up the Bible as the ultimate authority on what God demands of individuals. Although presumably the individual was still free to interpret the Book, it is notorious how as a matter of fact, not only *the* Book, but textbooks in general came to enslave the minds of children. So it was that Protestantism, whatever its religious and political effects, made no immediate or indigenous innovations in educational philosophy. Except for a slight shift in emphasis, the philosophy underlying Protestant education was as authoritative as the Aristotelian-Thomistic philosophy.

Similarly, Protestant Christian education accepted with modification the main tenets of the Thomistic conception of the fallen nature of man. The most notable alteration in this doctrine was that made by John Calvin (1509–1564). He reasoned that man's nature is not only originally corrupt but utterly corrupt. Only God's omnipotence can save man; and since God is also omniscient, it must already be known to him—hence foreordained—who is to be saved. Those who are saved enhance his mercy; those who are damned enhance his justice; both alike enhance his glory. This depressing doctrine of Calvin's occupied a very prominent place in the thinking of the Puritans who settled in America. It is small wonder, therefore, that the educational theory undergirding early colonial schools in New England viewed children as "limbs of Satan" and hence sought to inhibit many of their natural appetites and interests as inclinations toward evil.

In other respects Protestantism seems to have taken over the Aristotelian-Thomistic view of education quite completely. It took its ultimate aim of education from man's immortal destiny. The proximate ends of both Lutheran and Calvinistic education were vocational and civic. Perhaps, if anything, Protestantism was a little quicker than its Catholic parent in making explicit the educational implications of the Christian doctrine of the fatherhood of God, for it insisted on schooling for all children. John Knox (1505–1572), the great leader of Calvinism in Scotland, even laid down the ethical injunction that "No father of what state or condition whatever he may be, may use his children at his own fantasy, especially in their youth, but all must be compelled to bring up their children in learning and virtue."[17]

[17] Quoted in P. Monroe, *Founding of the American Public School System* (The Macmillan Company, New York, 1940), p. 24.

NATURALISM

The second and more fundamental shift away from the Aristotelian-Thomistic basis for educational philosophy was that engendered by the growing naturalism of the seventeenth and eighteenth centuries. The spearhead of naturalism was the new and rapidly expanding interest in science. The scientific interest was considered nominalistic and a trend away from the Aristotelian-Thomistic world frame, for it leaned heavily on the knowledge reported by man's senses. This departure was the more radical in that in these centuries accumulating scientific evidence was seriously contradicting much that had previously been regarded as authoritatively established about the world.

To be sure, Aristotle and St. Thomas Aquinas had reserved an important role for the senses in learning, but unfortunately the senses were hobbled by certain predilections and preconceptions. For one thing, the medieval mind had a predilection for such immaterial and therefore insensible concerns as a knowledge of God. Likewise, the Humanism of the Renaissance had a predilection for man rather than nature. For another thing, the Aristotelian-Thomistic method centered in an inquiry into the purpose or form of a thing and an assignment of it to a place in a preconceived hierarchy leading to pure form. The startling thing that the new sensory data of science revealed was that relations in the world of nature did not as a matter of fact square with ancient preconceptions. The planets, for instance, instead of revolving in perfect circles, as the preconception of a God of pure and perfect form demanded, moved in elliptical orbits. Obviously there was need for a new world frame to synthesize the novel data. This need was heralded by the publication of Francis Bacon's *Advancement of Learning* and *Novum Organum*. It was only gradually and through numerous writers, however, that the dimensions of this new world frame became evident in their bearings on educational philosophy.

The first dimension to be established in the new naturalistic philosophy of education was the importance of conducting education in accordance with nature. Earliest to give extension theoretical consideration to this orientation was Johann Amos Comenius (1592–1670), the great Moravian educator. As a Protestant clergyman he entertained the conventional Christian conviction as to the fallen nature of man. Yet he did not, on this account, hold nature in low esteem, as was usual in most Protestant and Catholic thinking. On the contrary, in his most renowned educational work, *Didactica magna,* he declared, "If we wish to find a remedy for the defects of nature, it is in nature herself that we must look for it, since it is certain that art can do nothing unless it imitate nature."[18] Like his predecessor Wolfgang Ratke (1571–1635), therefore, Comenius sought an educational procedure that, instead of doing violence to natural processes, cooperated with them.

SENSE REALISM AND EMPIRICISM

The second dimension of the naturalistic philosophy of education elaborated by Comenius was an emphasis on learning through the senses. It is they that are the clue to the natural method of learning. In contrast to the highly verbalistic education of seventeenth-century Humanism both Comenius and Ratke emphasized the importance of sense experience of things. First the thing and then its exposition was Ratke's advice to teachers, while Comenius urged that thing and symbol should accompany each other. Comenius drove the point home most effectively in his famous textbook, *Orbis pictus*. Here, capitalizing on the sense of sight, he wrote the first text utilizing pictures.

In spite of the advance that Comenius represented in educational theory, he was far from stating an experimental philosophy of education. The scope of his educational outlook included much more than teaching a knowledge of natural phenomena through sense impressions. He wanted to teach all knowledge, and his plan for doing so has been called "pansophism." Integrated in this plan was much that was still Scholastic in character. According to Comenius, a true knowledge of things could only be had by understanding how they came into existence. Each thing, he held, came into existence according to its "idea." In nature these things differed in their accidental manifestations. Nature was thus an ectype of God, who was the archetypal idea. Unlike many later scientists, Comenius still had hopes of knowing the ultimate nature, or quiddity, of things.

Further theoretical support for educational emphasis on the senses was received from Pietism. Pietism in Germany—Methodism in England—was a reaction from rationalism in religion toward religion as a vital inner experience or light. This validation of religion by an inner sense of faith found outward educational expression in a learning process also validated in sense experience. The chief leader in this Pietistic educational development was August Hermann Francke (1663–1727), and the chief educational embodiment the *Realschule*

[18] M. W. Keatinge, *Comenius* (McGraw-Hill Book Company, New York, 1931), p. 52.

(*Realien,* German for "real things" or science) inaugurated by one of Francke's pupils and later to become the leading German school with a mainly scientific curriculum.

The sense dimension of the new naturalistic philosophy of education was given still further definition and grounding in the empiricism of John Locke (1632–1704). Locke seems to have been the most notable philosopher-educator to try to clear up common misunderstandings by concentrating not on an explication of what knowledge is about but on an analysis of how human knowledge is learned. In his *Essay concerning Human Understanding* Locke proposed the theory that all knowledge in the mind derives from the observation of the facts of sense experience. Positing that the mind is like a *tabula rasa,* or blank tablet, at birth, he described learning as the impressions made thereon by report from the senses. The rigor of this psychological doctrine he mitigated only slightly by conceding that the mind has a faculty for discriminating, comparing, and generalizing its sense impressions. In spite of this concession, there can be no doubt that this empiricism was a powerful prop for the naturalistic philosophy of education which was in the making.[19]

If Locke's analysis of the structure of human understanding was right, it marked the definite end of certain long-standing educational presuppositions. Principally, it put an end to any lingering forms of the Platonic notion that man was born with innate ideas. Ideas about God, the sense of right and wrong, logical propositions like the principle of contradiction, and mathematical axioms, which hitherto had been thought to be self-evident and unlearned, were claimed by Locke to be learned through the senses. Proof of his claim he found in the observed fact that they were not always self-evident to people of every period or every locality. Indeed, Locke went so far as to attack the Christian notion of the corruptness of human nature, contending that children were good or evil according to their education.

While Locke's empirical theory of knowledge was implicitly the one that science had been employing to explore the world of nature, its educational application was much more passive. Instead of utilizing the senses as the adventurous scouts of a contriving mind, as did the scientists, educators employed them for more purely cognitive purposes. Mind, too, was treated cognitively by educators and largely made into a registry of sense impressions. Learning became receptive rather than active. At best, activity was but a tag end to provide drill or to complete forms already outlined.

[19] For a fuller psychological treatment, see *infra,* pp. 143–145.

RATIONALISM

A third dimension of the naturalistic philosophy of education is to be found in the new and preeminent importance assigned to reason and its naturalization in the eighteenth century. In spite of the new physical world that the senses revealed to science, it became no less evident that the senses were not wholly or invariably reliable. Had not Nicolaus Copernicus, for instance, shown that our senses deceive us when we think that the sun revolves about the earth? And had he not by a gigantic effort of reason based on painstaking observation come to the opposite conclusion, namely, that the earth revolves around the sun, and this against all authoritative statement to the contrary? It was reason again that enabled René Descartes and especially Sir Isaac Newton to go further than Copernicus and replace the Aristotelian hierarchy of essences with mathematical formulas that described the physical relations of the universe with a uniformity and simplicity that has won the admiration of history.

The marvels performed by reason on the new data afforded by the senses led in the eighteenth century to what has been called the "age of reason." What is novel and significant about this age of reason is the overwhelming confidence that it engendered in human reason unaided by the authority of the classics or by Christian revelation. The ability of man to stand independently, on his own reason, led to a new conception of him. Hitherto a concoction of the physical and spiritual worlds, he was now for the first time considered a product of nature alone. Search was instituted for the natural laws of his behavior. Man being a creature of nature, it was thought he must be governed by uniform laws, like any other aspect of nature. Far from depreciating his worth, this new inclusion of man in nature actually enhanced his dignity in a manner quite different from the Christian tradition.

More than any other, it was the great Swiss educator Johann Heinrich Pestalozzi (1746–1827) who was first successful in predicating educational theory and practice on an observation of what he took to be the uniform laws of human nature. While his approach to education was probably scientific—and we have Herbart's word for it that Pestalozzi did not intend to introduce the ideas of critical philosophers into his conclusions—there is no doubt that his implicit theory was naturalistic. Thus, he had a conception that the course of nature is undeviating, wherefore there could be but *one* sound pedagogical method. Furthermore, in his writings he frequently used such phrases as "psychological necessity," "the mechanism of human nature," and "the mechanical form of all instruction." These phrases, together with his own "object" method of instruction, show the extent to which Pestalozzi was trying to bring education into harmony with the scientific naturalism of his day.

The effect of rationalism was also evident in the social theory of education. This is clearest in the thinking of Claude Adrien Helvétius (1715–1771), the French philosopher. If man is governed by natural laws, then their discovery will enable him to direct his education toward progressively improving social conditions. Helvétius thought he had the main law for this improvement in Locke's empiricism. Indeed, he went further than Locke and claimed that nothing is in the mind, not even such powers as comparison and generalization, save as it is introduced through the senses. From this it was but a step to the further conclusion that man is nothing but the product of his education.[20] Inequalities among men are due, therefore, not to any Aristotelian hierarchy of social class or to divine ordinance but to unjust laws and inequalities of educational opportunity. Thus, in one bold leap of the imagination, social institutions, too, are seen to be subject to the critical methods of rationalism and empiricism. Henceforward, institutions are to be judged rationally by their effect on man rather than by authority and superstition. In order to ensure the maximum educational development of man, social institutions must be kept flexible and progressive.

Yet what was the naturalist's norm of educational progress? Unlike the immutable aim of the Aristotelian-Thomistic philosophy, the French revolutionary the Marquis de Condorcet (1743–1794) hazarded a belief in the "indefinite perfectibility" of man. In other words, as far as one could see, progress had no end save further progress. Does this mean that the naturalistic philosophy of education took no account of religion? No, but the religion of naturalism was deism, the religion of reason. In deism, God is not so much transcendent as immanent in nature and responsible for the harmonious and orderly laws that according to Newton's mathematics nature observers. It was upon some such ultimate ground as this that the American educator Horace Mann (1796–1859) rested his belief in public education

---

[20] Ian Cumming, *Helvetius* (Routledge & Kegan Paul, Ltd., London, 1955), p. 176. The Welsh industrial philanthropist Robert Owen (1771–1858) is reported by John Griscom to have entertained a similar view in the school he established for the children of his factory workers. "All you have to do, therefore, is to surround him [man] with circumstances exactly adapted to the dispositions and habits he ought to possess, and he would become just what he should be. His evil propensities would be either entirely suppressed, or they would be rendered harmless, by the irresistible weight of the good example around him." E. W. Knight, *Reports on European Education* (McGraw-Hill Book Company, New York, 1931), p. 104.

when he declared himself confident that the right of every child to education is a principle of natural law "clearly legible in the ways of Providence as these are manifested in the order of nature."[21]

ROMANTICISM

The last dimension in the naturalistic philosophy of education, romanticism, was in many ways the most important of all. Certainly it was the one that probably most strongly influenced the succeeding nineteenth and twentieth centuries. Romanticism was a reaction to an excess of rationalism in the age of reason. Autonomous as reason had appeared in disclosing the new world of science and in attacking old social abuses, nevertheless it became evident that its emphasis was one-sided. Man does not live by dispassionate science alone. Moreover, Newtonian as nature may be, nature is more than mathematical relations. In addition to reason man has feelings, which are just as much a part of nature as reason is.

It was Rousseau's *Émile* that popularized this aspect of naturalism in educational philosophy. Himself a man of intense feeling and emotion, Jean Jacques Rousseau (1712–1778) laid his main emphasis on the voluntary impulses of children. The three main influences on education, he maintained, are nature, men, and things. Of the three, men and things can be consciously controlled, while nature is an independent datum, or given. Therefore, nature is the controlling consideration to which the other two influences must be subordinate for a complete education. "The spontaneous development of our organs and faculties constitutes the education of nature," said Rousseau.[22] Nature must have free play; it must be uninhibited.[23] Not only are native sentiment and impulse the point of departure for educational theory and practice; they are also the norm. Rousseau definitely broke with what had hitherto been Christian educational philosophy in affirming that child nature is fundamentally good, not

[21] M. Mann, *Life and Works of Horace Mann* (Horace B. Fuller, Boston, 1868), vol. 3, p. 533.

[22] R. L. Archer, *Rousseau on Education* [Edward Arnold (Publishers) Ltd., London, 1912], p. 56.

[23] In a remarkable passage Martin Luther seems to have had some insight into this matter. "Now since the young must leap and jump, or have something to do, because they have a natural desire for it which should not be restrained (for it is not well to check them in everything), why should we not provide for them such schools, and lay before them such studies? By the gracious arrangement of God, children take delight in acquiring knowledge." [F. V. N. Painter, *Luther on Education* (Lutheran Publication Society, Philadelphia, 1889), p. 198.]

fallen. "Everything is good," he wrote in *Émile,* "as it comes from the hands of the author of nature."[24]

The romantic naturalism of Rousseau's educational theory will perhaps stand out more clearly if it is distinguished from some of its forerunners. One must be careful, for instance, to distinguish what is novel in Rousseau's emphasis on education through such organs of nature as the senses. On this point he was preceded by Comenius and Locke. While Rousseau in his turn emphasized the importance of the senses for cognitive learning, however, he went further and stressed their sensuous enjoyments, too. Knowing the tingle of his own senses so well, he insisted that education capitalize on this vital motivating force. The prominence of motivation or interest in all subsequent educational philosophy owes much to this romantic origin.

Again, there is nothing entirely novel in Rousseau's emphasis on the instinctive activity of the child. Aristotle had already made activity the distinctive characteristic of the soul, and St. Thomas Aquinas had even declared that learning is fundamentally self-active and self-assertive. What shows the importance Rousseau attached to self-activity was his unwillingness to interfere with its spontaneous expression. In the Aristotelian-Thomistic philosophy of education, self-activity was bridled by good habits or virtues. Rousseau, on the contrary, recommended the habit of having no habits. He was distrustful of the artificiality of human conventions. While, as he said, "everything is good as it comes from the hands of the author of nature," he also added, "everything degenerates in the hands of man."[25]

Consequently Rousseau's romanticism led him to what many have thought an antisocial theory of education. Depreciating the education of man the citizen governed by artificial or degenerate conventions, he tended to idealize the education of man in a pure state of nature. Hence the romantic reverence for the noble savage as an educational norm. Hence, too, the idealization of education in a rural rather than an urban environment. Yet it would be a grave misreading of *Émile* to think that Rousseau did not contemplate Émile's entrance into social relationships. As a matter of fact, he gave much space to it even if he did not finally and completely resolve the question of how man's natural spontaneity is to be preserved where it conflicts with a similar spontaneity in others.

IDEALISM

So far in the history of educational philosophy there had been little or no doubt in the minds of men from Socrates to Rousseau that the learner could come to know the world as it really exists.

[24] Archer, *op. cit.,* p. 55.
[25] *Ibid.*

To be sure, there were differences of opinion among educational philosophers as to the nature of the world and the way in which the learner acquires knowledge. Yet there was no doubt that, with persistence and refinement of effort, accurate knowledge of reality could be acquired. This happy confidence was severely shaken toward the end of the eighteenth century.

Oddly enough, the trouble began with Locke. Relentlessly pursuing Locke's empiricism to its logical conclusion, the Scottish philosopher David Hume (1711–1776) refused to accept as valid any knowledge for which he could find no antecedent sense impression. By turning this criterion on such a common notion of everyday life as causation, for example, he showed that the only perceptible relation between cause and effect was priority in time and contiguity in space. Cause and effect were not an observed event but an inference based on custom. The transformation of the power or agency of cause into mere temporal antecedency and spatial proximity was so contrary to notions of common sense that many came to be seriously skeptical over the possibility of acquiring accurate knowledge of reality.

The skepticism of Hume aroused the German philosopher Immanuel Kant (1724–1804) to a line of reasoning that not only stirred up the so-called "Copernican revolution" in philosophy but also profoundly influenced educational philosophy in the nineteenth and early twentieth centuries. Conceding the cogency of Hume's logic, Kant admitted the impossibility of learning to know objective reality as it really is—*das Ding an sich*. Nevertheless, he set about the task of giving a defensible account of common-sense notions about the world, which had been so seriously undermined by Hume. Here he came to the startling and revolutionary conclusion that phenomena like causation, time, and space are a priori categories of the mind. The mind is so constituted that it can understand the world only in terms of these categories. Traits hitherto thought to belong to objective reality were now seen to belong to the human mind. Instead of mind conforming to objective reality in the learning process, reality or the world was assimilated to the mind. In short, the mind imposed its subjective categories upon the world.

This reorientation of epistemology, or the theory of knowledge, had extensive effects upon educational philosophy. Most notably, it required a reconstruction of the spectator theory of mind and education. Since the assumption up to this point had been that reality could be known, most philosophies had treated the mind of the learner more or less like an intricate photographic process. Its function was to make a copy of reality. All this would have to be changed if the Kantian analysis was sound. Instead of copying the world, each learning mind would now have to build from within itself its own idea of the world. Hence this educational philosophy has been known as "idea-ism," or idealism, the *l* being introduced for euphony.[26] Its emphasis on the inner state of mind or feeling of the individual bore an obvious resemblance to romanticism.

The greatest development of idealism in educational philosophy took place in Germany. Several sorts are to be noted, each varying with its author's inner sense of what was most real and important. The central theme of Kant's lectures on education was moral. This is definitely in line with his general philosophic writings. Children should be trained to act not as they want but as they ought. The sense of oughtness, Kant held, is the product not of experience but of the a priori structure of the will. Although this will has a native inclination toward righteousness, it is impeded in realizing itself by more immediate desires. Education, therefore, is a phase of aiding or training the righteous will to realize itself.

It is not enough, however, to have a good will; the will must also be given some clue as to the direction in which it may hope to realize itself. This Kant laid down in a practical imperative. "So act," he enjoined, "as to treat humanity, whether in thine own person or in that of any other, in every case as an end withal, never as a means only."[27] The statement is novel, but the ethic, of course, is at least as old as Christianity, if not older. It deserves added mention here because it became the essence of the later phrase "respect for personality" in democratic educational philosophy.

Kantian idealism was further developed in the philosophy of Georg Wilhelm Friedrich Hegel (1770–1831). Like Kant, Hegel gave relatively scant direct attention to educational philosophy. The broad outlines of his position, which Karl Rosenkranz[28] (1805–1879) later elaborated in detail, however, are easily to be seen in his passing remarks on education as they are embedded in a more general philosophical context. Hegel objected to predicating the phenomena of experience on some thing—like the Kantian unknowable *Ding an sich*—that lay behind experience. To him a mind was predicated on nothing save its own experiencing or thinking. The process of thought was itself the basic reality; nothing lay behind it, beyond it, or outside it. Absolute Mind, Idea, or Spirit was continually evolving in self-consciousness of the plan its own development set forth. This development was objectified in nature and, even more important for education, in social institutions. Indeed, the history of social institutions was no more than successive stages of the Absolute realizing

[26] Kantian idealism in educational philosophy should not be confused with Platonic idealism. The base for Platonic idealism was more metaphysical, while that for Kantian idealism was more epistemological.

[27] I. Kant, *Metaphysics of Morals*, part I, book II, chap. 1, sec. 25.

[28] K. Rosenkranz, *Pedagogics as a System* (R. P. Studley Co., St. Louis, 1872).

itself. The child mind achieved self-realization by participation in social institutions, that is, by participating in the Absolute Mind realizing itself. Yet, in spite of his great emphasis on process, Hegel did not conceive that man's self-realization stretched on indefinitely into the future, as did Condorcet. More like Aristotle, he allowed only latitude for creative self-realization within the limits of an already complete and self-realized Absolute.[29]

It is in analyzing the process of self-realization that one can best see the educational bearing of the foregoing, for, to the Hegelian idealist, education is essentially a process of self-realization. The dynamics of self-realization consist basically in a dialectical process of reconciling opposites. Educationally one commences with the thesis that the child begins his life in bondage to nature. He is a creature of subjective sense, feeling, and impulse. The opposite, or antithesis, of a life in bondage to nature is the free life of objective mind or spirit. To reconcile or achieve a synthesis of these opposites, "self-estrangement" is necessary. Self-estrangement is a break the child makes during adolescence from the whim of feeling and impulse. He comes to realize the inadequacy of all experience that is merely individual. Consequently, he begins to reach out for that which is universal in the life of imagination and thought. Indeed, obedience to the universal, to the Absolute, is the beginning of wisdom according to Hegel. The school is of preeminent importance as the social agency through which the universal is brought within reach. And in the school the universal is most accessible in the literatures of Greece and Rome. Subordination of the self in reverence for the spiritual accomplishments of the past does not thwart but frees the self in the course of its realization. After this pilgrimage in self-estrangement, the youth returns to himself enriched with the spoils of culture and filled out at the points that formerly seemed incomplete in his life. Henceforward, he continues the process of self-realization as a citizen of the state, which, as already mentioned, is the highest or latest phase of the Absolute realizing itself.

While Kant and especially Hegel for the most part gave incidental rationalizations of the educational practice current in their day, it was in the educational philosophy of Friedrich Wilhelm August Froebel (1782–1852) that idealism made its most notable innovation in education. In *The Education of Man* Froebel started with the eternal unity of all things. This unity, stemming from God, finds

---

[29] Yet, referring to the difficulty he as a headmaster experienced in accurately estimating a pupil's scholastic ability and achievement, Hegel is on record as stating, "The uncertainty which reigns in this world of becoming shows itself strikingly in this connection." [M. Mackenzie, *Hegel's Educational Thought and Practice* (Swan, Sonnenschein & Co., London, 1909), p. 179.]

equal expression in the laws of both physical nature and human spirit. In fact, the development of each parallels the other. The aim of life and education is for each person to develop and realize the indwelling divine unity within himself. The inner, or a priori, nature of the child is already shaped to this end, for its essential character is that of a striving self-activity. Mark well, the child does not possess activity; he is activity. Neither does he need to be stimulated to act, for he is already spontaneously self-active. On the one hand, activity is an observing and taking in by the senses, as in the theories of Pestalozzi. On the other, it is even more a giving out, a positive expression of will, as in the idealism of Johann Gottlieb Fichte.[30]

The romantic reverence that idealism led Froebel to have for the inner law of the child's self-development also enabled him to be the first to perceive the educational significance of children's play. Play, which previous educators had almost always neglected as unimportant, and which the Puritans often thought even sinful, was by Froebel given a serious philosophical justification. He attached educational significance to play as the natural mode or outlet for the expression of self-activity. Play, he reasoned, is the outward expression of the inward endeavor to achieve self-realization. The more the child establishes the connectedness between his inner striving and its outward expression, the more he exhibits in his own life the divine unity that rules the world. Not unlike the theory of Hegel, education consists in reconciling or mediating opposites.[31] This is why Froebel, in true a priori idealistic fashion, constantly refers to the child's "making the inner outer and the outer inner." Consequently, Froebel was not content to find educational significance merely in the happy exuberance of play. Instead, he was ever on the watch for evidences in play that symbolized the awakening of the divinity of the child's inner nature. In fact, he chose and designed games and toys that he thought had just this symbolic significance for children.

Of course, the child's inner nature was not awakened all at once; there were stages. Between these stages there was a connectedness and unity, just as there was between the inner and outer worlds. Each succeeding stage grew out of the preceding one according to inner law. Thus education was a process of development, or, as Froebel called it, of "unfoldment." "All the child is ever to be and become," he wrote in *The Education of Man,* "lies—however slightly indicated—in the child and can be attained only through development

---

[30] R. Eucken, "The Philosophy of Friedrich Froebel," *Forum,* 30:172–179, October, 1900.

[31] For the application of this principle in the kindergarten "gifts," see *infra,* p. 216.

from within outward."[32] Incidentally, herein lay the basis for Froebel's symbolism: the appearance of earlier stages in a developmental series was supposed to foreshadow or symbolize the later fully developed ones. The theory of education as unfoldment Froebel rested not on a mere analogy but on what he believed to be an actual parallel to growth in plant life. Such a theory was by no means new with him, being found in the work of contemporary biologists and even earlier educators like Comenius. Yet Froebel was the first to organize a school on the theory that it was a garden of children, a *Kindergarten*, wherein the educational growth of children could be compared to the growth of plants. In spite of his romantic and religious respect for the free and unencumbered unfoldment of what was originally enfolded in the a priori nature of the child, Froebel did not, like some of his followers, lend approval to any and all unrestrained expressions of nature. Again leaning on biological analogy, he advanced the educational theory that undesirable native impulses could and should be atrophied by starving them on an opportunity to grow and unfold.

Although Froebel's idealistic philosophy added great impetus to the activity and developmental theories of education, it is well to observe here that his originality lay not so much in his advocating these theories as in his pointing to play as a vehicle of their expression. As already stated in connection with Rousseau, the activity theory of education was as old as Aristotle. Not only that, but Aristotle had worked out a developmental theory of education, too, to which, indeed, Froebel's theory of unfoldment bears obvious resemblances. For both philosophers, development is teleological; the final end, or product, is foreshadowed in the germ.

While the idealistic philosophy of education during the first half of the nineteenth century had its most notable development in Germany, it was not without its representatives in America. Forerunners were the transcendentalists Bronson Alcott[33] (1799–1888) and Ralph Waldo Emerson[34] (1803–1882). Both had a romantic regard for pupil individuality. But the man who more than any other was instrumental in grafting German idealism on American education was William Torrey Harris (1835–1909), United States Commissioner of

---

[32] F. Froebel, *The Education of Man* (D. Appleton & Company, Inc., New York, 1887), p. 68.

[33] D. McCuskey, *Bronson Alcott, Teacher* (The Macmillan Company, New York, 1940), chaps. 2–5. *Cf.* J. B. Wilson, "Bronson Alcott, Platonist or Pestalozzian?" *School and Society*, 81:49–53, February, 1955.

[34] R. W. Emerson, *Essay on Education* (Houghton Mifflin Company, Boston, 1909).

Education at the end of the century.[35] Philosopher as well as educator, Harris was a thorough Hegelian in outlook yet an enthusiastic Froebelian in kindergarten theory.

In Harris it is perhaps clearer than in the writings of earlier educational idealists how readily the philosophy of developmentalism can be accommodated to the Christian tradition. Thus he saw education as a process of pupil self-realization, which, in turn, is one aspect of the Absolute working out its self-realization in the objective world. If this is the case, education is obviously more than a process of imparting information for a mere temporary mundane existence. It is also an integral and necessary stage in the development or complete unfoldment of the Absolute. Such a complete development is hardly possible during the human life span. Hence education points to a development that requires immortality for its completion. What is this theory more than a recondite account of the Christian story of the pupil as a child of God destined for eternal life with him? Certainly, Protestant educators of the late nineteenth and early twentieth centuries leaned heavily on this interpretation for the philosophical basis of their educational efforts.

The most prolific writer on the idealistic philosophy of education in the twentieth century was Herman Harrell Horne[36] (1874–1946). At a time when idealism was already fast fading as the dominant American theory of education, Horne managed to draw together the various strains of idealism into their more systematic educational exposition. In addition to much that is already familiar he made two points of his own. One is his emphasis on volition and effort in learning. The pupil is like the plant, he agreed with Froebel, in that his response is self-active. But the child is unlike the plant, Horne continued, in that he can withhold his response. Hence the ultimate responsibility for getting an education rests on the will of the pupil. All education, therefore, is self-education; it is the result of voluntary effort put forth by a self-active mind. If effort is aided and abetted by interest, well and good. If not, then, like Kant, Horne urged that the pupil in any case put forth effort in obedience to what he ought to do.

A second and perhaps more notable point in Horne's exposition is the fact that he did not make any significant alteration in the developmental theory of education in the light of the Darwinian theory of evolution, which was introduced to the world after the deaths of Hegel and Froebel. To be sure, Horne saw that evolution had made the developmental process irreversible and unrepeatable, in con-

---

[35] His chief work in educational philosophy was *Psychological Foundations of Education* (D. Appleton & Company, Inc., New York, 1901).

[36] See especially *The Philosophy of Education* (The Macmillan Company, New York, 1905, revised 1927).

trast to the Aristotelian pattern of matter endlessly reproducing the cycle of changes demanded by its form. The Absolute, however, had no difficulty in assimilating this new theory of development, for Horne could still say that the Absolute is; only the finite becomes. Pedagogically speaking, this seems to mean that through education the child still becomes in time what he was eternally meant to be.

REALISM

Appealing as the idealistic philosophy of education was to the mind of the nineteenth century, it by no means had a monopoly on professional attention. In the very generation of Hegel and Froebel was another equally famous educational philosopher, Johann Friedrich Herbart (1776–1841), whose point of view had a realistic rather than an idealistic orientation. Strangely enough, Herbart took his point of departure from Kant, as had his two illustrious contemporaries. Concurring with the Copernican revolution in men's thinking brought on by Kant, Herbart agreed that we cannot know the world as it really is, that is, the Kantian *Ding an sich*. Though we cannot go behind appearances, phenomena, to know that experience is really "of," yet of one thing Herbart was certain in his own mind, that experience is of something more than itself, as had been the idealistic contention.

Speculating on this "something more" than experience itself, Herbart came to the conclusion that reality is composed of a plurality of independent "reals" not unlike the "monads" of the German philosopher Gottfried Wilhelm von Leibniz. The individual self or soul is just one real among others. It is the propensity of all reals in their contacts with each other to preserve their indigenous character against the adverse influence of other reals. In fact, it is just this interaction or reaction of reals upon each other that gives rise to what we know as experience. The effects of reactions between reals remain in experience as ideas and so affect the way in which we maintain ourselves in contact with later reals. This process is the basis for the whole Herbartian psychology of apperception, learning the new in terms of the old.[37]

The philosophy of education that grows out of the foregoing considerations is definitely realistic. Educational experience is a matter of contact between the soul as a real and other reals. As a process it is managed by presentation to the soul of these other reals. Obviously, educational outcomes are controlled by the choice of the reals that are presented. The way experience is ultimately organized depends

[37] For an elaboration of these psychological implications, see *infra,* pp. 145–148.

on the preparation made for it. In the realistic philosophy of education the emphasis is on factors external to the individual. In the idealistic, especially the Froebelian, the emphasis is from within out. Indeed, the Herbartian educational theory rested so definitely on manipulation of the reals with which the soul comes in contact that it was criticized for being mechanical and deterministic. But, after all, if the pupil had such freedom of the will as to be able arbitrarily to accept or reject the pedagogical efforts of the teacher, Herbartians felt that they could put little heart and enthusiasm into their work.

In selecting what reals should be presented in the curriculum, Herbart did not take his criteria from nature, as Rousseau had done. "To leave man to nature, or even to wish to lead him to, and train him up in nature," protested Herbart, "is mere folly. For what *is* the nature of man? To the Stoics and Epicureans, it was alike the convenient peg on which they hung their systems. Human nature, which appears to be suited for the most diverse conditions, is of so general a character that its special determination and development is entirely left to the race."[38]

Instead, like Hegel, Herbart leaned heavily on history in selecting his curriculum. Not the one to initiate the culture-epoch theory, Herbart was the first to give it educational importance. In the naturalistic philosophy of education, rationalists like Helvétius stood ready to reduce the past to a *tabula rasa* and to start afresh with new social institutions based on reason. Against this notion were those who claimed that the train of historical events could not be uncoupled like a train of cars. Hegel, for instance, asserted that there was an inherent continuity of institutional life, indeed, that history was the progressive realization of the Absolute. The stages or culture epochs through which mankind had passed on the road to its corporate destiny, therefore, appealed to Herbart as the proper course to be repeated in the instruction of the young. Later Herbartians derived further support for the culture-epoch theory of education when embryological research revealed that the successive stages in the growth of the embryo of a species tend to recapitulate the various stages in the evolution of the species itself. Hence, the culture-epoch theory of education came to be known also as the "recapitulation theory."

PRAGMATISM, INSTRUMENTALISM, AND EXPERIMENTALISM

The popularity of both the idealistic and the realistic philosophies of education was short-lived. On the whole they were too speculative and too conservative to suit the temper of the twentieth century.

[38] J. F. Herbart, *Science of Education* (D. C. Heath and Company, Boston, 1892), pp. 135–136.

Both Hegelian and Herbartian philosophers lent themselves too easily to education for the *status quo*. The opening decades of the twentieth century in America were decades of social protest and reform. The reconstruction of educational philosophy was predicated on science and scientific method. After its nineteenth-century detour into metaphysical speculation, educational philosophy returned to a more naturalistic course. The new movement was known by various names, earliest of which probably was "pragmatism." Later it was known as "instrumentalism" and still later as "experimentalism." The popular title of this new philisophy was "progressive education," its high priest John Dewey (1859–1952), and its text his *Democracy and Education*.

As the names pragmatism, instrumentalism, and experimentalism imply, Dewey's philosophy of education paid great attention to the nature and role of knowledge in education. In developing his theory of knowledge, Dewey was much influenced by the implications of Charles Darwin's theory of evolution. From Aristotle to Hegel educators had looked upon reason or intelligence as something primordial. Hence its exercise or its education was an end in itself. According to the Darwinian hypothesis, human intelligence was a relative latecomer on the world scene. It emerged as a means of making superior adjustment to a precarious environment. Following this lead, Dewey worked out a theory of education in which people are taught to think, not just because thinking is a good in itself, but because it is a means or instrument for solving problems of adjustment in a precarious world.

The preeminent method for solving problems is pragmatic and experimental. To test the truth of an idea or hypothesis one must act on it as if it were true and note what practical difference the idea or hypothesis makes. Here, then, is a new activity theory of education. Physical activities are to be undertaken not just for their own sake or because they are developmental of inner capacities, as Aristotle, St. Thomas Aquinas, and Froebel thought, but chiefly because active operations have a critical function to play in the process of inquiry. Knowledge, in place of being a condition precedent to instruction, is now the outcome of it, as in any case of inquiry.

The pursuit of truth in Dewey's philosophy of education is not that of the Truth which is the source of all lesser truths. With him the pursuit of truth through problem solving in the schools is a much more piecemeal affair. In fact, it must be such an affair, since the face of the world is changing so continually and unexpectedly as to foreshorten the range of events for which the educator can deliberately provide. In such a world universal concepts, instead of being endowed with the inherent form of truth, are never free from the jeopardy of restatement in the light of emerging novelties. In fact, education is defined by Dewey as the continual reconstruction of experience.

Change and novelty, obviously, played a role in Dewey's educational philosophy which was different from the place they occupied in any preceding system. Outstanding is the fact that Dewey accepted change and novelty at their face value. Earlier philosophies had looked behind the experience of change and novelty for some remote cause or final end to which they were subordinate. Plato, it will be remembered, thought of change as the mere appearance of an underlying reality that never changed. Aristotle conceded the reality of change but confined it to the change of matter in the realization of forms that were changeless. There was change or development within a form or species, but the form or species itself was eternal. St. Thomas Aquinas followed Aristotle in treating change as a passage from potentiality (matter) to actuality (form). Hegel and Froebel were not much different from Aristotle. Hegel treated change or development as the objective realization of an already self-realized Absolute, while Froebel's developmentalism was an unfolding of what was already enfolded in germ.

This whole pattern of thinking was shaken to its foundations by the publication of Darwin's *Origin of Species* in 1859. The startling claim of this book was, as its title implies, that species are not final and immutable. On the contrary, species are constantly evolving. Thus change is freed from subordination to the changeless. Indeed, the only course of change now to be detected in nature is the multiplication and diversification of change itself.

Dewey's was the first educational philosophy to give systematic expression to this dynamic aspect of Darwinian evolution. Thus, the continuous growth and diversification found to be the law of nature Dewey assigned as descriptive of the norm of education as well. Education was said to be all one with growing. Moreover, the end of growth is further growth. There is nothing to which education is subordinate as end save further education. Thus, Dewey was persistently disappointing to those who sought the end or measure of growth and education outside the processes of growth and education themselves. He particularly refused to find the criteria of education outside the dimensions of nature bounded by the here and now. For similar reasons he preached that education should not be a preparation for life but should be life itself.

Of course, an education that is so dynamic and throbbing with growing life is naturally progressive. Yet, though evolution is the rule of life which supports the progressive theory, Dewey was far from thinking that progress was automatic. Such a view is more readily applicable to the educational philosophy of the rationalists and naturalists of the eighteenth century or to the views of Herbert Spencer[39] (1820–1903) in the nineteenth. With Dewey progress was contingent on the exercise of human intelligence and on the cultivation of individual differences. Hence, progress was a piecemeal affair just as in the case of truth. It could be measured along specific lines, but no net calculation of it could be made.

This does not mean that the Dewey philosophy of education had no ideals. To be sure, the ideal is no longer a haven or heaven in which one can take refuge with the calm assurance that it alone is the supremely and immutably real which shields one from all tempests of change. Instead, the ideal is seen by Dewey to be merely a projection of human aspirations in the form of tentative hypotheses as guides to practical measures for the amelioration of current living. Indeed, all educational values, like truth, are determined instrumentally. They are gauged by the practical difference they make in life.

The Darwinian evolutionary hypothesis was also fruitful for Dewey in enabling him to overcome many of the problems that had plagued educational philosophers before him. Like Hegel, to whom he acknowledged a considerable intellectual debt, Dewey had a penchant for stating educational problems in terms of mutually opposed alternatives.[40] Look at the titles of some of his early writings, *Interest and Effort, Child and Curriculum, School and Society*. But there were many other conflicting educational terms, such as knowing and doing, culture and vocation, work and play, mind and body. Rather than make an "either-or" or a "both-and" resolution of the dilemmas created, Dewey attempted to look at these problems from a fresh point of view. Usually this involved seeing a "continuity" between the opposing terms. For this continuity he was indebted to the genetic, or evolutionary, mode of thought.

Of especial importance is the continuity between the individual and society. To Dewey the social process is all one with the educational process. Both rest in communication between individuals. In fact, the educational measure of a good society is the extent to which its individual members share or communicate cultural resources among its various members. The greater the cultural interpenetration and interdependence, the greater the resources within reach of any one individual in cultivating his unique individuality. And the more individuality developed, the more to exchange and share in the group.

[39] K. D. Benne, "The Educational Outlook of Herbert Spencer," *Harvard Educational Review,* 10:436–453, October, 1940. See also J. Herbst, "Herbert Spencer and the Genteel Tradition in American Education," *Educational Theory,* 11:99–110, April, 1961.

[40] W. J. Sanders, "The Logical Unity of John Dewey's Educational Philosophy," *Journal of Ethics,* 50:424–440, July, 1940.

The importance of individuality is further reflected in the importance Dewey attached to freedom both as an educational method and as an educational end. Yet freedom was not to stand in antithesis to social control. Rather was mastery of the social heritage a chief means to freedom.

THE AFTERMATH

For the first quarter of the twentieth century Dewey's philosophy of education met little opposition and received much support, abroad as well as in the United States.[41] During his heyday conservatives seem to have underestimated the momentum Dewey was gathering. Or, loyal to their tradition, they seemed insensitive to Dewey's well-directed attack on it. By the fourth decade of the century, however, a more sturdy opposition began to form. Conservatives started to rouse themselves from their philosophical lethargy or inertia. Indeed, opposition kept accumulating till by the post-World War II period Dewey had become almost a *cause célèbre*. Arrayed behind him were most of the professionals in public education. Arrayed against him were many academic professors, especially in the humanities, and many lay critics of the schools.

The issues between the two camps were many.[42] But principally—after the "freewheeling" twenties, the depressing thirties, the war-torn forties, and the uneasy postwar fifties—they were reduced to the main fact that a large portion of the American public was in no mood for progressive theories of education which were so experimental as to be relativistic. Filled with anxieties provoked by the "cold war," people turned for relief to "essentialist" philosophies of education in which progress could be calculated against more permanent aims and the curriculum was based on the enduring values of the past.[43] As a result there was a revival of idealist and realist philosophies of education, especially that of Scholastic realism. Some found security in a reassertion of Plato's idealism.[44] Others put their confidence in the rugged qualities of realism.[45] But leading the van

[41] W. W. Brickman, "John Dewey's Foreign Reputation as an Educator," *School and Society,* 70:257–265, October, 1949.

[42] J. S. Brubacher, *Modern Philosophies of Education,* 3d ed. (McGraw-Hill Book Company, New York, 1962).

[43] W. C. Bagley, "An Essentialist Platform for the Advancement of American Education," *Educational Administration and Supervision,* 24:241–256, April, 1938.

[44] R. Livingston, *Education and the Spirit of the Age* (Clarenden Press, Oxford, 1952), pp. 22–32.

[45] J. Wild, "Education and Human Society: A Realistic View," *Modern Philosophies and Education,* Fifty-fourth Yearbook (National Society for the Study of Education, Chicago, 1955), part I, chap. 2.

of resurgent conservatism by far were the neo-Aristotelians, especially the president of the University of Chicago, Robert M. Hutchins (1899–   ).[46]

Hutchins attacked the naturalism of the progressive-education position. His objection was to the romantic and anti-intellectualistic character of its naturalism rather than to naturalism itself. In its stead he favored a naturalistic philosophy of education based on natural law. By observing the uniformities of nature, education could be stabilized, he maintained. Uniformity is determined in Aristotelian fashion by distinguishing that which is essential to a thing's constitution from that which is merely an accident of its individuality. While the particular is not to be neglected in education, neither is the universal to lose its position of chief importance. The Aristotelian influence is clear also in Mortimer J. Adler (1902–   ).[47] Not only did he define education as Aristotle did as the habituation of native capacities in virtue, but his confidence in the unchanging nature of man led him to assert that the aim of education should be the same for all men in all times and in all places.

Delighted as were Catholics to see Aristotle put in opposition to Dewey, they thought that Hutchins and Adler did not go far enough.[48] They had a complaint against the naturalism of Dewey's instrumentalism and experimentalism that carried against the naturalism of Hutchins as well. Conceding the importance of following the natural order in many educational practices, Catholics rather objected to predicating educational theory exclusively on nature. For them it must be predicated on the supernatural order too, as with St. Thomas Aquinas.

Not a few had become weary of the philosophical stalemate centering in Dewey. In their judgment the end of World War II and the beginning of the second half of the twentieth century invited new emphases in educational philosophy. One of the earliest new trends was reconstructionism.[49] Itself an offspring of Deweyan progressivism, it none-

[46] R. M. Hutchins, "The Philosophy of Education," in R. N. Montgomery (ed.), *William Rainey Harper Memorial Conference* (The University of Chicago Press, Chicago, 1938), pp. 35–50.

[47] M. J. Adler, "The Crisis in Education," *The Social Frontier,* 5:141–144, February, 1939; "The Chicago School," *Harper's Magazine,* September, 1941, pp. 377–388.

[48] W. J. McGucken, "The Catholic Philosophy of Education," *Philosophies of Education,* Forty-first Yearbook (National Society for the Study of Education, Chicago, 1942), part I, chap. 6. See also J. D. Redden and F. A. Ryan, *A Catholic Philosophy of Education* (The Bruce Publishing Company, Milwaukee, 1942); H. Guthrie, and G. G. Walsh (eds.), *A Philosophical Symposium on American Catholic Education* (Fordham University Press, New York, 1941), pp. 16–26.

[49] T. Brameld, *Toward a Reconstructed Philosophy of Education* (Holt, Rinehart and Winston, Inc., New York, 1956).

theless distinguished itself from it. The progressive philosophy of education was suitable to a fairly stable society where changes were largely amendments to the existing scheme. But reconstructionists regarded the uneasy balance of atomic power between East and West as so volcanic as to require an educational philosophy prepared for revolutionary changes. If this prospect required utopian thinking, the educational reconstructionists did not blanch before it. With them the future was so real as to be part of their ontology.

Exitentialism provided another new trend.[50] With roots in the nineteenth century this philosophy had a burst of popularity during and immediately after the war. Its popularity is not difficult to appreciate since existentialists see man's predicament as one of loneliness and anxiety. Indeed, war or no war, man dreads most the possible annihilation of his existence. Unsure of what meaning life holds for him, he faces the future with understandable disquietude. With these premises the only assured meaning in life is to be found by making commitments to action and undergoing the consequences. While this philosophy may be a way of enduring war, its advocates had difficulty in adapting it to education.

Making the most considerable departure was linguistic analysis. Like existentialism this movement, too, had its origin outside education. Its main characteristic was an attempt to score philosophy in a "new key." This new key took its point of departure from the disappointment many felt in the inability of philosophy, after centuries of effort, to achieve any cumulative consensus on its principal problems. Positivists tried to resolve this difficulty by accepting only two kinds of statement as having dependable cognitive meaning: statements of empirical fact and statements of logic or mathematics which could be confirmed by calculation. This all but limited philosophy to scientific statements. By restricting syntactical statements of fact to the same severe standard, linguistic analysis imposed approximately the same limits on philosophy. While this was an interesting logical exercise for academic philosophers, educational philosophers had some difficulty in applying it to the problems of schoolteachers.[51]

[50] G. F. Kneller, *Existentialism and Education* (Philosophical Library, Inc., New York, 1958). See also H. Soderquist, *The Person and Education* (Charles E. Merrill Books, Inc., Columbus, Ohio, 1964).

[51] B. O. Smith and R. H. Ennis, *Language and Concepts in Education* (Rand McNally & Company, Chicago, 1961).

6 Educational Psychology

Of all the persistent problems in education perhaps none has been more perennially difficult than that raised by inquiry into the precise way in which learning takes place. It is easy to see why this problem should yield its secrets so grudgingly. To explain learning requires an inquiry into the complexities of human nature itself. This involves turning the lens of the mind upon itself, a task only a little less difficult than expecting the eye to see itself. What investigators have seen while peering into the inner recesses of the human mind has been very intricate, so intricate, in fact, that even scientists— let alone philosophers—have been unable to unite on a common description of what takes place there. Several closely related problems confront experts, and they can agree on none. What is the nature of the psyche of which psychology aims to make a logical study? How does the psyche function? Especially, how does it function in learning? How is it motivated? Are there individual differences in learning? Can these differences be measured? Is there a norm of functioning that can be made the basis of a hygiene of the mind?

FACULTY PSYCHOLOGY

The earliest and for many centuries the principal approach to the problem of learning was speculative and philosophical. Plato (427–347 B.C.) seems to have been among the first to ask himself just how new ideas enter the mind. Facing the perennial problem of Greek thought—whether or not virtue can be taught—he saw two alternatives. Either virtue was a gift of the gods,

137

or it was a type of conduct that could be acquired through education. In other words, either the tendency toward virtue was innate, or it was the result of instruction. Indeed, one might go further and say that here is a very early statement of what came to be a contest between heredity and environment, nature and nurture. The environment, or nurture, alternative presented insuperable difficulties to Plato. If one had no previous knowledge of virtue, how would he know where to turn to get it or in what way to identify it if he should accidentally find it? Unable to answer this question satisfactorily, Plato leaned in the direction of the heredity, or nature, alternative, that learning must be a development of latent capacities from within.

Speculating along this line, he put forth the theory that ideas are innate at birth. Though innate, they are not, however, fully developed. Rather are they vague and indistinct replicas of the perfect ideas that exist in the eternal realm whence the child is born into this world. In making the transition between the two spheres, the original perfection of ideas is somehow greatly dimmed, probably by the soul's entering the body. From this point on, learning consists in a process of reminiscence, of trying to remember or recapture knowledge once possessed in full. Impressions received through the senses serve to arouse corresponding ideas that have been slumbering in the mind since birth.[1]

It is notable that in Plato's psychology he drew a sharp distinction between mind and body. The mind's contribution to learning was ideas; the body's contribution, sensations. More significant was the relative importance Plato assigned to the component parts of the dualism. From the foregoing theory of learning as reminiscence it is clear that Plato thought that the source of error in learning was the body's being a handicap to the mind. Hence he exalted the role of the mind in learning and discounted that of the body. Although this dualism of mind and body was not original with Plato, it is significant that he helped to fasten it upon educational psychology as one of its most persistent problems.

Aristotle (384–322 B.C.), greatest of Plato's pupils, continued this dualism but went much further with the analysis and description of the psychological nature of the learner. Central in this nature, according to Aristotle, was the soul. It should be noted in passing that it is the Greek word for soul, ψυχή (English psyche), that has lent psychology its name. Aristotle's major work in this field was Περὶ ψυχῆς (*De anima* in Latin). In the twentieth century, when psychology has been said to have "lost its soul" and scientific psychology has been trying

---

[1] That the theory still lingered in the twentieth century may be seen in J. L. Mursell, "The Miracle of Learning," *Atlantic Monthly,* 155:733–741, June, 1935.

to free itself from its philosophical origins and implications, it is all too easy to forget that psychology commenced as the study of the soul.

It is noteworthy that in his psychology Aristotle did not entertain the later popular notion of the soul as a substance. Instead, he described the soul in straightforward terms of function. To state Aristotle's theory as simply as possible, the soul was the principle of life. But the soul was not only the principle which endowed the organism with life; it was also the principle which caused the organism to bring to fulfillment the unique characteristics which were latent within it. This final form of growth and development was conceived as a causal principle operating from the beginning of an organism's growth to direct it throughout to its final development.

The soul as an active principle had the potentiality, or faculty,[2] of functioning in various ways. Aristotle ascribed five faculties to the soul. These were (1) the vegetative, the faculty, or capacity, of the organism to develop and maintain itself; (2) the appetitive, the faculty, or tendency, to desire what is satisfying and good; (3) the sensory, in which Aristotle included our faculty for the aesthetic; (4) the locomotive, the faculty, or capacity, to move about; and (5) the rational, the faculty, or ability, to reason. Of the five faculties obviously the last is most important for education. It is because of its existence that Aristotle could say that man has an innate desire to know.

This rational faculty Aristotle further subdivided into the active and the passive intellect. A notable feature of the active intellect as a faculty of the soul was the fact that it was separable from the body and survived it after death. It entered man's body from the great reservoir of primordial mind that initially gave form to the universe and to this reservoir returned on the death of the body. The potential quality of intellect, or mind, therefore, was the same in all people, old and young. In absorbing Aristotle into their thought structure, the Christians eagerly seized upon his doctrine of the immortality of the soul and gave it a theological as well as a psychological meaning. This process of acculturation between Greek and Christian thought greatly complicated the future development of psychological thinking and led to very sharp controversies in later attempts at objective analyses of the learning process.

Describing the psyche, or soul, in terms of what it could do, that is, in terms of its functions, of faculties, was a method that found wide support in the centuries following Aristotle. So described, it was the psychology of the medieval Scholastics, including St. Thomas Aquinas (1225–1274), and in large part still remains the psychology

---

[2] A faculty, it will be remembered from its Latin root *facultas,* means a capacity, or power, to act.

of Catholic education. Furthermore, it was the most widely accepted psychology during the Renaissance and post-Renaissance periods. The chief controversy during this long period centered not in the principle of faculty psychology but in the number of faculties and their precise description. Some insisted that there was only one faculty; others, like the phrenologists of the nineteenth century, that there were upward of two dozen. Whatever their number, it was during this period that the five faculties of Aristotle were reduced to the three most generally accepted faculties of knowing, feeling, and willing. It was also during this time that more was heard of the faculties that have become most familiar to educators, namely, those of judgment, memory, imagination, and observation.

Coincident with the multiplication of the faculties were two other tendencies that require mention. One was the tendency to reify the faculties, that is, to conceive of them as entities or substances. It was the phrenologists of the nineteenth century who went furthest in this regard. They localized each faculty in a particular part of the brain, in some cases even under a particular surface of the cranium.[3] A frequent concomitant of reification was the further tendency to conceive of the faculties as being more or less independent of each other. This tendency, of course, was a definite departure from Aristotle, who thought of the soul as a unity. Both medieval Scholastics and Neo-Scholastics followed Aristotle on this point and insisted again and again that the faculties are merely aspects or phases of a single unitary soul.

After having described human nature in terms of the powers, or faculties, of a soul whose primary characteristic is activity, it is logical to expect that learning will consist in the exercise of those powers, or faculties, particularly the rational, or cognitive, faculties. According to Aristotle and later St. Thomas Aquinas, the rational, or cognitive, faculty was not self-initiating. It required sense experience to start it performing its characteristic function. This accounts for that oft-quoted medieval Latin dictum *Nihil in intellectu quod non prius in sensu* (There is nothing in the intellect that is not first in the senses). Once under way the rational faculty performed in several fashions, each of importance to learning. For one thing it was capable of abstraction; that is, it could regard aspects of its object of attention as if they were independent of it. For another it could act discoursively; that is, it could order experiences and concepts into systems.

---

[3] In America this theory was propounded by O. S. Fowler, *Memory and Intellectual Improvement Applied to Self-education and Juvenile Instruction* (O. S. and L. N. Fowler, New York, 1844), vol. 3. The European originators were F. J. Gall and J. K. Spurzheim, *Introduction au cours de physiologie du cerveau* (Paris, 1808).

A third capability was "intellectual intuition," grasping axioms that could not be demonstrated. Highly significant of this rational process was the fact that Aristotle claimed it occurred not gradually, bit by bit, but all at once. According to this theory and not unlike gestalt psychology of a later day, learning at this level came in a flash of insight.

The great educational risk of faculty psychology was its tendency to magnify the role of the intellect in learning at the expense of that of the senses. This overemphasis seemed excusable to the educators of the ancient and medieval worlds since the knowledge derived from sense impression was notoriously variable and unreliable while that of the intellect, being of the essence, was stable and dependable. But the attempt to take the citadel of knowledge by frontal assault on the intellect with only a feint at outflanking the senses made the campaign of education during childhood a most difficult one for all concerned.

First to attempt to restore the educational balance between the intellect and the senses was Johann Amos Comenius (1592–1670), the great Moravian educator of the seventeenth century. Although he has sometimes been called the first modern educator, it is notable that he accepted the faculty psychology current in his day. Accepting also the scholastic dictum *Nihil in intellectu quod non prius in sensu,* he made his chief psychological contribution by taking seriously the temporal priority suggested in it. It was educational labor lost, Comenius contended, to try to strengthen the faculty of will before that of reason, to sharpen the faculty of reason before that of imagination, and finally to exercise the faculty of imagination before training the senses. In predicating educational method on the priority of the senses, as, for instance, in publishing the first picture textbook, he greatly aided children in securing a footing on the bottom rung of the ladder of learning.

FORMAL DISCIPLINE AND TRANSFER OF TRAINING

The foregoing analysis would make it appear as if the exercise of the faculties was primarily in the interest of acquiring knowledge. Faculty and sense team up to distill wisdom. There are, however, repeated references in educational literature from Plato onward which seem to point to a psychological doctrine that education consists in the exercise of these faculties for their own sake. The content learned was deemed unimportant, but the strengthening or sharpening of the faculties was regarded as all-important. One of the clearest early statements of this position is to be found in Quintilian's *Institutes of Oratory*. "As regards geometry," stated this greatest of Roman teachers, "it is granted that portions of this science are of value for the instruction of children: for admittedly it exercises their minds, sharpens their wits, and generates quickness of perception. But it is considered that the value of geometry resides in the process of learning, and not as with other sciences in the knowledge thus acquired."[4]

Two different theories of learning thus grew out of and became predicated on the faculty conception of psychology. Although faculty psychology is not necessarily or inescapably to be identified with either of them, there can be no doubt that the one instanced by Quintilian enjoyed the greater historical popularity. In the course of time this theory came to be known as the doctrine of "formal discipline." Improvement from the exercise of a faculty like memory was supposed to be generally available, not just in the specific area in which memorization took place. Increase in power from the exercise of a faculty in one field of endeavor was thought to "transfer" automatically or at will to endeavor in other fields. Indeed, certain subjects in the curriculum, notably Latin, Greek, and mathematics, came to have the reputation of being peculiarly well suited to disciplining the mental faculties.

The man who has most often been selected by educational historians as the archrepresentative of the doctrine of formal discipline is John Locke (1632–1704). Several of his writings have tended to identify him with the disciplinarians. In the opening pages of his *Thoughts concerning Education* he remarked, "As the strength of the body lies chiefly in being able to endure hardships, so also does that of the mind."[5] As the humorist Mr. Dooley was to say two centuries later, it matters little what a child studies as long as he does not like it. There is clearly implicit here the theory that the mind is capable of a general training which later can be applied in any direction.

Disciplining the mind through the study of the hard and disagreeable brought religion to the support of psychological theory. The ascetic strain in Locke's statement just quoted was in part a legacy from the mind-body dualism already found in Plato and Aristotle and later continued in Christian teaching. The quality of mind being the same in all according to Aristotle, the failure of the child to learn must be due to a willful disinclination of the flesh. Hence the age-old belief that the intellect can be expedited to learn by corporal punishment. The Hoosier schoolmaster's primitive notion of transfer, that "lickin' and larnin' go together," thus had theoretical as well as empirical justification of long standing.

[4] H. E. Butler, *Quintilian, Institutes of Oratory* (G. P. Putnam's Sons, New York, 1921–1922), vol. 1, p. 177.

[5] J. Locke, *Some Thoughts concerning Education* (Cambridge University Press, London, 1889), p. 21.

But it was when Locke recommended the study of mathematics in the curriculum of the young gentleman that he seemed most unequivocally to espouse the doctrine of formal discipline. "I have mentioned mathematics," he wrote, "as a way to settle in the mind a habit of reasoning closely and in train; not that I think it necessary that all men should be deep mathematicians, but that having got the way of reasoning, which that study necessarily brings the mind to, they might be able to *transfer* it to other parts of knowledge as they shall have occasion."[6]

Over against this clear-cut and unambiguous commitment to the doctrine of formal discipline are other writings of Locke's that seem to commit him just as unequivocally to an opposite view. In spite of what he wrote about accustoming the mind to difficult tasks, he also was very eager that learning should be made pleasant, that it should not be imposed as a task since children learn so much more quickly and effectively when they have a "disposition" for it, and that teachers should watch for the time when children are "in tune" for learning. Furthermore, he was quite utilitarian in his attitude toward the curriculum. In spite of his praise of mathematics he did not confine himself to a few disciplinary subjects but recommended a wide variety of them and always for the uses to which they could be put. In fact, he had little or no confidence that a faculty, or power, as he preferred to call it, of memory could be strengthened by use. To him the quality of memory was an innate endowment, and he gravely doubted that it could be improved, for example, by memorizing Latin.

EMPIRICAL PSYCHOLOGY

Even more contradictory of Locke's being a formal disciplinarian were his psychological conceptions. His conception of mind and the learning process was, if anything, at the opposite pole from that of faculty psychology. To appreciate how sharp was the contrast in psychological conception between Locke and his predecessors, it will be well to recall for a moment the predicament in which Plato found himself in trying to explain learning. Unable to understand how new ideas could enter the mind from without, Plato had put forward the theory that learning was really a remembering of ideas with which the learner was familiar before birth. Learning was thus a development from within of innate ideas. The faculty psychology of Aristotle was similar in that faculties were also innate. Senses played the subordinate role of "tipping off" the ideas, or faculties. Yet, in spite of the maxim *Nihil in intellectu quod non prius in sensu,*

---

[6] J. Locke, *Conduct of the Understanding,* sec. 7 [italics mine].

some types of knowledge were thought to be both innate and independent of sense. Knowledge of God was a case in point; certainly his existence and attributes could not be learned through the senses.

Flying in the face of these long-standing tenets, Locke put forward the startling premise that the mind of a child is a blank at birth and that whatever he learns comes into the mind through the senses. This is his famous *tabula rasa* theory of psychology, and with it he swept away the whole theory of innate ideas and faculties. With them he also swept away the idea of learning as the development of innate potentialities, or faculties. In their stead he formulated a theory of learning that emphasized the acquisition of knowledge from without. So for the first time appeared a psychology that stressed nurture rather than nature, environment rather than heredity.

Locke's transition from rational, or faculty, psychology to empirical psychology was not, however, so complete as it might appear at first sight. If the mind was just a passive receptacle of sense impressions, what was to prevent these impressions from accumulating in a most disorderly and confusing array? Aware of this possible difficulty Locke found it necessary to posit that the mind was not a complete blank but that it had means of its own for dealing with incoming impressions. Among these means was its ability to compare impressions, discriminate between them, and generalize them. While these abilities were not of the order of the external senses, yet they were sufficiently like them, Locke thought, to be called a sort of "internal" sense. Sometimes he called them "powers" in order to distinguish them from faculties, which they seemed to resemble.

But even this last similarity to rational, or faculty, psychology was wiped out by certain of Locke's enthusiastic French followers. Claude Adrien Helvétius (1715–1771) and Étienne Bonnot de Condillac (1715–1780) in particular carried Locke's sensational empiricism to its most extreme conclusion. They made even the powers of the mind the result of sensations and thus their own psychology completely empirical. Helvétius reached this conclusion by finding it impossible in his mind to separate a power from some sensation. Thus, the power to discriminate one shade of color as deeper than another, he claimed, was itself the report of a sensation. Obviously, if such a thoroughgoing empirical psychology were true, then would man be nothing but the product of his education.

In any event, it almost goes without saying now that the empiricism of Locke's psychology could hardly be consistent with a disciplinary theory of education. The educational product, in which Locke was interested, was not an isolated cultivation of mental powers but the acquisition of information through the senses with the organizing aid of these powers.

It is an ironical fact of history, however, that once learning through the main avenue of the senses became firmly established pedagogy, it was not long before teachers turned to a formal training of the senses similar to the formal training or discipline of the faculties. Thus, instead of continuing to concentrate on the content of experience brought in through the apertures of sense, they began to train the senses for such qualities as quickness, acuity, and accuracy. Even an educator with such remarkable insight into learning as Johann Heinrich Pestalozzi (1746–1827) seems to have thought that formal training of the senses would "transfer" in the same way formal training of the faculties was supposed to.

ASSOCIATION AND APPERCEPTION

To Locke educational psychology is indebted for one further contribution, the phrase "association of ideas." Although Locke coined the phrase, the idea behind it was not original with him. For the source of the idea one must go back to Aristotle. In searching for the key to memory, Aristotle was the first to note how recollection of a given time could be facilitated by trying to remember some other item closely connected with it. In fact, he laid down four kinds of connection that would facilitate memory: contiguity of one idea with another, succession of ideas in a series, similarity of ideas, and contrast of ideas. Four secondary conditions of association were added by the Scot Thomas Brown (1778–1820) early in the nineteenth century. These made recollection, or association, depend also on the duration of the original sensation, its liveliness, or intensity, its frequency of occurrence, and its recency.

Aristotle's observations on the functioning of memory remained a relatively neglected portion of his psychology till the time of Locke and after, but from then on there was great need of it. Taking up where Locke left off, the great skeptic David Hume (1711–1776) carried Locke's sensationalism to one unexpected but very logical conclusion. Upon introspection into his own mental life he found nothing there but a succession of sensations or mental states. Of any unity holding these sense impressions or mental images together, as the soul, or psyche, was supposed to do, he found no trace. At this point the principles of association came in very handily indeed to afford some continuity to experience.[7]

[7] The continuities of contiguity, succession, and the like, however, were not enough for Immanuel Kant (1724–1804). His epoch-making reaction to Hume's destruction of the unity of psychological experience was to confer on the mind a priori synthetic powers of its own. The effect of this convenient device was felt more strongly in educational philosophy than in educational psychology. See *supra*, p. 123.

In spite of considerable activity in the text two centuries in exploring the bases and limits of associationism, it was not till the early nineteenth century that associationism's promising implications for educational psychology were enunciated. First to see these implications clearly was Johann Friedrich Herbart (1776–1841), the German philosopher and psychologist. Gathering them together with considerable originality, he formulated them into a theory of learning known as "apperception," a term he borrowed from that intellectual giant Gottfried Wilhelm von Leibniz of a century and more previous. But before proceeding to explain the theory of apperception it will be well to understand Herbart's description of the psychological constitution of the learner.

Herbart's psychology started with his metaphysics. The basic nature of the world he claimed to be constituted of a large number of independent "reals" not unlike the monads of Leibniz's philosophy. The soul, or psyche, of the learner was but one among these many other reals. As a real the soul was a simple unity and almost utterly colorless; it had no idea, feeling, or will. Yet, though deficient in these important respects, it did possess the one positive characteristic of being able to preserve itself in competition with other reals. This is important to remember, for the stress and strain attendant upon the collision of the soul with other reals in the environment was what gave rise to one's sense of feeling and one's consciousness of ideas. Idea, feeling, and will, thus excluded by Herbart in the presupposed nature of the soul, were reintroduced by him as resultants of the contact of the soul with its environment.

Furthermore, according to Herbart, ideas and sensations that entered the mind in this fashion always remained there to influence later learning. Those ideas which gained the focus of consciousness or attention and were able to maintain themselves there of course had the greatest influence. Those ideas which failed to gain attention slipped below the threshold of consciousness, whence, though momentarily forgotten, they continued to strive to reenter consciousness. The struggle for the forestage of consciousness generally was decided in favor of the ideas with the greater force. Command of superior force was brought about in one of two ways. In the first place, those ideas in the mind which were similar had a tendency to associate together and reinforce each other. So far the resulting composite bore considerable resemblance to conventional associationism. But, in the second place, those ideas which were dissimilar tended to repel each other. Either gaining attention, or consciousness, therefore, was a matter of combining with other similar ideas till enough strength was built up to command attention, or it waited on a weakening or repressing of dissimilar ideas already there.

What particular combination of ideas happens to be predominant at any given time will have much to do with determining what a person will pay attention to in his external environment. The name that Herbart attached to this selective process was "apperception." For anything to stand out clearly from its background was for that thing to be apperceived, and the combination, or association, of ideas in the mind that favored this condition of clarity was called an "apperceptive mass." This apperceptive mass was tremendously important as the synthesizing agent of experience, which associationists ever since Hume had had difficulty in finding.

The psychology of apperception and the apperceptive mass was, if anything, even more important in the field of education. There the Herbartian doctrine of apperception showed how it is the background already in the mind that makes possible the assimilation of new ideas. Reduced to its simplest terms, apperception may be stated in a phrase, which has become increasingly familiar, of learning the new in terms of the old. The doctrine especially directed the attention of teachers to the importance of commencing the learning process at the point where the child's past experience placed him. In fact, the first step in teaching and learning was to get that past clearly in mind so as to facilitate the apperception or association of the second step, which was the presentation of new reals, that is, new experience. For that matter, the doctrine of apperception led to the idea of a curriculum that was nothing more than a succession of presentations wherein the child constantly passed from familiar to unfamilar but closely associated subject matter.[8]

The Herbartian doctrine of apperception not only provided a common-sense general theory of learning but also was useful in simplifying a number of other psychological problems in education. Heading the list and probably including all the rest was the perennial problem of enlisting the child's active cooperation in accomplishing the task of education. Previous psychologies had located the source of activity in innate or a priori faculties, powers, and senses. Unfortunately, the child, endowed with free will, often did not will to exercise these capacities or to put forth the effort to achieve the educational ends set by his elders. Because of this capriciousness teachers had only indifferent success in winning attention and interest. The pedagogical result was that teachers rested their instruction on interest, if they could get it; if not, they insisted on effort without interest.

The doctrine of apperception, however, permitted a novel reinterpretation of the foregoing situation. In the first place Herbart completely dispensed with the theory of faculties as the basis for the

---

[8] For a more extended account of the instructional methods Herbart predicated on his educational psychology, see *infra,* pp. 212–214.

dynamics of educational psychology. As already indicated, he explained the dynamics of learning as the resultant of reals or ideas endeavoring to preserve themselves as they clashed against each other. Thus those dynamic forces which motivate conduct, such as feeling and will, have their origin in ideas. In fact, it was difficult for Herbart to draw a sharp line between will and idea, volition and understanding. Rather was the idea father to the action. Here were all the ingredients for the later-day theory of ideomotor activity.

This analysis is of particular importance for that special instance of motivation, interest. In terms of apperception, interest, like will, is a function of ideas. Or, like desire, interest arises from a strong and vivid presentation of ideas that are able to maintain themselves above the threshold of consciousness. To state the thought in yet a different way, interest is the hospitality of old ideas toward similar new ones. From these statements it is obvious that Herbart did not think of interest as superficially amusing or diverting but rather as a serious ingredient of learning. To Herbart this ingredient had two facets. On the one hand, he used interest as the outcome of instruction when he referred to the pleasing feeling that arises from the association of old and new ideas of a like nature. On the other hand, he used it as the means rather than the end of instruction when he employed past associations to facilitate apperception of current materials.

To teachers the attractive feature of Herbart's apperceptive psychology was the control it seemed to give them over the educative process. Lesson plans that hitherto were uncertain of fulfillment were now apparently brought within the limits of empirical control. All the teacher had to do was to build up the right sequence of ideas, and the desired conduct followed. Peculiarly enough, this feature of apperception, which recommended itself so strongly to most teachers, was at the same time the basis for one of the most serious criticisms of it. Some feared that it made education mechanical, that it was a threat to the pupil's freedom. In spite of this reaction, after his death Herbart's psychology enjoyed wide popularity in both Europe and America. In fact, just before the opening of the twentieth century a group of prominent American educators formed themselves into an association called the National Herbart Society for the Scientific Study of Education.

The most significant paper ever read in this society was an early one by John Dewey (1859–1952), in which, after criticizing Herbart's conception of interest, he proceeded to set forth his own psychology of interest. Dewey has become so closely identified with the field of educational philosophy that it is easy to forget that some of his best early writing was in the field of psychology. His chief objection to the apperceptive theory of interest was that it made out of interest a passive reflex of the clash or association of ideas. Consequently, as he interpreted Herbart, interest could be only an outcome of instruction. It could never be a means or a motive.[9]

Passing to the positive statement of his own views, Dewey put forward a more biological psychology, which described original nature as spontaneously impulsive rather than passive. Moreover, the dynamics of impulse were not the result of the environment impinging on the self. On the contrary, Dewey thought of impulse as a spontaneous outgoing of the self. Hence interest was a function of this native self-propulsive quality of life. It was not stirred by an object but itself picked the object out and attached itself to it. Objects were picked out not because they possessed the quality of being interesting but because they were seen as instruments for realizing some purpose of the learner. "The genuine principle of interest," wrote Dewey in his paper, "is the principle of the recognized identity of the fact or proposed line of action with the self; that it lies in the direction of the agent's own growth, and is, therefore, imperiously demanded, if the agent is to be himself. . . . The gist of the psychology of interest may, accordingly, be stated as follows: An interest is primarily a form of self-expressive activity—that is, of growth through acting upon nascent tendencies."[10] Many not convinced of this view by Dewey were finally won over to it in the twentieth century by the importance Freudian psychoanalysis focused on innate biological drives.

As for effort, conventionally thought of as the antithesis of interest, Dewey proposed that it should be considered an ally of interest. He counted it absurd to think that uninteresting disciplinary tasks call forth greater effort from a child than do vitally interesting ones. An effort of will is not something just expended when there is an absence of interest. Rather does the expenditure of effort indicate the strain that has been placed on interest because some obstacle lies athwart the path to the goal of one's ambitions. Hence, the greater the interest, the greater the effort.

[9] Dewey further criticized Herbartian psychology for its social implications. To him it was "a schoolmaster's psychology, not the psychology of a child. It is the natural expression of a nation laying great emphasis upon authority and upon the formation of individual character in distinct and recognized subordination to the ethical demands made in war and in civil administration by that authority. It is not the psychology of a nation which professes to believe that every individual has within him the principle of authority, and that order means coordination and not subordination." ("Interest as Related to the Training of the Will," *National Herbart Society Yearbook*, 1895, 2d supplement, p. 29.)

[10] *Ibid.*, pp. 9, 15.

GENETIC PSYCHOLOGY

The introduction of a biological note into Dewey's educational psychology may be taken as indicative of changes of much wider scope that were taking place in educational psychology by the end of the nineteenth century. During the last quarter of this century psychology changed from a philosophical to a scientific discipline. As Herbart may be said to have been the last of the great philosophical educational psychologists, so perhaps G. Stanley Hall (1846–1924) may be said to have been the first of the new generation of scientific educational psychologists. Trained at the University of Leipzig under the direction of Wilhelm Wundt (1832–1920), founder of the first psychological laboratory, Hall returned to America to introduce in the last decades of the nineteenth century the new approach to psychological problems.

Hall's chief contribution to educational psychology was in his promotion of the child-study movement. Although not the originator of this educational movement, he may be fairly said to have given it the descriptive phrase by which it subsequently became known. He called it "paidocentric," and from that time on into the twentieth century the cliché "child-centered" became a rallying cry of great power. The center of his interest in the child was not so much in theories of interest, attention, forgetting, and learning as in a more adequate account of the content of children's minds. While, as already stated, the child-study movement was older than Hall's interest in it, the movement really began to gather momentum with his publication of *The Contents of Children's Minds on Entering School.*

The material for this study he gathered by a novel technique at the time, the questionnaire method. Although this method is now known to have been handicapped by such serious inaccuracies as those introduced by hearsay and untrained introspection, at the time it afforded valuable new light on the way to more careful scientific studies in the twentieth century by students of his like Arnold Gesell (1880–1961), to say nothing of a host of followers influenced by him.

Much more significant than his method of gathering data was Hall's genetic theory of interpreting it. Here it is necessary to bear in mind that Hall, like Dewey, was profoundly influenced by the biological thought of his day, especially the Darwinian theory of evolution. Believing that there is no psychosis without neurosis and learning from embryology that various stages of organic evolution are recapitulated in the gestatory period of the human embryo, Hall projected the further theory that the social stages in the history of the race were also recapitulated in the child's educational development after birth. Accordingly, for each stage in man's progress from savagery to civilization there was supposed to be a corresponding stage in the development of childhood. Thus the child must be a hunter at one stage and a builder at another. The teacher had to be a close student of the time when each of these stages appeared so that he could take advantage of the nascent opportunities for learning it offered at the crest of its power.

Moreover, if recapitulation is complete, the teacher must expect the appearance of types of conduct, such as fighting, which, though historically useful as a mode of adjustment to the environment, are no longer approved. Yet, when they appeared, instead of inhibiting them, Hall advocated that they be allowed to run their course. This was his famous theory of catharsis. By permitting expression for these tendencies at the normal time for their natural development, he believed that they would spend themselves and disappear before finding harmful expression in later life.[11]

Probably Hall thought his reputation as a psychologist rested on his genetic theory of recapitulation. The theory did have its heyday but then was discarded in the light of more accurate scientific evidence, which showed that nature often takes short cuts instead of recapitulating. In fact, the more enduring phase of Hall's genetic psychology was his monumental study on *Adolescence*. Not the first to recognize the fact of adolescence, he was the first to describe its characteristics with any scientific accuracy. He noted the rapid physiological growth during this period, together with its psychological counterparts, especially sexual differentiation and maturation. Both these developments were seen to underlie a rapidly changing estimate of the individual by himself as well as by others. The data Hall brought forth greatly influenced educators and led to an extensive reconstruction of educational offerings for this age group.

FUNCTIONAL PSYCHOLOGY

Another to be influenced by Darwinian evolution and to press even further the incorporation of the biological viewpoint into educational psychology was William James (1842–1910), the American pragmatist. In his ever-popular *Talks to Teachers on Psychology* he made an early lecture the occasion for asking teachers to lay aside the classic tradition of rational psychology and invited them to adopt with him the biological approach. This exchange involved several innovations. To begin, James gave psychological phenomena a new philosophical orientation. Instead of conceiving of a primordial mind whose role was purely to know, he conceived of mind as a latecomer

[11] *Cf. infra,* p. 296.

in the evolutionary series whose role was to aid man in making better practical adjustments to his environment.

After identifying mind with biological adjustment to the environment, James went a step further to point to the organic basis of psychological life. Having taken his first professional study in medicine, he was especially sensitive to the possibilities of a close connection between psychology and the sister sciences of physiology and neurology, a connection that German investigators had already well explored. Speculation on this point had been indulged in from the time of Plato. With remarkable insight Plato had located the seat of the psyche in the brain, but his support of a mind-body dualism had greatly limited this physiological relation. Aristotle's mislocation of the psyche in the heart[12] was not so significant for the later career of the mind-body dualism as was his already noted assertion that the active intellect was freed from the body and survived it after death, which greatly retarded the subsequent development of a monistic theory of the mind-body relation. By the latter half of the nineteenth century, however, scientific psychologists were making some progress in this direction, as witness Hall's association of psychosis with neurosis. In addressing his psychological remarks to teachers, James boldly committed himself to much the same theory, although anxieties about its materialism were raised in the minds of his audience.

Yet he begged off from the obligation of offering any exact explanation of what the mind-body relation was. In place of such an explanation he suggested that teachers content themselves with a description of the way psychological life functions. Thus he was one of the early founders of the school of functional psychology. His description of the way in which the mind functions, however, was the least original part of his functional psychology. Even his famous phrase "the stream of consciousness" was only a more graphic description of the succeeding or passing states of mind earlier described and analyzed by David Hume. Besides, the focus and margin that James attributed to the stream of consciousness resulted in a concept that was but a less sharply defined adaptation of Herbart's threshold of consciousness. Because of such antecedents as these it is no surprise that James further described mental functions in terms of the already familiar concepts of association and apperception. To improve the schoolboy's memory, for instance, James recommended observance of the laws of association, especially those of contiguity and similarity.

More novel in his treatment of functionalism was James's discussion of instincts. He took issue with psychologies that viewed the learner as a sort of passive receptacle for impressions. On the contrary, he

---

[12] This mislocation may account for the phrase "to learn by heart."

adhered to the principle of no reception without reaction, no impression without expression. Moreover, he held that certain reactions or powers to express oneself were unlearned and part of native endowment. While the educational psychologies of Locke and Herbart had emphasized nurture and environment, James returned to Aristotle and the faculty psychologists to emphasize nature and heredity. Yet, in delineating the functioning of native capacities, James described them not as faculties but as instincts. Faculties and instincts have this in common, that they are both concerned with inherent functions of the learner, but they differ markedly in the categories under which the various functions are classified. Among others, faculties had been distinguished into the functions of reason, memory, imagination, and attention because of the preeminence of the rational factor in learning. James's list of instincts, however, was made up with biological categories more generally in mind. Thus he enumerated such native functions, or instincts, as fear, love, curiosity, imitation, pride, ambition, pugnacity, ownership, and constructiveness.

Instinct psychology differed notably from faculty psychology also in the manner in which it figured in learning. In faculty psychology, learning occurred through exercise of the faculties. In the case of instincts *"every acquired reaction is, as a rule, either a complication grafted on a native reaction, or a substitute for a native reaction, which the same object originally tended to provoke."*[13] In explaining learning in this fashion, James remarkably anticipated the subsequent development of learning as "conditioning" or "associative shifting." Since the teacher's art consists in grafting acquired reactions onto unlearned ones, it becomes of the utmost importance for him to be well acquainted with the pupil's original equipment of unlearned responses.

The outstanding functional psychologist in education during the first quarter of the twentieth century was Edward Lee Thorndike (1874–1949), a former pupil of James. Thorndike first came into prominence with his experimental studies in animal learning. By observing the animals' efforts to escape from a puzzle box constructed for them, he came to certain notable conclusions about the nature of the learning process. Central was his theory that learning the right response was largely accidental, a matter of trial and error. Progress in learning, that is, in the reduction of the number of errors and the increase in the number of successes, could be plotted in the form of a learning curve. To state this differently, learning was a matter of connecting the right stimulus with the right response. Hence,

[13] W. James, *Talks to Teachers* (Henry Holt and Company, Inc., New York, 1899), p. 38. *Cf.* G. Maciuszko, "Talks to Teachers on Psychology," *Educational Theory*, 7:53–55, April, 1957.

Thorndike's educational psychology has often been known as "connectionism" or "S-R bond psychology."

Going a step further, Thorndike reduced learning as the formation of bonds, or connections, to a set of laws. The principal laws of learning he declared to be the laws of exercise and effect. The law of exercise stated that when a connection between a situation and a response is exercised, the strength of that connection is increased. Conversely, when it is not exercised, the bonds, or connections, tend to weaken. The law of effect stated that the individual tends to repeat or learn quickly those bonds whose formation and exercise are accompanied or reinforced by a satisfying state of affairs. Conversely, again, the individual tends to weaken connections that are accompanied by an annoying state of affairs. The latter of these laws was reckoned the more important because it gave a plausible account of why some connections, or bonds, are eliminated and some are retained.

Among several subsidiary laws of learning it will be enough to mention here the law governing "associative shifting" or, as some have come to call it, "conditioning." This law states the circumstances under which a response originally connected with one situation, or stimulus, can become shifted to or associated with another stimulus so that in the future the second stimulus will become connected with it to call it forth. This shift is brought about, according to Thorndike, by simultaneously presenting the new stimulus with the old one. In this way bonds are formed to connect both stimuli with the initial response. When this has been accomplished, the old stimulus can be withdrawn and the new stimulus alone will call forth the old response.[14]

Here we have elaborated in detail James's theory of education as grafting new responses on native or unlearned ones. While pausing to note this historical connection, it may be well to note several other antecedents of Thorndike's inspiration. One of these stemmed back to Alexander Bain (1818–1903), the English inspiration of James's thoughts on habit formation. In the mid-nineteenth century Bain had already put forth a theory of learning that commenced with multiple random actions from which those which brought satisfaction were retained and fixed through repetition. But it is to Thorndike's credit that he gave clear formulation to this theory, based on experimental evidence. As to Thorndike's indebtedness to association and apperception psychology, the very conception of associative shifting is probably sufficient witness. Yet again, it was his clever

[14] The Russian physiologist Ivan Petrovich Pavlov is perhaps most famous for experimental work on the conditioned-reflex type of learning in animals.

and experimental use of old ideas that entitled him to front-rank recognition as an educational psychologist.

In addition to his contribution to general learning theory, Thorndike shed considerable light on several more specific learning problems. In spite of its theoretical criticism and rejection by Locke and Herbart, faculty psychology continued right into the twentieth century to enjoy wide popularity. That educational corollary of faculty psychology, the theory of formal discipline and transfer of training, particularly retained a strong grip on laymen and teachers with little or no training in psychology. Thorndike, in cooperation with Robert S. Woodworth and followed by a long line of other investigators, set up experimental situations to test the actual extent to which improvement in one field of activity would spread or transfer to other fields.[15] The upshot of most of these studies was to discount severely the traditional broad claims for transfer, which ran close to 100 per cent. Some investigators went to the other extreme of claiming that their results showed no transfer at all. Thorndike in his conclusions made the more moderate claim that there was evidence of transfer but only to the extent that there were identical or similar elements in the two situations under which practice took place.

The results of these studies not only shook confidence in the theory of transfer but also cast further doubt on the validity of the whole faculty conception of educational psychology. The effects of learning, instead of resulting in the general improvement of a faculty, were now seen to be very specific. One learned precisely what he practiced doing. Indeed, in so far as one acted, he became modified, and in so far as he become modified, he learned. Innate functions there were, to be sure, but it was as instincts rather than as faculties that they were modified or improved by later learning. At first Thorndike followed his former teacher James in distinguishing a long list of instincts. His later tendency, however, was to see that much of what was formerly thought instinct was really absorbed from the culture in which the learner grew up. Moreover, instincts came to be regarded as very plastic and capable of numerous modifications both as to the nature of their stimuli and as to the form of their response.

The theory of the specificity of learning led to many studies of how bonds, or connections, were formed in very specific learning situations. Thorndike led off with studies in the psychology of arithmetic and vocabulary. He was followed by others who investigated such specific problems as the best way to add and subtract, diagnosis

[15] E. L. Thorndike and R. S. Woodworth, "The Influence of Improvement in One Mental Function upon the Efficiency of Other Functions," *Psychological Review*, 8:247–261, 384–395, 553–564, May, July, November, 1901.

of most common number-combination errors, and the influence of age and sex. Charles Hubbard Judd (1873–1946) and others did pioneer work on the psychology of reading which later led to such important discoveries as the way in which eye movements and perception span function in learning to read. In the course of time nearly all the subjects in the elementary and secondary school curricula received similar psychological attention.[16]

BEHAVIORISM

In spite of the progress it made, functional educational psychology was not without its contemporary critics. There were many, for instance, who thought that functional psychology was using a very dubious analogy in predicating its learning theory to such an extent on animal learning. Broadening this criticism, they even expressed skepticism about whether or not data drawn so largely from a study of bodily behavior rather than the field of consciousness could properly be called psychology. Undaunted by this reappearance of the old mind-body dualism, some functionalists just before the First World War magnified the behavioristic approach into a school of educational psychology known as "behaviorism."

The distinctive feature of behaviorism was its identification of all psychological phenomena with patterns of motor response. Even the phenomena of consciousness like mental imagery and purpose were reduced to some form or other of bodily response. "Muscle-twitch psychology" was the name given to behaviorism by its critics. Thinking, for instance, was described as a laryngeal or subvocal habit. Furthermore, behavior as habit formation was exalted at the expense of instinctive behavior. In fact, John B. Watson (1878–1958), the leader of the behavioristic movement, found only three functional propensities at birth—love, fear, and rage. This finding greatly increased for him the range of controlled behavior.

Two important advantages were claimed for the behavioristic approach to psychological problems. For one thing, it freed psychological study from the subjective methods of investigation through introspection. Reducing psychological phenomena to overt instances of behavior, therefore, brought nearer the day when educational psychology could be studied as objectively as other sciences. For another thing, behaviorism, like previous educational psychologies emphasizing nurture rather than nature, held out great hopes to educators, doctors,

---

[16] For example, see W. H. Gray, *Psychology of Elementary School Subjects* (Prentice-Hall, Inc., Englewood Cliffs, N.J., 1938); H. B. Reed, *Psychology and Teaching of Secondary School Subjects* (Prentice-Hall, Inc., Englewood Cliffs, N.J., 1939).

politicians, and businessmen for controlling human conduct. Indeed, Watson went as far as to make the educational claim that, given a normal healthy baby at birth and given control over his subsequent conditioning environment, he could train the baby to become a "doctor, lawyer, artist, merchant-chief, and, yes, even beggarman and thief, regardless of his talents, penchants, tendencies, abilities, vocations and race of his ancestors."[17] Needless to say, at this point behaviorism was ceasing to be a psychology of education and was rapidly becoming a deterministic philosophy of education.

GESTALT PSYCHOLOGY

Other contemporaries of the functionalists made an even more radical departure from the functionalist theory of learning expounded by Thorndike. Their quarrel with functionalism, particularly as a child of the earlier associationism, was that it took too analytical a view of learning. It made the order of learning appear to be a matter of linking, or associating, bits of experience. Learning was a matter of going from part to whole. This new group of psychologists made the radical suggestion that the study of learning should commence with the whole. In making this suggestion they were definitely reflecting a similar movement in other cognate fields—"holism" in philosophy, "field theory" in physics, and the "organismic" approach to biology. Hence much of the twentieth-century emphasis on the education of the "whole" child.[18] In fact, gestaltists went so far as to claim that the mind was so constituted as to react to the total pattern or configuration of the situation. This school of psychological thought took its name from the German word for pattern, or configuration, *Gestalt,* since much of the initial experimentation on the idea was done in Germany. It had its heyday among progressive educators in the two decades preceding the Second World War.

The pith of gestalt psychology can be quickly gained from one of their figures. For instance, draw a triangle omitting portions of each side. Although the figure has been drawn with gaps in it, imagination seems to have an inescapable tendency to ignore or close them and thus complete the triangle. This tendency toward closure is characteristically gestalt. One reacts to the total situation, to undisclosed but thinly veiled elements, as well as to the fully disclosed ones. To employ a favorite word of the gestaltists, learning involves

[17] *Cf.* J. B. Watson, *Behaviorism* (The People's Institute Publishing Co., New York, 1925), p. 217. For a similar statement by Edward L. Thorndike. see "The Contribution of Psychology to Education," *Journal of Educational Psychology,* 1:6, January, 1910.

[18] Even functional psychologists were not unmindful of the importance of the whole, as witness their attention to "concomitant learnings."

"insight." After surveying all the factors in a situation, suddenly these factors seem to shake down into a pattern, or configuration.

Take the famous case of Wolfgang Köhler's apes. One chimpanzee, after learning to seize food beyond his reach with the aid of a stick, was given two sticks neither one of which was long enough to reach the food but both of which, if fitted together, brought it within reach. The solution of fitting the sticks together occurred to the chimpanzee after more than an hour of trial-and-error behavior. When it came, it was not the result of random accidental motor behavior. It came so suddenly, was attended with such new liveliness, and was remembered so well the next day that it left no doubt in Köhler's mind that learning had occurred through genuine insight.

The gestalt theory of learning through insight was not intended to be regarded as just another kind of learning in addition to trial-and-error theory. Gestalt psychology regarded learning as doing something new. Newness, it contended, could not be understood by analyzing the situation alone. On the contrary, newness consisted in a reorganization of the situation so as to bridge the gap between the situation and one's goal. This gap is bridged when the situation is suddenly seen as a pattern including and leading to the goal.

COGNITIVE LEARNING

Also reacting to the importance of the larger learning situation but not necessarily in the manner of the gestaltists were other important movements in educational psychology. One principal group consisted of those interested in very complex forms of learning, such as the forms involving thinking, problem solving, and creativity. Early in this field was Dewey himself. But when he wrote *How We Think,* he may more likely have been writing a logical rather than a psychological treatise. Perhaps, therefore, it was Boyd H. Bode (1873–1953), a fellow pragmatist, who tried to analyze cognitive learning in more precisely psychological terms. Although not a psychologist, Bode felt called upon as a philosopher to intervene among the "conflicting psychologies of learning."[19] He conceded that the educational psychologist must commence with a striving, purposing individual reacting to stimuli. But the secret of purposive learning, as he saw it, was the ability of the individual to keep reconstructing the stimulus as he got "feedback" from the consequences of acting on it. In Bode's mind the reconstruction of the stimulus was connected with the theory of meaning. When a thing is used as a sign of something else, it

[19] The title of Bode's first book on educational psychology was *Conflicting Psychologies of Learning* (D. C. Heath and Company, Boston, 1929). Later this was revised under the title *How We Learn* (1940).

may be said to mean the latter. Now, to use a thing as a sign alters it. The alteration arises from the fact that there is usually a difference between the object as suggested or meant and the object as actually perceived later on. When this difference has been noted, it becomes necessary to remake the meaning or stimulus to conform to fact. When this has been done, the learner is ready to react to the reconstructed stimulus and use it to suggest future meanings. This process goes on continually and is especially useful in explaining complex problems of learning. It fits in very well with Dewey's theory of education as the constant reconstruction of experience.

Moreover, Bode's theory of learning afforded a neat account of that higher learning known as "concept formation." Thus Bode said, "This process of relating the present thing to the thing meant in such a way that the latter is recognized as a suggested object is tied up with the process of concept formation. In order to form a concept the thing meant must not only be contrasted with the present thing so as to become a suggested object, but must further be detached from the present thing altogether so that it can be dealt with independently."[20] When detached, it becoms a concept.

The analysis of cognitive learning fairly leaped into large importance after the Second World War. To catch up with the Russians, when it became evident that Americans were trailing them in space exploration, doubled and redoubled effort was expended not only on space technology but on ways of developing creative minds that would improve the technology. One attack on this problem went back and took up where the old theory of transfer of training had been derailed. Transfer had not so much been disproved, claimed Jerome S. Bruner (1915–   ), as it had been badly stated in terms of faculty psychology. To him there was every evidence that massive transfer could be achieved by the appropriate management of learning. The key to proper management was twofold. On the one hand, it involved structuring the curriculum so that the interrelatedness of its parts could be clearly grasped and transfer expedited.[21] On the other, it involved organizing instruction so that children would themselves discover relationships rather than depend on the teacher to point them out. The great merit of this device was that success in discovery was self-rewarding.[22] Children would thus be intrinsically motivated to learn and so confirm Aristotle's belief that man by nature desires to know.

[20] *Ibid.*, p. 257.

[21] J. S. Bruner, *The Process of Education* (Harvard University Press, Cambridge, Mass., 1960), pp. 6–9.

[22] J. S. Bruner, "The Act of Discovery," in R. Gross and J. Murphy (eds.), *The Revolution in the Schools* (Harcourt, Brace & World, Inc., New York, 1964), pp. 144–156.

The emphasis on discovery in learning theory was no isolated academic phenomenon. On the contrary it was reinforced by the international competition to excel in aerospace exploration. Both Russian and American educators spurred the study of how creative students could be spotted and creativity cultivated. While creative students generally had high IQs, it was clear that a high IQ was no guarantee of creative capacities. Often teachers seemed to favor students with high IQs and too often were annoyed with creative ones because their capacity for imagination and invention tended to lead to divergent rather than convergent thinking.[23]

FREUDIAN PSYCHOLOGY

Perhaps nowhere in psychology is the impact of the whole more clearly seen than in the impact of Freudian psychology on education. Psychoanalysis was originally a therapy the Viennese physician Sigmund Freud (1856–1939) worked out for treating patients with marked neuroses. Freud's therapy of psychoanalysis consisted in getting his patients to talk out their troubles with him. The more he succeeded in getting his patients to recollect and release the most intimate and confidential facts about their pasts, the more successful he was in enabling them to understand and overcome their neurotic conduct.

After much experience with the technique of psychoanalysis, Freud came to certain theoretical conclusions. Perhaps basic was the fact that all conduct is motivated by the primitive biological drives of the individual. When these drives fail to function normally and an awkward maladjustment to the environment results, neuroses are likely to occur. This is especially the case when the social environment may hold unacceptable the normal functioning of some native propensity like sex and demands its repression. Only less important are situations in which normal desires are left unfulfilled by the environment. The danger is that these native or primitive desires when repressed or unfulfilled seek release under other guises. Freud and his followers identified a number of these, such as the "defense mechanism," "rationalization," "compensation," "logic-tight compartments," the "inferiority complex," and others.

Most important for education, Freud noticed that a great many neuroses have their origin in childhood. Gaining secure lodgment in the child's past before he is able to understand what is going on, these neuroses become mainsprings for adult conduct whose origin

[23] J. W. Getzels and P. W. Jackson, "Educating for Creativity," in R. Gross and J. Murphy (eds.), *The Revolution in the Schools* (Harcourt, Brace & World, Inc., New York, 1964), pp. 170–183.

is lost in the past and whose original motives are hidden even from their owner. The establishment of this fact has been a great spur to giving much more careful attention to wholesome living and educational conditions for the years of early childhood. It has been no less useful in analyzing the behavior difficulties of older problem children.

It should also be mentioned that psychoanalysis was a force in the mental hygiene movement. The attention paid by schools to physical hygiene at the end of the nineteenth century was, in the twentieth, expanded to include mental hygiene as well. For long, pioneer workers on the frontiers of medicine, criminology, social work, education, and even religion had been aware of the need to diagnose and care for the mentally ill. The rapid growth of both psychoanalysis and psychological testing in the twentieth century so advanced the study of the mentally abnormal that preventive work came to take on equal importance with therapeutic. Maintenance of the normal mind through mental hygiene thus became as important a function of the school as the diagnosis and remedy of the abnormal mind.[24] In order to assume some of this work, visiting teachers, teachers of special classes, and guidance counselors took on quasi-psychiatric functions.

SOCIAL PSYCHOLOGY

The more educational psychology became interested in wholes, the more it moved from a study of the individual learner to a study of the learner in a social situation. Among the first to point to the importance of social psychology in learning theory was George Herbert Meade (1863–1931). Perhaps as a legacy from the soul theory of psychology it was long thought that the child is born with a self, but according to Meade this is not so. Selfhood is a product of social interaction. At first the baby does not differentiate himself from his family or those about him. This is something that he has to learn to do. Out of his early random activities he selects those habits and attitudes whose expression his group rewards. He learns to play the role which his family, his neighborhood, his gang, his schools, his church, and other organizations expect. If he fails to live up to these norms of behavior, he will suffer from the disappointment of the groups from which he draws his social sustenance. Ultimately his personality and even his reputation will be structured by the tension of these social forces.

---

[24] See W. H. Burnham, *Great Teachers and Mental Health* (D. Appleton-Century Company, Inc., New York, 1926).

Another close student of the social aspect of learning was Kurt Lewin (1890–1947). By background he was peculiarly suited to this task. On the one side he early belonged to the school of gestalt psychologists, describing his own brand as "field theory," and on the other he had a strong interest in motivation. The advent of World War II caused him to focus both of these interests on what he later came to call "social dynamics." A notable study which he pioneered examined the kind of behavior generated in class when the teacher conducts himself democratically, autocratically, or in a laissez-faire manner. As one might expect, from Meade if no other, the student practices the kind of habits and attitudes exhibited by the leader. Later the development of group learning was studied through role playing, and lines of social force were plotted through the sociogram.

In looking back on the development of educational psychology in the twentieth century, one sees that points of view have had a tendency to appear, disappear, and reappear. Some theories are disproved, some just neglected, and some, if they reappear, usually do so after a degree of transformation. Thus, though no one talks of apperception any more, it persists in associationism, and associationism is involved in transfer, conditioning, and the newer cognitive learning. Gestalt psychology, at first the lone critic of atomism in educational psychology, has had to share its limelight with such other holistic movements as psychoanalysis and social dynamics. As a result educational psychology by mid-century, instead of presenting the profession with several thoroughbred schools of thought, seems to be crossbreeding.

MEASUREMENT AND INDIVIDUAL DIFFERENCES

Not least among the twentieth century's rich and varied contributions to educational psychology was the progress made in the psychological measurement of individual differences. Though a beginning in the accurate scientific measurement of these differences was not undertaken till the end of the nineteenth century, the differences themselves had been noted all through the history of education. To mention but a few cases, Plato in his *Republic* sorted children out and prepared them to become philosophers, warriors, or artisans according to whether they were possessed of golden, silver, or leaden talents of mind. In preparing boys to become Roman orators, Quintilian granted that some boys surpassed others in ability but claimed that dull and unteachable ones were as rare as those born with monstrous deformities. Frankly facing individual differences, the Renaissance's great schoolteacher, Vittorino da Feltre (1378–1446), encouraged none to expect education for careers beyond their capacities. Later, John

Locke observed that children have such different natures that little or nothing may be done to make the pensive child gay or the sportive one restrained.

A theory of the mind like Locke's *tabula rasa* has been used historically both to support and to contradict the existence of individual differences. Although his theory reduced all minds to a blank at birth and therefore apparently to equality, Locke himself did not hold them equal. Impressions made on a mind like wax, he realized, would not endure like those made on a mind like brass or steel. His French followers, however, disregarded this analogy and proceeded on the assumption that minds were not only a blank at birth but possessed of the same sensibility. The patent differences that minds exhibited were due, therefore, to exposure to different sorts of environment and different types of education. But whatever the source of these differences, whether of nature or nurture, the only comfort offered was the widely held belief that a principle of compensation governed their distribution. Thus, slowness of wits might be compensated by fleetness of foot, beauty of voice, or strength of arm.

It was one thing to note these differences but quite another to assay them. For long, the conventional method of assaying differences was the recitation or examination. By these devices teachers early learned to separate the sheep from the goats in both intellectual aptitude and scholastic achievement. The origin of their units of measure or grades is obscured in the remote past. There is evidence in eighteenth-century America, however, of the use of such descriptive terms as *optimi,* second *optimi, inferiores,* and *pejores* (best, second best, inferior, and worse). There is further evidence that early in the nineteenth century this fourfold method of marking or grading was translated into a numerical system by which students were rated on a scale ranging from 1 to 4. Later on, to recognize more than four grades of work, decimals were introduced, as 2.4 or 3.5. Other multiples of 4 were also used, including 100, which finally became the most popular.[25] But, in the long run, serious doubt arose in teachers' minds as to the dependability of such fine discriminations in pupils' achievement as marking on the basis of 100 permitted and encouraged. Instead of 100 grades, one reaction reverted to the earlier plan of distinguishing just 4 or in some cases 5 grades. For these they instituted letters, usually the first four or five in the alphabet, to indicate grades of work from excellent to failing. Some teachers trebled these grades by optionally adding a plus or a minus to each

[25] *Cf.* M. L. Smallwood, *An Historical Study of Examination and Grading Systems in Early American Universities* (Harvard University Press, Cambridge, Mass., 1935).

grade. Another reaction directed its attention to the subjective quality of all grades, whether letter, number, or descriptive. It pointed to the notorious variability among teachers even when they read the same student's examination paper in mathematics.[26]

It is not surprising, therefore, that in the course of time a demand should arise for a more exact measurement of individual differences and their educational products. The first educational psychologist to try to achieve precision by casting psychological data in mathematical terms was Herbart. In his psychology, it will be remembered, the dynamic quality of life manifested in idea, feeling, and will was supposed to be the result of the mutual attraction or repulsion of reals as they assailed each other. Just as Sir Isaac Newton formed the mathematical equation for the gravitation of heavenly bodies toward each other, so it seems to have been Herbart's hope to state a similar equation for his doctrine of apperception. Lacking objective or experimental evidence for his conclusions, he made no headway whatever toward a science of psychometrics.

A more profitable clue to the measurement of differences came from the Englishman Francis Galton. Influenced by Charles Darwin and biology more strongly than by psychology, Galton was early struck by the great hereditary differences in men. In publishing his pioneer studies in this field, he made his conclusions the more cogent by the application of novel statistical devices, which he developed. What Galton did to point out hereditary biological differences, the American J. McKeen Cattell did to call attention to psychological differences in reaction time, keenness of eyesight and hearing, perception of pitch, and the like. Wundt, the father of experimental psychology, had tried to minimize such differences or hide them in averages. But Cattell insisted that deviations from the average could be as significant as the average itself.

A quite different and still more promising approach to measurement was that of the Frenchman Alfred Binet (1857–1911) and his assistant Théophile Simon, who were the first to devise a practical yardstick for measuring intelligence. They were commissioned by their government to work out a test whereby authorities might know more precisely which children were of such low intelligence that they should be committed to an institution. After experimenting with a variety of tests, some of them anthropometric, they finally evolved their famous scale. This scale was made up of a series of well-selected questions to test common sense and judgment within a field of experience common to all children of a given culture. By giving the test

[26] For example, see D. Starch and E. C. Elliott, "The Reliability of Grading High School Work in Mathematics," *School Review,* 21:254–259, September, 1913.

to numbers of children, Binet and Simon were able to establish norms for children of various chronological ages. Children whose intellectual age, as indicated by performance on this test, fell below their chronological age were noted as retarded. The degree of retardation was determined by subtracting the intellectual age from the chronological. Only later was it seen by another investigator that a more constant relation between the two factors could be gained by dividing the intellectual by the chronological age. This gave the intelligence quotient, or IQ, so widely used to measure normal and accelerated children as well as retarded ones. Of course, the test had to be revised to tap the common experience of the children of different nations. In the United States this was most popularly accomplished in the Stanford revision of the Binet-Simon test.[27]

But the man who made educators measurement-conscious was Thorndike. At the turn of the century he offered what was probably the first university course in measurement. It consisted for the most part in an application of statistics to education. Statistics was no new thing, the mathematical theory of large-group phenomena having already been well launched by the Belgian Lambert Albert Jacques Quételet (1796–1874) in the early nineteenth century. The possibility of applying statistics to education, however, was not perceived till Thorndike and his followers familiarized American educators with such concepts as averages, means, sigma scores, probable errors, correlations, and the like.

Nevertheless, there were many early doubters who thought that psychological data were too spiritual, too inaccessible, and too varied to be measured exactly. They saw no possibility of transmuting qualitative differences into quantitative terms. The proponents of measurement retorted that what could not be measured could not be known and was therefore of doubtful value. This bold retort rested on the assumptions that whatever exists at all exists in some amount and that what exists in amount can be measured. Attacking these assumptions, Dewey pointed out that education was concerned not so much with what existed as with what did not yet exist, that is, with emergent learning. In spite of the controversy over presuppositions, the measurement movement won a secure place in American education. If it was not so exact as the more exact sciences, its pragmatic significance became well established. Indeed, the rise of democracy with its empha-

---

[27] It is interesting to note that after 1930 the Russians banned the intelligence tests of "pedologists" as a bourgeois prejudice restrictive of educational opportunity. Lately, however, this antipathy has been undermined somewhat by the decline in official prestige of the geneticist Trofim Denisovich Lysenko, who claimed, contrary to learned opinion, that acquired characteristics could be inherited.

sis on numbers made the statistical study of numbers almost a necessity.[28]

From this point on the momentum and scope of measurement increased continually. Progress was made in group as well as individual tests of intelligence. The group tests proved of special use in mobilizing America for both the First and the Second World War. Besides attention to intelligence, whole batteries of achievement tests were fashioned and standardized. By these, schools all over the country were able to judge themselves in terms of national norms. Tests to measure differences of aptitude and even personality traits were devised. Great progress in gaining professional confidence and overcoming popular prejudice was made when the Character Education Inquiry made extensive use of measurement techniques.

Before the measurement of differences took on a scientific character, there was a popular notion abroad not only that good and bad traits were mutually compensated but that individuals could be classed into distinct types. One of the chief things that measurement revealed, even as early as Galton's studies, was the absence or, perhaps better, the overlapping of types. When large enough numbers were taken into account, it was seen that differences were distributed in a continuous gradation from one extreme to another. In other words, individual differences fit the Gaussian normal-distribution curve. Even in measuring the differences between two sexes or races, the amount of difference was found to be very slight as compared with differences within a single race or sex. Turning from differences between individuals to differences between traits within a given individual, investigators found that ability in one trait tended to be highly correlated with a like ability in other traits. This finding disposed once and for all of the traditional notion of compensation.

[28] H. M. Walker, "Democracy and Statistical Method," *Teachers College Record*, 32:599–607, April, 1931.

7 Methods of Instruction

How to transform the child's ignorance into understanding is the problem beyond all others that has stood most persistently at the educator's elbow throughout the long course of educational history. In simplest terms, this problem has taken the form of determining the most effective things the teacher can do in order to get the child to modify his ways of behaving. In a more advanced state, it has taken the form of working out a method of exposition so that the child will not only change his ways but also comprehend what he is doing. In yet another form, the problem of instructional method is a matter of devising ways to motivate learning so that it will occur easily and be remembered.

The development of instructional method has not taken place in isolation. On the contrary, it has been intimately caught up in developments in other phases of education. As might be suspected, instructional methods have been unusually sensitive to change in the psychological theory of how learning takes place. Furthermore, the philosophical conception of the nature of man and the world in which he lives is a potent determinant of educational method. No less significant are the aims of education and the particular form of social and political organization under which the child is reared. Change any of these factors, and the method of instruction must change correspondingly.

IMITATION AND MEMORIZATION

The chief anxiety of primitive and even early civilized cultures concerned survival. In those days survival was precarious at best, so little known or so

167

misunderstood were the contingencies that surrounded people. Consequently, these cultures counted themselves successful if they reproduced themselves. They did not aim to survive by experimenting with the precarious but were content if they lost none of the experience of their ancestors. The method of instruction that early men found most appropriate to such circumstances was imitation. Children commenced to imitate their elders first in play. Toys and games were miniatures of adult activities. As children grew older, they imitated their elders more closely by participating directly in the hunt, in agriculture, in domestic duties, and in civic and religious ceremonies. The more advanced the culture, the more it was perpetuated by story and oral tradition. Naturally, before writing had been perfected, stories, traditions, and myths had to be memorized to ensure their conservation and reproduction.

Even after the development of writing and the recording of the folkways had ensured them against loss, methods of instruction continued to depend upon imitation and memorization. Among the Chinese, for instance, it was customary for the teacher at the lower levels to read a line from the traditional texts to his children and then have them repeat it after him. When the children returned to their seats, they committed the line to memory by continuing to repeat it aloud. Indeed, loudness of repetition was supposed to make the impression on memory the more emphatic. In any event, the practice explains why ancient Chinese schools were very noisy places. After committing the line to memory the pupil was expected to "back his book," that is, turn his back on his book and recite his lesson from memory.

This simple test of learning was followed at the end of one's schooling by the public examinations for appointment to posts in the civil service. As might be imagined from the kind of preparation the Chinese made for this examination, the highest marks were given to those candidates with the greatest powers of retention and reproduction. Examinations were marked for literary excellence as well as factual content, but even in the matter of literary form, where some originality might have been expected to count in a candidate's favor, his success was judged by his ability to conform to the style of the ancient and acknowledged masters of literary style.

A method of instruction that laid so much store by repetition and conformity naturally tended to become formal. Great teachers like Confucius (551–478 B.C.) were not unaware of this risk. Confucius particularly warned against memorizing the Chinese classics without understanding them or without habituating oneself to act upon them. "Learning without thought," he announced, "is labor lost, and thought without learning is perilous."[1] Another Chinese sage had

[1] Quoted in M. M. Dawson, *Ethics of Confucius* (G. P. Putnam's Sons, New York, 1920), p. 20.

the penetrating insight to advise the schoolmaster that "He ought to incite, animate, and urge his pupils, but never press them, still less force them."[2] Yet another advised the master not to pass too quickly from one subject of instruction to another or try to explain several things at once. The supreme art of teaching, ran a last maxim, lies in getting the pupil himself to ask questions.

In ancient India educational method was a similar mixture of wise precept and practice. There, too, great emphasis was laid on memorization of the sacred texts. Preferably, the texts were to be memorized with understanding, but all too frequently memorization was all that was achieved. The failure to understand the significance of what was learned often made learning a very dull if not soul-destroying experience. Consequently, there was an ever-present inclination on the part of teachers to resort to severe disciplinary measures to keep their pupils at their lessons. But the sage Manu declared, "Good instruction must be given pupils without unpleasant sensations, and the teacher who reverences virtue must use sweet and gentle words."[3] Yet even Manu recognized occasions when the instructor would have to punish faults with severe words and even threaten blows should the offense be repeated.

The educational methods found appropriate in Oriental China and India proved no less appropriate among peoples closer to the beginnings of the Occidental educational tradition. Thus it is interesting to note that in Hebrew שָׁנָה (*shānāh*), the word "to repeat," is also the word meaning "to teach." Hence learning the Mosaic law, the chief item in the Jewish curriculum, was largely a matter of rote memory. In turn, rote memory produced conformity to the law. The Biblical injunction of Jehovah, "What thing soever I command you, observe to do it: thou shalt not add thereto, nor diminish from it," discouraged any spontaneity of initiative.[4]

Conventionally, methods of instruction among the Jews were as barren in their formality as they were among the Orientals. The Talmudic writings, fortunately, did not ignore this shortcoming. One finds there a number of observations for improving instruction. Perhaps chief is the importance attached to understanding the material to be memorized. But understanding always seems subordinated to memorizing, as witness the injunction "First learn by heart and then know."[5] Another directive begins "The teacher should strive to make the lesson agreeable to the pupils by clear reasons, as well as by

---

[2] Quoted in S. S. Laurie, *Historical Survey of Pre-Christian Education* (Longmans, Green & Co., Inc., New York, 1900), p. 145.

[3] *Ibid.,* p. 176.

[4] Deuteronomy 12:32.

[5] Laurie, *op. cit.,* p. 95.

frequent repetitions" but concludes with the inevitable "until they thoroughly understand the matter and are enabled to recite it with great fluency."[6]

A more ominous ambiguity than that contained in the word that means both "to repeat" and "to teach" is offered by the Hebrew word מוּסָר (*mūsar*), which means both "instruction" and "chastisement." Thus the Biblical warning, "Despise not the chastening of the Lord," may be equally well translated "Despise not the instruction of the Lord." From this disciplinary angle Jewish methods of instruction were quite severe, especially in early Jewish history. With the Jews as with their early oppressors, the Egyptians, the rod was the symbol of instruction. The Book of Proverbs manifests its faith in the rod when it says, "He that spareth his rod hateth his son: but he that loveth him chasteneth him betimes" and "Foolishness is bound in the heart of a child; but the rod of correction shall drive it far from him." Again, "The rod and reproof give wisdom: but a child left to himself bringeth his mother to shame."[7] The Book of Ecclesiasticus further supported the rod by stating that "He that loveth his son will continue to lay stripes upon him that he may have joy of him in the end. He that chastiseth his son shall have profit of him, and shall glory of him among his acquaintance. . . . He that maketh too much of his son shall bind up his wounds; and his heart shall be troubled at every cry. An unbroken horse becometh stubborn; and a son left at large becometh headstrong. Cocker thy child, and he shall make thee afraid; play with him, and he will grieve thee. Laugh not with him, lest thou have sorrow with him. . . . Give him no liberty in his youth, and wink not at his follies. Bow down his neck in his youth, and beat him on the sides while he is a child, lest he wax stubborn, and be disobedient unto thee: and there shall be sorrow to thy soul."[8] Should the rod fail, there was even authority in Deuteronomy that a son be put to death.[9]

In contrast to such severity later Jewish methods seem more temperate. The Talmud even recommended that older pupils be not compelled to undergo corporal punishment lest it instill a rebellious spirit in them. Moreover, punishment should be meted out only to such younger pupils as have the capacity to respond by improving their learning performance. If they are congenitally dull and incapable of learning, the Talmud says they should not be punished. Even when

---

[6] *Ibid.*, p. 96.

[7] Proverbs 13:24, 22:15, 29:15.

[8] Ecclesiasticus 30:1–13. As late as the seventeenth century in colonial America the rod of correction was recognized in the town of Dorchester, Massachusetts, as a divine ordinance of God in the education of children.

[9] Deuteronomy 21:18–21.

punishment is indicated, the Talmud directs, "Children should be punished with one hand and caressed with two."[10]

The educational methods of imitation and memorization also pervaded early Greek education. During Homeric times and for a long time afterward the great man of noble example was held up for the young to imitate. With the emergence of the city-state as the central feature of Greek life, the laws provided the pattern that had to be memorized. In either case, the method of instruction aimed to affect conduct. There was no divorce of word and deed. The young were constantly under the surveillance of their elders. Whether under the eye of the parent, the Spartan "inspirer," or the Athenian pedagogue, a young man was continually being directed or reminded that "this is just and that is unjust; this is honorable, that is dishonorable; this is holy, that is unholy; do this and abstain from that. And if he obeys," added Protagoras, "well and good; if not, he is straightened by threats and blows, like a piece of warped wood."[11]

It is noteworthy that flogging was imposed not only to correct the wayward but also, especially in Sparta, to teach endurance of pain. As such, indeed, it was just another hardship like hunger, cold, and heat and hence ideal training for a society that, like Sparta, was constantly on a war footing. If voluntary floggings before the alter of Artemis are any evidence, Spartan boys liked rather than disliked such discipline.

SOCRATIC METHOD

The glory of Greek education is that it did not continue indefinitely to perpetuate Greek culture through imitation and memorization. By the fifth century B.C., methods of instruction that produced strict adherence to customary folkways began to give way for the first time to more critical procedures. Preeminent in the development of these procedures was the philosopher Socrates (469–399 B.C.), one of the greatest teachers of all time. In fact, the method of teaching that he employed has ever since borne his name. Briefly, the Socratic method aimed to teach not so much by transmitting knowledge as by inquiry into what might be accepted to be valid knowledge. This inquiry was carried on through the give and take of conversation, which Socrates guided by a cleverly put sequence of questions.

The details of this brief sketch of the Socratic method should be expanded under several headings. For one thing, Socrates did

[10] Quoted in G. Compayré, *History of Pedagogy* (D. C. Heath and Company, Boston, 1885), p. 10.

[11] B. Jowett, *Works of Plato* (Tudor Publishing Company, New York, n.d.), vol. 4, p. 157.

not approach the instructional situation as if he already knew the answers. Rather he approached it full of questions. One having obtained a tentative answer, he would proceed to put further questions to test its validity. The usual answers were little more than restatements of the uncriticized traditional or conventional thought of the day. Often Socrates would propose his own answer but even then usually in the form of a series of further questions. He always seemed to be feeling his way along, to be teaching by continually casting himself in the role of a learner.

Many thought the Socratic method of instruction to be quite ironic. That is, Socrates seemed initially to accept the responses made to his opening questions at their face value but then revealed his initial irony by proceeding to demonstrate the logical inadequacy of the response elicited by his interrogation. Any irony in the Socratic dialogues is perhaps more evident ex post facto to the reader than it was to Socrates himself. He genuinely did not claim to know. He did not claim to be σοφός, wise, as did the Sophists. Rather did he claim to be a φιλόσοφος, a lover of wisdom, which is the original meaning of our word "philosopher."[12]

Socrates's own version of his method was that it was maieutic. Modestly and reluctantly claiming to be possessed of wisdom himself, Socrates was more forward in claiming to recognize wisdom in others. He therefore took it as his peculiar function as a teacher to help others to give birth to the truth that was in them. Hence, on several occasions he referred to himself as an intellectual midwife. Viewed from this angle, his famous method of questioning was used like an obstetrician's forceps to deliver ideas. The most famous instance of such a delivery is recounted in Plato's *Meno*. There Socrates at random chose a boy off the street and by clever leading questions led him to demonstrate a geometrical theorem in spite of the fact that nothing had been further from the boy's whole experience the moment previous to Socrates's interrogation.[13] It should not be over-

---

[12] Story has it that Socrates was amazed that the Delphic oracle declared him the wisest man in Greece. Hence, he engaged any and all in conversation in search of one wiser than himself. Finding the wisdom of others to be mostly pretense, he finally agreed with the oracle but on the ground that he was the only man in Greece who did not think he was wise.

[13] It is interesting that in the nineteenth century Johann Heinrich Pestalozzi, whose method was also principally one of oral questioning, did not think the Socratic method appropriate for children because they lacked a background knowledge of both fact and linguistic expression to make it work. [R. R. Rusk, *Doctrines of the Great Educators* (Macmillan & Co., Ltd., London, 1918), p. 6.] The French educator and historian Gabriel Compayré took a similar view, asserting that the Socratic method might work for logical subjects like mathematics and grammar but not for content subjects like geography, history, and science. (Compayré, *op. cit.*, p. 24n.)

looked that the Socratic method squares with Plato's psychology of learning as a kind of recall of ideas once known but later lost in the recesses of memory.[14] Perhaps this theory also explains how the Latin verb *educere*, meaning "to lead forth," came to have the derivative form *educare* which later served as the origin of our English word "education."

The didactic questions that Socrates asked in his teaching-learning quest for knowledge in the course of time became a dialectic. The method of the Sophists with their cliché "man the measure of things" had emphasized what was individual and unique in human experience. Socrates was unwilling that learning should stop with such mere opinions or half thoughts, as he called them. Confident that true knowledge lay in the congruity or consistency of men's thoughts rather than in their uniqueness and diversity, he insisted on talking problems through till concepts could be formed that would undergird or generalize the differences revealed in discussion.[15]

Both Plato (427–347 B.C.) in his Academy and Aristotle in his Lyceum employed the dialectical method of instruction. Of the two perhaps Plato leaned a shade more heavily on the authority of the teacher. Not so dogmatic as the Spartan Pythagoras, whose *Ipse dixit* settled controversies for his pupils, Plato nevertheless did favor considerable control in the rearing of children. Pupil freedom he favored only after appropriate habits had been formed to warrant it. Yet he did not go so far as to countenance compulsion in learning, for he had grave misgivings that learning under compulsion would not have a lasting grip on the mind. Moreover, a freeman should not be treated like a slave in the acquisition of knowledge.

In expressing his anxiety about excessive freedom, Plato could almost be mistaken for a mid-twentieth-century writer on the subject. Unrestrained liberty, he feared, "will make its way into the home, until at last the very animals catch the infection of anarchy. The parent falls into the habit of behaving like the child, and the child like the parent: the father is afraid of his sons, and they show no fear or respect for their parents, in order to assert their freedom. . . . To descend to smaller matters, the schoolmaster timidly flatters his pupils and the pupils make light of their masters. . . . Generally speaking, the young copy their elders, argue with them, and

---

[14] For a fuller development of this theory, see *supra*, p. 138.

[15] John Dewey summarizes learning under the Socratic method as a search for opinions held by all men in common. Therefore dialectic is the means of finding agreement. There are three elements of such a dialectic: (1) an objective universal as the proper object of knowledge, (2) the implication of this universal in all particular opinions, and (3) the possibility of its discovery by systematic comparison of particulars. [P. Monroe (ed.), *Cyclopedia of Education* (The Macmillan Company, New York, 1912), vol. 3, pp. 373–374.]

will not do as they are told; while the old, anxious not to be thought disagreeable tyrants, imitate the young and condescend to enter into their jokes and amusements."[16]

Aristotle (384–322 B.C.) was generally opposed to dogmatic methods. The only way to learn to do things, he contended, was to do them. Therefore the only way he thought pupils could learn to think and organize their thoughts was to do their own mental tailoring. The teacher who would present the student with ready-to-wear thoughts deprived him of learning the art of cutting out and fitting together his own mental garments. Hence Aristotle was opposed to the instructional methods of the Sophists, "for," said he, "they used to hand out speeches to be learned by heart. . . . And therefore the teaching they gave their pupils was ready but rough. For they used to suppose that they trained people by imparting to them not the art but the products."[17]

Aristotle's chief improvement on the Socratic dialectic was that he perceived more clearly than his predecessors the role of concrete experience in teaching method. He believed that the Socratic method was moving in the right direction in striving to reach universals by induction. But the universal, he pointed out, was always implicit in the particular and concrete. Hence the implied importance of the teacher's going from the concrete to the abstract and from the particular to the general or universal.

Rapid educational progress might have followed on the further development of this now obvious educational truth of Aristotle's. But the generations of teachers who followed Aristotle were too dazzled by his principles of deductive logic. Consequently, they taught by deductively elaborating the implications of the works of the Greek masters and for long centuries seriously neglected Aristotle's inductive principles. Indeed, it is a singular circumstance in the history of educational method that, when teachers switched from teaching truth as something to be found out to something already perfected by the master and to be transmitted from teacher to pupil, the golden age of Greek education came to a close.

RHETORICAL METHOD

The Romans were no innovators in educational method. Yet, much as they copied from the Greek, they seem never to have copied Greek methods of instruction in their most creative phase, the dialectic of Socrates. In fact, Roman educational methods never rose much

---

[16] F. M. Cornford, *The Republic of Plato* (Oxford University Press, New York, 1953), p. 289.

[17] Aristotle, *De sophisticis elenchis,* quoted in R. McKeon, *The Basic Works of Aristotle* (Random House, Inc., New York, n.d.), p. 211.

above copying. They were thus a throwback in an advanced civilization to the procedures characteristic of early cultures, the procedures of imitation and memorization.

Like the Jews, Roman boys were expected to memorize the law of their people as set down in the Twelve Tables. Like the Greeks, they were set noble examples of manhood to imitate. Their own progress toward manhood, however, was under the supervision not of a pedagogue, who often was a slave, but of their fathers. Thus a Roman youth was his father's frequent companion in forum, camp, and field. He learned the Roman virtues of fortitude, prudence, earnestness, honesty, and piety not only by imitating the heroes of legend and history but also by observing these virtues in his father and his father's associates. It was even an adage, mentioned by Rome's greatest schoolmaster, Quintilian (35–100), that the way of learning by precept was long and difficult but by example was short and easy.

Yet later, when Rome extended its political dominion over Greece and Greece retaliated by captivating Rome with Hellenic culture, there was a steady infiltration of Roman education by Greek methods and materials of instruction. The education of Roman youth, for instance, became more literary in character. More time was spent on the grammar and rhetoric of effective speech. The method that was probably common in both countries for introducing the young to their letters was well stated by Dionysius of Halicarnassus. "When we learn grammar we take up first the names of the elementary sounds, called letters; then the forms and values of the letters. After we have learned these, we pass to syllables and their changes and, these having been mastered, to the parts of speech—nouns, verbs, and connectives, together with their affections—long and short quantities, accents both acute and grave, genders, cases, numbers, modal endings, and a thousand other things of that sort. After we have compassed the knowledge of all these, and not till then, do we begin to write and to read."[18]

By the time the Greek or Roman youth had learned enough to commence the reading of approved authors, a more advanced method of instruction was employed. Selected passages from these authors were analyzed and discussed. The Greek Protagoras (481–411 B.C.) was the first to initiate this method of instruction, but it was another Dionysius, Dionysius of Thrace, who gave precision to this procedure by dividing the analysis into six parts. The teacher first was to give the selected passage an exact reading with particular regard to pronunciation, punctuation, and rhetorical expression. Then followed an

---

[18] J. W. H. Walden, *The Universities of Ancient Greece* (Charles Scribner's Sons, New York, 1909), p. 21n.

explanation of any poetic figures of speech. Similarly, the teacher made an exposition of unusual references, historical or mythological. After the teacher had commented on the author's choice of words and given the etymology of any rare ones, he directed attention to the grammatical forms employed and ended with a literary critique of the passage as a whole. Thus were the Greco-Roman youth taught to express themselves forcefully and artistically.

The chief and perhaps only systematic expositor of instructional method among the Romans was Quintilian. On the whole, his methods were similar to those of the two Dionysiuses, departing from them chiefly to adapt them to the specialized training of the orator. Even so his carefully matured exposition in his *Institutes of Oratory* was built not so much on independent criticism as on the cornerstones of memory and imitation. There he referred to the capacity to memorize and to imitate as the traits in a boy that gave the greatest promise of successful preparation for a future career. All else seems a means of facilitating and promoting these two traits. To spur boys on, Quintilian was not averse to appealing to a boy's ambition and even envy. In the same spirit he would set boys in competition with each other although he was not unaware of the attendant vices of such a procedure. Anxious that children should not develop a distaste for education, he was free in dispensing praise. Indeed, he was even ready to enlist amusement and play in order that the young should not lose their interest in school. Finally, the beneficial influence of an occasional holiday on learning was not lost on him.

As for stimulating the student's educational output through flogging, Quintilian resolutely set himself against this practice in spite of the fact that it was common in his day. Indeed, so common was it that the phrase "to withdraw the hand from the rod" was an idiomatic expression to denote closing school.[19] The reasons for his opposition Quintilian stated very clearly. In the first place he held flogging fit only for slaves. In the second place he feared that its final effect would be only to inure the boy to blows. And in the third and last place be disapproved of punishment because it is futile when a child is grown and no longer amenable to threats and blows.

Much of Quintilian's great success as a teacher arose from his recognition that boys were not all alike and that different methods were appropriate for different natures. Jewish teachers had vividly described four types of students resulting from their emphasis on memorization—the sponge, the funnel, the sieve, and the winnower. Yet, so far as appears from the record, they had not varied their methods accordingly. Quintilian was more generally inclined to distinguish between students on the basis of the quickness with which

[19] Laurie, *op. cit.,* p. 343.

they learned. Some, he recognized, learned through steady and continued application to their studies and others through rapid and intense concentration. If Quintilian, like many of his profession, was a trifle impatient with the slow, he was no less suspicious of the precocious. In either case, he was quick to sense that some of his pupils required the spur while others needed to be reined in with the bit, that some could be spurred by fear while others were paralyzed by it. On the whole, he preferred the boy whose powers were cultivated under the lash of ambition and whom reproach stung to the quick.

CHRISTIAN AND SCHOLASTIC METHODS

One of the greatest teachers of antiquity was one whose principal interest was not in education at all. This was Jesus. Although he was primarily a great religious and moral leader, he often exerted his leadership in the role of teacher. Many of his precepts are introduced in the Bible by the expression "and he taught them, saying. . . ." Moreover, his closest followers were known by their educational relationship to him, that is, as disciples, a term which stems from the Latin *discipulus,* meaning "pupil."

There are a number of features that distinguish the methods of Jesus as a master teacher. The feature that apparently impressed his followers most was the fact that "he taught them as one having authority."[20] In this respect he differed markedly from Socrates. But though the two approached the teaching of truth from different angles, both were utterly fearless in the teaching of it, as witness the fact that both paid for their courage with their lives. Jesus's authority as a teacher rested in part on a thorough command of Jewish lore and in part on a cogency of presentation that exercised great persuasion upon the mind of his day and of all later times.

Perhaps most cogent in his art of instructing the masses who followed him was his use of the simile and parable. His materials were always drawn from the familiar background of his listeners, and so pertinent and incisive were his figures that only the dull or obtuse could miss the point. He encouraged questions but often anticipated them in the minds of his disciples before they were even asked. Not least in accounting for the success of his methods as a teacher was the fact that he loved children, as witness one of his most frequently quoted passages addressed indirectly to them, "Suffer the little children to come unto me and forbid them not for of such is the Kingdom of God."[21]

[20] Matthew 7:29.
[21] Mark 10:14.

In propagating the Christian viewpoint in the centuries immediately following the death of Jesus various methods were employed. As Christianity appealed at first chiefly to the lowest social classes, among whom previous education was at a minimum, it should not be surprising that the methods of instruction were largely narrative and exhortatory. Christian doctrine was taught quite dogmatically since a high value was set on orthodoxy in the instruction of these ignorant people. Conformity was achieved by a catechetical form of instruction, a system of oral questioning not unlike the Socratic method yet markedly different in that answers were fixed in advance. In training the body as well as the mind, ascetic and disciplinary methods were the rule.

Later, when Christianity became well established, with followers from the upper as well as the lower classes, more literate and hence more conventional methods of instruction came to prevail. But toward the end of the Roman Empire conventional education was rapidly becoming formal and lifeless. Too much emphasis was being placed on the letter and too little on the spirit of instruction.

None among the Christian leadership protested more vigorously against this decline than did St. Augustine (354–430), one of the early church fathers. He favored remedying the situation by putting greater emphasis on deeds and less on words. Thus he would have grammar taught not from rules but by association with men of correct speech, and in teaching rhetoric he would emphasize not so much a study of rules as a study of great orations. No study should be done, he claimed, under compulsion, "for no man does well against his will though that which he does be good."[22] Again, St. Augustine would encourage questions from the student so that the teacher could gauge the student's comprehension of his work and also shape the further direction of the discourse. Apparently, he hoped to develop an inquiring state of mind, for he derisively inquired, "Who is so stupidly curious to send his son to school in order that he may learn what the teacher thinks?"[23]

The times in which St. Augustine lived toward the end of the Roman Empire, however, were too decadent to pay much attention to his caveat. The basic political and economic conditions favorable to educational development continued to deteriorate till the nadir of the Middle Ages was reached. Had it not been for the Catholic Church, literacy might have all but disappeared. With the inroad into the Empire of the barbarians from Northern Europe, culture

[22] St. Augustine, *Confessions* (G. P. Putnam's Sons, New York, 1931), book I, chap. 12.

[23] St. Augustine, *De magistro* (Appleton-Century-Crofts, Inc., New York, 1938), p. 55.

was reduced to such a low ebb that the main problem of educational method became that of cultural survival, as it had been in early and primitive cultures. Consequently, memorization and imitation found reinstatement as the basic educational methods of monasticism and chivalry, the principal religious and secular educational stereotypes of the medieval period. To a greater or lesser degree asceticism supplemented these methods of teaching the vigorous but unruly populations of Northern Europe amenability to discipline.

Although progress in educational method was marking time during the medieval period, it would be a mistake to conclude that the methods employed were lacking in vigor. The training of both monks and knights was thoroughly realistic. Each was an apprenticeship in doing. The young page or squire, for instance, learned the accomplishments of a knight by becoming a kind of attendant to the lord of the castle. There under his surveillance and that of his lady the candidate for knighthood learned horsemanship and the use of arms as well as the knightly code and polite manners. Similarly, the monk learned his religious duties, often together with some craft like farming or copying manuscripts, from older, more experienced brothers, all under the supervision of the abbot.

The more systematic development of educational method did not go forward again till the end of the Middle Ages and the rise of the medieval university. This, it will be remembered, was the great period in which the Catholic Church was busy absorbing into its doctrine the philosophy of Aristotle. The precise way in which Greek and Christian viewpoints should be accommodated to each other raised many profound issues for medieval pupils and teachers, who were then known as "Schoolmen." One of the most famous of these Schoolmen, the monk Pierre Abélard (1079–1142), attracted a great following of students by propounding these subtle issues not in the form of dogmatic answers, as was conventional among his contemporaries, but in that of open questions. A list of these questions without any hint of their proper answers Abélard published under the famous title *Sic et non*. Perhaps his own unorthodoxy led him to devise this method as a means of warding off official censure.

However that may be, there can be little doubt that Abélard's was one of the most challenging of teaching devices. It left its mark even on the method of the much more famous Schoolman St. Thomas Aquinas (1225–1274), whose teaching became the very source of Scholastic orthodoxy. According to St. Thomas Aquinas, one learns either independently through his own discovery or through being dependent on someone else to instruct him. But even in the latter case the teacher does not, as is so often thought, transfer his knowledge bodily to the student. On the contrary, St. Thomas maintained that in learning by instruction, just as in learning by discovery, the teacher must regard the learner as the primary agent. There is no teaching without learning, and learning is a self-active process the learner must initiate. Hence the proper method of the teacher is not to transmit his knowledge to the pupil but with the cooperation of the pupil's potentialities to generate knowledge which will be similar to that already in the teacher.

More immediately and particularly, the way to elicit knowledge from the pupil's potentialities is through the logical demonstration of the syllogism. Here St. Thomas followed Aristotle very closely, for he thought the syllogism represented the actual way in which the mind worked. And since the quality of mind is the same in all, the syllogism was the best method of exposition for the young as well as for the mature student. This method is seen at its best in the way in which St. Thomas wrote his *Summa theologica*, to this day the great canon of Scholastic or Catholic orthodoxy. There, like Abélard, he introduces his material in the form of a question similar to the *Sic et non*. But, not content, like Socrates and Abélard, to stimulate the pupil's thinking by leaving the object of inquiry open, he proceeded in a series of logical syllogisms to review the authorities, propose the correct solution, and refute all objections to it. Holding to the philosophy of education that he did,[24] St. Thomas would hardly have believed in digging a ditch before his pupil without later on filling it up so that the student could successfully cross to the other side.

Students in the medieval universities not only had the curriculum presented and explained to them in a series of syllogisms but were themselves expected to gain considerable proficiency in the method of the syllogism itself. The technique for teaching this was the disputation. Just as the masters, or professors, disputed among themselves over such problems as were set in Abélard's *Sic et non,* so medieval students disputed among themselves. Theses were proposed and maintained against each other. The success of defense and attack depended on one's knowledge of dialectic and on the nimbleness with which one could manipulate the formal rules of the syllogism.[25] The importance of the disputation as a method of instruction is best revealed in the fact that, just before getting his degree, the medieval student

[24] *Supra,* pp. 109–114.
[25] For an example of what was long required, see F. Winterton, "The Lesson of Neo-Scholasticism," *Mind,* 13:398–400, July, 1888. See also D. Potter, *Debating in the Colonial Chartered Colleges* (Bureau of Publications, Teachers College, Columbia University, New York, 1944), chap. I; C. Meriwether, *Our Colonial Curriculum 1607–1776* (Capitol Publishing Company, Washington, D.C., 1907), chap. 8.

had to engage in a disputation in which he successfully maintained a selected thesis against all comers, including his professors in the guild of masters.

Employment of the syllogism caused the method of St. Thomas Aquinas to lean heavily upon instruction through words. But words, he claimed, conveyed greater meaning to the learner than could the things that the words symbolized. A concrete perceptible object conveyed no more to the learner than the limited attributes it possessed as an accidental instance of the class of objects to which it belonged. Words, however, did not suffer from such a limitation. They could symbolize all the attributes of a whole class of objects. To state this in other terms, words more nearly approximated generalized universals and therefore conveyed a wider scope of knowledge to the student than did things.

THE LECTURE

Also inclining methods of instruction to a highly verbal character was the custom of professors at medieval universities to lecture to their students. The growth of the lecture method can be directly attributed to the great scarcity of books at these budding institutions of learning. Since the first printed book was still some centuries off, the Middle Ages and even the Renaissance had to depend on the art of the scrivener for the copying of books by hand. Because the teacher at the medieval university was usually the only one who possessed a book, he fell into the habit of teaching by reading his book while the students took notes. So common did this habit or custom become that the Latin word meaning "to read," *legere* (past participle *lectus*), became synonymous with "teaching." Often the reading, or lecture, amounted to little more than dictation. And even dictation required frequent repetitions. When and where books became more abundant, the lecture turned from dictation and exposition to *commentatio* and *summa,* that is, to a summary of authors or a commentary on them.

Whether books should hold an important position in the art of instruction was an old bone of contention. Two of the greatest Greek teachers appear to have been somewhat jealous of the encroachment of books upon the precincts of oral instruction. Isocrates (436–338 B.C.), master of rhetoric, placed the book beneath the lecture in effectiveness because it deprived the reader or student of the author's force of presentation as conveyed by the teacher's voice and rhetorical manner. Plato's criticism of books extended even further. He attacked them for weakening habits of memory since they encouraged the student to rely on what is written down for recollecting pertinent information. Plato further indicted books for their inflexibility. Thus, the book cannot, like the teacher, detect when the student fails to understand and offer further explanations. Hence, in addition to the book, the constant need for the exercise of dialectic. It has already been observed how the medieval university fulfilled this need by supplementing the lecture and the text with exercise in disputation. Further evidence of inflexibility Plato found in the fact that books could not make allowances for individual differences among readers. Teaching, he declared, is like farming; different soils require different crops. So, in a way not open to the book, the teacher can in oral presentation adjust instruction to different types of mind.[26]

But in spite of such telling arguments books continued to grow in importance as instruments of instruction. Indeed, by the time of the medieval university, books became revered because of the uniformity and authority with which they invested instruction. Some texts might even be said to have had a canonical prestige. Thus in philosophy the books of Aristotle, in law the Justinian Code, and in medicine the writings of Hippocrates and Galen came to be universally accepted as the authoritative texts in their respective fields.

With the invention of printing the pedagogical importance of books was established beyond question. The printing of books at last freed instruction once and for all from the necessity of the method of personal communication from teacher to pupil. The extent and rapidity with which instruction could be propagated were enormously increased. Moreover, the control of thought, which had been relatively easy as long as the multiplication of books was done by hand, was now rendered far more difficult. Indeed, it is probably not too much to say that the astonishing versatility of modern civilization and education is in large part due to the development and spread of printing.

The University of Halle, which has often been called the precursor of the modern university, was the first to make important amendments in the lecture system of the medieval university. It transformed the lecture from an exposition and interpretation of accepted texts into the systematic presentation of a growing field of knowledge. Ultimately this change in the form of the lecture led to a similar alteration in the form of the disputation. By the time of the founding of the University of Berlin at the opening of the nineteenth century the disputation had given way to the dissertation. The candidate for a university degree still had to defend a thesis in oral argument. But the thesis, instead of aiming at the syllogistic elaboration and consolidation of some accepted canon of truth, had become a hypothesis

[26] K. Freeman, *Schools of Hellas* (Macmillan & Co., Ltd., London, 1922), pp. 204–207.

on which the student had endeavored to collect new experience to see whether the hypothesis could be verified.

HUMANISTIC METHODS OF INSTRUCTION

The lecture and the disputation were largely for teaching mature students attending the professional faculties of law, theology, medicine, and arts in the medieval university. In reviving the Greco-Roman ideal of liberal education, the Renaissance, to which the medieval period gave way, appealed to a younger group of boys. This shift in school clientele required a shift in methods. Moreover, since it was necessary to carry on the pursuit of the liberal arts in the Greek and Latin tongues, pedagogical method naturally shifted from a dialectical base in logic to one in grammar and rhetoric. Hence, there was a return to the methods of memorization and imitation. Indeed, the formula for instruction in the humanities was epitomized in the three Latin words *praecepta, exempla,* and *imitatio.* An excellent formula, it degenerated when narrowly limited to the style of just one classical author, Cicero, as was too frequently the case.

The spirit of the Renaissance at its best was marked by an endeavor to enjoy life more abundantly. It should not be surprising, therefore, that the best Humanistic teachers of this period attempted to make the educative process an attractive one. The Dutch scholar Desiderius Erasmus (1466–1536) has left the best written instructions on how to accomplish this end. At the very outset he carefully noted in *De pueris instituendis* the limits that the "innate capacity" and the "native bent" of the child set to what could be accomplished through instruction. Indeed he realized that no pupil was endowed with aptitudes in every direction, in fact, that very few had exceptional talents in even three or four directions.

In teaching the humanities, that is, Latin and Greek—their grammar and the culture locked up in them—Erasmus in the main employed the methods already tried and systematized by the great teachers of antiquity, with whose pedagogical writings he was undoubtedly quite familiar. In *De ratione studii* he recommended studying classical authors in much the same manner that Quintilian had and that Dionysius of Thrace had outlined before him. But Erasmus would have the teacher commence with an appreciation of the author under consideration, giving the important facts about his life and surroundings and an estimate of his talents and the characteristics of his style. Side by side with a consideration of the author's point of view, Erasmus would have the teacher comment on his diction, metaphorical and allegorical figures and the peculiarities and elegancies of his style.

Lastly he would have the teacher give what none of his predecessors had recommended, a moral evaluation of the passage.

His method for overcoming difficulties of exposition Erasmus summed up in a few simple directives: "First, do not hurry, for learning comes easily when the proper stage is reached. Second, avoid a difficulty which can be safely ignored or at least postponed. Third, when the difficulty *must* be handled, make the boy's approach to it as gradual and as interesting as you can."[27] To besetting the pupil with difficulties merely as difficulties Erasmus attached no merit at all. In another counsel he enjoined, "The master must not omit to set as an exercise the reproduction of what he has given to the class. . . . A literal reproduction of the matter taught is, of course, not required, but the substance of it presented the pupil's own way. Personally I disapprove of the practice of taking down a lecture just as it is delivered. For this prevents reliance on memory which should, as time goes on, need less and less of that external aid which note taking supplies."[28] The further improvement of memory he summed up in three added simple directives, "Understand, arrange, repeat."[29]

Erasmus's introduction of some independence and individuality into the learning of lessons was most welcome in an age addicted to rote memory and a slavish imitation of the literary style of Greek and Roman masters, especially Cicero. In this departure he had the support of the French essayist Michel de Montaigne (1533–1592) in the generation following his own. Montaigne deprecated teachers who behaved as if teaching were pouring knowledge into a funnel, the small end of which was in the pupil's ear. In writing *The Education of Children,* Montaigne exhorted the teacher not to insist on repetition of the lesson but to let the pupil "put it to the test, permitting his pupil himself to taste things, and of himself to discern and choose them, sometimes opening the way to him, and sometimes leaving him to open it for himself; that is, I would not have him alone to invent and speak, but that he should also hear his pupil speak in turn. . . . Let him make him put what he has learned into a hundred several forms, and accommodate it to so many several subjects, to see if he yet rightly comprehends it, and has made it his own."[30] As an instance of what he meant by having the pupil learn by experiencing himself, Montaigne suggested that "whatever

---

[27] *De pueris instituendis,* in W. H. Woodward, *Erasmus concerning Education* (Cambridge University Press, London, 1904), p. 217.

[28] *De ratione studii,* in Woodward, *op. cit.* pp. 177–178.

[29] *Ibid.,* p. 216.

[30] *Cf.* L. E. Rector, *Montaigne: The Education of Children* (D. Appleton & Company, Inc., New York, 1899), pp. 28–29.

there is singular and rare near the place where he is, let him go and see it; a fine house, a noble fountain, an eminent man, the place where a battle has been anciently fought."[31]

Both Erasmus and Montaigne were ahead of their times in seeking such independence for the individuality of the pupil. Thus, Montaigne's great English contemporary, Roger Ascham (1515–1568), no doubt more accurately portrayed the professional convictions of the time when he proclaimed that "Learning teacheth more in one year than experience in twenty; and learning teacheth safely when experience maketh more miserable than wise."[32] Again, in spite of the fact that he enjoyed some renown as an innovator in classroom method, Ascham really only made contemporary methods of language instruction more efficient. What he proposed as a method of ensuring accuracy in translating Latin was that the pupil should render a passage into English and then, after a lapse of time, render his translation back into Latin. A comparison, later, of the final product with the original would afford an accurate measure of his command of the language.

On study and making it more interesting Erasmus had several things to say. Instead of trying to stir up new energies in the pupil, he endeavored to motivate the curriculum by coupling it to drives already spontaneously operating. Thus, he sought to teach the humanities not through grammatical rules but through informal conversation about the boy's concerns at play and work with his fellows. Like Quintilian, he took full advantage of the social situation in appealing to ambition and emulation in the boy.

To those who would have the teacher resort to the rod as directed by the Old Testament, should gentler motivations fail, Erasmus frankly countered that, however advisable such a prescription might have been for the Jews of old, he doubted its suitability in the sixteenth century. And if the teacher must take up the rod, "Let us see to it," said Erasmus, "that the rod we use is the word of guidance or of rebuke, such as a free man may obey, that our discipline be of kindness and not of vindictiveness." For guidance he would warn the delinquent pupil "of the fate of those who by neglect of high wisdom have sunk into contempt, poverty, disgrace, and evil life." Only after "unwearied pains" at praise and blame would the great Dutch master have the teacher finally resort to actual corporal punishment; and then, he said, "Let the rod be used with due regard to self-respect in the manner of it." If asked what to do with boys who respond to no other spur, Erasmus would have them put out

---

[31] *Ibid.*, p. 41.
[32] S. S. Laurie, *Studies in the History of Educational Opinion since the Renaissance* (Longmans, Green & Co., Inc., New York, 1900), p. 80.

to work. " 'Yes,' says the master, 'but I want my fees.' There," Erasmus would reply, "I cannot help you: your duty is to the boy. But I fear that this matter of profit lies at the root of the whole matter."[33]

Both Ascham and Montaigne had similar views on discipline. Both would do away with forcing learning under the threat of violence. Indeed, Ascham wished the relation between master and pupil to be so free and easy that the pupil having difficulty with his lessons would be prompted to seek aid openly from the master rather than illicitly from his mates. Moreover, Ascham had neither frown nor chiding for the pupil who failed after he had done his best. To levy penalties for such a failure, he claimed, was an undeserved punishment of nature itself which risked a continuing dislike of studies throughout life. Urging a discipline of "severe mildness," Montaigne added the wise advice that, if one wishes a child to be sensitive to shame and chastisement, one should not harden him to them. Inure him to the hardship of heat and cold and wind and rain but never to that of punishment.

While a few rare teachers like Vittorino da Feltre (1378–1446), Erasmus, and Ascham were able to teach the humanities humanistically, the great majority fell far short of such achievement. Lacking in the learning of these men and in their insight into human nature and confronted with many a lad of only mediocre ability and ambition, the average run of teachers felt they could only succeed by the harsh strategy of enforcing learning through punishment. That conditions on the whole were bad in many places is witnessed by the sort of conditions against which Martin Luther (1483–1546), the leader of Protestantism in Germany, inveighed. Thus he wrote disapprovingly of the teacher "who should only know how to beat and torment his scholars," "whose schools were nothing but so many dungeons and hells, and themselves tyrants and jailers."[34] Again, when he thought he detected a slight improvement in conditions, he indirectly revealed their previous low state by being thankful that "our schools are no longer a hell or purgatory, in which children are tortured over cases and tenses and in which with much flogging, trembling, anguish, and wretchedness they learn nothing."[35]

Much of the cruel discipline of the period was due to the Christian conception of the fallen nature of man. The waywardness of children both at and away from their studies was laid at the door of original

---

[33] *De pueris instituendis,* in Woodward, *op. cit.,* p. 209.

[34] F. Eby, *Early Protestant Educators* (McGraw-Hill Book Company, New York, 1931), p. 32.

[35] F. V. N. Painter, *Luther on Education* (Lutheran Publication Society, Philadelphia, 1889), p. 198.

sin. The Devil being at the bottom of it all, many pious teachers thought it literally necessary to beat the Devil out of their children. In spite of the fact that Martin Luther became increasingly inclined to tilt at the Devil as the author of human woes, it is notable that his own views on correction were tempered with restraint. Commenting on the words of St. Paul, "Fathers, provoke not your children to anger, lest they be discouraged,"[36] Luther claimed that this was not an injunction against the punishment of children but an injunction to punish them in a spirit of love. "He who governs in anger," he remarked elsewhere, "only adds fuel to the fire."[37]

THE PRELECTION

The teaching of the humanities reached its most brilliant phase in the famous schools of the Jesuits founded at the time of the Counter Reformation and extending long into the post-Renaissance period. The instructional methods that enabled the Jesuits to merit the reputation earned by their schools were matured from a composite of the best contemporary methods and the best methods of antiquity. The central feature of the Jesuitical method of instruction was the prelection. As one may surmise from an etymological inspection of the word, the prelection was a variety of the lecture method. In brief, it was a sort of preview of a passage from a selected author who was being read by the students. To guide the students before they studied the passage themselves, the teacher himself gave an extended and carefully prepared prereading of the passage. The student meanwhile took notes to enable him subsequently to remember the salient points of the prelection.

While the Jesuits varied the prelection in detail for different subjects in the curriculum, it will be noticed that its divisions and the order

---

[36] Colossians 3:21.

[37] Eby, *op. cit.*, p. 33. Luther seems to have had an almost psychiatric appreciation of the child's fears. "A child who has once become timid, sullen, and dejected in spirit," he wrote, "loses all his self-reliance and becomes utterly unfitted for the duties of life; and fears rise up in his path, so often as anything comes up for him to do or undertake. But this is not all—for where such a spirit of fear obtains the mastery over a man in his childhood, he will hardly be able to rid himself of it to the end of his days. For if children are accustomed to tremble at every word spoken by their father or mother, they will start and quake forever after, even at the rustling of a leaf. Neither should those women who are employed to attend upon children ever be allowed to frighten them with their tricks and mummeries and, above all, never in the nighttime. But parents ought much rather to aim at that sort of education for their children that would inspire them with a wholesome fear; a fear of those things that they ought to fear, and not of those which only make them cowardly and so inflict a lasting injury upon them." (*Ibid.*, pp. 23–24.)

of their treatment had much in common with the method of Erasmus, of Quintilian before him, and of Dionysius of Thrace even earlier. What the Jesuits did was to take this method, tried by centuries of experience, and bring it to the highest polish it had ever received. Generally, according to the Jesuits' *Ratio studiorum,* the instructor first read through a selection from a chosen author without interruption. Then he went back to repeat and expand on his first reading. On this occasion he made sure that everyone understood the meaning of the selection. Thereafter he would analyze each part of the selection, relate it to other parts, discuss its appropriateness, and call attention to its rhetorical quality. His next step was to cite similar examples of style or argument either from the same author or from different authorities. Incidentally, here the teacher took occasion to comment on mythological or historical references found in the selection under consideration. Finally, he interposed a word on the uses to which the passage might be put and then concluded with an estimate or résumé of the whole.[38]

Obviously, teaching of this sort demanded careful preparation by the instructor. As the *Ratio studiorum* stated, "It will help much if the master does not speak on the spur of the moment without preparation, but reads carefully what he has thoughtfully prepared at home."[39] It must be that most Jesuit teachers took this suggestion of the *Ratio* to heart, for it is well known that many a prelection was a literary gem in its own right. Indeed, no less a critic of the Jesuits than Voltaire confessed that he never listened to any but good instruction while being educated by the Jesuits. As long as education remained Humanistic, that is, as long as it aimed to cultivate taste in reading and writing the Greek and Latin tongues, the prelection remained preeminent as a method of instruction. Yet there were restrictions on the adaptability of the method to modernizing forces. The *Ratio* itself forbade prelections of modern authors. Even more serious, the prelection proved inadequate for instruction in that most modern of modern subjects, science. Here a new method had to evolve.

If the teacher had to put much thought into the preparation of the prelection, the student had to work no less arduously in learning it after it had been delivered. For the most part, learning the prelection meant memorizing it, if not verbatim, at least the substance of it.

---

[38] The prelection is the origin of the German *Vorlesung* and the French method of *explication de texte.* For examples of the prelection, see R. Schwickerath, *Jesuitical Education* (B. Herder Book Co., St. Louis, 1903), pp. 468–474.

[39] E. A. Fitzpatrick, *St. Ignatius and the Ratio Studiorum* (McGraw-Hill Book Company, New York, 1933), p. 201.

Of course some learning was rote memory, but not all, for the *Ratio* would not permit the student to take down verbatim notes on the prelection. "If anyone can teach without dictating," the *Ratio* advised, "yet in such a way that the pupils can easily tell what ought to be written down, it is preferable for him not to dictate."[40]

In any case, one of the strongest features of Jesuitical instruction was the way in which it ensured learning through a continual review of old material. Each day the work of the preceding day was reviewed, each week the work of the past week, and each month the work of that month. At the end of the year an examination was set in which the student was examined for a knowledge of the books read during the year, for ability to translate the vernacular into Latin or Greek, and for familiarity with the various rules involved. In addition, he had to present some composition of his own creation.

The student's examiners were three in number, the prefect of studies and two teachers. Prior to the examination they reviewed the student's record; after the examination, while it was still fresh in their minds, they met again to make a final disposition of the student. The directions in the *Ratio* for their deliberations indicate that the faculty mind is pretty much the same in every generation. "If anyone is clearly unfit to make the grade," the *Ratio* records, "let there be no room for entreaty. If anyone is scarcely able, but still it seems that he should be advanced because of age, the time he has been in the same class, or some other reason; in such a case, unless something prevents, if the master approves his industry but little, let him be sent back to a lower class, but his name not added to the list. If there are some who are ignorant and it is not fitting to promote them, and no gain is to be expected in their own class, let them on consultation with the Rector be allowed no place at all, and let their parents or guardians be civilly notified to this effect."[41]

In studying his notes for review the student was to mark any possible objections to points made in the prelection. If he could not solve these objections himself, he was to bring them to the attention of the master or reserve them for a disputation. The disputation, however, was chiefly employed in the advanced classes, where philosophical or theological authors were being read.

The advice of the *Ratio* on conducting disputations will hold for most present-day discussion methods. It directed the teacher to "pre-

[40] *Ibid.*, p. 152.

[41] *Ibid.*, p. 184. Elsewhere the *Ratio* gives an interesting definition of "mediocrity," that border line between passing and failing. It obtains where a student "is able to understand and grasp what he hears and studies and to give an account after a fashion" but short of having made "sufficient progress." (*Ibid.*, p. 129.)

side in such a way that he may himself seem to take part on both sides; he shall praise anything good which is said, and call it to the attention of all; if some unusually difficult objection is proposed, he shall make a brief suggestion to support the defender or direct the objector; he shall not keep silent too long, nor yet speak all the time, but let the pupils set forth what they know; he shall . . . not permit an objection which is practically answered to be pressed too far, nor an answer which is unsound to stand too long; after a discussion, he shall briefly define and explain the entire matter."[42]

The competition involved in disputation was the main device that the Jesuits employed for motivating studies at all levels of instruction. The device was not new, however, having been the main dynamic that Quintilian used with Roman boys. What the Jesuits did was to divide their classes into halves as nearly equal in ability as possible. The two halves were then set to competing to see which could catch the other in some error of recitation. Further, each student was matched against some particular student in the opposite half, each to try to detect the other in some mistake. By this means students were easily incited to almost prodigious efforts of scholarship.

Other devices that the Jesuits used to enliven and enrich instruction included one of the earliest efforts at grade classification of pupils. In fact, the prelection demanded this. The master giving a prelection certainly could not properly deliver it to students who ranged in ability and training all the way from the bottom to the top of the school. Consequently, the Jesuits did some pioneer work in dividing their students into classes. Furthermore, even at this early date they made a practice of having a teacher move along with his class from grade to grade. Again, the Jesuits were clever enough to supplement their prelection not only with the disputation but also with dramatization. Thus, the dramas of Greek and Latin authors were performed as well as read.[43] Finally, none realized better than the Jesuits that all work and no play makes a dull scholar. Hence every day had its period of recreation.

In trying so earnestly and with such versatility to make instruction attractive, the Jesuits were rewarded by having fewer disciplinary troubles than in other schools of the time. In fact, their schools were noted for their milder discipline. As a sample, "Let there be no haste in punishing, nor too much in accusing," cautioned the *Ratio*.[44] Again, where admonition was necessary, the *Ratio* enjoined

---

[42] *Ibid.*, p. 154.
[43] It is notable that Puritanical influences in England discouraged dramatization as a method of instruction for its tendency to make "scholars playboys."
[44] *Ibid.*, p. 206.

that the one in fault should be addressed in no other way than by his own name. In meting out discipline, it was suggested that the addition of some literary task in excess of the daily assignment might sometimes be preferable to corporal punishment.

A student was often appointed to be monitor over the conduct of his fellows and report but not punish infractions of the rules. "On account of those who have been at fault either in respect to their application to their studies or in those matters which pertain to good morals, and for whom good words alone and exhortations are not sufficient, a Corrector (not of the Society) shall be appointed, who will hold the boys in fear and will chastise them with whatever punishment is needed and is suitable. When neither words nor the office of the Corrector avails, and a mending of his ways is not hoped for and he seems to be a stumbling block to others, it is better to remove him from the school than to keep him where he himself will profit little and where he may harm others."[45] But such an extreme judgment was left to the rector, especially in cases in which perhaps even expulsion was insufficient to expiate the student's scandalous conduct. Yet here even the rector was cautioned to act in a spirit of leniency and charity toward all.

In spite of the generally recognized effectiveness of Jesuitical methods of instruction, there were those who took exception to them. Chief among these were the Jansenists. At the bottom of their divergence from the Jesuits were theological disputes, which need detain us here only in so far as they led to different educational methods in the Jansenists' Little Schools of Port Royal. The Jansenists called their schools "little" in contrast to what they thought were pretensions upon the part of the Jesuits to rival institutions of higher learning. Similarly, the Jansenists condemned the Jesuits' use of rivalry to spur boys forward in their studies, for rivalry also led to pretense and ultimately to the sin of pride. Furthermore, the Jansenists were modernists rather than strict classicists. While the *Ratio studiorum* of the Jesuits frowned on the study of contemporary or modern authors and almost altogether neglected the study of the vernacular, the Jansenists made the initial approach to the classical languages through the vernacular, or mother tongue.

Although agreeing with the Jesuits in blaming the fallen nature of the child for his educational shortcomings, the Jansenists were more generally inclined to rely on divine grace for overcoming them than were the Jesuits, who put greater emphasis on discipline. To ensure upright character the Jansenists exercised careful and almost unceasing

[45] *Ibid.*, pp. 112–113.

surveillance over their pupils. Constant attention to the language and conduct of children was made possible by never assigning more than a half dozen to any one teacher and by then having him be their constant companion even to the point of sharing the same bedroom with them. With difficult children their rule was to endure much and pray still more.

Not least of those with Jansenist sympathies was François de La Mothe-Fénelon (1651–1715), the French prelate and author. His *Education of Girls* was not only a pioneer work in a day when educational efforts were almost exclusively expended on boys but also contained some excellent observations on methods of education applicable to boys as well as girls. He took the basic position that the less formal lessons were, the better. Instead of always being didactic, Fénelon thought lessons should frequently take their point of departure from the child's curiosity. Consequently, he advised teachers not to be annoyed by children's questions but to seize upon them as opportunities for facilitating instruction.

One great defect Fénelon noted in all education was that "all the pleasure is placed on one side, all the irksomeness on the other—all the tediousness in study, all the enjoyment in amusements. What can a child do but endure this rule with impatience and rush eagerly after sports? Let us, then, try to change this arrangement; let us make study agreeable, let us conceal it under the guise of liberty and pleasure, let us allow children to break in upon their studies sometimes with brief sallies of amusement. They need these distractions to refresh their minds."[46] Studies should be forced on the child only at intervals and then with a laughing face or accompanied by reasons why the student ought to apply himself, such as: This is to prepare you for your future vocation; this is to form your judgment; this is to accustom you to reason justly upon all the affairs of life.

In spite of these liberal views, Fénelon did not expect to be able to dispense with fear as a means of controlling the more intractable children. But even in their case he would not resort to fear till all other methods had been patiently tried. "Never reprove a child in its first excitement, nor in yours. If you chide in yours, the child will see that you are actuated by temper and hastiness and not by reason and affection; you will lose your authority irretrievably. If you reprove the child in its first excitement, its mind will not be calm enough to confess its fault, to subdue its passion, and to realize the value of your advice; you will even expose the child to the danger of losing respect due you. Show always that you are master of yourself; nothing will better prove this than your patience. . . . Do not speak

---

[46] F. Fénelon, *Education of Girls* (Ginn and Company, Boston, 1891), p. 38.

of a defect to a child without adding some method of overcoming it that may encourage the attempt, for the mortification and discouragement that cold correction produces must be avoided."[47]

RULES OF DISCIPLINE

So far in describing the historical development of methods of instruction, major emphasis has been laid on such problems as the structure of the lesson or the order of exposition, with only minor emphasis on discipline. Those who were to give major consideration to discipline and give it one of the most detailed statements in educational history were the Institute of the Brothers of the Christian Schools, or Christian Brothers, as they are known today. This teaching order was originated by St. Jean Baptiste de la Salle (1651–1719) about a score of years after the suppression of the Jansenists and their Little Schools of Port Royal in the middle of the seventeenth century. As Jesuit schools were controlled by rules set forth in the *Ratio studiorum,* so the schools of the Christian Brothers were managed by rules meticulously codified in de la Salle's *Conduct of the Schools.*

The general atmosphere that these rules aimed to create in the school was one of great seriousness. This seriousness consisted not in the teacher's wearing a severe or austere mien or in his becoming angry and lashing out with harsh words but rather in his putting on a manner of great reserve. Thus the teaching brother was cautioned not to descend to the level of the pupil, as in laughter, or on any account to suffer pupils to become familiar with him. Furthermore, when children began to assemble in the morning in front of school there was to be no playing or crying out that might disturb neighbors. Once in school, silence was the rule, not only for the pupils but as far as possible for the master as well. Directions for recitation and study were given by a sign rather than by word of mouth.

As in the case of the Jesuits, student inspectors were appointed to report on discipline during any absence of the teacher. Student supervisors, of whom two were to watch the conduct of the inspectors, were also appointed. Punishment for infractions, however, contrary to the practice of the Jesuits, was in the hands of the teacher. Five levels were recognized by the *Conduct of the Schools.* At the first and lowest level was reprimand, but this was not employed extensively, for a maximum of silence was enjoined on the order. At the second level was penance. Here such punishments might be meted out as maintaining a kneeling posture or learning a few extra pages of the catechism. The next level introduced the ferrule, which by prescription

[47] *Ibid.,* p. 34.

had foot-long leather thongs attached to a handle. It was administered for failure to attend class or even for being tardy. Next in severity was the rod. This was laid on for not heeding the lesson, for fighting with comrades, and for refusal to obey. Finally came expulsion from school.[48]

When correction was necessary, it was administered in an inconspicuous part of the school. Even here the *Conduct of the Schools* detailed the proper procedure: "While the pupil is making ready to receive punishment, the teacher will prepare himself inwardly to administer it in a spirit of charity, and with his thoughts fixed on God. Then he will gravely and sedately leave his place. When he reaches the place where the pupil is, he may say to him a few words to dispose him to receive the punishment with humility, submission, and the intention of correcting himself. . . . When he [the teacher] has been thus obliged to constrain a pupil to receive punishment, he will manage in some way at some later time to make him recognize and admit his fault. He will make him reflect and will bring him a strong and sincere resolution never to let himself yield again to a similar obstinacy. After the pupil has been punished, he will go and kneel decorously in the middle of the classroom in front of the teacher, to thank him for having punished him; and he will then turn toward the crucifix to thank God and to promise him at the same time not to fall again into the fault for which he has been punished."[49]

To ensure that punishment would be beneficial, St. Jean Baptiste de la Salle laid down certain criteria. Among other things he stated that punishment should be disinterested, that is, that it should be given by the teacher not in a spirit of personal vengeance but rather for the glory of God and to fulfill his holy will. Furthermore, it must be charitable; it must be motivated by an interest in the salvation of the pupil's soul. And, needless to say, punishment must be just. Accordingly, it is necessary to examine carefully beforehand whether the incident under consideration is a fault and, if so, one that deserves

[48] The Magdeburg School Ordinance of 1553 provided for punishment in school in the following order of severity: warning, reproof, memorization or copying of lines, wearing the *signum ignorantiae,* the rod, fines, imprisonment, and expulsion. The best-known *signum ignorantiae* was the dunce's cap. The term "dunce," interestingly enough, derives from the name of the great Scholastic teacher Duns Scotus, whose followers were known as "Dunses." "Duns" became "dunce" when the Dunses opposed the transition from Scholastic to Humanistic studies. Anyone who could not see the value of the new studies was called a Duns. Later a dunce was any dull person or child. The conical-shaped hat was merely his badge of ignorance, his *signum ignorantiae.*

[49] F. La Fontainerie, *The Conduct of the Schools of Jean Baptiste de la Salle* (McGraw-Hill Book Company, New York, 1935), pp. 186–187.

correction. In addition, the punishment must be proportioned to the fault both in nature and in degree. In proportioning punishment it is better that any error be made on the side of moderation. Again, punishment must be peaceable, that is, it should be administered and received "with great tranquility of mind and outward restraint." To ensure this result and to avoid doing anything of which the teacher might later repent, it may often be wise to defer punishment till such time as the teacher no longer feels emotionally disturbed.

In addition to these criteria, the *Conduct of the Schools* also pointed out the most common faults to be avoided in meting out discipline. It warned against punishment from which the pupil does not learn and which is given purely as an example for others. It also cautioned against punishment that is physically harmful. Thus the ferrule should never be used on the head or body but only on the palm, and the left palm at that, to spare the right for writing, an art in which the Christian Brothers have always excelled. Moreover, insulting words should never be spoken during punishment. Another mistake to be avoided was to fail to distinguish between the stubborn child and the one of timid disposition, the ill bred and the stupid. If the foregoing rules seem overly severe, one may take comfort from the fact that at the opening of the nineteenth century the whole *Conduct of the Schools* was revised in the direction of greater leniency.[50]

THE DISCIPLINARY METHOD OF INSTRUCTION

So far in the course of the development of educational method, discipline has been a method of social or moral control in the school and sometimes a method of prodding or quickening learning. But there is yet another method of instruction, frequently called "disciplinary." This method is to tax the student's abilities to the utmost by setting him difficult, even disagreeable, lessons and then, by holding him strictly to their accomplishment, to expect him to achieve a worthy discipline of his mind. According to this method of instruction it is not so important *what* the student learns as *how* he learns. The curriculum is not so important on its own account as it is as a barrier to balk the student and thereby to lead him to discipline himself, to impose habits on himself which will be useful no matter what the future barrier that obstructs his way.

---

[50] The 1811 revision of the Christian Brothers' *Conduct of the Schools* states, "With the view to adapt our education to the mildness of the present state of manners, we have suppressed or modified whatever includes corporal correction and have advantageously replaced this, on the one hand, by good marks, by promises and rewards, and on the other by bad marks, by deprivations and tasks." (Quoted in Compayré, *op. cit.,* p. 264.)

The man who is supposed to have given the greatest impetus to this method was John Locke (1632–1704). "As the strength of the body lies chiefly in being able to endure hardships," said Locke at the beginning of *Some Thoughts concerning Education,* "so also does that of the mind."[51] In writing these words he but uttered a thought entertained by minds in many centuries previous to his own. But just as it has already been seen that these words do not have the psychological import that they seem to have,[52] so it must now be shown that his method, too, did not have quite the disciplinary character usually ascribed to it.

It is obvious from the oft-quoted passage above that Locke clearly perceived the fallacy which lay in cheap rewards for study. The child should have what pleases him only if there is a rational need for it. But neither did Locke go to the other extreme of endorsing the coercion of learning. Over and over again in his essay on education he stated his disapproval of such a policy. Coerce a child to spin a top and he will grow to dislike it. Conversely, Locke realized children learn "three times as much" when interested, or "in tune," as he put it, than when indisposed. Yet, while Locke would not compel learning as a task, he did think it well if a child could learn to turn from something he was intent upon to something else, for in so doing the mind gained a desirable dominion over itself. Locke's middle-of-the-road position is classically stated in his remark, "He that has found a way, how to keep up a child's spirit, easy, active, and free; and yet at the same time to restrain him from many things that are uneasy to him; he, I say, that knows how to reconcile these seeming contradictions, has, in my opinion, got the true secret of education."[53]

Furthermore, Locke saw no peculiar virtue in constructing the lesson with extra-high hurdles. In fact, he suggested that the teacher should not plan for his pupil to advance by large strides. Rather, each next step should be "as nearly conjoined with what he already knows as is possible; let it be distinct but not remote from it: let it be new, and what he did not know before, that the understanding may advance; but let it be as little at once as may be, that its advances may be clear and sure. All the ground it gets this way it will hold."[54] Thus, apropos of language instruction, Locke would

---

[51] J. Locke, *Some Thoughts concerning Education* (Cambridge University Press, London, 1889), p. 21.

[52] *Supra,* p. 142.

[53] Locke, *op. cit.,* p. 30.

[54] J. Locke, *Conduct of the Understanding* (Clarendon Press, Oxford, 1890), p. 85. This passage is a remarkable anticipation of Johann Friedrich Herbart, *infra,* pp. 212–214, though it lacks Herbart's specific steps.

have the ancient as well as the modern languages taught through the method of conversation and their formal grammar mastered only after proficiency in speaking had been gained.

Like Fénelon, Locke recognized the curiosity of children not as an annoyance but as an asset to the teacher or parent. Indeed, he would have curious things put in the way of children to excite their inquiry and then publicly commend them for exhibiting curiosity. Moreover, he would have a father talk to his son about important matters as soon as possible, for a boy will become a man most quickly and surely by being treated like one.

The problem of punishments and rewards also occupied a large portion of *Some Thoughts concerning Education*. The main object of Locke's method here was to gain a measure of rational freedom. The child must first submit to the reason of others as a preparation for submitting later on to his own. Hence Locke would appeal to the child's desire for esteem and his sense of disgrace because their very mildness tended to encourage the child to control his conduct in the light of reasonable alternatives. Though Plato thought that reason appears relatively late in children, Locke argued that children should be allowed a degree of freedom suitable to their capacity for reason at a given age. Long philosophical discourses on conduct he distinctly thought unsuitable to the age of children. Yet he would have them understand that rewards and punishments follow as the moral consequences of their actions.

The child's reason should not be guided by too many rules, Locke thought, for fear he will almost certainly forget many of them and forgetting will lead to too frequent punishments. Instead, Locke would have but a few rules and these observed without fail. Yet, mild as he was in his views on punishment, he did not sidestep the possible necessity of giving a boy a thrashing. He mentioned two occasions as warranting such treatment, obstinacy and lying. Thus, if a boy openly defies his father in such a way as to raise the issue as to whose authority is supreme, a thrashing is in order. In the case of lying none but frank and honest excuses should serve to avert punishment. A thrashing, when administered, should never be carried beyond the point at which good might be expected to come from it. Beyond this point, Locke confessed, a father can only pray for his son.

8 Methods of Instruction— Continued

Most of the foregoing chapter has been occupied with a description of the growth of the best thought and practice in educational method down into the seventeenth century. Regrettably, however, the best thought and practice in each century have only rarely become prevalent or achieved general acceptance. This failure has occurred in spite of the fact that many of the observations quoted in the preceding chapter on the management of learning would still constitute good advice to beginning teachers in the current century. Some of these wise observations—as, for instance, that the teacher should insist on the student's understanding as well as memorizing the lesson or that he should be patient in exposition and gentle in discipline—have failed to influence practice even though iterated and reiterated century after century.

Aristotle and St. Thomas Aquinas had each had a glimpse of what was needed here, a method that was based on the nature of the child.[1] They had described this nature as composed of *both* bodily and mental faculties. They had even gone as far as to declare that there is nothing in the mind that is not first in the senses—*Nihil in intellectu quod non prius in sensu.* But the prevailing mind-body dualism resulted in teachers' interesting themselves almost exclusively in mental rather than bodily activity, as witness their emphasis on the lecture and dialectical forms of in-

[1] *Supra*, pp. 105–106, 109–110.

structional method. In addition, man's educational shortcomings, flowing from the Christian doctrine of original sin, were blamed more heavily on the material body than on the spiritual mind.

The cue to the development of educational method in the three centuries following the seventeenth is to be found in the way in which method more and more extensively capitalized on bodily or sensual activities as well as intellectual ones. This cue in turn, it should be noted, was increasingly associated with the evolution of methods for teaching young children. Progress in method down to the seventeenth century was made largely in the instruction of those of adolescent years and over. In the eighteenth and nineteenth centuries emphasis was on the preadolescent.

THE METHOD OF SENSE REALISM

If the senses and bodily activities are to take on enlarged importance for instructional method from here on, the inquiry may well arise as to why a consideration of the influence of John Locke (1632–1704) on method does not open this chapter rather than close the preceding one. The answer is simple. To be sure, in his educational psychology Locke did set the style of stressing the senses as the exclusive portals giving access to the *tabula rasa* of the mind.[2] Yet, profoundly as this thought has influenced subsequent innovators of educational method, it is interesting that it found no lodgment in *Some Thoughts concerning Education.* Even though Locke published this work after his *Essay concerning Human Understanding,* there is apparently no connection between the two. Evidently he was so much absorbed in the epistemological significance of his psychology that he failed to realize its potentialities for educational method.

The man who has most often been called the first modern educator was Johann Amos Comenius (1592–1670). Although he died before he could bring Locke's psychological ideas to the support of his own educational methods, it is nevertheless to his credit that he was earliest to contrive specific methods for instruction wherein bodily organs would be brought to the aid of the intellect. His most outstanding achievement here was his writing of the first textbook to employ pictures as a teaching device. In this book, the *Orbis pictus,* he brought the bodily organs of sight to the support of the struggling intellect. Here the beginner in Latin was helped to an understanding

---

[2] For a more extended account of Locke's psychology, see *supra,* pp. 143–144. If education (Latin, *educere,* to draw out) is appropriate to the Platonic theory of innate ideas, instruction (Latin, *instruere,* to build in) is appropriate for Locke's theory of mind, *tabula rasa.*

of Latin words by having the printed words accompanied by pictures illustrating their meaning.[3]

The *Orbis pictus,* however, was but a particular instance of Comenius's generalized conception of the teacher's method. In his monumental *Didactica magna* he laid down the general rule that everything should be taught through the medium of the senses. Further, one should try to employ more than one sense at a time, for senses like hearing and seeing will then reinforce each other. Imagine trying to teach physics without recourse to sensory experience at all. Yet Comenius lamented that it was common practice in his day to learn physics by merely reading Aristotle. Naturally opposing such a tradition, he advised the teacher to start with the senses because they stand nearest to the child's present state of understanding. Furthermore, to commence with the senses is to go from the easy to the difficult. Therefore, after a secure sense impression has been registered, the teacher may proceed to memorization, from memorization to comprehension, and thence to judgment.

In similar vein Comenius—Komenský in his Czech vernacular —urged that the order of the lesson be things before words and examples before rules. First teach the general idea of a thing before noting its exceptions. From this last remark it is clear that he did not intend the teacher to neglect generalization. Comenius could easily have gone to the extreme of emphasizing sense to the neglect of intellect, just as the adherents of the Aristotelian-Thomistic philosophy of education had overstressed the intellect to the disadvantage of the senses. But, on the contrary, he showed his indebtedness to this philosophy by stating it as one of his educational guideposts that nature always begins with the universal and ends with the particular. Deduction as well as induction, therefore, is a dimension of the teacher's method.

The confidence which Comenius displayed in the method of teaching through the senses was warranted, he thought, by the brilliant discoveries that science was beginning to reveal about the real nature of the world when investigators followed the lead of empiricism. For centuries people had adopted Aristotle's rational methods of describing phenomena in terms of their form, or purpose, and showing how each fitted into the grand hierarchy of form leading to pure form, or God. In the sixteenth and seventeenth centuries people began to employ new methods, which were first stated by Francis Bacon (1561–1626) in his *Novum Organum.* What was new in this book as compared with the *Organon* of Aristotle was the emphasis that Bacon placed on inductive rather than deductive logic. He stressed

---

[3] See A. W. Holland, "A Famous Book," *Contemporary Review,* 154:599–607, November, 1938.

the collection of data through sense observation and the conclusion by induction therefrom as to the exact nature of reality and the world in which we live. Though Bacon seems to have been well aware of the significance of his *Organum* for science and philosophy, his reference of educational problems to the Jesuits, whose practices he admired, shows how little he appreciated its novel implications for instructional methods.

Happily Bacon had a profound influence on Comenius. What Bacon either failed to see or saw but dimly Comenius perceived with great clarity. In fact, he caught a vision of educational method that quite transcended the mere use of induction through the senses as a pedagogical device. As the method of the *Novum Organum* had aided scientists to the discovery of the invariant laws that govern the movement of the heavenly bodies, so, thought Comenius, it might also reveal the laws that govern the classroom. "As soon as we have succeeded in finding the proper method," he declared, "it will be no harder to teach schoolboys, in any number desired, than with the help of the printing press to cover a thousand sheets daily with the neatest writing. . . . It will be as pleasant to see education carried out on my plan as to look at an automatic machine of this kind, and the process will be as free from failure as are these mechanical contrivances, when skillfully made."[4]

In a method so frictionless and so free from error there would, presumably, be no cause for disciplinary action. Indeed, changing his educational analogy from the machine to the musician's instrument, Comenius thought that for the teacher to strike a child for an error was akin to a musician's striking his instrument for producing the wrong note. Instead, the teacher should, like the musician, apply his pedagogical skill the more diligently in order to get better results.

It would be a mistake to think that Comenius's contributions to educational method were solely improvisations on a theme by Bacon. As a matter of fact, Comenius was also much indebted to the thinking of Wolfgang Ratke (1571–1635), who was a score of years his senior[5]

---

[4] M. W. Keatinge, *Comenius* (McGraw-Hill Book Company, New York, 1931), pp. 50–51. *Cf.* Johann Heinrich Pestalozzi, whose confidence in finding the scientific law of nature governing method led him to try to "mechanize" method. Ernest Horn in the twentieth century was of the opinion that progress in method had advanced to such a point by that time that the efficacy of teaching subjects like writing, spelling, and reading was on a scientific par with diagnosis in medicine.

[5] Ideas like those of Ratke and Comenius seem to have been in the intellectual atmosphere of the time. They appear vaguely in the *Positions* of Richard Mulcaster (1531–1611) and even in the work of the Humanist John Milton (1608–1674), who wrote, "Because our understanding cannot in this body found itself but on sensible things, nor arrive so clearly to the knowledge of

and also infected with the notion of teaching by a new method that would instruct all quickly, easily, and surely. The key to his method was also to follow the course of nature. The course of nature he expected to find under the guidance of his motto, *Per inductionem et experimentum omnia* (Everything through induction and experiment). Thus, he advocated that the lesson deal with matter before form, the thing itself before its rule. Having put concrete experience first, he further enjoined that nothing be learned by rote. Continuing his emphasis on the concrete, he tried still further to guard against the learning of meaningless words by insisting that everything be put in the mother tongue first.

As much as Ratke seems to have anticipated Comenius, it is no injustice to him to say that Comenius was the greater man. The influence of Ratke was curtailed by the fact that he tried to make his method a sort of carefully guarded trade secret and even more by his failure to institute a successful school built on his principles. Comenius, on the other hand, through his *Orbis pictus* achieved wide and long practical success. In the next generation the ideas of both men were carried forward and expanded most notably in the early *Realschule* founded by Johann Julius Hecker (1707–1768) at Halle. This school derived its name from the fact that its teachers employed *Realien,* the German word for "real things," to facilitate instruction. On the one hand, instruction took place through such *Realien* as the school's collection of plows, churns, and models of buildings and ships. On the other hand, instruction through *Realien* consisted in field excursions, such as expeditions into the country for botanical specimens or visits to artisans to see how their goods were produced.[6]

The absorption in *Realien,* while it did not eliminate the problem of discipline, did at least work in the direction of mitigating the severity of conventional school discipline. In instructions to his teachers on this subject Francke was much moved by a Christian spirit of love and sympathy toward children. The teacher's attitude, he thought, should be cordial and kind like that of a father. Patience, forbearance, and affection he especially enjoined upon young teachers because they are most likely to be lacking in paternal solicitude and

---

God and things invisible, as by orderly conning over the visible and inferior creature, the same method is necessarily to be followed in all discreet teaching." [*Tractate of Education* (Macmillan & Co., Ltd., London, 1911), p. 4.]

[6] The philosopher, mathematician, and statesman Gottfried Wilhelm von Leibniz (1646–1716) recommended that students study man in anatomical theaters, chemistry in the apothecary's shop, and botany and zoology in botanical and zoological gardens. He would also have schools build up collections or museums of rarities as further *Realien.*

Christian gentleness. Yet careful as Francke would be about disciplining children for little faults inherent in their nature or for dullness of nature not their fault, he was equally careful that the teacher should not become the sport of the children.

In the eighteenth century the pedagogy of appealing to the senses through concrete objects in the child's environment came to have revolutionary social significance. The type of education that had been useful in attacking the inaccurate presuppositions of Aristotelian science was expected to be equally useful in attacking the shams and iniquities of the established social order. Particularly was this the case in France, where during the early eighteenth century were sown the seeds that at the end of the century sprouted into social revolution. "Almost all our philosophy and education can be expressed in these few words," declared Louis René de La Chalotais (1701–1785) in his *Essay on National Education:* "It is the things themselves that it is important to know. Let us turn to the true and the real; for in itself truth is nothing other than what is, what exists, and in our minds it is only the knowledge of existing things."[7] Obviously this exhortation applied to teaching subjects with political significance like history and geography as well as subjects like the natural sciences.

So oriented, La Chalotais insisted that any method which begins with abstract ideas is not made for children. For himself, he wished nothing to be taught them except facts that were attested by the eye, whether the student were seven or thirty-seven years of age. Moreover, he would have children confronted with a great variety of objects under various circumstances. Their memories, he held, could never be overburdened with useful facts. Indeed, the edifice of learning could not be securely built till one had first collected the incontestable facts and observations later to be assembled into its foundations.

Yet another Frenchman, Étienne Bonnot de Condillac (1715–1780), no less a friend of learning through the senses, cautioned against instruction that relied too much on memorization. "I grant," he wrote, "that the education which cultivates only the memory may make prodigies, and that it has done so; but these prodigies last only during the time of infancy. . . . He who knows only by heart, knows nothing. . . . He who has not learned to reflect has not been instructed, or, what is still worse, has been poorly instructed."[8] Continuing in the same vein, Condillac added, "True knowledge is in the reflection, which has acquired it, much more

[7] F. La Fontainerie, *French Liberalism and Education in the Eighteenth Century* (McGraw-Hill Book Company, New York, 1932), p. 74.

[8] G. Compayré, *History of Pedagogy* (D. C. Heath and Company, Boston, 1885), p. 317.

than in the memory, which holds it in keeping; and the things which we are capable of recovering are better known than those of which we have a recollection. It does not suffice, then, to give a child knowledge. It is necessary that he instruct himself by seeking knowledge on his own account, and the essential point is to guide him properly. If he is led in an orderly way, he will acquire exact ideas, and will seize their succession and relation. Then, able to call them up for review, he will be able to compare them with others that are more remote, and to make a final choice of those which he wishes to study. Reflection can always recover the things it has known, because it knows how it originally found them; but the memory does not so recover the things it has learned, because it does not know how it learns."[9]

INFLUENCE OF ROMANTICISM ON METHOD

Much as sense realism contributed to modern methods of instruction, it was only one facet of the complex surface of nature with whose grain Comenius and others had succeeded in lining up the educative process. Another important facet of nature and one closely related to sense was that of feeling. Conforming educational method to this further aspect of human nature was chiefly the work of Jean Jacques Rousseau (1712–1778), outstanding eighteenth-century romanticist. Rousseau believed as heartily as did Comenius in the method of instructing through the senses and to the support of this method brought a reading of Locke. But while Comenius and Locke had been chiefly interested in the senses as the portals through which knowledge entered the mind, Rousseau inclined to think true education consisted less in knowing than in doing. Hence, he went on to include within his method those inner senses or springs of action better known as feelings. In making this inclusion he introduced a romantic note into educational method, the effects of which have not worn off even in the twentieth century.

According to Rousseau the central feature of the teacher's strategy should be to maneuver the pupil into wanting to learn. "Give the child the wish and . . . any method will then be suitable," he wrote

[9] *Ibid.*, p. 318. See also the remarks of a French *émigré* to America at this time; Pierre Samuel Du Pont de Nemours (1739–1817) had less confidence in facts, claiming that "The real aim of education is less to give the children positive facts than to keep them constantly developing, working themselves and by themselves to observe and understand. For that wonderful habit once made part of their lives will never be lost and will grow with the growth of their minds." [*National Education in the United States of America* (University of Delaware Press, Newark, Del., 1923), p. 24.]

in his *Émile*.[10] The inner drive that will carry the child furthest along in his studies is some present interest. So important were interest and inclination to Rousseau that he depended upon them rather than upon constraint to teach a child sustained attention and perseverance in the face of difficulties and distractions.

An important corollary of Rousseau's doctrine of interest made pupil freedom an essential part of the teacher's method. This freedom extended all the way from an injunction to dress small children in loose-fitting garments inviting the quick and easy uncoiling of native springs of energy to an approval of the child's pursuit of his own inclinations. If a child were restless, Rousseau would not thwart him but would rather treat this manifestation of energy as a necessary apprenticeship in learning. Unless the child gets about, how is he to learn about space or objects which lie at a distance? An even more important basis for giving the child freedom was Rousseau's belief that each individual was born with a distinctive temperament. A serious fault he found with the methods of his day was that all children were indiscriminately set the same exercises, thus destroying any special bent they might have and leaving a dull uniformity. Yet freedom was not an absence of restraint, as many of Rousseau's critics have reported his saying. Liberty gives children not more but less right to command others, Rousseau declared.[11] Freedom requires children to learn by depending more heavily on their own resources. In doing this they will learn to limit their desires to their capacities to fulfill them.[12]

Implicit in this last remark is Rousseau's theory of negative education, or learning through the natural consequences of one's acts. While he expected the child to complain if his teacher hemmed him in with commands or crossed him with prohibitions, there was one curb to the child's freedom against which Rousseau expected no murmuring whatever. This was the curb or limit placed upon the child's actions

[10] R. L. Archer, *Rousseau on Education* [Edward Arnold (Publishers) Ltd., London, 1912], p. 120.

[11] *Ibid.*, p. 85.

[12] The romantic idealist philosopher Immanuel Kant, in some lectures on education that show the influence of Rousseau, stated, "One of the greatest problems in education is how can subjection to lawful restraint be combined with the ability to make use of one's freedom?" Answering his own question he made the following points: (1) From earliest childhood the teacher should leave the child free in everything except what might injure the child. (2) The child must be shown that he can attain his aims only as he permits others to reach theirs. (3) The child must be shown that he is only under such constraint as will lead him to the use of his own freedom—that he is educated so that some day he may be free, that is, independent from the foresight of others. [E. F. Buchner, *The Educational Theory of Immanuel Kant* (J. B. Lippincott Company, Philadelphia, 1904), pp. 131–132.]

by the physical necessities of nature. If Émile fails to appear on time for a field trip, let the tutor depart without him, says Rousseau. If he breaks a window, let him sit and study in a cold room. In brief, let him learn through experience. But the shortcoming of this method of instruction, as La Chalotais and many subsequent critics have pointed out, is that, on the pretext of affording children their own experience, teachers deprived them of the benefit of the experience of other people past and contemporary.

The most important general rule that Rousseau enjoined on the teacher was not to accelerate education—*"not to gain time, but to lose it."*[13] "Hold childhood in reverence," he pleaded "and do not be in any hurry to judge it for good or ill. . . . Give nature time to work before you take over her business, lest you interfere with her dealings."[14] Perhaps no point in Rousseau's educational outlook has been the object of such perennial attack by his critics in the nineteenth and twentieth centuries as has this romantic regard of his for the subtle forces of nature finding expression during the period of childhood.

As Rousseau said, if the infant sprang at one bound from his mother's breast to the age of reason, the kind of education offered by the eighteenth century would have been quite suitable. The tendency of that century was to look for the man in the child, to see the child as a little adult, as if viewing him through the wrong end of a telescope. Mind was thought to have the same quality whether found in the child or the adult. Hence, the same rational methods of instruction sufficed for both. The immaturity of childhood, therefore, was a void to be filled up as quickly as possible. It was against this view that the romanticism of Rousseau protested. According to him, childhood has its own distinct character, its own laws of inner development, to which the teacher's method must conform. One important difference Rousseau noted was that while the child did not have the judgment of an adult, he did have the senses, which were fully as acute. Since a child begins to learn when he begins to live, education at the level of sense should begin at once. Education along rational lines should be postponed till he is mature enough for it.[15]

---

[13] Archer, *op. cit.,* p. 98.

[14] J. J. Rousseau, *Émile* (J. M. Dent & Sons, Ltd., Publishers, London, 1911), p. 71.

[15] Since Kant rejected the spectator theory of mind and held to the more romantic notion that the mind must build forth from within itself its own idea of the world, *supra,* p. 123, it is not surprising to find him endorsing the maieutic aspect of the Socratic method, *supra,* pp. 172–173, to teach rational knowledge; for, as he said in his educational lectures, rational knowledge is "drawn out of" and not "introduced into" children. (Buchner, *op. cit.,* pp. 183–184.)

To the parent who expressed the fear that then his child would spend his early years doing nothing, Rousseau romantically replied, "What! Is it nothing to be happy, nothing to jump and run all day? He will never be so busy again in all his life."[16]

The first to make a serious effort to translate Rousseau's romantic methods into practical classroom procedures was Johann Bernhard Basedow (1723–1790) in an experimental school that he called the "Philanthropinum." This was perhaps the first school in educational history that was opened with the deliberate intention of setting traditional educational procedures aside and launching forth altogether on the basis of "improved principles." To capture the freedom of nature in the spirit of Rousseau and to show a proper regard for childhood on its own account, the pupils in the Philanthropinum were dressed like children and not like little adults, as was the contemporary vogue. Their hair was cut short, and their garments were designed to be open and free at the throat. Latin was taught conversationally, and games were employed to motivate this process. Thus, when an object was hidden, the children tried to guess its identity by naming various objects in Latin. Handicraft, gymnastics, and field trips were also employed in the same spirit of method.

Unfortunately, Basedow was himself a poor teacher and tempermentally unsuited to the task of tactfully devising means to achieve his aims, aims that were widely acclaimed when published in a prospectus. Owing to his shortcomings and to the criticism of the Humanists, well entrenched in tradition, the Philanthropinum came to an early end shortly after Basedow's death. Besides ridiculing the school as mere child's play and hardly a fitting preparation for the subsequent study of authors like Cicero, the Humanists regarded the realism and utilitarianism of the Philanthropinum's methods as hostile to the spiritual values of their own more rationalistic methods.

OBJECT LESSONS

Although the first seed to spring up from Rousseau's *Émile* withered away, fortunately other seed from the same sowing was about to germinate more successfully. Indeed, the first half of the nineteenth century was to harvest one of the most bountiful crops of reforms in educational method ever seen in the history of education. In such

---

[16] Rousseau, *op. cit.,* p. 71. It is interesting to add that, while Karl Rosenkranz (1805–1879), Georg Wilhelm Friedrich Hegel's educational interpreter, thought that it was the nature of the child to be indolent, Philipp Emanuel von Fellenberg, an exponent of Pestalozzi's views, took the opposite position, holding that indolence in the child was the result either of a constitutional defect or of previous training.

quick succession that their lives overlapped appeared three of the greatest men in the whole of educational history, Johann Heinrich Pestalozzi (1746–1827), Johann Friedrich Herbart (1776–1841), and Friedrich Wilhelm August Froebel (1782–1852). First to succeed, but only after the hardest kind of trial-and-error process, was Pestalozzi, the famed Swiss educator.

Ever since the social culture had been reduced to written symbols and education had taken the social short cut of vicarious learning through the written or printed word rather than through direct experience, one of the most persistent aberrations of education had been that the oncoming generation had often memorized the literary form of their social culture without always comprehending its actual meaning. Of this difficulty reformers of nearly every century had been aware. Yet, though many had urged that comprehension and memorization go hand in hand, little or nothing had been done to mark out the steps in facilitating understanding. Few teachers realized, as Pestalozzi so clearly did, that "When a third person, to whom the matter is clear, puts words into my mouth with which he makes it clear to *people in his own condition,* it is not on that account clear to me, but it is and will remain his clear thing, not mine, inasmuch as the words of another cannot be for me what they are to him—the exact expression of his own idea, which is to him perfectly clear."[17]

The only way to correct this misunderstanding between teacher and pupil, according to Pestalozzi, was for the teacher to commence with sense impressions of the object of the lesson. Only after time for these impressions to take effect had elapsed should the teacher proceed to the naming of the object. Once named, the object could be studied as to its form; that is, its various qualities could be discussed and compared. Finally, with the abstraction of its essential as against its accidental qualities, the object was ready for definition. This, in brief, is what Pestalozzi so frequently refers to as the essence of his method, teaching everything through number, form, and language. In this way language and observation or experience are always so closely linked that education should henceforth be well on its way to eliminating forevermore rote memory without comprehension.

Obviously, from the foregoing, activity of the pupil is an essential part of learning. Without activity he can hardly get lively sense impressions. It will behoove the teacher, therefore, not to develop the lesson in the spirit of dogmatic exposition. On the contrary, he will conduct the lesson as to encourage the pupil to exert his own powers. Teaching, instead of creating vicarious experience for pupils, will

[17] L. F. Anderson, *Pestalozzi* (McGraw-Hill Book Company, New York, 1931), pp. 75–76.

have to create opportunities for firsthand experience itself. For the same reason Pestalozzi early abandoned emulation as a way of motivating learning. He held that the child should learn to feel pleasure in exercising his own powers for the discovery of truth rather than in comparing himself with others.[18]

Pestalozzi's lay public did not always see eye to eye with him on his activity program. While he was trying to develop children's potentialities by an exercise of their capacities, the public was anxious about how well the children knew their ABC's. While he was interested in how children were learning to think, feel, and act, they are inquisitive about what the children knew of their catechism. This difference in outlook led many to say that while Pestalozzi's method was probably good enough, it was only suitable for children of the well to do, who could afford the time necessary for children to learn at such a slow rate of progress. This criticism Pestalozzi denied, for he claimed that human nature was the same in all social classes and that therefore a method based on nature was equally applicable to all.[19]

The Pestalozzian method of object instruction put a much greater burden on the resourcefulness of the teacher than did the old recitation method. Formerly the teacher had called children up to his desk one, two, or three at a time to hear them recite their lessons. If he asked any questions, there was no uncertainty about the answer, for there was a book to arbitrate between pupil and teacher. All this was changed in the classroom run according to Pestalozzian principles. There the teacher taught the whole group at once. Standing before them, he framed his questions about the object under considera-

[18] The English sociologist and philosopher Herbert Spencer (1820–1903), although he gave an original twist to notions about curriculum, showed no originality whatever in the methods by which he would have his curriculum taught. In method he followed Pestalozzi implicitly. Pestalozzi's proceeding from the simple to the complex, from the concrete to the abstract, from the empirical to the rational, Spencer found highly compatible with his own notion of the social process as a movement from an indefinite homogeneity toward a more definite heterogeneity. Indeed, he proposed that object lessons "should not cease with early childhood, but should be kept up during youth, as insensibly to merge into the investigations of the naturalist and the man of science." Furhtermore, he favored Pestalozzi's learning as a process of self-activity. Children should be *told* as little as possible and induced to *discover* as much as possible, he maintained. In proportion as instruction became self-instruction and was accompanied by pupil satisfaction, he was confident it would not cease when school days were done, as happened too frequently in traditional schooling. [H. Spencer, *Education: Intellectual, Moral, and Physical* (J. M. Dent & Sons, Ltd., Publishers, London, n.d.), pp. 69, 80–83.]

[19] How similar these criticisms are to those made of progressive education in the twentieth century!

tion in the light of the understanding evinced by answers to preceding questions. The outcome of such a lesson could hardly be a foregone conclusion. Yet, though the teacher had to extemporize in his interrogation and exposition, he could hope to do so successfully only by the most careful preparation before entering the class. Preparation of this sort involved not only a much more extensive knowledge of subject matter than the traditional teacher possessed but also a knowledge of the art of skillful questioning and group management.

The sequence of the Pestalozzian lesson from objects to definitions ultimately found its way into the method by which textbooks were organized. One of the most popular of these texts in America was Warren Colburn's *First Lessons in Arithmetic on the Plan of Pestalozzi*. In this text the author sought to banish difficulties in arithmetic that arose out of the fact that children had been accustomed to memorizing and carrying out abstract rules which they did not comprehend. Commencing at the opposite end, Colburn (1793–1833) based his book on the assumption that the concept of number is first acquired by observing sensible objects. Hence, number ideas, number names, and mental operations with numbers were given the right of way over rules and figures, which received no mention in the first fifty pages of the text.[20]

The order of the Pestalozzian lesson has often been called going from the simple to the complex. Brilliant as was this insight, it was not without its abuses. One prominent type of abuse was thinking that the simple is arrived at by analyzing or breaking down a subject into its elements. Thus, children were introduced to reading by first learning their letters, next by putting letters together into syllables, then syllables into words, words into phrases, and finally words and phrases into sentences. Consequently, the much simpler method of learning to read by commencing with whole words or even with phrases or short sentences was long overlooked. It took some time for teachers to become aware of the fact that to go from the simple to the complex does not necessarily mean to commence with the logically simple, for the logically simple is often quite complex to the child.[21] Rather should the teacher start with the psychologically

---

[20] What Colburn did for arithmetic, other pioneers accomplished for other subjects in the American curriculum. Arnold Guyot (1807–1884) introduced the Pestalozzian point of view into geography, and Lowell Mason (1792–1872) did this for music.

[21] The mistake made in reading was repeated in various other subjects. In music, notes and scales were often made to precede learning to sing a tune. In writing, children were taught to make endless vertical lines and circles as preparation for forming letters whose parts, on analysis, are found to be composed of either straight or curved lines.

simple, that is, with what is already familiar to the child whatever its degree of logical complexity.

Another sort of abuse of the dictum to proceed from the simple to the complex was the tendency of some of Pestalozzi's followers to teach facts or definitions carefully compiled by an expert observer. These teachers attached so much importance to the child's learning an exact definition that they minimized or even skipped over the sensory experience of the child as likely to be immature and inaccurate. No one has excoriated the formalism of such a procedure more mercilessly than the English novelist Charles Dickens in his story *Hard Times*. There a little girl, a member of a circus troupe and well acquainted at first hand with horses, was caused endless embarrassment because she could not give the formal definition of a horse supplied at once by another pupil with little or no knowledge of horses. This pupil rattled off in one breath, "Quadruped, gramnivorous, forty teeth, namely: twenty-four grinders, four eyeteeth, and twelve incisive. Sheds coat in the spring, in marshy countries sheds hoofs too. Hoofs hard, but requiring to be shod with iron. Age known by marks in mouth."

Interesting the pupil in his work, Pestalozzi claimed, was largely a matter of the teacher being interested himself. Therefore, if the teacher failed to interest a child or even hold his attention, he should first look unto himself for the explanation. And certainly he should not resort to punishment where he or his method was to blame. In any event, discipline was mild and gentle in Pestalozzi's school. Not only was such control supposed to be more consistent with the nature of the child, but it was supposed to be more like the rule of love in the home, the spirit, of which Pestalozzi tried to capture.

MONITORIAL METHOD

The current innovation in educational method with which Pestalozzianism found itself chiefly in competition, expecially in England and America, was the simultaneous, or monitorial, method popularized independently by Andrew Bell (1753–1832) and Joseph Lancaster (1778–1838), both Englishmen. The essence of their method was for the master to instruct monitors, who in turn instructed the boys under them. As might be expected, the device was very popular where exceptionally large numbers of children were to be taught by a single master. For the same reason the method is more significant as a scheme of administration than as a method of instruction. As a matter of fact, neither as a scheme of administration nor as a method of instruction was the monitorial system of Bell and Lancaster anything new. Instruction through monitors dates back at least to

Comenius in the seventeenth century, if not to someone earlier, and had already been put in operation by the Christian Brothers, who called it the simultaneous method. What Bell and Lancaster did was to succeed in popularizing the notion.

If there was any novelty in their method of instruction, it consisted chiefly in ingenious contributions to the paraphernalia of the schoolroom. Here their ingenuity was stimulated by an endeavor to effect financial economies so that as many poor children as possible might be instructed at the expense of a single master. To this end, they invented wall charts from which children grouped in front of them could learn to read. They also added the sandboard and the slate for writing. Beyond these innovations, however, instruction was quite conventional in its methods. If, accordingly, there was a good deal of straight imitation, rote memory, and recitation in the master's instruction of his monitors, these methods were even more pronounced when the monitor turned to relay his instruction to the children in his charge.

The monitorial system of instruction did not survive long in competition with Pestalozzian object lessons. On a comparison of their educational merits, all the advantage in flexibility and insight into child nature lay with the Pestalozzian method. The chief historical service that the monitorial system performed was to win the public to the support of schools, for it appeared at first glance as if public education would be quite inexpensive. This service once performed, the monitorial system rapidly sank out of sight, for the public was soon persuaded that if it was going to support education, it might as well have the best.

HERBARTIAN METHOD

The advantage of the Pestalozzian method, it will be remembered, was that even better than Comenius's *Orbis pictus* it enabled the teacher to assist the child to a clear understanding of words. The Pestalozzian method did not abandon verbal learning, but it did inseparably tie verbalization or conceptualization to sense perception. Yet learning is not complete with the formation of a clear concept even when that concept is based on sense perception. Just as Pestalozzi indicated the proper steps for the teacher to take in proceeding from sense perception to definition or conceptualization, so it now remained for Herbart, second of the trio of great educational reformers of the first half of the nineteenth century, to point out to the teacher how to proceed from one concept to another, how to assimilate new concepts to old ones.

In this task Herbart was exceptionally successful, for, more effectively than any of his predecessors, he rested his method squarely on a clear-cut theory of the psychology of learning. His theory, it must be recollected, grew out of association psychology and was known as the doctrine of apperception. According to this doctrine one learned the new in terms of the old. The child did more than just perceive an object; he apperceived it as well. That is, ideas or concepts already stored away in his mind from previous contacts with his environment helped to condition the manner in which his mind received new presentations of the environment.[22]

To ensure apperception in the classroom Herbart analyzed the process into four distinct steps, which the teacher was to follow. Herbart died without attracting much attention to these steps, and it was not till several decades later that a follower of his revived them and recast them in the better-known five steps, in which form they became famous. The five steps are as follows: (1) Preparation. In this step the teacher commences the lesson with something he is sure is already familiar to the class. That is, he starts where Pestalozzi left off, with concepts that are clearly held in mind because based on previous observation or sense perception. Failing in this, he might have to begin with sense observation itself. (2) Presentation. Here the teacher presents the new material to be learned for the day. (3) Association. This is probably the most important of the steps, for here the teacher leads the pupils into a comparison of the materials of the preceding two steps, to note what in the new presentation is already familiar in the stage of preparation and what is an advance beyond it. The more carefully the teacher knits the new into the old by this comparison or association, the more securely is psychological apperception achieved. (4) Systematization or generalization. Here the teacher presents the class with other instances of the same kind of novelty first brought to their attention. With the aid of these the class is able to generalize what has been learned or apperceived in the third step. (5) Application. Here the teacher will probably tell the children to take the next ten problems or translate the next dozen lines. Application is thus an assignment of further examples of the day's lesson for each child to solve by himself according to the rule of generalization developed.

While these five steps give an excellent rationale of the art of explanation, they need to be supplemented with directions on how the teacher is to motivate the lesson as well as explain it. On this point, also, Herbart showed considerable ingenuity. Ordinarily, teachers try to interest pupils so that they may learn. The opposite is pedagogically correct, according to Herbart. Instead of being the inception interest should be the outcome of instruction. Pupils should learn so as to establish an interest for later learning. Interest, in

[22] For a more complete exposition of Herbart's educational psychology, see *supra,* pp. 145–148.

other words, is the pleasurable accompaniment of the way in which already acquired concepts or ideas attract or assimilate new but similar concepts or ideas. It is a result of apperception. Stated in terms of Herbart's psychology, interest is a function of the way in which the apperceptive masses operate. Therefore, Herbart and his followers in their method paid much attention to the sequence and breadth of materials in the curriculum in order to build up in the pupil a "many-sided" interest that would be subsequently available both to facilitate exposition and to ensure and promote motivation.

From the foregoing it will be seen that gaining the child's interest was a serious business to Herbart. It was far more than aiming to amuse or divert the child. With a gentle but steady hand the Herbartian teacher was to steer a course between the Scylla of turning instruction into play and the Charybdis of turning it into drudgery. This is naturally a very difficult passage, and Herbart did not expect that it would always be navigated successfully. "The fact should not be overlooked, however," wrote Herbart, "that even the best method cannot secure an adequate degree of apperceiving attention from every pupil; recourse must accordingly be had to the voluntary attention, that is, to the pupil's resolution."[23] True to his system Herbart advised the teacher to win the child's resolution, or will, to the side of his lessons by previously instilling in him the right ideas, which will ensure the right will or responses rather than to depend too heavily on rewards and punishments.

Herbart's doctrine of apperception also directed him to one brilliant insight far ahead of his times, namely, that there is no use in trying to restrain undesirable activities in a child unless some new activity is supplied to take the place of the one inhibited. Consequently, the teacher was advised that the best method of government in the school is to keep children occupied even if the immediate purpose of the activity is to avoid disorder rather than to instruct. If worse came to worst, Herbart was not one to shy away from corporal punishment so long as it did not injure the child's self-respect and was not overused. He would prefer to substitute some deprivation of freedom but never expulsion, for expulsion solved nothing and merely passed the disciplinary problem on to someone else.

SELF-ACTIVITY

The seeds of romanticism sown by Rousseau's *Émile* flowered more luxuriantly in the pedagogical method of Froebel than they did in that of either of the other outstanding educational reformers of the

---

[23] J. F. Herbart, *Outlines of Educational Doctrine* (The Macmillan Company, New York, 1901), p. 71.

early nineteenth century, Pestalozzi and Herbart. As just seen, Herbart appreciated the importance of the pupil's self-activity, but he was quite dubious about cultivating its spontaneity. Instead he preferred to exercise careful control over the channels in which it flowed. Pestalozzi, too, regarded self-activity highly, but to him it was a necessary accompaniment of gaining sense impressions of objects in the environment.

Froebel, on the other hand, took much more seriously Rousseau's injunction to reverence the child and to allow himself to be guided by rather than to be the guide to the course of development prompted by the child's nature. Hence, he took the view that the teacher's or parent's method should be more protective than prescriptive. That is, the teacher or parent should be careful not to interfere with nature's laws of self-expression or self-development. On the contrary, every effort should be made to create an educational situation in which the inborn forces of the child's nature would have every opportunity to unfold freely and naturally. The aim of the teacher's method should be to bring out rather than to put in. It should be creative rather than merely imitative.

The device par excellence for encouraging spontaneous self-development and self-expression Froebel thought was play. This was an innovation among educators. Prior to Froebel many different attitudes had prevailed with regard to play. These attitudes ranged all the way from regarding it as a harmless out-of-school diversion to the Puritanical one of suppressing it as a temptation of the Devil for idle hands. A few educators, of whom Locke was one and Basedow another, employed well-known children's games as a sugar coating to induce children's swallowing some incidental learning. Froebel's contemporary, Georg Wilhelm Friedrich Hegel (1770–1831), a teacher before he became a world-famous philosopher, thought play education a mistake, for in it the teacher descended to the childishness of the pupils instead of raising them to the level of serious realities. An even more renowned philosopher, Immanuel Kant (1724–1804), showing the influence of Rousseau in his lectures on education, valued play because the child pursues it so earnestly that he willingly imposes self-discipline on himself.

It remained for Froebel to perceive that play is in itself educational. He did not justify the teacher's use of play as a means to discipline or to teaching academic subject matter. Neither did he justify it for recreational purposes. On the contrary, he took the serious view that play is the best means at the teacher's disposal to release the child's inner powers. It holds this position because it is the natural way in which the child expresses himself when unrestrained by adult conventions.

If play is in part what a child does when unrestrained by adults, it follows that its conscious employment as an educational method involves an educational context in which the child is consciously allowed to go unrestrained to a much larger extent than according to any previous method. Yet this romantic freedom, which Froebel introduced into his method from Rousseau, was nothing whimsical. Froebel based it carefully on philosophy,[24] just as Herbart had rested his method on psychology and Comenius and Pestalozzi had used more general scientific analogies. To Froebel freedom was not a gift bestowed by the teacher or even by God himself. Freedom was something which had to be achieved, and that by self-activity. Froebel's native but autocratic Germany was very skeptical about the political and social consequences of a classroom method so highly imbued with freedom. As a result, it was in democratic America rather than in Germany that his methods received their greatest fulfillment.

Before turning to the introduction into America of the European educational innovations of the eighteenth and nineteenth centuries, one further aspect of Froebel's method should be considered. This concerns the way in which he incorporated Pestalozzian object instruction into his own methodology by means of his well-known "gifts and occupations." Pestalozzi used a great variety of objects and expected children to exercise their sensory powers to become acquainted with them. Froebel, on the other hand, used a more limited range of objects and at that only those which had a certain formal quality about them. He was interested not so much in the immediate knowledge yielded by sensory observation as in a more remote symbolic knowledge suggested by the formal quality of the object, or gift.

Thus, an important object in the Froebelian kindergarten was the ball. This was given to the child to play with, not just so that he might learn about its sphericity, as Pestalozzi might have employed it, but rather in the expectation that its sphericity would suggest to him the concept of divine, all-inclusive unity. Another important gift was the cube. Its importance lay in the fact that its rectangular lines and flat sides were the very opposite of the ball, or sphere. This opposition was significant to Froebel, for he thought learning occurred through the reconciliation, or mediation, of opposites.[25] The object, or gift, that mediated the ball and the cube, of course, was the cylinder. All this is an elaborately indirect approach to the well-attested truth that one cannot avoid simultaneous teaching of antithetical qualities like hardness and softness, length and breadth, the true and the false.

[24] For a more complete account of Froebel's educational philosophy, see *supra,* pp. 124–125.
[25] For the educational philosophy behind this theory of opposites in Froebel and Hegel, see *supra,* p. 125.

A further most important instance of Froebel's search for unity—even in opposites—was to be found in the social group constituted by the kindergarten children. Pestalozzi had tried to utilize social forces in his method by endeavoring to assimilate his classroom to the kindness and sympathy of the home. But Froebel was the first to propose social tactics in the classroom that were based on a definite strategy. His great emphasis on arranging children in the never-to-be-forgotten kindergarten circle was, like the sphere, to symbolize all-inclusive unity. But this sense of unity was to grow from the children's entering into social relationships as well as from their formal arrangement into a circle. In this sense the kindergarten was but a continuation of social relationships already well developed from the very early intimacy between mother and child. In the social environment of the school the child was to learn that he himself was both a whole and a part within a whole. All this, again, was excellent pioneering in educational method if the elaborate symbolism were not made to loom too large.

Although all these instances are taken from the kindergarten, the kindergarten was not, in Froebel's mind, the limit of the application of the activity principle. As a matter of fact, he conceived this principle the proper method in later years of schooling as well. Unfortunately, he had neither the early success nor the length of life to develop his method at the higher levels. That development was undertaken by his American followers in the twentieth century.

STATUS OF METHOD IN MID-NINETEENTH-CENTURY AMERICA

The innovations in instructional technique inspired by Rousseau and worked out in practical detail in the first half of the nineteenth century by the contemporaries Pestalozzi, Herbart, and Froebel did not reach America in force till the second half of the century. Before tracing the introduction of these innovations into American education, it may be well to pause a moment to note the status of educational method in mid-nineteenth-century America just prior to the impact of new ideas from abroad.

Ten years before the mid-point of the century, when Henry Barnard (1811–1900) was surveying conditions in Connecticut, he noted that a variety of instructional procedures were in use. Among these was the lecture method. This medieval device[26] evidently had had the vitality not only to survive in the higher institutions of learning but to spread into the lower ones as well. If the lecture method

---

[26] For a fuller account of the lecture method, see *supra*, pp. 181–183.

survived there, we may be sure that its first cousin, the prelection,[27] persisted in Jesuitical institutions of learning as they came to be founded in this country.

The most prevalent method Barnard found in the common schools was that of the recitation, which consisted in calling pupils up to the master's desk "to say their lessons." The lesson was cited in the book, and the children recited it—gave it back. Sometimes pupils were summoned individually and sometimes in groups. In the latter case their lessons might be said in unison. Unison, however, was not always possible, for children frequently did not possess copies of the same book from which to memorize the lesson. The difficulties besetting the teacher from a multivariety of texts were attested by Barnard's further survey, which noted some 200 different books in use in just the half-dozen main subjects in the curriculum. In whichever way children were called up, Horace Mann (1796–1859), Barnard's distinguished collaborator in Massachusetts, quoted an estimate that this method afforded each child about 20 minutes of the teacher's time each half-day—40 minutes of instruction daily and 320 minutes of sitting still.

This sort of instruction terminated at the conclusion of the school year in a public examination. At this time the children orally answered questions put by the teacher or the school committee before the assembled parents and such of the public as cared to attend. Such an examination, however, did not always provide a fair estimate of a school's achievement. A skillful teacher by asking the right questions of the right pupils could always make the school look better than it really was. Conversely, some children, embarrassed by the situation, often failed to show what they were capable of doing. The beginning of the end of this sort of examination was foreshadowed in Boston in 1845, when the school committee, anxious to appraise educational conditions in the whole public school system, substituted a written examination for all. In support of the change several arguments were put forward. The new examination was impartial, for each child had to answer the same questions and that without any leading help from the teacher. It was also more thorough in that it covered more ground for each pupil. And, not least, it could be made a matter of record so that a comparison could be made in succeeding years.[28]

---

[27] For a fuller account of the prelection, see *supra,* pp. 187–189.

[28] For the results when the same Boston examination was given again in 1919, see O. Caldwell and S. A. Courtis, *Then and Now in Education* (World Book Company. Tarrytown-on-Hudson, N.Y., 1924). For similar comparisons, see J. L. Riley, *The Springfield Tests—A Study in the Three R's* (Holden Patent Book Cover Co., Springfield, Mass., 1908); D. E. Lawson, "Historical Survey of Changes in Aims and Outcomes of School Examinations," *Educational Administration and Supervision,* 26:667–678, December, 1940.

At its best the prevalent method of teaching threw the pupil on his own initiative to interpret and organize a vicarious experience broader than his own. At its worst, as an anonymous schoolmaster put it, it was the sure method by which dullness could be taught. The large amount of memorization done at the behest of an often dogmatic and authoritarian teacher created its share of motivational and disciplinary problems. These were not diminished but aggravated by the furnishings of many schoolrooms. There a lively and sensitive child was often "stuck upon a bench full of knot-holes and sharp ridges, without a support for his feet or his back, with a scorching fire on one side of him and a freezing wind on the other; and a stiff Orbilius of a master, with wooden brains and iron hands, orders him to sit perfectly still, with nothing to employ his mind or his body, till it is *his turn to read*. Thus confined for hours, what can the poor little fellow do but begin to wiggle?"[29] Or whisper, play pranks, or indulge in stolen glances or in any of a dozen other nuisances in the schoolboy's bag of tricks?

Add to this situation the authoritarian conception of discipline that reigned in the schools of the period and a very explosive atmosphere was bound to result. The common thought of the time was that the parent or teacher was superior and the child inferior by virtue of a relation which God himself had ordained. Therefore, the child owed obedience to his superiors. "Obedience," so a current definition ran, "is doing anything because another, having competent authority, has enjoined it. The motive necessary to constitute an act of obedience is reference to the will and authority of another. The child receives as true what his parents say, because they say it; so he does as right what they command because they command it. . . . The pupil must be taught and made to believe that all school regulations and laws are based on authority—authority vested in the office of the teacher. . . . Nor is severe punishment to be regarded as the last resort. When it may be inflicted at all, it is the first resort and the true remedy."[30]

[29] E. W. Knight, *Reports on European Education* (McGraw-Hill Book Company, New York, 1931), pp. 312–313.

[30] P. E. Harris, *Changing Conceptions of School Discipline* (The Macmillan Company, New York, 1928), p. 79. The concept of discipline enunciated here was given excellent philosophical statement by no less a one than Immanuel Kant. The obedience owing from a child, he held, was twofold—to the absolute will of the parent or teacher and to the universal moral law. If obedience derived from constraint, it was absolute; if from confidence or voluntary acceptance, it was rational. Kant held that while due attention should be paid to the inclinations of children, there were many things children must do because prescribed by duty. Transgression of a command constitutes lack of obedience and therefore entails punishment. Punishment may be either physical or moral. But in no event should the child's will be broken (Buchner, *op. cit.*, pp. 188–

No doubt much of the early difficulty with school discipline arose from an excessively long school day. Not infrequently, ancient schools commenced at sunrise and continued till sunset. Under such circumstances, it would be remarkable if children's surplus energies did not rebel against such long periods of close application to their studies. The principal relief against the monotonous succession of long days at school was the designation of some days as holidays. Holidays originally seem to have been holy days. The Greek boy's school year was punctuated by some ninety such occasions. If this number seems excessive, it must be remembered that the Greeks did not observe the Sabbath, as later became the custom under Judaeo-Christian influence. Many other holy days in the Christian calendar, of course, added to the welcome vacation period from school. The chief difficulty in having holidays coincide with holy days was that the latter were not evenly distributed throughout the school year. Consequently, a custom grew up in medieval Europe of making Thursday a holiday in any week in which no holy day fell. In fact, even to the present day some European countries still observe a Thursday school holiday rather than the Saturday holiday prevalent in the United States.

Of course, pedagogues had long recognized that all study and no play made a boy a dull pupil. In spite of this fact, the total number of days spent in school seems to have depended on factors of transportation and economic competence rather than on theories of pedagogy. In colonial America the long summer vacation appears to have grown out of an agrarian economy in which children were needed to work on the farms during the summer months. Where schools were held in the summer, it was usually because of transportation difficulties during the winter. The predominance of an industrial economy in the twentieth century, however, has enabled the summer school and the summer camp to make inroads into this customary long summer vacation.[31]

The surcharged atmosphere of this total situation—much memorization with little exposition, crude school furnishings, and authoritarian discipline—did explode at frequent intervals in the invocation of corporal punishment. In one school of 250 pupils that Horace Mann

---

192). But the strictness of this view was already weakening in the next generation, for Hegel, one of Kant's successors, noted that it had ceased to be the custom in families to demand absolute obedience for obedience's sake. [M. Mackenzie, *Hegel's Educational Thought and Practice* (Swan, Sonnenschein & Co., London, 1909), p. 175.] See also J. P. Jewett, "The Fight against Corporal Punishment in American Schools," *History of Education Journal*, 4:1–10, Autumn, 1952.

[31] For a more extended account of vacations, see R. Byrns, "About School Vacations," *School and Society*, 57:175–178, February, 1943.

visited he reported that there had been 328 separate floggings in one school week of five days, or an average of nearly 66 each day. Apparently, the teacher thought that the hickory stick was the only board of education. One wonders how the teacher found time to teach in a day punctuated by so many disciplinary cases. Yet, on the whole, the public approved the practice and would have looked askance at withholding the rod of discipline as contrary to the injunctions of the Old Testament.[32]

In spite of the perversity of human nature to which wiggling, whispering, and pranks were ascribed, a new attitude toward child nature was beginning to be evident around the middle of the nineteenth century. This was due in part to the romanticism of Rousseau, in part to a general humanitarianism, and in part to the leaven of new political conceptions of democracy. A view gradually began to take hold that a child who grows up under subjection to an authority that requires obedience merely for the sake of obedience is not free and therefore is ill prepared for citizenship in a state based on the principles of liberty.

As a result, new principles of discipline gradually began to make their appearance. Although they were exceptional, men like Bronson Alcott (1799–1888) did try to train children for their responsibilities in a republic by making provision in the schoolroom for learning the art of self-government. Horace Mann, for instance, insisted that the guiding consideration in discipline should not be securing outward conformity to rule or code but enlisting the inner motive of the child. Discipline should be proportioned, therefore, not to the offense but to the intent from which it sprang. Similarly, some claimed that it was not enough that the teacher secured diligence in study and good order in the classroom. To them the vital question was: To what motives did the teacher appeal?

Turning inward to the motivation of children led to a reassessment of their restless energies. Those with wit to see began to realize that this abundant energy was not an outcropping of the Devil but a manifestation of curiosity or of the desire to manipulate. Given interesting instructional activities to engage it, this energy would be so readily absorbed that there would be no superabundance with which to transgress the school routine. Those who perceived this truth were the first to realize that good instruction and good discipline are one and the same thing. For centuries they had been looked upon as separate activities of the teacher. Now at last a new day was dawning—but it was only the dawn.

[32] For a more complete account of this ancient discipline, see *supra,* pp. 170–171.

The timid and reactionary were even apprehensive of the dawn. No one offered a rebuttal of their fears better than Ralph Waldo Emerson. Apropos of his injunction, "Respect the child," he said, "But I hear the outcry which replies to this suggestion:—Would you verily throw up the reins of public and private discipline; would you leave the young child to the mad career of his own passions and whimsies, and call this anarchy a respect for the child's nature? I answer—Respect the child, respect him to the end, but also respect yourself. . . . The two points in a boy's training are, to keep his *natural* and train off all but that:—to keep his *natural,* but stop off his uproar, fooling and horse-play;—keep his nature and arm it with knowledge in the very direction in which it points. . . ."[33]

EFFECT OF EUROPEAN INNOVATIONS ON AMERICAN EDUCATION

Barnard must have seen the new era dawning, for in his survey of instructional methods in Connecticut, already mentioned, he also noted tendencies to adopt some of the newer European procedures, especially the Pestalozzian. He also mentioned mutual, or monitorial, instruction, but of its value he took a very moderate and restrained view. About Pestalozzian methods Barnard was much more enthusiastic. So, too, was Mann, who did everything possible to introduce them into Massachusetts schools. David Perkins Page (1810–1848), however, whose *Theory and Practice of Teaching* was perhaps the most popular text for teachers at this time, warned teachers against being swept off their feet by either monitorial or object instruction. He seemed to treat them both somewhat as current fads and frills.[34]

[33] R. W. Emerson, *Essay on Education* (Houghton Mifflin Company, Boston, 1909), pp. 19–20.

[34] As to his own positive view of method Page stated that the teacher could ask no question more important than what the "natural order" of presenting a subject is. In supplying an answer to this, however, he was very vague compared with Pestalozzi. He was more distinctive when he gave one of the best early critiques of motivating schoolwork through prizes, a policy to which he was much opposed. Prizes, he contended, give undue prominence to comparatively unworthy objects, engender an undesirable spirit of rivalry, and stimulate only the few who may hope to gain them, leaving the rest indifferent. Besides, there is much difficulty in awarding prizes because there is an inequality in the external conditions of home study, to say nothing of their rewarding success rather than effort. Finally, study motivated by prizes may well cease when the prizes are withdrawn. [D. P. Page, *Theory and Practice of Teaching* (A. S. Barnes and Co., Inc., New York, 1847), chap. 8. *Cf.* Colonel Francis W. Parker a half century later in his *Talks on Pedagogics* (The John Day Company, Inc., New York, 1937), pp. 276–277.]

Nevertheless, in spite of Page's lukewarm attitude, Pestalozzianism steadily continued to gain favor. The way in which it capitalized on children's activities rather than repressed them appealed to teachers as the basis of both good instruction and good discipline.

Steady as was the spread of Pestalozzian method, it took its major spurt in the United States with the establishment of the Oswego Normal School in New York, coincident with the outbreak of the Civil War. The moving spirit at Oswego was Edward A. Sheldon (1832–1897), who had drawn his inspiration from the English branch of the movement, which tended to magnify the object aspects of Pestalozzi's method. Sheldon was so deeply impressed by a large collection of such objects in an educational museum in Canada that he introduced the idea at Oswego. Being a good promoter as well as a good schoolman, he was not long in making Pestalozzianism a vogue that became known in this country as the "Oswego movement."[35] Prospective teachers came to Oswego from far and near and when they graduated carried Pestalozzian object instruction to all parts of the country.

Wherever these teachers went, they generally started school museums, many of which are still to be seen. But object instruction did not stop with museums. It was also embodied in other instructional techniques, which have since become commonplace. Field trips, which began as a means of acquiring specimens for school museums, have since become a valued teaching device on their own account. Another application of object instruction of long standing is shopwork. Earliest to see that the shop and the farm are ideal environments for the Pestalozzian method was Philipp Emanuel von Fellenberg (1771–1844), the Swiss nobleman and educator. His application of Pestalozzian principles found its way into this country through the manual-labor movement on which many of our early colleges were founded. The introduction of physical, chemical, and biological laboratories into the schools are also partly, though not exclusively, to be credited to the same principles.

Another popular form that Pestalozzian object instruction took in America about the turn of the century was the inductive lesson. In such a lesson the teacher's method aimed to help the child to form concepts based on observation. The teacher would begin by aiding the child to gather a stock of primary sense impressions and conclude by helping him in inductively arriving at a classification and conceptualization of them by analysis and comparison. But it should not be thought that the inductive way of teaching was a one-way street going from percept to concept. As a matter of fact, the child was

[35] N. H. Dearborn, *The Oswego Movement in American Education* (Bureau of Publications, Teachers College, Columbia University, New York, 1925).

best taught when he learned to reverse this process as well. In reverse, learning started with a concept as a guide to what the child was to expect in contacting an object. When teaching moved in this direction, from concept to percept, it was often known as a "deductive" lesson. Some thought this was a separate kind of lesson, but it was really only the natural corollary of the inductive lesson.

The Herbartian method of instruction did not receive much attention in the United States till a score of years after the conclusion of the Civil War. Then it made its entry largely through young Americans returning from graduate study at German universities. These men promulgated the Herbartian five steps as a "general method" applicable to teaching all subjects because it embodied *the* logical way in which the mind learns.[36] Normal schools, quickly convinced of this claim, recast their model lessons on Herbartian lines. The five steps were followed strictly—as they should be if they constituted a general method. But this very strictness gave birth to a rigid formalism. In time, general method was attacked by skeptics of the theory that the mind learns in only one way and by proponents of "special methods" for particular subjects like reading or for particular aspects of the lesson like drill.

Enthusiasm for Herbart was at high tide in the decade before the turn of the century.[37] Yet, although it ebbed from then on, at least one notable American educator of the twentieth century continued to cling to the Herbartian pattern as an important method of instruction. He was Edward Lee Thorndike (1874–1949), outstanding pioneer in the scientific study of educational psychology. Since his theory of learning as conditioning or associative shifting bore such a direct resemblance to Herbart's doctrine of apperception,[38] it is not surprising to find that when Thorndike came to translate his scientific conclusions into a practical classroom method, he took over the Herbartian five steps with only slight modification.[39]

The Froebelian ideas of instruction made their first appearance in the United States with those freedom-loving Germans who, disap-

[36] See C. A. McMurry, *Elements of General Method* (Public School Publishing Company, Bloomington, Ill., 1892), one of the more notable books introducing Herbartianism in the United States at this time. The German Herbartian Wilhelm Rein (1847–1929) thought nature admitted of only one method of instruction. See his *Outlines of Pedagogics* (Swan, Sonnenschein & Co., London, 1893), p. 136. The idea is an old one. See *supra*, p. 179.

[37] For the spread of Herbartianism, see C. A. Harper, *Development of the Teachers College in the United States* (McKnight & McKnight Publishing Company, Bloomington, Ill., 1935), chaps. 14–17.

[38] *Supra*, pp. 145–148.

[39] E. L. Thorndike and A. I. Gates, *Elementary Principles of Education* (The Macmillan Company, New York, 1930), pp. 247–250.

pointed in the abortive revolution of 1848 in their native land, emigrated to America. These ideas were at first practiced only in private kindergartens. After the Civil War they gained access to the public schools largely through the leadership of William Torrey Harris (1835–1909), then superintendent of schools in St. Louis but later United States Commissioner of Education.

For long the method of self-activity was limited to preprimary education. Ultimately, however, it escaped this narrow confine in two directions. One was into the manual-training movement, the handicraft of which was seen as an excellent embodiment and extension of Froebel's gifts and occupations. The other was into the primary and upper grades of the elementary school, to which Froebel had always thought his method applicable. The educator most influential in making this extension was Colonel Francis W. Parker (1831–1902), who was a great admirer of Pestalozzi as well as of Froebel. Seizing upon Froebel's idea of self-activity, Colonel Parker became the most effective leader in putting motor expression to the fore at all levels of the elementary school. He did not restrict himself to formal or symbolic patterns of self-expression, as did Froebel,[40] however, but developed self-expression on its own account in a variety of forms, such as gesture, speech, music, modeling, painting, drawing, and writing.

With all his emphasis on motor expression it is obvious that Colonel Parker could not put up with the traditional conception of schoolroom order as stillness. If it is the child's will or tendency to motor expression that is to be trained, then Colonel Parker was ready to anticipate a certain amount of apparent disorder. The primary gift of God to man is choice; and since no one can choose the truth for another, a certain amount of commotion can be expected to be attendant on the exercise of choice by the immature minds of children. To be sure, if a child commits a crime against the routine of the school, immediate punishment may settle the case and bring quietness, if that is the end sought. But such discipline does not educate the child. Deprived of choice under the compulsion of fear, he acquires no habits of learning to rule himself.[41]

[40] Maria Montessori, working with subnormal children, also devised a method employing various kinds of objects and apparatus for the formal training of children's motor capacities. Achieving considerable success, she later adapted her procedures to normal children as well. Although some rated her methods superior to kindergarten methods, the general professional conviction has been that the methods of the modern kindergarten are quite superior. See M. Montessori, *The Montessori Method* (Frederick A. Stokes Company, Inc., New York, 1912).

[41] Hegelians like United States Commissioner of Education Torrey Harris, Colonel Parker's illustrious contemporary, arrived at the same conclusion but through a characteristically Hegelian terminology and ideology. To the

The most romantic extension of self-expression and self-activity as a pedagogical method in the twentieth century was made by certain members of the "progressive-education" movement. Their deep commitment to activism found expression in various forms such as the "activity" school, child "activity," and the "activity" curriculum. Their even deeper commitment to freedom as the only proper context in which activism could develop its full potentialities was almost reverential. In fact, among this section of progressive educators freedom for a while reached the proportions of a cult.[42] To these educators freedom was not only the end of the educational process but its proper method as well. They used it to particular advantage in teaching the arts, where they gave wide scope for children to express their individualities. Children were encouraged to express their deepest inner emotions as freely as possible in such media as painting, modeling, dancing, and literary composition. But freedom was invoked in other directions as well, for children's initiative was also solicited in planning the daily curriculum and in evaluating its final outcome.

In part, the romanticism of the methods of progressive education was due to the expanding momentum of the Froebelian influence, which, suppressed in Germany, found the democratic America of *laissez faire* most congenial to its propagation. In part, the activism of progressive methods of instruction was merely the educational phase of a coincident expressionism in the arts generally. The forces that were producing the "new" music and the "new" art were also producing progressive education, sometimes called the "new" education.[43]

Hegelian, freedom is achieved through subordination of self to moral law which, when achieved, composes the unity of the school. Such unity is a Hegelian synthesis of a thesis, the narrow whim of the individual, and its antithesis, the moral law embodying the broader social experience. (For the philosophic exposition of this triadic process, see *supra,* p. 125.) If by his misdeed the student breaks this unity of the school, he must restore it. But if he is coerced by punishment to restore it, his will is arbitrarily usurped by the teacher. The disciplinary situation should preferably be handled so that the child independently wrestles with his own misdeed and freely resolves or achieves a synthesis of his own conflict. See A. Tompkins, *The Philosophy of School Management* (Ginn and Company, Boston, 1895), pp. 157–183; J. S. Roberts, *William T. Harris* (National Education Association, Washington, D.C., 1924), pp. 197–205.

[42] Probably the most extreme employment ever made of freedom as a method in the schools was by Count Leo Tolstoy (1828–1910), the great Russian pacifist. Children were free to come or stay away from his school, to learn their lessons or refrain from them. Children were to feel only under the constraint of spontaneous interest. See W. A. McCallister, *Growth of Freedom in Education* (Richard R. Smith, New York, 1931), pp. 390–391, 398–399.

[43] I. L. Kandel, *The End of an Era* (Bureau of Publications, Teachers College, Columbia University, New York, 1941), chap. 2.

But the theory that supported this romanticism was changing in the twentieth century. In place of the philosophic idealism of the nineteenth century, scientific notions rose to undergird it.[44] Of most general scientific significance at the opening of the century was the emergence of dynamic concepts of educational psychology. The instinct psychology of William James (1842–1910) and Edward Lee Thorndike[45] gave great impetus to educational methods predicated on enlisting these native drives to pull the load of the school curriculum. Prior to these men G. Stanley Hall (1846–1924) had familiarized educators' minds with the notion of catharsis[46] (letting bad inclinations freely dissipate themselves) and had supported the cliché "No impression without expression." More startling yet, perhaps, was the force lent the methods of activism and freedom by the theory of psychoanalysis put forward by Sigmund Freud (1856–1939), great Viennese physician and psychologist.[47] According to Freud much mental ill-health stems from the thwarting of instincts whose repression is demanded by social convention. One result of his therapy of psychoanalysis was to encourage some relaxation of inhibitions and to permit a freer rein for native drives. The use to which such a theory could be put in education and the arts needs no further elaboration.

As the Old World ideas gradually spent themselves in their impact on American education, American teachers were stimulated to efforts of their own in the field of educational method. Grateful as they were for the improvements introduced from abroad, they had long had leaders who expressed misgivings about America's borrowing too extensively from the German educational tradition. Earliest to voice distrust was none other than Horace Mann, who himself had been greatly inspired by what he had seen when he visited Prussian schools. Yet in borrowing from Prussia he urged the greatest care to screen out any devices that smacked of passive obedience to arbitrary authority.[48] Similarly, Colonel Parker and John Dewey (1859–1952) were skeptical of the adaptability of Herbartian methods to the American scene. Both men detected a lack of freedom for the individual in the Herbartian pattern and the tendency of that pattern to subordinate the individual to the initiative of the teacher.

[44] For a fuller exposition of the educational philosophy of idealism, see *supra,* pp. 122–129.

[45] For a fuller development of the psychology of these men, see *supra,* pp. 150–156.

[46] For a fuller development of catharsis, see *supra,* p. 151.

[47] For a fuller development of psychoanalysis, see *supra,* pp. 160–161.

[48] J. S. Walz, *German Influence in American Education and Culture* (Carl Schurz Memorial Foundation, Philadelphia, 1936), p. 32.

THE PROBLEM METHOD

The most indigenous and original American contribution to educational method was made by John Dewey. In general principle, he identified himself with that great educational tradition which believed that the teacher's method should capitalize on the inborn active propensities of children. Like those of his predecessors, his method capitalized on these propensities in two directions, that of clarifying and ensuring understanding and that of motivating studies. His handling of each of these uses will now be taken up in turn.

Dewey's unique contribution was in the amendment he made to the employment of the activity principle as a means of clarifying the child's understanding of his lessons. To the idea of learning by doing he gave a hitherto unthought-of educational application. The direction of his thought may most easily be understood by noting the way in which Dewey himself distinguished his views from those of Pestalozzi and Froebel.[49] In exercising the child's native capacities for action, Pestalozzi used objects and Froebel "gifts" to acquaint the child with their properties. The fallacy in this method, according to Dewey, is that it assumes that objects must first be known before they can be used. Reversing this method, he held that objects usually become known, and senses incidentally exercised, in the course of using objects to achieve some end.

Dewey made much the same distinction in comparing his own ideas with those of early educators like Aristotle (384–322 B.C.) and Locke. In the case of Aristotle, the pupil activity aimed at by the teacher was preferably internal and mental because rational activity is most nearly akin to pure activity, its highest form. Dewey insisted, on the other hand, that activity must involve at least some kind and amount of overt doing. Growth in knowledge cannot germinate inside the head alone, he said. To learn or find out, one has to do something; one has to alter physical conditions outside the head to see whether what happens is what the head predicted would happen.[50]

If Dewey differed from Pestalozzi, Froebel, and Aristotle, all of whom were activists of one sort or another, he differed even more widely from Locke, whose sense empiricism he criticized for its failure to accord an active role to the senses. "It would seem," said Dewey, indirectly attacking him, "as if five minutes' unprejudiced observation of the way an infant gains knowledge would have sufficed to overthrow

---

[49] J. Dewey, *Democracy and Education* (The Macmillan Company, New York, 1916), p. 233.

[50] *Ibid.*, pp. 321–322, 393.

the notion that he is passively engaged in receiving impressions of isolated ready-made qualities of sound, color, hardness," and the like.[51] On the contrary, Dewey held that the child's restless reaching for and manipulating of objects were undertaken not to learn their isolated qualities but to see what changes in these objects could be expected if certain things were done to them. Hence, to the old dictum "Teach things rather than words" Dewey responded, "Teach not so much things as the meaning of things."[52]

It hardly needs remarking that from these contrasts a new concept of activity was emerging. Before summarizing the concept more pointedly, however, it must be said that Dewey did not overlook what had been so emphatically stated by other activists, namely, that all learning must involve doing because doing is central in the very nature of the child, whether one approach that nature philosophically, psychologically, or biologically. That provision must be made for the proper kind and amount of exercise and activity to ensure mental vigor and bodily health, Dewey himself readily conceded. At the same time he was fearful lest this sort of activity degenerate into mere random or formal exercise. In other words, activity in the abstract or for its own sake is not enough, for then one cannot tell whether activity is boisterous, thoughtless, mechanical, and perfunctory or purposeful, efficient, intelligent, and orderly.[53] To distinguish this one must have some perspective.

Summarizing and epitomizing his own views, Dewey defined activity as a series of changes definitely adapted toward accomplishing an end.[54] Thus, he would have objects and materials used at school in both work and play as a means of achieving ends suggested by the child's impulsive activities.[55] In striving to achieve his ends he would have the child act on his environment and then note the consequences in terms of his objective. Obviously, this is just the opposite of dictated exercise or "busy work." To Dewey self-activity would demand opportunity for investigation and experiment, for trying ideas out upon things.

Dewey's instrumentalism and experimentalism stand out in almost

---

[51] *Ibid.,* pp. 317–318.

[52] J. Dewey, *How We Think,* rev. ed. (D. C. Heath and Company, Boston, 1933), p. 236.

[53] J. Dewey, in *The Activity Movement,* Thirty-third Yearbook of the National Society for the Study of Education (Public School Publishing Company, Bloomington, Ill., 1934), part II, pp. 81–86.

[54] J. Dewey, in P. Monroe (ed.), *Cyclopedia of Education* (The Macmillan Company, New York, 1912), vol. 1, pp. 33–34.

[55] J. Dewey, *Democracy and Education* (The Macmillan Company, New York, 1916), pp. 180–181.

every phrase of his remarks on activity.[56] Of what practical classroom method, therefore, could Dewey more appropriately be the author than the problem method? The steps in this method he clearly outlined in his well-known volume *How We Think*. It requires little or no perspicacity to perceive that they are the same as in the scientific method. (1) The student must sense a difficulty. Preferably he must feel balked in some activity in which he is engaged so that the problem arises of how to restore its continuity. (2) Having once sensed a problem, he must next explore and clearly define it. (3) Once the situation has been thoroughly surveyed and analyzed, he must hunt data as to how the continuity of his initial activity can be restored or reconstructed into a more adequate form. (4) Next the student reasons out the implications of his data in terms of hypotheses. Then he dramatizes in his mind what the consequences of each hypothesis would be if acted out. (5) Finally he tests the hypothesis that seems most likely to achieve his ends by acting on it.[57]

While the whole approach is novel, it is at the fifth step that Dewey makes his unique contribution to activity pedagogy. His deliberate provision in this step for physical activities in accord with the hypothesis selected both tests whether the implications theoretically suggested by the hypothesis actually occur and at the same time provides participation in an experience wherein the pupil can hardly fail to come to an understanding of the terms and materials involved. Here then Dewey affords a startlingly new reason for the activity program of the laboratory, the shop, and the field trip. More than just to exercise the senses, more than to know objects concretely or symbolically, and much more than to gain relief from academic routine, the pedagogy of activity is to learn truth by testing it, to acquire by inquiry.

To many there has seemed to be historical kinship between the Herbartian five steps and Dewey's five steps. Doubtless there are similarities, but the differences are much more important. Dewey himself put his finger on the strategic difference when he said, "the Herbartian method makes no reference to a difficulty, a discrepancy requiring explanation, as the origin and stimulus of the whole process."[58] True, in the second step of presentation Herbart introduced new materials into the lesson but not so much as a problem as data to be assimilated in the next step of the method. To Dewey data are not "presented" in the normal life situation but dug up

---

[56] For a fuller discussion of Dewey's philosophy of education, see *supra,* pp. 130–134.

[57] J. Dewey, *How We Think* (D. C. Heath and Company, Boston, 1910), chap. 6.

[58] *Ibid.,* p. 204.

to solve a problem. Furthermore, data are not formally assimilated in the presence of old data recollected in the first step of preparation but are learned incidentally to overcoming the original discrepancy. No wonder Dewey concluded, "it often seems as if the Herbartian method deals with thought simply as an incident in the process of acquiring information, instead of treating the latter as an incident in the process of developing thought."[59]

The differences do not end here. A vast further difference lies between the Herbartian step of application and the Dewey step of testing, steps that superficially may look much alike. Application but puts to work a principle already known to the teacher and subtly insinuated into the children's minds in the steps of assimilation and generalization. In the very nature of testing a hypothesis, however, the outcome is more or less precarious and uncertain. Under such circumstances the teacher can only offer advice and guidance as progress is made toward the solution of a problem. He can hardly take the central position in the classroom that the Herbartian teacher has always been able to command.

So much for Dewey's conception of the role of activity in clarifying understanding. In turning now to his conception of activity in motivating learning, it will be seen that this phase of his thinking was not so novel. Yet even then, when portrayed against a background of the National Herbart Society, where he read his now famous paper "Interest as Related to the Training of Will," his ideas were novel enough to provoke a great debate.[60] Dewey found difficulty in Herbart's theory of interest because it treated feeling as an outcome or result of instruction, not as a phase of primitive impulse or feeling. For himself Dewey advised the teacher to motivate studies by making them instrumental to the pupil's realization of his own natural proclivities. Hence, the teacher who realizes that interest is simply the inner zestful realization of outgoing energy will cleverly engage the child's interest by hitching instruction on his native tendencies to action.

Dewey is careful to caution the teacher not to be deceived into thinking that because the child adopts certain external postures as those of attention or effort, he is necessarily interested. He also cautions against the artificial quality of schoolwork that has to be sugar-coated or "made" interesting, as he puts it. If instruction is calculated to enlist native drives, interest will be spontaneous and fictitious inducements or postures will be unnecessary. Furthermore, effort will flow much more freely if native impulses have been genuinely

[59] *Ibid.*

[60] *National Herbart Society Yearbook,* 1895, 2d supplement. See also *supra,* p. 149.

challenged than it will if effort is stimulated by a rational and un-emotional appeal to duty.

The problem method, as Dewey presented it, seems to have a very logical order of development. But interest, as he would have the teacher employ it, seems to indicate a more psychological order of the lesson. In Dewey's thinking the logical and the psychological are not opposed, however, but mutually dependent. To him there is no single invariant logical pattern to the lesson, as had been implied by the advocates of "general method" and by some advocates of the method of going from the simple to the complex. On the contrary, to Dewey logical order is a function of a person's familiarity with the materials under consideration and the purpose for which he wants to use them. Naturally, therefore, a teacher will organize his field differently if he is conducting research from what he will if he is going to teach beginners. He will arrange it logically if he is planning to add new facts to the field but psychologically if he is interested in seeing how his own knowledge of subject matter may assist in interpreting and promoting a beginner's needs and activities.[61]

It finally remains to note how Dewey gave a social setting to his problem method. Discarding Froebel's symbolism, he took a very common-sense view of the school as a social organism. Thus, he took the view, especially in his experimental school at the University of Chicago, that the school could prepare children for future social life only when it was itself a miniature cooperative society. This point of view affected not only the grouping of children within the school but the bonds of the school to the family and the community as a whole. It was particularly noteworthy that in Dewey's school the Pestalozzian objects and Froebelian formal gifts and occupations gave way to informal domestic and industrial activities taken from the community with which the children were already familiar, such as cooking, sewing, and carpentry.[62] In finding problems in these media children were given responsibility for selecting materials and using them in such a way as to accomplish plans conceived by them under the general supervision of the teacher.

Dewey's concepts of activity and the social process thoroughly permeated his attitude on the matter of classroom discipline. In the school he had in mind he expected that there would be greater noise and disorder than in the conventional one, but this did not trouble him. He believed that the standard of order where talking and moving

[61] J. Dewey, *The Child and the Curriculum* (The University of Chicago Press, Chicago, 1903), pp. 25–35.

[62] J. Dewey and E. Dewey, *Schools of Tomorrow* (E. P. Dutton & Co., Inc., New York, 1915).

about were done by children engaged in finding ways and means to solve a common problem is bound to be different from that where children sit silently at desks till released by the teacher to do something. In the latter case the teacher unhappily finds himself forced into a position where his standard of discipline requires him to be constantly on the alert against failures to conform to the school routine or rules. But in the former case the teacher's time can be devoted to noting and encouraging positive habits of growth, for such rules as exist are made and enforced by the children themselves in order to expedite the work all are interested in carrying forward.

THE PROJECT METHOD

New wine that Dewey's problem method was, it was not always poured into new bottles. There were many conservatives who tried to make it serve the old formalism. They saw no reason why the problem method could not be used to teach the old problems of the traditional curriculum. Just when, at the end of the First World War, the problem method seemed on the verge of being ensnared by the old formalism, William H. Kilpatrick (1871–1965) attempted to rescue it by reconstructing it as the project method.

The idea of the project was not altogether original with Kilpatrick, as it had already been in use in teaching courses in agriculture. There the project was an application on the farm at home of principles learned at school. As such, it had many of the characteristics of the problem. In fact, one might say it was a problem located in a concrete natural setting in such a way that the learner had to size up the situation, conceive a plan of what needed to be done, devise ways and means of manipulating materials to execute his plan, and check the results.

The project variation of the problem method enjoyed popularity elsewhere than in the United States. In Germany it was called *Gesamptunterricht*, the name emphasizing the fact that separate subjects were subordinated and incidental to undertaking some practical activity. In Russia this kind of instruction went under the name of the "complex." It seemed to operate satisfactorily in the early days of the revolution, when there was a less sharp demarcation between formal and informal education and when interests of the adult community were brought into the school from the factory or farm. Subsequently, when the needs of industry and agriculture became more urgently pressing, however, there was disappointment in the results. After the announcement of the New Economic policy the Central Committee overhauled the curriculum of the schools, reinstituting separate subjects of instruction and condemning the "complex" as anti-Leninist.

Seeing the vitality that the problem method possessed in the form of a project, Kilpatrick conceived of using the project as a much more general method of teaching than its narrow application had hitherto given it currency. In addition to extending its scope, he added a certain motivational character that has almost overshadowed its other characteristics. In his own words, he described the project as "any unit of purposeful experience, any instance of purposeful activity where the dominating purpose, as an inner urge, (1) fixes the aim of the action, (2) guides its process, and (3) furnishes its drive, its inner motivation."[63]

It is further interesting that Kilpatrick conceived of the teacher's method as having a wide as well as a narrow aspect, a division, however, that in no way corresponds to the old issue of general and special method. Kilpatrick's distinction grew out of his psychology of learning, in which he noted that learning hardly ever occurs singly. Almost always there are what he called "concomitant" learnings. Thus, while a child is learning arithmetic, he is also learning to like or dislike it, to be persistent or lackadaisical in his study of it, and to develop other similar habits and attitudes. The teacher who operates on this psychology will constantly have the wider aspect of method in mind as he teaches.[64] In doing so he will readily be reminded of the old adage that the verb "to teach" takes a double accusative. The teacher does not simply teach arithmetic: he always teaches John or Mary arithmetic.

The attention that Kilpatrick's broad aspect of method called to attitudes and emotional dispositions served also to give added recognition to another type of lesson that became increasingly popular in the twentieth century. This was the lesson that aimed at aesthetic appreciation. The problem-solving method was satisfactory in its place, but many claimed that method in art emphasized emotional feeling rather than a problem-solving attitude of mind. Problems perhaps could be assigned in the classroom, but feelings, never. The essence of teaching appreciation, therefore, lies in having the teacher learn to reveal his own feelings to children in such a way that children will catch them by contagion. One of the most effective ways of spreading such contagion was through encouraging the children to be productive themselves, all the way from painting and dancing to composition and dramatization.

[63] W. H. Kilpatrick, "Dangers and Difficulties of the Project Method and How to Overcome Them—A Symposium," *Teachers College Record*, 22:283, September, 1926.

[64] W. H. Kilpatrick, *Foundations of Method* (The Macmillan Company, New York, 1925), chaps. 8–9.

ECLECTICISM IN METHOD

The great popularity of the problem and project methods caused some to think that they marked the passing of the recitation.[65] This conclusion can only be accepted with considerable qualification. If by recitation was meant the rigid assign–study–*re*-cite–test classroom procedure, no doubt the recitation was passing as recommended classroom tactics. But even if unrecommended, it continued to be used by many out of sheer inertia. For others, however, the recitation was not so much passing as undergoing revision and improvement.

Some, for instance, who were inclined to pass from the recitation to the problem method, were skeptical of the romantic dependence on "inner urge" with which Kilpatrick had infused the project. They conceded the attractiveness of a method predicated on the moral autonomy of the pupil, but they were dubious as to whether teachers were adroit enough to preserve this autonomy and still bring children's achievement up to public expectations. Bent on the mastery of subject matter, Henry Morrison (1871–1945) proposed a "unit" plan based on a formula to ensure command. This formula was to "pretest, teach, test the result, adapt procedure, teach and test again to the point of actual learning."[66]

Morrison's tactics of teaching had a different nomenclature but even so were transparently Herbartian. He too had five steps: *exploration,* in which the teacher through oral question, discussion, and even testing acquaints himself with the apperceptive base which the class already possesses for the work about to be proposed; *presentation,* in which by lecture or demonstration omitting details the teacher gives the main outlines of the unit to be studied in such a manner as to arouse interest in it and then tests to find out which students have not understood; *assimilation,* in which the student collects the detailed data from sources indicated by the teacher in order to come to a full understanding of the unit; *organization,* in which the preceding two steps are carried to a point of a logical statement of conclusions; and *recitation,* in which the student presents either orally or in written form the final results of his work on the unit.

Another weakness in the recitation which had led to complaint was the fact it made no allowance for individual differences. In oral classroom instruction, as commenced by Pestalozzi and continued by Herbart, the exposition of the lesson was the same for all. This procedure, together with annual promotions. seemed to many for-

[65] V. T. Thayer, *The Passing of the Recitation* (D. C. Heath and Company, Boston, 1928).

[66] H. C. Morrison, *The Practice of Teaching in the Secondary School* (The University of Chicago Press, Chicago, 1931), p. 81.

ward-looking educators an insufferable educational lock step. With the encouragement of educational psychologists, who were just beginning to outline with exactness the contours of individual differences, a number of experiments began to appear in the individualization of methods of instruction.

Frederic L. Burk (1862–1924) at the San Francisco State Normal School was the first to make any notable advance in solving the problems involved in permitting children to proceed through school at individual rates of progress.[67] More notable and more widespread, however, was the Dalton Plan, in some places known as the "contract" plan. Under this plan the teacher made a contract with the pupil in which the latter undertook an assignment in his various subjects which would run for several weeks. Having undertaken it, the pupil was free to budget his time in completing the contract. His only limitation was that he could not receive another contract until he had finished every part of the one on hand. Group activities were not neglected, but it was the individualization of method that caught professional attention. Under this plan classrooms became laboratories or conference rooms, and teachers became consultants.[68] Meanwhile, children were put on their own initiative and resources in a way far surpassing the old recitation method of the nineteenth century.

Another plan that received widespread attention was that instituted at Winnetka, Illinois, where the superintendent had earlier been under the influence of Burk. The Winnetka Plan recognized not only that children proceed at different rates but also that the same child proceeds at different rates in different subjects. Consequently, diagnostic tests were given each child to determine what goals and tasks he should undertake. When, after working at his own rate of speed, the child thought he had accomplished his goals, he took a self-administered test to see whether he was ready for testing by the teacher and for undertaking of new goals and tasks. The Winnetka Plan emphasized group activities even more than did the Dalton Plan, for it devoted half of both the morning and the afternoon to such activities as plays, music, self-government, and open forums.[69]

Not only had there been no allowance for individual differences

[67] For the treatment of individual differences as a problem of educational administration where the method of instruction remains unaffected, see *infra*, pp. 374–379.

[68] H. H. Parkhurst, *Education on the Dalton Plan* (G. Bell & Sons, Ltd., London, 1922).

[69] National Society for the Study of Education. *Adapting the Schools to Individual Differences*, Twenty-fourth Yearbook (Public School Publishing Company, Bloomington, Ill., 1925), part II, pp. 77–82. See also C. W. Washburne and S. P. Marlon, *The History and Significance of an Educational Experiment* (Prentice-Hall, Inc., Englewood Cliffs, N.J., 1963), chap. 1.

in the old recitation but the recitation had been conducted in a very authoritarian manner, a manner at odds with the democracy of the times. Pupil spontaneity had had little chance. The domination of the teacher was not only evident in a method of instruction like the Herbartian but also disclosed itself in the etiquette of the old classroom. There children were required to stand when the teacher entered the room and to address him as "sir." Furthermore, the teacher's desk dominated the classroom from a raised dais in front of the room.

In the democratic era, which was blossoming in the first decades of the twentieth century, it became a problem how to make classroom teaching an occasion by which children would learn qualities of initiative and cooperation, which were so much in demand in a democracy. Obviously, some way had to be found to reduce the dominating position of the teacher without reducing his inherent authority so that pupil spontaneity would have an opportunity to develop. The thought occurred to some that this might be done by giving the children greater responsibility for the recitation. Thus, in reciting, children were taught to face the class rather than the teacher. Sometimes, in place of the teacher interrogating the class, the children asked questions of each other. This was especially valuable where children in small groups had previously been working on different parts of the assignment. Some teachers, to reduce their own formal prominence still further, moved their desks to the side or even to the back of the room.

More formal schemes of socializing the recitation involved organizing the class on the pattern of some political institution like Congress or a nominating convention. This attached a greater importance to each individual pupil so that he would be encouraged to participate more freely in class activity. Various forms of student government were especially useful here in improving the quality of school discipline. Success crowned this effort at the socialization of discipline in spite of the fact that William Torrey Harris, United States Commissioner of Education, had opposed the notion of a "school city" and the learning of civic functions by performing them.

An exceptionally popular form of the socialized recitation was the instance in which the class resolved itself into an informal discussion group. This has been particularly useful for instruction in controversial issues from literature to politics and economics. Here the discussion technique has been given a great development. This technique, however, has grown into much more than a revival of the Socratic method[70] or the disputations of the Middle Ages.[71] The discussion

[70] For a fuller discussion of the Socratic method, see *supra,* pp. 171–173.
[71] For a fuller discussion of the disputation, see *supra,* pp. 180–181.

technique is much more a group process than either of the earlier methods mentioned. The teacher's method is dialectical, to be sure, but it aims to get creative responses on the part of the children and perhaps even some kind of conjoint group decision.

With all the emphasis various modern methods laid on the initiative and self-reliance of the pupil, it became increasingly evident that there was a vast difference among children in their study habits. Under the old rigid recitation of assign-study-*re*-cite-test the second step of study had usually been unguided memorization of assigned homework. Even superficial examination, however, revealed that home conditions for study varied greatly. Some children had individual rooms in which to study at home, but many did not. Some children had moral encouragement from their parents, but again many did not. At first, educators tried to remedy this situation by administrative devices. Thus study halls were set aside in school, and study periods in which to use them. Later a long classroom period was arranged so that part of it might be devoted to the recitation and the other part to study under the supervision of the teacher. In addition, a literature appeared with explicit instructions on how to attack the lesson and make it part of one's experience. The first text on how to study followed more or less the lines of Dewey's problem-solving technique.

Perhaps no step in the assign–study–*re*-cite–test sequence has received greater improvement than that of the assignment. For long teachers had been in the habit of making rather crude assignments, such as the next ten pages or the next ten examples. With the introduction of the Herbartian method, however, they could make thoughtful preparation for the assignment. The last step in this method, "application," often was an assignment of work in which students could practice or apply the principle learned in the preceding step of "generalization." Again, as psychological evidence mounted for individual differences, teachers began to make differentiated assignments—a minimum assignment for all and a longer one to enrich the curriculum of the more able. The impact of Dewey's problem method brought further changes in the assignment, such as the addition of study questions and guides, suggested field trips, experiments, and the like. Even the socialized recitation had its influence, as witness inviting students themselves to formulate questions and problems for study.

The faculty counterpart of the socialized recitation was team teaching, developed in the post-World War II period. In team teaching the student had the advantage of the best talents of several teachers in a given learning enterprise. Specialization, which had long been common in the high school, spread to the elementary school as well.

Team teaching, however, not only permitted specialization but encouraged interdisciplinary activity as well. And not the least of its advantages was the release of the master teacher to concentrate on teaching while he delegated the more prosaic aspects of the classroom, such as keeping records and the like, to interns or even cooperating lay personnel.

EDUCATIONAL TECHNOLOGY

By the mid-twentieth century, it is now obvious, the advancing forces in method prominent at the opening of the century had pretty well spent themselves. Educators had settled down to making minor improvements along main lines already laid out. If the recitation had passed, so too had the period when teachers gave exclusive allegiance to some one method, such as the Herbartian or the Deweyan. Teachers had become eclectic in their choice of method, adapting their choice to different aims, different kinds of curriculum, and different types of students. If there was any point on the frontier of method where a novel break-through might occur, it seemed to be that of educational technology.

The rapidly growing interest in educational technology was the educational counterpart of automation in industry, which claimed larger and larger parts of the national economic life in the second half of the twentieth century. To some, educational technology seemed a *deus ex machina,* another kind of monitorial method, in its promise to cut rising school costs caused by the mounting school enrollments which were the by-product of the high birth rate of the war period.

While the most novel and startling device in educational technology was the teaching machine, this machine was hardly the first instance in which physical science and engineering technology had collaborated to smooth the way to improved methods of instruction. Two of the most notable instances had occurred long before the twentieth century. Perhaps the first was the invention of paper and ink in the ancient world, and the second was the invention of the printing press in the fifteenth century. In the twentieth century two further technological marvels made a tremendous impact on teaching method. One of these was sound recording, and the other photography. If Comenius's *Orbis pictus* put a powerful new tool at the disposal of the teacher, one might almost gasp at the new resources the teacher had in the phonograph, radio, movies, and television.

It is notable, however, that these great mass media had their technological development with commercial rather than educational ends in view. As a result there had been a problem of how to adapt them to instructional purposes. The problem was somewhat different in the case of the teaching machine. Here it was possible to design the "hardware" of educational technology with greater regard for the psychological theory of learning. Interestingly enough the teaching machine gave new importance to stimulus-response psychology.[72] Hitherto teaching had concentrated on the stimulus, but the teaching machine was successful in large part because it gave new attention to the response. Three characteristics of the machine attest to this. In the first place it involved active participation on the part of the learner. In the second the machine provided an immediate "feedback" or confirmation. And, third, it enabled the individual to progress at his own rate.

Designing the hardware, it needs saying, was only half the task of taking advantage of the vast possibilities of this new method of instruction. The other half was designing the program to be fed into the machine. The success of "programming" turned on providing many small, overlapping steps as the student progressed through a learning sequence. Just how many steps were needed seemed to be not just a logical matter, as with Herbart or Dewey or even Socrates in the *Meno*, but a matter for empirical investigation.

Over the horizon some foresaw vast possibilities for the aid which computers might give to the educational process. The ability of this electronic device to store and retrieve information was sure to prove a boon to school staffs. By employing this device the performance of students on teaching machines could be recorded and later studied by teachers and counselors to locate learning problems. And this is to say nothing of the revolution the computer would work in library science.[73]

By the mid-twentieth century it became clear that American education had the potentiality for mass production in education as industry had already had for a century in producing goods. Yet, except in rare instances, there had been no drive to actualize these potentialities. Nor was there one till 1955, when the Ford Foundation with its ample financial resources gave a sharp impetus in that direction. Happily the time was ripe for the impetus. There was at the moment not only a great shortage of teachers but conventional methods of teacher preparation were under severe criticism.[74] In addition, Russia's

[72] Two historic documents heralded this invention: S. L. Pressey, "A Machine for Automatic Teaching of Drill Material," *School and Society,* 25:549–552, May, 1927; B. F. Skinner, "The Science of Learning and the Art of Teaching," *Harvard Educational Review,* 24:86–97, Spring, 1954.

[73] D. D. Bushnell, "Computers in Education," in R. Gross and J. Murphy (eds.), *The Revolution in the Schools* (Harcourt, Brace & World, Inc., New York, 1964), pp. 56–72.

[74] *Infra,* pp. 488–492.

Sputnik had fired the opening gun in the race between the Soviets and the United States in education as well as aerospace exploration.

To get the neotechnology in education "off the ground" the Ford Foundation approached influential opinion makers, such as the Learning Resources Institute and the Educational Facilities Laboratories. Often it detoured around the professional "establishment," deeming it unlikely to break the cake of custom which it itself had fashioned and revered. In a short while there were experiments like "stratovision" and "continental classroom." Indeed, with all these devices there were some who thought that education was on the threshold of its first automated classroom, and that without dehumanizing education or making factories out of schools.[75]

---

[75] J. D. Finn, "Technology and the Instructional Process," in R. Gross and J. Murphy (eds.), *op. cit.,* pp. 13–31.

9 *Curriculum*

Outcroppings of curriculum evolution appear at many points in these pages. Hardly a major change has occurred in the underlying factors conditioning education that has not made an impress on the form and content of the curriculum. This is true whether the factor be political, economic, philosophic, or scientific. Thus far, however, no systematic account has been given of curriculum development in particular. What are the persistent problems that tend to recur again and again? The principal problem doubtless is: How shall the curriculum be selected? Shall it be according to conditioning sociological factors of nationalism, form of government, methods of making a living? According to theories of the nature of man, of the way in which he learns? According to the aims of education? In any event how shall one define the curriculum or conceive its nature? Shall it be stated in terms of mental discipline or socially useful habits?

ORIGIN OF THE "TRADITIONAL" CURRICULUM

If one goes back in history far enough, it is probably safe to say that he will nearly always find that the curriculum has had a functional genesis. Whether one goes back to the Egyptians, the Babylonians, or even the ancient Chinese, the story is likely to be the same— the curriculum, whether formal or informal, took its origin in the daily activities of the people. Each succeeding generation, in order to become competent to assume the tasks of adults, had a particular curriculum of training to undergo. The would-be artisan had his craft to learn, the warrior skill at arms, and the priest his arts and sciences. This concept of functionalism was put very laconically by Agesilaus, King of Sparta, who, when asked what he thought most proper for boys to learn, replied, "what they ought to do when they come to be men."

The civilization whose culture, handed down through the curricula of succeeding centuries, has continued to function most persistently in the Western world is that of the Greeks. They it was who not only literally created some of our principal current subjects of instruction but also worked out a functional curriculum that for inclusiveness and balanced proportion has rarely been equaled in subsequent educational history. This curriculum combined the intellectual, physical, moral, and aesthetic aspects of life in a most unusual degree of harmony.

On the intellectual side the Greeks laid the basis for what have ever since been known in the curricula of the world as the seven liberal arts. It will be well here to divide their consideration, as was later done, under the headings of the trivium and the quadrivium. The former was composed of grammar, rhetoric, and logic, or dialectic, as the Greeks and medievalists called it. This trivium, or trio of subjects, had its genesis in the daily civic life of the Greeks, especially the Athenian Greeks. Being democratically inclined, this great people tended from early times more and more to manage its civic affairs through the medium of public discussion. In order to speak more effectively in public assemblies men soon found it profitable to analyze literary practice so that it yielded its secrets of structure, motivation, and cogency. Thus, it was to teachers like the Sophist Protagoras (481–411 B.C.) that long generations of school children owe thanks for inaugurating the linguistic discipline of grammar. It was he who early taught men to be more precise in their speech by recognizing its parts, naming them, and defining the rules of their usage. What Protagoras did for grammar, Plato (427–347 B.C.) and more particularly Aristotle (384–322 B.C.) did for dialectic, and still others for rhetoric.

The genesis of the trivium was not, however, exclusively justified by its political usefulness. The Greeks also saw these three disciplines as the tools by which the teacher, like a sculptor, might shape the soul or intellect of the child according to the inherent law of its own structure. Plato, for instance, made dialectic fundamental in the curriculum, not just to gain a decision in debate or even to elucidate some particular truth, but rather because it was basic to the intellectual comprehension of any truth whatsoever. Indeed, in subsequent centuries it was this insight, that the trivium stated the laws of the mind itself, which became the preeminent and perennial justification for its inclusion in the curriculum.

The quadrivium, the other division of the early intellectual curriculum, was composed of arithmetic, geometry, astronomy, and music. Of these the two branches of mathematics were regarded most highly. Their practical value in the various crafts and in domestic economy, of course, spoke for itself. But Plato saw an even wider significance for mathematics in that it sharpened the mind; in fact, even students who were slow at mathematics, he thought, "have their general intelligence much increased by studying it."[1] Perhaps best of all, mathematics enabled one to reason in the abstract without reference to concrete reality and thus led one most directly to the realm of true being.

In addition to astronomy Pythagoras (580–500 B.C.), formulator of the Pythagorean theorem in geometry, wished to include in the curriculum such other sciences as geography, physics, and medicine. Yet, despite the functional value of astronomy in keeping track of time and the seasons, the scientific aspect of the quadrivium never loomed very large in the educational thinking of the Greeks. The pursuit of science involved the study of concrete objects and so had to employ the senses as well as the intellect. But the senses were notoriously inaccurate reporters of the truth because the concrete reality they reported had accidental variations which beclouded the undeviating essentials of truth in the abstract.[2] Therefore, as merely the appearance of pure being, the sciences and their study were doomed to a position of secondary importance in the curriculum till the rise of modern science in the sixteenth and seventeenth centuries.

This early inequality in the relative importance of the trivium and quadrivium—linguistic and scientific studies, Humanism and naturalism—received endorsement from Socrates (469–399 B.C.), at least as reported by Plato. When twitted by Phaedrus for never venturing outside the walls of Athens, Socrates retorted, "I am a lover of knowledge, and the men who dwell in the city are my teachers, and not the trees, or the country."[3]

The preference for the trivium over the quadrivium ultimately sprang from the dualism between mind and matter. This dualism arose from a further dualism between mind and body. And yet, in spite of the preference for mind over body in this dualism, the Greeks were great believers in physical education. Bodily appetites or faculties might be inferior to mental ones, but they were not to be neglected. Nor were they neglected by the Greek masses. Indeed, there was

[1] K. Freeman, *Schools of Hellas* (Macmillan & Co., Ltd., London, 1922), pp. 106–107.

[2] For a more complete exposition of the underlying educational philosophy here, see *supra*, pp. 104–105.

[3] B. Jowett, *Works of Plato* (Tudor Publishing Company, New York, n.d.), vol. 3, pp. 383–384.

a constant danger among the Greeks of an overemphasis on physical training, leading toward athleticism and professionalism.[4]

The curriculum of Greek physical education consisted of a number of notable games, which reached their highest point of development in the Panhellenic Olympic festival, a festival still celebrated in the modern world of sport. The principal games in which the Greeks excelled were running, jumping, wrestling, boxing, and throwing the javelin and discus. Originally these games had a functional military significance; javelin throwing, for instance, definitely prepared men for war. In the course of time, however, the Greeks came to play these games for moral and aesthetic ends as well as for military ones. In fact, physical fitness came to be secondary to strength of character. So firmly did the Greeks believe that the practice of their sports strengthened resolution and will power that they were more than half convinced that physical beauty was an index of moral beauty.

While the Greeks viewed physical exercise as the antidote for indecision and weakness of character, they also recognized that there could be too much as well as too little training in sports. Excessively strenuous physical education, Aristotle thought, tended to brutalize the young just as too little made them soft and effeminate. Moderation, therefore, was to be the rule. The Greeks, furthermore, sought proportion not only between too much and too little sport but also between the sports. Thus, they reserved their greatest praise for the all-around athlete, the man who not only had the well-developed legs of the runner but also the well-developed arms of the javelin thrower. Of all the sports probably the one most favored was wrestling because more than any other it afforded a balanced development of the whole body.

Just as the aesthetic quality of Greek education demanded balance and proportion between the activities of physical education, so too it demanded the same relation in the curriculum between physical education and intellectual education. The subject, perhaps, on which the Greeks most relied to mediate this proportion was music. Broadly, music was any art presided over by a muse. More narrowly, it was essentially rhythmic. It was involved not only in learning melodies on the lyre and the lute but also in the dance and in the lyrical aspect of literature, especially poetry. Music was thus a sort of common denominator of the physical and intellectual aspects of education and imparted to both a sense of its own rhythmic symmetry and harmony.

While the Greeks fully realized that one could learn to appreciate music without learning to play it, nevertheless they favored a child's

---

[4] T. Woody, "Professionalism and the Decay of Greek Athletics," *School and Society,* 47:521–528, April, 1938.

taking up an instrument just as long as he did not practice it too much. To spend too much time on an instrument would be just as reprehensible as to spend too much time at sport. To achieve professional competence in either was to vulgarize oneself and to debase the liberal quality of education.[5] The moderation advocated in time spent at practice Aristotle also extended to the kind of tunes played. Here he definitely preferred restrained melodies rather than tumultuous ones. The advantage to be gained in learning to play music as well as to appreciate it lay, as Aristotle also said, both in being able to amuse oneself and in being able to judge the playing of others. Plato, on the other hand, thought music was more important for its contribution to virtue.

Of the four aspects of Greek education—intellectual, physical, aesthetic, and moral—the moral was far from being the least important. Without trespassing on the more extended account of moral education reserved for treatment elsewhere,[6] it may be wise to point out here how harmoniously moral instruction was blended with other aspects of the curriculum, such as musical and physical education. Morals, especially under the Sophists, were taught as a separate discipline but never without reference to their effect on the whole man.

Finally, there was one interesting contradiction in the curriculum that profoundly affected all curricula subsequently predicated on Greek culture. The Greek curriculum neglected vocational education, and that in spite of the fact that the Greeks waxed exceptionally prosperous from industry and trade. The reason for this contradiction is not far to seek. Greek industrial arts were too closely connected with the ancient institution of slavery and therefore were unable to escape a servile stigma for the freeman. Moreover, their pursuit deprived a freeman of the leisure necessary to exercising at the gymnasium, or palaestra, and to performing the duties of citizenship. All this is to say nothing of the further sedentary nature of many crafts, which tended to stoop the spine and prevent the realization of an aesthetically well-formed body. Yet, while vocational education found no recognition in the formal curriculum of Greek schools, it was cared for informally through apprenticeship.[7] In fact, one of the laws of Solon exonerated children from failing to support their parents in the latter's old age if the latter had not taken the pains to bring their children up in a trade.[8]

[5] For a fuller discussion of liberal education, see *infra,* pp. 445–455.

[6] *Infra,* chap. 11.

[7] L. F. Anderson, "Some Facts Regarding Vocational Training among the Ancient Greeks and Romans," *School Review,* 20:191–201, March, 1912; W. L. Westermann, "Vocational Training in Antiquity," *School Review,* 22:601–610, November, 1914.

[8] The Jewish parent was enjoined to teach his son a trade as well as the Mosaic law. Note that Jesus was a carpenter, and St. Paul a tentmaker.

The curriculum that was good enough for the Greeks was, on the whole, good enough for the Romans, too. Dedicated to the educational ideal of the orator,[9] the Romans found the Greek studies of grammar, rhetoric, and logic especially to their liking. In borrowing these arts from the Greeks, the only addition to the curriculum that they had to make was the study of the Greek language itself in order to unlock its treasures. Under the title of grammar, thus, the Roman boy was expected to read widely not only in his mother tongue but in a second tongue as well. In this way, bilingualism made a recognized entry into what in modern times came to be known as the "traditional" curriculum.

CHRISTIAN INFLUENCE ON THE CURRICULUM

While the preoccupation of the Romans with the trivium of grammar, rhetoric, and logic did not lead them to omit the more scientific studies of the quadrivium or to be insensitive to the moral and aesthetic content of the curriculum, it did lead them to the relative neglect of these elements. The failure of the curriculum to strengthen moral fiber became particularly glaring toward the end of the Roman Empire, when both public and private virtue fell to their lowest levels. There is no telling how much further moral disintegration would have gone had it not been for the stabilizing effect of Christianity.

While even a façade of Roman culture remained, the effect of Christianity on the traditional curriculum was slow to make itself felt. With the collapse of Rome and the emergence of the Catholic Church in the Middle Ages as the strongest force for social stability in the Western world, religious and moral materials gained an ascendancy in the curriculum. These materials consisted largely of the catechism, psalmody, and the writings of the early church fathers. In fact, so deeply preoccupied did Christians become with the expectation of an early end of the world and the second advent of Christ that the curricula of Christian schools concentrated on religious and moral studies to the neglect and often positive exclusion of former secular ones.

Physical education, for example, gave way to asceticism. Monks, if not knights, reasoned: Why cultivate the body when it is the seat of the baser appetites and when, on account of its material nature, it fails to survive death, as does the immaterial soul? Far from developing the body, therefore, the Middle Ages tended to suppress and curtail its natural propensities. Again, the liberal arts of grammar, logic, and rhetoric all but disappeared under the interdiction of the more zealous religious leaders. Feared for the strength they lent to pagan philosophy, these subjects not only fell into disuse but were

[9] For a further development of the ideal, see *supra,* p. 5.

actually avoided. Where they did survive in spite of aggressive opposition, they took such epitomized and abbreviated form in the digests of the time that it was difficult to recognize their former glory.

Only toward the end of the Middle Ages did churchmen come to appreciate that the strength of the old Greco-Roman trivium could be captured as an ally for Christian philosophy. Consequently, they gradually conceded space in the curriculum to grammar and particularly to logic. But even so the curriculum of Christian schools remained narrowly religious and moral. In fact, so long did it retain this narrowness that Francis Bacon (1561–1626), that early herald of the scientific method, criticized it severely not only for sticking so closely to logic but for limiting itself to Aristotle's logic at that. Contrary to Socrates, Bacon seems to have had a higher regard for a curriculum based on nature than for one based on the mind of man, "For the wit and mind of man," he wrote, "if it work upon matter, which is the contemplation of the creatures of God, worketh according to the stuff, and is limited thereby; but if it work upon itself, as the spider worketh his web, then it is endless, and brings forth indeed cobwebs of learning, admirable for the fineness of thread and work, but of no substance or profit."[10]

RISE OF THE HUMANITIES (CLASSICS)

The balance between the intellectual, physical, aesthetic, and moral aspects of the curriculum was not restored till the Renaissance, which extended roughly from the fourteenth to the sixteenth century. In fact, the ideal of a well-rounded curriculum had so generally dropped out of sight during the Middle Ages, when trade and commerce and large-scale civil administration were at a standstill, that it was all but forgotten. Nor was the ideal remembered again till political and economic conditions in Europe approximated the sort that had sustained it earlier in Greece and later in the heyday of the Roman Empire. Such conditions first appeared in the cities of northern Italy. There the revival of trade and commerce again made possible stable political life and gave rise to a wealthy and leisured class of people for whose sons the narrow curriculum of the Middle Ages no longer possessed particular functional value. The attention of these young men focused more and more on mundane affairs and less and less on the supermundane, as had been the case in the medieval period. In the light of this more secular reorientation they had to seek new educational criteria for the life well spent.

It was only a matter of time till scholars like Petrarch (1304–1374)

[10] F. Bacon, *The Advancement of Learning* (Ginn and Company, Boston, 1904), pp. 31–32.

rediscovered such criteria in the literary remains of Greece and Rome, the manuscript evidence of which had to be literally recovered from medieval garrets and forgotten scrap heaps. In the culture of these civilizations men found a measure of life so superior and so far in advance of the times in which they themselves lived that the study of what the Greeks and Romans had thought and done became an all-absorbing vogue. But the account of this thought and action was locked in a purer Latin than the corrupted tongue of the Caesars inherited from the Middle Ages and was even more securely locked in Greek, which was almost unknown in Italy at the time. Quite logically, therefore, the study of Latin and Greek became the condition precedent to a life of culture and refinement. Because it required centuries for the Renaissance world to catch up with the excellence of the Greeks and Romans in arts, letters, and science, Latin and Greek held undisputed sway in the curriculum of the better schools down to the very opening of the twentieth century.

Latin and Greek did not supplant the ancient trivium; they merely became the medium through which grammar, logic, and rhetoric were taught—and for the same reason, to form the mind. This central position of the classics also earned them their older and more perennial name of the "humanities." Since mind, according to Aristotle, was the unique excellence of man[11] and since the classic languages had peculiar value in forming the mind of man, "therefore," wrote Battista Guarino (1434–1513), a Renaissance educator, "our forefathers called them *'humanitas,'* the pursuits, the activities, proper to mankind."[12]

It may appear that the Renaissance curriculum was as one-sided in its emphasis on the humanities as the medieval one was in its stress on religion and morals. This, however, was not intended to be the case. The intention, rather, was that the Humanistic curriculum should give the same well-rounded training as the classical literatures portrayed for Greco-Roman youth. That the Humanistic curriculum was headed in this direction is borne out by the aim that governed it, the development of *sapiens atque eloquens pietas,* wise and eloquent piety.[13] This popular Renaissance cliché indicates attention to three of the four important aspects of the Greek curriculum, the intellectual (*sapiens*), the aesthetic (*eloquens*), and the moral (*pietas*). Add to these the fact that the courtier, the educational ideal of the period,[14] was expected to become proficient in such manly exercises as fencing,

---

[11] For a fuller exposition of this theory of man, see *supra,* pp. 105–106.

[12] W. H. Woodward, *Vittorino da Feltre and Other Humanist Educators* (Cambridge University Press, London, 1897), p. 177.

[13] For further discussion of this education aim, see *supra,* p. 9.

[14] W. H. Woodward, *loc. cit.*

swimming, wrestling, and horsemanship, and one has before him again the traditional ideal of a balanced and well-proportioned curriculum.

To the foregoing might also be added training in polished manners. In part, this training was but a portion of the Renaissance heritage from Greek and Roman culture. The chief points in manners that Greco-Roman youth were taught to observe were modesty and reverence. Greek youth, for example, were taught never to sit in the presence of their elders, who themselves rarely sat because to do so was the mark of a slave. In part, Renaissance training in politeness was a legacy from the medieval training of chivalry. In order to become a knight the young squire had to learn the etiquette of proper deportment in the presence of ladies as well as chivalrous conduct toward an opponent in battle. During the Renaissance the code of chivalry gave way to the conduct of the courtier, and this in time merged with the manners of the gentleman.

Among the intellectual studies the trivium was still preeminent. If logic was somewhat less important than it had been during the medieval period, rhetoric, which had been relatively neglected then, was now restored to the importance it formerly enjoyed. But more important than either logic or rhetoric during the Renaissance was grammar. The Italian Vergerius (1370–1445) declared grammar to be the foundation of every other subject,[15] and Guarino opined that unless grammar be thoroughly learned the house of knowledge is built on treacherous ground. The quadrivium, if anything, enjoyed a somewhat lower esteem than it did among the Greeks. This is an almost startling statement when one stops to realize that the late Renaissance is the beginning of the period of great scientific discovery. This was the time of Galileo and Christopher Columbus, of Nicolaus Copernicus and Johannes Kepler, and yet none of these men were prepared for his great discoveries by any science he learned in the schools.

In examining the Humanistic curriculum more closely from the moral and aesthetic points of view, it appears that its aesthetic potentialities received greater attention south of the Alps while its moral resources roused greater enthusiasm north of them. To the south in Italy the humanities were the means of enjoying life more fully. The style of the ancient masters in poetry and prose was the special object of study. Boys used these masters as models for improving their own oral and written speech. The grace sought in speech was also sought in deportment of the body. Dancing as part of the curriculum of the courtier, however, held a somewhat doubtful status since there were "divines" even in that day who were apprehensive that dancing might be injurious to a young man's virtue.

[15] *Ibid.,* p. 107.

To the north of the Alps, especially in Germany, the Humanistic curriculum was a means to religious and social reform. What caught the imagination of the northern European in Greek and Latin literature was not so much the elegance of its style, though that was still important, as the critical and independent quality of mind revealed there. With an increasing number of minds trained to a fine edge of discrimination by wide reading of classical authors, Germany almost inevitably became the spearhead of the Protestant Reformation. Critical minds grew impatient with religious and social abuses and consequently demanded their reform. Participation in this reform, which in the centuries ensuing spread from religion to politics and economics as well, required training through a curriculum drawn from Christian and pagan sources and rich in its comprehension and analysis of human values.

DECLINE OF THE HUMANISTIC CURRICULUM

There can be little doubt that at the height of the Renaissance the classical, or Humanistic, curriculum of Latin and Greek had a high functional value. The study of these ancient tongues had such undisputed vitality that students needed no artificial inducements from the teacher to learn them. In the post-Renaissance period this happy pedagogical state of affairs began to deteriorate. As greater and greater numbers of students were attracted to the study of the humanities, it was almost inescapable that a larger and larger number appeared who lacked the native ability and aptitude to master the culture implicit in them. Consequently, teachers, among whom, too, a greater and greater proportion was undoubtedly inadequate, felt the task too great to teach an intimate understanding of classical culture. They therefore contented themselves when they succeeded in teaching just the languages without the culture. It was not long thereafter before teachers were contenting themselves with a job well done if they succeeded in teaching just the grammar of the language. Moreover, Latin and Greek grammatical usage was not all of equal merit. Therefore, teachers narrowed the Humanistic curriculum still further by confining themselves to just one author as a model, Cicero. Paradoxically enough, in this effort to keep the content of the curriculum as pure as possible, the humanities reached the narrowest and most barren stage of their degeneracy.

More fundamental sociological factors were also at work to account for the decline of the humanities in the curriculum. Although cultivated Latin long remained the language of scholarship and diplomacy, of the church and the courts, it was not long in meeting keen competition from the vernacular tongues. Kings, in their endeavor to build national states at the expense of the former feudal nobility, found the encouragement of the vernacular tongue a strong ally of national cohesion. Much later, in the eighteenth and nineteenth centuries, the democratic and industrial revolutions with their emphasis on the common man so elevated the importance of his vernacular as to encroach even more ominously on the monopoly of the humanities as the main avenue to culture. The humanities, moreover, suffered from refusing to move over and make room in the curriculum for the great advances of science during the seventeenth and eighteenth centuries.

In spite of the way in which these powerful underlying forces were slowly but surely changing the face of the curriculum, Greek and Latin managed by the very weight of their long-standing prestige, if by nothing else, to maintain top rank. This example of cultural lag in the curriculum prompted two different reactions. One was to accept the fact that the content of the classics was definitely outmoded but to justify their continued inclusion in the curriculum on the ground of their disciplinary value. The thought here was that close application to a highly inflected tongue with a complex syntax like Greek or Latin would yield beneficial results even if the content of those languages did not.

But here it must be noted that the disciplinary theory of forming the mind through literary studies was quite different from the classical theory of forming the mind. The classical theory sought to form the mind through its mastery of a worth-while content of subjects like grammar and logic, which were thought to state the very rules of mental operation. The disciplinary theory, on the other hand, cared little about the content of the curriculum as long as it was difficult enough to breed habits of persistence and industry, memory and reasoning. As evidence of this fact stands John Locke (1632–1704), great English educational essayist, who thought mathematics quite superior to Latin as the whetstone of the mind.[16]

There was nothing especially new about the disciplinary theory of the curriculum. Although it perhaps received classic exposition in the seventeenth, eighteenth, and nineteenth centuries, it was at least as old as China. At a very early date a difference had grown up there, too, between the literary language of scholars and the vernacular language of the common folk. There was also a time when Jewish youth had been plagued by the requirement that they study the Pentateuch in a Hebrew dialect that was already archaic. And even the Romans, in adopting the culture of the Greeks, had taken occasion to justify certain elements of it as disciplinary long after their original applicability to Roman conditions of life had worn thin.

[16] For a psychological account of the disciplinary theory of learning, see *supra,* pp. 141–143.

The other reaction to the cultural lag manifested by Greek and Latin in the post-Renaissance period was to try to make the Humanistic curriculum more realistic. John Milton (1608–1674), the great English poet and author of the *Tractate of Education*, was a leader in this movement. Holding that no nation had sufficient experience in its own past on which to predicate the education of its youth, he took the view that it was necessary to supplement such a limited background by including languages describing the unique experience of other civilizations. But in going back to the literatures of Greece and Rome he insisted that selections be made which had a definite functional bearing on the times in which he lived. This view is often called "Humanistic realism." It had little effect, however, for the tide of social events had already set too strongly against the humanities in their old form.

Another realistic approach to the curriculum has gone under the title of "social realism." The French essayist Michel de Montaigne (1533–1592) was perhaps the foremost exponent of this revision of the curriculum. Thoroughly schooled in the humanities himself, he favored their continued incorporation in the curriculum but in a subordinate position to travel and social contact. His view is well epitomized by the couplet

> *How much the fool that's sent to roam*
> *Excels the fool that stays at home.*

Hence by going abroad and rubbing elbows with men in diverse cultures Montaigne hoped to infuse a realism into the traditional curriculum that had been sadly lacking.

It will be well at this point to postpone for a moment the consideration of a third and more radical type of realistic reconstruction of the curriculum, that based on "sense realism," and instead to say a word about the effect on the traditional curriculum of an eighteenth-century move to revitalize Humanism known as "neohumanism." Neohumanism differed from the Humanism of the preceding centuries in its greater attachment to Greek. Hitherto, the Humanistic curriculum had been primarily a Latin curriculum; Greek had been of distinctly secondary importance, having been taught principally as a means of reading the New Testament in its Greek original. In the eighteenth century, however, the importance of Greek in the curriculum was made to rest upon the ideal of life it afforded, the serenity of this ideal when confronted with the inevitable limitations of life, and the central position it accorded to free intelligence in achieving a symmetrical development of the individual within these limits.

Perhaps neohumanism had its chief effect on the curriculum in the nineteenth century. The importance, for instance, that the great

German educator Johann Friedrich Herbart (1776–1841) attached to Homer's *Odyssey* as a vehicle for moral education undoubtedly stems from the influence that neohumanism had on him. Later in the century, William Torrey Harris (1835–1909), one of the most outstanding of United States commissioners of education, returned to the old Greek view of the importance of grammar in the curriculum. "Grammar," he wrote, "opens to the child his view of the inner workings of the mind of the race, and helps him insofar to a comprehension of his own spiritual self."[17]

The hypodermic of neohumanism wore off too rapidly for all but a relatively few select minds among most student bodies. Before the nineteenth century was out, many teachers were again depending heavily on the disciplinary value of the classics for their justification. But in the twentieth century they were deprived of even this long-standing stimulant. Psychological studies then cast grave doubt on the chief tenet of the disciplinary theory, namely, that such powers of concentration, memory, and reasoning as are developed by the study of Latin or Greek are automatically transferable to other studies like history and mathematics or to any professional or vocational choice a student might make.[18] Friends of the classics fought and ridiculed this scientific evidence but in vain. In the well-subsidized and carefully conducted *Classical Investigation,*[19] the results of which were published shortly after the First World War, supporters of the classics finally conceded that the disciplinary theory must be discarded or at least seriously qualified. If they were to have a leg left to stand upon, they would have to teach the classics better and for more functional reasons. As a result of the report much progress took place in just this direction, particularly in the attractiveness of textbooks. Yet, though large numbers continued to study the classics, their relative proportion continued to decline.

EMERGENCE OF SCIENCE IN THE CURRICULUM

It is necessary now to return and consider the more radical reconstruction of the curriculum suggested by the sense realists of the seventeenth and eighteenth centuries. The sense realists derived their name from the fact that they laid great store by knowledge predicated on sense experience. Prior to the sixteenth and seventeenth centuries most knowledge in the curriculum was verbal and based on the authority of the ancients, for the most part on the authoritative word

[17] W. T. Harris, *Psychological Foundations of Education* (D. Appleton & Company, Inc., New York, 1898), p. 322.
[18] For a psychological account of this study, see *supra,* p. 155.
[19] (Princeton University Press, Princeton, N.J., 1924.)

of Aristotle. Good early scientist that he was, Aristotle made many inferences about the nature of things according to what the end or purpose of each might be.[20] In the seventeenth and eighteenth centuries dependence on sense observation rather than speculative purpose revealed that many of his conclusions stood in need of revision. From trying to anticipate nature, as ancient science had endeavored to do, modern science turned to following nature as her humble servant.

Enthusiasts for the new method of investigating nature through the senses, like the Englishman Francis Bacon and the famous Moravian educator Johann Amos Comenius (1592–1670), saw visions of a new encyclopedic curriculum largely reconstructed by science. An encyclopedic curriculum had been a constantly recurring ideal ever since the time of the Greeks. In fact, their seven liberal arts were an early attempt at an encyclopedic curriculum of what was worth while for a freeman to know. Aristotle more than any other man in ancient times personified this ideal. In fact, so wide and varied were his writings that during the Middle Ages he was known as the "master of those who know." In the seventeenth century the new optimism generated by science emboldened Bacon to assert, "I have taken all knowledge to be my province." Influenced by Bacon, Comenius sat down and wrote his famous *Didactica magna* to set forth the art of "teaching all things to all men."[21] This ambitious revival of encyclopedism passed under the title of "pansophism." Yet little did either Bacon or Comenius realize that the new science would not merely simplify existing knowledge but also so expand its extent that never again could one man, like Aristotle, hope to comprehend its bounds within the limits of one brain.

In spite of this entrancing vision, Aristotle continued to tyrannize over most curricula. Most teachers continued on their traditional way of emphasizing verbalization rather than sense impression. Indeed, Humanism rather than naturalism was destined to rule the curriculum till the nineteenth century was already well spent. Nonetheless, a few eighteenth-century schools, like the *Pädagogium* of August Hermann Francke (1663–1727), the *Realschule* of Johann Julius Hecker (1707–1768), and the *Philanthropinum* of Johann Bernhard Basedow (1723–1790), did essay to introduce the new scientific culture into their curricula. In addition to astronomy from the old quadrivium, such new subjects as mechanics, geography, natural history, and drawing began to appear. The classroom paraphernalia of instruction began to enlarge. Globes, microscopes, and compasses made their appearance. The *Realschule,* just mentioned, included a botanical garden and scale models of ships, plows, and churns, novel

[20] For a fuller account of the philosophy involved here, see *supra,* p. 106.
[21] See the full title of this work.

additions beyond the conventional bookish curriculum, to say the least.

The adherents of science in the curriculum took further heart from the reshuffling of social values attendant on the French Revolution. Political radicals, bent on redrawing the social order closer to a pattern of justice inherent in nature, felt a real kinship with educators who wished radically to reconstitute the curriculum on the observed uniformities in nature. The same kinship obtained in America, too. In proposing the kind of education he thought most suitable for our infant republic, itself just born of revolution, Samuel Smith (1752–1839), runner-up in a prize-essay contest on this theme, proposed a national curriculum strongly favoring naturalistic science.

Science recommended itself to the curriculum makers of the nineteenth century for its utilitarianism as well as its realism and naturalism. The utilitarian necessity for making a place in the curriculum for science became most evident in England, the home of the Industrial Revolution. There the proponent of putting science in the schools was Thomas Henry Huxley (1825–1895), great expounder of the Darwinian theory of evolution. He took the general line that it was an extremely shortsighted policy for a great colonial nation like England with vast industrial and commercial interests to fail to give instruction in physics and chemistry, on which its industrial and commercial greatness rested. The ever-increasing competition of international trade finally caused England to accept this point of view, as did other great industrial nations like Germany, France, and the United States from the middle of the nineteenth century onward.

It should be mentioned here that science and its ally industry were instrumental in conferring new significance on the place of mathematics in the curriculum. During the reign of Humanism in the Renaissance, mathematics had been more or less overlooked. In the preceding period of the Middle Ages it had been even more generally neglected. Yet at that, mathematics had never suffered quite the loss of prestige that scientific studies had. The saving feature of mathematics lay in that it was an abstract mental discipline which could be carried on without getting too heavily entangled in the accidental qualities of nature. For this reason, as Plato had remarked, mathematics was the supreme subject in enabling one to speculate on the nature of pure being. With the rise of modern science, however, the worth of mathematics turned not on its speculative philosophical value but on its usefulness in scientific calculation. Kepler, for example, in coming to his elliptical hypothesis of the movement of heavenly bodies rested heavily on mathematical calculation, as did also Sir Isaac Newton in computing his law of gravity. As the secrets of science became the stimulus of the Industrial Revolution, there was even greater need for instruction in mathematics. Consequently, in the nineteenth and twentieth centuries mathematics came to occupy a most respectable place in the curricula of nearly all schools.

Although the arguments of utilitarianism and naturalistic realism both favored a scientific curriculum, the proponents of science were oddly uneasy about the claims of the Humanists and classicists as to the superior mental discipline afforded by linguistic studies. Not to be outdone, Herbert Spencer (1820–1903), another great English propounder of the scientific point of view with a considerable following in the United States, went as far as to claim that science not only equaled but excelled language as a discipline of the mind. "While language familiarizes with nonrational relations," he proclaimed, "science familiarizes with rational relations. While the one exercises memory only, the other exercises both memory and understanding."[22] As if he had not claimed enough for science as a superior mental discipline, Spencer went on to declare it also a superior moral and religious discipline.

RIVALRY BETWEEN HUMANISM AND NATURALISM

This rivalry in the curriculum between Humanism and naturalism, literature and science, was, of course, one of long standing. As already seen, it dated back at least to the distinction made in the seven liberal arts between the trivium of linguistic studies and the quadrivium of largely scientific ones. Socrates, it will be remembered, was an early humanist, preferring the study of man to the study of nature. Conversely, Bacon, it will be remembered, was inclined to favor realistic rather than Humanistic studies. He felt that a curriculum secured in the uniformities of nature was superior to one subject to the variability of the human mind. This rivalry, never very acute as long as the humanities were the overwhelming favorite in the curriculum, became increasingly keen as modern displaced ancient science. As a world view predicated on modern naturalistic science more and more conclusively demonstrated the need for fundamental revisions in the world view predicated on Humanism, the Humanists increasingly took alarm. From a position of security in the curriculum the humanities ultimately found themselves on the defensive.

The conflict between Humanism and naturalism in the curriculum raged all through the eighteenth, nineteenth, and even twentieth cen-

[22] H. Spencer, *Education: Intellectual, Moral, and Physical* (J. M. Dent & Sons, Ltd., Publishers, London, n.d.), p. 39.

turies.[23] Why did not Humanism early ease the conflict by gracefully making concessions to naturalism? Perhaps something of an answer to this question is to be found in the attack made by Humanists on Basedow's Philanthropinum toward the end of the eighteenth century. The Philanthropinum was a school designed to test the naturalistic educational theories of the time.[24] It not only included scientific materials in the curriculum but also employed methods of instruction predicated in part on the sense realism of Comenius and in part on the romantic naturalism of Jean Jacques Rousseau (1712–1778), author of *Émile*.

The first complaint in the Humanistic indictment of the program of the Philanthropinum was that its realism and naturalism led to a narrow utility. The Humanistic curriculum, on the other hand, was governed by the endeavor to achieve a general culture. Consequently, while naturalism was merely filling the mind with useful knowledge, Humanism was aiming at the broader result of strengthening and disciplining the mind in its basic functions. A related fault, for which the Humanists further indicted the Philanthropinum, resided in the great breadth to which a naturalistic curriculum had to stretch in order to cover everything of utility. In contrast, the Humanists praised their own curriculum for its relatively few subjects, which gave such a general exercise to the mind as to enable it to transfer its powers in any later direction. The next complaint of the Humanists went very deep. They pointed out that while the curriculum of naturalism and sense realism was composed of things, their own was composed of ideas. Naturalism, sense realism, and utilitarianism all led to materialism. Humanism, on the other hand, emphasized the immaterial, the spiritual. Consequently, it claimed a more intimate relation with moral values, a concern allegedly foreign to naturalism and science.

Unhappily, the closer the competition between the humanities, or classics, on the one hand and science on the other, the wider the rift between them. This seems unfortunate, since at least Plato among Greek educational philosophers did not originally think of Humanism and naturalism as being opposed to each other. On the contrary, he thought that one could not know man and his end apart from a knowledge of nature and its governing end.

The question then arises: Why did the first rift occur and later widen between Humanistic and naturalistic studies? There were various reasons. Perhaps, to commence, one might call attention to the fact that the Romans, who went to school to the Greeks, were interested not so much in the conquest and control of nature as in the con-

---

[23] For a twentieth century statement of the conflict see N. Foerster, *The American State University* (The University of North Carolina, Chapel Hill, N.C., 1937).

[24] For a fuller account of this educational philosophy, see *supra*, pp. 116–118.

quest and control of men. Much of what was necessary for an understanding and control of men the Romans found in Greek literature.
To this literature they added their own; and thus when Northern
Europe went to school to Greco-Roman culture, it, too, was tutored
in a literary tradition.

The interest in the understanding of man rather than in the conquest
and control of nature also stemmed from certain philosophical perplexities. Nature always presented itself in the concrete, but nature
in the concrete seemed to defy understanding because its properties
seemed so accidental. Trees, for example, have a great variety of
sizes, shapes, leaves, barks, and the like. But whatever its size, shape,
pattern of leaf, or quality of bark, a tree is nevertheless a tree.
The essence of a tree resides in the idea of a tree and not in any
purely accidental qualities of size or shape, leaf or bark. Now ideas not
only do not suffer from the variability of things but, when verbalized
or reduced to verbal symbols, seem to add an economy and comprehensiveness to the reach of learning far beyond what a concern with
individual things can do. Or, as St. Thomas Aquinas (1225–1274)
intimated, knowledge is more likely to result from a curriculum of
words than of things "inasmuch as words are symbols of intelligible
content."[25]

The linguistic curriculum received additional strong reinforcement
in the Middle Ages and again at the time of the Protestant Reformation. In both these periods the materials of study were drawn from
an authoritative body of truths recorded in literary documents rather
than from a contemporary firsthand study of nature or society.
Further, the deductive part of Aristotle's logic was taken and adapted
to transmitting the ready-made materials of both the early church
fathers and the Christian Bible. Hence, the method of defining, classifying, and elucidating an accepted literary tradition gained a centuries,
head start over Aristotle's neglected logic of induction and the later
naturalistic methods of inquiry, discovery, and invention. Consequently,
an early drawback to the inclusion of the new sciences in conventional
curricula was the absence of a well-tried method for teaching things
rather than ideas.

In addition to positive arguments for Humanism there were negative
ones against sense realism and naturalism. Militating against science
and against including concrete objects in the curriculum during the
seventeenth and eighteenth centuries was the fact that these innovations principally satisfied the needs of skilled artisans, merchants,
and military technicians. Consequently, the age-old stigma that had
attached to the working classes came to be transferred to the scientific

[25] M. H. Mayer, *The Philosophy of Teaching of St. Thomas Aquinas* (The
Bruce Publishing Company, Milwaukee, 1929), p. 58.

curricula that served their interests. Equally unfortunate for the position of science in the curriculum was the fact that, as science was instrumental in shifting power from the landed aristocracy to the new captains of industry, it became the handmaiden of capitalism. As such the new science seemed to have only technical lessons to teach the leaders of the Industrial Revolution and no moral ones. This merely confirmed the Humanists in their claim that science was materialistic and devoid of regard for moral values, to which the literary curriculum was so sensitive.

Yet not everyone took an intensely partisan either-or position in the controversy between Humanism and naturalism. Fortunately, there were a few who took a more moderate both-and point of view. Some neohumanists, for instance, tried to come to terms with the romantic naturalism of Rousseau by contending that his ideal of education, the natural man,[26] could be found best in a study of Greek culture, for this was the finest example of nature at its best. In the first half of the nineteenth century the German Herbart, whose educational views were later to have such influence in the United States, lent his weight to this view. Expanding this view further, he laid it down that the curriculum should be composed of two main elements, a knowledge of men and a knowledge of things.[27] And the Englishman Matthew Arnold (1822–1888), whose writings were also read in this country, later corroborated Herbart when he stated that different men have different talents. "This one's special aptitudes are for knowing men—the study of the humanities; that one's special aptitudes are for knowing the world—the study of nature. The circle of knowledge comprehends both, and we should all have some notion, at any rate, of the whole circle of knowledge."[28]

Herbart's dictum came to be prevailing opinion in the curricula of the twentieth century. Not only did the twentieth century show progress by including both Humanistic and scientific studies in the curriculum, but it also took steps toward breaking down or bridging the dualism between the two. Thus, the introduction into the curriculum of such social sciences as anthropology, economics, and sociology created a body of materials which, because they connect man's life with natural conditions, could not be neatly subsumed under the heading either of Humanism or of science.

---

[26] For a further account of this ideal, see *supra*, p. 14.

[27] For an interesting American elaboration of this view, see W. T. Harris, *op. cit.*, p. 340.

[28] M. Arnold, *Higher Schools and Universities in Germany* (Macmillan & Co., Ltd., London, 1874), pp. 175–176. Note also that the Jesuits in the 1832 revision of their famous Humanistic curriculum added a considerable amount of science. R. Schwickerath, *Jesuit Education* (B. Herder Book Co., St. Louis, 1903), pp. 194–198.

INTRODUCTION OF THE MODERN HUMANITIES

The forces of nationalism and democracy, which had had the negative effect of undermining the monopoly of the humanities, or classics, in the curriculum, also had positive influence in introducing new subjects, which some have called the "modern humanities." In addition to such studies of man as those already mentioned—anthropology, economics, and sociology—these newer humanities included two subjects that especially deserve consideration here, modern languages and history.

The rise of modern, or vernacular, languages in the curriculum was in part a by-product of the rise of sense realism and naturalism. Just as the sense realists thought that learning could be made more accurate and interesting by introducing concrete objects into the curriculum, so too they thought that it could be made more clear and vivid by using the native vernacular as the vehicle of instruction. To them a true understanding of the world was oblique and difficult enough without conducting instruction, as was the custom, in a second and less familiar tongue like Latin. Again, since the truths of science had difficulty in establishing themselves against the misconceptions of the world perpetuated in classical literatures, the supporters of science began to show hostility not only to the misconceptions but to the Greek and Latin languages whose great prestige seemed to protect and entrench them. To promote the claims of modern as against ancient science, it seemed necessary to form an alliance with modern vernacular languages against the ancient classical ones.

Not a few radicals went so far as to claim that, even as models of the art of writing, of eloquence, or of poetry, classical authors no longer enjoyed their former superiority over modern ones of the eighteenth century. To the pleas that a dead language should be included in the curriculum because it is more difficult and will presumably, therefore, give greater mental discipline, the Frenchman Jean d'Alembert replied, "It is more difficult to write and speak one's own language well than to speak and write well in a dead language."[29]

At first the modern, or vernacular, tongues made more rapid progress in being accepted as the language of instruction than as subjects in the curriculum. That is, the vernacular became the vehicle of exposition in the classroom some time before its literature became an object of instruction. This second step, the incorporation of modern foreign languages into the curriculum, did not occur until the nineteenth century, when they were carried in on the rising tide of nationalism.[30]

[29] Quoted in I. L. Kandel, *History of Secondary Education* (Houghton Mifflin Company, Boston, 1930), p. 183.

[30] For a more complete account of nationalism and education, see *supra,* chap. 3.

Until then, Latin had been able to maintain itself in the curriculum partly because Europe had kept alive the idea of a social order in which all men might hope to have political as well as religious unity. In the Catholic Church and in the Holy Roman Empire Latin achieved something of the status of a universal language. At the opening of the nineteenth century, however, it soon became evident that only a fraction of society, the nation, was to become the center of social cohesion. Once the trend of events set in this direction, each nation found it advantageous to promote its own local vernacular in order to enjoy the strength that arose from communication and mutual understanding among its people.

In large part the upsurge of modern vernaculars in the curriculum was romantic as well as nationalistic. If rationalism had been characteristic of the period leading up to the American and French Revolutions, it was the feelings of romanticism that characterized the post-revolutionary period of the early nineteenth century. To catch the distinctive spirit or feeling of any country's nationalism, the child was sent through the curriculum to the folkways, the folk literature, and the folk songs of that country. Backed by the powerful motive of patriotism, he was soon using the classics of his mother tongue as the measure of humanity. At least, in being humanized by his education, the student now had a choice of proceeding to his goal through the classic or vernacular languages, the ancient or modern humanities.

It also needs pointing out that the late-eighteenth- and early-nineteenth-century interest in the common man was democratic as well as nationalistic and romantic. With political power gravitating into his hands, it was only natural that the principal language of the schools should become the language of the common man. The American patriot Benjamin Rush (1745–1813), for instance, decried Latin and Greek because for a democracy their study was confined to too few people. A republican form of government, he intimated, could be preserved only where knowledge was universally available in the common mother tongue.

Just as romantic nationalism took much of its color from the long-standing folk literature of the people, so too it was not long in employing history for the same end. Prior to the nineteenth century, history had practically no independent status in the curriculum. In the preceding few centuries the only history that was regarded as worth knowing was that of the Greeks and Romans, and that was picked up incidentally through a reading of Greek and Latin literature.[31] Even after the vernacular had crowded the classics to a less

[31] In the Jesuit method of instruction through the prelection, historical materials were often introduced in the step of *eruditio*. See *supra*, p. 188.

conspicuous place in the curriculum, history still remained a phase of the vernacular literature. Thus, the American lexicographer Noah Webster (1758–1843) in the complete title of one of his school readers described it as "calculated to improve the minds and refine the taste of youth, and also to instruct them in the geography, history, and politics of the United States."[32]

Under the driving requirements of nationalism and democracy, however, history finally split off from literature and achieved independent status in the curriculum of the latter nineteenth century. Benjamin Rush, to cite him again, thought that above everything else the future guardians of American institutions should be instructed in history, especially that of "ancient republics, and the progress of liberty and tyranny in the different states of Europe."[33] To political reasons for establishing history in the curriculum Herbart added a moral one. For Herbart the chief end of education was moral, and literature and history were the two chief sources of a knowledge of man, which, together with a knowledge of things, composed his curriculum.

The further endeavor to make citizenship a part of the curriculum dates from earliest times. The Roman boy, for example, was expected to memorize the basic law of his people, the Twelve Tables. In colonial times the famous Massachusetts law of 1642 enjoined selectmen to be sure that children were well read in the capital laws of the colony.[34] At the time of the French Revolution, French youth were required to be instructed in "republican ethics and morals." In nineteenth and early twentieth centuries American courses in civics achieved considerable popularity but seldom went beyond an analysis of the structure of government. It was not till after the first World War that the average curriculum concerned itself with the vital problems of citizenship.

But the curriculum no sooner came to grips with such vital problems than it found itself in the area of delicate controversial issues. Controversial issues, of course, there had been since time immemorial, but they did not pose a special problem till the era of the public school sponsored by the emergent nationalism and democracy of the nineteenth century.[35] Thereafter the maintenance of unified support was constantly jeopardized by any attention the curriculum chanced

---

[32] *An American Selection of Lessons in Reading,* etc. (Thomas & Andrews, Boston, 1793), part III.

[33] Quoted in A. O. Hansen, *Liberalism and American Education in the Eighteenth Century* (The Macmillan Company, New York, 1926), p. 56.

[34] For twentieth-century legislative prescriptions of the curriculum, see J. K. Flanders, *Legislative Control of the Elementary School Curriculum* (Bureau of Publications, Teachers College, Columbia University, New York, 1925).

[35] For a longer account of the growth of public schools, see *infra,* chap. 17.

to pay to controversial issues. The policy followed by the United States in the nineteenth century deliberately excluded from the public school curricula such controversial topics as religion and slavery. Later, in the early decades of the twentieth century, the same policy kept out divisive questions of politics and economics, but the latter clamored so persistently for admission to the curriculum that after the First World War they were given a trial. Their retention there became more and more assured as the American people came increasingly to realize that their national and political stability depended on rearing children in an educational atmosphere of free discussion.

Perhaps a final word is in place here about geography. Ever since the great voyages of discovery there had been a demand that the up-to-date curriculum include geography. In its early form, however, geography was little more than a discipline in locating places and defining boundaries. All this was much improved when in the nineteenth century geography felt the touch of nationalism and industrialization. It then became a study of human geography, of man's relation to his physical environment. In this more humanized form geography came to take its place in the curriculum as one of the respected modern humanities.

THE EXPANSION OF PHYSICAL EDUCATION

Another subject in the curriculum to which nationalism and democracy gave great impetus was physical education. To see how this came about, it will be necessary to appreciate the new interest in physical development that Rousseau aroused. His romantic and naturalistic interest in childhood led him to recommend great freedom for the child to romp, jump, and climb to his heart's content. To facilitate freedom of movement Rousseau advocated simple, loose clothing for the child, quite an innovation in a day when it was customary to dress children like little adults.[36] The end product of this release of energies was to be a sturdy and robust body inured alike to extremes of heat and cold. The idea of hardening the body Rousseau no doubt borrowed from John Locke and *Some Thoughts concerning Education*. Locke's recipe for achieving a sound mind in a sound body—*mens sana in corpore sano*—called for accustoming them both to difficult tasks.

---

[36] In Rousseau's day mothers still wrapped babies in swaddling clothes to straighten limbs that they did not realize nature would straighten anyway. The new confidence in nature, however, led Immanuel Kant to remark, "It is very remarkable that children are taught how to walk just as though man would never have learned it without being taught." E. F. Buchner, *The Educational Theory of Immanuel Kant* (J. B. Lippincott Company, Philadelphia, 1904), p. 143.

Rousseau's ideas on physical education received their first trial in Basedow's Philanthropinum at Dessau. Though the Philanthropinum failed, it had imitators and it was at one of these in Schnepfenthal that the new naturalistic emphasis on physical education had a growing success. There a young German by the name of Johann Christoph Friedrich Guts Muths (1759–1839) introduced a system of exercises that he and later generations came to call "gymnastics." Guts Muths's contribution lay in his implementing with apparatus the running, jumping, and climbing that Basedow had carried over from Rousseau. Thus, to provide opportunity for climbing he introduced ropes, ladders, and masts. It is to be set down to his credit that he sought to establish a relation between the theory and practice of gymnastics and the theory of physiology and medicine. But gymnastics was not the whole of his curriculum in physical education; manual training, gardening, field excursions, and games were also part of his program.

If Guts Muths was the grandfather of German gymnastics, Friedrich Ludwig Jahn (1778–1852) was its father. Yet while the former tried to conform his gymnastics to nature, as disclosed in physiology and anatomy, Jahn also tried to harness gymnastics to the cause of patriotism. Suffering from the humilitating Prussian defeat at the Battle of Jena, Jahn longed for the day when the Napoleonic yoke would be thrown off.[37] His own plan for that day was to build a generation of vigorous, physically fit men who would be able, when the tocsin sounded, to wrest Prussia's freedom back from her oppressor. The first step he took in this direction was to gather the boys in his charge after school hours and lead them in outdoor gymnastics, athletics, and "hikes," much as did Guts Muths. When the weather turned inclement, he continued this extracurricular program of gymnastics indoors.

Physical fitness and national fitness were closely identified in Jahn's mind. But so too were fitness and a freedom-loving spirit. There was no set program in his *Turnplatz* or his *Turnhalle*.[38] Freedom of action and individual initiative were the order of the day. Boys improvised feats and then challenged their friends to duplicate them. Moreover, they chose their own games. Jahn did not aim at hardening the body, as did Locke, but rather regarded physical exercise as an opportunity for the growth and development of one's natural powers. The freedom sought by Jahn through physical education he wished everyone to enjoy. Hitherto the physical exercises, which had been revived at the time of the Renaissance, had been part of the

---

[37] To relate the nationalistic phase of physical education to the broader problem of nationalism and education, see *supra*, chap. 3.

[38] German for "gymnasium." The German word *Gymnasium* means a "classical secondary school."

curriculum of the courtier or the gentleman only. The democratic political implications of gymnastics for all, therefore, startled not a few of the conservative ruling classes and ultimately led to the temporary discontinuance of this part of the school program.

As already seen, Jahn's program of physical education was more or less extracurricular. The man who succeeded in getting physical education accepted as a regular part of the school curriculum was Adolf Spiess (1810–1858). One thing had to be done to accomplish this end, and Spiess did it. This was to grade exercises for different abilities, not only of age but of sex. To enable such a program to be carried out at all times, Spiess further recommended that a *Turnplatz* and a *Turnhalle* be connected with every school. It is also to him that physical training owes marching exercises and executing gymnastics in class formation, elements that in the end lent themselves to military discipline.

It was in Sweden rather than in Germany that the more precise lessons of anatomy and physiology for physical education were spelled out. There Per Henrik Ling (1776–1839) founded a system of gymnastics based directly on his study of these two sciences of the human body. The unique feature of his Swedish gymnastics lay in that his system was designed for the weak as well as for the strong. Similarly important, therefore, was his insistence that exercise should be prescribed for the individual rather than for the group. Much as Ling was interested in the therapeutic value of physical training, he was also inspired, it should not be overlooked, by the same sort of patriotic motives as was Jahn.

Both German and Swedish gymnastics crossed the Atlantic and had their heyday in nineteenth-century American curricula. More popular here after the Civil War, however, was a system of calisthenics introduced by Diocletian Lewis (1823–1886). In his calisthenics Lewis dispensed with nearly all the heavy apparatus ordinarily associated with gymnastics and gymnasiums. In fact, one of his main objectives was to disabuse the American mind of the idea that the physical strength promoted by drill on such apparatus was a mark of physical well-being. Instead, Lewis tried to develop organic vigor and graceful posture by calisthenics, that is, free movements of the arms, legs, and trunk. Limiting himself to such light equipment as Indian clubs and dumbbells, he popularized the notion that a curriculum of physical training could be carried out in quarters much less pretentious than formal gymnasiums. Neither athletic sports nor military training could take the place of calisthenics in Lewis's mind, for neither one could be counted on to give systematic and balanced exercise to every part of the body.

Whether or not Lewis was right in his opinion of sports, the fact remains that the American temperament was much better suited to sports than it was to either gymnastics or calisthenics. Gaining momentum in the latter half of the nineteenth century, American sports in the twentieth century became so immensely popular as almost to sweep formal physical exercises aside. In assigning to sports or athletics the most important part of the curriculum of physical education in this country, America clearly showed its English ancestry. Formal gymnastics had been introduced in England, too, but they never managed to get the upper hand over the long tradition of school games. In both countries it seemed that the qualities of initiative, resourcefulness, teamwork, and fair play that games induced were peculiarly congenial to their democratic political institutions.

Coincident with the spectacular expansion of sports in the American curriculum and extracurriculum was the development of a program of health education. Physiology made its entrance into the curriculum after the Civil War and was followed later by hygiene. But both subjects remained rather arid since they never seemed to get beyond an anatomical naming and locating of bones, muscles, and organs. As a result of the campaigning of the Woman's Christian Temperance Union, nearly every state in the American Union enacted statutes requiring schools to include information in their curricula on the harmful effects of habit-forming drugs and alcoholic beverages.

In the twentieth century, with new data from dietetics, dentistry, mental hygiene, and the like, a much more functional curriculum in health education came to supplant the old courses in physiology and hygiene. Medical and dental inspection came to be a regular part of school programs. Yet, in spite of such advances, the draft statistics of the First World War revealed an appalling amount of physical disability in the generation of military age. In 1929 President Herbert Hoover called a White House conference on child health and welfare, which produced a "children's charter" defining what a democracy thought its obligations were to the health of its children. The draft statistics for the Second World War showed some improvement but still much room for further advancement in health curricula.

THE ROLE OF WORK IN THE CURRICULUM

Of the great social forces—nationalism, democracy, and the Industrial Revolution—that transformed the traditional Humanistic curriculum of the Renaissance into the more modern one of the nineteenth and twentieth centuries, the Industrial Revolution so far has received relatively little attention. It has been seen, to be sure, how the rise of science stimulated the Industrial Revolution and how that revolution in turn promoted science to front-rank importance in the curriculum

But it yet remains to be seen how the revolution of power-driven industry combined with naturalistic democratic forces to alter the whole face of work in the curriculum.

To understand how this transformation came about, it is necessary first to recollect the status of vocational education prior to the Industrial Revolution. Owing to slavery and serfdom in the long centuries preceding this social upheaval, vocational education rarely if ever occupied a place in the traditionally respected curriculum of the schools. On the contrary, if given at all, training in commercial and industrial arts took place through apprenticeship outside the regular schools. This sort of training reached a particularly high level of development during the guild system of the late Middle Ages and the Renaissance. In England and later colonial America apprenticeship was the course of instruction not only for the various vocations but often for the various professions as well. Articles of apprenticeship generally obligated a master to teach his apprentice two things, the secrets, or "mysteries," of his trade and such items of general education as literacy and morality. As the apprentice usually became a member of his master's household, his deportment was also subject to his master's oversight.

The advent of the Industrial Revolution shifted production from the home to the factory, from handicraft to power-driven machinery. Such a radical shift in methods of production demanded radical readjustments in trade or vocational education. The hand worker used to become acquainted with the entire course of manufacture, from the procurement of raw material to the distribution of the finished product. The machine worker, on the other hand, seldom became acquainted with more than a fraction of the total process of machinofacture. Moreover, in place of a master pledged to oversee his general and moral education, he had for an employer an industrial capitalist who felt no particular obligation to look out for the personal education of his employee.

The exact form of readjustment in vocational education to which the Industrial Revolution pointed did not become evident at once. Slowly, however, two trends began to appear. In the first place, as vocational education ceased to be an incident of production and therefore a responsibility of the producer, it became necessary for the first time to look to the school to take this orphan into its curriculum. In the second place, since the machines of industry operated on complicated scientific principles and since the economics and politics of industrial capitalism became correspondingly intricate, it became necessary to elevate vocational training to the dignity of a formal school subject.

While these trends were making themselves manifest, the forces of sense realism and naturalism were also instigating a new role for work in the curriculum. The sense realists, it will be remembered, tried to revitalize the highly verbal Humanistic curriculum of the seventeenth century by putting greater emphasis on a study of concrete objects or things. What was more natural than to include among these things not only models of buildings, ships, chests, and the like but in addition the tools that skilled artisans used in making their artifacts? From thus making the curriculum more realistic it was only a short step to making it more vocational as well. Indeed, Hecker, who was responsible for putting realism into the German *Realschule,* stated it as the aim of this school "to develop the tendencies of such young people as are not destined for studious pursuits but whose talents would fit them for business, for agriculture, for the industrial and fine arts, etc., and to afford them an introductory training for these pursuits."[39] Something of the same spirit seems to have animated the American academy, which took its rise about the time when Hecker was introducing the *Realschule.* Not only did the academy offer such practical subjects as navigation, surveying, and bookkeeping, but one of its principal aims was to prepare boys for life rather than for college.[40]

The initial effect of Rousseau's naturalism was to reinforce the vocational tendencies of the realistic curriculum. His naturalistic attitude toward work he revealed in his assertion that "of all pursuits by which a man may earn a living, the nearest to a state of nature is manual labor."[41] And his realistic attitude toward manual education he disclosed in his claim that Émile "will learn more by one hour of manual labor, than he will retain from a whole day's verbal instructions."[42] Furthermore, said Rousseau, "If, instead of making a child stick to his books I employ him in a workshop, his hands work for the development of his mind. While he fancies himself a workman, he is becoming a philosopher."[43] But Rousseau had social as well as individual ends in view in making Émile's curriculum partly manual. "It is important to learn a trade," he added, "less for knowing the trade than for overcoming the prejudices which despise it."[44]

Again, as in the case of science and physical education and as

[39] Quoted in L. F. Anderson, *History of Manual and Industrial School Education* (D. Appleton-Century Company, Inc., New York, 1926), p. 43.
[40] For a further account of the academy, see *infra*, pp. 405–408.
[41] J. J. Rousseau, *Émile* (J. M. Dent & Sons, Ltd., Publishers, London, 1911), p. 158.
[42] J. J. Rousseau, *Emilius and Sophia* (Becket & Hondt, London, 1763), vol. 2, p. 64.
[43] J. J. Rousseau, *Émile* (J. M. Dent & Sons, Ltd., Publishers, London, 1911), p. 140.
[44] R. L. Archer, *Rousseau on Education* [Edward Arnold (Publishers) Ltd., London, 1912], p. 169.

a result of nationalistic impulses, Basedow's Philanthropinum was the first to offer trades in its curriculum. More successful, however, was Johann Heinrich Pestalozzi (1746–1827), the great Swiss educator. In his first gropings toward his later famous method of "object instruction,"[45] Pestalozzi went through an early period in which he thought a vocational course of instruction the best means of alleviating the condition of the poor, in whom he was greatly interested. Unfortunately, however, to simplify the learning of industrial occupations, he turned down the blind alley of analyzing their physical operations into such natural motions as striking, pushing, twisting, and swinging. A curriculum of such activities, Pestalozzi expected, would prepare for all possible crafts, even the most technical. Such a curriculum, obviously, was not many degrees away from one based on formal discipline.

Still more successful in harnessing the naturalistic impulses of the child to industrial occupations was Philipp Emanuel von Fellenberg (1771–1844), a Swiss nobleman and educator. On his estate he instituted a school where trades and agriculture were actually taught at first hand. He had the idea, following Pestalozzi, that object instruction nowhere so enlisted the native activities of the child as when objects were the tools and materials of the shop and the farm. Fellenberg's school was a great success, not only in the vocational curriculum it offered, but in its being economically self-sustaining. Later it bore further fruit in being the means of enriching the lives of children suffering from the defects of blindness and deafness and often of redeeming delinquents from a life of degradation.

Transplanted to the United States, Fellenberg's idea took root chiefly in the manual-labor college. The object of this college, however, was not so much to incorporate manual labor into the curriculum as to provide a means of self-support during a period of study devoted to the more conventional academic curriculum.[46] More important for the future history of vocational education in this country were the mechanics' institutes that came forward to meet the breakdown of the apprenticeship system. These institutes generally housed libraries on vocational topics and cabinets of models and minerals. Not infrequently they were the scene of lectures for the advancement of ambitious young mechanics. In the last half of the nineteenth century these institutions made way for the much superior technical institute, of which Cooper Union, Pratt, and Drexel were excellent examples. The technical institute not only helped to solve the knotty problems created

---

[45] For a fuller account of object instruction, see *supra*, pp. 207–211.

[46] The manual-labor idea seems also to have been part of the contemporary interest in physical education through gymnastics. See E. W. Knight, "Manual Labor Schools in the South," *South Atlantic Quarterly,* 16:209–222, July, 1917.

by the Industrial Revolution but also aided in racial adjustment in this country. Hampton and Tuskegee for Negroes and Haskell for Indians were outstanding institutes in this regard.

The inspiration of Rousseau's naturalistic reason for including work in the curriculum did not entirely spend itself in promoting preparation for earning a living. There were some who saw manual training as of educational value quite apart from economic sustenance. Before Rousseau's time Locke had recommended that even the sons of gentlemen should learn a trade, for, in addition to its usefulness, it was good exercise and a pleasant diversion. But it was Friedrich Wilhelm August Froebel (1782–1852), the great exponent of the educational values of play, who received most of the credit for developing the purely educational value of work.

Froebel followed Rousseau in believing that it was the central nature of the child to be self-active. Furthermore, just as play was the natural form which a child's spontaneous activity took,[47] so too, at a more mature level, work was just as natural a form for this activity to take. In his *Education of Man* Froebel cried out, "The debasing illusion that man works, produces, creates only in order to preserve his body, in order to secure food, clothing, and shelter, may have to be endured, but should not be diffused and propagated. Primarily and in truth man works only that his spiritual, divine essence may assume outward form. . . . The young, growing human being should, therefore, be trained early for outer work, for creative and productive activity. . . . Lessons through and by work, through and from life, are by far the most impressive and intelligible."[48]

The chief application that Froebel gave to his theory of the educational significance of work was in his gifts and occupations,[49] particularly the garden to be cultivated in connection with every kindergarten. The play so stimulated, Froebel maintained, was the child's work. The Finn Uno Cygnaeus (1807–1881) thought that Froebel's practice was good as far as it went for young children but that a further extension of it was necessary for older ones. Hence he worked out the "sloyd"[50] system of manual arts to be part of the curriculum of this latter group. But he was emphatic in demanding that none of these arts be conducted as trades. The educational outcomes he rather sought were neatness and exactness of execution, training the eye for good form and shape, and training the hand to be the obedient servant of the brain. As in the case of Pestalozzi, given such an analysis the sloyd curriculum was constantly in danger

[47] For a fuller development of Froebel's theory, see *supra,* pp. 125–127.
[48] F. Froebel, *Education of Man* (Sidney Appleton, London, 1905), pp. 33–34.
[49] For a further development of this notion, see *supra,* p. 216.
[50] The word "sloyd" is related to the English "sleight" and means "adroitness."

of being overtaken and underwritten by a theory of formal discipline.

Work as a cultural rather than as a vocational aspect of the regular curriculum made its way to American shores in the last two decades of the nineteenth century. The Workingman's School of Felix Adler (1851–1933), later to become the Society for Ethical Culture, was one of the earliest American expositions of the idea. It remained for the educational philosopher John Dewey (1859–1952), however, to give this idea its twentieth-century form and content.

Dewey followed in the historical tradition of Rousseau and Froebel in believing that the primary root of educational activity lay in the child's instinctive propensities for action. Yet, unlike Froebel, he did not hold that the educational significance of work lay in man's creating in outward form his own inner divine essence. Instead of burdening the curriculum with merely formal occupations symbolic of inner spiritual stirrings, Dewey invigorated it with the very realistic occupations of home and industry—cooking, sewing, weaving, carpentry, and the like. Moreover, for the first time he gave them a central position in the curriculum. A people's culture, he believed, takes much of its coloration from the manner in which it makes a living. Therefore, work should be one of the main axes of the curriculum. But work should enjoy this prominence as a liberal rather than as a purely vocational study. The erstwhile academic studies should be integrated with it.[51] Studies like history, geography, and mathematics should enlarge the understanding of work, which in turn should give concrete application to the significance of these studies.

In spite of the advances made by incorporating industrial arts into the curriculum through the technical institute and by giving them liberal status, there was still a shocking lack of trained workers in this country. A Federal commission investigating the situation just before the entry of the United States into the First World War revealed that less than 1 per cent of the country's workers had had technical training for their occupations. This situation obtained in spite of the product of the technical institutes, the agricultural colleges inaugurated by the Morrill Act,[52] the private business colleges that commenced offering commercial subjects toward the end of the nineteenth century, and the specialized high schools of trade and commerce that were just beginning to make an appearance. The result was the enactment of the Smith-Hughes Act of 1917, which extended a Federal subsidy to vocational education. Yet it is still interesting to note that the American Federation of Labor was anxious that this important step

[51] For concrete proposals to center the elementary school curriculum in the industrial arts, see F. G. Bonser, *The Elementary School Curriculum* (The Macmillan Company, New York, 1921).

[52] For a fuller account of this act, see *infra*, p. 442.

should not result in a narrow form of vocational education that would mark their children with a class stigma.

PLACE OF THE FINE ARTS

It would be a mistake to give an account of the entry of industrial arts into the regular school curriculum without some mention of how the fine arts also were included. As already seen, the fine arts through music had a very early foothold in the ancient curriculum of the seven liberal arts. If drawing was not included, it was not because Aristotle had not recommended it, for he thought it valuable in making people judges of beauty in the human form. Unfortunately, however, the Greek interest in the fine arts did not long survive in the curricula of subsequent ages. Perhaps this was due in part to the fact that the Greeks drew a distinction between the liberal and the industrial arts according to the social-economic class that practiced them. The fine arts, being liberal and therefore the occupation of freemen as contrasted with slaves, who practiced the industrial arts, tended to become the luxury of the upper classes. It was then but a short step to regarding them as a relatively superfluous part of the curriculum.

Hence from Greek times to the nineteenth century the fine arts almost disappeared from the regular school curriculum. Instruction in the fine arts did not cease during this period but did practically cease to be a function of the formal schools. What music continued to be taught during the Middle Ages, for instance, was to be found in special song schools established by the church to recruit its choirs. And what was taught of design was usually derived from apprenticeship to master craftsmen or artists of the time.

By the nineteenth century, however, forces were afoot that seemed to require the curriculum of the schools to take notice of the fine arts again. The nascent nationalism of this century, it has already been mentioned, thrived in part on the romantic interest in folk songs. Singing these songs in the schools soon became one of the chief ways in which national states forged the bonds of patriotism. And in the field of design the Industrial Revolution not only radically changed methods of production but also radically altered the source of their designs. Prior to the Industrial Revolution design was something that an apprentice learned as part of his over-all understanding of his trade. In the change to power-driven machinery this over-all training gave way to subdivision of the whole job and the specialized training of men for each part. But since industrial capitalists at first found no way in their factories to train their employees, as masters had trained apprentices in their households, there soon arose an urgent cry for schools whose curricula would provide some training in design. While nationalism and industrialism were promoting the restoration of the fine arts to the curriculum of the schools, romanticism was making an independent contribution of its own. The romantic interest of Rousseau in the spontaneous impulses of the child ultimately found one of its major outlets in the fine arts. On this point Comenius had already preceded him in the previous century by advocating painting as one means of developing a child's "internal senses." But it remained for Rousseau's followers, particularly Pestalozzi and Froebel, to win extensive practical support for a curriculum of fine arts predicated on the theory of their appropriateness for developing the child's native powers.

At first, drawing seems to have ridden into the curriculum on the tails of another pupil activity, writing. The two activities not only both involved the hand but often had the same end, for, as John Locke pointed out earlier and Horace Mann repeated later, a person may by drawing a few well-chosen lines convey what a whole page of prose might fail to tell. Modeling, too, seems to have entered the curriculum in association with geography. Thus, Pestalozzi used it as part of object instruction, in forming clay to represent the earth's contours. Froebel tried for greater spontaneity, as witness his remark that "at the present time art *alone* can truly be called free activity, but every human work corresponds more or less with creative activity, and this is necessary in order to make man the image of his Divine Creator—a creator on his own part in miniature."[53] Yet, in spite of this declaration, the drawing that Froebel prescribed was very formal, consisting largely of geometric lines and figures. Of course, on Froebel's behalf it must be said that it was these very mathematical or geometrical forms that to him symbolized the free divine essence.

Toward the end of the nineteenth century there was a gradual emancipation of art education from symbolism and formalism. The arts-and-crafts movement, which built upon Cygnaeus, who was indebted to Froebel, was one escape to greater initiative and individuality. Then, too, after the Columbian Exposition color received greater attention, and art for art's sake definitely supplanted the commercial motivation. In the twentieth century, progressive education pushed further with creative art, and art appreciation as well as art production became an important phase of the curriculum.

Singing, which was the chief form of music in the curricula of the nineteenth century, was joined in the twentieth by the dance and by instrumental music as well. School bands and orchestras be-

[53] Quoted in J. L. Hughes, *Froebel's Educational Laws for All Teachers* (D. Appleton & Company, Inc., New York, 1897), p. 259.

came regular features of many school curricula. Furthermore, the inventions of the phonograph and the radio brought within reach of school curricula unparalleled opportunities for teaching music appreciation. Art for art's sake came to be the ruling spirit in the rhythmic as well as the visual arts.

In fact, in the twentieth century it seemed that not only had there been a recovery of the ground lost since the Greeks but that modern curricula had gone beyond them. Perhaps no one had better stated the position of art in the modern curriculum than John Dewey. "There has been great loss," he wrote, "in relegating the arts to the relatively trivial role which they finally assumed in schooling, and there is corresponding promise of gain in the efforts making in the last generation to restore these to a more important position. Viewed both psychologically and socially, the arts represent not luxuries and superfluities, but fundamental forces of development.[54] . . . Art—in the aesthetic as distinct from the technical and industrial sense—is to be regarded as a perfected expression of any crude or primitive mode of activity which has gained a recognized social value. It is essentially a *consummation,* a refinement and idealization of what is originally done and acquired from more direct practical motives. It represents the end to which all other educational achievements should tend—its perfected goal."[55]

EVOLUTION OF THE EXTRACURRICULUM

In the nineteenth and particularly in the twentieth century American education witnessed a great development of a curriculum of informal student activities outside and parallel to the curriculum of more formal studies. Thus, while during school hours students were poring over their mathematics, languages, history, and science under the eye of the teacher, after school hours they found relief from their academic labors by voluntarily organizing, in addition to gymnastics and athletics, such extracurricular activities as debating, drama, school journalism, photography, and radio.

Extracurricular activities such as these, it should be said in all fairness, while they had their spectacular growth in the two centuries just mentioned, put forth their first roots much earlier. Some of them, athletics and debating, for instance, date from Greco-Roman times. In fact, in those ancient times both these activities, far from being the informal pursuits of boys in their out-of-school hours, were parts of the regular curriculum. The Greek boy paid just as regular and

[54] J. Dewey, in P. Monroe (ed.), *Cyclopedia of Education* (The Macmillan Company, New York, 1912), vol. 1, p. 224.
[55] *Ibid.,* vol. 2, p. 22.

conscientious attention to physical culture as he did to mental culture. And the Roman youth, because his educational ideal was that of the orator,[56] had declamation as the very core of his curriculum. In medieval times the disputation[57] was as central in the curriculum of the monk as physical exercises were in the chivalric training of the knight. Again, the curriculum of the courtier during the Renaissance gave prominence to both eloquence of speech and litheness of body.

In the American soil, to which these roots of European culture were transplanted in the post-Renaissance and Reformation periods, some plantings atrophied and some bore a new species of fruit. Physical culture, for example, failed to take root in the early American curriculum. The conditions of a frontier society required so much hard physical labor that there was no want of opportunity for physical development. Exercise directed to purely educational ends and disregarding practical ones would have seemed ridiculous and wasteful, if not positively immoral. Physical exercise carried on for its own end would have been sport, and sport did not suit the Puritan mind. For long, therefore, athletics not only were excluded from the curriculum but were frowned on outside the curriculum as well. Nevertheless, in spite of official frowns, boys continued to play their games. By the nineteenth century, economic conditions had been so greatly improved and religious orthodoxy so greatly relaxed that student athletics, though not readmitted to formal standing in the regular academic curriculum, were widely tolerated as a so-called "extracurricular" activity.

Debating had a somewhat different evolution. The medieval disputation with its syllogistic handling of religious theses readily found acceptance in the American college curriculum. This is not at all surprising since one of the chief purposes of that curriculum was to train clergymen. In the eighteenth century, as America turned its zeal from religious to political controversy, the place of the syllogistic disputation in the curriculum came to be taken by the forensic oration. But, by the nineteenth century, faculties were having difficulty in keeping life in even this part of the curriculum. The reason for this was that the contemporary growth of debating clubs outside the curriculum diverted interest from the formally recognized forensic oration. Faculties, notoriously slow to read the signs of the times and probably a little jealous of formal curriculum interest, permitted the forensic oration to die out but did nothing to replace it with debating and thus draw on the reservoir of interest located in spontaneous extracurricular activities.

[56] For a fuller account of this ideal, see *supra,* p. 5.
[57] For a fuller account of the disputation, see *supra,* pp. 189–190.

Space forbids a sketch of each of the many extracurricular activities that gained recognition during the nineteenth and twentieth centuries. In general, however, it may be said that the extracurriculum grew up in protest against the inadequacy of the regular, narrowly prescribed curriculum. Thus, athletics and debating, whatever their ancient standing, in the nineteenth century represented the answer to a demand by students for a type of training they were not getting in the regular curriculum. A similar story could be told of music. Originally one of the seven liberal arts, music found its way back into the liberal arts college through such extracurricular forms as glee clubs, mandolin clubs, and later bands and orchestras. Again, journalism and dramatics appeared in response to a protest against a too narrowly conceived Humanistic, or classical, curriculum and a demand for an outlet for students' own creative activities.

Even fraternities and sororities grew up originally as a response to real student needs. The communal character of the colonial college, it will be remembered, resulted in a close supervision that more or less confined students to the bounds of the college.[58] As a result, students came to satisfy their instincts for greater social activity by intensive cultivation of their own number. To this end, they formed secret Greek-letter societies. It was often in the program of these societies, too, that outlet was found for student literary and musical tastes that found no satisfaction in the regular curriculum. First of this sort of society or fraternity was Phi Beta Kappa, founded in 1776. A general suspicion of secret societies as a threat to democracy forced Phi Beta Kappa in the nineteenth century to give up its secrets.[59] Although it thereafter became an honorary scholastic society, many other social fraternities took its place as soon as the public sentiment against them had subsided. In addition to their bond of fellowship these fraternities through their houses did much to meet another urgent need, the need of the colleges for dormitories.

Often, at their inception, extracurricular activities had no more formal connection with the regular program than that the participants or a majority of them were members of the same college or school. In the long run this lack of connection between the curriculum and the extracurriculum led to grave difficulties. Not only did the extracurriculum compete with the curriculum for the major share of the students' time and interest, but not infrequently extracurricular activi-

---

[58] For the early history of the college, see *infra*, pp. 435–437.

[59] The three Greek letters ΦΒΚ, standing for the Greek words Φιλοσοφία Βίου Κυβερνήτης, mean "Philosophy, the guide of life." Making philosophy rather than religion the guide of life may have reflected the rationalistic deism of the time. See O. M. Voorhees, *The History of Phi Beta Kappa* (Crown Publishers, Inc., New York, 1946).

ties directly or indirectly involved the name of the school or college without the latter's having any real control. After some rivalry and strife at these points, college and school authorities managed to gain the upper hand in the situation. The spirit of rivalry remained, however, till authorities came to take a more constructive view of the entire curriculum problem. But there were great advances in the theoretical understanding of the curriculum in the twentieth century, and most educational authorities finally realized that the extracurriculum should be viewed not as the competitor of the regular curriculum but as its growing edge. Offshoots from the regular curriculum were to be expected. All that was needed was to see to it that the fruit of these offshoots be brought back into the regular curriculum to enrich it.

10 Curriculum— Continued

By the second half of the nineteenth century, as can be seen from the previous chapter, a wide and varied array of subject matters was receiving greater or less attention at the different levels of the educational ladder. In fact, there was hardly a phase of the social heritage from which a selection of materials had not been made and formulated into a subject matter for the schools. With the ever-accumulating capital of civilization outstripping the capacity of the curriculum to contain it all, the educational problem that lay ahead was to determine the most essential things with which to fill the limited years of a child's schooling. Intricately bound up with this problem were several others that greatly agitated the professional minds of the twentieth century—not only how the curriculum should be selected but how it should be organized. A solution to this problem had in turn to wait on the further problem of how the nature of the curriculum should be conceived.

"WHAT KNOWLEDGE IS MOST WORTH?"

In seeking historical answers to these questions it may be well to commence by disentangling and summarizing the theory of curriculum selection that had been implicit in the centuries preceding. For an almost indefinite period the chief criterion for judging studies had been Humanistic. The Humanistic criterion raised aloft the nature of man. Accordingly, the measure of the worth of studies derived from the hierarchy presumed to rule in man's nature. This hierarchy was ruled by a dualism wherein man's rational faculty was supposed to govern his animal appetites.[1] From this it seemed logical to conclude that the greater the rational content of studies, the more valuable they must be. Conversely, the more strongly studies appealed to feeling and sense, the less important they were. Furthermore, according to the mind-body dualism, sense suffered from being materialistic, while intellect benefited from being immaterial and spiritual.[2] Reinforcing the order of studies based on a hierarchy in man's nature was the hierarchy inherent in a society predicated on aristocracy. Intellectual studies and the upper classes, presumably, had a peculiar affinity for each other because both had a directive function to perform, the one over sense and the other over the lower classes, who were largely motivated by sense.[3]

No long-standing claim was made, it will be noted, that intellectual studies like the trivium of grammar, logic, and rhetoric were more useful than studies, like science and trade, that involved sense. The value of intellectual studies arose not from any use to which they might be put but rather from the relation they bore to the intrinsic nature of man. They were therefore valuable in and of themselves. Their value was inherent, self-contained. Useful studies were of a lower order because use would imply that a study was a means to an end, that its value was in part determined by the end which it subserved. Obviously, a study whose value was not self-contained could not rank so high as one whose value was self-contained. Furthermore, for a study to derive its value as a means implied that it was somewhat menial in nature. To be a means to some other end was too much like being a slave to a master. Therefore, as long as society formed an aristocracy, in which the merit of an upper class resided intrinsically—if accidentally—in its being well or nobly born, utility was necessarily an inferior measure of the worth of studies.

With the advent of modern science in the seventeenth century and particularly with the coming of the democratic revolutions toward the end of the eighteenth century, the criteria for the worth of studies began to undergo modification. The brilliant success which science experienced from relying on sensory verification was the first breach in the theory that intellectual studies were intrinsically superior to those which were sensory or sensory as well as intellectual. The whole theory collapsed when social revolution declared the intrinsic worth of not a few but *all* men. The most devastating weapon the revolu-

[1] For a fuller account of this view, see *supra,* pp. 105–106.
[2] For a fuller account of this view, see *supra,* pp. 103–104.
[3] For another account of this view, see *supra,* p. 83.

tionaries used against the citadels of privilege, whether of a privileged social class or of privileged subjects in the curriculum, was the test of reasonable utility.

Among the first to make a clear and considered statement of a utilitarian theory of the relative value of various subjects in the curriculum was the Englishman Herbert Spencer (1820–1903). A little after the middle of the nineteenth century Spencer published an essay, *What Knowledge Is Most Worth?* that was widely read not only in England but in the United States as well. Greatly influenced by English utilitarianism and perhaps by Darwinian evolution, Spencer arranged studies in the order of their use in aiding a society to survive. Thus, he arranged studies into "(1) those activities which directly minister to self-preservation; (2) those activities which, by securing the necessities of life, indirectly minister to self-preservation; (3) those activities which have for their end the rearing and discipline of offspring; (4) those activities which are involved in the maintenance of proper social and political relations; (5) those miscellaneous activities which fill up the leisure part of life, devoted to the gratification of the tastes and feelings."[4]

It goes without saying that this proposal was regarded at the time as very radical. Not only was a utilitarian criterion of value just the opposite of the traditional one, but the hierarchy of studies itself was turned upside down. Literary studies, which had long held first place under Humanism, were now at the bottom of the list. Anticipating this criticism, Spencer went on to add in his essay, "We yield to none in the value we attach to aesthetic culture and its pleasures . . . [but] . . . *as they occupy the leisure part of life, so should they occupy the leisure part of education.*"[5]

The seed from Spencer's thought did not bear fruit till the following century, and then it was a spore blown across the Atlantic that brought the best return. Before reaping that crop, however, it may be well to make a brief examination of the way in which the American educational soil was being prepared. In the last decade of the nineteenth century two famous committees of the National Education Association, the Committee of Ten and the Committee of Fifteen, made reports which recommended that steps be taken to shorten the period of elementary education. This recommendation grew in part out of increased demands for time by the secondary school and in part out of a mounting awareness on the part of educators that the curriculum had accumulated considerable deadwood that

[4] H. Spencer, *Education: Intellectual, Moral, and Physical* (J. M. Dent & Sons, Ltd., Publishers, London, n.d.), p. 7.

[5] *Ibid.*, pp. 30, 32.

needed to be chopped out.[6] For a long time new demands on the curriculum has been met by simply adding supplementary materials without subtracting anything to make room for them. It was high time now, thought these committees, that the excessive accumulation of materials be made to undergo a critical review.

In the first decade of the twentieth century a number of individual efforts were initiated to sift out the materials which no longer were important or relevant to the times in which children then lived. As the movement grew in public significance, the National Society for the Study of Education appointed a notable committee to report on economizing time through a determination of minimum essentials in the elementary school curriculum. This committee rendered three reports between 1915 and 1918.[7] In compiling its reports the committee made an inventory and tabular analysis of contemporary textbooks and courses of study. Its criterion for determining minimum essentials was frankly utilitarian. "Whatever is included must minister to the social needs common to ordinary American children," it said.[8] To ascertain these needs with some degree of objectivity the committee employed some new devices. For one thing it obtained a consensus of men in the field as to what were minimum essentials in some subjects. For another, as in vocabulary and spelling, it rested its minimum list of words on a count of the frequency of their occurrence in newspapers, magazines, and the like. On the whole, however, the final upshot of the work of this committee went little further than the elimination and rearrangement of old materials.

This, of course, was only a start in the direction of scientifically building the curriculum on the basis of the new measuring devices that were just beginning to gain professional acceptance at this time. As the devices improved and professional confidence in their efficacy increased, even bolder efforts at curriculum reconstruction were projected. "Pruning out the dead wood," vigorously declared the Department of Superintendence in a yearbook shortly after the First World War, "selecting minimum essentials from total possible content, adding supplementary material—tinkering with the curriculum—will

[6] For the effect of other economies of time recommended by these reports, see *infra,* pp. 379–380, 417–419.

[7] National Society for the Study of Education, *Minimum Essentials in Elementary Subjects,* Fourteenth Yearbook (The University of Chicago Press, Chicago, 1915), part I; *Second Report of the Committee on Minimal Essentials in Elementary School Subjects,* Sixteenth Yearbook (Public School Publishing Company, Bloomington, Ill., 1917), part I; *Third Report of the Committee on Economy of Time in Education,* Seventeenth Yearbook (Public School Publishing Company, Bloomington, Ill., 1918), part I.

[8] National Society for the Study of Education, Fourteenth Yearbook, *op. cit.* p. 15.

no longer answer the need. A complete revision is demanded by both educators and laymen."[9]

In starting the reconstruction of the curriculum from the ground up, it became of preeminent importance first to determine the aims of education. Here, too, the new measuring techniques were useful in making a sociological survey of the existing educational aims of contemporary society. Many were so enthusiastic over these scientific results that they were ready to allow science not only to state what *were* the aims of education but to dictate what they *should be* as well. Naturally, such a conclusion would have been nonprogressive and would have fastened the social *status quo* on both the aims and the curriculum of the schools. Educational philosophers were not slow to point out that while science could properly ascertain what educational aims were actually held, it was the province of educational philosophy to determine what aims should ideally control the selection of the curriculum.[10] The predominant educational philosophy of the day, to which reformers turned for their aims, was that of John Dewey (1859–1952). Consequently, curriculum reconstruction for the next two decades was profoundly influenced by his pragmatism, or instrumentalism.

In the lead among those who, starting with the aims of education, sought a complete rather than a patchwork revision of the curriculum was Franklin Bobbitt (1876–1952). From the outset, he was aware that fundamental thinking about the curriculum was confronted with "two antagonistic schools of educational thought. On the one hand are those who look primarily to the subjective results: the enriched mind, quickened appreciations, refined sensibilities, discipline, culture. . . . On the other hand there are those who hold that education is to look primarily and consciously to efficient practical action in a practical world."[11] For himself Bobbitt, following Dewey, chose the latter school of thought.

To arrive at sound educational objectives and thence at an effective curriculum Bobbitt proposed to make an "activity analysis" of the broad range of human experience into its major fields. After a wide examination of materials ranging from newspapers to the *Encyclopaedia Britannica* and from literature to science, he proposed ten major fields. In arriving at these ten he was apparently no little influenced by the *Seven Cardinal Principles of Secondary Education,*

[9] *Research in Constructing the Elementary School Curriculum,* Third Yearbook of the Department of Superintendence, National Education Association (Washington, D.C., 1925), p. 10.

[10] For a further discussion of the evolution of aims, see *supra,* p. 19.

[11] F. Bobbitt, *The Curriculum* (Houghton Mifflin Company, Boston, 1918), p. 3.

which preceded his own list by a half-dozen years; these principles in turn bore an obvious resemblance to Spencer's *What Knowledge Is Most Worth?*

Bobbitt[12] *(1924)*	Seven Cardinal Principles[13] *(1918)*	Spencer[14] *(1859)*
Language activities	Fundamental processes	Self-preservation
Health	Health	Procuring necessities of
Citizenship	Home membership	life
General social contacts	Vocation	Rearing children
Keeping mentally fit	Citizenship	Social and political re-
Leisure occupations	Leisure time	lations
Religious activities	Ethical relationships	Culture
Parental responsibili-		
ties		
Unspecialized practical		
activities		
Vocational activities		

Once these major objectives were established, the next step, as another pioneer in curriculum construction, Werrett W. Charters (1875–1956), so well pointed out, was to formulate principles stating how to get from aims to curriculum content. His own suggestion was to take one's major objectives or ideals and break them down into subgroups of minor objectives. By continuing to break objectives down into more and more minute parts one would come ultimately, as did Bobbitt, too, in the end, to specific immediate activities to be performed. These activities, then, were to be arranged in the order of their social usefulness, particularly in the order of their usefulness for children. Of course, there would not be time enough to give instruction in all these activities; therefore, a further selection of the more important ones had to be made in terms of the time available. These activities, finally, were to constitute the curriculum.

Activity analysis took a variety of later forms. In one direction it became "job analysis," the analysis of the activities in which one would have to perfect himself to prepare for a particular job or post. In another direction it took the form of an examination of pupil errors and difficulties in learning in order to make curriculum

[12] F. Bobbitt, *How to Make a Curriculum* (Houghton Mifflin Company, Boston, 1924), pp. 11–29.
[13] National Education Association, Commission on the Reorganization of Secondary Education, *The Cardinal Principles of Secondary Education*, U.S. Bureau of Education Bulletin 35, 1918.
[14] *Supra*, p. 281.

selections that would avoid or correct them. In some instances analyses were made of the social activities of a particular community or of a group in the community, such as the consumers.[15]

While men like Bobbitt and Charters were devoting their energies to the evolution of principles for the revision of the whole curriculum, others were engaged in more limited operations. Committees to review the curriculum from the perspective of particular subject-matter fields had been popular ever since the Committees of Ten and Fifteen. The results of most of the early committees, however, were composite committee judgments and affected selection principally in terms of the relative amount of time that should be spent on different subjects and what grade placement they should have. But the reports of later committees like *The Classical Investigation, The Modern Foreign Language Study,* and the *Report of the Commission on the Social Studies of the American Historical Association* went much further and employed experimental studies to authenticate their final conclusions.[16]

Although practically all curriculum reformers of the second quarter of the twentieth century were instrumentalists, or pragmatists, none was quite so radically instrumental in his approach to the curriculum as was Dewey himself. Unlike Bobbitt, Dewey did not think of educational aims as being drawn up in advance and independent of a problem demanding learning. To him lists of objectives, like those of educators from Spencer to Bobbitt, were chiefly useful to determine scope and proportion in the whole course of study. For Dewey, curriculum reconstruction was one with the continual reconstruction of experience itself. The curriculum, therefore, literally emerged from the process of adapting and readapting past experience to achieve aims that themselves were formulated and reformulated as the best way of solving the changing problems of the learner.

This view of Dewey's gave the interests and needs of the child greater weight as a criterion for selecting studies than Bobbitt or even Charters had given them. The Committee on Economy of Time had recommended that studies be selected which were within the *capacity* of the child, but here was a demand that the curriculum be selected on the basis of his *wants*. This raised a whole chain of questions, the questions of the relative importance of adult and child interests, of immediate and deferred values in the curriculum,

---

[15] For example, H. Harap, *The Education of the Consumer* (The Macmillan Company, New York, 1924); *The Technique of Curriculum Making* (The Macmillan Company, New York, 1928).

[16] For a bibliography of the more important curriculum surveys in this period, see J. M. Gwynn, *Curriculum Principles and Social Trends* (The Macmillan Company, New York, 1960), pp. 150–155.

and of the nature of the learning process itself.[17] Indeed, thorough-going curriculum revision even raised profound questions of social philosophy. In forming the curriculum from its foundations, for instance, the question arose whether the new curriculum should be governed by objectives consistent with current society with all its inadequacies or by objectives contemplating a radical reformation of society itself.[18]

SUBJECT MATTER VERSUS THE ACTIVITY CURRICULUM

The question of whether the curriculum should be child- or adult-centered was one of at least nineteenth-century origin. One of the earliest expressions of this tension was the conflict over whether the curriculum of secondary and higher education should be prescribed or elective. In early days the main business of children was to become adults. What was more natural, therefore, than to employ adult standards in selecting the curriculum leading to adulthood? Indeed, it was a kindness to children that those most familiar with the demands of later life should economize children's learning efforts by prescribing the choicest and most significant things for them to learn.

Commencing in the second quarter of the nineteenth century a strong reaction set in against the rigidly prescribed curriculum. In its stead the elective curriculum began to gain favor, becoming especially strong at the end of the century. The great champion of the elective principle was Charles W. Eliot (1834–1926). It reached the height of its development and acceptance at colleges like Harvard, where Eliot was president, and in the report of the National Education Association's Committee of Ten, in which all secondary school subjects were declared of equal worth if pursued for an equal length of time under equally competent instruction.

Popular as the elective curriculum became, it never completely smothered the prescriptive principle. As the twentieth century wore on, interest in some sort of prescribed core of studies began to revive. Such a core first showed strength by being able to force a truce with the elective principle. Some subjects were to enjoy a privileged position in the curriculum, as if protected by an educational tariff wall; other subjects were made elective and thus thrown on their

---

[17] See the reactions to these and other problems in curriculum theory of a top committee of curriculum experts in National Society for the Study of Education, *The Foundations and Technique of Curriculum-construction*, Twenty-sixth Yearbook (Public School Publishing Company, Bloomington, Ill., 1930), part II.

[18] For a theory of curriculum revision taking this view, see P. E. Harris, *The Curriculum and Cultural Change* (Appleton-Century-Crofts, Inc., New York, 1937).

own resources to survive in the competition to attract students. The precise formula for this compromise was to arrange the curriculum so that it would provide for both "concentration" and "distribution." In some curricula this took the form of a system of major and minor studies. In others it took the form of prescribed groups of studies with election permitted within each group.

At a deeper theoretical level the prescription-election controversy posed the question of whether to conceive the curriculum as composed of activities or of subject matter. Through the ages, the curriculum had been organized about subject matter. Indeed, so long had subject matter held sway that its acceptance had come to be quite uncritical. People had either forgotten or were quite unaware of the implications of the traditional conception of subject matter till the child-centered or activity curricula, emerging in the late nineteenth and early twentieth centuries, forced a critical examination of curriculum theory.

Originally, of course, the curriculum was a phase of the social heritage. It was the stock of meanings or past problem solutions which the group prized so highly that it prescribed their learning as a condition of adult membership in the group. The enlargement of society's store of meanings, which came with the passing of time, would have become very unwieldy had it not been for the systematic classification of these meanings into such subdivisions of subject matter as mathematics, grammar, and history. This classification of the whole field of knowledge, as well as the organization of each subdivision of subject matter within it, was highly logical. This was to be expected, for both ancient and modern science long held to a theory of knowledge which believed that objective reality had a logical structure which could be known and stated.[19] With such a premise it was quite reasonable to conclude that the logical organization of subject matter was more than a mere convenience of the human mind, that somehow it conformed to the stubborn facts of reality, to an invincible order in nature.

Such a view of subject matter naturally made a Procrustean bed of the curriculum. The curriculum was fixed in advance. As the child alone was pliable, he was made to conform to it. No wonder this sort of curriculum well earned its later epithet of "subject-matter-set-out-to-be-learned." Learning became either a mastery of the logically organized subject-matter account of the world as it was or, if subject matter was out of touch with contemporary reality, a discipline of the mind by honing it on the abrasive of cultural lag. Under these circumstances the textbook—which, too, was logically organized—was usually the curriculum. Or if the teacher was eclectically inclined to draw on several texts, scissors and paste would easily produce a composite one.

[19] For a further consideration of this philosophy, see *supra,* pp. 104–105.

Such was the almost exclusive theory of the nature and organization of the curriculum from earliest times down to the end of the nineteenth century. Indeed, it still retained strong supporters in the twentieth century as well. In these two centuries, however, this theory was to meet its first serious challenge. It was the Swiss romanticist Jean Jacques Rousseau (1712–1778) who first suggested a radically new approach to the curriculum. To him the child reflected the order of nature as well as the curriculum. Indeed, a sentimental and almost reverent regard for the child caused him to assign the child the more commanding place in the hierarchy of nature. Consequently, in his famous book *Émile,* far from subordinating the child to the curriculum, Rousseau did quite the reverse: he subordinated the curriculum to the child. He gave the drives that were urgent within the child the first claim on his attention in selecting and organizing the curriculum.

While Rousseau fired people's imaginations, he accomplished nothing practical himself. It therefore remained for another romanticist, the German idealist Friedrich Wilhelm August Froebel (1782–1852), the author of the kindergarten, to start educators on the road to effectually building their curricula around the nature of the child. To Froebel the goal of education was self-realization.[20] Following the idealistic philosophy of Immanuel Kant, Froebel looked upon the child as having an a priori self-active nature that was constantly striving to assert itself.[21] In fact, the education of the child, far from being only a product of the outside world, was an active impressing on the outside world of an unfolding inner nature. According to this view the curriculum was not something that originated exclusively outside the child. On the contrary, learning started from within; it was a working from within out, a process of realizing an inner self. In order to accord with this fact, therefore, the selection and organization of the curriculum would have to take the dynamic nature of the child into account.

Froebel's great emphasis on the inner self-active nature of the child should not lead to the conclusion that he neglected the social culture. In fact, he realized full well that the child was in large measure dependent on the outer world—the experience of others—in order to give effective direction and form to his inner nature. Hence, only by reaching out to make the outer inner could the child hope to give outward expression to his inner nature. Thus, in the form of a good Hegelian triad Froebel achieved an integrated learning experience, a synthesis of the thesis of inner nature with the antithesis

[20] For a further consideration of this aim of education, see *supra,* pp. 15–16.
[21] For a further consideration of this educational philosophy, see *supra,* pp. 125–126.

of external social culture. Yet note that the outcome of this synthesis did not make knowledge or subject matter the center of the educative process. Rather was the outcome a further stage in the self-realization of the child. The social culture or subject matter was but the nutritive material on which the self grew and realized itself.

Not all those who oriented the curriculum to the nature of the child did so out of sympathy with Froebel's idealistic philosophy. In America many arrived at such a curriculum by relying on the new dynamic, or functional, psychology of William James (1842–1910) and Edward Lee Thorndike (1874–1949), which was just beginning to establish itself at the turn of the century.[22] In two ways this educational psychology was enlisted in the service of a child-centered curriculum. On the one hand, it stated positively as a matter of empirical observation rather than philosophical speculation that the child at birth was organically possessed of a sizable list of instincts and impulses. The dynamic, propulsive nature of these native propensities led many educators to exactly the same conclusion as that of the Froebelians, that the curriculum must be fashioned to give expression to these assertive capacities. The fact that these educators arrived at this conclusion on scientific rather than philosophical grounds, however, frequently did not make them any less romantic or sentimental than the Froebelians in their regard for child nature.

On the other hand, negatively it greatly discredited the old theory of learning as formal discipline, the theory that the important thing in learning was not so much the content learned as the general mental power developed.[23] In its place dynamic educational psychology gave wide currency to the notion of the specificity of learning, that one learned specific ways of responding to specific situations. If this latter theory were the true one, then the content of the curriculum would have to be restored to importance. The curriculum would have to be stated in terms of the specific responses or activities that it was found desirable for children to learn.

The more specific effect of these ideas on the curriculum was to state the curriculum not so much in terms of logically organized subject matter about the world and adjustments to it that adults had learned as in terms of the activities of children themselves. Naturally, this was easiest to do in the kindergarten, which concerned itself with the education of children below the age when conventional subject matter was ordinarily introduced. There the curriculum consisted of songs and play, the spontaneous activities of all children.

[22] For a further account of this educational psychology, see *supra,* pp. 151–156.
[23] For a further account of this psychological theory, see *supra,* pp. 141–143.

But the Froebelian yeast soon began to leaven the subject-matter curriculum of the elementary grades as well, as Froebel certainly intended it to do.

An early instance of this leavening process was to be seen shortly after the Civil War at Quincy, Massachusetts, where Colonel Francis W. Parker (1831–1902), strongly influenced by Froebel, first gave promise of the distinguished career he later enjoyed. To bring the curriculum closer to the native activities of the child Parker tore out the partitions which logical organization had almost necessarily erected between various subjects in the curriculum. Thus, reading was taught not as an independent subject but as a means of acquiring information about history, science, and the like. Writing was taught not as an isolated art but as a means of communication. Spelling was handled incidentally to writing instead of having a separate status. At the turn of the century John Dewey, one of America's leading educational innovators, went even further in his experimental school at the University of Chicago. There he instituted a curriculum which gave a central position to such activities as cooking, sewing, and carpentering, activities with which the child was already familiar in the community. Subject matter was taught, too, but in conjunction with these activities rather than in the conventional fashion. Later some schools like the elementary school at the University of Missouri abandoned traditional subject matter altogether in favor of a fourfold curriculum of observation, play, stories, and handwork.[24]

LOGICAL VERSUS PSYCHOLOGICAL ORGANIZATION[25]

The activity, or child-centered, curriculum was not long in coming into open conflict with the traditional logically organized subject-matter curriculum. The defenders of tradition were sure the sentimentalism of this new education could result in nothing but a pampering of the child. The advocates of the child-centered curriculum in turn went as far as to assert that whatever was inert, mechanical, routine, and formal in the schools resulted precisely from a subordination of the child's interests and needs to the adult social demands of logically organized subject matter. The conservatives backing the traditional idea of "subject-matter-set-out-to-be-learned" retorted that one could hardly expect anything but a whimsical and capricious curriculum when it was predicated on the ephemeral and self-centered

[24] J. L. Meriam, *Child Life and the Curriculum* (World Book Company, Tarrytown-on-Hudson, N.Y., 1920).

[25] Since methods of instruction are also concerned with organization of the curriculum, chaps. 7 and 8, but especially the latter, should be reviewed in connection with this section.

impulses of the child. The adherents of the child-centered curriculum rejoined that at least their curriculum had the virtues of interest, spontaneity, and free initiative, to which the defenders of the traditional subject-matter organization made the surrejoinder that theirs preserved a sense of vigor, discipline, and order. The conflict was carried even into teacher-training institutions, the one group demanding teachers with a sympathy for children cultivated through a study of child psychology; the other, teachers fortified in scholarship through a curriculum ensuring an adequate command of subject matter.

The clash of these antithetical points of view generated much heated controversy. In the end, the heat grew so intense as to burst into a flame which happily illuminated the area in which a resolution of the conflict was to be found. The chief source of light on this conflict came from the direction of John Dewey, one of the parties to the controversy. In part, his fame rests on a little brochure entitled *The Child and the Curriculum* that he wrote at this time. In this brochure he deplored both depreciation of the immaturity of the child and the sentimental idealization of him. The weakness in both tendencies, he thought, stemmed from a common fallacy, the fallacy of taking a fractional view of child development. The supporter of traditional subject matter, repelled by a glance at the crudity and immaturity of the child, turned so quickly to dependence on the mature and ordered experience of adult subject matter that he failed to appreciate the promise of growth contained in the child's early strivings. The supporter of the child-centered curriculum, carried away by the promise of spontaneously budding capacities, shortsightedly confined his attention to child growth as if it were a completely self-contained and self-explanatory principle.

Constructively, Dewey saw these two points of view as complementary rather than contradictory. "Abandon the notion of subject matter as something fixed and ready-made in itself, outside the child's experience [he said to the one group]; cease thinking of the child's experience as also something hard and fast; see it as something fluent, embryonic, vital [he said to the other group]; and we realize that the child and the curriculum are simply two limits which define a single process. Just as two points define a straight line, so the present standpoint of the child and the facts and truths of studies define instruction. It is continuous reconstruction, moving from the child's present experience out into that represented by the organized bodies of truth that we call studies."[26]

To state this somewhat differently, the child-centered curriculum and the subject-matter curriculum had a common denominator, experi-

[26] J. Dewey, *The Child and the Curriculum* (The University of Chicago Press, Chicago, 1903), p. 16.

ence. Both were essentially activity curricula. The child-centered curriculum was professedly activistic, and the subject-matter curriculum on analysis turned out to be so too. What was grammar, for instance, but a way of acting when one wants to speak accurately? Or what was the π formula in geometry but a way of acting when one wants to square a circle? The nub of the curriculum controversy, therefore, was not how to conceive the nature of the curriculum. The real point at issue was how to organize it.

The traditional subject-matter curriculum, as already seen, was logically organized. It was, therefore, made up in advance and set out to be learned. The expectation was that the child would appropriate it or learn it as presented. Logically sound as this organization might have been for the adult, it was, as Dewey pointed out in *The Child and the Curriculum,* psychologically unsound for the child. The child, because he is a beginner, is not ready to start with the completed experience of the adult. Consequently, the teacher must organize the curriculum, not in a logical order to suit adult purposes, but in a psychological order to capitalize on the child's present experience and capacity. "A psychological statement of experience," declared Dewey, "follows its actual growth; it is historic; it notes steps actually taken, the uncertain and tortuous, as well as the efficient and successful. The logical point of view, on the other hand, assumes that the development has reached a certain positive stage of fulfillment. It neglects the process and considers the outcome."[27]

In the last analysis, then, the order in which the curriculum was organized was determined by what function it was to perform, whose purposes it was to serve. There was nothing final about the logical organization of subject matter, as had long been thought. On the contrary, logic was instrumental. It was a tool that could be shaped to serve the ends of adults or children. In a larger sense, therefore, according to Dewey, logical order was a phase of psychological order.

Hence, subject matter was not opposed to child experience but in fact must be incorporated into his experience. Or, to summarize in Dewey's words, "Every study or subject has two aspects: one for the scientist as a scientist; the other for the teacher as a teacher. These two aspects are in no sense opposed or conflicting. But neither are they immediately identical. For the scientist, the subject matter represents simply a given body of truth to be employed in locating new problems, instituting new researches, and carrying them through to a verified outcome. To him the subject matter or the science is self-contained. He refers various portions of it to each other; he connects new facts with it. He is not, as a scientist, called upon to travel outside its particular bounds; if he does, it is only to get

[27] *Ibid.,* p. 25.

more facts of the same general sort. The problem of the teacher is a different one. As a teacher he is not concerned with adding new facts to the science he teaches; in propounding new hypotheses or in verifying them. He is concerned with the subject matter of the science as *representing a given stage and phase of the development of experience.* His problem is that of inducing a vital and personal experiencing. Hence, what concerns him, as teacher, is the ways in which that subject may become a part of experience; what there is in the child's present that is usable with reference to it; how such elements are to be used; how his own knowledge of the subject matter may assist in interpreting the child's needs and doings, and determine the medium in which the child should be placed in order that his growth may be properly directed. He is concerned, not with the subject matter as such, but with the subject matter as a related factor in a total and growing experience. Thus to see it is to psychologize it."[28]

It may be well to cast the instrumentalism of Dewey's logic in the larger context of his instrumentalistic, or pragmatic, educational philosophy.[29] Profoundly influenced by Charles Darwin's theory of evolution, Dewey, it will be remembered, thought of education as a constant reconstruction of experience in order to adapt and readapt it to a changing environment. Successful adaptation of experience depended on being able to enlarge the implications of present experience by bringing one's own and others' past experience to bear on it. In the light of the larger experience, then, the most appropriate adaptation could be made. Under such circumstances the funded experience of the past had an instrumental function to perform; it was learned incidentally to solving a problem. The social heritage—subject matter, knowledge, information, facts—was to be learned not for its own sake or as an end in itself. Hence, the curriculum could no longer be made out in advance. Rather did the teacher and pupil have to make it on the spot when a problem of adjustment arose and when it became clear just what sort of subject matter would be needed for a solution.

This did not mean that the teacher could not plan for the curriculum in advance. Long-range planning, however, was consigned to the course of study. The terms "curriculum" and "course of study," which many educators used interchangeably or even synonymously, thus came to have different meanings for some who followed Dewey's analysis of the curriculum problem. The term "course of study" they applied to a suggested program of possible and even probable experiences

---

[28] *Ibid.,* pp. 29–30.
[29] For a fuller account of Dewey's educational philosophy, see *supra,* pp. 129–132.

which the child might have, all arranged so that the teacher could at any time judge the coherence and comprehensiveness of what the child was learning. The term "curriculum" they reserved for the sum total of all *actual experiences* of the child, growing out of his scholastic activities.

When it was published in 1903, Dewey's *The Child and the Curriculum* seemed like a reasonable resolution of the curriculum controversy to which it addressed itself. In fact, most of the progressive educators of the century took it as the basic theory of their curricula. Yet there was still a significant number of other progressive educators beyond the first quarter of the century who continued to employ an activity curriculum based on a highly romantic and sentimental regard for the child's interests and needs. Opposite and contemporary to them remained an even more significant number of "essentialists." who still insisted on a place for the "exact and exacting studies" of logically organized subject matter.[30] From their extreme positions on the flanks of the curriculum problem these two groups continued to snipe at each other until the middle of the century. Many of the shots from both sides fell short and thus unfortunately included within their target educators who followed in the more moderate footsteps of Dewey.

CULTURE-EPOCH AND RECAPITULATION THEORIES

In seeking defensibly logical or psychological organizations of the curriculum a number of schemes were turned up that enjoyed greater or less popularity from time to time. Two of the most important of these schemes stemmed from the nineteenth century. One was the culture-epoch, or recapitulation, theory, and the other the theory of correlation and concentration.

The theory of culture epochs was predicated on a philosophy of history. A slight reading of history will reveal to almost anyone that mankind has passed through various epochs of culture. Professing to discern a cosmic design in the progression from epoch to epoch, some authorities claimed that each generation had to repeat this progression epoch by epoch in order to achieve cultural maturity in its own day. This theory was already ages old long before it was popularly invoked in the latter part of the nineteenth century as a principle for curriculum guidance.[31] There is even evidence that

[30] For example, W. C. Bagley, "Is Subject Matter Obsolete?" *Educational Administration and Supervision,* 21:401–412, September, 1935.

[31] C. C. Van Liew, "The Educational Theory of the Culture Epochs," *National Herbart Society Yearbook,* 1895, pp. 74–98.

some early church fathers had recourse to this doctrine to persuade Christians of the necessity for studying Greek culture and not skipping it as pagan. Their argument was that since God had led mankind through the culture of the Jews to that of the Greeks and thence to Christianity, the contemporary curriculum could do no better than to select and arrange its subjects so as to repeat these stages or epochs.

Echoes of this argument were still to be heard in nineteenth-century German philosophy. There it was part of Georg Wilhelm Friedrich Hegel's absolute idealism to point to history as the record of the way in which the Absolute was working itself out in the affairs of men. The modern educational application of this theory was made in the writings of Johann Friedrich Herbart (1776–1841), particularly as they were interpreted and adapted by his follower Tuiskon Ziller (1817–1882) to formulate the modern statement of the culture-epoch theory. According to Herbart and Ziller the genesis of knowledge in the individual had to accord both in mode and in arrangement with the course the genesis of knowledge took in the history of the race.

The culture-epoch theory derived no little of its popularity in the nineteenth century from the scientific reinforcement it seemed to receive from the promulgation of Darwin's evolutionary hypothesis. Evolution, as a moment's thought will indicate, was itself a theory of history, a theory of the natural history of biological forms. A careful examination of the course of evolution or natural history revealed a tendency for nature to recapitulate itself. This tendency is particularly clear in the science of embryology. The embryos of most species in their development from conception to birth have been found to recapitulate much of the evolution of the species to which they belong. As can well be imagined, men were not long in recognizing the parallelism between the culture-epoch theory and evolution as revealed in embryology. Many at once jumped to the conclusion that this biological theory clinched the case for the culture-epoch theory; in fact, many changed its name to the "recapitulation" theory, by which it is still frequently known.

But granted now that curriculum makers should be guided by the culture-epoch, or recapitulation, theory, just what were the specific stages of cultural development to be incorporated in the curriculum? Here again there were two theories. According to one, the materials of the curriculum were to be arranged in the order in which the human faculties unfolded. Thus the teacher was to begin with physical objects on which the child could exercise his senses of perception. Next, when the child's imagination was awakening, the teacher would present different materials, such as myths and poetry. Still later he would proceed to memory work and finally to subjects requiring reason.

According to the other and more popular theory, curriculum materials were to be arranged according to socioeconomic epochs in the unfolding history of the race. Following this lead, the teacher commenced with a study of nomadic peoples. (Doubtless this is how the Indians and Eskimos originally entered the curriculum, where they have stayed well into the twentieth century.) After studying nomadic culture, the teacher passed on to pastoral peoples and thence to the more settled culture of agrarian civilization and finally wound up with a study of the industrial epoch.

Some held to the culture-epoch theory so rigidly that they thought the curriculum should recapitulate each epoch without fail. The author of the kindergarten, Froebel, was one of these. "Each successive generation," said he, "and each successive human being, inasmuch as he would understand the past and present, must pass through all preceding phases of human culture."[32] Furthermore, he wrote, "If the moment of the natural budding of the new subject of instruction has been missed, every later attempt arbitrarily to introduce the subject lacks interest. . . . The distinctive character of a natural and rational life-stirring and developing system of instruction lies in the finding and fixing of this point. For when it is truly found, the subject of instruction grows independently in accordance with its own living law."[33] The great educational psychologist G. Stanley Hall (1846–1924) took much the same view. Indeed, he even went further to contend that such a view provided a "catharsis" for the child, that it early purged him of long since outmoded types of racial behavior which if not eliminated now, might later manage to gain expression under very embarrassing circumstances.[34]

The culture-epoch theory was the vogue in American curriculum construction for several years before and after the turn of the twentieth century. Obviously it required an alert teacher to detect what period of race history happened to be in the ascendant in a child's growth so that the appropriate curriculum could be presented to coincide with this nascent tendency. Even if teachers were astute enough to arrange for this happy coincidence, there were some, like the educational philosopher John Dewey, who doubted that the culture-epoch theory had any factual basis in child nature. He not only challenged the theory's proponents to prove it but insisted that, even if they

---

[32] Quoted in J. L. Hughes, *Froebel's Educational Laws for All Teachers* (D. Appleton & Company, Inc., New York, 1897), p. 261.

[33] *Ibid.,* p. 64.

[34] For the psychological treatment of this view, see *supra,* p. 151.

could, they could verify it only by examining the child's current activities, which in any event formed a more reliable point of orientation for the curriculum than did remote epochs in the past. For Dewey the past should not fix the direction of present growth but rather should be a resource for aiding in the release of impulses clamoring for expression in the present. But more of this presently.

CORRELATION AND CONCENTRATION

A quite different but not unrelated approach to the selection and sequence of subjects in the curriculum was that represented by the theory of correlation and concentration. As Herbart saw the curriculum of his day, it was highly atomistic. Each subject seemed to be on a different shelf in the school. Indeed, he marveled at how the student could take each one down independently for a short while each day and then repeat the process day after day with as little resulting confusion as occurred. The multiplication of subjects that the nineteenth century witnessed greatly aggravated the atomism and pluralism of the curriculum.

The remedy that Herbart and later Ziller worked out for this situation was a plan integrating subjects through "correlation and concentration." The basic idea in correlation and concentration was to arrange subjects in the curriculum so that instruction in one was made to bear constantly on instruction in the others. Thus, in teaching geography it was very convenient to show its bearing on history, and in teaching history to enrich it by reference to literature. These subjects were rarely found separate in the life outside of school, Herbartians argued; why should they not be correlated in school?

There were, in fact, even more fundamental reasons for correlation. At bottom, the justification for the correlation of subjects was psychological. Correlation was really a special case of Herbart's doctrine of apperception.[35] Simply stated, it will be remembered, apperception was the doctrine that the child learns the new in terms of the old. If this was true within a given subject like history or geography, then why might it not be true between such subjects as well? Thus, Herbart and Ziller and their followers recommended using not only familiar historical facts as a background for learning new historical facts but familiar geographical data for the same purpose. Moreover, correlation could be counted on not only to make learning richer in meaning but to make it more interesting as well. Recognizing the new as something already familiar is a pleasure that has long been attested by the experience of old and young alike.

[35] For further background in the psychology of correlation, see *supra*, pp. 146–148.

Carrying out the logic of Herbart's theory on correlation, Ziller came to the conclusion not only that appropriate subjects should be correlated but that there was probably some one subject which should form the core for correlating all the others. This theory of close or intensified correlation was known as the "theory of concentration." For himself Ziller selected history as the core of concentration. Agreeing with Herbart that the chief end of education was moral, he naturally selected history because he followed Hegel in viewing it as the record of the unfolding purpose of a divine Absolute. Colonel Francis W. Parker, eclectic American educational innovator, was skeptical of weighting history so heavily for fear that, as in Germany, it would be made an instrument for entrenching the social *status quo*. The McMurrys, Frank (1862–1936) and Charles (1857–1929), perhaps the leading American Herbartians, made geography instead of history the core of concentration. Others took science, and still others the social life of the school.

Correlation as a vogue outlasted the culture-epoch theory. In fact, many who talked of an integrated curriculum in the decade before the Second World War really were thinking in terms of a correlation not very different from the Herbartian concept. The Herbartian theory of correlation, however, was not without its difficulties. A moment's reflection will disclose that all subjects did not readily reinforce each other. The correlation of science and literature, for instance, while natural at a few points, was often forced in order to give the learner a unitary experience. But this forcing of correlation beyond the connecting logic of apperception was clearly arbitrary. It was like trying to make trees by gluing boards together.

INTEGRATED, BROAD-FIELDS, AND CORE CURRICULA

Although the Herbartian theory of correlation and concentration disclosed weaknesses and limitations, the idea of endeavoring to achieve some integration of the curriculum into units larger than the old individual subject-matter divisions steadily mounted in importance in the twentieth century. Most radical here was the innovation that attempted to work out a curriculum where the child's own experience was the integrating factor. This conception contrasted sharply with Herbartian correlation, in which integration was achieved not so much by the child as by the teacher, who presented his pupil with knowledge already correlated and integrated. Such a result was about what one might expect from a realistic educational philosophy that bordered on the mechanistic.[36] Advocating the child as the nucleus

[36] For a more extended consideration of Herbart's educational philosophy, see *supra*, pp. 129–130.

agent for integration was Froebel. Indeed, what could be more logical for an idealistic educational philosopher who believed that knowledge was formed by a priori categories of the mind?[37] Dewey's pragmatism came to similar conclusions, for there, too, the individual exercised great initiative in planning adjustments and in systematizing his subsequent experiences. The later gestalt psychologists also ranged themselves with Froebel and Dewey and against Herbart—and against Thorndike, too, to the extent his educational psychology was mechanistic—for they accepted integration as an initial datum of personality. Such a strong array of influences naturally worked for integration in the curriculum from quite a different angle from correlation.

Curricula integrated in terms of child experience or community life went by various names. They were known as "integrated," "experience," "activity," "unit," and "project" curricula. In every case, however, the curriculum originated in the immediate life activities of the children themselves. The activities of life, of course, are never simple, nor do they present themselves sorted out with labels like "arithmetic" and "geography." On the contrary, life situations are usually very complex and cut clean across conventional subject-matter lines. Consequently, in taking up life at the point of some ongoing activity of the child a great variety of resources from the social heritage might be necessary to supply his needs or fulfill his purposes. As the child mobilized these resources and finally organized them to achieve his objectives, he achieved a personally tailored integration quite different from any ready-to-wear garment of logic that the Herbartian teacher might have presented him with. In such a situation, naturally, no course of study integrated and planned in advance would be adequate. Yet neither would a curriculum of a purely extemporaneous and occasional character give definite assurance of an adequate scope of experience at the end of a school year or even at the end of several school years. Hence, to ensure against gaps or disproportion in the curriculum, the integrated, experience, or project curricula had to give very special attention to the "scope" and "sequence" of studies.

Such a program for integrating the curriculum, though not uncommon in many progressive schools, was rather too advanced for most American school systems of the twentieth century. Generally, these fell back on some sort of compromise between it and Herbartian correlation. Among such compromises were the "broad-fields" and "core" curricula. The broad-fields curriculum sought greater unity by lumping logically related subject matters into a few major fields, such as the physical sciences, life sciences, social sciences, fine arts,

---

[37] For a more extended consideration of the idealistic educational philosophy, see *supra*, pp. 122–129.

and humanities. Although a few major fields took the place of many subdivisions of subject matter, each field had a greater area than that of the combined subject matters it represented. Characteristic of the broad-fields curriculum were such courses as "general science," "general mathematics," and "general language." Here too occurred experimentation with "survey," "orientation," and "exploratory" courses.

In the decades preceding and succeeding the Second World War the core curriculum was probably most popular. No doubt much of its popularity derived from the variety of ways in which it could be worked out, all the way from the prescribed curriculum of the nineteenth century to the integrated-experience curriculum of the twentieth. Although it had no uniform pattern, the core did try to avoid the atomistic quality of the elective curriculum by pulling together such subject matters as were cognate to it. As the core, therefore, was usually larger than any single subject-matter area, it might require longer than the usual class hour to encompass it. Indeed the core curriculum could be so broad and diverse that no single teacher was prepared to handle it alone. Hence the growth of "team teaching" to do cooperatively what none can do well singly.

On the whole, however, one must say that there has been evidence of arrested progress in curriculum development in the post-World War II period. In its heyday progressive education seemed on the point of resolving the long-standing tension between individual and social demands on the curriculum. It was poised on the threshold of a rationally planned diversity predicated on a scientifically calculated way of dealing with heterogeneity. Not only that, but it was poised to rescue such intangible learnings as the power to think and create from the mere status of concomitants to mastering facts and academic skills. Unfortunately the conservative attack on the schools unleashed by the "cold war" put a damper on all this, insisting instead on a frontal attack on solid subject matter in the manner of the "conventional wisdom."[38]

The conventional wisdom in curriculum matters had, however, one interesting frontier, the so-called "mid-century explosion of knowledge." The explosion not only vastly added to the total storehouse of knowledge but occasioned rethinking of what were the major elements to be taught in each field in order to keep creatively abreast of it. Consequently greater emphasis came to be placed on the basic structure of a discipline and the way in which its key concepts were interrelated. Mathematics was so revamped, for example, that many a parent was surprised to find he was unable to help his child with

[38] Hilda Taba, *Curriculum Development: Theory and Practice* (Harcourt, Brace & World, Inc., New York, 1962), pp. 4–5.

his homework. Naturally only those with profound subject-matter competence were capable of redesigning the curriculum along such lines.[39] This meant that the college professor of academic subject matter was once again in favor in curriculum councils. In the nineteenth century he had been the acknowledged leader in writing school as well as college texts. In the first half of the twentieth century he lost his preeminence to schoolmen, who, if they knew less subject matter, excelled him in their understanding of children. Now in the second half of the century the explosion of knowledge had catapulted the academic professor back into an esteemed, if not leading, position on national curriculum committees.

ADMINISTRATION OF THE CURRICULUM

The evolution from a subject-matter to an activity curriculum, from a logically organized to a psychologically organized one, and from the principle of a prescribed curriculum to that of an elected one had important implications for the administration of the curriculum as well. The traditional, prescribed, logically organized subject-matter curriculum for long derived its authority from the top of the administrative hierarchy. If changes were contemplated, the superintendent, principal, or supervisors usually originated them. Once decided upon, they were passed on to the teachers, who paid them out into the currency of instruction.

During the nineteenth and twentieth centuries the gradual shift to an activity curriculum, psychologically organized, with elective provisions for individual differences—in short to a more generally pupil-centered curriculum—was but the educational aspect of a broader shift in the center of gravity of authority. The larger social issue concerned a shift in control from external to internal authority. Hitherto, the authoritarianism of the Christian Church had been challenged by the Reformation and that of the monarchistic state by the French and American Revolutions. To many the times seemed opportune, because the forces of educational psychology and educational philosophy seemed to conspire, to introduce into education the same democratic shift in control that Thomas Jefferson had sought to make in government.[40]

Educational administrators first began to share the responsibility of curriculum revision by appointing representative committees of teachers to take the matter in hand. The great majority of teachers, however, had no part in the planning. Their turn came when the

[39] *Cf. supra,* p. 159.

[40] *Cf.* S. E. Morison, *Three Centuries of Harvard* (Harvard University Press, Cambridge, Mass., 1936), pp. 343–344.

activity conception of the curriculum began to take hold, when people began to make a distinction between the broad list of activities suggested by the course of study and the actual activities that occurred in the school and constituted the curriculum. Under such a theory every teacher was almost necessarily involved in curriculum construction all the time. Indeed, as teachers consulted the interest and needs of children in the make-up of the daily program, one might add that the pupils themselves came to have a share in curriculum revision.

The base of authority became even broader after the First World War. When course-of-study revision passed from tinkering with the old course to building entirely new ones, there were lay and expert interests to consult as well. Thus, many committees responsible for large-scale revision had extensive representation from the lay public as well as from the teaching staff. But this was not the first time that the lay mind had made its wishes known about the composition of the curriculum. Ever since the nineteenth century, state legislatures had from time to time taken occasion to prescribe what public schools ought to teach, from the Constitution of the United States to the harmful effect of habit-forming drugs and tobacco.[41]

Reconstructing the curriculum and course of study from blueprint to the finished house of knowledge was often no mere local affair. In some places, like Virginia and California, revision became a state-wide program. Curriculum experts were called in, not so much for the actual revision as to act in an advisory capacity. Many educational systems derived so much professional stimulation from fundamental state or local curriculum revision that they decided to keep their curricula under constant revision. This practice not only kept the curriculum from falling out of date but proved to be an excellent supervisory device for the in-service training of teachers.

[41] See J. K. Flanders, *Legislative Control of the Elementary School Curriculum* (Bureau of Publications, Teachers College, Columbia University, New York, 1925), pp. 65, 98.

11 Religious and Moral Education

Religious and moral influences on education have been noted at a number of points in these pages. They have made themselves felt in educational aims, curriculum, methods of instruction, educational philosophy, and the issue of public versus private schools, to mention but several topics. The treatment at each point, however, has been merely incidental. It is only proper that influences felt at so many points as religious and moral ones should now receive comprehensive and systematic historical treatment on their own account.

Furthermore, religious and moral education has problems of its own. Among the most persistent of these problems has been the question: To what extent is the formation of good character a function of nature and to what extent a function of nurture? Obviously, much depends on how educators have conceived of nature and nurture. Does human nature commence its educational career with the taint of original sin upon it? If so, can nurture or education do anything to correct the effects of that taint? Can good character be attained through a secular moral education alone, or must moral education be supplemented by religious education as well? Should there be a union or a divorce of church and state for the purposes of religious and moral education? If a divorce, how shall the responsibility for religious and moral education be divided between them?

FOLKWAY RELIGIOUS AND MORAL EDUCATION

The moral education of most early peoples was folkway, or customary, in character. Among the ancient Greeks the best early account of folkway morality was to be found in the Homeric poems. From the *Iliad* and the *Odyssey* the Greeks drew lessons in such virtues as piety, hospitality, courage, temperance, and self-control. Of these the cardinal virtue was piety, especially filial piety. Formal and informal educational agencies, the school and public opinion—all united to inculcate and enforce these moral virtues. Religion, too, added its sanctions, but it is notable that religion among the Greeks was a thing of beauty rather than fear. Its educational appeal was more ceremonial and mediatory than doctrinal and moral. Children learned their religion not only through participation in religious ceremonies but also through dances, games, and dramas that celebrated religious festivals. Although, as stated, there was nothing terroristic about Greek religion, it bears observing that the Greeks did not hesitate to employ fear and corporal punishment as wholesome incentives to conformity to the folkway standard of morality.

Early Roman moral education was also of a folkway, or customary, character. Indeed, the early Romans had an unusually deep sense of duty to the statute and moral law and a keen awareness of spiritual powers external to man that conduct had to take into account. The wealth of Latin words laden with moral meaning that the English language has taken over is perhaps a small measure of Roman alertness to the moral quality of conduct. Thus Roman youth were taught to accent in their conduct the easily recognizable virtues of *fortitudo, constantia, gravitas, pietas, patientia, honestas, prodentia,* and *temperantia.* The religious observances that backed the moral virtues centered chiefly in the household *lares* and *penates.* As a high standard of observance was maintained here, the religious education of children in the home was very effective.

Religious and moral education among the early Jews, whose tradition the later Christians took over and extended, had the same basis in custom that the practice of the Greeks and Romans had. As the early Greeks drew the moral precepts of their religion from the Homeric poems, so the Jews drew theirs from the Mosaic law. Other sacred writings were important, too, but they did not alter the fundamentally legal character of religious and moral instruction. With the Jews religious sanctions suffused education in manners as well as education in morals. Thus note the Biblical injunction, "Be not wise in thine own eyes: fear the Lord, and depart from evil."[1] Here,

---

[1] Proverbs 3:7.

as frequently in early Jewish literature, "The fear of the Lord is the beginning of wisdom."[2]

CRITICAL RELIGIOUS AND MORAL EDUCATION

Almost without exception religious and moral education through the folkways was authoritarian. Children learned folkway morality in the very act of being required to be obedient to it. Deviation from or criticism of the norm of conduct had no standing as part of the educational process. The Greeks, however, were the first to make a notable break in this rigidity of religious and moral education. As Greek political and economic influence spread over the Aegean area, men became increasingly aware of a wide diversity in the social conventions that reigned in moral education. As an outgrowth of this awareness there arose a group of teachers known as "Sophists" who tried to teach morality through a critical analysis of custom and convention.[3] Conservatives, feeling insecure because they were uncertain where the unrestricted criticism of convention might lead, looked very much askance at this radical departure. Accustomed to think of virtue as an innate gift of the gods, they seriously questioned whether it could be acquired through training of the intellect in reflective criticism.

The great advocate of teaching morality reflectively was Socrates (469–399 B.C.), the moral gadfly of Athens. In his mind, knowledge and virtue went hand in hand. To know the right, as he said, was to do it. To state this somewhat differently, Socrates claimed that no one would knowingly do the wrong. If one did evil, it was merely because he was ignorant of the right or good. The good, according to the Sophists with their motto of "man the measure of things," was a matter of individual opinion. Much as Socrates was devoted to making moral education a rational process, he was unwilling to go so far as to shift the basis of moral education from social convention to individual opinion. Opinions, he insisted, were only "half thoughts" about the good. To think oneself through to the whole truth about the good, one must not only approach it from many different individual angles but proceed on the presupposition that the human mind is the channel for universal reason.

If moral education in its folkway form had neglected the rational element, there were many who thought that Socrates overemphasized it. Chief among his critics was Aristotle (384–322 B.C.). To possess

---

[2] Psalms 111:10.
[3] For an elaboration of the political and philosophical significance of the Sophists in Greek education, see *supra,* pp. 26–27, 99–100.

knowledge about morals, Aristotle claimed, was not enough; one must practice morals as well. One must form moral habits. To know the good was important, but unforutnately it did not create a desire for the good. Stating his own position, Aristotle claimed that education in moral virtue is like an art. As an art it is predicated on three components. The first component is nature. Nature provides the potential raw materials out of which virtuous habits can be formed. It does not, however, endow man with virtues innate at birth, which was the early contention of the conservatives. Yet, while Aristotle did not think that virtue was a gift of the gods, he did not deny that the proportionate contribution of nature to moral education is dependent not on man but on some divinity. The second component of moral education as an art is habit. Here nature is exercised in the practice of the good. With the help of the teacher the child tries to actualize his potentialities for good. When these good habits became well established, Aristotle called them virtues and the sum total of these habits character. The third component of moral education is rational instruction. The function of rational instruction, of course, is to decide the good to which nature is to be habituated.

In forming moral character Aristotle assigned a special place in the curriculum to music. It was his contention that rhythms and melodies, if properly selected, were capable of arousing in the hearer feelings of anger, courage, and affection that, for intensity, were little short of genuine provocation. Hence, by changing the music from one mood to another, Aristotle believed that corresponding moral changes could be brought about in the listener. In this way he hoped, according to his famous theory of catharsis, to purge people of vicious feelings and strengthen them in virtuous ones.

In Greece the transition from a customary moral education to a critically rational one was not seriously obstructed by the religious beliefs of the people. In a religion like that revealed in Greek mythology there was obviously little dogma to be learned by children. Indeed, in the course of time the myths about Hellenic heroes and deities took such a variety of forms that any orthodoxy about them was all but impossible. Even so, Plato (427–347 B.C.), the pupil of Socrates and the teacher of Aristotle, took exception to including many of these myths in the curriculum of the school because of the immoralities they portrayed. Interestingly enough, he did not object to myths about the gods because myths were fictional. All he wanted to ensure was that if fictions were to be used, they should be ones which would promote and not impede the growth of the child in moral stature.

While Plato was willing to employ fictions for whatever good uses they could serve, he never desisted from relentlessly probing the boundary line between appearance and reality.[4] In fact, it was largely due to the freedom with which he and Socrates and Aristotle fearlessly attacked problems of metaphysics and ethics that learning in the Western world was emancipated from the position of handmaiden to religion it long had held. But then perhaps this bold inquiry would never have been possible had it not been for the fact that the Greek mind had always been predominantly secular. The Greek priests never became a dominant body or even a permanent class, for they were often elected and their return to private life was not unheard of.

This unabashed curiosity and penetrating inquiry of the Hellenic mind resulted in a religious and moral education whose sanctions were largely aesthetic in character. Thus, it became widely accepted that the basis for the good life lay not in duty but in happiness, happiness being defined as the satisfaction of one's natural impulses and instincts. This eudaemonistic basis for moral education, however, was qualified by two very important considerations that must not be forgotten. At first the standard by which the Greek measured happiness was not that of the individual but that of the community or city-state; measurement was not by the part but by the whole. It was only after the coming of the Sophists that the welfare of the state gave way to personal happiness as the basis of morality, and even then it was over the protest of men like Plato and Aristotle. Again, the eudaemonism of even personal happiness was not without its checks and balances. To guide the individual's self-assertiveness Aristotle had cautioned "nothing too much." Thus, one should be brave, but not so brave as to be foolhardy nor so wanting in bravery as to be cowardly.

CHRISTIANITY

Although the Romans were more legally and less aesthetically minded than the Greeks, no significant innovations in religious and moral education occurred till the rise of Christianity. This new religion posed some radically new outlooks on life, which resulted in profoundly altering the development of religious and moral education in the Western world. The Greco-Roman, or pagan (as it came to be called in the Christian era), world looked upon life here and now as its main opportunity. Man's worth was largely determined by membership in the secular state. Even at that, only a small percentage of the population enjoyed citizenship, a much larger group composed of women, slaves, and foreigners being excluded from it altogether. Opposed to this view was the Christian one wherein the

[4] For a fuller account of the significance of this problem in educational philosophy, see *supra*, pp. 103–104.

life here and now was seen as merely a temporary and probationary period prior to a period of eternal punishment or reward. An individual's worth took its origin not in his civic status but in his being a child of God. In fact, all mankinds of whatever sex, whether bond or free, and of whatever pigmentation of skin were regarded as brothers because owning the common fatherhood of God.

This radical reorientation of human outlook also had a new ethic, the ethic of love. This ethic was regarded not as a mere human product but as a norm established through divine revelation. Instead of narrowly seeking one's personal happiness, the new ethic commanded men to love each other as brothers. In a period of gross public and private immorality, it summoned people to renounce their lusts and embrace an austerely simple and pure manner of life. The decision to become a Christian and radically reorient one's life to Jesus became an act of the utmost gravity. It took its character from the Scriptures, where it was stated that, save as a man be born again, he shall not enter into the kingdom of Heaven.

Preparation for this regeneration involved several significant educational features. For one thing, regeneration was not to be achieved through mere intellectual instruction in Christian morals. One had to live and habituate himself in the Christian way of life as well as intellectually assent to its principles. Like Aristotle, St. Paul was skeptical of the Socratic theory of moral education that to know the right was to do it, for, he pointed out, though we know the better we often do the worse. The reason for this perversity the Christian found in human nature. While man's nature had been whole and in a state of order in the Garden of Eden, his expulsion from that paradise because of disobedience had resulted in a human nature in less than full control of its former faculties and one possessed of somewhat disorderly inclinations. This weakened nature, which Adam's sin visited upon the human race, came to be the chief presupposition of all Christian religious and moral instruction.

Fortunately, the means for overcoming this educational handicap were at hand. Through the grace of God and by learning to follow the example of Jesus, the only begotten son of God, who gave himself as a sacrifice that others might gain eternal life, the hope was held out for regaining paradise. In fact, as the aim of the Christian religion was the restoration of man to the paradise that his progenitor, Adam, had forfeited, so the aim of Christian religious and moral education was the restoration of man in the image of God that he had lost. To set the educational process in operation toward this end, there must be a repentance of sin. The new life was then unfolded through catechetical instruction, which gave a more or less detailed account of its main tenets. Coincidentally, there was to be continual practice in disciplining one's disorderly inclinations and in habituating oneself in Christian virtues of charity and forgiveness. The remarkable success of the early Christians in using psalmody to stir appropriate emotional attitudes to accompany their religious and moral instruction was eloquent testimony in support of Aristotle's recommendation of music for that purpose.

Christianity not only reoriented the aim of religious and moral instruction and restated the theory of human nature and its remaking but also tended to exalt the church rather than the state as the principal educational agency. This is not surprising since, according to Christian principles, the worth of man was made to depend on his relationship to God rather than his relationship to the state. Even more significant was the claim of the Christian Church to having been divinely instituted as a teaching agency. It claimed to derive its educational authority and jurisdiction from Jesus's own mandate to his disciples, "All power is given to me in heaven and earth. Going, therefore, teach ye all nations. . . . Teaching them to observe all things whatsoever I have commanded you: and behold, I am with you all days, even unto the consummation of the world."[5] With the collapse of the Roman Empire and the emergence of the Christian Church as the most stable social agency in the Western world, the ecclesiastical control of education extended itself to secular subjects as well as religious and moral ones.

Doubtless this ecclesiastical assumption of control over education was altogether necessary at the time. Except for the support of the church, the lamp of learning, which burned low enough during the Middle Ages, might well have been extinguished in the western half of the old Roman Empire. But ecclesiasticism brought problems of its own. When Christianity became the official religion of the Empire, the church was finally in a position in which it could have all pagan schools either closed or changed into Christian institutions. While it is easy to understand the laudable motives of the church in wishing to possess a monopoly of education, it cannot be overlooked that as a result religious and moral instruction risked becoming more dogmatic and authoritarian. Moreover, because some still clung to the imminence of the second advent of Jesus, the otherworldly ideal of religious and moral education came to prevail almost to the exclusion of any attention to the secular one.

Not least among the difficulties of an ecclesiocentric religious and moral education was its effect on the child. For him religion and morals tended to recede from the simple everyday character they

[5] Matthew 28:18–20 (Douay Bible). For a twentieth-century exposition of this mandate, see Pius XI's encyclical "The Christian Education of Youth," *Catholic Educational Review*, 28:133–134, March, 1930.

had enjoyed in the early Christian home when Christians were still known not for their doctrine so much as for their purity of life. The dogmatic religion of ecclesiasticism became a religion mainly for adults. It could reach the child only through the authoritative teaching of the catechism. In this form it was usually taught to children before they were really old enough to assimilate it. Hence, religious and moral education came to lay undue emphasis on memory at the expense of understanding. Words and symbols were exalted over concrete religious and moral experience.

During the Middle Ages there was little or no change in this pattern of religious and moral education. Instruction, such as it was, kept its eye steadily on eternity and supermundane affairs. Education based itself on faith first and on critical reason only second. Not only would a second coming of the Lord, expected at any moment, render reason relatively unimportant, but there was considerable uneasiness about a reason not subordinated to faith. It was such an inordinate confidence in human reason that had held the citadel of Greco-Roman paganism, and Christianity did not soon forget the difficulty of dislodging it from pagan schools.

Between the end of the Middle Ages and the full flowering of the Renaissance a very important process of acculturation went on between the Christian religion and the pagan philosophy of the Greeks. Indeed, peace had no sooner been established between the two by St. Thomas Aquinas (1225–1274) in his *Summa theologica* than a great wave of interest in ancient Greek and Roman culture swept Italy. A strong reaction set in against the gloomy outlook of the medieval period. Interest in mundane affairs supplanted interest in the supermundane. Human nature, which had been so greatly depreciated in the medieval period, became appreciated in the Renaissance. Educationally, it found expression in the study of the humanities, especially belles-lettres. Though still under the cloak of Christian orthodoxy, men began to look for the sound development of character through furnishing the mind with stirring moral sentiments drawn from the pagan literatures of Greece and Rome.

THE PROTESTANT REFORMATION

The prominence of belles-lettres in the curriculum divulges the essentially aesthetic character of the Renaissance in Italy. North of the Alps the Renaissance took on a much more critical and reformist mood. In the sixteenth century, in fact, under the leadership of Martin Luther (1483–1546), this mood reached the proportions of an open revolt against the authority of the traditional Christian Church. As a result, a great schism cleft Christianity. Those who continued their allegiance to the traditional church became known as Roman Catholics, and those who took issue with her as Protestants.

The central point in this controversy was the right of the individual to understand God's revelation in Scripture in terms of his own intelligence without the necessary intermediation of the church. Obviously this principle implied a radically different approach to religious and moral education. It attached an importance to training in individual judgment that ecclesiasticism was in danger of smothering in its over-anxiety to lead the individual to correct judgment as certified by the church. Yet even Protestants thought the judgment of individuals needed some instruction, and to this end Luther issued a popular catechism. Hitherto, catechisms had been intended chiefly for the guidance of the clergy. Luther's catechism proved so enormously popular that Catholics were soon giving similar catechetical instruction to their laity. In addition, the Protestant emphasis on the Bible led to the innovation of its inclusion as a prominent part of the curriculum. Similarly, the Sunday sermon, which took on great significance under Protestantism as an exposition of Scripture or doctrine, also became part of the educative process. Indeed, children learned to expect to be quizzed on the sermon next day in school. In other respects, Catholics and Protestants continued to predicate their educational theory and practice on much the same principles. Both assumed the fallen nature of man. Both continued to agree on the educational need for disciplining his unruly nature and habituating it to good aims.

Another difference between Catholics and Protestants belongs particularly to Calvinism and concerns Calvin's doctrine of the nature of man. The pagan theory of man, it will be remembered, put confidence in man's unaided resources to instruct himself for his own improvement. Catholic, or traditional Christian, theory took a less optimistic view of human nature. It held that man's nature had been wounded in its fall from grace but could still cooperate in rising again and, with the help of the church, regaining its rightful heritage. John Calvin (1509–1564) took an even less optimistic view of the situation, in fact, a thoroughly pessimistic one. He found human nature not just wounded by its fall but totally incapacitated to rise again except through God's intervention. The confidence that the pagan and, to an extent, the Humanist had in being able to lift themselves by education alone, Calvin could only look upon as vain conceit and pride. Human nature being not only impotent to save itself but positively inclined toward evil, he saw no hope in religious and moral instruction except as one put complete faith in God's will and mercy. Even then educational prospects were none too good since the predestination of some to be lost meant that not all could expect to be saved in spite of their educational efforts.

As in the medieval period, both Luther and Calvin set faith above reason, will ahead of understanding. Religious and moral knowledge gained by the intellect alone they considered inferior to that higher knowledge of those sacred interests which springs from faith and divine revelation. Doing good works, learning good habits, was important, but faith and creed were the final criteria of spiritual achievement. Hence the Reformation, as already implied, was essentially a battle of creeds. It is small wonder, therefore, that religious and moral education among both Protestants and Catholics leaned heavily on the catechism and catechetical methods of instruction.

It is particularly important to understand the somber presuppositions of Calvinism, for they formed the background of the Puritans and their educational theory and practice when they set up schools and churches in colonial America. There children grew up in an atmosphere perpetually saturated, weekdays as well as Sundays, with Calvinistic pessimism. The fateful consequences of dying became the constant companion of their thoughts. Jonathan Edwards, New England's outstanding Puritan preacher at this time, though on the whole kindly disposed toward children, did not escape adding to the gloom hanging over them by referring to them as "young vipers and infinitely more hateful than vipers to God."[6]

In the course of time Protestantism came to suffer from a formalism born in part of its own overemphasis on doctrine and creed and became relatively lifeless. An attempt to revitalize this lifeless shell of Protestantism began toward the end of the seventeenth and the beginning of the eighteenth centuries. This movement was known in Germany as "Pietism" and in England as "Methodism." In both cases new importance was attached to the inward emotions of the individual. Concern was shown not so much about what God's thoughts are toward man as about what man's feelings are toward God, not so much about what God does for man as about the sentiments that originate in and emanate from man. Had it followed the genius of Protestantism, this movement might have recognized a wide range of religious feeling. Instead, however, it turned aside to lay stress on a particular set of emotional experiences culminating in sudden and dramatic conversions like that of the founder of Methodism himself, John Wesley (1703–1791). It is small wonder, therefore, that conversion soon became the acknowledged goal of both evangelism and religious and moral education.

[6] Quoted in C. A. Hauser, *Teaching Religious Education in the Public School* (Round Table Press, Inc., New York, 1942), p. 64.

Pietism and Methodism seem to have had the inviting possibilities of introducing a note of spontaneity into the highly verbal and formal catechetical instruction of the time and of making a sympathetic gesture in the direction of the child. Instead, at least Methodism continued to take the dark view that child nature was inclined to be rebelliously disobedient to divine will. "Break your child's will in order that it may not perish," Wesley advised parents. "Break its will as soon as it can speak plainly—or even before it can speak at all. It should be forced to do as it is told, even if you have to whip it ten times running."[7]

One last influence of the Protestant Reformation on religious and moral education must not be overlooked—Luther's invitation to the state to assume some responsibility for such education. The arrangement entered into was one in which the church generally gave and supervised instruction provided by the state. In Greece and Rome religious and moral education had the sanction of the state. During the Middle Ages and the Renaissance the church had regarded itself as the proper fount of religious and moral education and at least the guardian protector of secular education as well. But Luther now inaugurated a joint partnership of these two powerful agencies. Little did he foresee the educational difficulties that were to arise from commingling the things that are Caesar's with those that are God's.[8]

In Calvin's theocracy a similar and, if anything, even closer partnership between state and church was effected to carry on the educational enterprise. Connecticut, following the precedent of Massachusetts, illustrates Calvinistic policy perfectly. There we find the state making it a civil obligation "That all masters of families do, once a week at least, catechize their children and servants in the grounds and principles of religion, and if any be unable to do so much, that then, at the least, they procure such children or apprentices to learn some short orthodox catechism, without book, that they may be able to answer the questions that shall be propounded to them out of such catechisms by their parents or masters, or any selectmen, when they shall have called them to a trial of what they have learned in this kind."[9]

---

[7] Quoted in W. James, *Talks to Teachers* (Henry Holt and Company Inc., New York, 1899), p. 182. This is a condensation from J. Wesley, *Works* (J. Emory and B. Waugh, New York, 1831), vol. II, p. 320.

[8] In his eighteenth-century *Treatise on Man* the Frenchman Claude Adrien Helvétius assigned the contradictions that existed among precepts on education to the fact that the educational enterprise was confided to both temporal and spiritual powers. See *Treatise on Man* (Vernor, Hood, and Sharpe, London, 1810), vol. 1, p. 36.

[9] E. P. Cubberley, *Readings in Public Education in the United States* (Houghton Mifflin Company, Boston, 1934), p. 19.

RISE OF SECULARISM

This Protestant innovation worked well enough where there was an established church and where the community was religiously homogeneous. But communities, especially in America, had a way of not remaining homogeneous. When they turned heterogeneous, the futility of insisting on religious orthodoxy more and more strongly pressed itself home on people's minds. Consequently, people began to cool in their religious zeal. What is more, in the eighteenth century a secular outlook on life born of science and political revolution began to compete very successfully with the religious outlook.

A forerunner of this secularism was the Englishman John Locke (1632–1704). Locke deserves to be mentioned here because in *Some Thoughts concerning Education* he had much to say on the formation of moral character, most of it without any reference to religious training. Perhaps this is because he was aiming at the manners as well as the morals of the young gentleman. Be that as it may, he left no doubt that he thought the way to form character was through discipline. Discipline, he wrote in an almost classically simple precept, consists in a man's being "able to deny himself his own desires, cross his own inclinations, and purely follow what reason directs as best though the appetite lean the other way."[10]

Of top significance in this statement is Locke's fresh appeal to reason. Not only did he depend heavily upon reason in the formation of character, but he was confident that an appeal to the child's reason was appropriate at a much earlier age than was ordinarily recognized. Yet, while he would reason with the child, Locke was careful to caution against burdening him with long discourses. Moreover, he urged avoiding abstruse philosophical reasoning because the child was probably too immature to act or reason in the light of remote principle. Much as he leaned on reason, he knew only too well how much easier it was to couch morals in words than to install them in conduct.

It is worth noting in passing that Locke was neither the first nor the last to seek moral values in a disciplinary theory of education. Such values were implicit in the restraint imposed by the moderation in Aristotle's golden mean; they were implicit in the self-control that Greek sports enforced; they were implicit in the self-negation that the rule of obedience imposed on the medieval ascetic; and they long continued implicit in the inhibitions that children had to suffer when compelled to follow a distasteful curriculum not for its content

[10] J. Locke, *Some Thoughts concerning Education* (Cambridge University Press, London, 1889), p. 21.

values but for the formal training of the mind that it was supposed to afford.[11]

Locke's emphasis on the role of reason in the formation of character was, in large part, a reflection of the new age to which modern science was introducing the world. In fact, in the eighteenth century this age was to be known as the "age of reason." People were tremendously impressed by the natural law and order that men like Nicolaus Copernicus, Johannes Kepler, and Sir Isaac Newton had discovered at work in the universe. The preestablished harmony that ruled there gave a new insight into the nature of God and his handiwork. From a position where it had been depreciated, if not despised, the world of nature moved into a position where it became the object of worship. Those whose religious thinking took this turn went by the name of "deists."

The natural law, which made the heavens appear so orderly, people came to seek in politics, economics, and education as well as in astronomy. None had a greater reverence for its operation in child nature than Jean Jacques Rousseau (1712–1778), the Swiss romanticist. The law of natural development, which he found operating there, he proposed as the norm by which to judge educational procedures. "Everything is good as it comes from the hands of the author of nature," he announced dogmatically in the opening sentence of *Émile,* his great educational treatise.[12] "Let us lay it down as an incontestable maxim," he wrote later in the same book, "that the first promptings of nature are always right. There is no original corruption in the human heart."[13] Here was a sharp break with Christian tradition, both Catholic and Protestant, which had long taken the view that original nature was desperately wicked. The implications for religious and moral education were profound. The Catholics thought the implications were profoundly erroneous and immediately put *Émile* on the *Index librorum prohibitorum.*

Although Rousseau did not find the original nature of the child corrupted, he did not hesitate to admit that the child had weaknesses because of which he was not strong enough to do without the help of others. Reason would help make up these deficiencies but not till the child was older. Here Rousseau parted company with Locke,

[11] In the nineteenth century, formal moral values were claimed for such subjects as manual training and handwriting. Thus, making a "true" joint in carpentry presumably taught fidelity, and vertical handwriting was supposed to symbolize moral rectitude.

[12] R. L. Archer, *Rousseau on Education* [Edward Arnold (Publishers) Ltd., London, 1912], p. 55.

[13] *Ibid.,* p. 97.

not on the efficacy of reason, but rather on how early it could be invoked. The age at which a child becomes capable of reasoning about his conduct Rousseau put relatively late. Prior to such evidence of maturity he claimed that a child's acts were amoral. Being amoral, they could not be blamed, and therefore the child was not to be punished during this period except by the natural consequences of his acts.

Rousseau was in no hurry, either, for Émile to be instructed in religion—he suggested age fifteen, though even that he feared was too early. The chief difficulty that he saw in religious instruction was the tendency of the child to develop an anthropomorphic religion. Unless religious instruction was given with great caution, the child could easily form preposterous notions, which would be very difficult to eradicate in later life.[14]

Obviously, to predicate religious and moral education on natural rather than supernatural principles was a long step in the direction of secularizing this branch of education. Other thinkers under the influence of the age of reason were moving in the same direction as Rousseau. The French revolutionary Charles Maurice de Talleyrand, for instance, lamented the way in which moral education had been predicated on the multitude of opinions which divide men. The result had been, he pointed out, to abandon morality to uncertainty and compromise. He himself believed that "Morality must be taught as a real science, whose principles will be demonstrated to the reason of all men, and to that of all ages."[15] And the Welsh industrialist and patron of education Robert Owen (1771–1858) took the extreme secular view that character depended not at all on the individual's exercise of will but rather on his external circumstances, that is, his environment. Therefore the difference between men of good and bad character is a function of differences in their education.

Surprisingly enough, eighteenth-century rationalism had a temporary effect even on the catechetical teaching of the Catholic Church. This was evident both in the content of the catechism and in the method of instruction in it. On the side of content, greater attention was paid to questions of morality than to those of doctrine. Matters like original sin and grace, because they did not readily comport with the rationalist's tendency to believe only what he could know by his unaided reason, were slighted. On the side of method, the same tendency undermined the church's traditional mode of authoritative

[14] The Catholic educator François de La Mothe-Fénelon (1651–1715) did not disapprove of children's learning of God as an old man with a white beard, for he expected them to reconstruct that notion later on.

[15] G. Compayré, *History of Pedagogy* (D. C. Heath and Company, Boston, 1885), p. 375.

and dogmatic exposition of revealed truth. Furthermore, it became common to question children on their catechisms as if the truth of religion were already implanted in them by nature and needed only to be called forth by the skillful interrogation of the teacher.

THE SECULAR PUBLIC SCHOOL

While science was shaping the minds of men for the secularization of education, political events toward the end of the eighteenth century were setting the stage of practical affairs for the same outcome.[16] Before following this train of events, however, it will be well to understand just how matters stood in America before the Revolution set them in motion. On the eve of the Revolution, it can be sweepingly stated that schools, wherever and under whatever public or private auspices held, included religious and moral education in their curricula as a matter of course. Such instruction, indeed, held first place as the backbone of civic morality, as witness those oft-quoted lines from the Ordinance of 1787, "Religion, morality, and knowledge being necessary to good government and the happiness of mankind, schools and the means of education shall forever be encouraged." Moreover, many colonies had statutes requiring religious tests for the certification of teachers. Some even delegated the supervision and administration of their schools to church authorities, and not a few had "established" churches, that is, churches that derived their revenues from taxes. This naturally made possible governmental support for church schools. For instance, in Massachusetts and Connecticut the Congregational Church occupied this privileged position; in Virginia, the Episcopal Church.

The results of the American Revolution necessitated fundamental changes in this pattern. While individual colonies approximated religious homogeneity and therefore could have an established church that ignored religious minorities, the aftermath of the Revolution joined these colonies into a national frame of government where homogeneity no longer obtained. Rather, religious heterogeneity prevailed on a national scale. Frankly recognizing this obvious fact, the First Amendment to the Federal Constitution, part of the so-called "Bill of Rights," declared in favor of religious freedom for all and enjoined against a privileged position for any religion. Practical necessity though this amendment was, it gave rise to no little anxiety on the part of many people as to what its effect would be on civic morality. Nevertheless, individual states one by one followed the Federal ex-

[16] Committee on the War and the Religious Outlook, *Teaching Work of the Church* (Association Press, New York, 1923), chap. 1.

ample and disestablished their local state churches, thus promulgating religious freedom locally as well as nationally.

The educational counterpart of the political divorce of church and state was the exclusion of religion from the public school curriculum. This secularization of public education did not occur immediately following the divorce of church and state, nor did it take the same course in each of the states. The developments in two states, New York and Massachusetts, however, may be taken as settling the issue for most of the others. In these states matters moved toward a crisis in the second quarter of the nineteenth century. In both the issue was forced not by the enemies of religion, such as atheists, agnostics, and freethinkers, but by its various sectarian friends.

What happened in New York State will be told in describing the growth of public education.[17] There the crisis was financial. The state had a limited amount of public funds to spend on education, which it was using to subsidize various church schools. As the number of churches seeking a share increased, the size of each share decreased. In fact, there was danger that the effectiveness of the state appropriation, which could have been quite considerable if concentrated on a single system of schools, would be dissipated. To avoid this outcome, the state decided in 1842 to discontinue its subsidies of private church schools and launch a public system of its own.

Church bodies, especially the Catholics, at once took strong exception. This, however, was of no avail. Just as the first Amendment to the Federal Constitution had won united support from the various sects by excluding the claims of any sect to special privilege, so in New York religion was excluded from the curriculum on the same grounds. Obviously, this arrangement was devised not in hostility to religious education as such but rather because the friends of religion could not agree among themselves how to teach it and preferred no religious instruction whatever in the public school to that of an opposing sect. Later, faced by the large Catholic immigration to America from Europe, the Protestant sects submerged their differences, decided to trust their Sunday schools for religious instruction, and became the loyal and staunch defenders of the public school as opposed to the Catholic parochial system.[18]

In Massachusetts the same result came about somewhat differently. There the controversy raged around Horace Mann (1796–1859), peerless leader of America's common school revival of this period. Because Mann steadfastly insisted on keeping controversial sectarian religious

---

[17] *Infra,* pp. 533–537.

[18] R. J. Gabel, *Public Funds for Church and Private Schools* (The Catholic University of America, Washington, D.C., 1937), p. 700.

materials out of the public school curriculum, he earned for himself the reputation of being the author of a godless public school system. As a matter of fact, he had no discretion in the matter. The policy was not of his making but had been determined by the Massachusetts Legislature a whole decade before he came into public office. In 1827, after a quarter century and more of bitter quarreling between orthodox and liberal interpreters of Calvinistic doctrine, the Legislature took steps to shield the public schools from this controversy by providing that school committees "shall never direct any schoolbooks to be purchased or used, in any of the schools under their superintendence, which are calculated to favor any particular religious sect or tenet."[19]

Again, this statute did nothing more than apply to public education the solution of the religious issue that had proved so brilliantly successful in the First Amendment to the Federal Constitution. Nevertheless, orthodox Calvinistic minorities were so inflamed as to attack Mann personally for this policy. They attacked not only his views on religious education but his general educational policies as well. Among the latter Mann had favored the introduction of Pestalozzian methods of instruction,[20] which, of course, were predicated on Rousseau's theory of child nature and were therefore anathema to Mann's Calvinistic critics. The same critics, moreover, sought to block the spread of these ideas by opposing one of Mann's favorite projects, the state normal school. But ultimately Mann won at every point.

In answer to the complaint that he was making the schools godless, Mann wrote his chief critic that he was not opposed to teaching religion in the public schools; but, he said, distinguishing his position quite clearly, "the religion of heaven should be taught to children while the creeds of men should be postponed until their minds were sufficiently matured to weigh evidence and arguments."[21] In taking this position, his critics answered, Mann was but enforcing upon the public schools his own brand of religion. In his youth Mann had strongly revolted against a strict Calvinism and in his mature years embraced a Unitarianism in which he was much influenced by the current philosophy of humanitarianism. What, therefore, was this "religion of heaven" but the eighteenth-century optimism that human nature could be redirected by good institutions and that good character could be assured through rational instruction in the moral virtues?

[19] Laws of Massachusetts, Mar. 10, 1827, chap. 143, sec. 7.
[20] For what these were, see *supra,* pp. 207–211.
[21] Quoted in R. B. Culver, *Horace Mann and Religion in the Massachusetts Public Schools* (Yale University Press, New Haven, Conn., 1929), p. 267.

Without pressing this controversy further, suffice it to say that William Torrey Harris, great Hegelian, leading superintendent of schools, and noted United States Commissioner of Education, carried on Mann's tradition during the second half of the nineteenth century.[22] Public school aims became predominantly civic and economic. By constitutional provision most states safeguarded public revenues from being diverted to sectarian religious instruction. The Massachusetts statute of 1827 became a model that many other states followed. Practically all religious instruction, not just sectarian, disappeared from the schools. The reading of the Bible alone remained; even in this case the decisions of state courts differed on whether this could be considered sectarian instruction.

THE SUNDAY SCHOOL MOVEMENT

When it became clear that the very existence of the public school depended on its being and remaining secular, the churches, particularly the Protestant, as already mentioned, turned to the Sunday school as the means for religious and moral instruction. By the time they reached this decision, the Sunday school was already a well-recognized institution. It had had its origin in England in the next to the last decade of the eighteenth century. Robert Raikes (1735–1811), its author, sponsored the idea as a means of combating the illiteracy, irreligion, and poverty that seemed to have joined forces to compass the degeneracy of the lower classes at the time. The education of these classes was particularly in need of attention, for one of the collateral results of the Industrial Revolution had been the disintegration of the apprenticeship system of education on which they had depended. As Raikes originally conceived the school, it primarily had the secular objective of teaching literacy and only secondarily a religious and moral objective. The school met on Sunday—from which fact it took its name—merely as a matter of convenience, for at this time, before child-labor laws had been passed, children were likely to be working in factories on weekdays.

At first there was considerable outcry against the Sunday school for profaning the Sabbath with its sessions in both morning and afternoon. This outcry subsided, however, when the churches early came to take the Sunday school unto themselves. Associations were formed to spread the Sunday school idea, an American Sunday School Union being established in the third decade of the nineteenth century. Before the century was out, an International Sunday School Association had

[22] N. G. McCluskey, *Public Schools and Moral Education* (Columbia University Press, New York, 1958), chaps. 3, 4, 7.

been formed, which in the twentieth century merged into the International Council of Religious Education. At first, under the churches, the Sunday school curriculum had been of the traditional variety, emphasizing the catechism. Before long, however, the Bible came to supplant the catechism in importance. As rote memory had been the method for studying the catechism, so now the memorization of verses became the approved type of Bible study. Apparently, there was no particular plan for what should be memorized, nor was much attempt made to explain the verses.

In the second quarter of the nineteenth century the American Sunday School Union led a movement for a series of selected lessons centering in the Bible. The series proved so successful that there was a rush among denominations for each to have one of its own. Such a variety appeared that they became known as the "Babel series." Order did not appear out of this chaos till shortly after the Civil War, when an International Lesson Committee was formed. This committee brought out what has since come to be known as the "uniform lesson plan." According to this, everyone, young and old, all over the world was to join in studying the appointed lesson for each Sunday in the year. The uniform plan was a great administrative convenience and had no little sentimental value in symbolizing a worldwide united Christianity. Its popularity went virtually unchallenged for the next score of years.

By the conclusion of the century, however, signs of a decline in popularity were in evidence. In a way, it is surprising that these did not appear sooner, for this was the period in which the secular schools were evolving their graded organization. At any rate, the demand grew more and more insistent that a "graded" series of lessons be brought out, one that would make greater concession to the immaturity of childhood. The International Lesson Committee finally brought out such a series early in the twentieth century, though it continued to regard its uniform series as more practical.

So far, Protestant Sunday schools have principally occupied attention. It needs pointing out that Sunday school practices found their way into Judaism and Catholicism as well. In fact, in the last quarter of the nineteenth century the Jews organized a Hebrew Sabbath School Union of their own to promote schools that on the Sabbath taught not only the principles and doctrine of Judaism but also the Jewish language and the Biblical and post-Biblical history of their people.

While the Catholics put great store by religious and moral education in their parochial school system, there were many parishes in the nineteenth century where such a system had not yet been established; there reliance had to be put on Catholic Sunday schools. The Catholic

Sunday school differed markedly on one point from the Protestant one. While the Protestant Sunday school during the nineteenth century had become a Bible school, the Catholic Sunday school remained a school of the catechism. Having a well-worked-out body of authoritative doctrine, the Catholics naturally placed greater emphasis on the verbatim transmission to the child of the intellectual framework of his faith. Indeed, for the very young memorization of the catechism was more important than understanding it, for Catholics held that exact familiarity with the text of the catechism was the basis for all later understanding.

The teachers who taught in Robert Raikes's Sunday school were paid for their efforts. The expense thus involved at first seriously threatened to interfere with the expansion of the good work the Sunday school was doing. Happily, John Wesley managed to solve this problem by appealing for volunteer teachers from his congregation. In solving this problem, however, he created another, that presented by a body of relatively untrained teachers. As time went on, the Sunday school suffered more and more severely under the weight of this second problem. Even Catholic Sunday schools, in spite of Catholic teaching orders upon whom demands were always in excess of supply, suffered from having to rely to a certain extent on untrained lay teachers. In America after the Civil War the cry for better teachers was met by Sunday school leaders resorting to the teacher institute, which Henry Barnard (1811–1900), Horace Mann's collaborator in Connecticut, devised for improving teachers in the secular school system.[23] The Chautauqua movement started out as just such an institute for the training of Sunday school teachers, but its astounding success later led to a broadening of its original purpose. By the next century the training of teachers and directors of religious education had become a regular part of university instruction.

By the opening of the twentieth century, Sunday school educators were agitated by problems that challenged the best-trained teachers. In fact, some of these problems had been clamoring for recognition for some time. A number of people had come to feel that religious and moral education was something more than just study of the Bible or the catechism. They wanted the addition of new materials, particularly from outside the Bible, materials on characters like Girolamo Savonarola and Luther or on movements like the missionary one. Others wanted to study materials that were being created by the new historical methods used in the higher criticism of the Bible. How else, in fact, could they participate effectively in the controversy that was currently raging between science and religion? Furthermore,

[23] For a more detailed account of the teacher institute, see *infra*, pp. 478–479.

up to this time the main aim of Protestant religious and moral education had been, as in the time of Wesley, conversion and the recruitment of church membership. In fact, the main effort of religious education so turned on evangelism and conversion that little or no energy was left for a religious and moral education that would exercise and improve as well as win new Christians. How was provision to be made for such activities? To be sure, the Christian Endeavor Society and the Epworth League provided some outlet for learning by doing, yet even so, a great shortcoming of the Sunday school movement had been its failure to understand the dynamic propensities of child nature. Clearly, to consider any of these problems effectively required a reexamination of the whole theory of religious and moral education.

RESPONSE TO SECULAR PEDAGOGICAL REFORM

As a matter of fact, all during the nineteenth century, while the Sunday school was adhering to its stereotype of religious and moral education, new ideas were fermenting in the minds of such distinguished educational reformers as Pestalozzi, Herbart, and Froebel. One ordinarily associates novel methods of pedagogy[24] with these men; yet it should not be overlooked that all of them had notions, either direct or by implication, about religious and moral education as well, particularly about moral education. For the most part American secular schools were quicker to respond to the pedagogical notions of these men than were the Sunday or church schools. Not infrequently, too, secular schools were first to respond to these reformers' suggestions on moral education. Nothing hindered them, for only religious instruction had been eliminated from public school curricula, while moral, or character, education, as far as this was separable from religion, had been left relatively undisturbed.

In discussing these men perhaps one should begin with the general philosophical reaction to the implications of Rousseau's naturalism in moral education. Much as a great philosopher like the idealist Immanuel Kant (1724–1804) was impressed by naturalism as a pedagogy, he was much more reserved in accepting it as a basis for moral education. The child's nature, that initial point of departure in all Christian religious and moral educational theory, Kant held to be neither good nor bad. Rather did the child become good or moral when his reason lifted him to the concept of duty or law. Natural propensity or desire, Kant thought, was unable to do this both because the end of desire was pleasure and because the feelings aroused by desire were too variable among people to be erected

[24] For a fuller account of their pedagogy, see *supra*, pp. 207–217.

into a universal law. Only reason was able to lay down a universal law that could command obligation without exception.[25]

But reason not only set the aim for Kant; it set the motive as well. The only thing in the world that he counted good without qualification was a will disposed to fulfill the duty commanded by the categorical imperative of universal law. This was the will of pure reason. Therefore, the highest objective of moral education was to follow the categorical imperative for itself alone. Of course, at first the child would begin by learning to obey the maxims or laws of his school, but ultimately he should learn to owe duty to laws as universal as humanity itself. To establish reverence for the moral law, Kant would not punish the child for any breach of it, for to Kant morality was so holy and sublime that it should not be degraded to a level with discipline.[26]

Kant's philosophy had a profound and widespread influence on nineteenth-century thought in Europe and America. On the whole, it reinforced, if it did not introduce, a dualism in moral education. One evidence of this dualism was the emphasis moral education came to place on obedience to abstract duty regardless of the motivation of organic desire. Thus it attached moral value to putting forth effort at one's studies even though they aroused no genuine interest.[27] Another evidence of this dualism was the way it made a distinction between the motive for action and the consequences thereof, between character and conduct. Motive and character came to be regarded as something purely inner and privy to consciousness, while conse-

[25] While the idealism of Georg Wilhelm Friedrich Hegel (1770–1831) differed in important details from Kant's, it agreed with his that moral education could not be left exclusively to nature. Hegel thought natural instinct too inflexible and in need of help from reflective morality taught both through the humanities and through direct instruction in such concepts as right, duty, and justice. Obedience by habituation to an external authority or law was to be the child's first step toward the moral autonomy of self-control. Hegel differed from Kant in that he condoned punishment as a means of showing the child his need to make impulse yield to the superior control of reason. See M. Mackenzie, *Hegel's Educational Thought and Practice* (Swan, Sonnenschein & Co., London, 1909), chap. 12, also pp. 169–170.

[26] E. F. Buchner, *The Educational Theory of Immanuel Kant* (J. B. Lippincott Company, Philadelphia, 1904), pp. 185–188, 210–213, 287. In these pages Kant says relatively little about religious education. But he is confident that, since religion requires theology and theology is too advanced for the child, one should commence moral before religious education. "Can anything be more perverted," he says on p. 233, "than to talk about the other world to children who have hardly begun life in this?"

[27] William Torrey Harris, United States Commissioner of Education at the end of the nineteenth century and a leading philosophical idealist, is a good example of this point of view. See J. S. Roberts, *William T. Harris* (National Education Association, Washington, D.C., 1924), pp. 199–202.

quences occurred outside the mind. Hence the teacher was often minded to discount the consequences of misconduct if by inner disposition the child meant well. Again, dualism evidenced itself in a distinction between moral knowledge and ordinary secular knowledge, the former being of a purer sort. This instruction in the two came to be given at different times of day, if not actually in different schools, as the history of the nineteenth century has just disclosed.

Kant's main influence, however, was on philosophy, not education. It was rather the famous Swiss reformer Johann Heinrich Pestalozzi (1746–1827) who, putting his main weight on education, first worked out a practical pedagogy of naturalism. The secret of his very successful object method of instruction lay in its enlistment of the child's native propensities for action. To acquire knowledge through sense perception of objects was just as easy and delightful as it was spontaneous, for the child did not have to be goaded into learning as the native curiosity of his senses actively craved the indulgence of exercise. Pestalozzi was confident that the same approach must be made in moral education. Moral education must stir the child's emotions. The child would never learn moral dispositions unless he actually felt them. Unfortunately, while Pestalozzi found the time to work out the ABC's, that is, the graded steps, of sense perception, he never did the same for emotions.

What Pestalozzi left undone, Johann Friedrich Herbart (1776–1841), Kant's successor at the University of Königsberg, managed to accomplish, but in a way different from what Pestalozzi probably would have chosen. According to Herbart's educational psychology the drive of will and emotion was a by-product of the apperception of ideas.[28] The idea was father to the act. Knowledge meant genuine power. Consequently, there could be no schism between knowledge and conduct or between moral and intellectual knowledge. For Herbart, not unlike Socrates, moral education was principally a matter of making the right moral "presentations" to the mind of the child. And, showing his obligation to the neohumanists of his day, he greatly emphasized the inclusion of literature and history in the curriculum as main sources from which to present moral ideas. Until the child had time to build up an effective apperceptive mass of moral ideas, Herbart thought he should be under the control of adults. This control, however, was to be gradually relaxed, for otherwise it would lead to moral tyranny rather than moral autonomy and freedom.[29]

[28] For a fuller account of this psychology, see *supra*, pp. 145–148.

[29] But Herbart would have none of Kant's transcendental freedom, for that would render uncertain the effect of moral education on the conduct of the child. It is further noteworthy that he rested the sanction for morals not so

The simplicity of Herbart's theory of moral education, as implemented by his five steps and his culture epochs,[30] had a wide appeal in both secular and church schools. This is not surprising, for Herbartian doctrine fitted into their existing pattern of lesson plans with a minimum disturbance of fundamental preconceptions. Without challenging the evangelistic theory of education as bringing saving truth to children in their otherwise lost condition, Herbart merely expedited the process of apperceiving the revealed truth. The only harm he did, if any, was to lull leaders into a false sense that the evangel was reaching its mark when it was intellectually comprehended by the child. After all, as Aristotle and St. Paul long ago pointed out, the ideal of making men good by making them intelligent was an oversimplification of the problem. Moreover, not only did modern psychology soon explode Herbart's ideomotor theory of behavior, but the tides of modern social forces often proved so powerful as to render a man impotent in spite of his knowledge of goodness.

Friedrich Wilhelm August Froebel (1782–1852), originator of the kindergarten, made a more religious approach to the problem of moral education. At the very outset, however, he parted company with conventional Christianity by refusing even to suspect child nature of evil inclinations. Nature was God's handiwork, and therefore to accuse it of evil was, to Froebel, blasphemous. Quite to the contrary, Froebel took the view that there was a spark of divinity in human nature which struggled to achieve a unity with the divine. The divine, however, was not so much supermundane as constantly revealed in the development of man and nature toward ultimate unity. Froebel made extensive use of anything in the child's environment that he thought symbolically suggested this unity to the child. The churches, from time immemorial addicted to symbolism, when they finally came to employ Froebelian ideas, found his educational use of symbolism peculiarly congenial.

The first germ of the child's religious and moral feeling Froebel looked for in the common unity, or community, of the family circle. Learning to be good there was a matter not of learning dogmas but of having an opportunity to be self-active, to grow according to the laws of nature into unity with humanity and ultimately with God himself. Evil Froebel treated not as something to be extirpated

---

much in religion as, like the Greeks, in an aesthetic sensibility of the child. He expected the child to recognize the inappropriateness of wrong just as he would the inappropriateness of a counterpoint in music that produced dissonance rather than harmony. See J. F. Herbart, *Aesthetic Revelation of the World as the Chief Work of Education* (George Routledge & Sons, Ltd., London, 1924).

[30] For further accounts of these devices, see *supra*, pp. 213, 294–297.

by punishment but as a tendency to activity that could be atrophied by having no opportunity to exercise itself. By nourishing good habits with praise, he hoped they would grow so lustily as to choke out the weeds of bad ones.

The first outstanding American educator to respond to these European influences was Colonel Francis W. Parker (1831–1902). He accepted Herbart's notion of presenting the best moral ideas to be found in history and literature but insisted on adding science as an additional source of moral knowledge. For moral dynamics, however, he went to Pestalozzi and especially to Froebel. From the latter he accepted the central position of the self-active nature of the child. The design of his nature having predominantly good tendencies,[31] moral education consisted in the working out of these tendencies through the child's self-effort. To turn this about and restate it, self-effort in the direction of the laws of growth is the essence of moral education.

If anything, Parker made Froebel's social emphasis in moral education even more explicit. *"The predominant condition, then, for moral training is community life, the society of the school,"* he said in his *Talks on Pedagogics.* "Here measures and gauges of history are acquired by actual experience; here civics is essentially practiced; the roots of afterlife, the springs of action, are all here. Home is the center; the church makes home better; but the common school is the place where the lessons gained in both may be essentially practiced. Here social classes learn to respect each other; the children of the rich and the poor, the intelligent and the ignorant, are fused and blended by mutual action and mutual love. The common schools present a perfect means of moral training; order, work, and play all tending to the cultivating of true manhood."[32]

From such broad premises it followed that *all* education was moral. Indeed, Parker was willing to go even further and state that methods of the secular school not adapted to the laws of child growth were positively immoral! To be specific, he indicted schools for immoral practices when they employed marks and prizes in such a way as to cultivate selfishness in the pupil; when they invoked corporal punishment, which resulted in degrading the spirit; when too great insistence on verbatim memorization work deprived the child of an

[31] Parker conceded there might be some evil in heredity. The Englishman Herbert Spencer (1820–1903) regarded any such evil tendency as akin to similar early tendencies in the race. See H. Spencer, *Education: Intellectual, Moral, and Physical* (J. M. Dent & Sons, Ltd., Publishers, London, n.d.), pp. 108–109.

[32] F. W. Parker, *Talks on Pedagogics* (The John Day Company, Inc., New York, 1937), pp. 258–259.

opportunity to be spontaneously original; and when history was falsely taught from the bias of religious creed, political partisanship, or national interest.[33]

What Parker took occasion to suggest in outline John Dewey (1859–1952), his friend, developed in considerable detail. Although Dewey found much in Froebel and Parker on which he could build, he also felt it necessary to clear the ground of Kantian obstructions before he could make his own additions. His chief objection to Kantian moral education was its dualism between impulse and reason. While Dewey was willing to go a long way with Kant in rejecting pleasurable impulse as a moral end, he was far from rejecting it as a means or motivation for conduct. The Kantian motivation of sheer intellectual effort he thought lacking in genuine motor power, such as only organic impulse and emotion can provide. Furthermore, it led to inconsistency and sentimentality. Sheer intellectual effort in attention to duty might enable a child externally to assume the formal indications of the correct moral attitude, but internally the attitude might be so greatly opposed to the child's real feelings that the moral result would be to teach him not a sense of duty but rather one of pretense and hypocrisy. Or, if one made the essence of morality inner motive— meaning well—rather than toeing the mark for the sake of appearances, then school morality ran the risk of becoming sentimental and even arbitrary.

As for the separation between moral and secular knowledge to which the initial Kantian dualism between reason and impulse led, Dewey was especially severe in criticism. "This separation, if valid," he trenchantly wrote, "is of especial significance for education. Moral education in school is practically hopeless when we set up the development of character as a supreme end, and at the same time treat the acquiring of knowledge and the development of understanding, which of necessity occupy the chief part of schooltime, as having nothing to do with character. On such a basis, moral education is inevitably reduced to some kind of catechetical instruction, or lessons about morals. Lessons 'about morals' signify as a matter of course lessons in what other people think about virtues and duties. . . . As a matter of fact, direct instruction in morals has been effective only in social groups where it was a part of the authoritative control of the many by the few. Not the teaching as such but the reinforcement of it by the whole regime of which it was an incident made it effective. To attempt to get similar results from lessons about morals in a democratic society is to rely upon sentimental magic."[34]

[33] *Ibid.,* pp. 271–272.

[34] J. Dewey, *Democracy and Education* (The Macmillan Company, New York, 1916), p. 411.

Abandoning any dualism in his own constructive thinking on moral education, Dewey stated his specifications very succinctly. "In truth, the problem of moral education in the schools is one with the problem of securing knowledge—the knowledge connected with the system of impulses and habits. For the use to which any known fact is put depends upon its connections. . . . What is learned and employed in an occupation having an aim and involving cooperation with others is moral knowledge, whether consciously so regarded or not. For it builds up a social interest and confers the intelligence needed to make that interest effective in practice. Just because the studies of the curriculum represent standard factors in social life, they are organs of initiation into social values. As mere school studies, their acquisition has only a technical worth. Acquired under conditions where their social significance is realized, they feed moral interest and develop moral insight."[35]

In this statement one will do well to note the continuity of Dewey's thinking with that of Froebel and Parker. Dewey, too, attached central importance to the spontaneous instincts and impulses of children. These, he furthermore agreed, must have an opportunity to exert themselves in a social situation. But in addition, he insisted, there must be opportunity for intelligence to exercise judgment, to evaluate work done, to discriminate and choose between the relative values of competing impulses. The role he thus assigned intelligence did not stand in sublime isolation. Rather, true to his pragmatism,[36] it operated as a biological instrument for the adaptation of impulse. Of course, Dewey expected that the directing of impulse would involve some constraint or inhibition of its spontaneity. Yet he saw no moral value in making inhibition a moral end in itself. Discipline, constraint, if it had any positive moral value, came from holding one's powers in line to concentrate on some job in hand rather than letting them discharge in random or irrelevant directions.

While Parker took great pride in the moral possibilities of the nonsectarian public school, Dewey professed to see in it even religious opportunities as well. "Our schools," he hopefully wrote, "in bringing together those of different nationalities, languages, traditions, and creeds, in assimilating them together upon the basis of what is common and public in endeavor and achievement, are performing an infinitely significant religious work. They are promoting the social unity out of which in the end genuine religious unity must grow."[37] Indeed,

---

[35] *Ibid.*, pp. 413–414. *Cf.* J. L. Childs, *Education and Morals* (Appleton-Century-Crofts, Inc., New York, 1950).

[36] For a fuller account, see *supra,* pp. 130–134.

[37] J. Dewey, "Religion and Our Schools," *Hibbert Journal,* 6:806–807, July, 1908.

so enamored was Dewey with the role of the school in social progress that he looked upon the teacher not only as a principal agent of this progress but "in this capacity as the prophet of the true God and the usherer in of the true kingdom of God."[38]

THE "RELIGIOUS-EDUCATION" MOVEMENT

At the opening of the twentieth century one might say that two theories of moral education were developing side by side, one in the Sunday school and the other in the secular school. In the former the curriculum of Christian faith and practice was considered as already known or revealed in the Bible. Christian nurture occurred through evangelism which brought the good tidings of religious and moral truths to the child and hopefully secured his acceptance and application of them. Church pedagogy, if not exclusively interested, was at least more deeply interested in God's approach to man through grace than it was in man's approach to God through education. It still looked on man more as a fallen angel than as a rising primate. In the latter, the secular school, the approach to moral character was educational rather than evangelical. There moral education took its point of departure in the ongoing experience of the child in a social situation. Moral knowledge was the result of choosing between alternate ends of conduct and evaluating them in the light of their outcomes or consequences.[39]

A mild crisis was developing. In 1903 a notable number of religious educators, public school men, and laymen—Catholic, Jewish, and Protestant—gathered together and formed the Religious Education Association.[40] Its constitution declared the object of this association to be "To inspire the educational forces of our country with the religious ideal, to inspire the religious forces of our country with the educational ideal, and to keep before the public mind the ideal of religious education, and the sense of its need and value."[41] This was an important statement, for, as one can see, it clearly made an educational rather than an evangelical approach to religious instruction.

What were the forces that led to this new emphasis? There were a number. To begin, this was a period of general dissatisfaction with

[38] J. Dewey, *My Pedagogic Creed* (Progressive Education Association, Washington, D.C., 1929), p. 17.

[39] Committee on the War and the Religious Outlook, *op. cit.,* p. 40.

[40] O. L. Davis, "A History of the Religious Education Association," *Religious Education,* 44:41–54, January, February, 1949.

[41] Quoted in A. A. Brown, *A History of Religious Education in Recent Times* (Abington-Cokesbury Press, New York, 1923), pp. 177–178.

and protest against existing conditions. Men were discontented with political and economic circumstances as well as with educational ones. Social reform was in the air, as witness the presidential campaigns from 1896 to 1912. Educational reform was not far behind. Experimental schools, which in the second decade of the century were to form the Progressive Education Association, were starting.[42] The scientific study of education through the new science of psychology was making marked headway in capturing the imagination of secular educators.[43]

Similar stirrings were not unnoticed in the churches. A scientific psychology of religion was coming into being. The higher criticism of the Bible in the light of modern historical study was demanding a reexamination of popular beliefs. Caught in the undertow of current political and economic reform, religion came to take greater interest in ethical than in metaphysical problems. There was more preaching of the social gospel. Spurred by new confidence in what man could do with his institutions by taking thought, numerous associations sprang up for the purpose of promoting moral education. Already toward the end of the nineteenth century Felix Adler (1851–1933) had formed the Society for Ethical Culture, and five years after the formation of the Religious Education Association the first International Moral Education Congress met in London.[44]

This new educational approach, indeed, had not been without its prophet in the evangelical nineteenth century. This prophet was the clergyman Horace Bushnell (1802–1876), a contemporary of Mann's and Barnard's. Just before the mid-point of the century Bushnell published a brochure, *Discourses on Christian Nurture.*[45] In this he took exception to the conventional evangelical view that the child, owing to the taint of original sin, must grow up in enmity to God till such time as he is mature enough to repent the evil of his ways and become converted to the Christian way of life. Quite to the contrary, he affirmed that the proper notion of Christian nurture is that the child should grow up with never a thought that he was going to become anything but a Christian. Becoming a Christian, in other words, could be a gradual process of nurture through education as well as the more abrupt, catastrophic one of revivalistic conversion.

[42] For a more extended account of this development, see *infra,* pp. 386–392.

[43] For a fuller account of this development, see *supra,* pp. 151–166.

[44] For a collection of the papers read on this occasion, see M. E. Sadler, *Moral Instruction and Training in the Schools* (Longmans Green & Co., Ltd., London, 1908).

[45] H. Bushnell, *Discourses on Christian Nurture* (Massachusetts Sabbath School Society, Boston, 1847).

Prophet of an educational approach though he was, Bushnell grasped the modern conception of education only very dimly. In fact, he flatly rejected the notion of education as developmental put forward by Froebel, his contemporary, whose work he probably did not even know at the time. Nothing was more unreasonable, he held, than the assumption that child nature was radically good and that therefore the work of Christian education had only to educe this good, give it an opportunity to express itself. To him growth in Christian virtue was no vegetative process but something still to be won through a struggle with and a result from evil. Yet what Bushnell did see clearly was that the church's theory of nurture had been suited to adults and stood in need of restatement for children.

The process of restating Christian nurture in more educational terms took several directions in the twentieth century. One was to incorporate into religious education the new pedagogical point of view of such secular educational innovators as Froebel, Parker, and Dewey. As Dewey had had an experimental school at the University of Chicago, so now an experimental Sunday school was opened at the Union Theological Seminary in New York. The man who more than any other tried to persuade the church schools to a new point of view was George Albert Coe (1862–1951), one of the foremost spirits in the Religious Education Association. In 1917, just a year after Dewey had brought out his famous *Democracy and Education,* Coe published his *Social Theory of Religious Education.*[46] This book set the progressive pattern for religious education that Dewey's ultimately did for progressive secular education.

As its title implies, Coe's book kept company with Froebel, Parker, and Dewey in making the central feature of religious education the growing experience of the child in a social situation. It proposed to awaken religious experience in children by having them live with people who had had and were having vital Christian religious experiences. It recommended that the term "religious instruction" be emptied of its traditional meaning of telling the child what to believe. Instead, it should be a matter of encouraging the child to develop his own religious experience by participating in a social situation in which people were at grips with problems the solution of which was bound to reveal religious values. This did not mean neglect of Biblical materials, whose transmission hitherto had been the core of the Sunday school program. Rather, it meant using the Bible as a constant source book for the enrichment and guidance of the ongoing and growing religious experience of the child. Consequently, there would be no fixed order of presentation of materials as in either the uniform or

[46] G. A. Coe, *A Social Theory of Religious Education* (Charles Scribner's Sons, New York, 1917).

graded lesson series. Instead, the inevitable social problems incident to changing social situations would furnish the best suggestion for the selection and order of presentation of Biblical materials.

By the end of the First World War the religious-education movement, inaugurated at the beginning of the century, had become a force with which to reckon. Its momentum was no little augmented by a strong contemporary movement to overhaul the secular curriculum of the public schools from top to bottom.[47] New techniques for curriculum revision, to say nothing of a rigorous application of functionalism, produced such striking results there that Sunday school leaders could hardly remain unaffected. The International Lesson Committee, whose uniform lesson series still ruled a wide favorite over the graded one, was not long in feeling the impulse to reexamine its procedures.

Two years after the end of the war the committee appointed a commission of seven, composed of both religious and secular curriculum experts, to study the situation. In two more years their report was ready. It recommended three kinds of lesson plans, a continuation of the uniform and graded series for those who still wished them and a new plan to be known as the "International Curriculum of Religious Education." This last followed the theory laid down by Coe. Taking its point of departure in the experience of the child in an ongoing social situation, it made much of the project method of organizing the curriculum.[48] Problems met in actual social experience became the vehicle for teaching religious values. Much was made of capturing religious values not by the frontal assault of "direct" assignment but by the flank attack of learning them "incidentally" in a social situation. Consequently, teachers were taught to be on the lookout for minor habits and attitudes formed as a by-product to learning major ideals. Churches, to provide physical plants adapted to the demands of this new program of religious education, built gymnasiums, recreation halls, and clubrooms.

The Catholics, though slow to respond to such a novel program, were not unaffected by notions of pedagogical reform that had been in the air for some time. Clinging throughout to the catechism as the central feature of their religious and moral instruction, they were always more or less sensitive to the danger that catechetical instruction might become aridly intellectual and formal. To prevent this happening, one group of German Catholics about the beginning of the twentieth century sought to base catechetical instruction on new psychological principles. For long, catechetical instruction had been dogmatic, following the threefold order of *propositio, explicatio,* and

---

[47] For a fuller account of this curriculum development, see *supra,* chap. 10.

[48] For a fuller account of the project, see *supra,* pp. 233–234.

applicatio. Now a new threefold method of "presentation," "explanation," and "application" was put forward. The current interest in psychology was most evident in the first step. The shift there was from commencing the lesson with an abstract statement in the catechism to starting it with reference to an experience of the child. This experience might arise from a concrete object like a sacred relic perceived by his senses or a dramatic story made vivid to his imagination. In the second step the catechist was to derive the catechetical principle implicit in the child's experience and explain it by correlating it with his previous doctrinal knowledge. The third step was an appeal to will to ensure that the fruits of the lesson would issue in conduct.

While the foregoing obviously reflects Herbartian educational thought, another innovation in catechetical instruction stemmed from Maria Montessori (1870–1952), the noted Italian educator. Montessori, too, was much impressed by the new psychological approach to education and laid great stress on the native proclivities of the child. Consequently, in catechetical instruction she proposed postponing temporarily the use of materials to be memorized. Instead, she preferred to let the child learn religion in a child's way, that is, by engaging in religious activities and having these explained in terms of the catechism as occasion subsequently arose. This attempt to build the supernatural edifice of truth and character on a more secure foundation in the natural order was a departure from traditional Catholic practices. Some Catholics feared it leaned too far in the direction of pedagogical naturalism; others thought that Catholic catechetical instruction had too long minimized the importance of the natural in intellectual and moral instruction.[49]

CHARACTER EDUCATION

Another direction taken by the restatement of Christian nurture in the twentieth century was that of scientific investigation. Of most outstanding significance here was the Character Education Inquiry. For long various methods had been proposed for the formation of character, but there was no scientific evidence to determine which had value and which had not. Upon the initiative of the Religious

[49] In America Fr. T. E. Shields (1862–1921) of Catholic University was among the first to introduce modern methods of catechetical instruction. "Love rather than fear, self-activity rather than regimentation, virtue rather than mere knowledge, development rather than cramming"—these were some of the characteristics of Fr. Shields,s methods. See G. Johnson, "Character Education in the Catholic Church," *Religious Education*, 24:56–57, January, 1929. More recently Fr. Alexander Schorsch of De Paul University has been noted for an interesting application of the "unit" method to religious and moral instruction.

Education Association backed by financial assistance from the Institute for Social and Religious Research, a very carefully planned inquiry was launched to throw light on this problem. After elaborate investigation over a period of years, the inquiry made its report just as the clouds of depression were darkening the land.[50]

It concluded that conventional ways of teaching character were on the whole ineffective. A principal cause of this ineffectiveness lay in the frequent contradiction between the abstract precept taught and the practical demands of the individual situation to which it was taught as applicable. Such circumstances not only made the teaching of consistent moral character difficult but often resulted in recommending inconsistency as the price of inward peace of mind. There was no use, moreover, in expecting many children to resolve this tension in favor of abstract ideals unless they had the force of public opinion behind them. In its own best judgment the inquiry took the view that "the building of a functioning ideal for society which may serve at once as a principle of unified or consistent response and as a principle of satisfactory social adjustment . . . must, therefore, be derived from the inherent nature of social life and growth as experienced by the child himself."[51] The thinking of Dewey and Coe is very obvious in this conclusion.

One interesting outgrowth of the wide discussion and investigation of character education was the rejection or at least serious qualification of the ancient notion of Aristotle that character was an aggregate of traits or good habits.[52] Coe early took occasion to point out that training in character or virtue was something more than a training in individual virtues. Thus, individual virtues such as bravery, fidelity, and honesty apply as well among a band of robbers as among a group of law-abiding citizens.[53] Hence character education, to be successful, must also train the child to organize his habits or virtues according to some fundamental or inclusive principle of consistency. Training of this sort involved an integration of the whole child around purposeful activity in a democratic social situation.[54]

The great interest that the character-education movement stirred up was most timely. The third decade of the twentieth century, being

---

[50] Character Education Inquiry, *Studies in the Nature of Character* (3 vols., The Macmillan Company, New York, 1930).

[51] *Ibid.*, vol. 3, p. 378.

[52] For a philosophical account of this theory, see *supra*, p. 106.

[53] G. A. Coe, "Virtue and the Virtues," *Religious Education*, 6:485–492, January, 1912. For a further criticism of this theory, see H. Hartshorne, *Character in Human Relations* (Charles Scribner's Sons, New York, 1933), chaps. 9–12; *Character Education*, Tenth Yearbook (National Education Association, Department of Superintendence, Washington, D.C., 1932), pp. 43–50.

[54] Hartshorne, *op. cit.*, chap. 13.

a postwar decade, witnessed a general moral reaction from the high idealism of the war period. In part, this reaction was a moral letdown, but in part also it represented a considerable change in moral customs that by many was mistaken for a moral letdown. Unrivaled economic prosperity in this decade followed by unrivaled economic depression in the next added further to the strain of keeping the nation's moral chin up. As a result a number of large-scale character-education programs such as the Iowa Plan, the Junior Red Cross, and the Knighthood of Youth were put in operation.[55]

The autonomy characteristic of trends in moral and character education in the twentieth century was distinctly a product of nineteenth-century liberalism. Between the two world wars, but especially in the thirties, doubt that liberalism could adequately meet the exceedingly severe political and economic strains of the day arose in the minds of many in both Europe and the United States. Totalitarian and collectivistic regimes arose to challenge seriously liberal capitalistic ones. The way in which the two rivals managed moral education is worth noting. On the one hand, the totalitarian and collectivistic regimes eliminated or suppressed every autonomous element in moral education which could weaken or interfere with the smooth running of the economic and political machine. Liberal capitalistic regimes, on the other hand, still permitted moral autonomy but prevented the strife of religious and moral systems from disrupting public endeavors by excluding them from the public school, which thereby of necessity became quite secularized.[56]

THEOLOGICAL REACTION

Praiseworthy as the new directions in moral and character education had proved, there were many who thought they suffered the fatal defect of neglecting religious and theological content. Early to sound this warning was Pius XI in his widely read encyclical *The Christian Education of Youth,* promulgated in 1929. In it he looked with dismay on the endeavor to do experimental research in the area of moral education. For him this subordinated the supernatural to the natural order. To draw conclusions about moral education from the latter when it properly concerned the former, therefore, was not only vain, false, and irreverent but positively dangerous. Indeed, generally speaking, the Pope condemned the reigning pedagogic naturalism. Not unexpectedly, therefore, he said, "Every method of education founded, wholly or in part, on the denial or

[55] *Ibid.,* chaps. 5–6.
[56] *Cf.* C. Dawson, *The Crisis in Western Education* (Sheed & Ward, Inc., New York, 1961), pp. 195–197.

forgetfulness of original sin and of grace, and relying on the sole powers of human nature is unsound."[57]

Many Protestants, too, were not far behind in expressing a want of confidence in what the religious-education movement had been able to accomplish. Among their misgivings was its lessened educational emphasis on the Bible and on the person of Jesus. Christology was often by-passed by the introduction of extra-Biblical materials which were sometimes regarded as important as Biblical materials themselves. Again there was misgiving that the religious-education movement took an entirely too optimistic view of human nature, as witness the belief of one notable investigator that, "Religious education can accomplish nearly anything it wants to do with human nature, if only it will gain an accurate knowledge of the laws of mental life, and have the grace to observe them."[58]

To the evangelical conservative such a claim amounted to unwarranted pride and conceit. In this judgment he seemed to be confirmed by the events of the day. The inhumanities practiced by the totalitarian regimes of Russia, Italy, and Germany caused many to forgo trust in man's native goodness or in his ability to work out his salvation. Another event, commencing about the fourth decade of the century, was the accentuated return to theology led by Karl Barth and Emil Brunner. Sin was now seen not just as a psychological or sociological phenomenon but as a disjointedness between man and God.[59] Consequently many regarded it as a snare and a delusion to expect man to lift himself out of the human predicament by his educational bootstraps.[60] Siding rather with St. Paul, the theologians claimed, "By grace are ye saved through faith: and that not of yourselves: it is the gift of God."[61]

After the Second World War a concerted effort was made to restore religious instruction to the curriculum of the public schools if this could be done without violating the century-old tradition of the separation of church and state. The principal vehicle by which this end was sought was the device of "released time." This plan called for the release of a certain portion of the school week so that children could receive religious instruction at churches or synagogues of their choice or religious personnel from these institutions could come to

[57] Pius XI, "The Christian Education of Youth," *Catholic Educational Review,* 28:148–162, March, 1930.

[58] E. D. Starbuck, *Religious Education,* 18:72–77, February, 1923.

[59] J. D. Butler, *Religious Education* (Harper & Row, Publishers, Incorporated, New York, 1962), pp. 115–117.

[60] H. S. Smith, *Faith and Nurture* (Charles Scribner's Sons, New York, 1941), pp. 131, 201–202.

[61] *Ephesians* 2:8.

the public school and offer instruction to members of their respective flocks.

Almost immediately this practice was brought under the scrutiny of the United States Supreme Court, which was asked to rule whether the practice infringed the First Amendment of the Constitution. The Court held that it did when the instruction was given on public school premises[62] but not when children were dismissed from public school to be instructed at churches and synagogues of their parents' choice.[63] The reasoning behind this decision took note of the fact that the First Amendment is double-barreled. It guarantees freedom of religious worship *and* enjoins the establishment of religion. Released time made no infringement of religious freedom because children could be excused from it, but it did run counter to the injunction against establishment when the time released was spent on public school premises. Here the public funds spent on the maintenance of public school buildings where religious instruction was in progress amounted to an establishment of religion.

The excitement which the Supreme Court stirred over its rulings on released time had hardly subsided when the public was rocked by another ruling on the First Amendment, this time on offering prayer in public schools. In New York the State Board of Regents had composed a prayer for the public schools so broad it was thought unexceptional to any sect. Nonetheless exception was taken and carried to the highest court of the land. There a divided Court struck down this public prayer and on the same grounds as released time. While the "regents' prayer" did not offend religious liberty, since students could be excused from participation in it, it did fall within the clause banning an establishment of religion, since the prayer was formulated by an agency backed by the panoply of governmental power.[64] Many members of the public were shocked, but those who were had forgotten the centuries-long history of the threat government has posed to religion in prescribing prayers, a history which Justice Hugo L. Black pointedly recalled in his decision.

These decisions revealed a sharp rift in the ranks of the supporters of public schools. While in the nineteenth century Protestants had almost solidly backed the exclusion of religion from the public schools, in the twentieth century they were no longer of a single mind. Consequently many friends of the public schools were not a little alarmed by the efforts of the supporters of released time and governmentally sanctioned prayers to whittle away the secular basis of the public schools. The wavering state of public opinion is shown by the claim

[62] *Illinois ex rel. McCollum v. Board of Education,* 333 U.S. 203 (1948).
[63] *Zorach v. Clauson,* 343 U.S. 306 (1952).
[64] *Engle v. Vitale,* 370 U.S. 421 (1961).

of some that the "wall of separation between church and state," which Thomas Jefferson and James Madison after him had advocated,[65] had never been complete or unsurmountable[66] and by the counterclaim of others that if it had not been, it was so intended.[67] Still others stanchly maintained that even with a "wall" the secular public schools were far from neglecting moral and spiritual values.[68]

[65] R. F. Butts, *The American Tradition in Religion and Education* (Beacon Press, Boston, 1950), p. 92. See also R. M. Healey, *Jefferson on Religion in Public Education* (Yale University Press, New Haven, Conn., 1962).

[66] W. K. Dunn, *What Happened to Religious Education? The Decline of Religious Teaching in the Public School 1776–1861* (The Johns Hopkins Press, Baltimore, 1959).

[67] R. F. Butts, *loc. cit.*

[68] John Dewey Society, *The Public School and Spiritual Values,* Seventh Yearbook (Harper & Row, Publishers, Incorporated, New York, 1944). See also *Moral and Spiritual Values in the Public Schools* (National Education Association, Educational Policies Commission, Washington, D.C., 1951).

12 Formal and Informal Education

Every now and then educators have to stop to remind themselves that there is much more to education than what takes place within the four walls of the school. They have to remind themselves that the child is getting an education from his experiences out of school as well as from those within—indeed, that sometimes his out-of-school education is more significant for his future development than his in-school education. Persistent and recurrent questions arise from this situation. What, for instance, has been the relative effectiveness of formal and informal education? How did the formal school come into existence? What social function did it evolve to serve? Again, what have been the vicissitudes of the family as an immemorial preschool educational agency? And what has been the success of the postschool education of adults?

THE TRANSITION FROM INFORMAL EDUCATION TO FORMAL SCHOOLING

The history of education has been principally the record of formal processes of education, particularly the formal processes resting on symbols of language and number. Indeed it has been chiefly these processes of which there is any written historical record. What was education like before this record began? If the primitive cultures which survive today are any index of prehistoric cultures, early education in that far-distant time must have been largely informal. As such it was probably little differentiated from the daily activities of the adult generation. It was something that occurred at odd moments during these activities and was incidental to them. The young learned such activities as hunting, making artifacts, and worshiping local divinities by participating directly and informally in these activities along with older and more experienced people. Even the play of children was in large measure an imitation of adult activities, their toys diminutive models of the implements of their parents.

But even as early (or late) as the culture of primitive society, education was losing its informality. This decrease in informality came about through the primitive initiation ceremony. It is common to stress this ceremony as a milestone in the life of the young. Occurring about the period of adolescence, the ceremony marked the transition from childhood with its immaturity and irresponsibility to adulthood with its privileges and duties. As a matter of fact, however, initiation was more than a ceremony to mark the passing of a milestone. It was, in addition, a period of intensified education. Often it lasted several days or even weeks, during which the candidate for adulthood was both instructed and tested. He was instructed in the special secrets and lore of his tribe and tested in his ability to endure pain, hunger, and fear. If he survived this ordeal, the event was celebrated with feasting and dancing.

In some cultures initiation rites continued long after the appearance of schools and their more formal kind of instruction. A number of factors seem to have conspired to bring formal schools into existence. One of the earliest appeared with the increase of the cultural heritage. As this heritage accumulated, it became so extensive that there was no longer time to transmit it informally. There was even danger that parts of it might become lost or forgotten. As a result, a special institution, the school, where such parts of the culture might be perpetuated, was gradually evolved. As thus evolved, the school was not directly concerned with life. Rather was it, as the sociologists have described it, a residual institution. Like a residuary legatee, it caught up and perpetuated the odds and ends of the social culture that no longer were transmitted directly through daily life experiences.

Even more significant in broadening the gap between life and education and necessitating the school was the increase in the complexity of the cultural heritage. The culture transmitted at the time of initiation was never so intricate that the youth could not understand it by direct and immediate participation in the adult activities prescribed. At a later time, however, the culture became so much more complex and difficult that an increasing number of adult activities lay beyond their comprehension. Youth's level of meanings was distinctly below that of the mature members of his group. Educational experiences had to be arranged in stages, therefore, like a system of locks in a canal, to lift the youth to a level where they could participate in adult activities with the same meanings that adults attached to them. In other words, the intricacies of culture had to be simplified for them into a series of graduated steps. But each of these steps placed education that much further away from the life activities for which they were preparatory. Although educational experiences were still selected and pointed toward life, obviously education had progressed far from the incidental informality of life toward the conscious formality of school.

Probably no single item of the complexity of culture made school more necessary than did the reduction of the social culture to written form. When this occurred in very ancient times, the youth had first to learn the symbols of a written language, to say nothing of its grammar, before he could partake of the adult culture. Naturally, this required a preparatory state, a stage apart from life itself. Moreover, it required that some adults make an adult activity of instructing youth in reading and writing and later on in the mysteries locked in the recorded culture itself. Thus the complexity imposed on the social culture by writing led not only to a formal school but to a group of formal or professional teachers as well.

Under the conditions of informal education, adults became *ad hoc* teachers as occasion might demand. Parents in their daily occupations continually stepped in and out of the role of teacher. In so advanced a culture as that of the Spartans every adult was responsible for the instruction of the young, regardless of blood relation. But as culture became more complex and especially as this complexity was due in part to recording the culture in written symbols, a division of labor gradually occurred in society so that some adults made it their special business to be teachers of the young. Naturally, they specialized in teaching the recorded culture of the past; but as this changed relatively slowly, teachers tended to get out of touch with active life, the culture of the present, which was constantly being reshaped on the anvil of daily experience. Thus again formal education became differentiated from informal, and school became differentiated from life.

It would be a mistake to think that the evolution of a formal school with a curriculum largely of written materials and later with a staff of professional teachers entirely supplanted the earlier process of informal education. As a matter of fact, informal education paralleled formal schooling right down through the ages into modern times. In quantity, if not in quality, it predominated in this long period. A boy developed into a hunter or fisher, a farmer or merchant, an artisan or priest by what he learned on the job. From earliest times right down to and beyond the period of the guilds of the Middle Ages, a more or less formal sort of apprenticeship education existed. In fact, it was the only kind of education that the great mass of mankind ever knew. Until the nineteenth and twentieth centuries only a very small percentage of the population had either need or inclination for the formal literary education of the schools. Even in the past century, with the coming of compulsory schooling for all, shrewd educators did not forget that children spent a greater number of hours out of school than in and that the informal education of those hours was often more effective than the formal education of schooling.

RELATIVE VALUE OF FORMAL AND INFORMAL EDUCATION

The question whether formal or informal education is superior has long been a favorite topic of debate among educational theorists. The Greeks, for instance, raised the question whether one could formally teach virtue—in their estimation the highest qualification of a citizen. In the old Greek education the young had learned virtue incidentally in the discharge of their duties as citizens. The norm of virtue, which they tried to emulate, lay embodied in the lives of great men past and present. In later Greek education a group of teachers known as "Sophists" claimed to teach virtue not so much by imitation as by theoretical discussion of it as an idea or ideal.

Naturally, these two views of education clashed. The advantage that lay with the older, more informal education was that virtue was ingrained or habituated in and through conduct. The advantage that lay with the Sophists, the "progressives" of their day, was that they were able to reconstruct the ideal or norm of virtue to meet the new and changing demands of their time. In a formal school, teachers could abstract the idea of virtue from the concrete context of its practice. In the abstract form of ideal they could be critical of it and reshape it in the light of criticism. The limitation of the old informal education was that it suffered from the conservatism of routine, from the inhospitality of habit to innovation. The limitation of the new formal education was that it was too intellectual. It lacked the involvement and commitment to be found in the informal education of life.

If the Greeks doubted that a satisfactory education could be obtained apart from life, Roger Ascham (1515–1568), the great English educator of the sixteenth century, seriously doubted that a good education could be had apart from school. He took little stock in the adage that experience is the best teacher. Rather he contended that "Learning teacheth more in one year than experience in twenty; and learning teacheth safely when experience maketh more miserable than wise."[1] This statement will indicate how far the formal conception of education had gained in prestige in the twenty centuries intervening between the golden age of Greece and the sixteenth century.

Yet it is statements such as this which mark the crest of the historical movement from life to informal education and from informal education to formal schooling. In fact, in the very act of teaching "safely" the crest of the wave of formal education overarched itself and came tumbling down. Formal education had been safe because it was identified with the written culture where were recorded the tried and true experience of the social group. But the experience was always past experience. Formal education in books was concerned particularly with the past. The greater the book, the longer the past seemed to dominate men's minds and the more the social culture represented by contemporary living was put at a discount. Because of this, one might say that the social culture recorded in books tended to be more inelastic than that which was grounded in the habits of daily living. Habits may change ever so slowly; but they are alive, and they do grow. The written culture should be able to criticize and renew itself, too, every time a new book is published. But, alas, instead of progressing with the slow changes in the daily course of living, the recorded culture too often fell behind. A cultural lag developed in which safety predicated on the past was gained at the risk of maladaptation to the present and future.

Instead of trying to determine the relative superiority of life or school as an educator, many recognized that each had its appropriate and distinct role to perform, that an education without the contribution of both was deficient. As far back as Biblical times the Jews made the formal education of words parallel the informal education of deeds. In Deuteronomy, Jehovah enjoined, "And these words, which I command thee this day, shall be in thine heart: And thou shalt teach them diligently unto thy children, and shalt talk of them when thou sittest in thine house, and when thou walkest by the way, and when thou liest down, and when thou risest up."[2]

The same idea is evident in the writings of John Locke (1632–1704), the educational mouthpiece of seventeenth-century England. In his essay *Some Thoughts concerning Education* he showed a high regard for the education to be had from books and gave careful attention to the fields to be studied. But he did not, on this

[1] S. S. Laurie, *Studies in the History of Educational Opinion since the Renaissance* (Longmans, Green & Co., Inc., New York, 1900), p. 80.

[2] Deuteronomy 6:6–7.

account, neglect the informal education of out-of-school experience. On the contrary, he recommended that a father should talk to his son about important matters as soon as his son's maturity and experience would permit. His underlying idea was that only as a boy is treated like a man will he become a man. And, vice versa, a father must treat a son no less like a man when the boy was the one to propose his boyish concerns for mutual discussion.

In eighteenth-century prerevolutionary France, Louis René de La Chalotais (1701–1785) made an even more striking balance between the contributions of formal and informal education, school and life. In his *Essay on National Education* he frankly stated, "All that needs to be known is not contained in books. There are a thousand things about which it is possible to learn by conversation, by usage, and by practice; but," he went on to point out, "only minds that are already somewhat trained can profit by this sort of instruction. . . . In society, the spirit of study and of business seem opposed to each other; but a man will not understand business well if he has not studied. The important thing is to acquire the main principles of the more uncommon kinds of knowledge; experience—which is the best teacher—will accomplish the rest."[3]

By the twentieth century the extent and complexity of civilization had increased to so great an extent that "uncommon" kinds of experience markedly outstripped the range of direct common experience. The environment to which the individual had to react became enlarged far beyond the immediate time and place in which he found himself. Consequently, the American William C. Bagley (1874–1946) was inclined to reverse the relative emphasis of La Chalotais on school and experience. He did not think raw experience so good a teacher as the school, for the school could provide a unique type of experience—vicarious experience. From his point of view the unique function of the school was that it enabled the pupil to transcend the limitations of raw or common experience. Through school studies like history and geography, the pupil was able to transcend the limitations of the time and place in which he lived and thus vicariously absorb experience otherwise quite uncommon to daily experience.[4]

In the writings of America's most eminent educational philosopher, John Dewey (1859–1952), neither school nor life was favored over the other; neither was one thought of as supplemental to the other. Instead, Dewey enunciated the doctrine that education and life were one. This was not, however, an exclusive return to the informal educa-

---

[3] F. La Fontainerie, *French Liberalism and Education in the Eighteenth Century* (McGraw-Hill Book Company, New York, 1932), p. 73.

[4] W. C. Bagley, "Education as a Unique Type of Experience," *Religious Education,* 18:35–37, February, 1923.

tion of life experience. The theory of the oneness of education and life sought rather to tear down any barrier between the two without destroying the identity of either. Thus, instead of confining itself to its four walls, the school was urged to avail itself of varied community resources for whatever educational value they might have. The school's getting outside its own walls might extend all the way from excursions into the community to making the school an adjunct of the farm and the factory. And to the extent that the school stayed within its four walls it was demanded that the curriculum pursued there be a form of living that is immediately significant.

EARLY BACKGROUNDS OF FAMILY EDUCATION

Of all informal educational agencies in the history of education the family has probably been first not only in point of time but also in point of importance. The quality of education in the family has depended on several factors. One is the status of the child himself, and another the social status of the child's mother. Yet another has been the number of years over which the family surveillance of education extends. A final but not least important factor has been the extent to which the family has found it convenient to delegate its educational functions to someone else.

In primitive societies the education of children in the family was of a relatively low order. In part, this was due to the fact that primitive children often did not enjoy the dignity of being regarded as persons. On the contrary, all too frequently they were treated as chattels to be disposed of or even killed at the will of the father. As the mother, too, was not infrequently regarded as a chattel, her stature as a teacher was not very impressive. Moreover, tribal sex antagonisms lessened her influence. Hence family education extended little beyond habituation in the mores of the tribe. Real education did not begin till puberty, when the boys, at least, were taken from the home and, as already seen, made into men through the educational experiences of initiation.

Though the ancient Greeks were responsible for some of the most prodigious advances made in the history of Western education, they were not notable for any great improvement of education within the family. To be sure, the status of children was improving in their time. Yet in spite of this fact the Greeks had not entirely outgrown the practice of infanticide. No doubt, they practiced infanticide with eugenic and therefore educational ends in view, but this circumstance does not completely excuse their obliviousness to the sanctity that Christians later attached to all human life, no matter with what handicaps it was born.

What advance the Greeks did make in their regard for individual personality—and it was undeniably very considerable—was chiefly in their conception of adult personality and adult male personality at that. Man might be the measure of things, as the Sophists opined,[5] but there was little thought that this dictum included women as well. So advanced a thinker as Plato (427–347 B.C.) might claim an equal status for women among men, but he had no support in public opinion and was contradicted in theory by his own pupil Aristotle (384–322 B.C.). Consequently, as might be imagined, the domestic status of the Greek woman was not very high either as wife or as mother. As a result, the formal education of women was neglected, and indirectly in consequence that of their children in the home. This low standard of home education was even further impaired by the practice in the more well-to-do classes of delegating the mother's function to a nurse.

The educational efforts of the Greek family, like those of the primitive family, were chiefly directed toward the inculcation of manners and morals. Indeed, it is said that the Greeks were more deeply concerned about their children's manners than they were about their letters. Thus Plato related that "Mother and nurse and father and tutor were quarreling about the improvement of the child as soon as ever he is able to understand them; he cannot say or do anything without their setting forth to him that this is just and that is unjust; this is honorable, that is dishonorable; this is holy, that is unholy; do this and abstain from that."[6]

Family spirit was very high within the precincts of the early Roman home. There in an atmosphere of great reverence father and mother joined in the sacred trust of rearing their children with rigorous simplicity in the hardy virtues of industry and self-control. The mother contributed the *educatio* and the father the *doctrina*. No finer example of this relatively high position of the Roman mother in the education of her children can be found than in the well-known story of Cornelia and her two sons, the famous Gracchi. Roman family discipline remained at a high level during the Republic and probably did not deteriorate much till imperial times. Even then the poet Horace bore witness to the great debt that he owed his father for the close attention paid to his education at home and after he had left home for school.

Family education among the Jews, who definitely influenced the later Christians, was also of a high order owing to the fact that the father's great power and responsibility in the education of his

[5] For a further account of the Greek concept of individuality, see *supra*, pp. 25–28.

[6] B. Jowett, *Works of Plato* (Tudor Publishing Company, New York, n.d.), vol. 4, p. 157.

child was shared to a large degree with the child's mother. The father had to teach his son a trade as well as give him moral instruction. But the mother was important, too, as witness the injunction of the Book of Proverbs, "My son, hear the instruction of thy father, and forsake not the teaching of thy mother."[7] The Jews, moreover, considered a well-bred child a credit to his parents and one badly reared as a source of shame.

Christianity reinforced and extended the Jewish domestic tradition in education. By holding that all people regardless of color, sex, or condition of servitude were the children of God and therefore equal in his sight, it maintained the highest possible ideal of womanhood. In the long if not the short run, this had profound significance for the training of children in the family circle. Thus the Christian ideal had to struggle with the same popular prejudice against the equality of women that Plato had met. In the end the Christian ideal won, though none too soon. The latter days of the Roman Empire saw family life at its lowest ebb. Parents who by reason of social position and education should have taken their responsibilities more seriously neglected the training of their children by turning it over to hirelings. Further, they debauched themselves by infidelity in marriage and the practice of infanticide. Except for the influence of Christianity, which consistently set its face against such conduct and steadfastly held out the hope of a spiritual rebirth, there is no telling to what depths family training might have sunk.

The Christian conception of the equality of human beings in the spiritual domain was not always matched by a similar equality in the temporal domain. As a result, it will be well to remember that during the Middle Ages and the Renaissance the exalted position of women among the nobility was not always enjoyed by their sisters among the commonalty. Necessarily, therefore, there was also considerable difference in the quality of home training afforded in the two classes. Yet, even though the upper-class mother might employ a nurse, it is interesting to note that she exercised close supervision over the formation of her child's speech, manners, and morals. In the matter of moral and religious education, indeed, the catechism enjoined solicitous care upon parents both high and low, rich and poor.

None attached greater importance to education in the family than did Martin Luther (1483–1546), the great Protestant who led the Renaissance in its aspect of moral reform north of the Alps. To Luther the parental education of children was a divine mandate. "Think," he cautioned in his catechism, "what deadly injury you are doing if you be negligent and fail to bring up your child to

[7] Proverbs 1:8.

usefulness and piety, and how you bring upon yourself all sin and wrath, meriting hell even in your dealings with your own children, even though you be otherwise ever so pious and holy."[8] Yet in spite of this heavy responsibility Luther was all too aware of the fact that the great majority of parents, even if not remiss in their educational duties, were quite unqualified to discharge them. Therefore he laid it down that "No one should become a father unless he is able to instruct his children in the Ten Commandments and in the Gospel, so that he may bring up true Christians."[9] But, he lamented, many enter the state of holy matrimony who cannot even say the Lord's Prayer.

In the upper classes of the seventeenth and eighteenth centuries there was a renewed tendency not only to delegate the training of young children to nurses but to abandon it to them. As the age was one of increasing wealth, well-to-do mothers slipped into the evil habit of looking on time spent on the education of their children as an intrusion upon their pleasures. When the highborn child outgrew his nurse, it was usual to continue his education at home by engaging a tutor. This is what the English philosopher John Locke recommended although he advised the lad's father to maintain close supervision of the operation. Even the outspoken enemy of eighteenth-century artificiality, that advocate of romanticism, Jean Jacques Rousseau (1712–1778), and his *Émile* prescribed a tutor for his ideal child of nature.

In spite of his recommendation of a tutor, Rousseau is still justly famous for the ringing summons he gave to mothers to take a re-awakened joy and interest in their children. Prior to Rousseau, even those parents who were not neglectful of their children had become so deeply imbued with the dispassionate rationalistic spirit of the times that they were on guard against indulging their feelings toward their children. The beginnings of such a reserved attitude are to be seen in the warning of Michel de Montaigne, the sixteenth-century French education essayist. "Mothers are too tender," he said, referring to the child reared in his mother's lap, "and their natural affection is apt to make the most discreet of them all so overfond, that they can neither find in their hearts to give them correction for the faults they commit, nor suffer them to be inured to hardships and hazards as they ought to be."[10] To mothers who had restrained their feelings the romantic Rousseau appealed for a fresh release of sympathy and

[8] Quoted in F. V. N. Painter, *Luther on Education* (Lutheran Publication Society, Philadelphia, 1889), pp. 118–119.

[9] *Ibid.*

[10] M. de Montaigne, *Of the Education of Children* (G. P. Putnam's Sons, New York, 1891), pp. 32–33.

affection. Maternal emotions, far from being harmful, he cried, were the law of nature. His appeal met with a hearty response. Mothers in their eagerness to be natural commenced at the very beginning of childhood education by returning to the nursing of their children instead of employing wet nurses, as had become conventional.

If Rousseau succeeded in precipitating the flow of a new spirit in the home training of children, it was the Swiss educator Johann Heinrich Pestalozzi (1746–1827) who succeeded in reducing Rousseau's inspiration to a practical pedagogy. This pedagogy he expressed in two books, each of which had a domestic setting, *Leonard and Gertrude* and *How Gertrude Teaches Her Children*. To Pestalozzi the home was the principal center for the education of children. As he conceived it, the school, the state, and the church were merely to supplement the education of the home. Indeed, the good school, he thought, should pattern itself on the good home. The principal features of the home offering educational advantages were its practical activities and its atmosphere of love and security. The practical activities offered opportunities for exercise of the senses in object instruction.[11] Apparently this had also been the earlier inspiration of the "school of the mother's knee" that Johann Amos Comenius (1592–1670), the great Moravian educator, had proposed more than a century earlier. Affection and security offered the advantage that, as Pestalozzi himself said, "where love and the ability to love are found in the home circle there one can confidently predict that the education it affords almost never fails."[12]

Close to Comenius and Pestalozzi, perhaps even excelling them in his appreciation of the significance of the mother as the earliest teacher of childhood, was Friedrich Wilhelm August Froebel (1782–1852), the romantic German idealist. To enrich the educational experience of the very early mother-child relationship, Froebel provided a significant literature, his *Mutter- und Kose-Lieder,* suggesting ways in which the two might sing and play together. Perceiving that the whole educational edifice rests on the foundation of home training, a few years before his death he called upon the state to establish institutions not only for the education of children but also for the education of parents and of those who were to become parents.

FAMILY EDUCATION IN AMERICA

Most of the foregoing theories and practices had more or less effect on family education in America from the seventeenth century

---

[11] For a further account of this method of instruction, see *supra,* pp. 207–211.

[12] L. F. Anderson, *Pestalozzi* (McGraw-Hill Book Company, New York, 1931), p. 117.

onward. At first, colonial America was under the influence of the Protestant Reformation. Following the admonitions of Luther not a few colonial legislatures enacted statutes requiring parents to give their children religious and vocational training and making it incumbent upon local officials, usually town selectmen, to enforce the law. Such was the famous law of 1642 in Massachusetts. Although two centuries later Massachusetts passed the first modern compulsory-attendance law, it did not shift the responsibility for its enforcement from the parent. Indeed, even the twentieth century made no alteration in the fundamental American policy that the primary obligation to educate the child rests with the family.[13]

Although in a frontier society like that of early America the economic value of women gave them superior social significance, their role was still definitely subordinate to that of men, as witness the marriage ceremony, in which the woman undertook to "obey" her husband. While in the eyes of the common law man and wife were one, to all intents and purposes the man was that one. His household was often ruled like a monarchy and not a dual monarchy at that—much less like a republic or a democracy. The eighteenth-century genteel ideal of frail womanhood reinforced rather than altered this situation. Offspring of this union, according to the religious notions of the time, came into the world with the great burden of original sin upon their souls. Consequently, in order to bring the satanic impulses under subjection, family discipline was very severe. The proper perspective on the place of the child in the family was that he should be seen and not heard.

If there was any division of the parental responsibility for the education of children, it was usually assigned to the mother to sway the heart of the child but to the father to inform its intellect. In either event, family education was something that extended well beyond a child's tender years. Thus Henry Barnard (1811–1900), leader of Connecticut's common school revival in the second quarter of the nineteenth century, pointed out that "The tone of conversation at table and at the fireside is of greater importance than many imagine: so are the books and newspapers read and thrown before the young. The father, at his workbench or behind his counter, while hoeing his corn or pursuing any other of our social forms of useful labor, may be communicating to his sons and other companions, lessons on an endless variety of useful topics; while the mother may ordinarily find still more frequent and opportune occasions to pursue a similar course with her daughters."[14]

---

[13] For a further account of compulsory attendance, see *infra*, pp. 529–531.

[14] J. S. Brubacher (ed.), *Henry Barnard on Education* (McGraw-Hill Book Company, New York, 1931), p. 61.

In the nineteenth and twentieth centuries the underlying sociological factors which conditioned family education began to undergo vast changes. The most potent factor producing these changes was the shift from small-scale domestic manufacture to large-scale industrial machinofacture. As this shift gained momentum, the home rapidly disappeared as a center of economic life. Such mechanical improvements as gas, electricity, and running water in the home, the telephone and the delivery truck, the bakery and the laundry, robbed the home of the chores that long constituted an important part of its educational discipline for children. This created the new and difficult problem of how to utilize the child's excess leisure time to advantage. Urban homes, especially where housed in city apartments, became little more than places to eat and sleep. Yet, in spite of its diminished functions, children had to stay under the parental roof longer, for the increase in the complexity of technology which followed later in the wake of the Industrial Revolution prolonged the period of social infancy, that is, the period when the child still had to be supported by his parents while he learned to deal with the increased intricacy of life.

With less to do in the home and with less and less time spent in the home not only by the father but by the mother as well, parents became less strict than formerly. As children learned less obedience, courtesy, and respect in the home, the school had to take upon itself the inculcation of these homely virtues. Of course, there were compensating advantages. Children learned more of initiative and responsibility perhaps than formerly, but whether this entirely made up for the loss of docility and obedience was a moot question in the minds of many of their elders.

The long-term effect of the Industrial Revolution resulted in an emancipation of parents no less than of children from the former drudgeries of the home. This was particularly significant for the status of mothers. Women began to have a little leisure to cultivate their minds and to reconstruct the traditional fireside stereotype of themselves. The eighteenth-century stereotype of frailty they exchanged for a nineteenth-century one of robust and informed womanhood. This gave rise to a feminist movement that in the twentieth century led to the political enfranchisement of women. From the nineteenth century onward a whole host of books and magazines addressed to parents, but especially to mothers, began to appear. These had the avowed purpose of informing women of the proper intellectual, moral, and physical training of their children.

In an age that was almost straining to make social progress perhaps none gave more lofty statement to the educational importance of the mother than did Catherine Beecher (1800–1878), preeminent nineteenth-century representative of her sex. "The success of democratic institutions as is conceded by all," she declared, "depends upon the intelligent and virtuous character of the mass of the people. If they are intellectual and virtuous, democracy is a blessing; but if they are ignorant and wicked, it is only a curse. . . . It is equally conceded, that the formation of the moral and intellectual character of the young is committed mainly to female hands. The mother forms the character of the future man . . . the wife sways the heart whose energies may turn for good or for evil and destinies of the nation. Let the women of a country be made virtuous and intelligent, and the men will certainly be the same. The proper education of a man decides the welfare of an individual, but educate a woman, and the interests of a whole family are secured. If this be so, as none will deny, then to American women more than to any others on earth is committed the exalted privilege of extending over the world those blessed influences which are to renovate degraded man."[15]

In spite of this lofty sentiment most mothers in the nineteenth and twentieth centuries, as in Luther's century, were nowhere equal to so noble a task. As Barnard himself said, "The family circle and the mother are unquestionably the school and the teacher of God's appointment, the first and best for young children. Were every home surrounded by circumstances favorable to domestic training and had every mother the requisite leisure, taste, and ability to superintend the proper training of the feelings, manners, language, and open faculties of the young, their early school attendance would not be an object of great importance. But whatever may be the fact in a few homes, and with a few mothers, there can be no doubt that in reference to many homes, so unfavorable" is the situation that most children can hardly leave for school too soon.[16]

What Barnard stated to the people of the nineteenth century was nothing novel. Utopians as far back as Plato had found the family wanting as an educational institution. In addition to the point made by Barnard, they complained that parents tended to be extreme with their children, either to spoil them with foolish indulgence or to treat them with needless severity. Some complained that parents thwarted the good influence of their children's teachers. Robert Owen (1771–1858), the Welsh reformer, claimed that children in the homes of the poverty-stricken working classes got under the feet of their parents and were addressed in terms anything but conducive to a wholesome education. And the French reformer Charles Fourier

---

[15] C. E. Beecher, *Domestic Economy* (Thomas H. Webb, Boston, 1842), pp. 36–37

[16] J. S. Brubacher, *op. cit.*, pp. 252–253. For a further discussion of the relative merits of the home and school as educational agencies, see *infra,* pp. 512–514.

(1772–1837) feared that family education might inculcate antisocial tendencies in children by encouraging them to acquire wealth by any means.[17]

Throughout history some reformers have claimed that the only remedy for the educational inadequacy of the family was to turn the child over to the state. The nineteenth and twentieth centuries, however, moved in a somewhat different direction. On the one hand, without supplanting the family by the state these centuries did evolve new schools for the very young, principally the kindergarten and the nursery school,[18] which supplemented the family at a number of points. On the other hand, strong movements were set afoot to realize at long last the oft-repeated cry of reformers for an improved parenthood. The first step in this direction was the inception of the child-study movement, which was the late-nineteenth century expression of the new interest in the importance of childhood that Rousseau had initiated. The organization of groups like the Child Study Association, the American Child Health Association, and the American Child Hygiene Association culminated in 1912 in the formation of the Federal Children's Bureau. Shortly after the First World War the American Home Economics Association brought child care within the scope of its interests. And in 1925 was called the first conference on modern parenthood, which resulted in the same year in the founding of the National Council of Parental Education. All these agencies were of great aid in publishing to interested parents the most recent information on child care.

ADULT EDUCATION

If the family has been the first and perhaps most important of informal types of education, adult education is certainly the last and yet far from least of them. What adult education covers depends to a large extent on what degree of informal life activities one wants to embrace. To include only formal adult education activities would leave out of account many of its most vital phases. Yet, on the other hand, to include all life experiences, because all life is educative, sets a task that space for discussion, if nothing else, forbids. Where to draw a line between these two policies, therefore, must be not only difficult but probably in the end arbitrary.

In ancient times the most significant education seems to have been carried on informally at the adult level. Socrates (469–399 B.C.), for instance, rated as one of the greatest teachers of all time, never

---

[17] G. Masso, *Education in Utopias* (Bureau of Publications, Teachers College, Columbia University, New York, 1927), pp. 8–9.

[18] For a more complete account of these schools, see *infra*, pp. 380–386.

really conducted a formal school. His famous dialogues, reported by Plato, were casual conversations held with such adults as he could draw into discourse with him. He was a teacher, if at all, by virtue of being a gadfly to the adult conscience of Athens. In his *Republic* Plato proposed to institutionalize the educational pursuit of truth that Socrates had carried on so informally. As he conceived his republic,[19] the systematic education of the guardian, or philosophical, class was to continue well into adult years. Jesus, on the other hand, was more like Socrates, an informal teacher of adults. He, too, instructed his disciples or the multitude that followed him on such occasions as presented themselves. After his crucifixion, the training preparatory to entering Christian fellowship, while perhaps a little more formal, was still largely at the adult level.

The great theological controversies of the Middle Ages might also be cited as an instance of early adult education. Many of these controversies were fought out in medieval universities to which youth and adults flocked like knights to a tournament. The theological controversies of the Protestant Reformation also had effects in a new form of adult education, the Sunday sermon from the pulpit. This weekly lecture to the laity kept them informed not only on doctrinal matters but not infrequently on politics as well. In the sixteenth and seventeenth centuries, indeed, the sermon was a much more significant form of adult education than the modern newspaper with its editorials.

In the eighteenth century the world caught a new glimpse of adult education pursued as a conscious end. Leaders of the French Revolution, with their almost unbounded confidence in the possibilities of education, conceived of education as the vocation not only of children but of adults as well. "Study," wrote La Chalotais, "should be the occupation of our youth and the relaxation of the rest of our lives to fill usefully the intervals of leisure."[20] His contemporary the Marquis de Condorcet (1743–1794) also held the view that "education should not cease when the individual leaves school. It should be of concern to all ages; for," he went on to voice the optimistic opinion, "there is no age at which it is not possible and profitable to learn."[21] Condorcet even made the practical proposal that on Sundays the local schoolteacher should give a lecture to the adults of his community on a topic they had had no time to pursue while in school.

What was little more than a vision with La Chalotais and Condorcet in the eighteenth century became a living reality in the next two centuries. Perhaps most successful in instituting education for adults

---

[19] For a more extended account of this utopian conception of education, see *supra,* pp. 103–104.

[20] La Fontainerie, *op. cit.,* p. 73.

[21] *Ibid.,* p. 325.

beyond the formal school of childhood and adolescence was Denmark. Following the inspiration of Bishop Nikolai Frederik Severin Grundtvig (1783–1872), Denmark set up its since famous folk high school. Seeing that the circumstances of the people of his day were depressed both materially and spiritually, Grundtvig proposed a curriculum for young artisans and peasants which emphasized national culture in both song and folklore. In addition to this stirring material there was instruction in the country's political institutions and economic resources. Above all the bishop insisted that instruction be oral, for he believed that the spoken word infused the curriculum with life, an insistence which stood in marked contrast to the dead languages of Latin and Greek so popular in the texts of the conventional schools of the day. This type of school proved a vast success; it spread widely throughout the country and attracted many foreign visitors, especially from the United States.

In eighteenth- and nineteenth-century America the tavern and the village store came to rival the church as forums of adult education. There arguments over abolition, temperance, and the like trained their adult participants not only in knowledge of their subject but also in rhetorical and logical skills. Often these discussions were continued in a variety of adult groups that were formed at this time for the mutual improvement of their members, such as the Junto, of which Benjamin Franklin was a member and founder, or, later in the eighteenth century, the American Philosophical Association. In the nineteenth century, women began to form clubs of their own. This movement proved a formidable phase of adult education, the significance of which could all too easily be lost in the laughter that was sometimes directed at the alleged superficiality of its programs.

Library resources through which individual adults might continue their education were quite meager in this country as late as the Civil War. At the conclusion of that grim event there was as yet no American library with as many as 200,000 volumes although there were a score of such in Europe. At this time, in fact, only six American libraries had half that number of volumes. Of the libraries that had collections of 1,000 books, the majority included items that had only the most limited appeal. If libraries of the day were few and poorly stocked, museums of science and art were nonexistent. Collections of art treasures at this date were still largely the possessions of private individuals. The next seventy-five years, however, witnessed a stupendous multiplication of all these facilities for the general adult public.[22]

While libraries were growing into great repositories of the social experience of the past to which the adult could go for self-improvement,

[22] See also S. Ditzion, "Social Reform, Education, and the Library," *Library Quarterly,* 9:156–184, April, 1939.

newspapers were rapidly taking their place in educating the adult about current affairs. Impinging on the adult at first largely through editorial policies and later through the medium of news, the press latterly has come to inform and instruct through advertising as well. Effective as the press has been, it has had the keenest competition possible in the twentieth century from the motion picture, and the radio, and television in shaping public opinion and forming the taste of the adult population.

In the nineteenth century, adult education, which up to that time had been largely informal, began to take on a more and more formal aspect. Early to achieve popularity were evening schools. Starting in the century preceding as opportunities for youth whose education for one reason or another had been all too meager, these schools naturally came to make a great appeal to ambitious young adults who wished to improve their spare time. Evening schools at first were at the elementary level of instruction but later were at the secondary level as well, where they included cultural in addition to vocational subjects. As in so many other educational enterprises, Massachusetts was first to pioneer with publicly supported evening schools, but Ohio was first with a free evening high school, established at Cincinnati just before the Civil War. When, in the opening decades of the twentieth century, America woke up to the vast hordes of foreign immigrants in her midst, the evening school was called to do yeomen service in their Americanization, both in respect to literacy and in respect to citizenship.

Ambitious young workers in the first half of the nineteenth century also made mechanics' institutes a very popular form of adult education. These institutes arose in many large factory centers where the apprenticeship system was breaking down under the impact of the Industrial Revolution.[23] They provided libraries and gave instruction through public lectures and evening classes both in technical subjects and in the common branches. Lowell Institute and Cooper Union, pace setters of the movement in the second quarter of the nineteenth century, were followed by other forms of adult workers' education in the twentieth century, such as the Rand School of Social Science, Bryn Mawr's summer school for women workers, and, among unions, the International Ladies Garment Workers' Union, with its educational program covering music, drama, and athletics as well as economic and labor problems.

Beckoning adults to cultural rather than vocational pursuits was the lyceum movement, which had its inception early in the second

---

[23] The vicissitudes of economic occupation as a type of informal education have been briefly sketched as part of the chapters on the curriculum rather than the current chapter. See *supra,* pp. 267–273.

quarter of the nineteenth century. This movement was the outgrowth of the experience of an obscure student of geology at Yale. While traveling to increase his store of geological informaton, he frequently addressed village audiences on geological topics. Finding his talks well received, he conceived the idea of organizing a whole system of popular lectures. These lectures, according to his announcement, were to advance the education of adults, improve the quality of the public schools, call into use neglected libraries, and encourage the building of new libraries and museums. The first series of lectures was opened in Millbury, Massachusetts. Under the name "lyceum," the institution soon excited such general interest that it grew into national proportions. Lyceums sprang up everywhere to satisfy the great popular demand for this sort of informal educational improvement. When audiences tired of local lecturers, lyceum managers brought in outside talent. Great names like those of Ralph Waldo Emerson, Henry D. Thoreau, Oliver Wendell Holmes, and Henry Ward Beecher came to grace lyceum programs. Although the movement died down somewhat before the end of the nineteenth century, popular lecturing from public platforms continued to hold adult interest well into the twentieth century.

Very similar to the lyceum as a fountain of popular adult education was the Chautauqua movement. The Chautauqua grew out of the old-time camp meeting, which in turn grew out of the necessity for having ministers of the gospel go on circuit. Settlements too sparse and scattered to warrant several stops by the circuit rider used to join together at some convenient point and camp there temporarily while they formed a single large congregation to which he might preach. One very popular such place was Lake Chautauqua in New York. There a decade after the Civil War the Methodists arranged to hold a summer institute[24] for the training of Sunday school teachers. The institute proved a great success. Indeed, so successful was it that Lake Chautauqua soon became a center for summer vacationists to pursue a great variety of cultural interests covering literature, science, and the fine arts as well as religion. Imitation Chautauquas soon came into existence elsewhere; some of these themselves went on circuit and thus became traveling Chautauquas.

One of the sturdiest descendants of the Chautauqua movement was the summer session, or summer school, which came to be a regular part of university calendars in the twentieth century. Summer schools of this type, revealing the Chautauqua influence, were originally designed to appeal to the general adult public as a form of popular university, without too much attention to academic requirements and academic degrees. In the course of time, however, they

---

[24] For a further account of teacher institutes, see *infra*, pp. 478–479.

became more and more generally geared to the college and university mill with its cogs of credits and prerequisites. Schoolteachers became the main body of the adult population patronizing summer schools, as they were eager to advance themselves toward graduate degrees.[25]

Enthusiasm for the Chautauqua idea was so intense that many adults thought the summer all too brief a time in which to make the most of it. To carry its spirit back to their homes and keep it alive there during the other seasons of the year two further types of popular education came into being. One was the reading circle. Through this device interested adults could keep up and advance their summer interests during the winter by reading more or less systematically from a carefully prepared list of books in the field.

Another was the correspondence school. The idea of taking up or continuing one's education by correspondence first appeared in Europe, but it took its most substantial root here in the United States, especially as an outgrowth of the Chautauqua movement. The lectures at Lake Chautauqua by William Rainey Harper (1856–1906) proved so popular that his listeners asked him to outline a continuation of their summer work for winter study. This he gladly did but, being a very busy man, could give it only a small amount of supervision. Several years later correspondence instruction was improved by making it more systematic and by charging fees that defrayed the expenses of an instructor specifically assigned to this task. When Harper became president of the University of Chicago just before the opening of the twentieth century, he was the first to make correspondence instruction a regular part of university extension work.

University extension as a form of adult education dates from the middle of the nineteenth century in England. There a tutor of Exeter College became sensitive to the fact there were numbers of adults who did not attend university lectures in their free hours principally because of the remoteness of the university. He conceived the happy idea, therefore, that if the adult student could not reach the university, the university ought to go to the student. The professor, like the clergyman, ought to go on circuit. Nothing much came of the idea till about the middle of the Victorian era, when a Cambridge professor started giving very successful extramural lectures of a popular nature on astronomy. Later he accompanied his lectures with a syllabus and concluded them with an examination. This was the germ that in a very few years grew into an officially recognized program of university extension at Cambridge.

In the United States university extension was first proposed at John Hopkins in the next to the last decade of the nineteenth century.

---

[25] For an account of summer schools as part of the teacher-training program, see *infra*, pp. 496–497.

At the opening of the last decade of the century a committee of colleges and universities in New York urged the University of the State of New York to take steps toward organizing university extension work. New York, however, was only one of more than twenty-five states and territories that soon took such action. Unfortunately, the seed of university extension fell on thin soil, for though it flourished at first it soon languished. The reason was that too much university extension instruction was second rate and at second hand. Second-rate instructors who did not know how to adapt their academic subject matter to the popular mind and its problems were assigned to the work of university extension. As soon as this mistake was corrected in the twentieth century, university extension revived and went on to become a most significant contribution of the university to advancing the education of adults.

The term "adult education" was first popularized after the First World War, when an effort was made to envision the manifold educational activities of adults as a whole. Leaders from various fields of adult education came together to promote their common interests by forming the Adult Education Association, with the *Journal of Adult Education* as its official mouthpiece. A rough estimate put 15 million adults as the number engaged at the time in one sort or another of formal or informal adult education. The enterprise was so tremendous and so pregnant with future possibilities that the Carnegie Corporation decided to invest some $3,000,000 in its study and promotion.

Part of this money was used to subsidize an important bit of psychological research into the learning capacities of adults. For long it had been a popular prejudice that teaching adults was about on a par with attempting to teach an old dog new tricks. The researches of Edward Lee Thorndike (1874–1949) definitely dispelled that notion. On the contrary, they supported the general conclusion that the curve of ability to learn constantly rises till it reaches a plateau at about twenty years of age, from which after a period of some years it slowly declines at the rate of perhaps 1 per cent a year.[26] But the decline is so gradual that no adult of fifty should be discouraged from trying to learn anything he needs to know. Naturally these findings gave scientific confirmation to the great hopes that had long been put in the education of adults.

With huge numbers of adults unemployed during the Great Depression following 1929 the Federal government tried to alleviate their sufferings to some extent by promoting adult education activities. In part, adult education was a phase of such New Deal agencies

[26] E. L. Thorndike, *Adult Learning* (The Macmillan Company, New York, 1928).

as the Agricultural Adjustment Administration and the Tennessee Valley Authority. The success of these governmental innovations depended to a degree on instructing the people about them. In part, too, adult education was a phase of the Works Progress Administration, where it was a means of relief for unemployed teachers. Somewhat different but still within the scope of adult education were such other government-instigated activities as the Federal Arts Theater and the Federal Writers' Project. This federal interest in the education of adults was far from being just an emergency matter. Through the Cooperative Extension Service of the U.S. Department of Agriculture the Federal government had long been running a rural, agricultural, and home economics program which was the largest in the country, perhaps in the world.

While the Federal government's was the single largest program, the variety and number of smaller ones were almost legion. Happily this interest in adult education continued after the Second World War, especially with the encouragement it received from the Ford Fund for the Advancement of Adult Education. On the more informal side perhaps the most notable innovation of this period was the widespread formation of clubs for the reading and study of the "great books." While one might have expected such clubs to be composed of college graduates, as a matter of fact people from all strata of society were to be found in them. Indeed it was supposed to be one criterion of a great book that it made an appeal to all levels of ability and all occupational categories. On the more formal side the university began to take a fresh look at its offerings. Realizing that there was an increasing number of agencies offering opportunities for adult education, it turned to examine what its own unique function in this field should be. It came to the conclusion, on the one hand, that the adult was a different breed of student from the undergraduate and that different requirements and offerings should therefore be designed for his degree. On the other hand, it came to see its own graduates as a new clientele. Consequently it began to offer work for them not to meet demands for an advanced degree but just to update them in general or professional training already obtained at the university. Hence, as the second half of the century advanced, education, as La Chalotais said it should, was well on its way to becoming "the occupation of our youth and the relaxation for the rest of our lives."

13 Elementary Education

The education of the very young has been a persistent problem in every society. When education has been left to informal forces, however, the form of the problem has been different from when it has been the concern of such a formal agency as the school. Under the reign of informal forces, every child from the earliest age unavoidably gets some kind of education just through the process of living. As soon, however, as formal schools make their appearance in educational history, perennially perplexing problems such as these arise: At how tender an age shall children commence attending school? Shall all children attend, or only some children? If children do attend, for how long a period shall they remain in school? What is the purpose of their going to school at this early age? And what shall they learn?

EARLY PATTERNS

Much can be learned about the character of early elementary education from the names borne by schools for the very young. It is probably no accident, for instance, that the first, or lowest, school attended by the Roman boy was the *ludus,* a name taken from the Latin word meaning "play." This may signify either or perhaps both of two things, either that the Romans did not make strict educational demands on the very young or that, like the Greeks, they viewed education as a form of leisure. While the Roman boy entered a *ludus,* the Greek boy entered a palaestra, which, as might be inferred from present usage of the term, had a curriculum including physical education. Coordinate with the palaestra was the *didascaleum,* the didactics of which concerned literacy and music.

The age classifications into which the Greeks divided the periods of education remained influential for many centuries. First there was a preschool period up to about seven years of age. Next there was the initial period of formal schooling, which lasted to some point in adolescence. Beyond this there were, finally, various types of post-adolescent education, which, in the course of time, became divided into secondary and higher education. Aristotle (384–322 B.C.) wanted to follow the poets and assign a seven-year span to each of these three periods, but Plato (427–347 B.C) wished to reconstruct practice by a scheme calling for many more than three periods and lasting till a man reached middle age. More significant for present purposes is the fact that Plato was the first to suggest that the periods from two to three and three to six years of age are not too early to commence deliberate consideration of the kind of adult a child is to become.

Among the Greeks it was common practice to leave the training of the child up to the age of seven to the direction of the mother. Toys and games together with fables were the chief materials of instruction. In the formal school that followed, the main object was to achieve literacy. After the rudiments of reading and writing had been mastered, the child started immediately on the best Greek literature, in which Homer, of course, held first place. Out of reading and writing grew some elementary instruction in grammar. Elementary notions of number were often taught along with letters. Thus, after a child had learned to identify the letters in a name like "Socrates," he was called upon to point out the fifth letter or tell how many letters there were altogether. Music and physical training completed the curriculum of this first level of formal schooling.

Like the Greek, Roman education had three stages. Although it was also common Roman opinion that formal instruction should not begin before seven, Quintilian (35–100), Rome's chief schoolmaster, thought it well at least to commence moral instruction before that time. If one could reconcile himself to not expecting too much in too short a while, Quintilian would even take the first steps toward literacy during this period. The sooner the child started, the more knowledge he could hope to amass by the end of his period of formal schooling. The object of the Roman *ludus,* like the Greek *didascaleum,* was the achievement of literacy. But here again Quintilian put in the caveat, "You will hardly believe how much reading is delayed by undue haste."[1] To clinch his point by analogy he reminded teach-

[1] H. E. Butler, *Quintilian, Institutes of Oratory* (G. P. Putnam's Sons, New York, 1921–1922), vol. 1, p. 37.

ers of the waste that follows from attempting to pour water too fast into a narrow-necked pitcher. For beginning readers, Aesop's *Fables* were most popular. Later, emphasis was laid on the Twelve Tables, stating the basic law of the land.

The Judaeo-Christian educational tradition was much the same as the Greco-Roman. Formal schooling for the Jewish boy commenced in a school attached to the synagogue at about six years of age, although Isaiah recommended that it begin at the time when a child is weaned. As in other ancient cultures, the first stage of formal Jewish education was devoted to achieving literacy and learning the Pentateuch, which set forth the basic customs of the people. Later, during the Christian period, the elements of the new dispensation were taught first in the catechumenal schools. These schools, however, marked a falling off in the quality of elementary instruction since they aimed not at literacy but only at a basic knowledge of Christian aspiration and conviction. The failure to include literacy as an objective of this school is easily understood when it is remembered that many Christians were converts who at that time came chiefly from the most underprivileged social classes.

THE MEDIEVAL VERNACULAR SCHOOL

During the medieval period, which ensued on the breakdown of the old Roman Empire, political and economic circumstances, and consequently educational conditions, too, underwent a vast deterioration. What survived of the educational traditions of Greece and Rome was perpetuated chiefly in Latin-language schools erected and maintained in connection with cathedrals, monasteries, guilds, and chantries. At this time Latin was the language not only of the church but also of the law courts, of civil government, and even of business. The chief need for it, therefore, was among churchmen, lawyers, magistrates, and the like. The great mass of the people, who had no such occupational responsibility and who in any case spoke only the vernacular, had no occasion for such schools.

Yet, as the circumstances of this part of the population improved toward the end of the Middle Ages, they found an increasing need for enough education to meet the requirements of their humble position. This was especially true of a social class below the burgher class and yet high enough to have need of reading notices or keeping small-business records. To meet this need there arose schools taught in the vernacular. These were known as "adventure" or "hedge" schools because they were usually private ventures and were held under such mean and impromptu conditions as behind hedges. Under these circumstances it is not surprising that these vernacular schools had an ephemeral existence.

The significant characteristic to note in this development is that a new distinction between elementary and secondary education was in the making. In the Greco-Roman tradition the difference had been one simply of age, marked by more advanced studies in the post-adolescent period. Out of the medieval period was emerging a distinction based on social class and the language of instruction. Thus secondary schools became the precinct of the upper classes where the classical tongues were both the object and the vehicle of instruction, while elementary schools were the province of the lower classes where the vernacular dominated instruction. Further emphasizing this class distinction between elementary and secondary education was the fact that the vernacular school ran concurrently with, that is, paralleled, the early years of upper-class education. Hence attendance at the elementary school of this and later times was never a preparation for secondary education. Indeed upper-class students got their fundamentals either privately or in the lower years of the secondary school. The idea of a single, rather than a dual, educational ladder extending from the ABC's to the university did not appear till the nineteenth century in America and the twentieth in Europe.

RELIGIOUS ORIGINS OF ELEMENTARY EDUCATION

The impetus that gave the vernacular school a more than ephemeral existence and firmly established it in educational history came from two sources, the invention of printing about 1450 and the Protestant Reformation in the next century. Indeed, many date the substantial origin of the modern elementary school from the Protestant Reformation rather than from some earlier time. The impetus imparted by the Reformation stemmed from the consequences of Martin Luther's break with the Catholic Church. At first Luther (1483–1546) appealed to individual reason to attack the authority of the church. Later, when this weapon was turned upon his own position, his confidence in individual reason weakened. In an endeavor to settle controversies he appealed to the Bible. Thus, his revolt ended in a new authoritarianism, the authority of the Bible being substituted for the former authority of the Catholic hierarchy.

The central position so accorded the Bible obviously had tremendous implications for education. Ultimately it meant that everyone would have to learn how to read in order to seek personal guidance from Holy Writ. Furthermore, the new Protestant church service stressed congregational singing and responsive reading, rituals both of which also required literacy. For these reasons, not a few Protestant principalities in Germany made the elementary education of their people compulsory. In spite of Luther's translation of the Bible into German, the elementary vernacular school probably would not have been able to carry the prodigious burden laid on it if it had not been for the even earlier invention of printing. It took both of these events to implement the Protestant Reformation. Together they determined the character of elementary education for the next several centuries.

It was an English version of this school which the Puritan colonists brought to New England shores in the seventeenth century. There it was often known as a "dame school," owing to the fact that it was frequently taught by some thrifty woman eager to turn a penny by teaching while at the same time engaged in spinning or some other convenient household occupation. These schools, however, were not always private ventures. Often they were parochial ones sponsored by different religious denominations, as in New York and Pennsylvania. In Calvinistic New England, where church and state were hand in glove, the state itself enjoined the establishment of elementary schools, which for long thereafter were known as "common schools." The common school, it should be noted, was common not in the sense of inferior, not as a school for the poor, but as a school open to all.

The tenor and content of instruction in these schools can perhaps best be gathered from a reading of the famous New England primer, of which the first edition appeared about 1690 and which long was the first book of colonial school children. This little book commenced with the alphabet; then came "easy" syllables, next one-syllable words, and then two-, three-, and four-syllable ones. Thereafter came the Lord's Prayer and the Apostles' Creed, and further on the catechism. Other reading materials in the primer usually had a definitely religious and moral tone, as for instance a poem whose first verse ran:

> *The Praises of my Tongue*
> *I offer to the Lord,*
> *That I was taught and learnt so young*
> *To read His Holy Word.*

Since a knowledge of reading was the chief gateway to an understanding of the Scriptures, reading was easily the most important of the three R's. Indeed, it was often taught when the other two were not. It is not surprising, therefore, that in these early times reading and writing schools were often separate. When the third R, arithmetic, was taught, it was usually in conjunction with the writing school. The aim was generally to teach arithmetic as far as the rule of three, or proportion, for this was very necessary in figuring the relative values of the various colonial currencies. Paper for writing and "ciphering," as arithmetic was often called, was scarce and of poor quality. Quill pens were still used, and much of the teacher's time was consumed in sharpening them for the children. In fact, sharpening quills, setting copies, dictating sums, "hearing" lessons, and, above all, keeping order absorbed so much of the teacher's time that he had little enough left for exposition.

CHARITY AND PHILANTHROPIC SCHOOLS

From the middle of the eighteenth century onward there was a noticeable change in the forces promoting education of elementary grade. For one thing, growing tolerance dampened the fires of sectarianism, which up to this time had been the chief dynamic of this sort of education. For another, economic, political, and nationalistic forces were beginning to crowd religion from its position as the focus of attention in men's minds. By the end of the century these three forces were making almost simultaneous demands on the education of young children.

Perhaps first to make itself felt in the provision for early formal education was the economic force. Throughout the seventeenth and eighteenth centuries the economic status of the lower social classes in Europe was distressing. Poverty and its attendant consequences were evident on all sides. The upper-class explanation of these conditions was that they arose from the laziness and lack of industry of the poor. To remedy or at least mitigate these conditions in England some of the more philanthropically minded persons among the favored or privileged classes turned to education.

Two sorts of schools were proposed. John Locke (1632–1704) was the author of one of them. While Locke is best known for *Some Thoughts concerning Education* (*of the Sons of Gentlemen* completes the title), he was also the author of quite a different plan of education for the children of the laboring people. For them he proposed "working schools." He would have had children from three to fourteen attend schools in which they would be instructed in such industries as were carried on in the parish. The produce of their work was to pay for their instruction and also, presumably, for their midday meal of a "bellyful of bread" and, in winter, "a little warm water gruel; for" added Locke, appealing to the frugality of his class, "the same fire that warms the room may be made use of to boil a pot of it."[2] On Sunday he would have these same children taken

[2] Quoted in H. R. F. Bourne, *Life of John Locke* (Henry S. King & Co., London, 1876), vol. 2, p. 384.

to church to be brought up in religion and morality as during the week they were brought up in industry. Upon leaving school they were to be securely placed in some local occupation.

Locke's scheme for alleviating the wretched condition of the lower classes through education remained largely on paper except in so far as it may have been an influence in determining the character of another sort of school, the "charity" school. This type of school, established and supported out of benevolences solicited from the more favored classes, was very popular in the eighteenth century. The Society for Promoting Christian Knowledge and its branch, The Society for the Propagation of the Gospel in Foreign Parts, which included the American colonies, were the chief agencies for making this philanthropy effective.[3] The schools of these societies aimed to teach reading, writing, and enough arithmetic to fit a child for an apprenticeship. But more important than the three R's was their aim to rectify irreligion and vice by teaching the catechism and discouraging lying, swearing, and the profanation of the Sabbath. Later it was recommended to the Society for Promoting Christian Knowledge that the curriculum include sewing, knitting, spinning, or other useful employments so that children would become self-supporting.

As the Industrial Revolution began to make itself felt, the educational provision for young children took a somewhat different turn. In the absence of child-labor laws at the beginning of the Industrial Revolution, children worked such long hours during the week that there was imminent risk that a generation would grow up which knew neither its letters nor its catechism. To meet this danger an English publisher by the name of Robert Raikes (1735–1811) established Sunday schools. He gathered the youthful victims of child labor together on Sundays and had them taught the indispensable elements of knowledge by teachers whom he paid out of his own funds. Although held on Sunday and not neglecting religious and moral instruction, the original Sunday school, it may surprise some to learn, was quite secular in both conception and support.[4] Raikes's promotion of the Sunday school was an immediate success, and when the idea was transplanted to America early in the nineteenth century, there was no interruption of its success.

Another educational attempt to snatch children from under the wheels of industry and give them a decent start in life was that made by Robert Owen (1771–1858), a Welsh millowner and

[3] For educational histories of these two societies, see W. O. B. Allen and E. McClure, *The History of the Society for Promoting Christian Knowledge, 1698–1898* (E. and S. B. Young & Company, New York, 1898); H. B. Binns, *A Century of Education* (J. M. Dent & Sons, Ltd., Publishers, London, 1908).

[4] For the religious development of the Sunday school, see *supra,* pp. 320–323.

philanthropist. He grieved for the children of five and upward who were apprenticed to him by the poor-law authorities of the communities near his mill. After these young people had worked out their apprenticeship with him, he saw them returning merely to swell the ignorant mass of the population. To make a beginning at forestalling such an outcome, Owen proposed taking children as early as three years of age and forming them into an "infant school." There he would provide an informal sort of education emphasizing health and physical exercise rather than books. Owen actually established such a school near his mill, and it was visited by people from far and wide. It was not long before a few similar infant schools were set up both in France and in America.

Still another type of first school for children that fitted congenially into the new industrialism was the monitorial school stemming in part from Joseph Lancaster (1778–1838) and in part from Andrew Bell (1753–1832). The essential feature of this sort of school was that one master could teach as many as 200 to 1,000 pupils at a time in a single large room. Such considerable numbers were handled by dividing them into groups of 10 students, with a decurion, or monitor, over each group. The master instructed the monitors, each of whom relayed the instruction to the 10 other students under his immediate charge. This scheme for mechanical quantity production was more successful in teaching subjects susceptible of rote memorizing than it was in teaching those requiring thought and discrimination. Nevertheless, its efficiency in reaching large numbers at little expense greatly appealed to its philanthropic backers in England and also in America, when it was introduced there in the first quarter of the nineteenth century.

The charitable, or philanthropic, interest in elementary education in nineteenth-century England and America should not be overrated. On the one hand, there was a quite uncritical optimism as to the amount of social uplift that could be expected from a mere mastery of the three R's embellished chiefly with religious and moral teaching. On the other hand, there seems to have been a definite limit to the height to which social uplift was to rise through this first level of schooling. The dominant conception of charity was still quite aristocratic, and few upper-class benefactors intended their benevolences to support elementary schools that would "put notions" in the heads of lower-class children.

One of the chief vehicles for such conservatism in America was the blue-backed speller put out by America's great lexicographer, Noah Webster (1758–1843). This book was a reader as well as a speller. The selections included materials chosen from economic and political contexts as well as from earlier religious ones. From these selections it is evident that people at this early period of our national history expected the elementary school to teach respect for property rights, the virtue of industry, and contentment with one's lot in life.[5]

This view of the obligation of the elementary school to underlying economic forces had not entirely disappeared as late as the early twentieth century. John Dewey (1859–1952) detected numerous evidences of its persistence when he examined the elementary schools of this period.[6] Some of this evidence he found in the opposition of influential members of the community to the expansion of the elementary school curriculum. With the exception of history and geography they tended to oppose additions to the curriculum as unwarranted "fads and frills." In the expectation of this group, when children had learned the three R's plus perhaps a little history and geography, the majority of them would leave school and go to work. In their minds elementary education was little more than a substitute for the old apprenticeship system of education. The elementary education of the masses was regarded as a kind of necessary concession rather than as a generous expectation.

NATIONAL AND POLITICAL ORIGIN OF ELEMENTARY EDUCATION

As already indicated, other forces than the economic were cooperating in the eighteenth and nineteenth centuries to shift the purpose of the elementary school slowly away from its earlier almost exclusively religious base. One of the most powerful of these forces was nationalism.[7] Nationalism as a passion of the upper classes was an old phenomenon in Europe, but nationalism as a passion of the masses was something new, introduced by the French Revolution of 1789. The leaders of that movement deliberately cultivated the feelings of nationalism in the masses to make them conscious of the liberty they had won through the revolution and to make them ready to defend it.

The instrument most ready to hand for attaching the masses to their newly won liberty was education—not the old education of the upper classes but a new education designed for the masses. This political motive for their education gave the school of this class,

[5] M. Curti, *The Social Ideas of American Educators* (Charles Scribner's Sons, New York, 1935), pp. 32–33.

[6] J. Dewey and E. Dewey, *Schools of Tomorrow* (E. P. Dutton & Co., Inc., New York, 1915), pp. 235–237.

[7] For a more extended account of nationalism and education, see *supra*, chap. 3.

the elementary school, a new dignity. Further, it drew to the support of the elementary school the strength and resources of the state. The purpose of preserving the people's liberties through their patriotic devotion could not be made to depend on the uncertainties and possible self-interest of charitable benevolence. Nothing less than the state itself would have to stand sponsor for such an education.

Nationalism and patriotism had several points of influence on the curriculum of the school for the masses. Perhaps chief was their effect on instruction in the vernacular. If formerly the vernacular had been subordinated to Latin, now it was made the principal channel for purveying the new elixir of patriotism. Folk tales and literature in the folk tongue were greatly emphasized. Indeed, in Germany, where nationalism was also rampant after the Napoleonic defeat of Prussia, the elementary school was called the *Volksschule* or folk school. Folk music was also made a source of patriotic instruction. Geography and history were introduced into the elementary school curriculum, too, in order to give nationalism a firm setting in the dimensions of space and time.

Almost inseparable from the nationalistic basis for elementary education, as already perceived, was the political one. The new impetus given to elementary education by the French Revolution was as important for political reasons as for nationalistic ones. Not only did the masses have to learn patriotic enthusiasm for their new liberties; they had also to learn how to exercise them. They had to learn not only the "rights of man" but his corresponding political duties as well.

The political implications of the American Revolution were even more important than the nationalistic ones for the aim of the common school in this country. If the people were to rule themselves, they needed to develop capacity for judging their own actions and the actions of others. For this they required an education that would free them from blind dependence on their leaders. They also needed to be as free from superstitious fear and prejudice as from chimerical hopes. Above all they needed to train their wits so as to be constantly alert to guarding freedom of opinion and conscience. That declamation gained a place in the common school curriculum in the early national period shows the eagerness of the people to prepare themselves for participation in the exciting innovation of launching the first great modern democracy.

While religion, economics, nationalism, and politics each in turn conditioned the rise and purpose of the elementary school, none of these large-scale social forces was entirely supplanted by the others that succeeded them. Although the force of each varied, their influence on the elementary school was exerted tandem or abreast right down to the twentieth century. Indeed, little if any change became noticeable even in that century. When in 1915 a national committee assumed the task of determining the minimum essentials of the various elementary school subjects, they used a criterion of elementary education still highly colored by its origins. It was their mature judgment that "the function of the elementary school is to provide those educational opportunities necessary to ensure, with the assistance of the other institutions of society, the acquisition on the part of elementary school children of those habits, skills, knowledges, ideals, and prejudices which must be made the common property of all, that each may be an efficient member of a progressive democratic society, possessing the power of self-support and self-direction, . . . the capacity and disposition for cooperative effort, and if possible the ability to direct others, if one is in a position of administrative responsibility."[8] In the next decade particular attention was given to specifying just what skills, knowledges, and ideals all children must possess. On the whole, specification followed religious, economic, and political aims already mentioned, to which were added command of the fundamental processes, worthy use of leisure, worthy home membership, and health.[9]

EXPANSION OF THE ELEMENTARY SCHOOL CURRICULUM

The process of multiplying and differentiating offerings in the common school curriculum went on throughout the nineteenth century. Basic in the elementary school curriculum during this entire period, of course, were the three R's, but even the three R's had growing pains. Of the three, probably reading was subdivided and expanded to the greatest extent. One direction taken by this development was the study of English grammar. This study of the structure of the vernacular was doubtless in part an influence of the secondary school, where Latin, especially Latin grammar, was the chief item in the curriculum. Another direction was the development of reading into declamation. Most early reading had been oral. Hence the step from the oft-repeated rereading of set selections in the reader to their oral declamation was a very short one. Toward the end of the century a wider selection of readings began to appear under the title of "litera-

---

[8] National Society for the Study of Education, *Minimum Essentials in Elementary School Subjects,* Fourteenth Yearbook (The University of Chicago Press, Chicago, 1915), part I, p. 15. See L. V. Koos, "Recent Conceptions of the Aims of Elementary Education," *Elementary School Journal,* 24:507–515, March, 1924.

[9] For a further discussion of these aims, see *supra,* p. 17.

ture." The Herbartian idea that the moral ends of education could be served by a study of literature[10] was no little responsible for this extension. The much later transition from oral to silent reading further reinforced the trend.

The expansion of the other two R's was not nearly so extensive. Although writing took on the fancy name of "penmanship" after the Civil War, it still remained the same basic skill. As social demands on the individual's skills increased, writing became almost as important as reading. Consequently, the importance of spelling increased proportionately. The same was true of arithmetic, although here the expansion was chiefly in the direction of mental arithmetic.

New additions to the elementary school curriculum were of several varieties. Among the first was geography. Its suitability to Pestalozzian object instruction[11] was one reason for inclusion, though its commercial and nationalistic significance was also recognized. History, too, was early added. Before the Civil War, history was largely absorbed incidentally through selections in the readers. After that war, however, it became an important study in the elementary school curriculum in its own right. Again the Herbartian employment of history to achieve the moral aims of education played a large part. Where political rather than moral ends predominated, history developed in the direction of instruction in civics.

Pestalozzian object instruction was also responsible for the introduction of nature study into the late-nineteenth-century elementary school curriculum. Yet some credit for this addition to the curriculum must go to Friedrich Wilhelm August Froebel (1872–1852), for an exceptionally important part of the equipment of every kindergarten was a garden of growing things. Elementary science gained admission with the ascendant star of science in industry. Emphasizing the child's sensory capacities and his propensities for action even more than science were the subjects of drawing and music, also introduced in this century. But also more often than science were they likely to be regarded as "fads and frills." Physical exercise was added, also, but the public was long skeptical about this, particularly in the face of out-of-school opportunities for exercise through work and play.

Of a more practical nature were several other innovations in the common, or elementary, school curriculum during this period. In the early part of the period, bookkeeping, which ordinarily was more likely to be found offered in the academy, received some recognition. Toward the end of the period, sewing and cooking for girls and manual training for boys began to enter the curriculum of the lower school. Their claims to attention, however, were not so much voca-

[10] *Supra,* pp. 325–326.
[11] *Supra,* pp. 207–211.

tional as pedagogical. Their pedagogical value seemed to lie in their being an excellent outlet for the exercise of youthful energies or, in the case of sloyd manual training, in their affording a kind of formal discipline. Where sloyd was advocated for its coordination of mind and body, it was sometimes offered to girls as well as boys.

TOWARD A GRADED SCHOOL

Originally the American common school, where the three R's were taught, was a one-room ungraded school. The number of classes that were "heard" by the single teacher in charge varied with a number of circumstances. The two principal considerations were the pupil's age and the subject taught. But as children's levels of achievement on entering school and their native capacities varied, the number of classes dictated by age and subject had to be multiplied. Worse yet, as this was the day before the vogue of uniform textbooks, classes had to be still further multiplied to make adjustments to the variety of books possessed by the families sending children to school. In consequence, the number of classes was usually so great as seriously to interfere with efficient instruction.

After the first quarter of the nineteenth century, arguments were persistently pressed for the improvement of instruction through the grading of the common school. The chief arguments for grading were pedagogical. The monitorial organization of schools obviously demanded grading. The Pestalozzian form of instruction, which came to supplant the monitorial, also required grading for its success. The teacher's oral questioning in connection with the observing and examining of objects could be effective only if the class was reasonably homogeneous.[12] A further professional argument in favor of grading was the division of labor it permitted among teachers according to their talents and training. Moreover, as the idea of grading became embodied in school architecture, so that the one-room school gave way to the multiroom building, grading made possible the assignment of each teacher to a separate room.[13]

Theoretically desirable as grading came to be acknowledged, it remained practically inadvisable, if not impossible, till the urbanization of our population brought about a sufficient concentration of families in one place. Even then, grading in this country began with founding

[12] For a discussion of the Pestalozzian method of instruction, see *supra*, pp. 207–211.

[13] Henry Barnard, Connecticut's great leader on the common school revival after 1838, had an excellent early grasp on the problem of grading. See J. S. Brubacher (ed.), *Henry Barnard on Education* (McGraw-Hill Book Company, New York, 1931), pp. 78–89.

and systematizing schools at different levels rather than with arranging grades within a given school. America had started with a two-class system of schools inherited from Europe and the Middle Ages. Above was one set of schools consisting of a Latin grammar school and a college for the social classes that aspired to leadership in church and state. Below was another set of schools of odd sorts and sizes for the general run of the population. In this set were the common schools, supplemented by various private-venture and philanthropic schools, such as the already noted dame and infant schools and monitorial schools. These two sets of schools were differentiated from each other not so much by being higher and lower rungs on the same educational ladder as by being patronized by higher and lower social classes.

A single educational ladder that reached unbroken by class distinction from the common school to the university had been the democratic ideal that Thomas Jefferson (1743–1826), author of the Declaration of Independence and third President of the United States, had proposed to the Legislature of his native state of Virginia.[14] But the idea was ahead of its time not only in Virginia but elsewhere. Much more closely representing the popular outlook of the day was the dual state system of schools actually set up in New York. There immediately after the Revolution a State Board of Regents was given oversight of secondary and higher education, but a "state superintendent of common schools" was not appointed till the second decade of the nineteenth century.

The various schools that had grown up at the elementary level were not at first organized systematically with reference to each other. Each had been founded to meet some particular need. Consequently, there was considerable overlapping of ages and services rendered. When population increased to a point at which school facilities needed to be enlarged, the early tendency was to establish another one-room ungraded school of the sorts already described. With the steady march of urbanization, however, cities began to try to meet the problem of expanding school facilities through grading. Not all cities had the same ungraded system at the start, and consequently the course of development toward a unified graded system of schools varied considerably from place to place.[15]

By the middle of the nineteenth century the pattern of the elementary system had begun to take definite shape. It consisted not always but frequently of three parts, the primary, intermediate, and

---

[14] C. F. Arrowood, *Thomas Jefferson and Education in a Republic* (McGraw-Hill Book Company, New York, 1930), chap. 7.

[15] For a sampling of various cities, see E. P. Cubberley, *Public Education in the United States* (Houghton Mifflin Company, Boston, 1934), p. 309.

grammar grades.[16] The division between the primary and upper grades stemmed in part from the differences between the infant and the common schools and in part from a distinction in the common school that reflected the old division between the reading and writing schools. Thus, in the common school there seems to have been a lower division emphasizing reading and an upper, or advanced, division in which reading was continued but writing was included along with arithmetic, spelling, grammar, geography, and sometimes bookkeeping. In many communities the upper division was called the "grammar school." But in not a few places the grammar school was further subdivided into the grammar grades proper and the intermediate grades, the latter between the grammar and the primary grades.

The length of time consumed in passing through the primary, intermediate, and grammar grades also varied in different communities. This was due in part to different allotments of time possessed by the three divisions of school before their organization into a single system. In New England a nine-year elementary school was not uncommon. In some places in the South and Middle West there was a seven-year elementary school. But in the course of time an elementary school of eight years came to be the norm. It is a moot point how much this result was the product of indigenous American conditions and how much an imitation of the Prussian eight-year *Volksschule,* which was much admired in the United States and the graded system of which was highly recommended as a model by returned American observers from abroad, like Horace Mann, Henry Barnard, and Calvin Stowe.[17]

By the post-Civil War period the graded elementary school was thoroughly established. Indeed, if one judges by the way in which the rest of the school program was organized on the basis of it, the course of study was carefully planned in detail, grade by grade. Textbook publishers followed suit with whole "graded" series of readers, arithmetics, and the like. Written examinations were the gates between grades, and these gates swung open and shut in a scheme of annual promotions. In fact, the administrative machinery was so

[16] The grammar grades, where English grammar was taught, are to be distinguished from the Latin grammar school, which was a secondary school.

[17] Quite a controversy was waged at one time over this point. See C. H. Judd, "Prussia and Our Schools," *New Republic,* 14:347–349, April, 1918; P. Monroe, "Further Consideration of Prussia and Our Schools," *School and Society,* 7: 691–694, June, 1918; C. H. Judd, "Shall We Continue to Imitate Prussia?" *School and Society,* 7:751–754, June, 1918; P. Monroe, "Shall We Continue to Advocate Reforms by False Arguments?" *School and Society,* 8:290–294, September, 1918. See also F. F. Bunker, *The Reorganization of the Public School System,* U.S. Bureau of Education Bulletin 8, 1916, pp. 19–28.

highly perfected that soon the elementary schools were caught in a lock step from which heroic efforts were to be necessary to extricate them.

PROMOTION

Attention was focused on the faults of the system when rumblings of discontent were voiced by Charles W. Eliot (1834–1926), Harvard's widely influential president. In 1892, he spoke before the National Education Association on "undesirable and desirable uniformity in the schools." He particularly complained of the way in which the system of grading and promotion suppressed rather than took account of individual differences. That this was the effect of grading and promotion is not surprising. Grading was originally recommended so that a teacher would be faced by children of similar age and scholastic attainment. It was logically to be expected, therefore, that the teacher's classroom efforts would be directed toward all alike and that promotions should be made in grade lots according to some uniform standard.

But the fact gradually forced itself on educators' minds that grading had not achieved as much homogeneity in the classroom as had been anticipated. In one direction this was felt in the great amount of retardation that tended to occur in the various grades. In another direction there was a feeling that the bright and capable child was not being advanced rapidly enough. A number of practices began to appear about 1890 that tried to remedy this situation by introducing greater flexibility into the scheme of promotion.

Even before 1890 the seriousness of this problem was recognized in a number of cities, notably, Quincy, Massachusetts, and St. Louis, Missouri. In these cities the trouble was thought to reside in the policy of annual promotions. An adjustment was therefore made by placing promotion on a semiannual or even quarterly basis. This more frequent reclassification of pupils was a great advantage to those failing of promotion, for it eliminated the necessity of repeating a whole long year's work.

Another scheme was widely known as the "Batavia Plan," taking its name from the community in New York where it had its origin. The school system there recognized two groups in the classroom, those making normal progress and those tending to lag behind. If the class was under fifty in number, the teacher was allowed to devote special attention to coaching the laggards. If the class was over fifty, an assistant teacher was appointed to take care of this group.[18] By this device both groups were brought along over the

[18] In North Pueblo, Colo., the assistant teacher was assigned the regular group.

same ground so that they could be promoted together at the same time.

In Cambridge, Massachusetts, the elementary school program was divided into two parallel courses, one of six and the other of eight years' duration. Both covered the same curriculum, but one faster than the other. At convenient points children could be transferred from one course to the other as their abilities seemed to warrant. The Cambridge Plan had the advantage over the Batavia Plan in that its emphasis was on pushing the bright ahead rather than on bringing the dull up to standard.

A further variation of the Cambridge Plan was one attempted in Santa Barbara, California, and Baltimore, Maryland. Here a six-year elementary school was organized in three parallel courses. The three, instead of covering the same ground at different rates, maintained the same rate but covered varying amounts of ground. The average child covered an average curriculum, the slow child a minimum curriculum, and the gifted an enriched curriculum in each of the six elementary years. All finished at the same time but with varying accomplishments.

This plan of grading and promotion took a further lease on life when the psychological-testing movement got under way after the First World War. The results of the new intelligence and achievement tests gave educators fresh confidence in being able to group children homogeneously. As a result, a number of ways of grouping children were tried. To cover the wide variety of plans conveniently, they were designated "*XYZ* ability grouping." Essentially, these plans centered in a curriculum readjustment rather than in a mere administrative arrangement. They aimed to separate children of a given grade into ability groupings so that each child might have a curriculum and rate of progress suited to his ability. While some benefit attached to this aim, it was not without drawbacks. Some thought it undemocratic. Others pointed out that no group was ever entirely homogeneous since the individual child varied in his own abilities. Therefore, a child could not be put in an *X, Y,* or *Z* group for all his school activities but would have to be constantly regrouped as the type of activity changed.

Most flexible of all was a plan tried out in Pueblo, Colorado, before the end of the nineteenth century. There each child was allowed to proceed at his own rate regardless of the progress of his fellows. Such a plan, of course, placed a considerable burden on school administration. The development of individualized methods of instruction described earlier[19] all worked hand in glove to make this burden of administration lighter.

Perhaps the most widely adopted scheme since the turn of the

[19] *Supra,* p. 236.

century has been one that left the conventional graded system relatively untouched. Treating flexibility in promotion more as an *ad hoc* problem, it plucked out victims of the system here and there and organized them into special classes. These classes have gone by a variety of names, "ungraded classes," "opportunity classes," and the like. Here have been placed overage children, children who have fallen behind because of absence through illness, those who need coaching in some special subject, and so on. Assignment to such classes is usually not permanent but merely till the child is ready to return to his regular grade. Such a scheme obviously serves the double purpose of relieving the regular grade of the burden of carrying a retarded pupil and at the same time affording the retarded pupil better instruction than he could obtain in his regular grade. On occasion, the device has been used to provide special opportunities for gifted children.

ECONOMIZING TIME

Another attack on the lock step of the graded elementary school was aimed at its length. This attack, even more notably than the one on inflexible promotion, was led by President Eliot. At the meeting of the National Education Association in 1888 he addressed himself to the question: Can school programs be shortened and enriched? He thought they not only could but must be shortened in order that the graduates of colleges and graduate schools might embark sooner on the task of earning their living. In Eliot's mind one way to lower the alarming rise in college entrance age was to reduce the program of the eight-year elementary school. He pointed in particular to arithmetic and the excessive time given to reviews as absorbing more than a justifiable proportion of the latter years of elementary education.

Eliot's address provoked much discussion in the next few years. The upshot of this discussion was the appointment of two famous committees by the National Education Association, the Committee of Ten and the Committee of Fifteen. The former, after studying the secondary school problem, reported in 1893. The latter, after studying possible economies in elementary education, reported two years later. Both reports recommended much the same plan of economy. Their plan called for shortening the elementary school offering enough to permit algebra to replace much of seventh- and eighth-grade arithmetic and Latin to take the place of English grammar in the eighth grade. These recommendations obviously had the interests of higher education in view and reveal the predominance of college professors in the composition of the committees.

In spite of this bias, the idea of economizing in the elementary school program caught the imagination of public school men. After the turn of the century they continued to discuss it from angles other than that of college preparation. For example, they wondered whether large numbers of pupils dropped out of school before reaching high school because the program of the seventh and eighth grades was at fault. The new study of the psychology of adolescence also raised the question of whether the line between elementary and secondary education should not be redrawn. For these and other reasons the principle that elementary education should be foreshortened by two years so as to include the ages six to twelve was gradually accepted. The period of secondary education, thus, was to commence two years earlier and include a span of six rather than four years of schooling.[20]

Impossible as it may seem, the curtailment of elementary education was to be compensated by an enrichment of its program. Yet there was no thought that this enrichment should be accomplished by cramming what had previously been given in eight years into the former span of six. To be sure, some compensation was sought in the prolonging of the school year, but the main effort at enrichment while curtailing the elementary school was sought in a different direction. This direction was to find out as scientifically as possible what were justifiable minimum essentials in each subject field in the elementary school curriculum.[21] To ensure further enrichment through more vital instructional procedures, a similar scientific analysis of methods of teaching elementary school subjects was also undertaken.[22] In fact, the general improvement of teacher training was collaterally promoted in order to give effect to Eliot's belief that the elementary school program could be both shortened and enriched.

THE KINDERGARTEN

Curiously enough, at the very moment when reasons of economy of time were dictating an abbreviation of the upper years of the elementary school, forces were already afoot to extend its lower years. The last two decades of the nineteenth century thus not only witnessed

---

[20] For a more complete account of how the last two years of the elementary school became incorporated into the junior high school, see *infra,* pp. 417–419.

[21] National Society for the Study of Education, *Fourteenth, Sixteenth,* and *Seventeenth Yearbooks,* being the first, second, and third reports of the Committee on Minimum Essentials in Elementary School Subjects (The University of Chicago Press, Chicago, 1915; Public School Publishing Company, Bloomington, Ill., 1917, 1918).

[22] National Society for the Study of Education, *Principles of Method,* Eighteenth Yearbook (Public School Publishing Company, Bloomington, Ill., 1919).

Eliot's demand for shortening the elementary school but also saw the growth of the kindergarten as a form of preprimary schooling. The historical account of this addition to the elementary school can best be begun by picking up again the development of the infant school, which has already been mentioned.

The idea of a school for very young children was entertained by Johann Amos Comenius (1592–1670), who advocated a school of infancy in conjunction with the home. There he wanted special attention given food, sleep, fresh air, and exercise in order to build up a body fit for the habitation of the soul. Robert Owen shared his idea of an infant school with a Frenchman, Jean Frédéric Oberlin (1740–1826), who originated the *salles d'hospitalité,* which in the course of time gave way to the *salles d'asile* and were finally incorporated into the French public school system as the *écoles maternelles.* Schools of a similar type in Germany were known as the *Kleinkinderbewahranstalten.* The object of all these schools, as of the infant school, was to emphasize health, physical exercise, and moral training for children of tender years and to "annoy" them as little as possible with books. This stress on the spontaneous activities of children favorably inclined Owen toward Pestalozzian methods,[23] which he was disposed to introduce into his school at New Lanark.

In the hands of Owens's successors the infant school became more and more formal, like the school for the age level just above where children were first formally introduced to the three R's. The change in spirit can be easily inferred from the testimony of a noted infant school master, Samuel Wilderspin (1792–1866), before a committee of Parliament studying this sort of school. It was his claim that before the age of seven a child educated in an infant school should be able to read any book in simple language, should know the first rules of arithmetic and many of the elements of geography and natural history, and should have a "tolerable" knowledge of the New Testament and sundry other items.[24] Such expectations were, of course, quite inflated. The infant school that made its way to American shores, while less ambitious than Wilderspin's, yet was more or less of the formal sort. Because of this it soon lost its identity in the primary grades of the common school, the work of which it tended to duplicate.

Not till the introduction of the kindergarten into the United States from Germany in the latter half of the nineteenth century did the original idea of a different sort of education for the very young of

---

[23] For a fuller account of these methods, see *supra,* pp. 207–211.

[24] Wilderspin made his chief exposition of the infant school in *A System for the Education of the Young* (James S. Hodson, London, 1840).

preprimary age receive the further exploration it deserved. Owen had stressed physical activity in the infant school for the important but rather limited purposes of health. Froebel, the founder of the kindergarten, went further and laid the basis of the kindergarten in physical activity for deep and broad philosophical reasons.[25] He felt that the core of the kindergarten curriculum should be the play activities of children. Instead of viewing games lightly, he thought of them as children's most serious occupation. Play he saw as the form that children's activities took in their quest for self-development toward the eternal unity that unites all things—God.

For example, Froebel made much of games played with a ball, for, from contact with the ball, he expected the child to develop a sense of unity. Similarly, when the child played with a large wooden cube divided into eight smaller cubes of equal size, he was supposed to be learning about the relation of whole and part. Again, the social organization of the kindergarten was expected to symbolize the same concepts about the whole and the part. To reinforce this notion, Froebel emphasized games in which children were arranged in a circle, which also conveyed the idea of unity. Drawing, painting, paper folding and cutting, and clay modeling were other natural forms of self-activity that he marked for inclusion in the kindergarten. But, true to his philosophy, he advocated a rather formal kind of art because of its supposed greater symbolism. Not least among the arts, singing, too, received great attention as a form of self-activity.[26]

The kindergarten, so radically different from the conventional primary grades of the elementary school, became increasingly popular in the United States after the Civil War. At first, individual kindergartens were set up under private auspices. Soon associations sprang up in the more important centers to spread the idea. The exhibit of kindergarten materials in 1876 at the Centennial Exposition in Philadelphia further stimulated the movement. Kindergartens were also established in connection with settlement and welfare centers. No little impetus was felt from a contemporary revival of the arts generally, which saw a natural ally in the kindergarten.

The first public kindergarten was in Boston, but there the seed fell on shallow soil and withered soon after springing up. The credit for the first permanent kindergarten, therefore, went to St. Louis, where Susan Blow (1843–1916) under the leadership of Superintendent William Torrey Harris (1835–1909), later United States Com-

[25] For a fuller account of Froebel's educational philosophy, see *supra,* pp. 214–217. For his method, see *supra,* pp. 125–127.

[26] See Froebel's *Mutter- und Kose-Lieder.* Note, too, how the role of the mother had been anticipated in Comenius's "school of the mother's knee."

missioner of Education, became one of the foremost kindergartners in America. The incorporation of the kindergarten into the public school system of the country was a slower process. Some communities were deterred by the expense of purchasing the kindergarten materials and also by the smaller pupil-teacher ratio required. Others were deterred by law, which gave a narrow definition to the limits of the common, or elementary, school.

Even where the kindergarten became a legal part of the public school system, it remained for long a separate institution in spirit. The primary teachers looked with suspicion on the kindergarten because they thought its curriculum of play activities was a poor preparation for the serious work and study of the primary grades. The kindergarten teachers responded with criticism of the procedures of the primary grades in the light of what they believed to be the superior educational philosophy of Froebel. In trying to extend this philosophy into the primary grades, they were but doing what Froebel himself planned to do. If the principle of self-activity in his philosophy was sound, then it undergirded not just the kindergarten but the upper grades as well. And this is exactly the direction in which it expanded. In the course of time the quarrel between the kindergarten and the primary grades subsided, and a considerable interpenetration of ideas took place. But in this interpenetration there can be no doubt that the influence of the kindergarten was the more marked.

The predominance of kindergarten principles, however, did not take place without a considerable modification in their scientific and philosophic support. After 1900, kindergartners divided into two camps. One was orthodoxly Froebelian and followed Miss Blow. The other was more heterodox and followed the restatements of kindergarten principles made by Patty Smith Hill (1868–1946). The latter was much influenced by the educational philosophy of John Dewey and the educational psychology of G. Stanley Hall (1846–1924) and Edward Lee Thorndike (1874–1949). They both perceived the main contribution of the kindergarten to lie in its activity program. This, they saw, could stand on biological, psychological, or pragmatic bases just as well as on Froebel's brand of philosophic idealism. Consequently, they quickly discarded Froebel's symbolism as too mystical, as lacking warrant in fact. Liberated from the cramping necessity of extracting certain symbolic effects from games, songs, and art activities, Patty Hill conducted the first modern kindergarten where these activities were enjoyed for their own sake. Freedom was accorded children in these activities in order that they might learn to adapt materials and activities to achieve purposes of their own. It was this conception of the kindergarten which came to predominate in the twentieth century.

THE NURSERY SCHOOL

The kindergarten extended the downward reach of the elementary school by only a year or two. That meant that in most communities there were four preschool years in which the home still served as the main educational agency. These years, however, did not escape the careful study of men trained in psychology and medicine. Preeminent in this investigation was Arnold Gesell (1880–1961) at Yale, who held degrees in both these fields. His research and that of others led many to adopt the conclusion that the first years of life were far more critical for the future development of the child than had hitherto been realized.[27] Many physical and mental maladjustments of later years, it was claimed, could be traced back to the growth and development that took place in these earliest years. Proper care and attention in this period might easily prevent the latter effects of communicable disease or dietary deficiency. Similarly, some of the worst types of phobia, inferiority complex, aggression, and repression of primitive impulses in adult years might easily be eliminated if action could be taken during infancy. Facts such as these cried out for some ounce of prevention before waiting for a cure that would have to be measured by the pound. About 1920, Yale and Iowa set up psychological clinics to minister to this urgent need.

Several years before this action, a new educational institution, the nursery school,[28] offered its services and grew rapidly in the next two decades. Such a school had already enjoyed nearly a decade of successful experience in England. The American nursery school opened its doors to children of prekindergarten age, accepting children as young as eighteen months and as old as four years. The daily program was largely composed of free-play activities to which the nursery school teacher paid close attention to see what attitudes and

[27] See A. Gesell, *The Pre-school Child* (Houghton Mifflin Company, Boston, 1923).

[28] See two significant statements of J. B. Watson. "Our own view after studying many hundreds of babies is that one can make or break the child so far as its personality is concerned long before the age of five is reached. We believe that by the end of the second year the pattern of the future individual is already laid down." (J. B. Watson and R. R. Watson, "Studies in Infant Psychology," *Scientific Monthly*, 13:494, December, 1921.) "I have come to the conclusion, possibly without sufficient experimental data, that the first few years are all-important ones for shaping the emotional life of the child. . . . I see no way of getting the information we so much desire except by the use of slow and intense experimental methods. . . . I suggest the establishment of an experimental nursery where fifteen to twenty children can be brought up during the first five years of life." H. S. Jennings, J. B. Watson, A. Meyer, and W. I. Thomas, *Suggestions of Modern Science concerning Education* (The Macmillan Company, New York, 1917), pp. 74–77.

habits were being formed. In addition, the children had a medical inspection on coming to school, and if they stayed to lunch, their diet and eating habits were also carefully supervised.

As will be seen, the nursery school program resembled that of the revised and modernized kindergarten, only at a lower level of maturity. It would be a mistake, however, to think that the nursery school was only a downward extension of the kindergarten. As a matter of fact, its much greater attention to physical and mental health definitely characterized the nursery school as an indigenous growth in the American educational system.

The nursery school at times has been confused with the day nursery. The antecedents of the day nursery were sociological rather than psychological and medical. Working conditions that drew the mother away from home gave rise to the need for some place where the mother might, so to speak, "check" her child during working hours. This was the idea behind the French crèche opened in Paris just before the middle of the last century. In the crèche, or day nursery, the child's physical needs were cared for during the mother's absence but nothing was undertaken with educational ends in view. The English nursery school movement, too, commenced more as a self-protective social measure or as a phase of public health. The psychological and educational aspects of the movement were rather meager.

But even where the psychological and educational aspects of the nursery school were prominent, as in the United States, there was still a sociological problem involved in the relation of the nursery school to the family. Clearly, the nursery school was encroaching on the preschool educational functions hitherto exercised by the home. The declared purpose of the movement, however, was not to supplant the home but to supplement it. Certainly, some supplement was necessary. The growth in technical knowledge of the preschool child had increased so rapidly since the First World War that few parents could keep abreast of it unaided. In this connection it is interesting to note that the Merrill-Palmer School at Detroit, in which a nursery school is very prominent, was founded with the avowed purpose of strengthening parental training. Another convenient supplement that the nursery school offered the home was an adequately equipped place where the prekindergarten child could play with others of his own age under skilled supervision.

Like the kindergarten, the nursery school had to start as a private enterprise. In fact, in the mid-twentieth century it was still largely in that phase. The anxieties that deterred the public adoption of the kindergarten arose again to hold back the public adoption of the nursery school. During the Great Depression of the 1930s the Federal government supported nursery schools, but chiefly to relieve unemployment among teachers. Incidentally, it hoped that the service rendered the community would be so great that popular pressure would be brought to bear on states and municipalities to continue the service once Federal aid was withdrawn at the end of the Depression.

INNOVATIONS IN METHODS AND MATERIALS

The criticism that found a target in the elementary school's regimented system of grading and promoting children was not long in making a further target of its curriculum and methods of teaching. These, as already noticed, early submitted to the forces of uniformity that mechanized grading and promotion. What the long-term effect of this submission had become is worth describing.

The average American elementary school at the turn of the century had a school term of considerably less than half a calendar year. Three-quarters of this time was spent on the formal subjects, which, on the whole, were taught in a very mechanical and frequently a disciplinary manner. The ready-made list of spelling words and arithmetic problems often bore no vital relation to the needs of the society in which the child lived. If he was fortunate in his reader, his selections were chosen from the best in English literature. If not, he probably fed from selections off the intellectual scrap heap of the past. Well drilled in the selections of his reader, the student often found difficulty in reading at sight, as the school committee of Quincy found to its sorrow in its famous examination of 1873. Similarly able to recite rules of grammar, he was frequently unable to use them in writing his own compositions. Furthermore, in "penmanship" few children of that period ever learned to write an easily legible hand. And in history and geography the pupils' knowledge was usually in the form of a skeleton outline from which some of the more important bones were missing.

Startlingly enough, a quarter of a century later painfully similar conditions were described as obtaining in *Middletown*, the average town of the United States. "The school, like the factory," ran the sociological description of this town, "is a thoroughly regimented world. Immovable seats in orderly rows fix the sphere of activity of each child. For all, from the timid six-year-old entering for the first time to the most assured high school senior, the general routine is much the same. Bells divide the day into periods. For the six-year-olds the periods are short (fifteen to twenty-five minutes) and varied; in some they leave their seats, play games, and act out make-believe stories, although in 'recitation periods' all movement is prohibited. As they grow older the taboo upon physical activity becomes stricter, until by the third or fourth year practically all movement is forbidden except the marching from one set of seats to another between periods, a brief interval of prescribed exercise daily, and periods of manual training or home economics once or twice a week. There are 'study periods' in which children learn 'lessons' from 'textbooks' prescribed by the state and 'recitation periods' in which they tell an adult teacher what the book has said; one hears children reciting the battles of the Civil War in one recitation period, the rivers of Africa in another, the 'parts of speech' in a third; the method is much the same."[29]

Paradoxically, in the very period when the great run of schools changed their procedures but little, more changes than ever before were being advocated. The first suggestions for change came from Europe, from which both Pestalozzian and Herbartian methods were introduced to leaven the American educational lump.[30] Though both methods had their heyday in this period, their vitality was soon spent, and they succumbed to formalism. In fact, once formalized, they did not so much continue to protest against as to conform to the inertia and mechanism so characteristic of the graded elementary school of the times. This was particularly true of the teacher-centered Herbartian procedures.

A more far-reaching and enduring reform of elementary school conditions was sponsored and tended by Colonel Francis W. Parker (1831–1902), who was called to Quincy, Massachusetts, to try to remedy the distressingly formal instruction revealed by the examination of 1873. Although he employed Pestalozzian and Herbartian procedures, Parker was much more deeply influenced by Froebelian ones. To him the center of the educational process was not objects of nature, as to Johann Heinrich Pestalozzi, or history and literature, as to Johann Friedrich Herbart, but the child himself. Believing wholeheartedly with Froebel[31] in the pedagogical principle of self-activity, Parker concentrated the work of the elementary school on self-expression, especially in the forms of reading and writing. All other subjects, like history and geography, he taught incidentally to these two. Thus, history and geography were sources in which one read for information, and writing was a means of expressing oneself. Other types of activity, which he developed at Quincy and especially later at the Cook County Normal School in Illinois, involved drawing, clay modeling, field trips, and the like.

---

[29] R. S. Lynd and H. M. Lynd, *Middletown* (Harcourt, Brace and Company, Inc., New York, 1929), pp. 188–189.

[30] For an extended discussion of these methods, see *supra*, pp. 207–211, 212–214.

[31] For a fuller account of Froebel and his ideas, see *supra*, pp. 125–127, 214–217.

It was not long before Quincy parents were criticizing Parker for turning their elementary schools into natural history museums and "mud-pie factories." They also expressed grave doubts that the three R's could be mastered when subjects were incidentally correlated to central processes of reading and writing. To settle the storm that was brewing, the Massachusetts State Board of Education conducted an examination of Quincy children in old-type subject matter. The results showed that the children surpassed those trained in traditional methods. Ultimately the fame of what came to be known as the "Quincy new departure" spread far and wide, and visitors from many parts of the country came to inspect it.

Another and contemporary new departure from conventional practice was the Workingmen's School launched by Felix Adler (1851–1933), founder of the ethical-culture movement. Into the curriculum of this school Adler introduced sloyd manual training and industrial processes. The idea behind this departure was not so much vocational as it was Froebelian. What better outlet for self-activity, thought Adler, than the opportunity for shaping objects to serve human ends. Hence, to learning through manipulating or playing with objects or gifts, as Pestalozzi and Froebel had recommended, Adler added learning through the actual construction of objects in the workshop.

THE ERA OF PROGRESSIVE EDUCATION

Parker and Adler, however, were merely the early or distant rumblings of the storm of protest that had been gathering over the schools, secondary as well as elementary. The storm broke in full force in the twentieth century. In the next two decades a great variety of indigenously American new departures sprang up. Other forces in the social subsoil seemed to unite to make the crop large and successful. For one thing, the scientific study of educational psychology was putting forth some of its earliest and most vigorous shoots at this time.[32] For another, educational philosophy was beginning to respond to the indigenously American philosophy of pragmatism.[33] For yet another, art, music, and literature were seeking new media of expression.[34] The spirit of protest and reform was abroad even in politics and economics as well as in the arts and education.[35]

---

[32] For a more extended account of this development, see *supra,* pp. 150–166.

[33] For a more extended account of this development, see *supra,* pp. 130–134.

[34] See I. L. Kandel, *The End of an Era* (Bureau of Publications, Teachers College, Columbia University, New York, 1941), pp. 41–48.

[35] For a more extended account of this development, see *supra,* pp. 46–47, 95–97.

This was the "progressive era" in American history when states were experimenting with social legislation such as the eight-hour day, with the popular recall of judges, and with the initiative and referendum. People seemed to have a renewed confidence that old abuses did not have to be endured and that by taking thought they could remold their institutions nearer to their hearts' desire.[36] The educational aspect of this period of protest and reform came to be known as the "progressive-education movement."[37]

The experimental elementary school directed by John Dewey at the University of Chicago after 1894 was one of the first and foremost examples of the new, or progressive, education.[38] Dewey thought it was an archaic practice for elementary schools to spend 75 to 80 per cent of their time on verbal studies. While such a proportion might have been proper before the invention of printing, in the twentieth century it amounted to forcing a middle- and upper-class education on the mass of the population. In place of such an education Dewey substituted one centering in occupations. His occupations, however, were not the symbolic ones of Froebel but the current social ones of the home and community with which the child was becoming increasingly familiar. Thus, Dewey's school started with household occupations. From here foods and textiles were later traced to the source of their production. Still later, occupations were seen in their historical setting. Number work was done incidentally to occupations like carpentry and cooking. Reading and writing began in the children's keeping of their own records. These and other activities were all conceived in a social context, for it was Dewey's idea that education was the regulation of a process whereby the child came increasingly to share in the social consciousness.

[36] *Cf.* eighteenth century rationalism, *supra,* pp. 35–37, 93, 95.

[37] For the use of the phrase "progressive education" prior to 1918, see R. R. Palm, "The Origins of Progressive Education," *Journal of Elementary Education,* 40:442–449, February, 1940. In Europe the movement was better known as the "new education," but this phrase, too, had an ancient usage. The Greek dramatist Aristophanes, for instance, entertained his audiences by ridiculing the "new" education of the Sophists in comparison with the "old," or traditional, education sanctioned by custom. Prior to the twentieth century the new, or progressive, education was chiefly a protest against the formal traditionalism of the day. It was not till the current century that progress became the basis of a positive, constructive theory of education. The best account of this twentieth-century movement is to be found in L. Cremin, *The Transformation of the School* (Alfred A. Knopf, Inc., New York, 1961).

[38] K. C. Mayhew and A. C. Edwards, *TThe Dewey School* (Appleton-Century-Crofts, Inc., New York, 1936). See also J. Dewey, *School and Society* (The University of Chicago Press, Chicago, 1900). For a more complete account of Dewey's philosophy of education and his influence on method, see *supra,* pp. 130–134.

Other experimental schools, such as Marietta Johnson's school at Fairhope, Alabama, in 1907, Caroline Pratt's Play School in New York City in 1913, and Margaret Naumberg's Children's School, also in New York City, in 1916, followed in rapid succession. Marietta Johnson endeavored to set up an organic type of education. The conventional conception of education for future ends or deferred values was abandoned in favor of one that concentrated on the growth of the child in the present. Assigned tasks and fixed requirements for promotion were shelved in favor of work that was suitable to the child's present level of growth. In the Play School, later the City and Country School, materials of instruction were used freely instead of symbolically as with Froebel or didactically as with Maria Montessori. Children undertook "jobs" and were allowed much freedom in devising ways and means to accomplish them. Margaret Naumberg's Children's School was dominated by psychological notions set in motion by Sigmund Freud (1856–1939), the founder of psychoanalysis.[39] She conceived the problem of weaning the child from his early egocentrism as a more complex emotional task than had been recognized hitherto. Conventional education, she thought, merely corrected symptoms of these deep emotional drives and therefore often resulted in unfortunate repressions. To bring the child's unconscious or subconscious to the surface in a worthy form of expression she held one of the major functions of her school. To this end great freedom was permitted, especially in art work, which was viewed as one of the best channels by which to bring out the child's inner life.

As can be seen, the emphasis in each of these schools was quite different. The import of progressive education for the elementary school, therefore, was not one uniform policy but a potpourri of policies that were sometimes even conflicting. The critics of progressive elementary schools, however, were not so discriminating. The two characteristics of which they saw all progressive schools possessed and the two which they made the chief targets of their attacks against all such schools were their increased emphasis on freedom and interest for the pupil. Many thought the increase excessive. Creative as this expressionism could be on the one hand, shoddy was the only term for its opposite results. Moreover, in the minds of many, preoccupation with the subconscious of children and the avoidance of neurotic repression became associated with the denial of authority. In order not to be identified with such extreme friends of freedom in the new education, Dewey found it necessary to distinguish his own position from theirs in the 1920s and again in the

[39] For a fuller account of Freud's influence in educational psychology, see *supra,* pp. 160–161.

1930s.[40] In spite of his care, critics like the "essentialists" continued to attack all progressives alike.

While the average American community was slow to modify its practices in the light of the experience of experimental schools, as *Middletown* bears witness, the infiltration of new ideas was very rapid in the two decades between the First and the Second World War. By 1937 a revisit in Middletown showed that it had gone "conservatively progressive" in its elementary schools.[41] This is a good phrase in which to describe the cautious spirit in which educational advance was made. Sentimental regard for uninhibited freedom in education made little headway against forces of social solidarity that became increasingly strong as the date of America's entry into the Second World War approached. On the other hand, such valuable contributions to elementary education as a regard for the "whole" child, attention to the attitudes learned as well as to the subject matter, the importance of emotions, great attention to individual differences, a greatly expanded and diversified curriculum, and a redirected emphasis on "activity"—all these seemed here to stay even in the more conventional schools.

When World War II ended, however, a new assault was mounted against progressive education which spread to education generally. In spite of the defeat of the fascist powers Americans still did not feel secure. The "hot" war with Germany was succeeded by the "cold" war with Russia. Instead of ascribing victory in the hot war at least in part to the schools where its heroes had been prepared, apprehensive critics wheeled about and made the schools the scapegoat for the frustrations of the cold war. The Duke of Wellington had ascribed the victory at Waterloo to the playing fields of Eton, and the Prussians had credited victory in the Franco-Prussian War to the Prussian schoolmaster. But Americans felt no such educational debt of gratitude.

The assault on the schools came on two fronts. On one front, it loomed as a renewal of the charge that the schools were guilty of a exaggerated romanticism. Furthermore, important as freedom and interest were, progressive educators were charged with emphasizing them to the neglect of drill in fundamentals. On a second front, critics had little patience with the complexities of learning which the scientific study of education posed to progressives. These complexities they simplified (countercritics thought oversimplified) by demand-

---

[40] See J. Dewey, *Art and Education* (The Barnes Foundation Press, Merion, Pa., 1929); *Education and Experience* (The Macmillan Company, New York, 1938).

[41] R. S. Lynd and H. M. Lynd, *Middletown in Transition* (Harcourt, Brace & World, Inc., New York, 1937), p. 204.

ing a return to traditional patterns. Reading was a good example. Disregarding much good scientific study of reading problems resulting in the whole-word or "look-say" method, they demanded a one-sided return to phonetics.[42]

Yet the criticism was not entirely negative. The conservatives seemed to have a positive rationale even if not always clearly stated or comprehended by them. This rationale took its cue from a Humanism trying to make a seeming last-ditch stand against the encroachments of the empiricism and relativism of progressivism. Since society does not value the kind of "basic education"[43] it ought to, conservatives recommended the kind judged good by a wise minority. It avoided a majority preference by pointing out that ours is not a democracy but a republic.

After a half-century of progressivism in education it is not surprising that a severe reappraisal was under way.[44] To this no one could take exception. But educators did become deeply resentful of sarcastic polemics directed against the schools[45] and venomous opportunistic propaganda aimed at undermining public confidence in the whole educational enterprise.[46] The amount of space given to charge and countercharge added up to the severest and most widespread critique of the schools in American educational history.[47] But more of the "cold" war on education in succeeding chapters.[48]

[42] For example, R. Flesch, *Why Johnny Can't Read and What You Can Do about It* (Popular Library Inc., New York, 1956).

[43] J. D. Koerner, *The Case for Basic Education* (Little, Brown and Company, Boston, 1959).

[44] H. L. Caswell, "The Great Reappraisal of Public Education," *Teachers College Record*, 54:12–22, 1952.

[45] For example, A. Lynd, *Quackery in the Public Schools* (Atlantic Monthly Press, Little, Brown and Company, Boston, 1953).

[46] For example, Allan Zoll's National Council for American Education.

[47] For a wider sampling of criticisms, see C. M. Hill and C. W. Scott (eds.), *Public Education under Criticism* (Prentice-Hall, Inc., Englewood Cliffs, N.J., 1954). For an analysis of this criticism, see M. A. Raywid, *The Ax-grinders* (The Macmillan Company, New York, 1962). See also W. Van Til, "Is Progressive Education Obsolete?" *Saturday Review,* February, 1962.

[48] *Infra,* pp. 424–426, 489–492, 559–560.

14 Secondary Education

Secondary education has been one of the most prized of all formal types of education. It has enjoyed esteem because it has been the rung of the educational ladder that has led to opportunity and preferment. On this account, educators and laymen have perennially paid close attention to the secondary school. Hence, what its aims should be, of what its curriculum should consist, and to what educational clientele it should appeal are questions that have grown more persistent with the years.

Of these questions the most strategic is doubtless the last. It can be raised more specifically in several ways. Shall secondary education be open to all or to just the few; shall it be universal or selective; shall it be predicated on equality of opportunity or on social status? Patently, one's decision on this point will largely determine what he thinks the aims of secondary education ought to be. Shall secondary schools be primarily preoccupied with preparation of youth for college or with preparation for immediate social competence in life; should their primary function be preparatory or terminal? The decision on this point together with the decision on clientele further determines the questions of curriculum. Shall the same secondary school curriculum be provided for all, or should provision be made for differentiation; should the curriculum be prescribed or elective? Again, should the curriculum at this level emphasize general or vocational education? Incidentally, how long a period should secondary education cover; what are secondary education's proper boundaries with elementary education below and higher education above?

CLASSICAL ORIGIN OF THE GRAMMAR SCHOOL

Pre-Christian Greek society was one of the first to feel the necessity of finding answers to the foregoing questions. The rapid rise of the Greeks to leadership in the economic and political life of the eastern Mediterranean made it imperative that they develop educational opportunities beyond the elementary level. As long as society was relatively simple and demanded only moral and physical education, elementary education was enough. The development of traits or virtues like courage, endurance, reverence, obedience, loyalty, and temperance could be accomplished through training or habituation. The accumulation of economic leisure and the acquisition of political hegemony, however, made new demands which gave rise to considerable self-examination among the Greeks. Curiosity about their social conventions led to inquiry into these conventions or institutions, and inquiry led to innovation. At this point it became clear that an education which consisted of mere training or habituation would no longer suffice. Something more intellectual was now in order.

Ability to participate in the public discussions of the day, whether of politics or philosophy—problems that were never far removed from each other in the Greek mind—required education beyond the ordinary. Especially, it required skill in expressing oneself clearly and cogently. Hence, it was not long before schools sprang up that offered to give students a mastery of the linguistic techniques of grammar, logic, and rhetoric that were indispensable to effective self-expression. Those fortunate enough to get such an education had by far the best chance for preferment and advancement whether declaiming in the courts, winning votes in the assembly, or making a telling point in philosophical discussion.

Two sorts of secondary schools beyond the elementary grew up to prepare Grecian youth for these wider opportunities. In one of these, philosophical interests predominated; in the other, rhetorical ones. Both offered basic training in grammar. But the philosophic secondary schools offered the grammar as a prerequisite to training for participation in subsequent logical and ethical discussions, while the rhetorical secondary schools required it as preparation for the very practical end of effective public oratory.

The Romans, possessed of little educational ingenuity, took over both these secondary schools from the Greeks after conquering them. Prior to this event Roman pretensions to literary education were slender indeed. But, as Suetonius remarked, how could it be otherwise at a time when Rome was so completely absorbed in the long series of wars to expand its imperial domain? When Rome emerged as a world power, however, secondary schools on the Greek models began to make an appearance to give the advanced training necessary for the rulers of empire. Yet in taking over these secondary schools the Romans did make some slight adaptations in them. With the Greeks the philosophical and rhetorical schools had been more or less coordinate; with the Romans the former school was somewhat subordinated to the latter. At Rome the philosophical school took on the more limited role of being a grammar school to which a boy went before attending the school of the rhetorician. The Romans, having little flair for philosophical speculation and having great genius for the management of public affairs, found this arrangement more suitable for the education of their civic ideal, the orator.[1]

It would be a mistake to think that so important a man of affairs as the orator had no more extensive education than might be contained in the formal rules of grammar and some well-known tricks of rhetoric. As a matter of fact, orators like Cicero and teachers of rhetoric like Quintilian (35–100) realized that the future rulers of empire needed in addition a wide background of general education. They needed, as the Roman historian Cornelius Tacitus, remarked, "to be armed at all points with the whole panoply of knowledge."[2] They needed to know the liberal arts of the Greeks—the quadrivium of arithmetic, geometry, astronomy, and music as well as the trivium of grammar, rhetoric, and logic. Especially did they need to be familiar with the style of the best authors of prose and poetry. This meant Greek as well as Roman authors and thus introduced bilingualism into education. But it was not enough to study the style of others; Roman youth had also to exercise themselves in compositions of their own. All this, in addition to accidence[3] and syntax, was the education that the grammar school—the school of the *grammaticus*— gave the Roman youth in preparation for entry into the school of the *rhetor*.

The vitality of the grammar school continued as long as oratory remained a vital instrument for affecting public policy. In the end, however, the transition from Republic to Empire concentrated political power in the hands of the Emperor, who ruled without responsibility to the formerly august Roman Senate. Consequently, oratory became an occasion for flattery or entertainment instead of persuasion; its form was cultivated at the expense of its content. With this demotion in the importance of oratory came a corresponding decline in the grammar schools. So alarming was the decline, not only in significance

---

[1] For a further account of this educational aim, see *supra*, p. 5.

[2] Tacitus, *Works* (Harper & Brothers, New York, 1889), vol. II, p. 439.

[3] "Accidence" was long the term used to denote a language's inflection, its declensions and conjugations.

but in numbers as well, that the Emperor found it necessary to subsidize them for the first time. The subsidy, however, was only a temporary check to the process of decline.

NARROWING OF THE GRAMMAR SCHOOL

In spite of its decline the Roman grammar school survived into the medieval period. Its survival was at first somewhat doubtful, for it had also to contend with the hostility of Christian leaders. To them the grammar school seemed the chief perpetuator of the pagan culture that had so stanchly resisted the spread of Christianity. For a considerable time, therefore, the teaching of grammar and associated liberal arts was a cause for censure in Christian circles. Confronted with a choice between a liberal education and the salvation of his soul the Christian had no hesitancy in choosing.

By the sixth century the long failure to cultivate letters had gone as far as to stir genuine anxiety over the imminent possibility of an illiterate leadership. Fortunately, by this time the conflict between pagan and Christian culture had about reached a resolution. The grammar school managed to survive by virtue of reconstructing its aim. Instead of preparing primarily for the worldly ideals of a successful man of affairs or of a loyal citizen of the state, it came now to put first the training of devoted and intelligent leaders of the church. In this reconstructed aim, even grammar, long out of favor because of its association with pagan literature, was discovered to have uses in combating heresy by ensuring the right translation and understanding of Holy Writ. Subsequently and secondarily, as leaders regained confidence in this school, it was able to resume the function of preparing for such public and private offices as required command of the written culture.

It was most opportune for secondary education that, as the Roman state in its progressive debilitation afforded less and less stimulus for the grammar school, the expanding requirements of the Catholic Church came more and more to demand just this sort of training. Prominent in responding to this demand were the monastic and cathedral schools. The former were conducted under auspices of the medieval monasteries, and the latter under the sponsorship of the bishop and in conjunction with his cathedral. Although intended chiefly for those planning to carry on the work of the church, these schools sometimes opened their doors to youth bent on secular careers. Collegiate schools of the period were much like the cathedral schools except that they were conducted under the sponsorship of secular canons. Yet another agency of secondary education was the chantry. Chantries were endowments left by testators to engage a priest to chant masses for the repose of the testator's soul. When not so engaged, these priests were frequently assigned teaching duties by their superiors. But not all medieval secondary education had ecclesiastical connections. In addition to the foregoing schools there were guild and burgher, or municipal, schools, whose very names indicate their secular origin and nature.

The curricula of these medieval secondary schools gave a large place to a new religious and moral literature that had grown up to supplant the obnoxious pagan literature but that nonetheless was somewhat modeled on its style. An especially popular book of this sort was Dionysius Cato's *Disticha de moribus*. In some places an effort was made to keep the liberal tradition alive, but not very successfully, for only digests of the liberal arts like Martianus Capella's *Marriage of Philology and Mercury* were at hand. Furthermore, in the famous trivium of grammar, rhetoric, and logic the medieval secondary school emphasized grammar. Unlike its Roman prototype, the medieval study of grammar was almost exclusively concerned with accidence and syntax. Since the times no longer demanded skill in oratory, rhetoric was studied only as a set of rules governing the writing of letters and official documents. In the quadrivium, only arithmetic received any general notice although astronomy and music, of course, had special relevance to the church. Yet, limited and one-sided as was this curriculum of the medieval secondary school, it was well suited to the needs of the times, which principally demanded a mastery of Latin as preparation for careers in church and state.

THE HUMANISTIC SECONDARY SCHOOL

The decadence of medieval secondary schools set in with the rise of the forces that produced the brilliant creative period of the Renaissance. On the political side these new forces were marked by much greater stability of legal institutions. On the economic side the revival of commerce and trade greatly improved the standard of living, especially for the rising middle class. The prosperity, peace, and security attendant on these new forces had a profound effect in changing people's outlook upon their times. This change was most notable in shifting the focus of their attention from the world to come to the world in being. In the preceding medieval period men had been preoccupied with the salvation of their souls in the hereafter. They now became equally absorbed in the exploration of every fact and potentiality concerning man in the here and now.

How to get greater enjoyment and meaning out of life—that was the pressing question. Obviously, the funded experience of the medieval period to be found in the literature of that day was entirely inadequate to gratify the gropings of the Renaissance. Ultimately, the full measure of these longings was not satisfied till the rediscovery and revival of the writings of the greatest Greek and Roman authors, especially the Roman. But in their humane letters, or belles-lettres, the people of the Renaissance did find a critique of life and an estimate by which they could satisfyingly judge their own times.

The almost unbounded enthusiasm that the cultivated leaders of Renaissance society felt for the literary remains of classical civilization was not shared by any of the educational institutions inherited from the medieval period. To be sure, the medieval university taught the liberal arts, but only for the practical preparation they afforded for such professional studies as law and theology. So, too, the main object of the various medieval secondary schools was to teach Latin—but again, only enough of the language to meet the practical needs of the clergy, civil officers, and rising middle class of businessmen. In the institutions of neither higher nor secondary education was there any interest in classical literatures considered from the humane or Humanistic point of view.

Because the portals of the older and established institutions of learning remained closed to the new intellectual interests of the Renaissance, the times cried out for a new type of school in which youth might study the Latin and Greek tongues and through them the wonderful culture of antiquity. A number of such schools, known as "Humanistic schools" because their curriculum was centered in a study of man in all his humanity, soon sprang up. Their main aim was individual development and personal accomplishment through learning to speak and write Latin elegantly. As they took their literary models from the best Roman literature, so they took their educational ideals from the greatest of Roman schoolmasters, Quintilian, and his *Institutes of Oratory*. The Humanistic secondary school of the Renaissance, therefore, was much more nearly the lineal descendant of the old Roman grammar school than of the Latin schools of the monasteries, cathedrals, guilds, and the like. It was this Humanistic school which, when the Renaissance spread beyond Italy, became the *collège* and the *lycée* in France, the *Gymnasium* in Germany, and the Latin grammar school in England and America. It is important to bear this genealogy in mind, for some of the most persistent problems of American secondary education in the twentieth century stem from this ancient lineage.

Boys entered the Humanistic secondary schools of the Renaissance at a very early age, at least as early as seven. The Dutch scholar Desiderius Erasmus (1466–1536) thought formal education should commence even earlier, and the English educational writer Sir Thomas Elyot (1490–1546) agreed with him. The Roman boy learned Latin as his mother tongue, but the English boy had to learn Latin as a second tongue before he could study what the Roman boy did. Therefore Elyot thought the education of the English boy would have to commence earlier if his subsequent achievement was to be comparable with the Roman boy's. It is noteworthy that students sometimes remained in the Humanistic secondary school till as late as their twenty-first year. This age span is eloquent of the relation that this secondary school bore to the university on the one hand and to the struggling vernacular, or elementary, school on the other. Having an age range of anywhere from seven to twenty-one, the Humanistic secondary school obviously overlapped and to a degree paralleled both its neighboring educational institutions.

In this situation lay a legacy that reached far into the future in influence. The difference between elementary and secondary education at this time was one not of age but of language.[4] The elementary school taught the vernacular; the secondary school taught Latin. This difference in curriculum was really indicative of an even deeper social cleavage between the two schools. Not everyone needed Latin, not even the narrowly practical sort taught in the medieval secondary schools. And the number who had the economic means to study Latin for the sheer aesthetic enjoyment it might afford was limited indeed. Hence, the Humanistic secondary school was from the first an upper-class school. And so it remained in spite of the fact that frequently a certain number of capable poor boys were admitted free.[5]

The curriculum of the Humanistic secondary school of the Renaissance was preponderantly taken up with the study of Latin and Latin authors. Greek was usually introduced only in the upper forms, or grades, of the school. The early years were engaged with accidence and syntax, but as quickly as possible these tools were employed in the reading of classical authors. In their widest scope these authors were read for informational and moral ends as well as aesthetic ones. Thus, they were relied upon for knowledge of science, history, and geography as well as for patterns of style, taste, and form. The schoolmaster's chief embarrassment arose from selecting the best authors when so many were of classic quality. Among Latin authors Terence, Vergil, and Cicero, and among Greek authors, Homer and Demosthenes, seem to have been most favored. This almost exclusive reliance on the literatures of Greece and Rome for a fuller knowledge of the nature of man and his potentialities led in the course of time to the designation of these two languages in the curriculum as the "humanities."

---

[4] *Supra,* p. 365.

[5] For further details on who were "poor" boys and to what extent schools were "free," see I. L. Kandel, *History of Secondary Education* (Houghton Mifflin Company, Boston, 1930), pp. 78–79.

A number of the Humanistic secondary schools of the Renaissance and post-Renaissance periods became famous enough to deserve separate mention here. First to achieve eminence was the Casa Giocosa of Vittorino da Feltre (1378–1446) at Mantua in Italy. The Humanistic secondary schools of the Hieronymians, or Brothers of the Common Life, must also be mentioned, for it was there that so much was done to lay the foundation for the modern organization of secondary education. It was they who introduced the classification of pupils into six to eight forms, or grades, with a graded course of study, a pattern that is still visible in secondary schools of the twentieth century. The great scholar Erasmus was a product of these schools, as was also Johann Sturm (1507–1589), who, through patterning his famed secondary school at Strasbourg after their model, spread their influence far and wide over Europe.[6] Another teaching order to achieve lasting distinction in the field of secondary education was that of the Jesuits. Drawing on the experience of all the foregoing, they incorporated their own experience into a *Ratio studiorum,* first published in 1599, which long stood for the best in Humanistic education.[7]

It remains to note that the Humanistic secondary school north of the Alps took on a somewhat different character from that located in Italy. North of the Alps, particularly in Germany, the revival of learning was less aesthetic and more critical. The Humanistic interest in man had stronger moral flavor. Study of the humanities, therefore, was used to promote moral reform. In pleading to the German mayors and aldermen for the establishment of Humanistic secondary schools, Martin Luther (1483–1546), the leader of the Reformation side of the Renaissance in Germany, rested his argument on both moral and aesthetic grounds. His major argument for the study of Latin and Greek was that they were indispensable as a protection against inaccuracies of translation and interpretation of the Holy Scriptures. But in a subsidiary argument he pointed out that the study of foreign tongues might add the same spice to the life of the mind as foreign spices added to more material tastes.[8]

[6] For the graded arrangement of his curriculum and that of Thomas Platter and Philipp Melanchthon as well, see P. Monroe, *Thomas Platter and the Educational Renaissance* (D. Appleton-Century Company, Inc., New York, 1904), p. 69.

[7] E. A. Fitzpatrick, *St. Ignatius and the Ratio Studiorum* (McGraw-Hill Book Company, New York, 1933).

[8] Luther also looked to the secondary school to provide leaders, which had long been the role of secondary education. In fact, he favored that all children attend school for at least an hour a day but that "the brightest pupils, who give promise of becoming accomplished teachers, preachers, and workers, should be kept longer at school, or set apart wholly for study." [F. V. N. Painter, *Luther on Education* (Lutheran Publication Society, Philadelphia, 1889), p. 200.]

Luther's main argument was also prominent in the minds of the Massachusetts colonists when they made their first provision for secondary education. Their reason for adopting the oft-cited act of 1647 was their announced anxiety that it was "one chiefe proiect of ye ould deluder, Satan, to keepe men from the knowledge of ye Scriptures, as in formr times by keeping ym in an unknowne tongue, so in these lattr times by perswading from ye use of tongues yt so at least ye true sence & meaning of ye originall might be clouded by false glosses of saint seeming deceivers."[9] In fact, so much was this the motivation of Humanistic education in Protestant countries that secondary education there was largely designed for youth preparing for college and the ministry. This domination of Humanistic education by vocational ends long remained to confuse the tradition of liberal education in American secondary schools and colleges.

As long as the secondary schools of the Renaissance and Reformation periods studied the humanities, later called the "classics," in order to enter into a richer appreciation of goodness and beauty, they prospered mightily. But when these schools began to find their principal model of eloquence in one author, Cicero, they began to show signs of formalism and decline. Furthermore, when they began to content themselves with the mere command of the Latin and Greek tongues or even with just a command of the grammar, their sun was beginning to set. As long as grammar held to its Roman connotation of including the liberal arts, the Latin grammar school of England and America had vitality. But when this school undertook little more than a narrow study of the word forms and constructions of grammar, its sun was already well below the horizon.

It should occasion no surprise that formalism and decay overtook the Humanistic secondary school. After all, to inspire the sons of the nobility, of country squires, merchants, and professional men with a love for culture on its own account required higher gifts of teaching than were possessed by the average teacher of the fifteenth to seventeenth or eighteenth centuries. Furthermore, correspondingly few students of these times had the intellectual or emotional make-up to be affected by any but the very best instruction. Consequently, the exalted aim of truly appreciating the riches of classical culture was achieved by only the more gifted pupils. For the rest the Humanistic school became little better than a dreary and exacting drill.

At that, there were those who managed to make a virtue of the results of decadence. They were teachers and laymen who favored the Latin grammar school not for its content but for the mental

---

[9] E. P. Cubberley, *Readings in the History of Education* (Houghton Mifflin Company, Boston, 1920), p. 299.

discipline that dreary and exacting drill afforded.[10] Not what one learned but how one learned was the critical question with this group. From the seventeenth to the nineteenth centuries there were yet others who, though they had little or no regard for the formalized Humanistic curriculum, nevertheless laid great social store on having the imprint of this stereotyped curriculum stamped upon a boy. Relatively few families could afford this sort of education for their boys; therefore, worthless as they thought it was in content, they valued its rarity as a badge of class distinction.

DEMANDS FOR REFORM

The Humanistic secondary school also owed its decline to its failure to keep its curriculum abreast of the changing climate of opinion in the seventeenth and eighteenth centuries. The demand for curriculum change came principally from two quarters. First, it came from the changing circumstances of the upper classes. As strong centralized monarchies arose at the expense of the feudal nobility, this nobility more and more began to find its significance not in its own local castles but at the court of the king. There the noblemen constituted not only the courtly society of the time but also the chief civil servants of the state. Thus the state came to be served by lay rather than by clerical personnel, as had frequently been the custom in earlier times. Obviously, neither the current Humanistic education of the clergy nor the former chivalric education of the nobility was adequate for the nobleman in his new role as courtier. The young man who planned a career as a soldier, statesman, man of affairs, and *galant homme* all in one had need of a quite new sort of training.

The demand for curriculum change also followed from the rise of science to new heights of importance. These were the centuries, it will be remembered, when such men as Nicolaus Copernicus in astronomy, William Harvey in medicine, and René Descartes in mathematics were making vast additions to human knowledge. Presumably, Humanism as the study of whatever concerns man should have included these new scientific interests, but all too often it did not. The Humanists thought scientific interests were naturalistic and therefore materialistic. The distinctive thing about man, the essence of his humanity, they thought, was just the opposite. According to the Humanists, man's essential spiritual or intellectual quality was non-materialistic.[11] Hence Humanism and naturalism, Humanism and sci-

[10] For a discussion of the educational psychology contemporary to this ideal of secondary education, see *supra,* pp. 141–143.

[11] For a fuller account of the psychology of education underlying this view, see *supra,* p. 138.

ence, humane letters, or belles-lettres, and science, soon developed an antagonism toward each other. As the medieval university out of obscurantism had closed the doors of its curriculum to the Humanism of the Renaissance, so now the Humanistic secondary school of the Renaissance refused to open its portals to the repeated knocking of science for admission to the curriculum.

The controversy between Humanism and naturalism was part of a wider controversy that raged during these centuries between the "ancients" and the "moderns." The issue between these two groups, as their names suggest, was whether the best standards in art, literature, philosophy, and the like were to be found in the cultural remains of Greece and Rome or whether Europe by the seventeenth and eighteenth centuries had developed a culture of its own that equaled or even surpassed them. Thus it was that the poetry and prose of the new vernacular literatures was pitted against the poetry and prose of the classical tongues, Renaissance painting and sculpture against the art of the ancients, modern science against the science and philosophy of Aristotle.

The obdurate refusal of the Humanistic secondary school to accommodate itself to these new demands of the times clearly indicated the need for some new form of secondary school, nor was it long before a variety of new forms began to make their appearance. In Germany two new sorts of secondary schools came forward, one the *Ritterakademie* and the other the *Realschule*. The former ministered chiefly to the ideal of the courtier, while the latter catered more generally to the scientific interest. In France these new interests found an outlet in the secondary schools of the Oratorians and Portroyalists. And, in England discontent was early expressed by upperclass fathers' engaging private tutors for their sons rather than sending them to the conventional Humanistic school. It was this sort of father to whom John Locke (1632–1704) addressed himself in *Some Thoughts concerning Education*. The schools that chiefly represented this sort of protest in England were the academies set up by Dissenters from the Church of England when they were excluded from contemporary Humanistic schools because of their Nonconformity.[12] The curriculum of this sort of school received its boldest statement in the famous *Tractate of Education* by John Milton (1608–1674), the great Nonconformist poet.

Each of these movements for the reform of secondary education struck out in a somewhat different direction. Yet, in spite of this diversity, some general trends were fairly well defined. Latin continued to be taught, but only so much as might be necessary to put one

[12] I. Parker, *Dissenting Academies in England* (Cambridge University Press, London, 1914).

at ease in polite conversation. Modern languages, including the student's own vernacular, made their debut. Science was studied not only in its abstract findings but also at the *Realschule* in the "machines of daily use." Closely allied were courses in mathematics and military science. In addition, history and geography found important places in the new curriculum. On the physical side these new schools included dancing, fencing, riding, and swimming. Yet, broader and more attractive as this sort of curriculum seemed to be, it made surprisingly slow headway against the traditional European secondary school curriculum, where the humanities remained entrenched for a long time to come.

THE LATIN GRAMMAR SCHOOL IN AMERICA

The settlers of the various American colonies, much as they may have intended to make a more or less fresh start in religion, politics, or earning a living on American shores, apparently had no intention of making a new start in their provision for secondary education. Instead of planting new seed, the colonists transplanted a full-grown European Humanistic secondary school to the New World. Since, naturally, they tried to disturb the roots as little as possible in transplanting the school, it will be well to indicate precisely what these roots were.

Most colonial secondary schools took their pattern from the English Latin grammar school. Because the founders of these schools at Boston and elsewhere had generally settled on the Atlantic seaboard in search of religious freedom, their secondary schools tended to follow the Reformation pattern of Humanistic education north of the Alps rather than the Renaissance pattern to the south. Lads were sent to the Latin grammar school, therefore, not so much to cultivate an aesthetic enjoyment of the humanities as to prepare themselves for the colonial college and thence for service in church and state. The main baggage of the curriculum was, of course, Humanistic rather than naturalistic, classical rather than scientific. Intended to be socially useful, frequently Latin and Greek became so narrowly grammatical that the chief advantage claimed for them was their formal discipline of the mind.

Boys entered the colonial Latin school as early as seven or eight years of age. Preferably they entered after they had learned to read, but in not a few cases the Latin school had to teach beginning reading as well. Perhaps this arrangement was necessary because there was no dame school in the neighborhood. More often, probably, it was a deliberate preference because at its inception in the colonies the Latin grammar school paralleled rather than followed the dame and common schools. These schools bore this relation to each other because in colonial times the difference between them was, as in Europe, one of advancement not in one's education but in one's economic class and social expectations. If a boy could afford to have expectations, he took his first formal instruction not in a dame or common school but in a Latin grammar school.

The Latin grammar school remained the typical colonial secondary school during the seventeenth and eighteenth centuries, but its roots never penetrated deeply into the social subsoil of the Atlantic seaboard. They grew lustily here and there but only under forced cultivation elsewhere. Massachusetts, for example, found it necessary to pass a statute requiring towns of a certain size to maintain Latin grammar schools. The penalty of a fine was attached for noncompliance, but many towns preferred to pay the fine rather than be put to the expense and bother of establishing such schools. Even where Latin grammar schools were established, there was doubt about their value. Very early in the eighteenth century a memorial of the selectmen of Boston complained that "many hundreds of boys in this town, who by their parents were never designed for a more liberal education, have spent two, three, four years or more of their early days at the Latin school, which have proved of very little or no benefit as to their after accomplishment."[13]

Apparently, the school served the needs of too small a percentage of the population. Besides, the population from which the secondary school clientele was drawn was not geographically concentrated in the town but tended to scatter widely. In time, this decentralization of population led to the subdivision of the town into school districts, no one of which was large enough to support a Latin grammar school and each one of which was so far removed from the center of town as not to care to support a secondary school there. In the South, support for the Latin grammar school was further weakened by the practice of the more well-to-do families sending their sons back to England for their education.

THE AMERICAN ACADEMY

In the eighteenth century, changing social conditions and the inability or unwillingness of the Latin grammar school to adjust itself to them called forth a new and competing form of colonial secondary education, the academy. Secular interests began to crowd religion out of the dominant position in people's minds. A marked increase in religious tolerance permitted greater prominence for the problems of

[13] Quoted in W. H. Small, *Early New England Schools* (Ginn and Company, Boston, 1914), p. 356.

reducing the hinterland and promoting commerce on the high seas. Furthermore, new political ideas were stirring. Unsatisfactory relations with England and the reading of prerevolutionary writings from France were shifting the focus of men's attention. In the eighteenth century particularly, American colonists began to take a keen interest in the scientific movement, which in the preceding century had already gained a considerable momentum in Europe.

The Latin grammar school, serving the religious needs of the Reformation, had little or nothing in its curriculum that prepared a young man for taking his part in these new movements. Various efforts to remedy this deficiency came to a head in the movement from the middle of the eighteenth century onward to found academies. Whether this movement was an American counterpart of the English one that led to the founding of the Nonconformist, or Dissenting, academies is not historically clear. At any rate the circumstances out of which both grew were remarkably similar.

Benjamin Franklin (1706–1790), scientist as well as statesman and philanthropist, proposed the first American academy, but it did not take secure hold on his fellow Pennsylvanians in the form he hoped. Furthermore, soon after its actual founding it was raised to the level of a college. Later in the eighteenth century the intellectual climate of Massachusetts proved more congenial to the academy idea than that of Pennsylvania. Chief, though not first, of the Massachusetts academies was that founded at Andover during the Revolution. The charter of Andover declared its intention to offer boys the conventional secondary school studies "but more especially to learn them the great end and real business of living."[14]

This last declaration of intent was something new in American secondary education. It forecast a curriculum that would be terminal, in addition to the conventional college preparatory one. Thus, at Andover in addition to Greek and Latin grammar it was planned to include English grammar together with practical geometry, logic, geography, and "such other liberal arts and sciences or languages, as opportunity and ability may hereafter admit."[15]

The curriculum that Franklin originally proposed for his academy was even more radically utilitarian in character.[16] Could he have had his way he would have dispensed with the ancient classics altogether and used English models for reading, declamation, and forming one's prose style. Even more practically he proposed the inclusion

---

[14] Quoted in E. E. Brown, *The Making of Our Middle Schools* (Longmans, Green & Co., Inc., New York, 1903), p. 195.

[15] *Ibid.*

[16] T. Woody, *Educational Views of Benjamin Franklin* (McGraw-Hill Book Company, New York, 1931), pp. 158–179.

of arithmetic, accounting, geometry, and astronomy. Obviously, these were basic for boys expecting to become mariners, surveyors, or merchants, three of the most important occupations of the day. In addition, Franklin did not forget natural science, geography, morality, and history. He dwelt particularly on the social uses to which a study of history might be put. His views, however, were too radical for his times. To get supporters, he had to make concessions to what he called the "ornamental" studies, the classics. In the end, therefore, it was the Andover program that prevailed as the model for the academy movement.

The steady and then later rapid growth in both the number of academies and the number of courses they offered is proof of the fact that the academy met a very urgent need in American life. The range of people's curiosity, as measured by the academy curriculum, seemed almost unlimited. Instruction was offered in subjects all the way from Greek to modern languages, from Biblical antiquities to United States history, from mercantile law to principles of teaching, from "penmanship" to painting, from natural philosophy to chemistry, and from arithmetic to trigonometry. No doubt many of these courses were short and superficial, but it must be remembered that this was a period of mechanical invention and social innovation. There was great optimism about the perfectibility of man and his ability to control his destiny. Great willingness was manifested to try the new, especially in a curriculum that offered training in whatever seemed useful in prying open the doors of opportunity.

The pace of the academy's growth during its first half-century was moderate but steady. Then in the second quarter of the nineteenth century it mounted by great strides to the apex of its popularity. In part, this rapid growth was due to the fact that while most academies were founded under private auspices, New York lent public support to the movement.[17] In part, it was also due to the founding of academies for girls. In view of the age-long prejudice against the education of women beyond the three R's, perhaps nothing in the academy movement so attested the period's optimism and confidence in human capacities or yielded such rich dividends as did the courageous provision for the secondary education of girls.

Improvement though it was on the Latin grammar school, the academy still was not a wholly adequate expression of indigenous American conditions. Contrasted with the definitely indigenous American high school that followed it, the academy was really just a transitional institution. It mediated between the period of depending on Old World traditions of secondary education and the time when

[17] G. F. Miller, *The Development of the Academy System in New York* (J. B. Lyon Company, Albany, N.Y., 1922).

people could see more clearly the unique form of secondary education the New World demanded. It may be put down to the credit of the academy, therefore, that it inaugurated a new ideal of secondary education that was terminal and not college preparatory in character, that it greatly expanded the secondary school curriculum, that it enlarged the secondary school clientele to include girls as well as boys, and that, in states like New York, it went far toward popularizing the notion of public secondary education.

Yet, though the academy did popularize secondary education more widely than did the Latin grammar school, it fell short of making secondary education thoroughly democratic. The expansion of the curriculum and the admission of girls were both steps in the direction of democracy. But, except for a state like New York, support was generally private and not public, as democracy would demand. Even when publicly subsidized, the academy catered to a select clientele. Consequently, there was a protest against taxing the many for the benefit of the few—an argument to be aimed shortly at the high school itself. Furthermore, the academy was not built directly on top of the common school as its logical extension. On the contrary, like the Latin grammar school, its lower grades paralleled those of the common school. Like its predecessor, the academy allowed boys to enter at seven years of age; even though later the entrance age was raised to twelve, it still was in competition with the common or elementary school grades.

The decline of the academy was coincident with the rise of the high school, which not only copied the democratic features of the academy but also managed to democratize secondary education at the points where the academy had failed to do so. In the last quarter of the nineteenth century, normal schools and state colleges also multiplied rapidly and took over many of the functions of preparing individuals for active life that had been such a distinctive feature of the rise of academies. In consequence, the other side of the academy program, the classical and college preparatory sides, came strongly to the fore in the academies that remained. And it was this feature that continued to distinguish private schools and academies right down to the middle of the twentieth century.

RISE OF THE HIGH SCHOOL

It is interesting that the high school made its first appearance in American education not after the academy had passed the peak of its popularity but at the opening of the academy's quarter century of greatest growth. The budding of the high school, therefore, did not grow out of disappointment in what the academy was trying to do, as the academy had grown out of the shortcomings of the Latin grammar school. On the contrary, the originators of the high school were so greatly attracted by the program of the academy that they wished to imitate and improve on its opportunities. This is clearly evident in the deliberations of the Boston School Committee, in which the high school idea was hatched. The committee was convened by public pressure to consider the advisability of setting up a school that should "furnish the young men who are not intended for a collegiate course of studies, and who have enjoyed the usual advantages of the public schools, with the means of completing a good English education, and of fitting themselves for all the departments of commercial life."[18] The adoption of such a program would make the academy program available (1) at public expense and (2) as the normal upward extension and completion of common school education.

After thorough consideration of the issue the committee recommended that just such a new school be set up. Further, it was of the opinion that the school could be established and maintained without materially augmenting the public tax burden. As it looked at the seven years ordinarily spent in the grammar grades of the common school, it was convinced that an economy of two years was possible without any loss of essential subject matter. The two years saved it proposed should become the first two of a new three-year school that would directly follow the common school and that would provide the necessary foundation for successful careers in both mercantile and mechanical pursuits. Such a proposal, it thought, would not only perfect the public school system but would also prove a boon to parents who were at double expense to pay school taxes and also tuition to send their sons to private academies out of town where this advanced education could be had.

The school that resulted from the school committee's deliberations opened its doors to the Boston public in 1821 under the name of the English Classical School. Almost at once, however, it became known as the English High School and subsequently, of course, as just the "high school." If not the first institution to bear the name "high school," since one or two Lancasterian[19] "high schools" are matters of earlier record, the Boston school at least was the first *public* high school. At that, while it was the first public high school in fact, it was not the first such school for which statutory provision was made. In the last two years of the eighteenth century, Connecticut passed a law that permitted the erection at public expense of schools

---

[18] Quoted in E. D. Grizzell, *Origin and Development of the High School in New England before 1865* (The Macmillan Company, New York, 1923), p. 42.
[19] For a fuller account of Lancasterian schools, see *supra*, pp. 211–212, 369.

of a "higher order," which were to offer English as well as Latin branches and to which pupils were to be admitted only on completion of a common school education. Only the fact that this law remained a dead letter on the statute books prevented Connecticut from receiving credit for having pioneered in the high school movement.

The first high school was an immediate success. Within six years after its founding the state of Massachusetts took notice of Boston's achievement by passing the first effective general legislation under which other high schools could be set up within the state. Surrounding New England states, particularly Connecticut, tried the new institution, and Pennsylvania and Ohio had high schools even before Connecticut. The high school idea proved especially congenial to the frontier states. Free land on the frontier made the people there too equalitarian to look with favor on a dual or parallel system of schools in which elementary and secondary education were distinguished from each other on the basis of a child's social expectation. These people, like democracy-loving people everywhere, took the high school to their bosoms because it provided for secondary education that was the continuous extension of the elementary school in what has become famous as the American single, or unitary, educational ladder. They liked it, furthermore, because it was open to the children of all the inhabitants at public expense and because it provided a curriculum predicated on the interests of the masses.

Yet, strangely enough, it was in the Middle West where the legality of the high school was most seriously questioned. In Kalamazoo, Michigan, objection was made to paying taxes for the support of a high school on the ground that it was not properly a part of the system of common schools recognized by law. The term "common school," it was claimed, historically applied only to schools of elementary grade. Moreover, education beyond the rudiments of the common school was a luxury of the few that should be paid for privately. The court, speaking through one of Michigan's greatest judges, Judge Thomas McIntyre Cooley, took an opposite view. It held that the state had ample power to provide an intermediate school between the common school and the state university. Indeed, it expressed surprise that any one should question the right of the state "to furnish a liberal education to the youth of the state in schools brought within the reach of all classes."[20]

The "Kalamazoo case," as it came to be called, had a wide effect in reassuring communities that hitherto had hesitated for legal reasons to set up high schools of their own. In fact, between 1870 and 1890 (the Kalamazoo case was decided in 1874) the number of high schools increased fivefold. In 1890 the number was just over

[20] *Stuart v. School District No. 1 of Kalamazoo,* 30 Mich. 69, 75 (1874).

2,500, with an enrollment of just above 200,000, and twenty years later there were well over 10,000 high schools, with a pupil enrollment of more than 900,000. In the next two decades the number of high schools jumped to just under 24,000, while the number attending high school more than quadrupled, and between 1900 and about 1940 the high school enrollment increased by 1,200 per cent while the high school population itself rose by only 60 per cent. Such growth was nothing short of phenomenal.

This phenomenal growth of the high school rode through the nineteenth and twentieth centuries on the crest of a great wave of accelerated social change. Basically, there was a vast upward trend of the American standard of living. This tremendous improvement in the economic lot of all classes grew chiefly out of the rapid exploitation of our prodigious natural resources after the Civil War. Before the war, Congress thought it would take centuries to dispose of the public domain at the contemporary rate of settlement. Only a mere quarter century after the war the public domain was gone and the frontier officially closed. Rapid industrialization after the Civil War enormously increased national wealth. The standard of living mounted to a point at which the fiscal problem of financing so stupendous an undertaking as secondary education at public expense was made to appear no problem at all.

Other sociological factors were also working in the direction of expanding the demand for high school education. The open class system promoted by social mobility on the frontier encouraged people to use the public high school to improve their chances of mounting higher on the social-economic ladder. The opportunity for native ingenuity in America's diversified industry and commerce was so great that no one wanted to fail to improve his talents by training. But it must not be overlooked that many went to high school, particularly after the Depression of 1929, because the extensive mechanization of both agriculture and industry had led to the technological displacement of labor. They went not to improve their opportunities but because during these years there was no other safe place for youth to go.

Rapid as was the high school's growth, it did not occur without growing pains. The diagnosis of these pains will be easier if at this point a glance is taken at the high school curriculum. This, as one might surmise from the inspiration the high school drew from the academy, was the least original of its initial features. The first high school, the Boston English Classical School, had a definitely academy curriculum. Its work in English included reading, grammar, composition, and declamation; in mathematics, arithmetic, algebra, geometry, and trigonometry; in philosophy, natural, moral, and political philosophy; and in history, ancient and modern history. In addition and in further imitation of the academy, it taught bookkeeping, navigation, and surveying.

The Latin and Greek of the academy curriculum, however, were missing. But they were not missing long, for they were mentioned in the high school law of 1827. Apparently the framers of this law anticipated that in many places the high school would be the only available secondary school and therefore designed it to prepare for college as well as for life. Not only were the classics added, but in the middle period of the nineteenth century the high school indulged itself, as had the academy, in a multiplicity of courses that often were short and superficial. As a result, the high school had to be lengthened to four years. By the end of the century, however, the high school curriculum began to contract. Subjects like evidences of Christianity, Biblical and classical antiquities, and ancient geography disappeared. So too did astronomy and geology. Some of these were replaced by such new subjects as industrial and household arts, agriculture, and an expansion of the older commercial subjects.

As can be seen from the Massachusetts law of 1827, the high school early chose the dual function of being not only a terminal institution but also a college preparatory institution. It is difficult to explain the inclusion of the classics, the college preparatory subjects par excellence, in any other way. At any rate, before the Civil War most high schools, like most academies, were offering two courses of study, one an English course preparing for life and the other a Latin course preparing for college. By the turn of the century the majority were offering a third course, usually commercial or industrial. By the end of the first decade in the twentieth century the average number of courses was six. After the First World War some high schools offered as many as a dozen or more separate courses.

Out of these parallel course offerings grew the idea of specialized high schools, that is, commercial high schools, technical high schools, and the like. As the numbers attending high school rose in almost geometric ratio, either old buildings had to be remodeled or new ones constructed. Many communities, following European precedent, chose to house different course offerings under separate roofs and separate administrations. But this practice of the first part of the twentieth century was not preferred in the decades following the First World War. Thereafter, the comprehensive high school with the various courses gathered under one roof and one administration was the most popular because it was reckoned to be more democratic.

While the primary purpose of the original high school may have been to prepare for life, before the nineteenth century was out its secondary purpose of preparing for college had begun to take on increased importance. This it did in spite of the opposition of men like Henry Barnard and Noah Porter. Though a great promoter of the public high school, Barnard thought it should not overextend itself into college preparation. Porter, president of Barnard's alma mater, Yale, was of a similar mind because he feared that if the high school became college preparatory, the college would be unable to control what was taught there. In spite of this and similar opposition, the high school was often the only secondary school in a community and hence to serve its constituency almost inevitably had to take on college preparatory functions. But as high schools were of very uneven quality and as colleges were very diverse in their entrance requirements, the articulation between secondary and higher education generated much friction and unrest.

In fact, the unrest became so acute that the National Education Association called into being a number of national committees to study and report on various phases of the problem. The twenty-five years between the report of the first committee, the Committee of Ten in 1893, and the report of the last one, the Commission on the Reorganization of Secondary Education in 1918, proved to be perhaps the most crucial in the career of the high school.[21] Up to this point, the high school had ridden the crest of a wave of public optimism. Now reefs loomed ahead. The American public had to do some hard thinking on how to avoid these reefs. They had now to think through to its logical conclusions their former somewhat haphazard and opportunistic idea of a high school and make such practical adjustments as might be involved.

THE ARTICULATION OF HIGH SCHOOL AND COLLEGE

One of the first reefs which the high school approached was that of its articulation with the college. Not originally designed to be college preparatory, the high school had to do a good deal of groping before it established a satisfactory working relationship with the college. During the stage when high schools were pushing up under local stimulation, they were very uneven both in the quantity and in the quality of their offerings. Consequently, completion of high school was a very unreliable index of fitness to proceed to college. The colleges made matters even more uncertain and confusing by differing widely among themselves in their entrance examinations. Besides, they defined their entrance requirements in terms of the degrees they awarded.

[21] The names of the more important other committees and the dates of their reporting were the Committee on College Entrance Requirements, 1899; the Committee on Articulation, 1911; and the Committee on Economy of Time in Education, 1912.

As long as they awarded only one degree, the B.A. degree, they showed an inflexibility in their entrance requirements that was inhospitable to the variety of courses offered in the high school.

A few years after the Civil War the University of Michigan took an early lead in trying to bring some order out of this chaos. It appointed a committee of its faculty that on invitation would visit high schools within the state. During its visit it would make a thorough study of the quality of the work done there. If it was satisfied with it, the graduates of that school were thenceforth admitted to the University of Michigan on the recommendation of the high school principal without examination. Indiana adopted much the same scheme shortly thereafter, except that the State Board of Education instead of the state university designated the high schools to be approved.

The accrediting system, thus initiated, greatly improved the articulation between high school and college in the states concerned, but it still left unregulated the differences in entrance requirements from state to state. The need for a larger regional control in the Middle Western states was met in 1894, when the North Central Association was formed.[22] Precedent for regional standardization of entrance requirements, however, had already been set by the formation a decade earlier of the New England Association of Colleges and Preparatory Schools, which in the next century became the New England Association of Colleges and Secondary Schools. The idea of regional control proved very popular, as witness the number of other associations that sprang up in various parts of the country.

In New England and the North Atlantic States standardization took two directions. On the one hand, it followed the Middle Western practice of dispensing with college entrance examinations through a system of accrediting. To this end, the New England College Entrance Certificate Board was formed. On the other hand, standardization took the form of getting colleges to accept the results of a single examining agency. Ultimately, this led to the formation of the College Entrance Examination Board at the turn of the century. The results of its examinations have since become the most widely accepted of any college entrance examining body in the country.

The Committee of Ten, whose appointment in 1893 has already been mentioned, looked forward to the day when colleges would be accessible to all secondary school graduates who had creditably accomplished their work, no matter what group of subjects they had studied. But, "as secondary courses are now too often arranged," it lamented, referring to the low quality of work in many high schools

[22] C. O. Davis, *A History of the North Central Association of Colleges and Secondary Schools, 1895–1945* (North Central Association of Colleges and Secondary Schools, Ann Arbor, Mich., 1945).

of the period, "this is not a reasonable request to prefer to the colleges and scientific schools."[23] Though the time was unripe for such an ideal relation, the committee did try to simplify the transition from high school to college by minimizing the differences in pupil purpose and subject-matter value that had created articulation problems. For one thing, it suggested that "every subject which is taught at all in a secondary school should be taught in the same way and to the same extent to every pupil so long as he pursues it, no matter what the probable destination of the pupil may be," that is, whether it be college or life.[24] Realizing that differences could not always be ignored, the committee further advised that differences be equated as far as possible, or, to quote, "all the subjects between which choice is allowed should be approximately equivalent to each other in seriousness, dignity, and efficacy."[25]

Not long after the Committee of Ten reported, the National Education Association appointed another committee to make a specific study of the effect of college entrance requirements on the high school. This Committee on College Entrance Requirements reported in 1899. Among a number of recommendations two particularly need to be mentioned here. One was the recommendation that the elective principle should receive at least partial recognition in the secondary school curriculum. By recognizing this principle the committee prevented the college entrance requirements from operating like a Procrustean bed. The other recommendation grew out of seed sown by the Committee of Ten. The equivalence of studies suggested by that committee was virtually reduced to a formula by the Committee on College Entrance Requirements. It recommended that "any piece of work comprehended within the studies included in this report that has covered at least one year of four periods a week in a well-equipped secondary school, under competent instruction, should be considered worthy to count toward admission to college."[26]

In this formula lay the germ of what later became the system of units, or credits, that has since formed the basis of practically all academic bookkeeping in the twentieth century. Some precedent for it already existed at the beginning of the decade. At that time the New York Regents inaugurated a system of "counts" by which they evaluated high school diplomas. In the first decade of the next

---

[23] *Report of the Committee of Ten on Secondary School Studies* (National Education Association, National Council of Education, Washington, D.C., 1893), p. 52.

[24] *Ibid.*, p. 17.

[25] *Ibid.*, p. 43.

[26] National Education Association, *Report of the Committee on College Entrance Requirements,* p. 38.

century the Carnegie Foundation for the Advancement of Teaching made use of the same system of accounting except that it replaced counts with "units." "A unit," it defined as "being a course of five periods a week throughout an academic year."[27]

In 1899 the Committee on College Entrance Requirements recommended ten units for college entrance—four in foreign language, two in English, two in mathematics, and one each in history and science. The National Education Association's Committee on Articulation in 1911 jumped the total number of units to fifteen, distributed into three for English and one each for social and natural sciences, together with two majors of three units each and one minor of two. Of the fifteen not less than eleven were to come from English, foreign languages, mathematics, and the sciences mentioned. These recommendations with minor amendments persisted well down to the middle of the twentieth century.

The spread of the progressive-education movement into the field of secondary education after the First World War created much impatience with even these requirements for college entrance. College entrance requirements were stated in terms of units of subject matter. The progressives were not primarily interested in subject matter; their main interest was in the ongoing experiences of children. Subject matter was only a means to enriching these experiences. With a curriculum organized about children's experiences rather than traditional subject matter, progressive secondary schools could not fulfill college entrance requirements precisely. Yet, though unable to fulfill the letter of the requirements, they felt that they could more than fulfill its spirit. To prove this, the Eight Year Study was undertaken. A number of colleges were persuaded to accept for a period of eight years students from certain progressive secondary schools without requiring them to meet conventional entrance requirements. At the end of this time the work of these students was compared with that of students more traditionally prepared. The results, published in 1942, indicated quite clearly that success in a liberal arts college did not depend so exclusively as had been thought on the student's study in secondary school of certain subjects for a prescribed length of time.[28] It looked at last as if conditions warranted acting on the ideal of articulation between high school and college for which the Committee of Ten was unready in 1893.

Many secondary school educators felt that the colleges of the country exercised more than their proper share of influence in working

[27] Carnegie Foundation for the Advancement of Teaching, *Annual Report,* 1906, p. 38.

[28] W. M. Aikin, *The Story of the Eight Year Study* (Harper & Row, Publishers. Incorporated, New York, 1942), chap. 6.

out the articulation between high school and college. The high school, they also felt, might have worked out its peculiar non-college-preparatory function more quickly and effectively if it had been left more nearly alone by the colleges. Perhaps this is so. Yet it would be a mistake to overlook the great benefit that college influence conferred on the high school. At a time before effective state supervision for secondary schools had been worked out, the colleges were practically the only standardizing agencies operating to advance the quality of secondary school instruction.

THE JUNIOR HIGH SCHOOL

One generally admitted improvement of the high school, which was abetted by the Committee of Ten and the Committee on College Entrance Requirements, was the movement to reorganize it into a junior and a senior division. This movement originated partly out of a feeling in the colleges that the four-year high school did not provide a long enough period in which to make the preparation necessary for college entrance. They felt that the pursuit of some secondary studies should commence in the last two years of the eight-year elementary school. The Committee of Ten, whose personnel and sympathies were strongly collegiate, echoed this feeling. It specifically recommended in its report that algebra, science, and foreign languages find lodgment in the last two years of the elementary school curriculum. The Committee on College Entrance Requirements came to the same conclusion and even went as far as to recommend the removal of the seventh and eighth grades to the high school building.

These recommendations originally grew out of an address by Harvard's renowned president, Charles W. Eliot (1834–1926), before the National Education Association in 1888. The question he put to his audience was: Can school programs be shortened and enriched? The question was a very pressing one to him, for he noted that the entrance age of Harvard freshmen had been rising steadily till it was then a month or more beyond nineteen. This situation, compared with the progress of European youth through their institutions of secondary and higher education, indicated that American youth were entering on the responsibilities of life about two years later than their European counterparts. Hence, Eliot made the proposition, later taken up and approved by the Committee of Ten and the Committee on College Entrance Requirements, that secondary education commence two years earlier than had been customary.[29]

[29] The Committee of Fifteen, which reported in 1895 on economy of time in elementary education, also endorsed this proposition. For a fuller account of this committee, see *supra*, pp. 379–380.

These recommendations led a number of communities to "departmentalize" the two upper grades of their elementary schools. That is, the seventh and eighth grades tried to approximate not only the curriculum of the secondary school but its methods and administration as well. Each teacher took charge not of a grade but of a department of study. Instead of teaching all the subjects of a grade, he taught the seventh and eighth years of some one subject such as mathematics or English.

A much more radical suggestion for the reorganization of secondary education came at the opening of the twentieth century from William Rainey Harper (1856–1906), the first president of the University of Chicago. Harper boldly suggested that the secondary school period should cover not only the eighth grade of the elementary school but the first two years of college as well. As if this suggestion were not bold enough, he went on to recommend that the work ordinarily covered in this stretch of seven years be done in six and even in five by the brilliant student. Radical as these suggestions were, they attracted much serious attention and study. In so far as these suggestions for the reorganization of secondary education included the lower years of the college, they were somewhat premature. But in so far as they looked to reorganizing the twelve years of elementary and secondary education into a six-six rather than an eight-four pattern, they caught the imagination of American educators.

In 1912 the Committee on Economy of Time in Education appointed by the National Education Association reported in favor of a six-year period of secondary education. In announcing its decision, it further recommended that this period have a junior and a senior division of three years each. It is these divisions which were embodied in junior and senior high schools. Yet even before the committee published its report various communities had already begun to experiment with the idea of a six-year secondary school. Once experimentation started, it spread rapidly. While most communities tended to reorganize their schools on a six-three-three basis, others tried out six-six, six-two-four, six-four-four, and six-three-five bases. After the mid-century some school systems experimented by including the sixth grade in the junior high school, thus making the latter a four-year school and in some cases calling it a "middle school."[30]

The unique feature of all these schemes was, of course, the intermediate school. By 1918, educators were able to think of many more good reasons for its existence than merely the provision of six instead of four years in which to get ready for college. By that date the

[30] See also *The Articulation of the Units of American Education,* Seventh Yearbook (National Education Association, Department of Superintendence, Washington, D.C., 1929), part III.

main argument in support of the school had become a psychological one. Studies in the psychology of adolescence indicated that children at this age were undergoing physical and psychological changes which demanded different sorts of social and educational opportunities from those provided in either the conventional elementary or secondary school. Other studies of a more sociological character indicated that there was a great leakage of students from the school system in the transition from the elementary to the high school. Doubtless this occurred because compulsory-attendance laws permitted children to go to work on completing elementary school. A junior high school of three years would be an advantage in such circumstances since it would encourage a child to stay in school at least a year longer. Then, if he had to go to work, it would provide him with a graceful exit.

A less pedagogical factor that favored the adoption of the junior high school idea in the second and third decades of the century was its happy coincidence with the period of extremely rapid growth in high school enrollments. These enrollments quite outstripped existing facilities to house them. New buildings of some sort simply had to be built. Why not junior high schools? Thus it was that pedagogical theory and physical necessity conspired to bring about a fundamental reorganization of secondary education that might otherwise have been very difficult to effect.

In many communities the necessity of adding to physical plant outweighed pedagogical advantage. This explains why many early junior high schools were junior high schools in name only. Pedagogically, of course, the junior high school involved much more than a convenient way to house the seventh, eighth, and ninth grades. The junior high school, in addition to continuing the integrating effect of elementary education, was planned to mark the beginning of differentiated education. With the help of a good guidance program the child was to have a chance to explore his talents with a view to selecting the career most suitable for him.

GUIDANCE

At its inception in the first decade of the century, "guidance" did not have the broad connotation it acquired later in the middle of the century. It started out as the much more limited enterprise of vocational guidance. The idea of such guidance had been maturing in the mind of Frank Parsons (1854–1908) for some years prior to 1908, when he managed to get philanthropic backing to open a counseling bureau in a Boston settlement house. Although this was the first bureau dispensing personal advice on vocations, there had long been a considerable literature addressed to people who were seeking economic success. Some of the literature sought to arouse the success motive, and some of it tried to give profitable hints about steps to such success. Such literature, followed ultimately by personal counseling, was a logical outgrowth of the American environment. America, the land of economic opportunity, certainly could not long be without guidance on how to estimate one's talents and seize one's opportunity. Moreover, in order to maintain a fluent and mobile American democracy, people woke up in the twentieth century to the obligation of seeking out and bringing to fruition the peculiar capacities of each individual.

It is surprising that vocational guidance was not the outgrowth of the efforts of industrial management or, for that matter, of the interests of labor unions. It is equally surprising that it did not arise as a phase of vocational education or even of general public education. Though vocational guidance did not originate in the schools, however, it quickly spread to them. Before the second decade of the century had been completed, it had spread in significant proportions from city to state and from state to nation. By the outbreak of the First World War a National Vocational Guidance Association had already been formed and was soon publishing a periodic bulletin.

In founding his vocational-counseling bureau Parsons operated on the belief that it was better to choose a vocation than to hunt a job. Choice of a vocation rested on two things, a survey of jobs and a self-analysis. Parsons's theory of self-analysis attached great importance to putting the analysis down on paper. In getting it down he freely used rating sheets and the technique of the personal interview. These implements of guidance were vastly improved as psychologists managed to perfect their scientific measurements of individual differences. Tests given to draftees in the First World War not only gave an intelligence rating for the first time on various occupations but also helped sift out men for special duties. On the whole, however, these tests have been more successful in identifying vocational interest than in measuring vocational aptitude.

As the psychological study of individual differences spread throughout the educational world, educators were quick to see the need for a guidance program much broader than mere vocational guidance. In fact, the beginning of educational guidance had already been visible in the number of "how-to-study" books that came off the press coincident with or following the time in 1910 when Dewey focused attention on method by publishing *How We Think*. But, in addition, educators were quick to perceive that the instruments of vocational guidance could be reshaped to their own ends. The idea behind exploratory and try-out courses, for instance, was readily adapted to the broad-fields curriculum, where the guidance possibilities of such courses as general science and general language could be exploited.

The enlargement of the scope of vocational guidance into educational guidance was completed by the enlargement of educational guidance into guidance as broad as education itself. Educational guidance was originally concerned only with a child's school career. This scope for the term was perhaps adequate as long as the curriculum confined itself to the traditional round of scholastic studies. As the curriculum came to be restated in terms of child activities and as the scope of these activities came to include not only those undertaken in school but a range of them as wide and complex as life itself, however, it was small wonder that some came to identify education and guidance.[31]

REAPPRAISAL OF THE COMPREHENSIVE HIGH SCHOOL

The enlargement of the scope of guidance was in part due to the enlargement of the functions of the high school itself. The original purpose of the high school, it will be remembered, was to prepare for life. This was also the view endorsed by the Committee of Ten. As the committee viewed the situation in 1893, only a few endowed private schools (presumably old academies like Andover) were properly situated to prepare for college. So insignificant a percentage of high school graduates went to college at this time that the committee stated that the high school's "main function is to prepare for the duties of life that small proportion of all the children in the country—a proportion small in number, but very important to the welfare of the nation—who show themselves able to profit by an education prolonged to the eighteenth year, and whose parents are able to support them while they remain so long at school."[32]

Accurate as the Committee of Ten's estimate of the role of the high school may have been at the end of the nineteenth century, times were changing more rapidly than it could foresee. The mounting tide of high school enrollments, which reached tidal proportions in the twentieth century, soon required a radical revision of outlook. While the Committee of Ten advised the membership of the National Education Association in 1893 to regard the high school as a selective institution, the Commission on the Reorganization of Secondary Edu-

[31] J. M. Brewer, *Education as Guidance* (The Macmillan Company, New York, 1932).
[32] *Report of the Committee of Ten on Secondary School Studies, op. cit.,* p. 51.

cation advised the same body in 1918 that high school must be provided for every normal boy and girl up to the age of eighteen. The transition from selectivity to universality in a quarter of a century was a veritable revolution.[33]

Although the revolution was generally accepted, the demand for democratization of the high school brought almost irreconcilable problems in its wake. Most of these problems came to a focus in the curriculum. The Committee of Ten had recommended that all subjects be taught in the same way and to the same extent regardless of the length of time the student stayed in school and regardless of whether he was going to college or out into a job. By the same reasoning the committee might have added that the curriculum should be the same no matter how many attended high school. Obviously it advocated the constancy of the curriculum on the theory of formal discipline.[34] If by the study of a few subjects, principally languages and mathematics, it is more economical and efficient to develop mental power which will transfer in any direction than to become specifically competent in many directions, then time spent, destination, and numbers are unimportant variables.

Insistence on this kind of curriculum, however, resulted in a high dropout rate among high school students. This was clearly inconsistent with the policy of universal secondary education voiced in 1918, the success of which would depend on improving the holding power of the high school. When shortly after the turn of the century psychological studies began seriously to undermine the validity of the theory of formal discipline,[35] members of the Commission on the Reorganization of Secondary Education were not unhappy to seek a new theory of curriculum selection. This they found ready to hand in the pragmatism of John Dewey, who two years previously had published his widely read *Democracy and Education*. Accordingly they outlined objectives for the high school, the "seven cardinal principles,"[36] wherein subjects would be chosen for their ability not merely to form the mind but to inform it.

Unfortunately the bid to democratize the clientele and curriculum of the high school had liabilities as well as assets. If nineteenth-century policies had favored the academic needs of a select few and neglected the mass of the high school population, the opening half of the twentieth century reversed the situation. Not only that, but academic

[33] L. Cremin. "The Revolution in American Secondary Education, 1893–1918," *Teachers College Record*, 56:295–308, March, 1955.
[34] *Supra*, pp. 141–143.
[35] *Supra*, p. 155.
[36] *Supra*, pp. 17, 283–284.

standards, which could be held high under the selective policy prevailing at the end of the nineteenth century, were necessarily lowered to accommodate the policy of mass secondary education enunciated a quarter of a century later, for in this mass were the reluctant and inert as well as the willing and creative. Indeed, a kind of academic Gresham's law seemed to operate. The standards set by the policies of 1918 tended to drive down the academic standards inherited from 1893.

The result of these twentieth-century changes in the high school curriculum was very disturbing to those who still entertained the traditional notion that secondary education should be liberal and Humanistic. Some tried to set American secondary education in perspective by comparing it with that in Europe.[37] None made the comparison better or in more epitomized form than I. L. Kandel (1881–   ). "While the European countries," he wrote, "nearly wrecked their systems of secondary education by a too rigid adhesion to a traditional faith in a limited number of subjects, which were presumed to contain in themselves all the educational values, the high schools of the United States were confronted with the danger of failure because of the absence of any clear-cut concept of liberal education, and because of a certain laissez-faire attitude which satisfied the intense popular faith in education by providing every boy and girl with the opportunity to attend high school."[38]

Perplexing as were the practical problems of the comprehensive American high school, logically there seemed to be no reason why the two policies, terminal and postsecondary education, could not be accommodated to each other under the same academic roof.[39] Yet in spite of this observation the practical problems persisted. The Great Depression of the 1930s put the principle of the comprehensive high school under particular stress. Unemployed youth presented such a serious problem at that time that a special study was made of their social and educational needs. The National Youth Commission, after examining the problem from all angles, reported that while 70 per cent of youth wished to enter white-collar occupations, the country could absorb only about 12 per cent in this way. Now, if 50 to 75 per cent of all remaining jobs required little or no technical training, the great majority of high school youth was not going to need to

[37] W. S. Learned, *The Quality of the Educational Process in the United States and Europe,* Carnegie Foundation for the Advancement of Teaching Bulletin 20, 1927.
[38] Kandel, *op. cit.,* p. 460.
[39] *The Functions of Secondary Education,* National Education Association, Department of Secondary School Principals, Bulletin 64, 1937.

go to high school to prepare for a job. This could mean that the vocational character of the high school's aim to prepare for life would have to be radically revised. The conclusion that the commission drew was that "The prime function, therefore, of universal secondary education is to provide liberal education for the common life of the whole population."[40]

Toward the end of the Second World War the Educational Policies Commission of the National Education Association began to plan for the years after the peace. Even before the war was over it issued a pamphlet on *Education for All American Youth*[41] which reaffirmed and updated for country, town, and state the aspirations of the report of 1918. Both of these documents were astute attempts to read the signs of the times. Both represented advanced thinking and set the pace for professional and lay opinion. While neither document seemed so far ahead of the public as to leave it obviously out of breath, there must have been a number of stragglers.

Very shortly after the War these stragglers seemed to find a rallying point at which to call a halt. At an educational conference in Washington a resolution was passed which, unremarked at the moment, in a few years became a favorite target of the critics of the high school. Noting that 20 per cent of the high school population was currently well cared for in college preparatory courses and another 20 per cent in preparation for skilled trades, the resolution deplored the fact that the remaining 60 per cent were ill served by current high school programs. The resolution then went on to demand a "life adjustment" curriculum for this 60 per cent. The aim of this resolution, and of the Commission on Life Adjustment Education appointed by the United States Commissioner of Education to implement it, on the surface seemed to take a different slant from that of the National Youth Commission but basically was probably quite in line with twentieth-century trends to find a suitable curriculum for the new masses flooding through the gates of democracy's comprehensive high school.

While its thesis may have been the same, accompanying circumstances were not. In the postwar jitters brought on by the "cold war" with Russia, many made the high school along with the elementary school the scapegoat of their frustrations. The principal indictment made against the high school pointed out its essential anti-

[40] H. P. Rainey, *How Fare American Youth?* (Appleton-Century-Crofts, Inc., New York, 1937), p. 47. See also National Society for the Study of Education, *General Education in the American College,* Thirty-eighth Yearbook (Public School Publishing Company, Bloomington, Ill., 1939), part II.

[41] *Education for All American Youth* (National Education Association, Educational Policies Commission, Washington, D.C., 1944).

intellectualism.[42] The life adjustment curriculum not only included "how-to-do-it" courses, of which driver education is a good example, but also emphasized courses like general mathematics and general science which were pointed toward specific applications. Worse yet and confirming the academic Gresham's law suggested above, superior students were inclined from pragmatic motives to elect these courses in preference to advanced studies in mathematics and science or other substantial subject matters.

Critics who made this indictment claimed not to be opposed to the democratization of the high school but rather wanted to know why democratic ends would not be better served by a return to substantial subjects like history, science, literature, mathematics, and foreign languages. The successful launching of the Russian Sputnik months ahead of a similar launching by the United States seemed to give almost crushing weight to the critics' argument. In their anxiety for the future security of the country many opponents of the existing situation were ready to return to traditional American patterns[43] or even to copy European designs of secondary education.[44]

Attack and counterattack followed each other till the protagonists of both recent and older kinds of secondary education reached a virtual deadlock. What was needed was an assessment of the situation by someone whose prestige was great enough to command respect from both camps of opinion. This man turned up in the person of James Bryant Conant, former president of Harvard. He held the confidence of public school men by virtue of his membership on the Educational Policies Commission and the confidence of academic and lay critics of the high school by virtue of having been president of America's leading university.

After wide visitation and study, made possible by a subvention from the Carnegie Corporation, Conant definitely endorsed the unique character of the comprehensive high school, that is, a high school endeavoring to serve "all American youth," the reluctant as well as the willing, the mediocre as well as the talented. Although he recognized the need of many students for diversified marketable skills, he recommended prescribed programs for all in English, history, mathematics, and science. Beyond that he laid special emphasis on programs for the academically talented, urging them to study the

[42] For example, A. Bestor, *Educational Wastelands* (The University of Illinois Press, Urbana, Ill., 1953); R. Hofstadter, *Anti-intellectualism in American Life* (Alfred A. Knopf, Inc., New York, 1963), chaps. 12–14.

[43] J. D. Koerner, *The Case for Basic Education* (Little, Brown and Company, Boston, 1959).

[44] H. G. Rickover, *American Education: A National Failure* (E. P. Dutton & Co., Inc., New York, 1963).

solid academic subjects, not for the outmoded discipline of the mind, but because their difficult intellectual content was necessary for personal fulfillment and national welfare and security. Better guidance, starting earlier, Conant recognized, would be needed to achieve these objectives.[45]

On the whole, Conant's report amounted to underscoring what was good in the present system. Not everyone was pleased with this outcome, but a measure of academic tranquillity returned to the high school. The pursuit of excellence[46] became popular, especially with the impending threat of Russian superiority in space. Philadelphia and New York City established special high schools for gifted students, and many secondary schools provided courses which would entitle their graduates to advanced placement when they entered college.

[45] J. B. Conant, *The American High School Today* (McGraw-Hill Book Company, New York, 1959).

[46] Rockefeller Brothers Fund, *The Pursuit of Excellence,* Special Studies Project Report V (Doubleday & Company, Inc., Garden City, N.Y., 1958).

15 Higher Education

Higher education is concerned with instruction in the more advanced phases of the social culture. It not only treats of the current culture in its most recondite terms but, being the most advanced stage of learning, occupies an uneasy yet exciting post on the frontier between the known and the unknown. The fact that higher education opens windows on areas of culture that are settled as well as areas yet unsettled poses one of its most persistent problems. This is the age-old issue of freedom for the human mind to follow an argument whithersoever it may lead, even beyond the present boundaries of knowledge. Should the university be a place where the mind is peculiarly free to appraise the known and explore the unknown? Closely allied is the question: Should the university be exclusively occupied with professional and research studies? Or should it also be occupied with giving a liberal education? Again, whether liberal education be a function of higher or secondary education, just how shall liberal education be conceived? However the foregoing questions are answered, should higher education be supported and controlled under public or private auspices? In spite of their age, none of these questions has lost any of its persistence with the passing of the centuries. In fact, if anything, these perennial problems of higher education are more pressing in the twentieth century than ever before.

HIGHER EDUCATION IN ANCIENT TIMES

Higher education in the Western tradition commenced with the Greeks. It had its origin principally in the impulse given to the study of philosophy by the Sophists. Informal schools of adult students soon grouped themselves around such great thinkers and teachers as Socrates, Plato, and Aristotle. In the course of time schools like Plato's Academy and Aristotle's Lyceum developed a continuity that spanned many generations of succeeding teachers. Still greater stability attached to these schools under Roman rule when it became the custom of emperors to subsidize the teaching of subjects like philosophy and rhetoric at such principal centers of learning as Athens, Rhodes, and Alexandria. It further became imperial custom to grant teachers such important privileges as exemption from taxation and freedom from military service. Yet, along with support, came a modicum of control, for sometimes emperors reserved to their persons the right to make appointments to particular chairs of instruction.

But even with this degree of regulation never was higher education in the ancient world more than a voluntary aggregation of teachers and students. Neither a governing nor an examining agency ruled over them. In fact, they had no corporate character whatever. Thus the centers of higher learning in the ancient world should probably not be called universities, as has sometimes been the case. A somewhat greater degree of organization seems to have obtained at the ancient seat of learning at Alexandria. There at least the Ptolemies had provided a handsome public building, with noble porticoes, in which instruction could be carried on. In addition, Alexandria had an unexcelled library reported to contain more than 700,000 individual items. Yet even at Alexandria there was no corporate university organization such as the medieval bequeathed to educational posterity.

The whole range of ancient knowledge was generally taught at these seats of learning. Very prominent, of course, were the liberal arts. The arts of grammar, logic, and rhetoric were taught, together with the arts of arithmetic, geometry, astronomy, and music. In addition, there existed chairs in the professional subjects of law, theology, and medicine. There was thus broad and diversified training for judge, advocate, senator, doctor, or priest. Apropos of this last category it is worth noting that many of the early fathers of the Christian Church taught and were taught at Alexandria. In no ancient city of the Roman Empire was intellectual life richer than in Alexandria, for no city was so favorably located at the crossroads of ancient culture. There the strains of Greek, Roman, Judaean, and Oriental cultures met and rubbed cultural elbows.

Even at this early time student life at these ancient seats of learning began to develop customs that seem to have been capable of spontaneous regeneration wherever and whenever the higher learning was later carried on. Thus there were already evident scorn and contempt for the beginning, or freshman, student. Already he was the butt of the pranks of older and more sophisticated students. Another custom which goes back to these times was the organization of student clubs and discussion groups. Apparently, it was customary then, as it was later in the medieval university, for students all too often to argue points of useless erudition. Clubs and discussions frequently led to rivalries and rivalries to brawls and riots, which, again, were only first in a long series of subsequent and similar disorders.

The higher learning of the ancient world had its ups and downs. Periods of formalism and sterility followed periods of intellectual vigor, only to be themselves succeeded by periods of decadence. Although the lamp of higher education burned low at times in the eastern half of the Roman Empire, it never nearly went out as in the western half. The reasons for its dimming were not far to seek. Stimulus though imperial support was to higher learning, it had its drawbacks. The price for imperial support was too frequently imperial control. The moment thought was no longer free to pursue an argument wherever it might lead, the higher learning started to flicker out. It was virtually snuffed out when the Christian Church came to suspect higher education as a beacon of paganism, and this in spite of the fact that great church fathers like Clement and Origen had taught the higher learning at Alexandria.

THE MEDIEVAL UNIVERSITY

Although the brillant culture of classical antiquity went into eclipse during the Middle Ages, the leaders in the Christian Church were able by dint of great effort to keep some learning alive. The chief centers for this learning were the cathedral schools that bishops encouraged in conjunction with the churches of their cathedral cities. The education given there, while the best the times afforded to keep the ranks of the clergy recruited, nevertheless was hardly to be ranked as up to the standard of higher education.

Yet it was out of the intellectual life that centered in the cathedral school that the medieval university ultimately emerged. Cultivation of a level of learning higher than that of the cathedral school only awaited the emergence of social interests complex and important enough to call it forth. The beginning of the end of the Middle Ages heralded just such a situation. This was the great theological controversy between the nominalists and the realists over the nature of universals. To the intellectual frontier represented by the controversy rushed young and vigorous minds from all over Europe. In order to participate effectively in the struggle, however, these minds needed training in dialectic as well as in theology. Many found that the best way to get this training lay in listening to the lectures and disputations of such leaders in the fray as Pierre Abélard. These men held forth in cathedral schools and particularly in the cathedral city of Paris.

The higher learning thus had a rebirth in Paris very similar to its first birth in Athens and Alexandria. Teachers and students came together informally to pursue their common interests. While at Paris, these interests were predominantly theological, in Bologna and Salerno, two other prominent centers of higher education in the Middle Ages, the chief intellectual preoccupations were law and medicine, respectively. This informal band of teacher and taught soon came to be known as a *studium generale*. It was not long, however, before a stronger organization was needed. In Paris the teachers, or "masters," as they were called, ran afoul of the chancellor of the cathedral of Notre Dame. The chancellor, because it was his duty to license masters, tried to exercise more far-reaching control over them than they were willing to accept. Consequently, they banded themselves together to resist his power. In Bologna it was the students who banded together to control the conditions under which instruction was given by their teachers, or "doctors,"[1] as they were called there. Frequently students and masters or doctors joined forces to protect themselves from the exploitation by the townspeople, upon whom they were dependent for food and lodging.

In the course of time this closer organization took the medieval legal form of a *universitas*. In twentieth-century parlance a *universitas* would be a "corporation."[2] In other words, medieval students and masters or doctors incorporated themselves, and this corporate organization of higher education came to be known as a *universitas magistrorum et scholarium*. Later it was convenient to shorten this title to its first term or its Anglicized form, "university." Because the university was a corporation, it had, like any modern corporation, to get a charter. It could get this from either the state or the church, as both were active in medieval times in fostering higher education.[3]

---

[1] Note the etymological derivation of doctor from *doctus,* the past participle of the Latin *docere,* to teach.

[2] The governing bodies of some modern universities, for example, Yale, are still called the "corporation."

[3] Universities like Oxford and Cambridge were even granted representation in Parliament by the sovereign. Following English precedent, the American College of William and Mary at first had a representative in the Virginia House of Burgesses.

The internal organization of the medieval university varied somewhat from place to place. Some features, however, were quite common. The students ordinarily organized themselves by nations. This was partly for sentimental reasons but more practically for purposes of protection. In medieval towns strangers were never very welcome and often were considered quite legitimate prey by the townspeople. The masters and doctors organized themselves according to their fields of specialization. For example, those having a faculty, or proficiency, in law came to be known as the "faculty of law." Four faculties were usually recognized, law, theology, medicine, and arts. Over each faculty presided a dean, who originally held this office by virtue of being the senior member. Over the whole university stood the rector, who in the course of time came to supplant the chancellor.

The course of instruction in the medieval university seems to have been organized into three levels. Since lectures and disputations were carried on in Latin, the first prerequisite of the medieval university student was a thorough command of Latin. Of course, he was expected to know some Latin when he came to the university, but nevertheless he usually spent his first year at the university perfecting his Latin while he also pursued the liberal arts—or at least their medieval epitome. On satisfactorily completing this training, the medieval student was admitted to the degree of bachelor of arts and to the second stage of his work, candidacy for the degree of master of arts. During this period he attended lectures chiefly in the dialectic, metaphysics, politics, and ethics of Aristotle. At the conclusion of this work he stood a test, which finally admitted him to the coveted master's degree. On gaining this degree he might or might not take a third period of training by entering one of the higher faculties, such as law or theology.

There were two principal ways in which instruction was carried on at the medieval university, the lecture and the disputation. Much of the instruction took the form of lecturing because of the great scarcity of books in this period before the invention of printing. On this account lecturing often amounted to nothing more than an instructor reading to his students out of his own book.[4] It should not be surprising, therefore, that most universities had regulations on the rate at which readings, or lectures, were to be given. There were precautions against such rapid reading that the students could not take adequate notes but also against lectures so slow that the teacher stretched out their number and thus received a larger fee. Lectures were also both ordinary and extraordinary. The ordinary lectures were given in the morning by the master or doctor himself. Extraordinary lectures were usually given at odd times by advanced students

[4] For another account of this method of instruction, see *supra,* pp. 181–183.

and consisted in a repetition of the master's lecture for the benefit of those whose notes were incomplete because of dozing or lack of diligence. Indeed, Oxford had a statute requiring its professors to repeat notable passages. This may have been less necessary later on when students were able at least to rent books which had been copied in scriptoria.

The great danger of the lecture was that it tended to become dogmatic. Some relief from the dogmatism of the book was achieved through the master's gloss. That is, in reading his book the master sometimes took occasion to comment on the text, to elaborate or amend it. A further Oxford statute actually required its professors to raise debatable points for discussion but only if relevant. Still further relief was gained through the disputation. Lectures provided weapons to enter the theological controversies of the time, but disputations provided an arena in which to practice them. Disputations were debates in which one student or master would maintain a thesis against another student or master. While the logic of the argument was judged by the rules of Aristotle's *Organon,* there was considerable latitude for a student to exercise his own ingenuity.

The supreme objective of university study was, of course, the award of the master's or doctor's degree. In the formal award the degree was granted, as it still is, "with all the rights and privileges pertaining thereto." Just what were these coveted rights and privileges for which the medieval student sacrificed so much? Chief was the right to practice his profession or teach in the field of his specialization. It was not only the right to teach that was coveted but the right to teach anywhere, the *jus ubique docendi.* The older universities easily attracted students because their degrees were recognized everywhere without question. The best way open to younger universities to overcome the handicap of their late founding was to take their charter from a universal sovereign, a pope or an emperor. The imprimatur of such a sovereign would, of course, command the respect and recognition that would entitle the degree holder to his rights anywhere.

The privileges that university degrees conferred upon their recipients were several. Principally they conferred exemption from taxation, exemption from military service, and exemption from trial in the courts of the civil magistrate. If the university students fell afoul of the law, they were privileged to have their cases tried within the jurisdiction of the university. At a time when a rather crude sort of personal justice was often administered by the local duke or baron, it was no mean privilege to be tried within a jurisdiction where men were learned in the study of law. It will be quickly recognized that the immunities regarding taxation and military service were not altogether new with the Middle Ages. Honorable and long-standing precedent for such privileges extended back to favors conferred upon teachers of higher education by the Roman emperors themselves.[5]

The social significance of this practice of bestowing privileges on the educated both in ancient and in medieval times was to encourage learning by placing a premium upon it. After the latter part of the Renaissance there was a marked tendency for sovereigns to withdraw these privileges or permit them to fall into desuetude. The fact that they did so is evidence that the higher learning had become so well established that there was no longer need to encourage it by civil exemptions. The exemptions from taxation, however, which was withdrawn from individuals, was still pretty generally allowed to attach to the property of the university as a whole.[6]

It should be noted that the bachelor's degree never carried the rights and privileges which were such an important part of the master's and doctor's degrees. This was because the bachelor's degree was originally just a permission to become a candidate for an advanced degree. Although at first the degree drew its significance almost entirely from the studies it opened up rather than the ones it concluded, later on the reverse became the case. Thus, the more students attended the university with no intent of doing more than completing their bachelor's studies, the more the bachelor's degree became a terminal one.[7]

The whole system of the medieval university with its hierarchy of degrees had its exact counterpart in the medieval guild system. Just as guilds were the form in which the various crafts organized themselves, so the universities were really guilds of the craft of scholars. The master of arts in the university corresponded directly in status to the master workman in one of the guilds. The bachelor of arts corresponded to the journeyman, and his degree indicated

[5] Note how these privileges were mentioned in the charter of the colonial college of Brown (1764): Thus, "for the greater encouragement of the Seminary of learning, and that the same may be amply endowed and enfranchised with the same privileges, dignities, and immunities enjoyed by the American colleges, and European universities, We do grant, enact, ordain, and declare, That the College estate, the estates, persons, and families of the President and Professors, for the time being, lying, and being within the Colony, with the persons of the Tutors and students, during their residence at the College, shall be freed and exempted from all taxes, serving on juries, and menial services: And that the persons aforesaid shall be exempted from bearing arms, impresses, and military services, except in case of an invasion." [A. O. Norton, *Readings in the History of Education* (Harvard University, Cambridge, Mass., 1909), p. 102.]

[6] It is interesting to note how American municipalities tried to encroach on even this privilege during the severe economic Depression from 1929 onward, claiming that universities should pay taxes.

[7] H. B. Green, "The Origin of the A.B. Degree," *Journal of Higher Education,* 17:205–210, April, 1946.

that he was serving an apprenticeship in the arts. The disputation in which the bachelor maintained a selected thesis against all comers as evidence of his qualification to be licensed as a master of arts corresponded to the piece of workmanship a journeyman might present to prove his fitness to be made a master of his craft.

The system of degrees was the means the university employed to hold high the quality of its membership. The discipline that this provided also enabled the university to present a united front to the townspeople when disputes arose between them. This was a very important asset, for strained relations between town and gown have been almost as old as higher education itself. Quarrels between the two have most often arisen over rents and the quality and price of victuals and drink. For long the university held the whip hand over the town through its threat to exercise the right of *cessatio,* that is, ceasing to hold classes in that particular town and resuming them somewhere else.[8] This right was easy to exercise when, as at Paris, the university met in an odd assortment of rented buildings on "Straw Street," so called because of the straw strewn on the floors where the students sat. Under such circumstances it amounted to little or nothing to pull up stakes and move elsewhere. When, however, the university became possessed of permanent buildings, this was not so easy to do, and thereafter the town faction was more able to wage equal combat with the gown. Occasionally, even as late as the twentieth century, these combats resolved themselves into riots or even pitched battles.

The term "gown" has been taken symbolically to refer to the university because many of the students were clerics and therefore clerical dress became customary for even those students who did not plan to seek ordination on the completion of their studies. This custom has persisted into the twentieth century, in which the cleric's gown or some adaptation of it constitutes official academic costume.[9] The clerical influence is easily detectable in the loose, flowing robe and hood. The many colors of the hood were added much later to designate the wearer's degree and the institution from which he took it. The cut of the academic costume in some European universities clearly shows the influence of Renaissance styles. At Oxford and Cambridge the wearing of an abbreviated gown is a daily custom, but in the United States academic costume is worn only on ceremonial occasions

---

[8] The right of *cessatio* corresponds to the modern strike. It was so powerful a weapon when wielded by an organized corporate body that it is small wonder that the right of masters and students to organize was at first fought as unlawful, just as were trade unions in their inception at a later day.

[9] M. Goeddeke, "The Evolution of Academic Costume," *Catholic Educational Review,* 36:358–359, June, 1938.

such as commencement. The ritual of this occasion, if studied closely, will also often reveal clerical origins. The academic procession and the order of awarding degrees not infrequently take their cues from ecclesiastical ritual.

ORIGIN OF THE COLLEGE

The age of students at the medieval university varied widely. The candidates for the arts degree at Paris, for instance, were considerably younger than the students studying law at Bologna. Fifteen was not at all an uncommon age for students at the former university. Naturally, there was great danger that youths of this age would be tempted to spend their time in sloth and riotous living rather than in diligent application to their studies. To offset this danger, colleges were founded. At first the college was just a hospice, hall, inn, or hostel under the charge of a master who enforced discipline based on rules not unlike those governing monasteries. Gates were closed at sundown. The industrious were encouraged, and the indolent were sternly reminded of their duties.

In the course of time, endowments began to accrue, and colleges became fixtures in university life. But, more important, the college began to take on educational significance. The master in charge began to assume tutorial functions. Moreover, colleges became obviously convenient places at which to give extraordinary lectures, or repetitions. Later, professors, too, took up residence in these colleges and even gave their ordinary lectures there.

Colleges never gained the importance at Paris or elsewhere in continental Europe that they did in England at Oxford and Cambridge. There by the sixteenth century the colleges had become almost autonomous. Ordinary lectures in the colleges virtually superseded university lectures when students no longer were required to attend the latter. In fact, the English university became a collection of communal colleges; the university still awarded all degrees, but the college took responsibility not only for training its members in the liberal arts but also for supervising them in moral discipline. Even the conventional college architecture of the quadrangle conformed to the communal character of the college.

When the Society of Jesus was founded as part of the Catholic Counter Reformation, it decided to cast its famous educational institutions in collegiate form. In organizing their colleges, however, the Jesuits distinguished between an upper and a lower college although the two were at first part of the same institution. In the course of time the lower colleges became differentiated and even separated as secondary schools, while the upper colleges continued to give instruction of university grade as they always had. The administrative pattern of the Jesuit college followed that of the medieval university. At the head was a rector, who was assisted by a chancellor, or prefect of studies, whose duty it was to organize the curriculum, direct disputations, and decide upon those fitted to receive degrees. The rector was further to be assisted by the deans of faculties. Yet in spite of such assistance the rector was not relieved by the *Ratio studiorum* from paying occasional visits to classes, even the lower ones, and to both public and private disputations.[10]

The seventeenth-century founders of Harvard, when they established this first of the nine colonial colleges in America, took the English college as their model. The college men among the founders were mostly graduates of Emmanuel College at Cambridge University, England. As Emmanuel College was strongly Puritan, it is more than likely that Harvard's founders intended to erect another Emmanuel in the town of Cambridge, Massachusetts. The founding of Yale in New Haven, Connecticut, at the opening of the next century followed the same pattern.

The chief features of these and other American colleges were like those of their English prototype. Thus, the distinguishing feature of the American college was its communal character. The college was, so to speak, a large boarding school for pupils of more mature age. Responsibility for moral oversight as well as academic instruction devolved upon the officers of the college for all in residence there. Regulations for the control of students' personal lives were prescribed down to such minutiae as misspending time and wearing improper garb. On the academic side these regulations were matched by close prescription of the collegiate course of study. All pursued the same fixed curriculum through the four-year college course. College work was further organized not by individual courses but by college classes, that is, by college generations—freshman, sophomore, junior, and senior classes. Not infrequently, the president taught the senior class.[11] Finally, all progressed toward the same academic degree of bachelor of arts.[12]

Although faithful to the communal character of the English college,

---

[10] E. A. Fitzpatrick, *St. Ignatius and the Ratio Studiorum* (McGraw-Hill Book Company, New York, 1933), pp. 114–117, 128, 138, 141.

[11] It was this arrangement, undoubtedly, which accounted in no small measure for the grip which presidents like Mark Hopkins at Williams and Timothy Dwight at Yale had on the undergraduates of their day. And usually it was that part of the senior course devoted to "moral philosophy" which gave the president his greatest opportunity to mold the mind of the next generation.

[12] For a nineteenth-century defense of this traditional college pattern, see N. Porter, *The American Colleges and the American Public* (Charles C. Chatfield & Company, New Haven, Conn., 1870), chaps. 8, 10.

higher education in colonial America did make one important innovation in its administrative organization. At Oxford and Cambridge controlling authority was vested in a bicameral body composed of the faculty on the one hand (the "lesser congregation") and of the graduates on the other (the "greater congregation"). Naturally, at its founding Harvard had no graduates to form a greater congregation. To overcome this inescapable handicap, an innovation in the control of higher education was instituted, and a board of overseers was appointed. At William and Mary, the equivalent group was a board of visitors. The main management of academic policies, however, was still vested in the president and fellows. As the Harvard faculty at first were accounted fellows, this type of control was not unlike the medieval pattern according to which the rector and faculty held much of the power. But the Harvard faculty later lost even this time-honored power when, after a protracted struggle, they were excluded from sitting on the governing board of fellows.

The innovation of unicameral rule by a president and fellows, who operated like a board of trustees, received its most popular demonstration at Yale, Harvard's great rival. There the fellows were a self-perpetuating body, at first drawn from the surrounding Congregational clergy. This clerical control should occasion no surprise, for it was a band of Congregational preachers who had been largely instrumental in starting the "collegiate school" in New Haven. For similar reasons, the board of control at Brown was composed of Baptist ministers and at Princeton of Presbyterians. As years passed and as secular interests occupied a larger share of men's thoughts, increasing numbers of laymen took places on these boards. Among these laymen a liberal number of alumni began to appear when colleges undertook to solicit financial support from their growing "greater congregations." But, whether control was lay or clerical, it was Yale's unicameral rather than Harvard's bicameral governing body that was copied by the newer colleges as they were founded.

PUBLIC VERSUS PRIVATE CONTROL OF THE COLLEGE

In spite of the clerical control and even clerical origin of many of the colonial colleges, few if any of these institutions were able to dispense with some financial assistance from their colonial governments. Yet, though the government subsidized the colleges it had chartered, it never assumed a relation toward them such as it did toward the state colleges and universities of the nineteenth and twentieth centuries. The state was willing to foster higher institutions of learning but not to assume primary responsibility for their support and control.

The gradual disestablishment of the various colonial churches by the states, commencing with Virginia in 1789, created a situation that required a readjustment of the relation of state and church in higher education. The secularism and democracy of French Revolutionary thought inspired many Americans to think in terms of public control of higher education. Any public encroachment on the prerogatives of the colonial colleges, however, was obviously destined to produce resistance. The American Revolution simplified the problem for New York. King's College ceased to exist, so that when the war was over the state could start afresh in its chartering of Columbia. In Connecticut the problem was more complicated. The state tried to exercise a modicum of control over Yale but was rebuffed. In retaliation it withdrew its annual grant-in-aid. After some years of disagreement public and private interests settled their differences by an arrangement that made the governor and lieutenant governor of the state ex officio members of the Yale corporation.[13] This solution also served to settle a later contest between Harvard and Massachusetts.

Yale and Harvard, however, merely compromised the issue of public versus private control of higher education. The real head-on clash between these two forces occurred in the case of Dartmouth College in New Hampshire. The Dartmouth charter was granted by the English crown to a self-perpetuating board of trustees just before the Revolution. No issue in the control of the college arose till the second decade of the nineteenth century. At that time the state of New Hampshire sought to reorganize the college as Dartmouth University. The trustees resisted and engaged no less a lawyer than Daniel Webster, an alumnus, to argue its case before the courts.

The case was first argued in the courts of New Hampshire, where the trustees lost. But on appeal to the Supreme Court of the United States this decision was reversed by a famous decision of Chief Justice John Marshall in 1819.[14] In his opinion the act of the state of New Hampshire was unconstitutional because it impaired the Dartmouth charter and therefore contravened the provision in the Federal Constitution that enjoined states from impairing the obligation of contracts. Such reasoning could hold only if Dartmouth was a private rather than a public corporation, and thus Chief Justice Marshall had to deal with this issue as well.[15]

---

[13] Yale's president, Ezra Stiles (1727–1795), was surprised and delighted that the "civilians" acquiesced to being a minority in the corporation.

[14] *Trustees of Dartmouth College v. Woodward,* 4 Wheaton 518 (1819).

[15] For an elaboration of this issue, see J. S. Brubacher, "A Reargument of the Dartmouth College Case," *Educational Trends,* 8:6–11, May-June, 1940.

Friends of the college took the view that it would be dangerous to regard the college as a public corporation because its fate would then become subject to the rise and fall of popular majorities. Moreover, future benefactors of the college might be alarmed, for they would have no assurance against interference with the objects of their bounty. Learned professors, too, might be deterred from a life of scholarship if title to their chairs were made to depend precariously on the popular will.

Friends of the state had just the opposite anxieties. They preferred to regard Dartmouth College as vested with a public interest. Indeed, they contended that the prosperity of higher education in the state depended entirely upon the public esteem in which it was held. Relieve the college trustees of responsibility to popular majorities and suspicion was bound to arise whether the college was being administered in the broad interests of public welfare or in the narrow interests of private, sectarian, or party benefit. Worse yet, once this suspicion got abroad, it would avail the college little, if at all, that palpable misconceptions ruled the popular mind.

As is well known, Chief Justice Marshall sided with the friends of Dartmouth College. Both he and Webster were members of the conservative Federalist party. In spite of the French and American Revolutions, or perhaps because of their excesses, these men lacked a thoroughgoing confidence in the judgment of the common man. Thomas Jefferson, however, father of American democracy, expressed grave anxiety over this want of confidence. "The idea that institutions established for the use of the nation cannot be touched nor modified," he wrote apropos of the Dartmouth College case, "even to make them answer their end, because of rights gratuitously supposed in those employed to manage them in trust for the public, may perhaps, be a salutary provision against the abuses of a monarch, but it is most absurd against the nation itself."[16]

In spite of this pointed criticism the Dartmouth College case came to be revered as one of the great bulwarks of academic liberties in the United States. Writing in his *Commentaries on American Law,* Chancellor James Kent no doubt expressed the popular estimate of the case when he said that it "did more than any other single act proceeding from the authority of the United States to throw an impregnable barrier around all rights and franchises derived from the grant of government, and to give solidity and inviolability to

---

[16] Quoted in C. Warren, *The Supreme Court in U.S. History* (Little, Brown and Company, Boston, 1922), vol. 1, p. 484. See J. M. Shirley, *The Dartmouth College Cases* (G. I. Jones & Co., St. Louis, 1879), p. 107.

the literary, charitable, religious, and commercial institutions of our country."[17]

INCREASE IN INSTITUTIONS OF HIGHER EDUCATION

The Dartmouth College case had a notable effect on the expansion of provisions for higher education in the period between its decision and the Civil War. During the colonial period, 9 colleges had been founded. In the period from the Revolution to the Dartmouth College case this number was augmented by only 12 new colleges. In the next period, however, some 500 colleges were founded. There were various causes of this tremendous effort to expand higher education. At least two of them can be associated with the Dartmouth College case.

Most notable of the influences of the Dartmouth College case was the severe setback it administered to public and secular interests that had sought to obtain some measure of control in the policies of the existing private colleges. Their reaction to this rebuff was to launch out in the direction of founding state institutions of higher learning. Only in the case of the University of Virginia, however, did this effort succeed both as a public and as a secular enterprise. In nearly every other instance strong religious pressures succeeded at least in delaying the secular state in its progress toward a secular state university.

As colonial colleges like Harvard and Yale exhibited English influences upon American higher education, so the University of Virginia exhibited French influences.[18] In the founding of this great state university secular purposes were as prominent as religious ones were in the founding of the colonial colleges. Thus, Jefferson made careers in agriculture, commerce, and industry concerns of the University of Virginia along with the more conventional interest of higher education in such careers as medicine, law, and theology. In its curriculum he gave prominence to mathematics and science along with the more usual classical languages. Also high among his objectives for the university was instruction in the principles and structure of government itself. And, not least, studies were to be elective.

[17] J. Kent, *Commentaries on American Law*, 12th ed., O. W. Holmes Jr. (ed.) (Little, Brown and Company, Boston, 1873), p. 419. Sir Henry Maine, the great English legal scholar, called the Dartmouth College case "the bulwark of American individualism against democratic impatience and socialistic fantasy." (Quoted in Warren, *op. cit.*, p. 491.)

[18] There were French influences at Georgetown, too, where many Jesuits, exiled from France, took asylum. See F. P. Cassidy, *Catholic College Foundations and Developments in the United States, 1674–1850* (The Catholic University of America, Washington, D.C., 1924).

Of the other state universities founded in this period perhaps the most successful was the University of Michigan. There German influences were pronounced. The hope was to have an institution that approached the quality and discipline of the German university rather than the English communal college. Indeed, voices in high places raised the question whether it was not time to discontinue the communal character of the college. At least it was proposed that Michigan experiment with boarding students about town so that its limited financial resources might be invested in the academic educational program instead of in dormitories. In the curriculum secular interests were to be played up and theological ones kept in perspective. Yet, in spite of these bold plans, progress was almost discouragingly slow. The heyday of this and other state universities did not really come till after the Civil War. Then the Federal munificence with which the Ordinance of 1787 endowed the systems of education in the new states cut from the public domain began to yield handsome dividends indeed.

Perhaps most active in founding new colleges were the various church denominations. After losing the long struggle to control the new state universities in the interests of religion, the churches finally bowed to the inevitable implications of the separation of church and state.[19] For them the chief implication was the necessity for founding denominational colleges. Fortunately, they could move confidently forward in this mission since the Dartmouth College decision assured them, as Chancellor Kent had remarked, of the "inviolability" of any charters they might obtain. The growth of denominational colleges fed readily on the vigorous religious evangelism of the time. This evangelism was particularly strong on the American frontier, and it was there that many of the new colleges held their first classes. In a sense, these colleges were advance agents of the church militant wherein each denomination was bent upon extending a sort of religious imperialism of its own.

Unfortunately for the tremendous increase in the number of colleges, the frontier was neither thickly enough settled nor possessed of a high enough standard of living to sustain the increase adequately. Many institutions commenced operating in such humble circumstances as to be called "log-cabin colleges." Many others sought to meet expenses in part by introducing Philipp Emanuel von Fellenberg's manual-labor program for students. Fellenberg had urged manual labor on grounds of educational theory,[20] but these frontier colleges seized upon it for its economic usefulness. In nearly every case the

---

[19] For example, see L. L. Gobbel, *Church-State Relationships in Education in North Carolina since 1776* (The Duke University Press, Durham, N.C., 1938).

[20] For a fuller account of this theory, see *supra,* p. 270.

necessary work was so arduous and time consuming that either the work program or the academic program had to suffer. The mortality among these colleges was therefore very high. But so it was among other denominational colleges as well. Denominational rivalry, internal dissension, unfavorable geographical location, disaster by fire—all were mortal enemies of these struggling colleges. In fact, of the 500 colleges founded during this period of denominational or other reasons only about 200 managed to survive as permanent additions to the country's list of higher institutions of learning.

State universities and denominational colleges were not the only institutions to be founded to swell the opportunities for higher education before and after the Civil War. This was also the period in which higher education of a technical nature first began in this country. The colonial colleges had been almost exclusively absorbed in a linguistic curriculum featuring Latin and Greek and preparing for the professions, especially the ministry. As the effects of the Industrial Revolution spread more and more widely in the nineteenth century, a demand arose for higher education that was technical in character. The first institution to offer such training was the Rensselaer Polytechnic Institute, founded in 1824 at Troy, New York. In the middle of the century Harvard and Yale followed suit, Harvard by setting up the Lawrence Scientific School and Yale the Sheffield Scientific School on their respective campuses. The Massachusetts Institute of Technology came into being in the year in which the Civil War closed.

When Rensselaer Polytechnic Institute opened, its courses in applied science included agriculture as well as mechanics. There was not much demand for advanced training in agriculture, however, till the decade before the Civil War. At the end of that decade President James Buchanan on constitutional grounds vetoed a bill sponsored by Senator Justin S. Morrill of Vermont that would have subsidized the states with land grants from the public domain to set up colleges of agriculture and mechanical arts. The problem of food supply during the Civil War led to a renewed demand for Morrill's bill, and it was finally passed in 1862 with the signature of President Abraham Lincoln, who had no constitutional scruples in signing it. The several states lost little time in taking advantage of this Federal munificence and early set up what since have become well known as our "land-grant colleges." In some cases, instead of chartering new foundations, the states used this endowment to establish schools of agriculture and mechanical arts in conjunction with institutions already flourishing within their borders. Many of these "A & M colleges" later expanded into the field of the liberal arts and sciences as well, a development anticipated in the original act. The social dividends from this legislation were so rich that at the close of the century the Federal government passed a second Morrill Act appropriating an annual cash subsidy to these institutions.

THE HIGHER EDUCATION OF WOMEN

Another new and important direction in which the facilities of higher education were expanded in the middle and latter part of the nineteenth century was in the provision made for the higher education of women. The pages of history prior to this century had not been devoid of instances of very well-educated women. One might, for instance, mention women like Héloïse, Catherine of Aragon, and Mary Wollstonecraft. Yet, women of this sort were distinctly exceptions rather than the rule. The popular attitude toward women's education was more truly stated by Jean Jacques Rousseau (1712–1778) when he described the education of Sophie, Émile's future wife. Her education was to be almost the opposite of Émile's in that she was not to be trained to lead an independent life of her own but rather to render her husband's life agreeable by subordinating herself to him.

Even then, Rousseau probably overstated the case for the education of women since the Sophie he had in mind definitely belonged to the upper strata of society. On the whole, the general notion was that woman's social function of childbearing and home management did not require and would not be improved by the sort of formal education offered in the schools. Because for long women had had no very intellectual function to perform for society, many people fallaciously concluded that women did not have the intellectual capacity to benefit by such an education even if it were offered to them. Others argued that even if women could profit by such an education, it would make them less refined. In the nineteenth century, statistics were adduced to prove that the fertility of women declined as the amount of their formal education increased. Many who made much of these figures overlooked the fact that they were equally true of men.

It was not until the nineteenth century that serious inroads were made into the popular prejudice against the education of women. In this century a happy combination of circumstances, however, advanced the cause of women's education to a rank on a par with that of men. Perhaps the two most important circumstances were economic: the Industrial Revolution and the settlement of the American frontier. In both these movements women frequently proved themselves of equal or nearly equal worth with men. These conditioning sociological factors fortified, and in turn were reinforced by, the democratic equalitarianism that had been stimulated by the American and French Revolutions. Religion blew both hot and cold on the further education of women. Its story of the eviction from the Garden of Eden fostered a notion of the moral inferiority of women, while its "new dispensation" greatly improved their status by making the sons and daughters of men equal in God's sight.

In the light of this latter insight, especially as interpreted by the Protestant Reformation, it became as necessary for girls to learn to read as it was for boys. Hence, in the common schools of the American colonies, coeducation was a not uncommon phenomenon.[21] While girls had no entree to the Latin grammar school, the academy movement in the eighteenth century included a few academies for girls. Many of these academies, however, never rose much above the level of finishing schools. In the nineteenth century the idea rooted and persisted in the minds of a few notable woman pioneers that there should be educational facilities for women, higher as well as secondary, which should be equal in every respect to those for men.

To three women in particular, Emma Willard (1787–1870), Catherine Beecher (1800–1878), and Mary Lyon (1797–1849), goes the credit for pioneering this idea.[22] Emma Willard and Catherine Beecher inaugurated seminaries, the one in New York and the other in Connecticut, which demonstrated quite clearly that, given an equal opportunity, girls could succeed in studies just as intellectually rigorous as those of their brothers. In 1837 Mary Lyon founded Mount Holyoke, a seminary too, but Mount Holyoke had the distinction before the century was out of being elevated to collegiate grade. Mount Holyoke was not the first women's college, that distinction going to Vassar, founded just after the Civil War, but it did enjoy a longer tradition.

While colleges like Mount Holyoke and Vassar were as strictly for women as colleges like Princeton and Dartmouth were for men, it is notable that in many of the new state universities of the Middle West the coeducation of men and women was practiced from an early date. Indeed, the capability of women to absorb the higher education of men had not long been established before the idea was broached that the old-line men's colleges open their facilities to the education of young women. Only a few like Harvard and Columbia listened to the plea, but even they refused at first to admit women

[21] For a history of coeducation, with emphasis chiefly on England, see L. B. Pekin, *Coeducation* (The Hogarth Press, Ltd., London, 1939), chaps. 5–7.

[22] For a fuller account of these women, see W. Goodsell, *Pioneers of Women's Education* (McGraw-Hill Book Company, New York, 1931). For the history of women's education in general, see T. Woody, *A History of the Education of Women in the United States* (2 vols., Science Press, Lancaster, Pa., 1929).

to the same classes with men. Instead, they made their libraries, laboratories, and faculty available for women through a separate college organization, a sort of "annex" to the main body. At Harvard this annex came to be known as Radcliffe, and at Columbia as Barnard. But as women came to prove their academic metal equal to that of men, they came to share the same classrooms and laboratories as their brothers.

THE GENTEEL TRADITION IN LIBERAL EDUCATION

Thus far the development of collegiate education has been traced with only incidental reference to the kind of education offered there. From the beginning, the American colonial colleges awarded the bachelor of arts degree. This fact will readily indicate that the curriculum was composed of the traditional liberal arts taught at the medieval university and inherited by it from classical antiquity. The ideal of liberal education, however, did not stand still from medieval to colonial times nor from colonial to modern times. In order to understand the changes that liberal education underwent in the American colleges it will be well to trace the ideal from its earliest origins among the Greeks.

Liberal education, as it took form among the Greeks, had several aspects. Perhaps the initial aspect to consider is the one revealed by the etymology of the word "liberal." This word takes its root in the Latin word *liber,* meaning "free." There are many conditions of freedom, but the one to which the Greeks referred in speaking of liberal education was political and economic in character. Liberal education, therefore, was the sort of education that was appropriate for a freeman or, as later centuries were to say, a gentleman in contrast to the sort that was appropriate for a slave. Obviously, the education of a freeman, who was a citizen, voted, held public office, and bore arms, would be widely different from that of a slave, who did none of these things. The education of a freeman would be further widely different because, living on the work of slaves, he had ample leisure to devote to education, an advantage the slave never possessed.

This early conception of liberal education was well stated by Aristotle (384–322 B.C.) when he wrote in his *Politics,* "There is a distinction between the liberal and illiberal subjects, and it is clear that only such knowledge as does not make the learner mechanical should enter into education. By mechanical subjects we must understand all arts and studies that make the body, soul, or intellect of freemen unserviceable for the use and exercise of goodness. That is why we call such pursuits as produce an inferior condition of body mechanical, and all wage-earning occupations. They allow the mind no leisure, and they drag it down to a lower level. There are even some liberal arts, the acquisition of which up to a certain point is not unworthy of freemen, but which, if studied with excessive devotion or minuteness, are open to the charge of being injurious."[23]

This statement of Aristotle's shows two further aspects from which the concept of liberal education must also be examined. First, liberal education should be broadly general rather than narrowly specialized. Indeed, the Greeks had a phrase for it, ἐγκύκλιος παιδεία, which was rendered into Latin as *encyclius disciplina* and the meaning of which might be caught in English by the phrase "all-around training" or "well-rounded development."[24] To the aesthetic Greek this ideal of liberal education implied a harmonious development of the physical, moral, and intellectual qualities of the individual.[25] To ensure this well-balanced development the Greeks evolved a curriculum, later known as the seven liberal arts, consisting of a trivium of grammar, logic, and rhetoric and a quadrivium of arithmetic, geometry, music, and astronomy.[26]

Second, although a chief dimension of liberal education was its breadth, it is also evident from Aristotle's statement that liberal education, if any of its ingredients preponderated, was more intellectual than anything else. The activities of a freeman, clearly, were many and diverse. It was necessary for educational purposes, therefore, to be able to arrange these activities in some hierarchy of liberality. The worth of anything, Aristotle contended, depended on the unique or distinguishing character of that thing. The unique or peculiar worth of man, for instance, was to be found in his intellect, his capacity to reason. His vegetative nature man shared with plants, his appetitive

---

[23] Aristotle, *Politics,* book VIII, chap. 2, in J. Burnet, *Aristotle on Education* (Cambridge University Press, London, 1913).

[24] See H. Parker, "The Seven Liberal Arts," *English Historical Review,* 5:424–425, July, 1890; see also W. Jaeger, *Paideia* (Oxford University Press, Fair Lawn, N.J., 1939), pp. 314–317.

[25] Overdoing any of these qualities impairs liberal education. The exaggeration of physical education has led to athleticism, of moral education to asceticism, and of intellectual education to scholasticism. See I. L. Kandel, *History of Secondary Education* (Houghton Mifflin Company, Boston, 1930), pp. 6–7.

[26] Although the number of liberal arts was conventionally set at seven, some classical authors mentioned a different number. In medieval times the number became fixed at seven after the Christian author Cassiodorus (490–585) pointed out that there was Biblical backing for the number seven. Reading in *Proverbs* 9:1 that "Wisdom hath builded her house, she hath hewn out her seven pillars," he concluded that there must be an identity between the seven liberal arts and the seven pillars of wisdom. See his *De artibus et disciplinis liberalium litterarum.*

nature with animals, but his rational nature he shared with none.[27] As a rational animal he was *sui generis*. Therefore, man's various activities as a freeman were to be measured by the extent to which they were more or less rational in character. By this standard the trivium was more liberal than the quadrivium because, with the addition of mathematics, the disciplines of grammar, logic, and rhetoric are the ones by which man orders thought.

It also follows from other writings of Aristotle that liberal education as intellectual education must be an education pursued for its own sake. To be truly liberal, education must be its own end. If it is a means to some other end, moral, political, or otherwise, it occupies a servile and therefore inferior status. If, on the other hand, education is pursued as an end in itself, for its own sake and with no ulterior end, then it is truly liberal. In other words, just as the freeman is served and is never servant, so liberal education must be a final and not a contingent end.[28]

The Romans perpetuated the ideal of liberal education without essential modification. Only an epitomized version of it, however, survived during the Middle Ages. Although a larger content of the liberal arts had been recovered by the time of the medieval universities, this content was quite narrowly subordinated to professional studies, particularly theology.

During the Renaissance the ideal of liberal education was revived more nearly in its former scope. Curiously enough, this revival occurred outside the walls of the universities and largely in association with the education of the courtier. Yet the ancient pattern was still visible through the words of two Renaissance educators. "We call those studies *liberal*," wrote the Italian Vergerius (1370–1445), "which are worthy of a freeman."[29] And the Frenchman Michel de Montaigne (1533–1592) drew up his remarks on education "for a boy of quality, then, who pretends to letters not upon account of profit (for so mean an object as that is unworthy of the grace and favor of the Muses, and moreover in it a man directs his service to and depends upon others)."[30]

As the scholars of the Renaissance had rediscovered the full ideal of liberal education in the writings of Greek and Roman authors, so it became customary to associate liberal education with a knowledge of the Greek and Latin literatures. These literatures came to be known

[27] For a fuller account of this distinction, see *supra*, pp. 83, 105–106.
[28] For the underlying philosophy of this distinction, see *supra*, p. 107.
[29] Quoted in W. H. Woodward, *Vittorino da Feltre and Other Humanist Educators* (Cambridge University Press, London, 1897), p. 102.
[30] M. de Montaigne, *Of the Education of Children* (G. P. Putnam's Sons, New York, 1891), p. 20.

as "humane letters," belles-lettres, or, in short, the humanities. Their Humanism, of course, stemmed from the fact that they were a portrayal of those acts and thoughts which were uniquely worthy of man. They reflected man in the full depth of aesthetic feeling, in the highest aspiration of moral purpose, and in the most brilliant sweep of intellectual speculation. Naturally, therefore, the humanities, or "classics" as they were later called in the United States, became the staple vehicle of the liberal arts curriculum.

The arts faculties of the medical universities, though at first they closed the doors of their classes to the new Humanism, became in the end as enthusiastic about it as were the typical secondary schools of the Renaissance. Hence the universities too, came to identify liberal education with training in the classical tongues. With the coming of the Protestant Reformation and its interest in reading the Scriptures from the Greek and Latin sources, it became evident that the new training in classical literatures was as useful in preparing clergymen as it was in training courtiers or gentlemen. Consequently, at a Puritan college like Emmanuel and particularly at an offshoot like Harvard the ancient ideal of liberal education became compounded not only with linguistic elements but with ministerial ones as well.

This better than anything else accounts for the frequent statement that the early colonial colleges in America were little more than professional schools for the ministry. No doubt a large percentage of the early graduates of American colleges did find their way into the ministry. Yet it would be a mistake to think that because the linguistic pattern of liberal education served the ministry so well, it served no broader purpose. As a matter of fact, it turned out whole generations of statesmen, jurists, doctors, and educators as well as clergymen. That liberal education never entirely lost sight of Aristotle's stricture against overspecialization is further attested by the fact that Yale College was founded specifically to train up men "fitted for public employment in church and state."[31] At its founding, King's College, too, gave large space to secular objectives.

The domination of the liberal arts college by the ministry was neither complete nor of long duration. What did endure for long centuries was the monopoly the classics held over the approaches to a liberal education. This monopoly, commencing in the Renais-

---

[31] A statement of President Thomas Clap of Yale in 1754 went furthest to confound collegiate with professional education. "Colleges," he wrote, "are *Societies of Ministers,* for training up persons for the Work of the *Ministry.*" [T. Clap, *The Religious Constitution of Colleges* (T. Green, New London, Conn., 1754).]

sance, was not seriously questioned till the nineteenth century. Hardly a quarter of that century had passed, as already seen, when a rising demand made itself felt for a more scientific and technological curriculum. This demand reflected a basic shift in popular interest. If in the seventeenth century the intellectual frontier had concerned religious controversy, in the eighteenth it had begun to shift to politics and in the nineteenth to industrial expansion. By the same token, if the classical tongues had been a necessity to participate in theological controversies and to a diminishing extent in political ones, their relevance to the new industrial era of the nineteenth century was seriously open to question.

As cultural lag seemed to overtake the general tradition of liberal education, two defenses, the one formal and the other substantive, tried to keep it abreast of the times. Chief protagonist of the former was a committee of the Yale faculty and corporation. "The two great points to be gained in intellectual culture," declared this committee, "are the *discipline* and the *furniture* of the mind; expanding its powers, and storing it with knowledge. The former of these is, perhaps, the more important of the two. A commanding object, therefore, in a collegiate course, should be, to call into daily and vigorous exercise the faculties of the student."[32]

In this defense, obviously, a somewhat modified conception of the traditional ideal of liberal education was emerging. According to this conception, liberal education consisted not so much in the cultural content of the classics studied as in the mental habits of persistence, memory, and judgment formed from their study. Yale's defense was no isolated affair for the Yale influence spread far and wide through her graduates of this period. So many of them were later involved in founding new colleges that Yale came to be known as the "mother of colleges."

There were many, however, who did not shift to the disciplinary defense of liberal education but who still stood steadfastly by the classics for the rich "furniture" of the mind they afforded. The classical literatures, not the natural sciences, they declared, afforded the best content for a liberal education. The great spokesman for this point of view was Matthew Arnold (1822–1888), the English school inspector, critic, and poet. For the man who wished to know himself and the world Arnold advised "that he acquaint himself with the best which has been thought and said in the world; . . . of this

[32] From a report adopted by the faculty of Yale College and published as "Original Papers in Relation to a Course of Liberal Education," *American Journal of Science and Arts,* 15:300–301, January, 1829. For the rise and decline of the psychological theory of discipline, see *supra,* pp. 141, 143, 155.

best the classics of Greece and Rome form a very chief portion, and the portion most entirely satisfactory."[33] In other words, the classical literatures were still the supreme products of the human mind. There, as nowhere else, could one get a sense of the human mind moving freely, without danger of imposition by prejudice or selfishness, malice or flattery, exaggeration or sophistry.

It remained for John Cardinal Newman (1801–1890) in his widely quoted *Idea of a University* to restate the genteel ideal of liberal education, not in terms of a literary or a scientific curriculum, not in terms of a psychological theory of mental discipline, but in terms of a theory of knowledge. It is common, he wrote, to speak "of a *'liberal* education' as the especial characteristic or property of a University and of a gentleman; what is really meant by the word? Now, first, in its grammatical sense it is opposed to *servile;* and by 'servile work' is understood, as our catechisms inform us, bodily labor, mechanical employment, and the like, in which the mind has little or no part. . . . And so in like manner, we contrast a liberal with a commercial education or a professional; yet no one would deny that commerce and the professions afford scope for the highest and most diversified powers of the mind. . . . Why this distinction? Because that alone is liberal knowledge, which stands on its own pretensions, which is independent of sequel. . . . Surely it is very intelligible to say, and that is what I say here, that Liberal Education, viewed in itself, is simply the cultivation of the intellect, as such, and its object is nothing more or less than intellectual excellence."[34] Newman's bias toward Aristotle stands out in nearly every word of this passage. Clearly he, like Aristotle, conceived of liberal education as genteel intellectualistic education.

DEMOCRATIZATION OF THE COLLEGE

The genteel tradition in liberal education, whether justified by its form or content, continued to be a powerful influence in twentieth-century American higher education. Yet, the erosion at work on it was not arrested, neither by the Yale report nor by Newman's strictures. Indeed, one might say that the erosion had a head start as early as the great revolutions at the end of the eighteenth century. At that time political and economic forces released by the American and French Revolutions, the Industrial Revolution, and the American frontier began a radical alteration of the underlying sociological condi-

[33] M. Arnold, *Thoughts on Education* (The Macmillan Company, New York, 1912), p. 243.

[34] J. Newman, *The Idea of a University* (Longmans, Green & Co., Ltd., London, 1919), pp. 106–121.

tions that ever since the time of Aristotle had given validity to the genteel ideal of liberal education. The growth of political democracy and the rise of the laboring classes seriously undermined the time-honored social system in which political power was restricted to a relatively small upper class and leisure was the privilege of the few. In a democratic society in which everyone enjoyed political freedom and in which this freedom gave new dignity to the labor of the common man, it became urgently necessary to reconstruct the traditional ideal of liberal education as the education appropriate to the political and economic interests of a small class of the population.

Affairs had come to such a pass by the middle of the nineteenth century that Massachusetts withdrew financial subsidies to Harvard when a special committee of the legislature reported, "The college fails to answer the just expectations of the people of the State because its organization and instruction are a quarter of a century out of date. . . . It should give the people the practical instruction that they want, and not a classical literary course suitable only for an aristocracy."[35] In like vein the president of Brown lamented, "Our colleges are not filled because we do not furnish the education desired by the people. . . . We have produced an article for which the demand is diminishing. We sell it at less than cost, and the deficiency is made up by charity. We give it away; and still the demand diminishes."[36]

An early remedy for these conditions was sought in two directions, the enlargement of the college curriculum and the establishment of the elective principle to permit choice among the new subjects offered toward one's academic degree. The chief studies that had notoriously been neglected in liberal education were the sciences. This neglect, as already seen, originated in the belief that the more naturalistic studies of the old quadrivium were less liberal than the more Humanistic studies of the trivium. By the nineteenth century, however, the natural sciences had made such startling progress that their continued neglect in the curricula of higher education amounted to nothing less than a scandal. The founding of colleges like Rensselaer Polytechnic Institute and the land-grant colleges was an eloquent protest against this scandal.

While it was the expected role of science to enlarge and enrich the content of liberal education, it is a bit unexpected that one of its chief champions, the English scientist Thomas Henry Huxley (1825–1895), not to be outdone by the classicists, also justified the

---

[35] S. E. Morison, *Three Centuries of Harvard* (Harvard University, Cambridge, Mass., 1936), p. 287.

[36] Quoted in F. A. Walker, *Discussions in Education* (Henry Holt and Company, Inc., New York, 1899), p. 82.

inclusion of science because of the formal discipline it afforded. "That man, I think, has had a liberal education," wrote Huxley, "who has been so trained in youth that his body is the ready servant of his will, and does with ease and pleasure all the work that, as a mechanism, it is capable of; whose intellect is a clear, cold, logic engine, with all its parts of equal strength, and in smooth working order; ready, like a steam engine, to be turned to any kind of work, and spin the gossamers as well as forge the anchors of the mind; whose mind is stored with a knowledge of the great fundamental truths of Nature, and of the laws of her operations; one, who, no stunted ascetic, is full of life and fire, but whose passions are trained to come to heel by a vigorous will, the servant of a tender conscience; who has learned to love all beauty, whether of Nature or of art, to hate all vileness and to respect others as himself. Such an one, and no other, I conceive, has had a liberal education; for he is, as completely as man can be, in harmony with Nature."[37]

The concession of a place to science in the college curriculum came more easily than did recognition of the principle of an elective curriculum. Thomas Jefferson worked for the introduction of electives at the University of Virginia, but it was not till Charles W. Eliot (1834–1926) came to the presidency of Harvard after the middle of the century that the elective principle made any real headway. In pressing for this principle Eliot was aided by the predominant laissez-faire liberalism of the century. Just as men sought freedom from excessive governmental regulation of private enterprise, so as an educational corollary they sought freedom from a too rigidly prescribed college curriculum. The utilitarianism often associated with laissez-faire liberalism also was a factor aiding the elective principle. To Eliot freedom was an indispensable condition for the capable student who knew what he wanted.[38]

Nothing helped liberalism and utilitarianism infiltrate the genteel notion of liberal education so greatly as did the mounting numbers of students who were applying for admission in the twentieth century. While at the turn of the century only 4 per cent of the youth of college age were attending college, by mid-century more than 30 per cent were in attendance, and the President's Commission on Higher Education had recommended that 48 per cent could well be enrolled for at least two years of college work.[39] In another decade

[37] T. H. Huxley, Science and Education (D. Appleton & Company, Inc., New York, 1894), p. 86.

[38] Morison, op. cit., pp. 343–344.

[39] President's Commission on Higher Education, Higher Education for American Democracy (Government Printing Office, Washington, D.C., 1947), vol. I, p. 41.

and a half the Educational Policies Commission of the National Education Association called for universal postsecondary education.[40] There was no reason to be startled by the increase, for it could have been predicted from the vast increase in high school enrollments which got under way before the end of the nineteenth century and reached its climax in the report of the Commission on the Reorganization of Secondary Education in 1918, which called for universal secondary education till the age of eighteen.[41] What remained now was to cap the democratic high school with a democratic college. This necessitated a restatement of the traditional ideal of liberal education so as to give voice to the needs and aspirations not only of those who by force of talent or socioeconomic status were heirs to the genteel tradition but also to those who by reason of more modest talents and economic circumstances were nonetheless ambitious to advance themselves and fill new responsibilities in an increasingly complex society.

Democratization of the college took two complementary directions: a restatement of the aim of liberal education and a reorganization of its administrative structure to include the junior or community college. In the first direction John Dewey (1859–1952), the great educational philosopher of democracy, made a notable theoretical attack on the traditional notion of liberal education. He never tired of pointing out how the distinction between "liberal" and "servile," cultural and vocational or professional education grew historically out of the presuppositions of Greek society, which was a two-class society composed of freemen and slaves.[42] Further, he took issue with the Aristotelian conception of intelligence or rationality. He rejected both Aristotle's notion of cultivating the intellect as an excellence in itself and the disciplinary notion of concentrating on mental habits. The conception of mind on which he predicated his own idea of liberal education was more Darwinian in character. Mind, instead of being something primordial to "discipline" or "furnish," was to Dewey a late-comer in the evolutionary series. Instead of being an end in itself, mind was an instrument to effect better adaptation to the environment.[43]

Obviously Dewey's point of view gave a definitely pragmatic turn

[40] *Universal Opportunity for Education Beyond High School* (National Education Association, Educational Policies Commission, Washington, D.C., 1964).

[41] *Supra,* pp. 421–422.

[42] See an article by Dewey on liberal education in P. Monroe (ed.), *Cyclopedia of Education* (The Macmillan Company, New York, 1912), vol. 4, pp. 4–6. See also his "Challenge to Liberal Thought," *Fortune,* 30:155–190, August, 1944.

[43] For a further exposition of Dewey's educational philosophy, see *supra,* pp. 131–134.

to liberal education. Yet it would be a mistake to infer from his critique that he advocated a metamorphosis of liberal into vocational education. As he himself said, "The problem of securing to the liberal arts college its due function in democratic society is that of seeing to it that the technical subjects which are now socially necessary acquire humane direction."[44] The opposition of the genteel tradition of liberal education to practical and technical studies arose in the pretechnical times when vocations were not only carried on by the lower classes but were largely empirical in character. By the twentieth century the Industrial Revolution had radically altered this situation. By incorporating scientific theory into their processes many trades and handicrafts had become technologies. Moreover, it became difficult to understand the social consequences of technology without drawing on history, economics, politics, sociology, and ethics. The motivation for the liberal study of these disciplines, therefore, became pragmatic rather than esoteric.

Not a few found such a democratization of the genteel tradition in liberal education distasteful. They did not doubt that a new kind of general education had to be worked out for the democratic masses seeking postsecondary education, but at the same time they thought it would be a confusing misnomer to call this new general education liberal. Liberal education had a unique historical connotation which they were unwilling to surrender. As a result a new title had to be found for liberal education as reconstructed along lines laid down by Dewey. This reconstructed liberal education ultimately came to take the title of "general"[45] education or, in some instances, "life adjustment" education.

This attempted democratic reform of liberal education did not go unchallenged. It was not long before twentieth-century descendants of Aristotle and Newman took alarm at what they thought were anti-intellectual tendencies in higher education. The counterreformation, if such it may be called, was led by Robert M. Hutchins (1899–   ), then president of the University of Chicago. Education rightly understood, Hutchins claimed, was a cultivation of the intellect, which, he further claimed, was the peculiar excellence of all men in all times and in all places.[46] The intellect was to be cultivated through studies of permanent worth. These were to be found in the

[44] J. Dewey, *Democracy and Education* (The Macmillan Company, New York, 1916), pp. 366–367.

[45] See W. S. Gray (ed.), *General Education* (The University of Chicago Press, Chicago, 1934); National Society for the Study of Education, *General Education,* Thirty-eighth Yearbook (Public School Publishing Company, Bloomington, Ill., 1939), part II.

[46] R. M. Hutchins, *The Higher Learning in America* (Yale University Press, New Haven, Conn., 1936), pp. 70–84.

great books of all time. A "great book" was one that is contemporary with any age. But in order to read great books the student must know how to read them. To learn this he must go back to a curriculum made up of the trivium of grammar, logic, and rhetoric together with some formal mathematics from the quadrivium.

Exacting as were Hutchins's standards, he did not limit liberal education to the few, as had the genteel tradition. On the contrary, the liberal education he had in mind was for the whole student population in so far as they had time to pursue it. To transfer his scheme from the realm of theory to that of practice Hutchins persuaded the faculty of St. John's College, Maryland, to install a curriculum built around the great books. This curriculum had the backing of a number of prominent educators.[47] But on the eve of the Second World War it seemed very doubtful that many higher educators wished to go as far as to reinstate Aristotle as the arbiter of liberal education.

Yet the counterreformation was not over. The "cold war" which ensued after World War II revived anxiety over anti-intellectual tendencies in undergraduate education. Nothing gave such impetus to this anxiety as did the Russian launching of Sputnik months ahead of any American capability to duplicate the effort. For many this was proof of a dangerous deterioration of higher education brought on by the democratization of the college. The direction in which this set men thinking, however, was not to turn their backs on the extension of postsecondary education to the many but to renew a realization of the importance of the talented few, who had more or less become the "forgotten," or at least the neglected, men while democratization was being effected. As a result a new emphasis was put on the "pursuit of excellence"[48] in colleges and universities to accelerate the intellectual advancement of the superior. This advancement was further augmented by provision for honors programs encouraging more independent and creative study for those capable of it.

THE JUNIOR COLLEGE

As already foreshadowed, the second direction in the democratization of the American college was the organization of the junior or community college. In reaching its mature stature it is clear that the American university was a hybrid resulting from the union of an English college and a German graduate school. In some universities during the twentieth century the English lineage was more pronounced;

[47] For example, M. Van Doren, *Liberal Education* (Holt, Rinehart and Winston, Inc., New York, 1943).

[48] Rockefeller Brothers Fund, *The Pursuit of Excellence*, Special Studies Project Report V (Doubleday & Co., Inc., Garden City, N.Y., 1958).

in others, the German. But, whichever predominated, in most cases the German graduate school had merely been superimposed upon the English college without much thought being given to what their unique relation to each other might be. William Rainey Harper (1856–1906), president of the University of Chicago at its founding, was the first to give serious consideration to this problem.

The original proposal for the reorganization of secondary education, as already seen,[49] involved the first two years of college as well as the last two years of the elementary school. While in the first decade of the twentieth century little attention was paid to this part of President Harper's bold suggestions, in the third and fourth decades much greater consideration was given to it. By that time the great tidal wave of students that was flowing through the high schools had reached the colleges. Their facilities, like those of the earlier high schools, became swamped. A demand arose not only for additional facilities for higher education but for facilities nearer home. To those inclined to satisfy this demand Harper's idea of detaching the lower two years of college from the upper two made a great appeal.

Committed to the idea of the preeminent importance of the graduate school, Harper proposed that a distinction be drawn between the first two and the last two years of the college course. In his initial thinking on the problem he referred to the first two years as the "academic college" and the latter two years as the "university college." These terms were later changed to "junior college" and "senior college," respectively. The idea in the back of Harper's mind was to make a distinction in the kind of work done in the conventional four-year college. As his original terms indicated, he thought of the last two years as more akin to graduate and professional education and the first two years as more like secondary education. Reconstructed in this fashion, the high school would become the place for general or liberal education, while the university would be the place for professional studies. The course that Harper was plotting here was not so novel as many Americans thought. It was, as has since been pointed out, merely a further upward extension of the high school— often called the "people's college"—which itself had originated as an upward extension of the common school. Furthermore, it had ample European precedent, for in nearly all Continental countries professional university studies commenced directly on completing liberal education in secondary school.

In practice, for the most part, junior colleges were established independently and housed separately from high schools. Their spirit partook more of the college, from which they were split off, than of the secondary school, toward which their founders wished to incline

[49] *Supra,* p. 418.

them. Like many early junior high schools, a number of junior colleges failed to develop unique programs of their own. Their ambition was rather to grow into full-blown four-year liberal arts colleges. Where unique programs were developed, the tendency was to extend the best traditions of the high school, that is, to prepare for life. Junior colleges thus were expected to be terminal institutions for most students. The curriculum, therefore, was composed of both liberal and technical studies, the former of which could be terminal or a preparation for the university and the latter a preparation for positions of junior responsibility in commerce and industry. In many instances junior colleges took over provision for adult education in the territory they served and thus became "community" colleges as well.

Through such a proposed distinction Harper helped others to foresee a number of resulting advantages. Many mediocre students would find it convenient to terminate their academic education at the end of junior college. This would enable the senior, or university, college to raise the quality of its preparation for the graduate and professional schools of the university. Furthermore, a junior college might attract many to attend a two-year college who would be kept from a four-year college altogether by the forbidding drain on economic resources. Again, a two-year college might encourage many secondary schools to undertake to offer work of junior college grade. The advantage here would be to relieve the pressure of numbers at university seats of learning. Perhaps, finally, many colleges with insufficient resources to offer four-year courses would prefer to become strong junior colleges rather than to remain weak conventional four-year colleges.

The development of the junior college was slow, but it subsequently fulfilled all the expectations of its founders. Up to the beginning of the Second World War hundreds of junior colleges had been established in the United States. The Middle and Far Western states, however, were more hospitable to the new college than were the Eastern states. In the former group California and Missouri had particularly significant developments of the junior college idea. In southern California the junior college had a lusty growth as a phase of rapid population increase and expanding metropolitan boundaries. In Missouri the firm establishment of the junior college was the outcome of the conversion of some declining colleges from four- to two-year programs.

MODERNIZATION OF THE UNIVERSITY

While the undergraduate college was struggling to define its aim and organization, notable changes were also taking place in graduate instruction at the university level. Up to the Civil War energetic young American scholars bent on graduate degrees had found it to their advantage to attend European universities, especially German ones. Why was this so? What did German universities offer that American universities did not? To answer this question we must go back and pick up the development of universities at the point where we left it to discuss the growth of the college and of liberal education.

It has already been mentioned that the medieval university was slow to respond to the Humanistic forces of the Renaissance. Opposition to the modernizing forces of the Renaissance was characteristic not only of the arts faculty but of the other professional faculties as well. In each of these, certain texts were lectured on perennially so that they came to have the force of canonical texts. In law, the canonical text was the Justinian Code; in medicine, Galen or Hippocrates; in theology and the arts, Aristotle. In the course of time, Aristotle came to exercise a veritable tyranny over academic minds. Indeed, there were not a few who, like Martin Luther when at the University of Wittenberg, rebelled against such academic tyranny. To escape similar tyranny in the next century English Dissenters from the Church of England had to set up their own academies when Oxford and Cambridge excluded members of Dissenting sects from admission. Furthermore, these ancient English universities were so out of step with the times that professional studies like law and medicine were more profitably pursued outside than inside their walls. The long-term effect of such conditions was to bring universities to a very low ebb.

By the end of the eighteenth century, with the exception of France, where universities were stricken down during the revolutionary period, universities were at flood tide again. Perhaps nothing had so much to do with this as the founding of the German University of Halle at the end of the seventeenth century. This institution of higher education became illustrious as the first modern university.[50] A number of novel features entitled Halle to this distinction. At the head of the list was its establishment of the *libertas philosophandi.* Here for the first time the study of Aristotle lost its orthodoxy and was superseded by the study of modern philosophy based on the advances that had been made in science and mathematics. The intellectual spirit of the university was expressed by the motto "nothing without sufficient reason."

This spirit pervaded the curriculum and the methods of instruction as well. Not only did the curriculum court the new sciences, but it reformed instruction even in the humanities. Instead of attempting a slavish imitation of the style of Cicero, Humanistic instruction at

[50] F. Paulsen, *German Education Past and Present* (Charles Scribner's Sons, New York, 1908), pp. 117–123.

Halle turned more critical and tried to recapture the free spirit of criticism characteristic of the Greeks. Another new departure was the delivery of lectures in the vernacular. Furthermore, the form and content of lecturing underwent change. Lectures, instead of being a *summa* or *commentatio* on accepted texts, were changed into a systematic presentation of the findings derived from inquiry. Disputations, from being a consolidation of established canons of truth, began to veer in the direction of an independent pursuit of learned studies.

It was in connection with the University of Halle, too, that steps were taken to differentiate and coordinate secondary and higher education. The first stage of work at the medieval university, it will be remembered, was a perfecting of the student's Latin so that he could take his bachelor's degree and apprentice himself for the master's degree. This preparatory work clearly belonged to secondary education. But at first, except for the cathedral schools, which were closely identified with the growth of universities, there was no other place to obtain this preparation. Later on, preparation might have been sought at the humanistic secondary schools of the Renaissance, had it not been for the early disregard the universities showed for Humanism. For several centuries, therefore, the Humanistic schools more or less paralleled the university in the age level of their pupils if not in the spirit of their instruction. By the time Humanism succeeded in pervading the universities, there was an overlapping in spirit as well. Halle was early instrumental in correcting this duplication of secondary education facilities. This it did by ceasing to offer work preceding or leading to the bachelor's degree and by accepting as a substitute for this work the product of the *Gymnasium,* the German Humanistic school. In taking this action it set the Continental precedent of making the university a strictly graduate and professional institution of higher education.[51]

At the opening of the nineteenth century and a little over a century after the founding of Halle, Germany again took a long lead in modernizing university education. Crushed to earth in its collision with Napoleon at this time, Prussia tried various means of resuscitating its national self-respect. One thing it undertook was the invigoration of its intellectual life. Top consideration here went to the founding of a new university, the University of Berlin. To make its establishment an outstanding event, a preeminent faculty was sought out. Endeavor was made to fill each professorial chair with that man who by virtue of his research would bring the greatest distinction to it. The idea

[51] In continental European educational systems liberal education is the objective of secondary education, not of higher education, as in the American college. Hence, the European student goes straight from his secondary school to graduate or professional study at the university.

that higher education should issue in research was as old as Francis Bacon (1561–1626) and Johann Amos Comenius (1592–1670), but it awaited the Universities of Halle and Berlin to take practical steps in that direction.

Selection of such a faculty naturally had a profound influence on instruction. The faculty's interest in research became the central feature of the instruction given. Each professor gathered his advanced students together into a seminary, where he supervised their first efforts in original research. As proof of his proficiency each student undertook an independent piece of research, the results of which he wrote and published in the form of a dissertation. For this new research emphasis in university instruction a new degree was awarded, the degree of doctor of philosophy (Ph.D.). The aim was to turn out scholars, not teachers, although as yet there was no doubt that a good scholar would be a good teacher.

Since the spirit of research can breathe only in an atmosphere of academic freedom, it is important to note how the University of Berlin did much to promote the famous German doctrine of *Lehr- und Lernfreiheit* (freedom both to teach and to learn). This German phrase for academic freedom was really a further development of the *libertas philosophandi* at Halle. At Berlin it was invoked particularly against state interference. Formerly, the state could exercise some control over the universities because they taught a well-defined field of subject matter. This could no longer be the case, however, when the university was engaged in research enterprises the outcome of which was bound to be uncertain. Consequently, the Prussian Minister of Education warned the state that it stood to gain most from the new university if it refrained from requiring it to serve any specific state interests.[52] Teaching and learning were to develop in an atmosphere of freedom to which the only limits were those imposed by the nature of the problem under investigation itself.

This ideal of academic freedom became one of the brightest stars in the crown of the German university system. In France the victorious Napoleon seems to have organized the universities on almost the opposite principle. Not infrequently in history one of the blessings of defeat has been an encouragement to freedom in education, while one of the liabilities of victory has been its tendency to freeze the educational *status quo* in the form that made victory possible. At any rate, there is no doubt that, in the nineteenth century, graduate instruction thrived in Germany as nowhere else.

---

[52] Note how Adolph Hitler and the Nazis took just the opposite view, contending that the pursuit of truth could not remain unbiased by the interests of the state. For a further account of academic freedom, see *infra,* pp. 594–607.

GRADUATE AND PROFESSIONAL EDUCATION
IN AMERICA

Prior to the Civil War higher education in the United States had nothing to offer that was comparable with instruction at the German universities. American higher education, following the English pattern, had developed along collegiate lines with a course of study culminating in the bachelor's degree. Obviously, higher education in this country was not on a par with that abroad, particularly in Germany, where universities had long since restricted themselves to work beyond the bachelor's degree. It is small wonder, therefore, that, in the nineteenth century, energetic young Americans were attracted to Germany for their graduate training.

American institutions of higher education had been slow to offer even professional study in law and medicine, let alone graduate study in the arts and sciences. In professional study, too, colonial policy had followed English precedents. Lawyers and doctors had learned their professions by apprenticeship rather than by attendance upon lectures under a faculty of law or medicine. In fact, as late as the twentieth century it was not at all unusual for a young man to prepare for the bar by reading law in the office of a practicing attorney. Law and medical schools did not become regular adjuncts of American higher education till the nineteenth century.

Indeed, one might go as far as to say that there were no *universities* in America prior to the nineteenth century. There were colleges but no universities in spite of the fact that a few institutions bore that title. At the end of the eighteenth century the idea of a national university had been entertained by a few leading minds. Both James Madison and Charles Pinckney moved for a national university in the Constitutional Convention, but the motion was lost. Benjamin Rush advocated the idea in an essay on a fitting system of education for the young republic. And the idea weighed so heavily on George Washington's mind that he left a bequest in his will for the founding of a national university. But nothing came of it. Presumably states' rights stood in the way.

Apparently the country's first President had several ends in view in making this bequest. One of the chief advantages he saw in a national university was that of an agency for developing a unified national spirit. An institution where the youth from various parts of the country could freely intermingle, he felt, would go far toward overcoming the prejudices and jealousies of localism that had so handicapped the prosecution of the Revolution. A national university would also be useful in a young republic as a center for the advancement of knowledge in the principles of politics and self-government. Furthermore, Washington conceived of a national university as cultivating not only belles-lettres but the sciences basic to agriculture, commerce, and manufacturing as well.

The men who immediately succeeded Washington in the presidency, John Adams and Thomas Jefferson, also favored the founding of a national university. So did President John Quincy Adams. Prior to the latter, committees of both houses of Congress had at one time or another reported favorably on a national university. The issue, however, went into eclipse during the slavery controversy, only to be brought forth again by the National Education Association after the Civil War. Congressional interest also revived at the end of the nineteenth century. Talk about a national university now centered in a graduate institution for research rather than in an institution of collegiate grade, as Washington probably conceived it. But still opposition balked favorable action on the floor of Congress. The immediate opposition came from the old-line private seats of learning in the Northeastern part of the country. But this opposition was only part of a general antipathy of the American public toward the nationalization of its educational system.[53]

The chief early period in which American universities were founded was the second quarter of the nineteenth century. Most of these were universities that came into being when, as already noted, the Dartmouth College decision made it clear that the public interest in higher education could not hope to control existing private seats of higher learning. Most state universities of this period, however, were really little more than universities in name only. Though the University of Virginia made an ambitious attempt to organize faculties of university scope and the University of Michigan bravely endeavored to imitate the spirit of the German universities, both these efforts fell considerably short of university grade, at least as measured by German standards. Conservative religious forces held Virginia back, and public governmental control was an obstacle in Michigan.

The first American university to approximate the model of the German universities was Johns Hopkins in 1876. Those who guided the destiny of Johns Hopkins managed to avoid the conservative restraining influences that had held back the universities of Virginia and Michigan. On the one hand, Johns Hopkins was to be private and independent of governmental control, and on the other no provision was made for a faculty of theology. Furthermore, to avoid the conservative influence of the undergraduate liberal arts faculty,

---

[53] For further details, see C. W. Tvedt, "A Brief History of the National University," *School and Society,* 33:42–47, January, 1931; E. P. Cubberley, *State School Administration* (Houghton Mifflin Company, Boston, 1927), pp. 67–75.

which tended to assimilate graduate instruction to itself, no undergraduate college of liberal arts was provided. Instead, as originally planned, Johns Hopkins was to be a strictly graduate institution for purposes of scholarly research. Although undergraduate studies were later added, this does not detract from the credit due Johns Hopkins for first supplying America with graduate instruction comparable with that in the best European universities. The first president, Daniel Coit Gilman (1831–1908), went about launching the university just as the University of Berlin had been launched. Instead of investing his capital funds in buildings, he first gathered together a nucleus of professors preeminent in research. Then with a picked group of graduate students, which among others soon included Woodrow Wilson and John Dewey, he established a university complete with seminaries, academic freedom, and learned publications. The occasion marked a new era in American higher education.

Before the nineteenth century was out, other new universities followed the lead of Johns Hopkins. Notable among these were Catholic University, the University of Chicago, and Clark University, the latter under the leadership of G. Stanley Hall, the educational psychologist. Indeed, the leaven of the German university began to be felt even in the old-line colleges. Harvard under the leadership of Charles W. Eliot rapidly became a leading university in fact, although under its articles of incorporation it still remained a college. Yale College, although twenty-five years earlier, in 1861, it had been the first American institution of higher education to award the degree of doctor of philosophy, only now changed its name to Yale University.

By the opening of the twentieth century, American higher education had come of age. But this was not without having experienced some of the difficulties attendant upon reaching maturity. The twentieth century was not very old before higher education began to feel itself in the grip of "the Ph.D. octopus."[54] Smaller and less important institutions, unable to attract professors already distinguished by their research, tried to compensate for this shortcoming by appointing to their faculties men who held the Ph.D. degree and who, therefore, were potentially capable of conferring prestige by some future piece of research. Thus, the Ph.D. degree came to have a tremendous value both for academic employment and for academic advancement.

Consequently, among the exceedingly large numbers who sought the degree were many who sought it for its prestige and for no other value. Many doctors were stillborn; they did no research beyond the dissertation that made them doctors of philosophy. Complaints

[54] W. James, "The Ph.D. Octopus," *Harvard Monthly,* March, 1903; reprinted in *Educational Review,* 55:149–157, February, 1918. See also E. W. Knight, "Getting Ahead by Degrees," *School and Society,* 53:521–528, April, 1941.

began to arise. Some proposed a two-year master's degree for those who wanted to teach or administer rather than do research, but this proposal never caught on. Others wanted to keep the doctor's degree but tried to find a substitute for the research requirement which would be of more pragmatic value to those who would not be engaged in research. But the Ed.D. degree as an instance of this effort ran a poor second to the Ph.D. in prestige value. Some complainants sought a relaxation of the language requirements; others, a reduction in the narrowness of specialization to which the Ph.D. was leading; still others, the preservation of research from encroachments of the public "service" function of the university.

Complaints continued after the Second World War, but they in no way diminished the vigorous growth of graduate instruction. On the eve of that war there had been 100 graduate schools granting Ph.D. degrees. Twenty years later there were 175. In the same period institutions granting master's degrees increased from 300 to well over 500. All this was in response to a 300 per cent increase in the demand for graduate degrees. Doubtless such a phenomenal increase would have been impossible had it not been for the Federal government's liberal research budgets. Involved as both cause and effect, of course, was the postwar "explosion of knowledge." The complaints which continued to be voiced were the same ones which had assailed the graduate school before the war. In addition, there was a substantial complaint that the time consumed in obtaining the Ph.D. degree was becoming excessively long. Yet, though there was considerable recognition of the pertinence of these complaints the undoubted popularity of the Ph.D. seemed so to outweigh its shortcomings that no one was inclined to make major alterations.

16 Professional Education of Teachers

It is a well-known fact of physics that a stream of water can never rise higher than its source. One is sometimes tempted to assert a similar dependence of the pupil on the teacher. To do so, however, would not be altogether true. If pupils did not rise above the educational level of their parents and teachers, as many actually do, social progress would indeed be an impossibility. Yet, in spite of this optimism, there can be no denying the fact that the quality of one's teachers will more often than not be the most important determinant of the height and rate of rise which each generation attains.

In a centuries-long retrospect, it appears that the quality of teachers has varied widely with the different answers given to certain fundamental questions. Thus, is it enough that a prospective teacher knows the content he is going to teach? Or must he also have special training and practice in the technique of teaching? This query raises the prior question: Can teaching be reduced to a well-defined technique or even to a science? Or is teaching just an art? Whether science or art, can teaching be regarded as a profession? If it can, why has the social-economic status of teachers on the whole and in the long run been so low? Why does their prestige vary, as it has so often, with the age level of those taught? Is it possible to improve the quality of teachers through a policy of public certification? Finally, should teachers organize to protect and improve their standards?

ANCIENT STATUS OF TEACHERS

Generally in the ancient world the chief qualification for teaching was knowledge of the subject matter to be taught. Consequently, the esteem in which the teacher was held depended in large measure on the importance of his subject area. In early historic times, when reading and writing were accomplishments of only the priesthood, who used them to record and interpret sacred and scientific lore, teachers stood in high regard. In fact, the priests themselves were usually the teachers. They taught both command of the symbols of language and what these symbols recorded of history, theology, astronomy, and meteorology. In ancient India, teachers even constituted an exalted caste, for Brahmans, the highest caste, enjoyed the exclusive privilege of being priests and teachers. In equally ancient China, teachers enjoyed a public respect second only to that paid public officials. Among the early Jews, too, teaching was a sacred office. If the Jewish boy was taught to honor his father and mother, he was taught to an even greater degree to honor his teacher as a sort of spiritual parent. The Greeks, unlike most ancient peoples, revered their poets, rather than their priests, as teachers.

Among the later Greeks, instruction in verbal symbols became a much more common possession than formerly. This circumstance resulted in a general lowering of the status of teachers, particularly teachers of the rudiments of literacy. The fees paid these teachers must certainly have been paltry, for even the poor of that day were usually able to afford some primary instruction for their children. In his *Laws* Plato (427–347 B.C.) assigned this level of teaching to foreigners. Indeed, it was not infrequent that the upper-class Greeks and later the Romans engaged slaves for this function. The name frequently attached to such a slave-teacher was *paidagogos,* a Greek word referring to the leading of children and giving us our modern word "pedagogue." Such practices, however, were discountenanced by the Spartans, who were exceptionally careful never to let their youth come under the supervision of people of low estate, such as slaves and foreigners. In addition to their regular teachers the Spartans charged every adult with responsibility for supervising the education of the young.

In spite of the example of the Spartans and in spite of the urging of Rome's greatest schoolmaster, Quintilian (35–100), that the utmost care be exercised in the selection of a child's nurse and teacher, the teachers of young children failed to improve in public esteem both in Greece and in Rome. In fact, in addition to meager pay, these teachers had also to submit to reproaches from disappointed parents who, though they paid but a pittance for education, expected the teacher to be letter-perfect in his knowledge even down to such insignificant details as the name of the nurse of Anchises. As the status of teachers deteriorated rather than improved in the ancient world, their lot came to be a veritable byword for misery. Thus, the Greco-Roman author Lucian made the claim that whom the gods hate they make schoolmasters. On another occasion, he thought no punishment in the afterworld better fitted to sins committed in this world than being compelled by poverty to teach the elements of reading and writing.

The status of teachers of the higher branches, such as philosophy and rhetoric, was considerably better. Rhetoricians like the Greek Isocrates (436–338 B.C.) or the Roman Quintilian enjoyed excellent incomes and highly respected positions among their people. Yet it must not be overlooked that the first teachers of these higher branches, the Greek Sophists, had a difficult time in earning public respect. Part of this difficulty grew out of their radical educational doctrines, but part arose from the fact that they accepted fees for their services. In a society that admitted only of freemen and slaves the acceptance of pay for services rendered immediately classified the Sophists, if not so low as slaves, at least as lower and less respectable than freemen. Hence, contrary to later educational history the social respectability of teachers hinged not on their professional but on their amateur status.

Other factors also militated against the public esteem in which even teachers of the higher branches were regarded. Lucius Annaeus Seneca pointed to one of these factors in his famous line *Non vitae sed scholae discimus.* That is, he says, teachers are too prone to teach school instead of life. Perhaps the aim and purpose of their teaching did originate in the demands of life outside school, but in the course of time their teaching became so routinized that they lost track of the fact that the demands of life had changed. Standing still while life moved on exacted its inevitable penalty in lowered esteem for the profession.

Charlemagne (742–814), leading royal patron of learning after the fall of the Roman Empire, pointed to another of these factors. Because of the darkened learning of the medieval period, he implored all who could to teach, ". . . for," he said, "although it is better to do than to know, yet it is necessary to know in order to do."[1] Attaching greater significance to a life of participation in the daily

---

[1] Quoted in F. V. N. Painter, *History of Education* (D. Appleton & Company, Inc., New York, 1886), p. 105. *Cf.* the modern quip, "He who can, does; he who can't, teaches; and he who can't teach, teaches others how to teach."

affairs of the community than to one spent in preparing youth for participation therein was nothing new. As already stated, highly as the Chinese rated their teachers, they nevertheless always rated them below public officials. The boys who passed highest in China's famous examination system were appointed to public office. Since the training tested by this examination was good only for places in the civil service, unsuccessful candidates found themselves not only without jobs but positively unfitted for any other occupation because it was unseemly that a learned man should turn to agriculture or commerce for a living. Hence, those who failed to gain the highest awards of the examination system turned to the only thing for which they seemed at all fitted, namely, teaching. Though the teacher's position was still one of honor in China, there was a notable origin here for the perennial remark that teachers are recruited from the ranks of failures in other walks of life.

Probably a final factor producing the low status of teachers in general during the Greco-Roman period was the retarded development of contemporary methods of instruction. At this time, great dependence was still placed on methods of memorization. The role of the teacher hence was little elevated above that of a taskmaster who punished failures to remember. Quintilian in his *Institutes of Oratory* had come nearer than anyone else to writing a manual for teachers, but the bulk of this work is concerned with describing the educational ideal of the orator, little or nothing being said about the teacher of the orator. The art of teaching seems to have been regarded as a gift. Certainly this idea prevailed in the time of Charlemagne, for he directed his plea for teachers to "all those who by God's help are able to teach."[2] The fact that ability to teach was so long regarded as a gift no doubt further postponed both a theoretical and an empirical study of how the technique of teaching might be improved.

MEDIEVAL PREPARATION OF TEACHERS OF HIGHER LEARNING

The professional education of teachers first became prominent at the medieval university, which was the first herald of a reviving intellectual life after the decadence of learning following the decline of Greco-Roman civilization. The spread of a reviving interest in law, theology, medicine, and arts, however, depended on raising up the learned teachers who had so long been lacking in these fields. Doubtless the most coveted aspect of the medieval university degree

[2] Painter, *loc. cit.*

was the right to teach conferred upon its recipient. While this was preeminently the situation in the faculty of arts, it was only a little less so in the faculties of law, theology, and medicine. Thus, it should be noted that the title of "doctor," conferred by the degrees of these last three faculties, originally meant "teacher," as witness its derivation from the Latin verb *docere,* to teach. The title of "master," awarded by the arts faculty, not only set an early precedent for making the master of arts a distinctively teaching degree but also long served to designate the teacher as a "schoolmaster"—and later a "schoolmistress."

The principal training provided for the teacher in the medieval university was in subject-matter fields. The doctor, or teacher, of law, theology, or medicine had primarily to know the professional subject matter of his special field. So, too, in the arts the chief prerequisite was a knowledge of the seven liberal arts as they had been handed down from antiquity. These arts themselves constituted the teacher's chief "mystery," as the people of medieval times called any intricate skill not at the command of the layman. As yet, little if anything was known of the mystery of imparting the arts; therefore, the future teacher received no formal instruction on this point. In the absence of such instruction, *docendo discere* was the rule; that is, the candidate for the arts degree was to learn to teach by teaching.[3] The chief opportunities he had for this were to give an occasional "extraordinary lecture" and to engage in disputations, the two principal media of instruction in the medieval university.[4]

As already mentioned, the great advantage of the university degree was the right to teach that it conferred on its recipient. The degree, thus, was tantamount to a license to teach. At first it was in the discretion of the chancellor of the cathedral, in the city where the university was situated, to license teachers. The interest of the church in deciding who should and should not teach is easily understood from its being the custodian of orthodoxy. As the demand for religious orthodoxy waned and as the force of secular interests waxed, the state came to be more and more generally responsible for licensing teachers. But whether the state or the church controlled the licensing, or granting of degrees, all degree holders wanted to be assured of

---

[3] It is noteworthy, however, that St. Thomas Aquinas (1225–1274) did drop a line on the theory of teaching to the effect that "Instruction implies perfect action of knowledge in the teacher or master." That is, "The teacher must have explicitly and perfectly the knowledge which he causes in another. . . ." For how else is the pupil to actualize his own potentialities fully? See M. H. Mayer, *The Philosophy of Teaching of St. Thomas Aquinas* (The Bruce Publishing Company, Milwaukee, 1929), p. 65.

[4] For a fuller account of these methods, see *supra,* pp. 180–183.

the *jus ubique docendi,* the right to teach anywhere without further examination.

The medieval period also affords the first instance of the professional organization of teachers. At the outset, universities were, as stated elsewhere, corporations of students and teachers organized for mutual protection.[5] In this respect, they were definitely patterned on the guilds of the time. Universities were just as particular about the admission of bachelors of arts to the standing of masters of arts as guilds were in making masters out of journeymen. Just like guilds, they tried to merit public confidence by keeping the standards of their own guild, or university, at a high level.

BEGINNINGS OF FORMAL TEACHER TRAINING

On the whole, the course of training offered in the universities assured the late medieval and Renaissance periods a supply of fairly competent teachers of the higher or professional branches of learning. Equally satisfactory general conditions apparently did not obtain at the secondary level. While a few Humanistic teachers like Vittorino de Feltre (1378–1446) and Johann Sturm (1507–1589) made outstanding reputations for themselves during the Renaissance and post-Renaissance periods, the general run seem to have been of inferior quality. In fact, so inferior were they that Sir Thomas Elyot (1490–1546) opened one chapter of his famous *Book Named the Governor* with the remark, "Lorde god, howe many good and clene wittes of children be nowe a dayes perisshed by ignorant schole maisters."[6]

Conditions, however, could not well be less than distressing when teachers, in addition to being ignorant, also possessed uncouth manners and perhaps were not always sober. Many abused the power which was vested in them as teachers but to which they were unaccustomed by birth or breeding. This abuse of power combined with a lack of self-control all too often resulted in unnecessary cruelty. Writing *Of Pedantry,* the French educational essayist Michel de Montaigne (1533–1592) complained not so much of the ignorant teacher as of the one surfeited with knowledge. Like a wick drowned in too much oil this sort of teacher was in danger of giving off a smudge along with his illumination. In similar vein, Montaigne accused teachers of a penchant for "using a certain method of high-flight and obsolete language quite different from the ordinary way

[5] For a fuller account of the organization of universities, see *supra,* pp. 430–431.

[6] T. Elyot, *The Book Named the Governor* (Ridgway & Sons, London, 1884), p. 40.

of speaking."⁷ "Pedigese" apparently was a habit of teachers even in that early day! His final indictment of teachers was the already familiar one of Seneca's, that their teaching was too far removed from life.

Under such circumstances it should not be surprising, as Montaigne noted, that teachers were often the butt of contemporary humor. Certainly, he remarked, no one would boast of having a teacher included among his ancestors. The nobility, moreover, were still so proud of their feudal tradition of fighting that they tended to look down upon learning as emasculating. It took a man like the great Protestant reformer Martin Luther (1483–1546) to couch his pen against the warrior's spear and claim that teaching unruly boys was as much of a challenge to a man's courage and ability as fighting in armor was. Indeed, he went so far as to add that, had he not been called to the ministry, he would have wanted to be a teacher. In spite of this boast, it is safe to state that the general esteem in which teachers were held had not improved noticeably since the times of Lucian.

Again it must be pointed out that this discouraging state of affairs was in part due to the absence of a theory or science of teaching. Even as late as the seventeenth and eighteenth centuries the idea still persisted that the ability to teach was a gift. Thus, the French educator Charles Rollin (1661–1741) observed, "When a teacher has asked and received from Jesus Christ, for the management of others and for his own salvation, the spirit of wisdom and knowledge, the spirit of counsel and strength, the spirit of learning and piety, and, above all, the spirit of fear of the Lord, there is nothing further to be said to him; this spirit is an internal teacher that dictates and instructs in everything, and that on every occasion will show him his duties and give him wisdom to perform them. A great indication that one has received it is when he feels an ardent zeal for the salvation of children; when he is touched by their dangers; when he is sensible to their faults; when he experiences something of the tenderness and solicitude that Paul felt for the Galatians."⁸

This situation was not so discouraging, however, that signs of improvement were altogether wanting, for the Renaissance was also marked by an early recommendation that a study of the art of teaching be approached empirically. Thus, the great Spanish scholar and teacher Juan Luis Vives (1492–1540) in *De tradendis disciplinis* stated that the way to acquire the art of teaching is to observe the work of those already masters of the art. In fact, he favored the

---

⁷ *Cf.* L. E. Rector, *Montaigne: The Education of Children* (D. Appleton Company, Inc., New York, 1899), p. 89.

⁸ Quoted in Painter, *op. cit.,* pp. 237–238.

observation of many different teachers to see if rules of teaching could be evolved from their combined experience.

Two teaching orders of the Catholic Church seem to have made the greatest progress along these empirical lines, the Jesuits and the Christian Brothers. As the members of these orders drew up a "rule" by which they lived, so too in the course of time they accumulated considerable practical experience in teaching, which they also formulated into a rule. The Jesuits summed up their rule in the *Ratio studiorum,* while the Christian Brothers stated theirs in the *Conduct of the Schools.* The Jesuits were particularly successful in producing good teachers for the Humanistic or secondary schools. Their success was due not only to their *Ratio* but also to the fact that the training to become a Jesuit might, under certain circumstances, involve a unique alternation of study and teaching. After a period as a novice and later another as a *scholasticus,* the candidate might spend a third period, his regency, during which as a teacher he went over the same ground he had just been over as a student. After his regency, the candidate returned to another period of study, following which he was admitted to the priesthood and sent back to teaching again. To make this system of preparing teachers even more effective the *Ratio* advised Jesuit provincials to put those likely to specialize in teaching under the supervision of a master teacher in order to give them practice in conducting classes. In this way it was hoped that a class "of good professors may be cultivated and propagated like a crop."[9]

If conditions at the level of secondary education cried out for better teachers, they cried out even more urgently at the elementary level. Circumstances there are perhaps best revealed by the sixteenth-century publication of Edmund Coote's *English Schoolmaster,* which was addressed: "To the unskillful . . . and *to such men and women of trade, as tailors, weavers, shopkeepers, seamsters, and such others as have undertaken the charge of teaching others.* [With this textbook] *thou mayest sit on thy shop board, at thy books or thy needle, and never hinder any work to hear thy scholars.*"[10] Surely nothing could be more eloquent of the social-economic status of elementary teachers in this period or of the kind of instruction they were prepared to give.

Yet even in the seventeenth and eighteenth centuries there were initial signs of a tendency to give serious and undivided attention to preparation of teachers of the rudiments. First to do so were

[9] E. A. Fitzpatrick, *St. Ignatius and the Ratio Studiorum* (McGraw-Hill Book Company, New York, 1933), p. 132.

[10] Quoted in F. Watson, *English Grammar Schools to 1660* (Cambridge University Press, London, 1908), p. 156.

the Christian Brothers. The founder of this teaching order, St. Jean Baptiste de la Salle (1651–1719), was inspired by an intense desire to improve the lot of the poor. This he proposed to do through education, but he early found that he could make little headway in his dominating purpose without giving the brothers associated with him preparation and practice in the art of teaching. Consequently, in addition to the rule of the *Conduct of the Schools,* which he wrote for his order, he instituted preparation of teachers according to this rule as one of the important activities of the order.

It is worth noting that in his rule St. Jean Baptiste de la Salle called the attention of the Christian Brothers to the chief faults and virtues of the teachers. The young teacher, he felt, was principally in danger of too great an itching to talk and of being preoccupied with his own embarrassment. To ensure balance and poise he counseled the beginning teacher against both the extreme of harshness and the extreme of lack of force in his relation with pupils. He advised him furthermore to beware of trifling, of becoming despondent, and of bearing malice. Perhaps most revealing of his insight into the educative process was St. Jean Baptiste de la Salle's awareness that the young teacher was all too prone to neglect the differences of character and disposition which children manifest. Most of the virtues he urged on teachers were simply such Christian ones as humility, prudence, piety, and generosity, but he did not neglect those having most to do with success in teaching: patience, gentleness, and restraint.

TEACHER TRAINING IN PRUSSIA

Of the various European nations it was doubtless Prussia that made the most rapid progress in the eighteenth and nineteenth centuries toward putting teacher training on a firm foundation. Since Prussian teacher training became the model for the later American normal schools, it will be well to examine wherein lay the excellence of the Prussian example. This excellence seems to have lain in two main directions, the backing given by the government and the patterning of teacher training in the nineteenth century on Pestalozzian principles.

The first institution for the training of teachers in Prussia was the Seminarium Praeceptorum, founded at Halle by August Hermann Francke (1663–1727), an important contemporary of St. Jean Baptiste de la Salle. The idea of a teachers seminary was principally taken up and perpetuated by Johann Julius Hecker (1707–1768), a student at the University of Halle who seems to have come under Francke's influence. Hecker carried the idea forward with such zeal that he won the support of Prussia's famous king, Frederick the Great. It was during this sovereign's reign that the first steps were taken toward requiring training at a seminary as a prerequisite to teaching. Unfortunately, however, Frederick fell short of his excellent intentions. He had a habit of pensioning his old soldiers by appointing them to teaching positions and in this way lightened the financial burden of both his military and his educational establishments.

Frederick's compromise of his ideals was only temporary, and by the first quarter of the nineteenth century much more stringent regulations were in force. By that time schoolteachers had definitely become public officials and their appointment had to have the approval of the state. Moreover, they were forbidden to increase their stipend from teaching, even though it was the bare minimum permitted by law, by simultaneously engaging in any other occupation that might lower the dignity of their calling or divert their attention from their main duties. With this regulation disappeared the monopoly that tailors in Prussia had enjoyed as teachers a century earlier. Further adding to the dignity and attractiveness of teaching as a career was the fact that promotions were provided for those who were faithful in their vocation and unremitting in self-improvement. A long life spent in self-improvement was rewarded by a pension, a practice that still further enhanced teaching and contributed no little toward making Prussian schools the best in Europe.

As already intimated, the Prussian teacher did not owe his prestige wholly to the backing given by the government. For much of this prestige he was in debt to the fine preparation he received at the *Lehrer-Seminarien* provided by his country. These seminaries were three-year schools with average enrollments of about sixty. Candidates were eligible to enter these training institutions upon completion of the elementary school. Since they were planning to teach in elementary schools, the chief staple of their curriculum was a thorough knowledge of the elementary school subjects that they were going to teach. Over and above these subjects it was expected that the candidates would learn gymnastics and some musical instrument. As for method, the aim was not so much to inculcate candidates with theory as "to lead them by enlightened observation and their own experience to simple and lucid principles."[11] To provide opportunities for observation—and practice teaching, too—it was customary to locate seminaries close to orphanages. Needless to say, the arrangement was mutually beneficial.

The Prussian seminaries reached the peak of their eminence when

[11] V. Cousin, "Report on the State of Public Instruction in Prussia," in E. W. Knight, *Reports on European Education* (McGraw-Hill Book Company, New York, 1931), p. 171.

the government decided to infuse them with the spirit of the pioneer work of the great Swiss educator Johann Heinrich Pestalozzi (1746–1827). The genius of his educational contribution lay in his removal of instruction from the realm of empirical rule of thumb to that of scientific and philosophical theory.[12] Although not the first to predicate the method of instruction on a theory of child nature, he was the first to let his theory be guided by what he actually observed. In the course of time his observations came to form a body of definitely technical data. Consequently, teaching grew in technical complexity. No longer was it sufficient for the teacher to know merely the content of the subject matter that he proposed to teach. In addition, he had now to become familiar with a rapidly enlarging field of pedagogics. Henceforward, society did not have to wait on the arrival of the natively gifted teacher. With the aid of pedagogics even the less gifted could now hope to become successful teachers. As pedagogics increased in complexity, it made growing demands on the abilities of prospective teachers. This resulted in an increasingly better selection of candidates and, in the long run, in an improved social-economic status for the elementary teacher.

Indicative of this improvement was the enrichment that took place in the curricula of the Prussian teacher seminaries. Psychology as the basis of pedagogics occupied a position of great prominence, but in addition to this technical subject there was an enlargement of the academic program as well. For background here the student was able to study both natural philosophy and natural history, in addition to extensive reading in literature and political history. Mathematics, music, and drawing also received considerable emphasis. The chief shortcoming of the program, however, was its lack of connection with secondary or higher education. Candidates for the Prussian seminaries came, as already stated, from the elementary school, which in nineteenth-century Europe was the school of the lower classes.[13] Consequently, the elementary school teacher's was a narrow orbit. Sprung from the elementary school, he returned to teach there without ever having the broader experience of going through secondary or higher education.

EARLY STATUS AND TRAINING OF TEACHERS IN AMERICA

Before tracing the influence that this Prussian precedent exerted in the United States in the nineteenth century, it will be well to

[12] For a fuller account of Pestalozzi's theory and practice, see *supra,* pp. 207–211.

[13] For a fuller account of the class character of the elementary school, see *supra,* pp. 364–365, 404–405.

picture the social status and training of teachers during the previous colonial period. Although social classes were exceedingly mobile in the American colonies, nevertheless three classes were roughly distinguishable, a lower class composed of indentured servants and slaves, a middle class possessed of some property and addressed as "goodman" or "goodwoman," and an upper class of gentlemen addressed as "mister" or "sir." Oddly enough, teachers belonged to all three classes. In most instances, much depended on the level of instruction in which a person was engaged. Famous and successful Latin grammar teachers like Ezekiel Cheever of New Haven and Boston no doubt were addressed as "mister." So also were college professors, who in the early days of the country were more than likely to be clergymen, too. Not infrequently clergymen—and doctors, too, for that matter—combined the teaching of Latin and Greek with their other duties because they were the only learned men in their communities. Teachers, moreover, who had to be able enough to substitute for the clergyman in case he was absent from the pulpit generally stood high in social esteem.

Teachers of the elementary or common branches, however, did not enjoy such elevated rank. In the early days a frequent source of these teachers was the class of indentured servants. Freemen who taught at this level instead of seeking to exploit the country's vast natural resources were thought to be weaklings who probably could succeed at nothing else. Although a caricature, Washington Irving's Ichabod Crane no doubt approximated a stereotype here. Few people looked on teaching the rudiments as a full-time job. Such teaching either was combined with church duties like those of the sexton, organist, or gravedigger or was a side occupation of some good dame while engaged in the sedentary duties of her household. Consequently, elementary teaching was only a little more respectable than manual labor. To the ambitious it was a steppingstone rather than a capstone in a career. There is evidence that some colonial schoolmasters exhibited such vicious habits as profanity and drunkenness, but on the whole it seems that the great majority were men of exemplary habits and sober conversation.

Beyond their education in subject matter, colonial teachers enjoyed no previous preparation for careers in teaching. Even their study of subject matter was not generally undertaken with a view to teaching it. College professors and tutors obtained their training in the colleges in a manner not much different from the medieval pattern already discussed. In fact, emphasis on subject-matter content was to remain the principal staple of their training down to the middle of the twentieth century. This sort of collegiate training was also the principal preparation of masters in the Latin grammar schools and the colonial academies. (It constituted the preparation even of most high school teachers in the nineteenth and twentieth centuries.) Teachers of the elementary, or common, branches might have had some secondary education, but frequently they had no more than the common branches themselves. At all levels of instruction in colonial times, training in the technique of instruction was conspicuous by its absence.

Interestingly enough, the great advance that the nineteenth century was to make in training American teachers in technique took place at the elementary school level. In the opening decades of that century an early restlessness and anxiety began to manifest themselves over the low state to which teaching in the common school had fallen. At the time of the War of 1812 Denison Olmstead gave a commencement oration at Yale in which he recommended a "seminary for schoolmasters." In it "the pupils were to study and recite whatever they themselves were afterward to teach, partly for the purpose of acquiring a more perfect knowledge of these subjects, and partly of learning from the methods adopted by the principal the best modes of teaching."[14] Later another Yale man, James T. Kingsley, put his finger on what he thought was the main difficulty when he pointed out that common school teachers had little or no training beyond the common school in which they themselves taught. To remedy this situation he suggested a school intermediate between the common school and the college where the prospective teacher could get a sufficiently advanced content to enable him to enrich his instruction in the common school. Going a step beyond Kingsley, the Amherst College faculty proposed raising education to the collegiate level of instruction, but neither Amherst nor any other college took this step till toward the end of the century and then only grudgingly.

To move from the world of theory to that of practice, Philadelphia in 1818 established a model school for the training of teachers in the rest of the city's school system. This school was put in the charge of Joseph Lancaster (1778–1838), great exponent of the monitorial system of instruction. Naturally, the technique of instruction that candidates for teaching learned there was the monitorial one. The teacher taught the monitors, and the monitors taught the rest of the students.[15] The main emphasis in training, consequently, was the conventional one on learning subject matter. Indeed, Andrew Bell (1753–1832), Lancaster's English contemporary exponent of monitorial instruction, is reported to have stated, "Give me twenty-four pupils today and I will give you back twenty-four teachers tomorrow."[16]

[14] Quoted in Carnegie Foundation for Advancement of Teaching Bulletin 14, p. 22.

[15] For a more complete account of monitorial methods, see *supra*, pp. 211–212.

[16] Quoted in J. P. Gordy, *Rise and Growth of the Normal School Idea in the United States,* U.S. Bureau of Education Circular of Information 8, 1891, p. 24.

While the Philadelphia model school lasted till the middle of the century, the preparation of teachers on the monitorial plan did not arouse any widespread enthusiasm. Much more popular as an agency for training teachers was the American academy. Designed to prepare for life as well as for college, it offered courses leading boys to such careers as surveying, navigation, and commerce.[17] What more appropriate, therefore, as the demand for trained teachers began to arise, than that a teacher preparatory department should be added to the academy? Here seemed an institution just waiting to offer the advanced sort of academic training that Kingsley had suggested. The idea was not long in catching public imagination. It took most secure hold in New York State, where the Legislature in 1834 actually subsidized private academies to train teachers for the state's common school system. Although ten years later the state started its first normal school, New York continued to rely on academies and high schools for some of its teachers till almost a century after 1834.

In spite of this popularity the academy was by no means an altogether satisfactory solution for the problem of securing trained teachers for the common schools. It supplied only one-tenth of the number of teachers needed. In part, this was due to the expense involved in attending an academy. As yet, the salaries paid common school teachers were far from yielding an adequate return on the investment necessary in order to attend a private academy. Perhaps because of this, those who attended stayed only one-third as long as required to complete the full teacher preparatory course. Another inadequacy of the academy was the fact that the higher branches occupied such a position of prestige that the review of the lower branches, which most candidates desperately needed, was neglected. In fact, teacher training was so largely subordinated to the interests of general education that, in effect, it occupied a lower and less dignified plane.

Obviously, the academy was best equipped to add to the subject-matter knowledge of the future teacher. But subject matter was not enough. Future teachers were also in need of a knowledge of classroom management and control. To supply this deficiency, Henry Barnard (1811–1900), one of the two principal leaders of the American common school revival in the fourth and fifth decades of the nineteenth century, conceived the idea of holding teacher institutes. These were short but intensive periods of training offered to fit a teacher with the minimum skills of his calling. They usually ran from a few weeks to a month or more. The topics for study covered a wide range. Should prizes be given for good work; should there be public examinations and exhibitions; can teaching be reduced to a science; should

[17] For a fuller account of the academy, see *supra,* pp. 405–408.

the laboring classes be educated; what are the common causes of failure in teaching—these were but a sample of the questions that enlivened institutes. While institutes aimed to be concerned with such professional problems, it was regrettably all too frequent that time had to be devoted to review and drill in subject-matter fields as well. Usually, an institute was incomplete without the appearance of some prominent and inspiring speaker on the program. Called into being as temporary expedients, teacher institutes, surprisingly enough, remained popular supplements to the regular normal school program well into the twentieth century.

RISE OF THE NORMAL SCHOOL

None of the foregoing improvisations to supply a body of trained teachers proved adequate in the long run. In neither quantity nor quality were they adequate. What was needed, so the friends of education claimed, was an institution wholly devoted to the interests of training teachers. Such an institution first appeared under private auspices in 1823, when Samuel Read Hall (1795–1877), author of the famous *Lectures on School-keeping,* set up a three-year seminary for teachers at Concord, Vermont. Though later he moved his seminary to Andover, Massachusetts, where he kept it open for a decade and a half, he had practically no significant private imitators. Apparently the need was for an institution which not only was wholly devoted to teacher training but also was initiated and maintained by the public.

Agitation for state support of a teacher-training program was most acute and also most successful in Massachusetts. There the drive for better teachers was part of the larger agitation for getting the common schools out of the doldrums into which they had settled. "As is the teacher so is the school" was the popular slogan with which Charles Brooks (1795–1872) stumped Massachusetts on behalf of a state normal school. The pattern that Brooks had in mind was the Prussian teacher seminary, which had received wide attention in this country through the reports of visitors to Prussia such as Henry E. Dwight, Calvin Stowe (1802–1886), and others. The publication of a similar report by the Frenchman Victor Cousin (1792–1867) and its translation into English also had a great effect on American opinion. Although all these men had the example of the Prussian seminary in mind, it is interesting that the normal school that Massachusetts inaugurated in 1839 owes its name to Cousin, who in his report used the French word *normal,* meaning "model," rather than the German word *Seminar,* or the English "seminary."

The Massachusetts legislation of 1839 established the first state normal school in the United States but not without grave misgivings on the part of the legislators. Indeed, the legislation might not have been forthcoming at all had not James G. Carter (1795–1849), perennial supporter of the idea of a state normal school, at the last moment secured a private offer of $10,000 for the purpose, conditioned on the state's matching it with an equal amount. Even then, with all the eloquent oratory of Horace Mann (1796–1859), Massachusetts' greatest secretary to its State Board of Education, the state normal school was launched for an experimental period of only three years. And at the end of that period only after a protracted legislative battle was it continued with a reduced grant of $6,000.

The opposition arose from various sources, some religious and some private. Many still thought the academy competent to serve all legitimate requirements of the state. Not a little of the opposition stemmed from the fact that the inspiration of the normal school was Prussian in origin. Particularly displeasing to the American mind was the fact that the Prussian seminary was expected to inculcate prospective teachers with a willing obedience to their superiors or masters. That good practices could be retained and undemocratic ones sifted out was evident in the first normal school established by Connecticut at New Britain. One of its early circulars made this observation about discipline: "The age of the pupils, the objects which bring them to a normal school and the spirit of the institution itself, *will, it is believed, dispense with the necessity of a code of rules.*"[18] Countering the fear of autocracy, also, was no less a person than a former president of the United States, John Quincy Adams. Shall republics, he cried out, be outdone by monarchies in their solicitude for popular education at the hands of trained teachers?

Indicative that fears of Prussian influence were easily exaggerated is the fact that the normal schools founded in this country before the Civil War were actually more like the American academy than the Prussian *Lehrer-Seminar*. With minor amendments the normal school curriculum was really the same as the so-called "English" course of the academy. In other words, normal schools were, so to speak, academies devoted wholly rather than partly to teacher training. In a number of cases normal schools were located in old academy buildings. In the case of the first normal school at Lexington, Massachusetts, its earliest title among its students was "Lexington Academy."

In addition to the English course composed of such ingredients as grammar, spelling, composition, arithmetic, algebra, geometry,

---

[18] Quoted in W. D. Agnew, *Administration of Professional Schools for Teachers* (Warwick and York, Incorporated, Baltimore 1924), p. 71.

physiology, Scripture, music, and drawing, the normal school also included lectures on the art of teaching and governing school. *Lectures on School-keeping* by Hall and especially *The Theory and Practice of Teaching* by David Perkins Page (1810–1848), first principal of the state normal school at Albany, were the type of text on pedagogics read by most of the students.[19] In large part their prescriptions were of the empirical rule-of-thumb sort. Strangely enough, these books seem to have been little impressed by Pestalozzian methods. Consequently, influenced as our normals were by the Prussian *Lehrer-Seminar,* they failed at first to make any outstanding adaptation of its single most successful feature, its Pestalozzian pedagogics.

Not till the establishment of the state normal school at Oswego, New York, in 1860 did a wave of Pestalozzianism sweep through American normal schools. But again, strangely enough, the Pestalozzian pedagogics introduced at Oswego by Edward A. Sheldon (1832–1897), its noted first principal, came by way of England rather than Prussia. Because the English emphasized the mechanics of Pestalozzi's object instruction, the pedagogics taught at Oswego tended toward the formal side. Students learned the technique of instruction through objects much more quickly than they gained understanding of the theory and spirit behind it. But even formal object instruction was so superior to the pedagogics which preceded it that the influence of Oswego on other normal schools was felt far and wide.

The second wave of educational theory to sweep American normal schools was the Herbartian, toward the end of the nineteenth century. Just as Oswego was instrumental in spreading Pestalozzianism, so the state normal school at Normal, Illinois, was the center from which Herbartian doctrines of apperception and correlation radiated.[20] There it was that the great American Herbartians Charles De Garmo (1849–1934) and the brothers Charles McMurry (1857–1929) and Frank McMurry (1862–1936) made their initial reputations.

By the turn of the century, normal schools made a wide offering in professional subject matter. One type of course was in basic educational theory. Under this title some normals offered philosophy of education, and nearly all offered educational psychology. The history of education was another type of course that was all but universal. In fact, more was known about the history of education than about any other branch of education at this time. A third, rather omnibus type of course was didactics, which instructed in the theory and art

---

[19] For the detailed evolution of work in pedagogics, see O. J. Williamson, *The Development of Professional Programs in Education* (Bureau of Publications, Teachers College, Columbia University, New York, 1936), chap. 2.

[20] For a fuller account of these technical developments, see *supra,* pp. 212–214.

of teaching. Last was work offered in the model, or practice, school. This, however, deserves separate mention.

The addition of a model school to the first normal at Lexington was a distinct improvement on the old academy. Historically, the model school served both as a place for the student to observe good instruction and as a place to get some practice of his own. Unfortunately, in Massachusetts, the model school soon languished and died because it was inadequately financed and because the regular staff of the normal school was too overburdened with work to give it proper supervision. This mistake was not repeated when New York opened its first normal school in Albany five years after the one at Lexington. Yet it remained an open question for the rest of the century whether the regular staff should supervise practice teaching or whether there should be specially appointed critic teachers. So, too, there was considerable debate whether the model, or practice, school should be under the control of the normal school or of the local public school system. Both sides, however, were in agreement that practice conditions should be as nearly like actual circumstances as possible.[21]

The normal school movement progressed rather slowly at the beginning. At the very outset, it had to overcome the skepticism of those who had opposed its founding. Not only were enrollments very small, but those who matriculated often failed to stay throughout the three-year course. New York tried to entice students to its first normal school by subsidizing them to the extent of their railroad fare. It was not till the great expansion of free public education after the Civil War, when the staffing of the common, or elementary, schools came to depend almost wholly on women teachers, that the period of rapid expansion of normal schools set in. It is notable that the Middle Western states met this expansion with much more liberal financial support than did the Eastern states. Their greater effort was in part due to public lands the income from which could be turned to support educational purposes and in part to an attempt to compensate themselves for the absence of a well-established system of secondary schools and colleges such as existed in the East.

In spite of the later rapid growth in numbers attending state normal schools, there was still a great dearth of trained teachers. To supply this deficiency large city school systems like those of Boston and New York commenced before the Civil War to recruit teachers from training classes operated in connection with their own schools. This sort of training often appealed to girls who did not want to go away from home to a state normal school. In addition, it had the great

---

[21] See also D. Fristoe, "Early Beginnings of Laboratory Schools," *Educational Administration and Supervision*, 28:219–223, March, 1942.

advantage of offering opportunities for practice under local conditions. Though many cities adopted this scheme, it was not without drawbacks, not least of which was its tendency to encourage inbreeding of teachers. This narrowness of pedagogical outlook was often made more glaring by the fact that the pedagogical staff at state normals was usually quite superior to that at local ones.

While the origin and growth of normal schools occurred chiefly under public auspices, it would be a mistake to overlook the growth that took place under private auspices. Most deserving of mention here is the effect the normal school movement had upon Catholic teaching orders. These orders had traditionally cared for the training of their members. Generally, training was undertaken in a period called the "novitiate." Before the Third Plenary Council of Baltimore in 1884 this novitiate was usually a year or more in length. The effectiveness of the novitiate as a period of teacher training, however, was diminished by the fact that much of it was devoted to religious discipline and by the added fact that frequently it was abbreviated because the demand for trained teachers was so very urgent. The Third Plenary Council took note of this situation and tried to rectify it by exhorting religious communities to give their members normal school training for a more adequate period of time. The stronger orders, eager to return to a longer period of training, did not wait for a second exhortation.[22]

TRANSITION TO THE TEACHERS COLLEGE

By the end of the nineteenth century the normal school had become a well-established part of the American school system. Not only had it become the principal agency for the preparation of elementary school teachers, but it had also begun to be a source of high school teachers as well. Being practically the only institution that offered technical training in teaching to large numbers of students, it was the logical place to look for the great increment in teachers needed to man the high schools, whose period of phenomenal growth was just beginning.[23] But there was one very important hurdle that the normal schools had to leap before they could enter freely and without objection this new field of service to the public. They had to raise the length and quality of their training so that high schools would not fail of being accredited by the accrediting associations because some of their teachers lacked college degrees.

[22] For an account of the founding of various teaching orders in the United States, see J. A. Burns and B. J. Kohlbrenner, *A History of Catholic Education in the United States* (Benziger Bros. Inc., New York, 1937), chaps. 2, 4, 6.

[23] For a further account of the high school's growth, see *supra,* pp. 410–411.

As matters stood about 1890, approximately 65 per cent of the entering normal school population had only an elementary school education, and only about 20 per cent had finished high school. Consequently, the period of normal school training lasted anywhere from one to four years, depending on how much high school work was offered in the normal school curriculum. In practically no cases did the normal school course extend more than two years beyond the usual four-year high school. Despite the attention given to the "technique" of teaching, a background such as this was far from adequate preparation to instruct in high schools that were preparing for college. Nor could normal school students altogether make up for this deficiency by being more mature—on the average, twenty years of age—or by being self-supporting and thus having habits of attention, industry, and perseverance which indicated that they knew the value of time and opportunity.

The whole predicament was further complicated by uncertainty as to the role to be played by colleges and universities in the preparation of secondary school teachers. These institutions had long given adequate academic training to qualify students to teach in secondary schools, but on the whole they had neglected the more technical phases of teaching. Some of them feared the competition that the normal schools might offer in academic preserves which hitherto they had themselves more or less monopolized. Others thought that it was high time the colleges and universities began to offer technical courses in education themselves. Whether or not colleges should undertake this work was the subject of heated and extended discussion at the 1889 meeting of the New England Association of Colleges and Preparatory Schools. Holding to the affirmative, that they should, was G. Stanley Hall (1846–1924), eminent educational psychologist and president of Clark University. Holding to the negative were the presidents of Harvard and Yale, Charles W. Eliot (1834–1926) and Timothy Dwight (1828–1916). The latter two advocated as an alternative the establishment of a "higher" normal school. As a matter of fact, the future developed along the lines of both these alternatives.

The idea of some higher development of the normal school appealed to the state of New York. Therefore, in 1890, it reorganized its first normal school at Albany into the New York State Normal College. Michigan improved on New York in 1903 and constituted its normal college at Ypsilanti the first state teachers college. In giving the normal school at Albany collegiate status, New York empowered the institution to grant degrees in pedagogy. This privilege betokened that the State Board of Regents apparently expected the institution to avoid instruction in conventional college subjects and to restrict itself to purely professional courses. Fifteen years later the regents, im-

Professional Education of Teachers

485

pressed by the increasingly exacting demands of scholarship made on high school teachers, authorized the college to draw up a four-year course of study in pedagogics *and* liberal arts. Students for this program were to be selected according to entrance requirements that approximated those of the best Eastern colleges and at the end were to be awarded the bachelor of arts degree. Furthermore, at this time Albany dropped the preparation of elementary school teachers and concentrated wholly on the preparation of high school teachers.

When the new normal colleges commenced awarding degrees in pedagogy, no particular exception was taken. But when the new teachers colleges commenced granting the arts degree, there was a definite outcry. Colleges of liberal arts particularly were prompted to object. They took the position that it was historically unwarranted to grant the B.A. degree, long associated with the tradition of liberal education, to graduates of professional schools. A more careful reading of history should have advised them, as already seen, that the arts degree in the medieval university originated almost exclusively as a teaching degree.[24]

The struggle between protagonists of liberal and professional education was waged not only between liberal arts and teachers colleges but between rival factions within the teachers college faculties themselves. On the whole it seems that the Western state teachers colleges were at first more favorably inclined toward liberal studies than were the Eastern ones. Like the West's more generous support of its normals, this inclination seems to have been due to its greater dependence on teachers colleges to augment the supply of higher education.

The evolution of normal schools into teachers colleges was by no means confined to the training of high school teachers. It spread to the training of elementary teachers as well, a development that had the endorsement of the National Education Association as early as 1908. Once this transition got under way, it moved quite rapidly. Thus, in 1920 immediately after the First World War there were in the United States 46 teachers colleges and 137 normal schools. Only eight years later on the eve of the economic Depression the proportion had almost reversed itself, there being then 137 teachers colleges and 69 normal schools. The chief problem presented by this rapid growth was to ensure that the normal schools reorganized into teachers colleges became colleges in fact as well as in name, that the addition of two years' work was more than a mere quantitative one.

The rapid growth of teachers colleges almost immediately posed a problem of standardization in order to keep requirements uniformly

[24] F. H. Swift, "The Teacher's Baccalaureate," *Teachers College Record,* 21: 25–50, January, 1920.

high. When the National Education Association gave its encouragement to the transformation of normal schools into teachers colleges, it suggested such standards as high school graduation for an entrance requirement, a four-year curriculum broad enough to cope with the new demands on teaching, and departments of educational research. Meantime, the normal schools and colleges had been measuring themselves against each other in their voluntary organizations.[25] A normal school department of the National Education Association, organized in the nineteenth century, and a National Council of Normal School Presidents, organized in the twentieth century, merged after the First World War into the American Association of Teachers Colleges.

This association in 1926 adopted an important set of standards for accrediting its members. It defined teachers colleges as institutions devoted exclusively to the training of teachers and offering at least one 4-year course for that purpose. Admission requirements were set at high school graduation, and graduation requirements at the conventional college standard of 120 semester hours of work. Prescriptions were also laid down with regard to the size of teachers college faculties, their degrees, and their teaching load. Moreover, teachers colleges were required to have training schools and proper libraries. The association even legislated on building standards and declared that indifferent financial support would be evidence of an inadequate educational program.

After the First World War there developed an increasing dissatisfaction with the curricula of the teachers colleges. Up to that time, teachers colleges had tended to imitate each other in the construction and reconstruction of their curricula. No one had examined the curriculum appropriate for teacher education from the critical point of view, which was just then beginning to yield such significant results in elementary and secondary school curricula.[26] To fill this gap was the purpose of the Commonwealth Teacher-training Study.[27] With a generous subsidy and a corps of assistants an elaborate analysis was made of the teacher's activities in class, in the extracurriculum, in the community, and the like. The results of this analysis were worked over into standards by which not only existing curricula could be evaluated but new ones set up.

The same year the Commonwealth study came off the press, the Great Depression added to the uncertainties of teacher education.

---

[25] A. L. Crabb, G. Poret, and T. E. Smith, "The Evolution of Teachers College Standards," *Sixteenth Yearbook,* American Association of Teachers Colleges, 1937, pp. 104–123.

[26] For a description of this curriculum development, see *supra,* pp. 279–286.

[27] *The Commonwealth Teacher-training Study* (The University of Chicago Press, Chicago, 1929).

In a short ten years the country had moved from an appalling dearth of teachers during the First World War to an unemployable surplus during the Depression. It became much easier to get teachers than to get money from legislatures for teacher training. The efforts of public and private institutions for training teachers overlapped. These difficulties were complicated by uncertainty as to how much time a prospective teacher should spend in training, how much time he should give to general and professional education, how much practice teaching he should have, and other problems. To get the facts necessary to clearing up these confusions a national survey of the education of teachers was undertaken in 1931, and its results were published two years later.

TEACHER TRAINING IN ARTS COLLEGES AND UNIVERSITIES

Note has already been taken of the mild crisis at the end of the nineteenth century when the question was debated whether the advanced training of teachers should go forward in "higher" normals or whether the time was ripe for colleges and universities to interest themselves in the professional study of education. How the idea of higher normals eventuated in teachers colleges has just been traced. It is in order now to follow the developments attendant on instituting courses in the professional study of education in already existing colleges and universities.

As already seen in the preference of Eliot and Dwight for higher normal schools, the old-line seats of learning did not at first want to be troubled with the professional study of education. This negative disposition was a bias of long standing and, although departments and schools of education at colleges and universities had become commonplace since the nineteenth century, had far from disappeared even at the outbreak of the Second World War. It is noteworthy, for instance, that, when at the Yale commencement already mentioned Denison Olmstead sounded an early clarion call for the better training of teachers, neither Yale nor any other college, for that matter, did anything in response. No doubt this apathy is easy to understand. Olmstead had the elementary, or common, schools in mind. Certainly no one expected the colleges to give more adequate instruction in the common school subjects, which apparently was the crying need of the day. Indeed, even academies, though their teacher training departments taught these subjects, thought such instruction somewhat beneath their dignity.

This situation improved little if at all with the introduction of the more technical subject of pedagogy. At first, pedagogy was so empirical and so unscientific that it seemed as far below the notice of college professors as did the common branches themselves. Even after the introduction of Pestalozzian and Herbartian notions, it still seemed far from the sort of technical "mystery" that was worthy to occupy a part of the college curriculum or the time of the professional mind. When a chair of pedagogy was under consideration at the University of Michigan, someone asked what technical literature could be the province of such a chair. The question was an embarrassing one, for in the decades following the Civil War there actually was a dearth of good professional literature, and what little existed was mostly in German. No doubt, President Eliot of Harvard spoke for a great many when he remarked that his faculty "in common with most teachers in England and the United States feel but slight interest or confidence in what is ordinarily called pedagogy."[28]

Eliot was right. Pedagogy did not enjoy the full and unqualified confidence of professional educators. In fact, in the twentieth century the term fell into such disrepute that it quite lost its currency. At the turn of the century, however, new philosophic and scientific movements in education led by John Dewey (1859–1952) and Edward Lee Thorndike (1874–1949) went far toward building new confidence in the professional study of education.[29] But the title of pedagogy, though still highly appropriate, remained a discredited term because of its associations.

Another source of the collegiate and university bias against the professional training of teachers was the low standard of scholarship that obtained in the academy and normal school training of teachers. Probably none deplored these low standards more than the normal schools themselves. Yet they were almost powerless to make quick and sharp improvements. The salaries of common school teachers were so low and the demand for teachers was so great through most of the nineteenth century that many left normal school long before they had completed the full prescribed course. As institutions of higher learning looked down the ends of their respectable noses at this indifferent product of the normal schools, it often seemed as if they failed to take into account the great difficulties under which the normals labored.

In spite of these serious handicaps, the professional study of education slowly but surely made its way into the academic strongholds of college and university. As already implied, it was the rising demand for trained secondary school teachers and the new dignity given to the technical study of education by science and philosophy that

[28] *Report of the United States Commissioner of Education, 1890–1891*, vol. 2, p. 1076.

[29] For an account of these movements, see *supra*, pp. 130–134, 151–157.

breached the academic walls. In 1852 Indiana University was the first to yield to the demand for adding education to the list of higher studies. The state universities of Iowa and Michigan were not far behind. After the Civil War the latter two institutions transformed their chairs of pedagogy into departments of education. Before the century was out, even old foundations like Harvard and Yale offered courses in education. Such beginnings, however, were frequently subdivisions of older and more strongly established academic departments, such as philosophy and psychology. By the first decade of the twentieth century most of the state universities of the Middle West had gone a step further and reorganized their departments of education into independent schools of education.

By far the most significant step for the future development of the higher study of education was the founding of Teachers College at Columbia University in 1892. This institution had originated three years earlier as the New York College for the Training of Teachers. It aimed to serve education at the same level that the better schools of law and medicine served their professions. From the very first, its supporters looked forward to the day when its principal work could be pitched at the graduate level. Indeed it soon took leadership at this level in creating a research literature in the history, philosophy, and science of education which had been so greatly lacking in the nineteenth century. The stimulus of this leadership can be seen in the fact that while in 1910 the number of Ph.D.'s awarded for educational research was reckoned in tens, after the First World War it was counted in hundreds.

THE GREAT DEBATE ON TEACHER EDUCATION

In spite of cumulative efforts at raising standards the teaching profession on the eve of the Second World War still failed to earn the full measure of respect due a learned profession. Too many laymen and academicians still agreed with Irving Babbitt, who, at the onset of the Depression, had flayed professors of pedagogy as humanitarians that "are held in almost universal suspicion in academic circles and are not infrequently looked upon by their colleagues as downright charlatans."[30] Worse yet, when the war was over, disgruntled critics subjected teachers and the preparation of teachers to perhaps the most severe attack in the history of education. The attack seemed to come in two waves. Immediately after the war the loyalty of public school teachers came under scrutiny. Hardly had they vindi-

[30] Irving Babbitt, "President Eliot and American Education," *Forum*, 81:1–10, January, 1929.

cated their patriotism before their professional competence was impugned.

Apprehension about the loyalty of teachers was a by-product of postwar uncertainties. Everyone had expected war to be succeeded by peace, and nearly everyone was disturbed that peace, when it came, was racked with instabilities. The spy scare, for one thing, led people to suspect their neighbors of being possible enemies. They particularly marked others for disaffection if the latter exhibited any marks of nonconformity. Consequently teachers who expressed liberal views, let alone subversive ones, were immediately suspect. As a matter of fact, extremely few teachers in the total population were proved to be disloyal. Yet incalculable damage was done to the confidence reposed in teachers merely by denouncing them even with a palpable lack of evidence.

Even though the spy scare turned up a negligible number of subversives among teachers, the public was still intent on finding a scapegoat to blame for the frustrations brought on by their general anxieties. If it was difficult to catch teachers in acts of disloyalty, it was much easier to blame them for the fact that Russian schools seemed to be a much more effective instrument of state policy than did American ones. Many thought the evidence on this score conclusive when Sputnik streaked into the stratosphere well in advance of a similar American effort.

Numerous complaints were leveled at teacher training, but they all seemed to focus in the claim that the training suffered from anti-intellectualism.[31] This anti-intellectualism was evident at two main points. In the first place, students intending teaching careers were woefully deficient in their knowledge of the liberal arts.[32] In the second place, the professional study of education had proliferated so many courses that they were thin and overlapping. Not only that, but too many of these courses were "methods" or "how-to-do-it" courses so greatly preoccupied with narrow practical recommendations that they involved no "mystery" at all; that is, they had no theoretical or intellectual content.

Indeed, so lacking in intellectual content were these courses that

---

[31] This criticism found its best-organized expression in the Council for Basic Education and a book by its former executive, J. D. Koerner, *The Miseducation of American Teachers* (Houghton Mifflin Company, Boston, 1963). For a critique of this council and this book, see M. A. Raywid, "CBE in Perspective: A Report on the Council for Basic Education," *Educational Theory*, 14:144–157, July, 1964. For a larger setting of the criticism of anti-intellectualism, see R. Hofstadter, *Anti-intellectualism in American Life* (Alfred A. Knopf, Inc., New York, 1963).

[32] *The Student and His Knowledge* (Carnegie Foundation for the Advancement of Teaching, New York, 1938), pp. 38–42.

not a few critics bluntly asserted that education was not a "discipline" in the first place.[33] Since education must draw on such well-established disciplines as psychology, history, philosophy, and sociology, it had no unique content or method of its own. Therefore it should be dropped from the catalogue. Robert M. Hutchins (1899–   ), president of the University of Chicago, set the pace by claiming that all one needed to teach was competence in the liberal arts and an opportunity to teach. What he had in mind was that the liberal arts would "double in brass"—on the one hand, they would provide a knowledge of the subject matter to be taught and, on the other, through the trivium of grammar, logic, and rhetoric, a knowledge of how to teach, for what is teaching but the art of expressing oneself grammatically, cogently, and persuasively? Although this view was a rude shock to those who had come to believe with Charles H. Judd at the end of the First World War[34] and Alexander Bain even in the nineteenth century[35] that education was well on the way to becoming a science, it was a very popular one with academic faculties hostile to the "establishment," as James Bryant Conant called the educational profession.[36]

Various policies were proposed and put into effect to remedy the anti-intellectualism of teacher training. A few institutions, like Yale, impressed by the belief that education had no standing as a separate discipline, continued to train teachers but did so by pulling the studies composing the foundations of education—educational psychology, educational philosophy, educational history, and educational sociology—back into their respective parent academic disciplines. This plan was logical enough except for the fact that men trained in academic subject-matter disciplines were too frequently not equally or even moderately well trained in problems of education.

Many other institutions either conceded that education was a discipline or, if not, that at least it was a professional field served by such basic disciplines as psychology, philosophy, history, and sociology. (Analogously, medicine is not a science, but there are medical sciences such as anatomy, physiology, and the like.) In either event the preparation of teachers was made an institution-wide responsibility, that is, a responsibility of the academic as well as the professional

[33] J. Walton and J. L. Kuethe, *The Discipline of Education* (The University of Wisconsin Press, Madison, Wis., 1963).

[34] C. H. Judd, *Introduction to the Scientific Study of Education* (Ginn and Company, Boston, 1918).

[35] A. Bain, *Education as a Science* (D. Appleton & Company, Inc., New York, 1879).

[36] J. B. Conant, *The Education of American Teachers* (McGraw-Hill Book Company, New York, 1963).

faculty. Cooperative endeavor here generally promoted mutual under-standing and tended to reconcile age-long animosities. Some institu-tions, like Harvard, designed a special degree for this cooperative enterprise, the M.A.T., or master of arts in teaching.

Yet another policy for increasing the intellectual content of teacher training developed somewhat fortuitously. To provide for the ever-escalating enrollments in the post-World War II period some states found it more convenient to enlarge existing physical facilities for higher education than to build entirely new colleges. As a result many decided to change their teachers colleges into state colleges or even state universities, thus transforming them from single- to multiple-purpose institutions. As these institutions added independent liberal arts faculties, they effected a balance between liberal and pro-fessional studies which had been lacking earlier. Thus came within sight the end of a strange historical paradox whereby academicians scolded professional educators for the absence of intellectual content when it was academicians who denied it to them by forcing teacher training in the nineteenth century from the college campus into normal schools which were obviously off the main trunk line of culture.

CERTIFICATION OF TEACHERS

The interest of the American public in having its teachers certified is considerably older than its interest in taking responsibility for having them trained. Thus, even in colonial times it was customary for public authorities, usually the school committee, to examine candidates for public employment as teachers. Probably the chief anxiety of the examiners regarded the candidate's religious orthodoxy, for in those days this was of paramount importance where the pliant minds of the young were concerned. In addition, inquiry was directed at what the candidate knew about the subjects he was to teach and especially at how well he could "govern" a school. Any certificates issued on the basis of such an examination were usually good only for the locality over which the school committee presided and generally for no longer than a year.

Satisfactory as local certification of teachers was for frontier com-munities, it soon showed definite weaknesses. Most obvious was the unevenness of certification from community to community and the inconvenience to which a teacher was put by having to stand reexami-nation every time he changed his location.[37] But also unfortunate was the lowering of standards that followed the breakdown of towns

[37] To assist candidates in passing any sort of examination, I. Stone published his *Elementary and Complete Examiner* (A. S. Barnes and Co. Inc., New York, 1869).

and counties into districts as the local units of educational administration.[38] These units were so small and often so isolated that they quite lacked broad educational ideals even if they had had the resolution to insist upon them.

This situation did not improve till powers of certification were returned to the town and county authorities. Yet even then there remained considerable unevenness of administration, which did not vanish till the state asserted its central authority to issue certificates. Salutary as the centralization of teacher certification in the hands of the state was, it was a policy that had been adopted by only a few states at the turn of the twentieth century and by only a little more than half of them in the first quarter of the century. Time, of course, was on the side of the state; for, with the increasing mobility of population brought on by improvement in transportation, teachers more and more wished to possess certification that enabled them to teach anywhere within state boundaries. In addition, the state had another attraction to offer, the substitution of approved training at a state normal school for the state examination leading to certification.

Public authorities were not long in learning to use certification not only as a prophylactic to protect the public but also as a positive instrument to improve the quality of teachers. The chief way in which they forged their instrument for this purpose was to grant different sorts of certificates, proportioning the time they ran to the amount of training taken to receive them. Henry Barnard was one of the first to recommend this practice. Most prized, of course, was the permanent, or life, certificate, which permitted its holder to teach anywhere in the state for the rest of his life. While the immediate effect of the life certificate was to raise the quality of teachers in the nineteenth century, its long-term effect on the twentieth century was seen to stifle professional growth. Consequently, toward the middle of the twentieth century there was a tendency to argue for temporary certificates so that the state could keep constant control of the qualifications of its teachers.

Latterly, differentiation in the certificates issued to teachers took another direction. Instead of certifying competence to teach for a certain length of time, the state commenced to certify competence in a particular field of teaching, such as the kindergarten or primary grades in the elementary school or some subject-matter field in the high school. Such specialization in certification was evidence of the great technical complexity that the professional study of education had achieved in the twentieth century. Consequently, by the Second World War neither competence in educational technique nor

[38] For a more complete account of the district system, see *infra*, pp. 544–547.

competence in subject matter was alone sufficient to qualify one for teaching in the public schools. Rigorous rules of certification laid down requirements in both. In addition to subject-matter specialization, they required at least educational psychology, principles of either elementary or secondary education, and a certain number of hours spent in practice teaching.

It needs pointing out historically that public certification has been required only of teachers in public schools. At times in the past there has been a desire but also a great hesitancy to demand certification of teachers in private schools as well. It may be said for the socially select private school that at its own instance it has usually set very high academic subject-matter requirements of its teachers, but also it may be said against it that it has tended to scoff at requirements in technical education. Indeed, there has even been a tendency to regard these latter requirements as the "racket" of a pressure group.[39] The private parochial school system of the Catholic Church, on the other hand, has traditionally accepted the idea of certification. Although the Third Plenary Council in 1884 made certification properly a function of the diocese, this policy has not worked out well. Instead, Catholic teachers have come voluntarily to seek state certification, leaving it to the diocese to make any further religious requirements it may wish.[40]

The positive and aggressive raising of standards of certification was seldom an easy task. The almost constant excess of the demand for teachers over the supply in the nineteenth and early twentieth centuries exercised continual restraint on those who wished to elevate requirements. If they had raised them to what professional standards demanded, they would but have made the existing shortage of teachers more acute. With the exception of periods of war, it was not till the severe economic Depression of 1929 that the country experienced

---

[39] Professor Robert A. Millikan, Nobel prize winner in physics, expressed a common academic attitude toward modern certification requirements when in the *New York Times* of December 28, 1930, he said, "I actually had a first-rate training for teaching physics, or, for that matter, for teaching any analytical subject; for in the high school, in the preparatory school, and in college I had excellent teachers of algebra, geometry, trigonometry, and analytics, who kept me hard at work solving problems from the time I was thirteen up to the age of twenty-one, and who gave me thereby vastly more sound training for teaching physics than I could have acquired by any number of courses in pedagogy. . . . Now, my comment is that I couldn't today break into, as I did forty years ago, the teaching of secondary school physics, because our states, many of them, have passed laws under the stimulus of teachers'-college labor unions, which actually are working, so it seems to me—and I know I am right in at least a few individual instances—to prevent the ablest and best trained of our younger minds from getting into secondary teaching at all."

[40] Burns and Kohlbrenner, *op. cit.*, p. 222.

for the first time an excess of the supply of over the demand for trained teachers. A number of states took advantage of this unusual circumstance to raise their certification requirements to a level at which they had long wished but had not dared to fix them.

After the Second World War the National Education Association made an intensive effort to improve the quality of teachers by setting up the National Commission on Teacher Education and Professional Standards (TEPS). Up to this time teacher certification had resembled the conditions of civil service. Licensure was controlled by the state, not the profession. The state laid down standards but did not prescribe a course of training. Indeed, it even accepted substandard teachers, a practice unthinkable in a profession like medicine. To make the training of teachers truly professional required that facilities develop programs which they then submitted for accreditation by a professional agency. To provide just such an agency the commission in turn set up the National Council on Accreditation for Teacher Education (NCATE). In spite of these notable efforts some dissatisfaction still remained, especially with the way dependence on such quantitative measures as the number of courses and credits taken tended to legalize mediocrity. In an endeavor to lay the unrest the Carnegie Corporation invited James Bryant Conant (1893–   ), former president of Harvard, to make a thorough study of the education of American teachers.[41] Minimizing both state and professional agencies, he recommended virtually localizing certification in the faculties of institutions training teachers. This might be an escape from mediocrity, but did it retain the nineteenth-century safeguard against laxity of local standards? The "establishment" was doubtful, but New York was willing to try Conant's ideas on a limited scale.

IN-SERVICE TRAINING OF TEACHERS

Although until the Depression of 1929 the practical demand for trained teachers outran the supply, with the consequent tendency for teachers to enter teaching before completing their normal training or with their normal training at a minimum, an early and commendable effort was made to help these teachers to make up their deficiencies while teaching. Henry Barnard in the mid-nineteenth century was among the first to make some simple suggestions toward this end. Among other things he urged teachers to visit each other's classrooms to see whether they could pick up any suggestions. In addition, he recommended that they subscribe to some good educational periodical in order to keep abreast of new developments. Ridiculous though this may seem, he even called upon them to buy a book on the

[41] Conant, *op. cit.*

problems of teaching. His teacher institutes, already mentioned, were perhaps his greatest contribution to the improvement of teachers already in the field.

Barnard's exhortation to teachers to become better read in their professional problems bore its richest fruit in the next to the last decade of the century. The Ohio State Teachers Association then took the lead in organizing a reading circle among teachers. The plan was to provide for teachers a systematic course of reading covering a period of anywhere from a year to three years. Happily, the reading lists contained books on science and literature as well as books of a more professional nature. The plan met an immediate and enthusiastic response, as witness its spread and adoption in every state of the Union except one. A number of states even legalized the circle, while others made arrangements whereby work accomplished in it was credited toward certification. An approving nod for the movement came from the United States Commissioner of Education himself. State memberships in these circles ran as high as 10,000 and reached their peak in the first decade of the twentieth century. Thereafter, the reading circle entered a steady decline as summer school and university extension became the more effective and popular means of in-service training of teachers.

The summer school that supplanted the reading circle was also the logical successor to Barnard's teacher institute. It was like the institute in that it offered a relatively brief intensive period of training, but it also resembled the normal school, college, and university in that its course of study was much more rigorous than that of the old institute. The idea of the summer school seems first to have hatched in the mind of Harvard's famous professor of zoology, Louis Agassiz (1807–1873). The effective study of zoology requires field-work; what better way to provide opportunities than to use the long summer vacation? The sponsors of the study activities centering at Chautauqua, New York, also popularized the idea of making a profitable use of the summer vacation period. Educational meetings on the Chautauqua model were soon held at Martha's Vineyard, Massachusetts, and Saratoga, New York.

It was not till after 1900, however, that summer schools for teachers received an organization and administration that coordinated them with the main trunk line of year-round teacher training. This started with states' counting summer work toward the renewal of temporary certificates. Later, ways were worked out so that summer study could be evaluated in terms of the regular winter program. Thereafter, it became possible for teachers eager to improve themselves to win advanced degrees by installments while still employed. Some public school systems stimulated the improvement of their teachers by offering salary increments for summer courses completed. State departments of education also gave great impetus to the summer school, for it became one of the most convenient means by which teachers could satisfy the gradually but steadily advancing requirements for certification. Taken all together, these influences built up a summer school clientele that alone reached a quarter of a million teachers just as the Great Depression at the end of the 1920s settled over the country. It was probably the greatest mass attempt ever known at professional self-improvement in service.

The university extension movement also lent itself effectively to the movement for improving teachers in service. As in the case of the summer school, university extension, though it got under way in the nineteenth century, did not reveal its possibilities for teacher training till the twentieth century. Then it developed a whole series of late-afternoon, evening, and Saturday morning classes both on and off campus. The off-campus course was particularly advantageous when practical fieldwork was involved. Its great disadvantage lay in the inadequacy of library facilities. Much the same considerations obtained when extension training was later carried on by correspondence.

PROFESSIONAL MAGAZINES

Professional periodicals, at the time when Barnard was urging teachers to read them, were only in their infancy. The first magazine devoted to the interests of teachers, the *Academician,* survived its birth in 1818 by only a few years. Other magazines took its place. Of chief interest were the *Massachusetts Common School Journal* started by Horace Mann and the *Connecticut Common School Journal* started by Henry Barnard. Both journals played a prominent part in the common school revival of the fourth and fifth decades of the nineteenth century. On the one hand, they were designed to arouse public interest in the schools and, on the other, to acquaint teachers in service with better practices. Particularly intended to be a scholarly compendium of the best current theory and practices here and abroad was Barnard's *American Journal of Education.* Of such monumental proportions did this prove to be that it earned Barnard the distinction of being virtually the creator of American educational literature.

It is a startling fact that none of these journals was self-supporting. Barnard almost impoverished his old age by sinking his personal fortune in his *American Journal,* and state departments of education, which followed the example of Massachusetts and Connecticut in having official journals, were not long in finding that their organs had to be either subsidized by the state or paid for out of state education association dues. Even in the twentieth century, voluntary subscriptions by teachers to professional magazines were in such small volume that many of these publications were unable to stay in the field without some kind of sponsorship, such as that of professional associations. The growing graduate schools of education, interestingly enough, gladly provided another of the principal sources of this sponsorship. Like other graduate faculties they counted scholarly publication one of the bright jewels in the crown of higher learning.

As already stated, early educational journals served the double purpose of improving teachers in service and of arousing the public to the needs of the schools. This latter purpose disappeared after the free public school system became firmly established in American affections. Thereafter, the principal magazines directed toward the lay public were those for parents, a type that continued to come off the press right down into the twentieth century. In that century, however, educational periodicals underwent a great diversification in order to keep abreast of the specialization occasioned by the tremendous accumulation of educational data that was stimulated by the new scientific and philosophical study of education. Separate magazines appeared for the different levels of the educational ladder. Each subject-matter field, too, such as English and geography, seemed to have a publication devoted to its interests. School superintendents and supervisors were served by several periodicals. Reports of scientific research in education found an outlet through various publications and reviews. New departures in education, pressed with the need of getting their cause before the lay and professional public, often sponsored journals. Again, educational news coverage was the forte of one magazine, social protest of another.[42] In addition to all these, the Catholics had periodicals of their own to keep their constituency informed of Catholic views on education.

EDUCATIONAL ASSOCIATIONS

Another powerful means of improving the quality and status of teaching was the formation of professional associations. The precedent for this movement in the nineteenth century was the American lyceum movement. The early lyceum started as a pressure group of lay and professional people bent on stirring the public to greater effort on behalf of the common schools. Contact with spirited laymen in these lyceums taught teachers much about the value and strategy of organizing to achieve their ends. It was not long, therefore, before teachers were organizing associations exclusively their own, some along local, some along national, lines.

[42] For example, see C. A. Bowers, "The *Social Frontier* Journal: A Historical Sketch," *History of Education Quarterly,* 4:167–180, September, 1964.

Local associations were of various sorts. In large urban centers like Boston and New York, city associations arose. It was in Massachusetts and New York, too, that the first state associations took form just before the middle of the nineteenth century. More regional in character was the American Institute of Instruction, which organized the New England area after 1830. The programs of this institute were of first-rate quality, as one might expect, considering that its membership catered only to the elite in the profession. It excluded not only common school teachers from its meetings but the public as well.

In 1849 an attempt was made to form a national education association under the title of the American Association for the Advancement of Education. This association had Horace Mann for its first president. It also had a large number of laymen in its membership. The first effort to establish a national organization exclusively for teachers occurred at Philadelphia in the next decade. As the result of a call of ten state teacher associations, seventy-five people met there in 1857 to form the National Teachers Association. This national organization did not thrive at first. Born on the eve of a war to test the unity of our nationhood, it could hardly have picked a less propitious birthday. In addition, the new association was not very popular because it limited its membership to men and to public school men at that. A few years after the Civil War the National Teachers Association still showed no outstanding evidence of growth, having a membership of only 300 or thereabouts.

In 1870 the National Teachers Association became the National Education Association (NEA), and from this date there commenced a more rapid and significant growth of a national organization of American teachers. The secret of the progress of the National Education Association lay in its expansion through federation. Thus, very shortly after its initial launching, other organizations like the American Normal Association and the National Superintendents Association affiliated themselves with the National Education Association and became departments in it. Augmented in this manner, membership increased to 2,500 by the opening of the next century. Membership became so large, in fact, that an inner National Council was organized for the abler and more active minds in the total organization, which, it was thought, was becoming heterogeneous and unwieldy. Yet, in spite of the gratifying growth to 2,500, it must be remembered that this figure was only a very small percentage of the total number of teachers in the United States at this time.

In the nineteenth century the National Education Association grew not only in numbers but in professional prestige as well. Nothing better indicates the professional eminence it attained than the famous committees it sponsored in the last decade of the century. Its Committees of Ten and Fifteen, to mention but two, returned reports that profoundly influenced the organization and curriculum of American schools in the next century.[43] Leadership in the association never drew on more eminent men than it did during this period, for this was the time when men like Charles W. Eliot of Harvard and William Torrey Harris (1835–1909), United States Commissioner of Education, were the sort of timber from which its presidents were cut.

Excellent as was this leadership, in the opinion of many it was too much drawn from college campuses. Others thought that the school superintendents exercised too much control. Although the National Education Association had long since admitted women to its ranks, as well as private and parochial school teachers, there were still others who thought that the voice of women did not weigh heavily enough in the association's policies. Another complaint cited that meetings of the association were too much influenced by the circumstance that a preponderance of the attendance came from the vicinity of the city where it met. All these criticisms culminated in a reorganization and democratization of the National Education Association immediately following the First World War. At that time a representative assembly was set up to govern the organization, and its membership was enlarged from 10,000 to about 200,000 in the years before the next world war. By 1957, the centennial year of the founding of the association, the membership had swelled to 700,000. This was a mighty increase, but the membership still included only half of all those teaching.

Meanwhile, the reorganized National Education Association exerted itself harder than ever to provide the country with national leadership in education. It set up headquarters at the nation's capital and also organized a research division. Most significant of all, however, was its formation of the Educational Policies Commission in 1935. Aided by a generous grant from the General Education Board, the association picked a committee of its top leaders to appraise current national trends in education, plan for the future, and disseminate its thought through a series of monographs.

Another attempt to organize all ranks of teachers nationally was the National Catholic Education Association. This organization got its start in 1903 and was somewhat similar to the National Education Association in that it bound together in one organization a number of separate Catholic education societies. While the scope of its purpose was larger than that of the National Education Association in

[43] For a more extended account of these committees, see *supra,* pp. 379, 413–415.

that it included religious as well as secular education, its numbers were necessarily somewhat smaller because of the sectarian character of the Catholic religion.

From the first, the National Education Association organized American teachers on the basis of their common professional tie. In 1916 a different sort of national organization of teachers made its appearance, the American Federation of Teachers. This federation was an attempt to organize teachers along labor union lines, to organize them on the basis of their common economic interests as well as their professional ties. It was no sooner set up than it naturally affiliated with the American Federation of Labor. The larger parent organization gained no control over the policies of the teachers' union, however, and the latter did not adopt the strike as an instrument of educational policy. Starting with a membership of 2,500, the American Federation of Teachers had grown to nearly 60,000 a decade after the Second World War. In its half-century of existence it has exerted an influence far out of proportion to its numbers. On the whole, this influence has been exerted in the direction of much the same sort of improvements that the National Education Association has sought, such as better child-labor laws, pensions, and academic freedom.[44]

In the early decades of the twentieth century there was an overwhelming public sentiment that it would be unethical for teachers to strike to implement policies for which their organizations stood. One indication of this sentiment was the fact that the American Federation of Teachers, when it was founded and when it affiliated with the American Federation of Labor, did not formally adopt the strike as a weapon to enforce its views. In spite of this forbearance, however, strikes did occur with increasing frequency after the Second World War. Indeed, apologetics were even offered in their defense.[45] But state legislatures, led by New York, countered with laws outlawing strikes by public employees in all categories and providing heavy penalties, such as loss of seniority and pension rights.

Although both the National Education Association and the American Federation of Teachers courted membership from faculties of higher institutions of learning, neither had marked success. College professors showed little or no sense of "vertical" solidarity with their colleagues in elementary and secondary schools. Instead they channeled their group solidarity into a separate and independent organization, the American Association of University Professors,

[44] A. Robinson, *A Critical Evaluation of the American Federation of Teachers* (American Federation of Teachers, Chicago, 1934), chap. 2.

[45] For example, M. Lieberman, "Teachers Strikes," *Harvard Educational Review,* 26:39–70, Winter, 1956.

founded in 1915. Even as late as 1960 its membership numbered only 42,000, a small fraction of the total number engaged in college and university teaching. This was somewhat surprising since the association had been a very effective instrument in safeguarding professors in their exercise of academic freedom.

The twentieth century also witnessed the formation of a number of other national organizations of teachers, which had more limited educational purposes than the four already mentioned. Among the few that can be mentioned here, certainly the National Society for the Study of Education deserves early consideration. This society was started in 1895 as the National Herbart Society for the Scientific Study of Education. Although from the first it was not bound by Herbartian doctrines,[46] the decline in Herbartian influence soon led the organization to change its name to the National Society for the Scientific Study of Education. But even this title proved too narrow for the objectives of the society, and therefore the word "Scientific" was dropped.

In spite of this last change of title a number of the members of the society felt that its yearbooks failed to take a sufficiently forceful stand on social issues which affected education. Failing to make headway on this point within the society, these members decided in 1934 to organize a new society, the John Dewey Society. The liberal social orientation of this society's yearbooks has been as pronounced as those of the great educator after whom the society was named. But the society had no more exclusive commitments to the educational philosophy of John Dewey[47] than the National Herbart Society had to Johann Friedrich Herbart.

Last but not least to deserve mention here is the Progressive Education Association, founded in 1918. The persons who met to form this organization were joined in common protest against the formalism of the sort of education inherited from the nineteenth century rather than in any commonly accepted positive philosophy of their own. The association was bent on encouraging new variations, and its spirit was very individualistic during the first decade of its existence. So individualistic was it that the association was roundly criticized at the beginning of the Depression of 1929 for having no social orientation. In the next decade the association almost overcorrected for this shortcoming, for it found itself accused of fostering socialism and collectivism.

As the Depression dragged to a close in the beginning of the Second World War, the country seemed to become surfeited with liberal innovations whether of the New Deal or of progressive educa-

---

[46] For a more complete account of these doctrines, see *supra,* pp. 212–214, 297–298.

[47] For a fuller development of this philosophy, see *supra,* pp. 130–134.

tion. It was not long, therefore, before the Progressive Education Association became a symbol not of optimism and hope but of caricature and abuse. As a result it fell into disfavor not only with the public but with professionals as well. Variety of outlook, which had been the growing edge of educational progress since the turn of the century, now became the source of frustrating schisms. What had been magic phrases like "self-activity" and "the whole child" became shibboleths and clichés. In an endeavor to escape mounting unpopularity without sacrifice of inner spirit the society decided in 1944 to change its name to the American Education Fellowship.[48] Some thought the association's work was done and that it was time to balance its books. Others thought that it was time for the enunciation of a new program. In spite of the change the movement continued to languish. In a final effort at resuscitation the American Education Fellowship returned to the old name of Progressive Education Association, but it was too late. In 1955 the association expired.

FEMINIZATION OF TEACHING

Note has already been taken of the complaint that women entered over the disproportionate influence exerted by men in the affairs of the National Education Association. This complaint focused attention on a long-term trend in the personnel of the teaching profession. Down through the eighteenth century, teaching had been almost altogether a man's job. In just one century's time, the nineteenth, it became a preponderantly woman's vocation. Indeed, nothing bears more startling witness to the profound transformation which took place than the fact that during this century usage substituted the personal pronoun "she" for "he" in referring to the teacher.

This transformation was compounded of many factors. Women seem to have made their first entry into teaching through the old dame school as early as the seventeenth and eighteenth centuries. The dame school, however, was the steppingstone to nothing in particular—not even to marriage, as teaching later became—and it opened no enviable career of its own. At the end of the eighteenth century the infant school seemed to beckon to women as its appropriate teaching personnel. This school was at least a little more challenging than the dame school.[49] In the next century Friedrich Wilhelm August Froebel (1782–1852) still further tended to project women into teaching by emphasizing the role of mothers in education.

[48] In Europe the progressive-education movement was known as the New Education Fellowship.

[49] For further accounts of the dame and infant schools, see *supra,* pp. 366, 381.

In the nineteenth century, however, fundamental sociological factors were working in favor of drawing women into teaching. This was the century, it will be remembered, when the Western frontier was opening up and when American economic life was beginning to respond to the Industrial Revolution. Both these movements gave new emphasis to the economic worth of women. The Civil War, too, so depleted man power that new demands and responsibilities were thrown upon women. Spurred by these forces, women moved rapidly down the road toward economic emancipation. In no avenue did they find the traffic less congested than down the avenue to teaching. For long, women had been in demand to teach schools kept during the summer, when men were in demand in the fields. But during the great educational awakening of the mid-nineteenth century, educators like Horace Mann and Henry Barnard depended on women to staff the winter terms of school as well. Not only did they depend on women, but they commended them as better qualified than men to teach the young. Woman teachers, Barnard thought, surpassed men in patience and sympathy and were even possessed of a moral nature superior to that of men. And, in addition, an attractive economic fact of no little importance, women were willing to teach at salaries considerably below those of men.

The influx of women into teaching became noticeable before the Civil War. Not long after that war they became a majority of all those teaching. Reliable figures indicate that, by 1880, 57 per cent of the teaching force of the country consisted of women. On the threshold of the next century they accounted for 70 per cent, and at the conclusion of the First World War just short of 85 per cent, of the total.[50] Moreover, women were crowding men not just in the ranks of teachers but in the commanding ranks of leadership as well. Thus, in 1911 the National Education Association elected as its first woman president Ella Flagg Young, the superintendent of schools in Chicago. So far had women come to take over the profession of teaching that some people began to express anxiety that men were being crowded out. Yet the only curtailment of their numbers in the twentieth century resulted from a rather widespread opposition to married women teachers, especially during the economic Depression of the 1930s when there were not even enough positions open for men. Since that time, however, married status has ceased to be a bar to teaching. In fact during and after the Second World War the shortage of teachers was so acute that married women were actually recruited to staff the classrooms.

[50] T. Woody, "Entrance of Women into the Teaching Profession," *Educational Outlook*, 2:72–88, 138–163, January, March, 1928.

SOCIOECONOMIC STATUS OF TEACHERS

The century following the establishment of the first normal school in Massachusetts witnessed a very marked enhancement of the socioeconomic status of teachers. This is clearly indicated in a careful study of teachers' salaries for the first seventy-five years of that period.[51] During that three-quarters of a century the cost of living increased but 30 per cent while teachers' salaries rose anywhere from 150 to 450 per cent. It is safe to reason from such figures that teaching steadily mounted in this period from a relatively unattractive to a relatively preferred occupation. Furthermore, at the end of this period able men and women were much more likely to choose teaching as a career than they were formerly. Not only that, but young men and women embracing teaching as a career could much better afford extended training in preparation for it.

The complexion of the foregoing statistics appears somewhat less roseate when teachers' salaries are broken down into the salaries of men and women in urban and rural areas as compared with wages of artisans and unskilled laborers. This breakdown reveals that at the beginning of the seventy-five-year period mentioned men received distinctly better pay than women and that city teachers received better pay than rural ones. Moreover, while the salaries of urban men teachers were in a class by themselves, the salaries of rural women teachers were similar to the wages of unskilled labor and the salaries of urban woman teachers were similar to the wages of skilled artisans. The principal change in this situation in the next three-quarters of a century ending about 1915 occurred in the salaries of women teachers. These not only improved relatively to the wages of laborers and artisans but also made gains in approximating the salaries of men teachers. The lot of urban men teachers improved least in this period. In fact, although their salaries continued to treble the salaries of artisans, they were relatively little better off in 1915 than they had been at the time of the Civil War.

Down to the twentieth century, teachers' salaries not only reflected the commonly accepted prejudices that men should be paid more than women and that teachers of the higher grades should be paid more than those of the lower but also the current economic preconception that salaries were a product of the law of supply and demand. Besides, teachers were not always paid in currency. Frequently, part of the expense of having a teacher was met by having the teacher board around among his patrons. In the twentieth century, however, salaries began to be predicated on a different set of pre-

[51] W. R. Burgess, *Trends of Schools Costs* (Russell Sage Foundation, New York, 1920), chaps. 2–4.

suppositions. Salaries were drawn up according to schedules that were based not so much on the current conditions of the market as on such factors as cost of living, professional degrees, and years of experience. Increments, according to the schedules, were provided for added training and experience—in some cases for professional excellence as rated by principals and supervisors. Many new salary schedules also broke with the past by adopting the "single-salary" principle, that is, having the same schedule for upper-grade as for lower-grade teachers. Owing in part to the feminist movement and the adoption of woman suffrage, some went as far as to extend the single-salary principle to mean equal pay for men and women for the same level of work.

How did this great improvement in both the amount and the method of compensation come about? Did the appearance of the normal school with its better-trained product come first and persuade communities to pay higher and more equitable salaries? Or did the public first commence to pay salaries that justified young men and women to invest in the longer normal school training? David Perkins Page, the first principal of New York's first normal school at Albany, discussed this perennial problem in his *Theory and Practice of Teaching.*[52] He concluded that the two factors must go hand in hand. If he permitted himself to assign priority to either factor, he perhaps thought improvement in teaching had to come first.

[52] D. P. Page, *Theory and Practice of Teaching* (Hall & Dickson, Syracuse, 1847), pp. 270–274.

17

Public and Private Education

Informal education takes place inevitably in both public and private life. Formal education, because it is deliberate, takes place under either public or private auspices at the option of the parent or society. How shall this option be exercised? This is truly one of the persistent problems of education. In fact, with the growth of the modern state—whether Communistic, fascistic, or democratic—it has become one of the more insistent, even inescapable, issues of modern education.

The problem of public and private education presents itself in various forms. In its earliest form and one that still occurs occasionally, the question arises whether to educate the child at home or outside the home. Today the great majority of children are educated publicly outside the home, since few parents are well enough trained to teach at home and since still fewer are wealthy enough to hire private tutors. Hence, the current form of the issue between public and private education concerns the question: Who shall bear the expense of education outside the home? Shall it be borne by the state out of taxes paid by the parent and other taxpayers or by the parent through tuition fees supplemented, perhaps, by income from private endowments? The problem of support is further complicated by questions of ends or aims. Are there grounds of public policy, for instance, that require a monopoly of education for the state? Or are there good reasons for allowing public and private schools to compete side by side? More particularly, what are the proper educational jurisdictions of the home, the church, and the state?

EARLY DISTINCTION OF PRIVATE
FROM PUBLIC EDUCATION

The ancient Greeks were among the first to sense the significance of different answers to the foregoing questions. The educational practice of Sparta was one answer, and that of Athens a somewhat different one. In both there was a high regard for the secular city-state. In its more primitive form the Greek so identified himself with the city-state that he did not think of his own interests as being separate from those of the state. Sparta particularly clung to this folkway view of the state. The individual being submerged in the state, it is small wonder that education was a state, or public, affair. The role of the state in Spartan education commenced with a public decision on the physical fitness of the newborn infant to survive. From then on, the nearest he came to private education was the first half-dozen years of his life, which were left in the charge of his mother. Thereafter he continued his education in public barracks, where he ate, slept, and mastered the skills and attitudes required of all adult Spartans. Here he was constantly under public supervision of adults in general and of public officials, such as the ephor and the *paidonomos,* in particular till the day he became an adult himself.

Athens commenced with the same primitive notion of the city-state. But, unlike Sparta, it early evolved in the direction of recognizing that the individual had some interests apart from the state. The recognition that the individual had a private as well as a public life opened up a sphere for private education. This distinction was observed from the very outset. The decision whether the newborn infant should be allowed to grow up was left to the Athenian father for private rather than public action. Later, education beyond a civic minimum was made dependent upon the financial circumstances of each family.

Apart from practice and on grounds of principle, both Plato (427–347 B.C.) and Aristotle (384–322 B.C.) favored public rather than private education. Aristotle in particular was very explicit on this point, saying, "Since the state as a whole has a single end, it is plain that the education of all must be one and the same, and that the supervision of this education must be public and not private, as it is on the present system, under which everyone looks after his own children privately and gives them any private instruction he thinks proper. Public training is wanted in all things that are of public interest. Besides, it is wrong for any citizen to think that he belongs to himself. All must be regarded as belonging to the state: for each is a part of the state and the treatment of the part is naturally determined by that of the whole."[1]

[1] Aristotle, *Politics,* book VIII, chap. 1, in J. Burnet, *Aristotle on Education* (Cambridge University Press, London, England, 1913), p. 106.

Rome, like Athens, evolved in the direction of differentiating the individual from the state and consequently of making education the private affair of the family. In well-to-do families this led to the practice of giving a boy his whole education at home, but Quintilian (35–100), Rome's greatest schoolmaster, sharply criticized the custom. He preferred "the broad daylight of a respectable school to the solitude and obscurity of a private education." He strongly rebutted the arguments of those who feared that a boy's morals would be contaminated at school and that his education would be neglected where the master had to instruct more than one pupil at a time. Morals, he claimed, were equally or more easily corrupted at home, for "that soft upbringing, which we call kindness, saps all the sinews both of mind and body."[2] Instruction in school, he declared furthermore, was quite superior to that in the home, because at home a boy could learn only what was taught him, while at school he could learn from the correction of others as well. All of this was to say nothing of the advantage of competition with other children.

Although Quintilian opposed private education in the home, it is not to be thought that the school education which he did not favor was to be at public expense. To him the opposite of private education was education outside the seclusion, the privacy, of the home. He favored having the child educated *in* public, not necessarily *by* the public. Yet even on the matter of expense it is noteworthy that Quintilian was subsidized by a handsome stipend from the Emperor. His contemporary, Pliny, did not favor this practice. The major portion of the expense of a teacher should be borne by parents, he thought. To make it a charge upon the public treasury seemed to him the wrong policy, "for where masters are paid out of public funds, which is the case in many places, inefficiency is generally the result."[3]

WEAK STATE AND GROWING CHURCH SUPPORT OF EDUCATION

Nevertheless, in spite of this protest, the older the Empire grew, the more necessary public subsidies of education became. The vital political situation, which ordinarily prompts people to seek education voluntarily, was lacking in the latter days of the Empire.[4] With the

[2] H. E. Butler, *Quintilian, Institutes of Oratory* (G. P. Putnam's Sons, New York, 1921–1922), vol. 1, p. 43.

[3] Quoted in W. Hobhouse, *The Theory and Practice of Ancient Education* (G. E. Stechert & Company, New York, 1910), p. 41.

[4] *Supra*, pp. 29–30.

final collapse of the Empire, public subsidies disappeared. Probably formal schooling would have disappeared with them had it not been for the appearance of a new private agency in support of education, the Catholic Church. The church took a private interest in education at first not so much to cultivate learning for its own sake as to train students for lay and professional duties in the church and also for the civil ones that devolved upon it with the disintegration of political authority. Later it was the monasteries whose private interest in education managed to keep the flickering light of learning from going out altogether. In addition to the song and cathedral schools under the auspices of the church and monasteries, there also grew up in the Middle Ages many private-venture schools such as the chantries. Except for brief moments like that in which the palace school existed at the court of Charlemagne, the splintered civil state of feudalism was too busy fighting wars to show a public concern with education.

As the Middle Ages gradually became transformed into the Renaissance, education still continued almost wholly private in character. The universities, which took root in the early part of this period, were supported almost entirely out of student fees. Guild schools, where they existed, were a charge upon the guilds or the members who patronized them. And the Humanistic schools, which in the middle part of this period nourished the revived interest in the Greek and Roman classics, were naturally an expense to the middle-class families wealthy enough to pursue culture for its own sake.

Yet, with the revival of learning, there was also a revival of the notion of a public interest in education. In fact, the most famous Humanistic school in this period, that of Vittorino da Feltre (1378–1446), was conducted at the court of the Prince of Mantua in Italy. This school must have had a quasi-public character, for in addition to the sons of the nobility many poor boys attended. Sometimes there were upward of threescore whose fees and even whose board and clothes were paid for out of the bounty of the Prince or his court. The great Humanistic scholar, Desiderius Erasmus (1466–1536) declared education a public obligation in no way inferior to that of ordering an army for the common defense, but he called upon both public and private agencies—statesmen, churchmen, and wealthy private citizens—to meet the obligation. Their support, he pointed out, was particularly needed in the case of boys whose parents were in modest circumstances. As yet the line between education as a charity and as a public enterprise was indistinctly drawn.

PROTESTANT ORIGINS OF PUBLIC EDUCATION

It was in the latter part of the Renaissance, when the energies of this movement found an outlet in the Protestant Reformation, that a more pronounced step toward the public support of education was taken. In making the Bible the authoritative guide for saving oneself, Protestants contracted the obligation of learning to read. Consequently, from the heads of families to the magistrates of cities and the sovereigns of states all those responsible for souls became charged in the name of their own salvation to favor popular education.

But this was a large undertaking—certainly much larger than the private family competent to manage. Martin Luther (1483–1546), prime mover of the Reformation in Germany, acknowledged that the great majority of parents were unqualified for the task even when they were not negligent in their duties. Popular education was even more of an undertaking than could be handled by the Protestant Church, itself newly established and in a country recently ravaged by the Peasants' Revolt. The Protestant Church lacked the wealth and trained personnel to carry out such an educational program. Hence, Luther appealed to the civil authorities of Protestant principalities to exercise the fullness of their powers on behalf of establishing and maintaining schools. The public provision of education, he reasoned, was a duty to ensure the welfare and stability of both spiritual and temporal institutions.

Luther's plea did not fall on deaf ears. A number of Protestant rulers acted on the conviction that his arguments carried. As early as 1524, Magdeburg set up a system of schools that followed Luther's suggestions. Before the century was out, Saxony and Württemberg took the leadership in adopting school codes calling for a system of schools for all the people. It was not till the next century, however, that Weimar went as far as to adopt the principle of compulsory education suggested by Luther. Unfortunately, these promising developments were greatly retarded by the Thirty Years' War, which comsumed most of the first half of the seventeenth century. State systems of education, indeed, did not gain momentum again till the eighteenth century, when Prussia emerged as the leader.

The Prussian legal code of 1794 indicates better than anything else the progress state or public education had made by this time in the home of the Protestant Reformation. That code promulgated that "All schools and universities are state institutions, charged with the instruction of youth in useful information and scientific knowledge. Such institutions may be founded only with the knowledge and consent of the state." Furthermore, the code provided that "all public schools and educational institutions are under the supervision of the state, and are at all times subject to its examination and inspection."[5] From an appendage of the church at the beginning of the sixteenth century the schools had become an appendage of the state in Protestant Germany by the end of the eighteenth century. Yet, in spite of this shift in the locus of control, the Protestant Church continued in fact to exercise a very considerable influence in education, for its clergy were usually the state officials exercising local inspection or supervision. In this way the church enjoyed a sort of junior partnership in the management of the schools.

RELATIVE ROLES OF HOME AND SCHOOL

In the nineteenth century, Prussia and Germany in general went on to assume undisputed leadership in the excellence of their state school systems. Public schools became a necessity for political and nationalistic reasons as well as religious ones. In spite of these powerful and compelling influences, there was considerable discussion of the proper role of the family in education. At first the great nationalist Johann Gottlieb Fichte (1762–1814) took the view that fundamentally the obligation to educate rested on the shoulders of parents. The state could enforce this obligation but could not direct that it be fulfilled according to any particular principles or at any particular schools, the schools of the state, for instance. Later, when he lost confidence in the doctrine that every man seeks his own good, Fichte went to the extreme of advocating the elimination of parental education in favor of an exclusive education by the state.

Others were more deeply interested in the problem with which Quintilian wrestled: Should the child be educated privately at home or away from home at school? Just before the opening of the nineteenth century the famous philosopher Immanuel Kant (1724–1804) answered this question much as had Quintilian. He favored sending the boy away from home in order to escape its faults and limitations. Education at home, he feared, not only revealed the home's shortcomings but even fostered them. The positive advantage of public education away from home lay in the opportunity it afforded the child to measure his powers against those of his fellows. Moreover, Kant believed that habits of citizenship were cultivated by the child's learning the limitations which the rights of his schoolmates imposed upon him.

Johann Friedrich Herbart (1776–1841), who succeeded Kant in

[5] Quoted in F. P. Graves, *A History of Education* (The Macmillan Company, New York, 1913), vol. 3, p. 284.

the chair of philosophy at Königsberg, took an opposite view. He perceived advantages in continuing education within the environment of the home. Within its private precincts the opportunity to individualize education was much greater, he thought. To be in charge of fewer children would enable the tutor to apply Herbart's doctrine of apperception more effectively. It would be difficult at best to teach the new in terms of the old—the doctrine of apperception—where, as at school, there were many children, with consequent diversity of background.[6]

The great reformer of childhood education, Johann Heinrich Pestalozzi (1746–1827), whom Fichte admired greatly, took a more compromising position. Being concerned with the education of small children, he gave considerable attention to the preschool education of the home. It was there in domestic activities and in parental feelings and attitudes that the child's first lessons were learned. Yet Pestalozzi realized very well that the best home had its limitations. Few parents had either the time or the resources to provide the child with all the opportunities that he should have—hence the need for school. But the role of the school, public or private, should be to supplement and reinforce the character and vocational education already going on there. It should continue to expand powers already under development.

The point of view of Georg Wilhelm Friedrich Hegel (1770–1831), virtually the court philosopher of the Prussian state, tended to coincide with that of Pestalozzi. Hegel, of course, couched his reasons in the terms of the idealistic philosophy for which he was famous. In the circle of the family, he conceded there might be room to cultivate the idiosyncracies of a child's individuality. But, unlike Herbart, he cautioned against placing too high a value on individuality. The teacher in school had no time for this. In school a new life begins for the child. There his mind must be brought to relinquish its peculiarities and to make its own what is common knowledge. It must seek the law and order of universal reason. In fact, Hegal thought no education worth the name unless it brought about this transformation of the mind.

Even within the family circle Hegel would not permit the parent to have the exclusive decision with regard to the education of his child. The state had a twofold interest in his education as well. On the one hand, the state might have to supervise the child's education in his own interests. Should his parents be too poor or too negligent, it would have to step in to ensure that he received the right sort of education. On the other hand, the state had an interest of its

[6] For the psychological doctrine of apperception see *supra,* pp. 145–148, and for its methodological application, see *supra,* pp. 212–214.

own in supervising the education of the child, this interest being the future recruitment of trained personnel to carry on the functions of government.[7]

THE FRENCH REVOLUTION AND PUBLIC EDUCATION

In France, it was the French Revolution rather than the Protestant Reformation that first raised the issue of private and public education in acute form. For some, like Claude Adrien Helvétius (1715–1771), the issue was not particularly novel. Helvétius stated it in the terms that Quintilian had employed. Like the great Roman, he favored public education, that is, education away from home. He came to this conclusion for much the same reasons that Quintilian had although he did adduce several further arguments. Chief among these was his conviction that teachers at school would know more about problems of instruction than would parents at home.

The French Revolution, however, was to promote public education in the more advanced form of state-supported education. The Protestant Reformation had solicited state support of education for both religious and secular ends; the French Revolution was to advocate a state system of schools on exclusively civil grounds. Rumblings of such doctrine were heard as early as the times of François de la Mothe-Fénelon (1651–1715). This great cleric, stylist, and educator claimed that "Children belong less to their parents than to the Republic, and ought to be educated by the state. There should be established public schools in which are taught the fear of God, love of country, and respect for the laws."[8]

By the time the French Revolution broke out, the novel preachment of Fénelon had become commonplace among writers on education. Nearly all followed Louis René de La Chalotais (1701–1785) in his *Essay on National Education* and recommended a state system of schools. More important, the constitution of 1791 made provision for education in the following terms: "There shall be created and organized a system of public instruction common to all the citizens and gratuitous in respect to those subjects of instruction that are indispensable to all men." Charles Maurice de Talleyrand at once proposed to the National Assembly an enabling act to give effect to this constitutional provision. This act would have made education definitely a function of the state and not of the church, but nothing

[7] For a further account of the home as an educational agency, see *supra,* pp. 346–354.

[8] Quoted in G. Compayré, *History of Pedagogy* (D. C. Heath and Company, Boston, 1885), p. 182.

came of it. The assembly dissolved before it had time to consider Talleyrand's bill.

In the days that followed, two oppositely radical proposals were made regarding the role of the state in education. The first was made by the Marquis de Condorcet (1743–1794) just before his death. In harmony with other radicals, he outlined a scheme of educational institutions to be set up and maintained by the state. But at the same time he prophesied that the time would come when the public establishment of instruction would become useless if not dangerous. Such a time would obtain when education was so widely diffused that men would find in their own education a weapon keen enough to repulse all charlatanry and expose all selfish exploitation. Of course, Condorcet conceded that such a utopian anarchy was still somewhat distant. Thus, while his immediate program called for education through the agency of the state, his long-range program hoped to dispense with it.

At the opposite extreme from this anarchistic proposal was a bill, which had the backing of Maximilien de Robespierre, to give the state complete control over education. According to this proposal children were to be educated at public expense in public boarding schools. Here the state would be responsible for food and clothing as well as instruction. Moreover, parents would not even have the option to educate their children privately; the state was to be the exclusive educator.

Neither of these radical proposals was enacted into law. Although both had some support in revolutionary circles, neither had enough to gain general assent. Surprisingly enough, the upshot of all these proposals was the enactment of a law that was more conservative than even Talleyrand's modest bill. The only gesture this final enactment made toward a state-supported system of schools was the remission of fees for indigent students. The private support of schools was too deeply entrenched to be easily overthrown by the imaginative proposals of revolutionary thought. Yet, if little progress was achieved in fact, much was gained in directing thought in new channels. It remained for the nineteenth century to translate revolutionary thought into concrete legislation. This legislation came in installments, most important of which were those from Napoleon, the July Monarchy, and the Third Republic.

PRIVATE EDUCATION AND *LAISSEZ FAIRE* IN ENGLAND

England was much slower than Prussia or France to move in the direction of public support of education. In fact, while those countries were exploring a state theory of education, England was giving classic form to the theory of noninterference by the state in education. To commence again with the question raised by Quintilian—whether to educate one's son at home or away at school—it is interesting to note that John Locke (1632–1704) came to the opposite conclusion from that of Quintilian. Unlike him and a long line of succeeding writers on education, Locke preferred that a young man be educated at home rather than away at school. It is there under the watchful eye of the father, he felt, that moral education can best be supervised. Locke appreciated that there was danger of developing shyness at home and that a certain sturdiness was developed in association with other boys away at school. He even conceded that the master at school might give better instruction in the boy's studies. Yet the master would not have the time the father would to give a constant surveillance to the lad's morals. Locke feared nothing more than the consequences of virtue once lost and the exceedingly great difficulty of recovering and rehabilitating it.

Perhaps Locke's point of view was but a protest against the schools of his time. His proposed method certainly could have been effective only in the relatively few families of the well to do. In spite of his protest, most boys of the wealthy were still educated publicly, that is, away from home and at school. If possible, no doubt, they attended one of the great English public schools like Eton, Harrow, or Westminster. But the word "public" applied to these schools merely meant that education was given there "in" public and "to" the public. It did not mean that education was provided "by" the public or "at" public expense. In America such schools are known as "private" schools.

In other words, the dominant English educational tradition favored private education. It was up to the family to decide whether to educate its children privately at home or away from home at a private school. Indeed, the family did not have to provide any education whatever if it did not want to. Certainly, in the old English common law the child had no remedy against his parents if they failed to give him schooling. He could compel them to provide him only with necessities. The common law recognized food, shelter, and clothing as necessities, but not education. The only compensation provided by the state to fill this void was to be found in the education incidental to compulsory apprenticeship permitted by the poor law of 1601.

In Puritan England of the seventeenth century there was some demand that the state assert itself in educational matters, a demand that was actually realized by the Puritans who emigrated to form the New England colonies of America. But with the passing of Oliver Cromwell and the Commonwealth, the demand lost its energy in old England. In fact, with the Church of England party back in control of the state, the Nonconforming sects now exerted pressure in the opposite direction and against state control of education. Naturally, they were suspicious of any state control of education where the state was under obligations to an established church. Hence Joseph Priestley, a Nonconformist of the next century, stated in his *First Principles of Government* that in the interest of freedom it was better not to have the state take a hand in education.

Later, toward the end of the eighteenth century and the beginning of the nineteenth, private education free from government interference received further elaboration and support on grounds of political theory. This was the period of transition from mercantilism to liberalism in English political economy. Under mercantilism a considerable amount of governmental regulation was customary to divert economic production and distribution into channels from which payments in precious metals would flow into the regulating government's treasury. The American colonies, it will be remembered, were victims of this artificial regulation of trade. The classic critique of mercantilist theory and practice is to be found in *The Wealth of Nations* published during this period. There the author, Adam Smith (1723–1790), made a plea for permitting trade and commerce to take the natural course that the self-interest of producers and consumers dictated. Independent individuals should be free to contract what relations with each other they found to their advantage. Furthermore, government was to derive its authority from contract, too. By resting government on compact and by restricting its sphere of action to the police powers necessary to preserve peace and to provide courts for the enforcement of contracts, a large residue of freedom was reserved for the individual. The freedom so secured became the basis for nineteenth-century liberalism and the famous theory of *laissez faire*.

Obviously, the argument for liberalism and *laissez faire* had a fertile field in education. There, together with religious reasons already mentioned, it was applied to make the English tradition of private education seem both just and reasonable. Thus, the initiative in providing education, like that in making a commercial contract, should wait till self-interest stimulated it. Both were subjects of free enterprise. Indeed, the middle class raised up by the Industrial Revolution feared the paralysis of individual enterprise, to say nothing of the destruction of the incentive to self-help, if the government were to provide schools. That many lower-class people were too poor or too ignorant to take the initiative to helping themselves did not disturb the English middle and upper classes. Consequently, the only education from which the lower classes benefited during this period was what private philanthropy—motivated by self-interest, of course—found to its advantage to provide for them.

Although the foregoing seems the logical implication of *laissez faire* for education, oddly enough Adam Smith himself seems to have lukewarmly favored a modest degree of public education. He conceived that the government might not only encourage but require all to gain the rudiments of an education. The expense to the lower classes would be but nominal since the schoolmaster would be "partially but not wholly, paid by the public; because, if he was wholly, or even principally paid by it, he would soon learn to neglect his business."[9]

The archdefender of the doctrine of *laissez faire* toward education was Herbert Spencer (1820–1903), Smith's fellow countryman. He seems to have attached almost scientific validity to the doctrine. In his *Social Statics* published in 1851, he contended that each man had a general liberty to exercise his faculties compatible with a similar liberty in others. This is the fundamental principle of equal liberty, which it is the duty and the only duty of the government to protect. If the state takes a man's property to educate his own or another's children, this is infringing on rather than protecting his general liberty in the use of his property. To this it might be returned that the state is justified in curtailing a man's general liberty in the use of his property in order to protect the general liberty of children, which, without education, might become impaired. Spencer's rebuttal here pointed out that failure to provide children with schooling was not an infringement of their previous general liberty. It diminished no liberty they already had. "Omitting instruction," he wrote, "in no way takes from a child's freedom to do whatsoever it wills in the best way it can; and this freedom is all that equity demands."[10]

The scope of a Socialist state designed to serve the public welfare extended farther than Spencer's limited vision could see. Indeed, it alarmed him into adding, "For if the benefit, importance, or necessity of education be assigned as a sufficient reason why government should educate, then may the benefit, importance, or necessity, of food, clothing, shelter, and warmth be assigned as a sufficient reason why government should administer these also. So that the alleged right cannot be established without annulling all parental responsibility whatever."[11]

Religious anxieties and devotion to *laissez faire* prevented a public education act in England till 1833 and even then led to public subsidy of existing private agencies. Not till the Forster Act of 1870 was

[9] A. Smith, *The Wealth of Nations* (Clarendon Press, Oxford, 1869), vol. 2, pp. 368–369. See also C. F. Arrowood, *Theory of Education in the Political Philosophy of Adam Smith* (published by the author, 1945).

[10] H. Spencer, *Social Statics* (D. Appleton & Company, Inc., New York, 1882), p. 361.

[11] *Ibid.*, p. 362.

a system of schools, supported by the state but provided and maintained by the locality, put on a stable basis. Thereafter public and private schools existed side by side. The policy underlying this practice is nowhere better stated than by John Stuart Mill (1806–1873) in his well-known essay *On Liberty*. There he declared, "That the whole or any large part of the education of the people should be in state hands, I go as far as anyone in deprecating. All that has been said of the importance of individuality of character, and diversity in opinions and modes of conduct, involves, as of the same unspeakable importance, diversity of education. A general state education is a mere contrivance for molding people to be exactly like one another; and as the mold in which it cases them is that which pleases the predominant power in the government, whether this be a monarch, a priesthood, an aristocracy, or the majority of the existing generation, in proportion as it is efficient and successful, it establishes a despotism over the mind, leading by natural tendency to one over the body. An education established and controlled by the state, should only exist, if it exist at all, as one among many competing experiments, carried on for the purpose of example and stimulus, to keep the others up to a certain standard of excellence."[12]

COLONIAL PRECEDENTS FOR A PUBLIC SYSTEM OF SCHOOLS

Parts of all three of the foregoing traditions—German, French, and English—have entered into the American evolution from private to public schools. In the colonial period, the predominant form of education was moral and vocational, administered through apprenticeship laws copied from the English. More formal education there was, too, but its importance and auspices varied widely in the different colonies. In the Southern colonies the English tradition of private education prevailed. This is well illustrated by Governor Sir William Berkeley's reply to an inquiry by his home government on what was being done for the education of children in Virginia. His oft-quoted reply was, "The same course that is taken in England out of towns; every man according to his ability instructing his children. . . . But, I thank God, *there are no free schools* nor *printing,* and I hope we shall not have them these hundred years, for *learning* has brought disobedience and heresy and sects into the world, and *printing* has divulged them and libels against the best government. God keep us from them both."[13]

[12] J. S. Mill, *On Liberty* (J. W. Parker & Son, London, 1859), pp. 190–191.
[13] W. W. Hening, *Laws of Virginia* (Samuel Pleasants, Richmond, Va., 1810), vol. 2, p. 517.

In the Middle colonies education other than apprenticeship was also predominantly private. There schools were adjuncts of the churches. Some sects maintained parochial school systems. In any event, the great diversity of sects in this area tended to delay the day of public schools. The only school the Middle colonies maintained at public expense was the pauper school. Here the state defrayed the educational expenses of those children whose parents did not have enough money to pay for their education privately and yet had too much pride to take the pauper's oath.

The principal early progress toward a public system of schools was made in the Northern, or New England, colonies. There Massachusetts took the lead with its notable enactments of 1642 and 1647. The first of these laws owed its inspiration to the English poor law. It charged the selectmen with the duty of ascertaining whether parents and masters were training their children in labor and other useful employments. If not, they were given authority to put the children out as apprentices. The law went significantly beyond the prototype of the mother country in also charging the selectmen with inquiring as to the ability of children to read well enough to understand the principles of religion and the capital laws of the colony.

The latter charge shows American indebtedness to the Protestant tradition in education, especially as it came down through John Calvin and the English Puritans. The joint interest of church and state in education was further expanded in the law of 1647. According to this legislation, towns of a certain size were to appoint a teacher to conduct school, and larger towns were to set up schools of an advanced character. It was left optional with each town whether to meet the expenses by taxation or to prorate them among the parents patronizing the school.

It would be a mistake to identify the educational provisions of these two laws with the public school system that took form in the nineteenth century. Yet it would be an equally grave mistake not to realize how this advanced legislation of the seventeenth century foreshadowed the future. Involved in these two laws were precedents and principles that were invoked again and again in American educational history.[14] First one should note that the obligation to provide education was put primarily on the shoulders of the parent. This much is clear and explicit in the law of 1642, nor did the law of 1647 shift this burden. The law of 1647 merely provided a place where the parent, his hands full with pressing back the frontier and fighting Indians, might discharge the obligation of educating his chil-

---

[14] G. Martin, *Evolution of the Massachusetts Public School System* (D. Appleton-Century Company, Inc., New York, 1902), pp. 14–15.

dren without being relieved of it. But, second, it should be noted that these laws recognized education as a vital public concern. They recognized education as essential to the well-being of the state and therefore that the state had an interest in enforcing the parent's obligation to educate his child. Moreover, they indicate that the state could determine the kind and minimum amount of education that its wards should have.

These were bold principles for the seventeenth century. Yet it is unlikely that the colonists fully appreciated their scope. Thus, in spite of vesting education with a public interest, it is notable that they made but a very faltering step toward the public support of education. Education might be important for the commonweal, but reliance was put on private initiative to secure it. Even where taxes were levied, the rate bill was usually a large item in financing the schools required by law. Under the rate bill the expenses of the school in whole or in part were prorated among patrons according to the number of children sent or the kind of curriculum pursued. Since so much of school costs was borne directly by patrons, it is not surprising that many parents patronized private-venture schools. At all times there seem to have been a considerable number of these in competition with the public schools.

The prominence of private initiative was not the only check to the growth and elaboration of the public school idea. After making a good start under the laws of 1642 and 1647, there was a lamentable decline in town or public schools before the seventeenth century was out. This was due in part to frontier conditions. The movement of population toward the frontier put great stress on the unified town control of schools. Ultimately, this control had to be decentralized and lodged in the districts of the town. As districts were small and frequently lacking in leadership, the public control of schools sank to a very low ebb.

In part, again, the decline of the public school idea was due to a decline in religious fervor. Indeed, the public school was animated not so much by a political ideal as by a religious one. To be sure, the laws of 1642 and 1647 were acts of the secular state; yet the state was largely the agent of the Puritan churches. And even though the law of 1642 expressed anxiety over children's knowledge of both the principles of religion and the capital laws of the colony, the main anxiety, as stated in the law of 1647, was "ye olde deluder Satan." Naturally, therefore, when the early religious zeal became tempered, there was a noticeable decline of interest in the public school it had sired.

In the eighteenth century the schools that prospered were the private ones, especially the line of academies that commenced with Phillips

Andover Academy. Much of this success was due to the private schools' more flexible curriculum. Dependent on patrons' fees, private schools were naturally more responsive to changing social demands.

IMPACT OF FRENCH AND ENGLISH LIBERALISM

Nevertheless, toward the end of the eighteenth century, writers began to explore the question of public education from a new angle. They were stimulated to do so by contemporary French liberalism, which was congenial to the revolutionary thought of both France and America. In contrast to the Puritan period the trend of this thought was almost wholly secular. To the state was assigned the duty of improving man's lot, for which the revolutionary period had raised such high hopes. Much of the expectation for achieving this end in France, as has already been noted, was pinned on a system of public schools. The same influence was early at work in America.

Shortly after the American Revolution and the setting up of the Federal frame of government, the American Philosophical Society offered a prize for the best essay on a system of education suited to the genius of the new political system. Both the winner of this contest, Samuel Knox (1756–1832), and the runner-up, Samuel Smith (1750–1819), proposed that the system should be a public one. Both strongly opposed private education. In his essay Smith showed familiarity with Quintilian's criticism of private education at home. After rehearsing the criticisms of the famous Roman, he went on to make one point of his own. Public education, he claimed, was the best means of freeing a child from prejudice; for prejudices are like hereditary titles, and error is never more dangerous than in the mouth of a parent.

To Smith's criticism of private education at home, Knox added a number of objections to education at private schools. First, he opposed private schools on democratic grounds. They did not, he pointed out, offer equal opportunity, which was the greater pity since talent was by no means a monopoly of those of means. Private schools he further held undemocratic since they tended to isolate their patrons from the rest of the community and thus set up double standards. In contrast he much preferred the public school, where friendships might cut across class lines. Again, it was a mistake in a democracy, he thought, to make education the concern of the few rather than of the many. Second, he opposed private schools on nationalistic grounds. He disliked their tendency to divide rather than unite the youthful nation. On this last point Knox received reinforcement from Robert Coram, one of the unsuccessful contestants. He too favored the social solidarity promoted by the public school since every citizen must suffer more or less for the failure of anyone to meet his social obligations.

To proceed from essays to concrete legislation, the most significant proposal was that made by Thomas Jefferson (1743–1826) for a public system of schools in Virginia.[15] Like the Frenchmen with whose writings he was so familiar, Jefferson advocated for his native state a public school system that was divorced from ecclesiastical control and that was universal and free at the elementary level. In only one respect did his recommendations differ from theirs. While they had proposed a national system of schools, he drew up his own law so as to lodge control of the schools in the local authorities. Yet, in spite of Jefferson's political stature and personal prestige, he was never quite able during a long life to carry the Virginia Legislature with him.

Apparently the time for such plans was no more ripe in late-eighteenth-century America than it was in the corresponding period in France. Indeed, it was English rather than French liberalism that in fact gripped American educational practice at this time. It was the doctrine of a laissez-faire liberalism learned from Adam Smith and later from Herbert Spencer that governed the actual provision of educational opportunity. The state held aloof, waiting for the self-interest of parents, churches, and philanthropic-minded agencies and persons to provide such education as they might. Only when paupers were to be educated or the rate bills of indigent children were to be defrayed did the state step in with a niggardly contribution.

GROWING DEMAND FOR PUBLIC EDUCATION IN AMERICA

Yet, in the very heyday of laissez-faire liberalism there was an insistently growing demand that the state take positive action in support of wider educational opportunities. At first, American states met this pressure with a variety of halfway measures. In some cases, the state went halfway toward a public school system by subsidizing private schools and philanthropically supported school societies. In other cases, it went halfway toward a tax-supported school system by allotting to the schools the revenues derived from excises, lotteries, and the sale of public lands. In yet other cases, it went so far as to pass permissive legislation so that local agencies could voluntarily tax themselves for schools if they wished.

But to go the whole way and establish free schools through the abolition of tuition fees and through levying a tax for schools con-

[15] C. F. Arrowood, *Thomas Jefferson and Education in a Republic* (McGraw-Hill Book Company, New York, 1930), chaps. 2, 7.

stituted a final barrier that proved most difficult to overcome. The transition from the liberal or laissez-faire theory of the state to a more welfare-oriented or Socialistic theory required a long period of public discussion. People habituated to thinking that government best which governed least could not easily and quickly accustom themselves to a government whose mark of merit was expanding services. Was free public education an unwarranted interference with liberty, or was it an indispensable ladder to bring democratic freedom within reach? This was the crucial educational issue of mid-nineteenth-century America.

Before examining the arguments pro and con, it may be well to take account of the pressures that were at work. The period was one in which the general cause of the common man was in the ascendant. There was a romantic, optimistic belief abroad that man was capable of indefinite perfectibility. All that he needed was to assume control over the form and functioning of his social institutions in order to provide the requisite opportunities. Thus the demand for public education was but part of a larger humanitarian movement to modify unsatisfactory institutions, including prisons and slavery. The general optimism was further heightened by unlimited economic opportunities on the frontier. In politics the trend of the times was reflected in an assumption of control of the national government by the common man, who ushered himself into office by electing Andrew Jackson president.

In looking more closely at the alignment of forces that was forming over the public school issue, it will be seen that the proponents of public schools were drawn from two classes. Leadership was drawn from the old middle-class families that had gained political and economic eminence during the commercial revolution of the Renaissance. Although their rule was giving way now to the rising industrial capitalist class, they still retained sufficient wealth to maintain them in their philanthropic and humanitarian interests. Accustomed to the more intimate relation of master and apprentice, they found their ideals antagonistic to those of industrial employers, who treated their employees more impersonally. It should not be surprising, therefore, that the old middle class made an alliance with the aggressive industrial working classes of the cities. The leadership of the one class together with the votes of the other certainly presented a very formidable pressure group.

The chief opposition to public schools was found in the rural areas. The increased demand for education, aroused by the Industrial Revolution, had not arisen as yet in rural communities. Besides, the farmer anticipated the burden of a school tax with apprehension since he was more likely to pay a direct property tax than the industrial city dweller. No doubt, there were other classes of taxpayers with a similar anxiety. Not an inconsiderable opposition was also formed by church groups that already supported parochial schools of their own. Naturally, these were joined by a small number of proprietors of private schools whose livelihood was threatened by the competition of public enterprise.

From the foregoing it would be easy to draw the false conclusion that the battle lines were drawn distinctly and exclusively. As a matter of fact, there was considerable confusion. Thus, it would probably be a mistake to think that all the industrial working classes were equally ambitious for educational opportunities. Closer to the truth would be the fact that the demand for public education was probably least in evidence among the working classes most in need of it. The movement for public schools was far from a proletarian uprising. Similarly, it would be an error to regard all members of the commercial middle class as uniformly in favor of public schools. In fact, there were a number who distinctly were not. So, too, it would be a mistake to class all industrial capitalists as opposed to public schools. Some of them frankly supported the cause for the protection it afforded property against social unrest.

The clash of argument between these forces covered a wide area. It was sharpest over the anticipated effect free tax-supported schools would have on the institution of private property. There were many, for instance, who thought that a tax for schools was an unwarranted interference with the individual's right to dispose of his property as he wished. It was unjust, they thought, that those with property and few or no children should have their property taxed to educate the children of others less well to do. In the rural idiom of the day, it was no more just to do this than it was to seize one man's plow to plow another man's field. In fact, there was even fear that such a practice might place a penalty on thrift and give encouragement to indolence.

There were others who thought that the proposed public schools were an unwarranted infringment on property rights already vested in private schools. Capital and forethought having gone to build up such institutions, it was claimed that the government had no business to set up schools which would compete with them and undermine their value and effectiveness. It even seemed to many that a public system of schools was directly or indirectly an unjustified interference between parent and child.

Of course, the protectors of private property were not unaware that all taxes constitute some invasion of property rights. More precisely stated, therefore, their position was that they were willing to be taxed for the preservation of their liberties but not for the support of benevolences. Echoing the past, they still counted education a luxury rather than a necessity. Education was for those with leisure; the poor had no leisure. Hence, public schools could only educate them beyond their social position for desires they would have no means to fulfill and thus for an unhappiness they would be powerless to avoid.

Still others were alarmed because they professed to see the specter of socialism as the basic principle immanent in the public school. This accurate surmise of what was taking place was not appreciated as a danger by the mid-nineteenth-century generation as it was by the generation at the end of the century. The latter raised the cry of socialism when it was proposed to make textbooks and high schools free and tax-supported as well as common or elementary schools.[16] The word "socialism" was enough of a bogey at the turn of the century to demand some explanation. A historian of the period, writing the history of the Massachusetts public school system, felt called upon to point out that the implications of the Massachusetts laws of 1642 and 1647 were "neither paternal or socialistic." "The child is to be educated," he argued, "not to advance his personal interests, but because the state will suffer if he is not educated."[17] This feeble distinction, however, hardly saved either the seventeenth- or the nineteenth-century movements from being Socialistic.

None advocated more clearly or more forcefully than Horace Mann (1796–1859), secretary of the Massachusetts State Board of Education, that property rights were not exclusively individual and private but social and public as well. Property, he claimed, was given by the Creator to all men, not to just a few or to any single generation. Hence each man in his generation was trustee of his property for the next generation. Consequently, mindful of this trust, man could not do with his property exclusively as he wished. One way of transferring this trust to the next generation was through taxes paid in the present for the education of the oncoming generation.[18] From this analysis followed the oft-repeated cliché that the wealth of the state must educate the children of the state.

Even a man of more conservative mold like Daniel Webster held that property was vested with a public interest on behalf of education. He voiced the New England tradition when he declared, "For the purpose of public instruction, we hold every man subject to taxation in proportion to his property, and we look not to the question, whether

---

[16] J. P. Munroe, "Certain Dangerous Tendencies in Education," *Educational Review,* 3:145–155, February, 1892.

[17] Martin, *op. cit.,* p. 16.

[18] *Tenth Annual Report to the Massachusetts State Board of Education,* 1846.

he himself have, or have not, children to be benefited by the education for which he pays. We regard it as a wise and liberal system of police, by which property, and life, and the peace of society are secured."[19]

This concluding remark of Webster's was often elaborated in popular form. Enlightened self-interest was implored to see that property rights would be enhanced rather than curtailed by free tax-supported schools for all. Specifically, the argument was that education would make children more productive and thrifty adults. If this proved the case, there would necessarily be a reduction in the amount of poverty and with a reduction in poverty would follow a reduction in crime. Such a chain of events not only would make the rights in property more secure and enjoyable but would also diminish the necessary public outlay for poorhouses and jails.

On more elevated grounds again, as was his wont, Mann even made the bold claim that public education for all might be expected to mediate the conflict between capital and labor. With great earnestness he stated that "Surely nothing but universal education can counterwork this tendency to the domination of capital and the servility of labor. . . . Education, then, beyond all other devices of human origin, is the great equalizer of the conditions of men—the balance wheel of the social machinery. . . . It gives each man the independence and the means by which he can resist the selfishness of other men. It does better than to disarm the poor of their hostility toward the rich: it prevents being poor."[20]

This theme of Mann's was also a popular political argument for public schools. It reminded one of the democratic equalitarianism of the French Revolution.[21] How could a democratic government achieve equalitarianism and thus preserve its own character unless it could mold youth in schools of its own design? The situation was the more urgent since existing schools were insufficient in number and often undemocratic in form. The pauper school was an excellent case in point. Intended for the poor, the poor frequently failed to attend it as they were often too proud to declare themselves paupers. Thus the school defeated its own end.

But worse yet, as already mentioned, public education was objected to because its benefits would be shared equally by the children of the profligate and the children of the industrious. Addressing himself

[19] *The Works of Daniel Webster* (Little, Brown and Company, Boston, 1885), vol. 1, pp. 41–42.

[20] M. Mann, *Life and Works of Horace Mann* (Horace B. Fuller, Boston, 1868), vol. 3, pp. 668–669.

[21] For a fuller account of democratic equalitarianism in education, see *supra*, pp. 43–45, 47–48.

to this objection in one of the proudest oratorical efforts of his career, the great statesman Thaddeus Stevens (1792–1868) told the Pennsylvania Legislature, "It ought to be remembered that the benefit [of public education] is bestowed, not upon the erring parents, but the innocent children. Carry out this objection and you punish children for the crimes or misfortunes of their parents. You virtually establish cases and grades founded on no merit of the particular generation, but on the demerits of their ancestors; an aristocracy of the most odious and insolent kind—the aristocracy of wealth and pride."[22]

Could such a distinction between children and their parents be the sort of unwarranted interference in the family relationship complained of by the opponents of public schools? It hardly seems so. By the same token it seems historically inaccurate to accuse the public school of trying to supplant the home. Henry Barnard (1811–1900), Connecticut's great educator, effectively refuted that notion. He admitted at once that the family circle and the mother were unquestionably the first and best school and teacher for young children. If every mother had had the leisure and training to superintend the early education of her children, Barnard would have been in no hurry to urge their attendance at public school. But, whatever the fortunate circumstances of a few homes and a few mothers, he was only too painfully aware that the great majority of homes were not so happily circumstanced. Many mothers lacked training, and most of those who had it lacked the leisure to employ it effectively. In view of these conditions Barnard recommended attendance at public school, not to supplant the home but to supplement it.[23]

Casting aside the practical arguments considered so far, Mann rested the philosophic argument for public schools on the natural rights of man so popular during the French and American Revolutions. "I believe," he proclaimed, "in the existence of a great, immortal, immutable principle of natural law, or natural ethics—a principle antecedent to all human institutions, and incapable of being abrogated by any ordinance of man—a principle of divine origin, clearly legible in the ways of Providence as these ways are manifested in the order of nature and in the history of the race, which proves the *absolute right* to an education of every human being that comes into the world; and which, of course, proves the correlative duty of every government to see that the means of that education are provided for all."[24]

[22] T. Stevens, "A Plea for Public Schools," *Report of the United States Commissioner of Education, 1898–1899,* vol. 1, p. 520.

[23] J. S. Brubacher (ed.), *Henry Barnard on Education* (McGraw-Hill Book Company, 1931), pp. 252–253.

[24] Mann, *op. cit.,* pp. 533–534.

In the end the arguments favoring a free public school system won. It was largely the urban industrial vote that carried the day. By the end of the Civil War the victory for free tax-supported schools was virtually complete. By that time the last rate bill had been abolished, and pauper schools were things of the past. In fact, progress was already well under way not only to make the schools free but to make textbooks free as well. In the twentieth century, free medical examinations and free transportation to and from school were further charged to taxes. The 100 years preceding the Second World War had witnessed a profound change in political philosophy. At the beginning of this period the state had limited itself to being the arbiter in the conflicting interests of its citizens and the protector of their lives and property. By the end of the period, it had expanded into a social welfare agency actively reaching out for the physical, moral, and intellectual improvement of its citizens.

COMPULSORY ATTENDANCE

In spite of the obvious requirements that industrialism and nationalism as well as political democracy made on the education of the masses in the nineteenth century, many children were failing to get the schooling necessary to meet these requirements. In considerable though diminished degree this failure continued even after the battle for free tax-supported common schools had been won in this country. Consequently, a move was set on foot to compel all children to attend school. The idea of compulsory attendance was not new.[25] On the secular side its parentage reached back to English apprenticeship practices originating in the sixteenth century and on the religious side to German precedents of the Protestant Reformation in the same century. The English of the sixteenth century, becoming alarmed by the growing vagabondage of the time, commenced the enactment of a series of laws that made apprenticeship education compulsory for those who might otherwise become vagrants. In the same century a few German principalities also arrived at compulsory-attendance legislation, but by the route of religion. The Protestant Reformation, coming in this century, so emphasized personal reading of the Bible that literacy almost became a prerequisite to salvation. Therefore, the German princes who felt responsibility for the literacy and hence the salvation of their subjects made education compulsory.

Martin Luther, the great inspirer of the Protestant Reformation in Germany, put the whole case for compulsory education very well

[25] J. W. Perrin, "Beginnings of Compulsory Attendance," *Educational Record*, 25:240–248, March, 1903.

in a letter to a German prince, the Elector John of Saxony. "Where there are towns, and villages which have the ability," Luther wrote, "your electoral grace has the power to compel them to maintain schools, pulpits, and parishes. If they will not do it from a consideration for their salvation, then your electoral grace, as highest guardian of the youth and of all others needing supervision, is to compel them to do so, just as they are compelled to render contributions and services toward bridges, paths, and roads, or other matters pertaining to the public interest. . . . If the government can compel such citizens as are fit for military service to bear spear and rifle, to mount ramparts and perform other martial duties in time of war; how much more has it a right to compel the people to send their children to school, because in this case we are warring with the devil."[26]

In the United States, Massachusetts pioneered in compelling attendance during the elementary school period. What made legislation urgent then was the confusion into which the Industrial Revolution threw long-standing provisions for apprenticeship education. Again it was Massachusetts that pioneered, commencing by enacting a child-labor law that made it illegal to employ a child under fifteen years of age unless he had attended an approved school for at least three months in the year preceding his employment. Sixteen years later, in 1852, Massachusetts followed this legislation with the first modern compulsory-attendance statute. In this it provided that all children between eight and fourteen years of age must attend school at least twelve weeks in the year, six of which must be consecutive. This law, unlike the one it succeeded, carried penalties for infraction.

Many improvements were made in this basic legislation in the next seventy-five years. Age limits were extended, and the school term was lengthened. Compulsory-attendance laws were coordinated with child-labor laws. The school census was tightened, and stricter measures of enforcement were taken. But in spite of these improvements the principle on which enforcement rested remained the same as the initial legislation of 1642. The principle in this early law, as well as in those which followed later in other states, was that the law must be enforced against the parent and not the child. The duty to educate his child rested as squarely on the parent's shoulders in the nineteenth and twentieth centuries as it did in the seventeenth. Hence, once a truant is reported, the modern truant officer goes at once not to the swimming hole or the ball park but to the child's home. Indeed, so important is the parent at this late date that, if he wishes, he may still educate his child at home rather than at

[26] F. V. N. Painter, *Luther on Education* (Lutheran Publication Society, Philadelphia, 1889), pp. 136–138.

school if the state thinks his particular home meets the minimum requirements of a school.

But, by the same token, the chief difficulty in enforcing the law was in the same place, the home. The chief obstacle to enforcement was the neglectful parent. Particularly negligent in sending their children to the common, or elementary, school were the parents of poorer classes who had urgent need of the earnings of their children to sustain their families. Not all opposition, however, grew out of penury. Some took exception to the principle of compulsion. Compulsory education, it was claimed, was monarchical in origin and therefore contrary to the exercise of free institutions. This sort of opposition high-lighted another interesting angle to this legislation. The people who promoted it at first were rarely educators. Rather were they people drawn from laboring and political groups. Indeed, one might say that early child-labor legislation sought the protection of adult rather than of child interests. Only later on did the welfare of the child become the predominating consideration.

The idea of universal compulsory education at the elementary level solved some problems but at the same time created others. It gave some assurance of national solidarity, civic competence, and even economic self-support, but at the same time it brought into the common, or elementary, school elements of the population that created new and difficult problems for educational policy and administration. It brought into the school the physically handicapped such as the crippled, the deaf, the chronic truant, the delinquent and incorrigible, the needy, and the foreign-born. In some states, in addition, as the age limit of the compulsory-attendance law was extended upward to cover the years of secondary schooling as well, it kept juveniles in school who either had no interest in school or were actively hostile to it. Not all teachers welcomed this new clientele with open arms. In any event, the new clientele required not only differentiation of courses at the elementary level but also new types of schools, such as those for the atypical and the wayward.

THE PERSISTENCE OF PRIVATE SCHOOLS

The victory for free compulsory education by no means terminated private education. But then the battle just recounted was not to eliminate private education; it merely sought to establish public education. As a matter of fact, in spite of the establishment of public education, private education continued to flourish. It flourished so lustily, indeed, that both Barnard and Mann mentioned it as one of the most formidable obstacles to the improvement of the struggling public school system. What were the reasons for the persistence of the private school? What social needs did it satisfy?

Doubtless many continued to patronize private schools in the nineteenth century—and the twentieth too, for that matter—because they did not accept equalitarianism in either politics or economics. Succeeding waves of immigration from European stocks other than those of the original settlers made these patrons even more firmly resolved not to have their children attend an equalitarian public school. They feared for the contamination of their children's language and health habits, to say nothing of their manners and morals. Of course, the socially select school served these ends very well. It was not that such parents did not accept democracy but rather that to them democracy meant respect for and freedom to develop differences, differences inherent in social class and in racial and national background.

Many parents who on principle would have preferred the growing public school were attracted to private schools because of the superior quality of instruction offered. As Henry Barnard pointed out, ordinarily such parents tried to improve the public school before resorting to private ones. They found this, however, a very slow and discouraging process. Apprehensive that improvement could not be brought about during the minority or school years of their children, they felt justified in withdrawing their children from the public schools in favor of private ones. Even so, some may have continued to agitate for better public schools. But, as Barnard so clearly saw 100 years ago, the heart and treasure of most such parents were with their own children in their private schools and consequently their interest in public schools lagged, if it did not eventually turn into open opposition. The pity of this evolution was that it deprived the public schools of their chief source of improvement—enlightened and energetic parents.[27]

On the whole, the parents casting about for superior educational facilities joined forces with those seeking the cultural protection of a socially select school. Particularly was this so in the case of the college preparatory schools that became so popular on the Atlantic seaboard and especially in New England from the Civil War onward. It needs pointing out, however, that a not inconspicuous number of the parents seeking better instruction were instrumental in setting up private schools to experiment with new methods and materials of instruction. It should never be forgotten that except for such pioneering persons innovations like the high school, the normal school, and the kindergarten might not have become successful parts of the

[27] Brubacher, *op. cit.*, pp. 112–114, 118.

American public school system. It was such persons, too, who sponsored the experiments of progressive education during the twentieth century.

GROWTH OF THE CATHOLIC PAROCHIAL SCHOOL SYSTEM

One of the chief reasons for the persistence of the private school was to satisfy the demand for religious and moral instruction beyond what could be offered in the public school. Prior to the general establishment of public schools, nearly all private schools included religious and moral instruction as a matter of course. While the private school could cater to sectarian preferences, the public school could not. Because the public school was the servant of the whole public, it had to exclude from its curriculum controversial topics like religion, the teaching of which might give offense to some segment of the population. As a result, to emphasize religion private schools not only persisted but were also energized to multiply by the inauguration of public schools.

Of this class of religious school the Catholic parochial system has been easily the most extensive and the most important.[28] When the agitation for public schools became general, Catholics found it necessary to form a twofold policy. At first, they tried to work out a means of securing Catholic educational aims within a public scheme of schools. Failing in this, later on they stirred themselves to a great expansion of the parochial schools outside the public system and directly under their own control.

Apropos of the first policy, the church took its initial moves under the able Archbishop John Hughes (1797–1864) of New York City. In that city it had been an early practice to distribute the state common school fund among various private agencies offering education to the public. Naturally, therefore, Archbishop Hughes made a claim for a subsidy to Catholic schools just as other denominations did for theirs. Legitimate as was the claim, it met great opposition because it revived old religious animosities. Furthermore, many feared that the disbursement of state funds would become increasingly ineffective as they were divided into smaller and smaller amounts among greater

[28] In 1847 the Presbyterians also attempted to establish a parochial system of schools. Before long they had organized 350 such schools in twenty-nine states of the Union. But the movement was virtually dead before the Civil War was over. The Lutherans were somewhat more successful in founding and maintaining parochial schools, contributing 180,000 of the 275,000 pupils attending Protestant parochial schools in 1936. See C. H. Moehlman, *School and Church* (Harper & Row, Publishers, Incorporated, New York, 1944), pp. 67–68.

and greater numbers of applicants. To settle the rising controversy, the New York State Legislature finally decided in 1842 to put all its eggs in one basket, that is, to put its funds behind one public system of schools. By the end of the century most states had statutes or constitutional provisions prohibiting expenditures of public funds to support private or parochial schools. Indeed, President Ulysses S. Grant publicly advocated this position. Thus came to an end the Catholics' first effort to promote their parochial schools within a framework of public responsibility for schools.

The next step by the Catholic Church was taken in Poughkeepsie, New York. According to a plan, which was inaugurated in 1873[29] and which became known as the Poughkeepsie Plan, the public school authorities rented a former parochial school building. In respect to curriculum, texts, and methods the school set up there was to be like any other public school and was always to be open to inspection and supervision by the local superintendent and board of education. Religious instruction was given before school formally opened in the morning, but none was given during official school hours. The teaching staff, it was tacitly agreed, might be drawn from Catholic teaching orders and were to retain their positions and be paid by the public authorities as long as they passed their examinations and did their teaching effectively. This plan worked satisfactorily in Poughkeepsie for more than twenty years. It was also adopted in other New York cities.

Even before it was clear what the outcome of this policy would be, the Catholic Church was beginning to redouble its exertions under its more familiar policy of promoting its own private, or parochial, school system. Indeed, the church set its face sternly against the public school movement as it became increasingly clear that in Europe as well as in the United States it was waging a losing battle in trying to win the new public school for religion. Alarmed by this trend of the times, Pope Pius IX made defense of the public school one of his famous *Syllabus of Errors* of 1864.[30] Consequently, a

---

[29] As a matter of fact, the plan was older than its employment in Poughkeepsie. See D. F. Reilly, *The School Controversy, 1891–1893* (The Catholic University of America Press, Washington, D.C., 1943), pp. 76, 76n.

[30] The errors in question were as follows: "47. The best theory of civil society requires that popular schools open to the children of all classes, and, generally, all public institutes intended for instruction in letters and philosophy, and for conducting the education of the young, should be freed from all ecclesiastical authority, government, and interference, and should be fully subject to the civil and political power, in conformity with the will of rulers and the prevalent opinions of the age. 48. This system of instructing the youth, which consists in separating it from the Catholic faith and from the power of the church, and in teaching exclusively, or at least primarily, the knowledge of natural things and

decade later an instruction, issued to the American bishops from the College of Propaganda at Rome, laid down as a principle of both natural and divine law that public school attendance be forbidden. The church authorities, however, did recognize that practice must fall far short of principle where no satisfactory Catholic schools had yet been erected.

The Third Plenary Council of the American hierarchy sitting in Baltimore in 1884 expanded the rudiments of this policy into specific directives: "I. Near each church, where it does not yet exist, a parochial school is to be erected within two years from the promulgation of this council, and is to be maintained *in perpetuum,* unless the bishop, on account of grave difficulties, judge that a postponement be allowed. . . . IV. All Catholic parents are bound to send their children to the parochial schools, unless either at home or in other Catholic schools they may sufficiently and evidently provide for the Christian education of their children, or unless it be lawful to send them to other schools on account of sufficient cause, approved by the bishop, and with opportune cautions and remedies. As to what is a Catholic school, it is left to the judgment of the Ordinary to define.[31] The twentieth century witnessed no essential change in this policy.

Many Catholic communities, however, found it very difficult to bear the double burden of taxation in which the decrees of the Baltimore Council resulted, one tax for the public school and another for the parochial school. To bring this seeming injustice forcibly to the attention of the American people and to try to win some relief from it was the task undertaken by a Western prelate of the Catholic Church, John Ireland (1838–1918), the great archbishop of St. Paul, Minnesota. Invited to speak to the National Education Association meeting in St. Paul in 1890, he addressed himself to the topic of state support for parish schools. To allay any fears in his audience that he might be insidiously seeking to destroy America's public system of schools he first spoke in eloquent praise of it, even of state laws enforcing compulsory attendance, which some Catholics were opposing at the time. Indeed, out of very love for the public school system he went on to wish it might be expanded and managed so as to include religious instruction and thus all the children of all the people. The proposal he laid before the association for what he called "Christian state schools" was essentially the Poughkeepsie Plan.

Archbishop Ireland not only spoke in favor of the Poughkeepsie

the earthly ends of social life alone, may be approved by Catholics." See P. Schaff, *Creeds of Christendom* (Harper & Brothers, New York, 1877), vol. 2, pp. 224–225.

[31] Quoted in J. A. Burns, *Growth and Development of the Catholic School System in the United States* (Benziger Bros. Inc., New York, 1912), p. 195.

Plan but went further and approved its introduction in two Minnesota towns of his see, Faribault and Stillwater. This action together with his speech raised a tremendous stir among Catholics. Many among the laity as well as among the clergy thought that Ireland's outspoken approval of public schools was squarely contrary to Catholic philosophy and policy. For long, Catholics had claimed that the right to teach belonged to the family and the church. While they welcomed material assistance from the state in providing schools and even recognized the right of the state to exact a secular curriculum along with the religious one, Catholics denied that the state had an independent right itself to educate.

In order to bring the learning of the church to bear on this controversial issue, James Cardinal Gibbons (1834–1921) of Baltimore, who was then primate of the Catholic Church in America and who was sympathetic to Archbishop Ireland's point of view, prevailed upon Thomas F. Bouquillon, eminent professor of moral philosophy at the Catholic University of America, to write a brochure on the problem. To the question contained in the title of his brochure *Education: To Whom Does It Belong?* he forthrightly answered. "The family, church, *and* state." Although he rested his conclusion on a long line of Catholic authorities, critics at once arose to challenge his interpretation of these authorities and to cite opposing ones. In part, the point of view of Dr. Bouquillon's critics, although couched in religious terms, was not unlike Spencer's theory that the state should take a laissez-faire attitude toward education.[32] At last to quiet the controversy the matter was appealed to Rome, whence finally issued a pontifical *tolerari potest;* that is, Archbishop Ireland's Faribault-Stillwater Plan was not ideal, but it could be tolerated.

But by the time this decision on policy was handed down, which was a year or more after the controversy started, the practical situation had become worse. Protestants in Faribault and Stillwater, fearing that Catholics might be gaining an advantage over them, brought

---

[32] See R. I. Holaind, S.J., *The Parent First: An Answer to Dr. Bouquillon's Query* (Benziger Bros. Inc., New York, n.d.): "Considering natural law only, parents cannot be compelled by the civil authority to send their children to an elementary school. . . . First, parents alone are judges of the material and intellectual wants of their children; the control is due to them in strict justice; an obligation of that kind is an abridgment of their control; and, therefore, a violation of justice. Secondly, the only reason why the state could interfere would be the violation of the right of the child; but all the child is strictly entitled to is to receive the education necessary to live in comfort in the condition of his parents. On the other hand, it is not universally true that the three R's are necessary to live in comfort; hence it cannot be proved by natural law alone that the parents can be compelled to give their children a knowledge of the three R's."

the experiment to an end. The Poughkeepsie Plan, too, reached its end about five years later. The state superintendent of public instruction in New York, on appeal to him in his quasi-judicial capacity, decided that it was against public policy for public school authorities to lease their buildings or to have nuns for teachers as under the Poughkeepsie Plan.[33] The policy of collaborating with the state having proved abortive, the church shelved it for the time being and concentrated on building up its parochial school system.[34] Accommodating about one-third of the Catholic children between the ages of five and seventeen in 1890, fifty years later this system had grown to the point at which it was caring for nearly one-half of the number of Catholic children in this age group.

PUBLIC EDUCATION—MONOPOLISTIC OR PLURALISTIC?

The development of the Catholic parochial system of private schools would seem to have been thoroughly in harmony with the American conception of religious freedom as embodied in the Federal Constitution. Moreover, the development would also seem to have been democratic, if democracy be taken to mean freedom to cultivate different cultural outlooks, as the patrons of socially select schools have claimed. But it must not be overlooked that freedom of this sort has also led to segregation among children and the isolation of some of them from others. Consequently, many friends of the democratic faith have been genuinely perturbed by the way in which private schools raise cultural barriers to democratic intercommunication.

Early to mention this difficulty was Colonel Francis W. Parker (1831–1902) in his *Talks on Pedagogics,* published just before the turn of the century. He feared that mistrust and suspicion which cultural division and isolation breed. Nor did he think that these attitudes were overcome even by the few who finally pursued studies together under the common roof of the university. Far more serious, however, was the antipathy shown minority groups after the First World War. Of interest here was the fact that this antipathy spread to the private schools by which some groups preserved their cultural uniqueness and integrity. The situation reached a crisis in the state of Oregon. There a law was passed in 1923 that made attendance at public schools compulsory for all children of elementary school

[33] *"Matter of the Appeal of Keyser v. Board of Education of Poughkeepsie* (1898)," *Judicial Decisions, 1822–1913,* University of the State of New York, Annual Report, 1914, p. 560.

[34] For a further account of religious instruction in the schools, see *supra,* chap. 11.

age. Without specifically mentioning private schools, this law quite effectually put them under a ban by giving the public school a monopoly on early education.

This was not the first time that an endeavor had been made to bring private and parochial schools under public control. California had tried it in 1874, and Massachusetts in 1888. France had put a ban on Catholic teaching orders in the law of 1904. In a surprisingly short span of history, education had moved from a condition in which nearly all education was under private auspices to one in which the public was making an initial bid toward becoming the sole educator. Coming at a time when the totalitarian theory of the state was being born, the Oregon law naturally proved crucial.

A case was made of it for the courts, where in the due course of time it came before the United States Supreme Court. After being upheld by the state and lower Federal courts, the law was held unconstitutional on final appeal. In its decision the Supreme Court of the land enunciated the view that "The fundamental theory of liberty upon which all governments in this Union repose excludes any general power of the state to standardize its children by forcing them to accept instruction from public teachers only. The child is not the mere creature of the state; those who nurture him and direct his destiny have the right, coupled with the high duty, to recognize and prepare him for additional obligations."[35]

This decision obviously declared that the state is but one among other agencies interested in the education of the child. Thus, the United States Supreme Court definitely committed this country to a pluralistic rather than a monistic or totalitarian view of public education. Furthermore, the decision was in line with the principles implied long ago in the Massachusetts laws of 1642 and 1647. It recognized, as they did, that the primary obligation to educate rests on the shoulders of the parent.

In what Oregon failed to achieve Benito Mussolini threatened to have more success. To forestall Fascist control of religious schools in Italy, Pope Pius XI in 1929 issued the papal encyclical *The Christian Education of Youth,* in which he made a definitive statement of the mutual relations of family, church, and state in matters of education.[36] There he stated that in the natural order the primary duty to educate rests with the family, while in the supernatural order its rests with the church. The family as educator, of course it was recognized, suffers from the limitations of the parents. It therefore needs the assistance and guidance of an educational agency that is sure and infallible in all things pertaining to man's last end. The family, it was conceded, is also supplemented in the natural order

---

[35] *Pierce v. Society of Sisters,* 268 U.S. 510, 535 (1925).
[36] *Catholic Educational Review,* 28:129–164, March, 1930.

by the educational offices of the state, for the state has a particular stake in the political, vocational, and physical education of its citizens. Yet, because the church considers itself the guardian of the natural right of the family to educate, the encyclical categorically enjoined the state not to be so zealous in education as to substitute itself for the family. Rather is it the function of the state to protect the educational initiative of the family and church and to remove public impediments that stand in their way. It is worthy of note that in coming to these conclusions the Pope cited the Oregon decision with approval.

It was not long before two instances occurred in which an American state, far from shouldering the church aside, was indirectly smoothing its way. One of these instances arose about the time of the depression. On that occasion the state of Louisiana construed a free textbook law to warrant free texts for parochial as well as public school children. A plaintiff took exception to this practice as diverting public funds for private purposes. But Chief Justice Charles Evans Hughes, speaking for the United States Supreme Court, held that the expenditure was for a public purpose, being for the children and not the private parochial schools.[37] The same reasoning governed a short while later when New Jersey chose to transport parochial school children to school at public expense.[38] Thus was born the so-called "child-benefit" theory of constitutional interpretation.[39]

Saved from the totalitarianism implicit in the Oregon legislation and then encouraged by the financial aid derived from the child-benefit interpretation of the Constitution, many Catholics were emboldened to lay claim to a share of Federal appropriations which increasingly around mid-century were thought necessary if the nation's schools were to meet the stresses of the postwar population explosion, the heightened technological competition of the "cold war," and the rising costs of postwar inflation. The country, however, was not ready to go quite this far. It was a question in the minds of many, even many Catholics, whether public moneys for private and parochial schools would not bring a state control in its wake which in the end might imperil the very victory won for pluralism in the Oregon decision.[40]

[37] *Cochrane v. Louisiana State Board of Education*, 218 U.S. 370.

[38] *Everson v. Board of Education*, 330 U.S. 1.

[39] For the view that the Supreme Court underestimates the benefit to private schools, see C. Spurlock, *Education and the Supreme Court* (The University of Illinois Press, Urbana, Ill., 1955), p. 78.

[40] R. F. Butts, "Our Tradition of States Rights in Education," *History of Educational Journal*, 10:30–34, 1959. See also I. Widen, "Public Support for Parochial Schools: Why the Issue Has Remerged," *History of Education Journal*, 4:58–72, Winter, 1953.

18
Educational Administration and Supervision

The preceding chapters have largely concerned themselves with the educational task from the instructional angle. They have considered the educative process as conditioned by such perennial factors as aim, method, and curriculum at the different levels of the educational ladder and also by results of psychological, philosophical, political, and economic thinking. In considering the persistent problems of instruction from these angles, relatively little attention has been given to the way in which the educative process is further conditioned by the practical details of administrative organization. These details must not be neglected, for the larger and more complex the educational enterprise, the more significant are these details. Not infrequently, indeed, the quality of the instructional program itself has depended on the efficiency with which the school or school system has been organized and administered.

The recurrent questions that these details of educational administration pose are various. How and where, for example, should the educational program be housed? More basic, doubtless, is the question of finance. How shall money for the educational program be raised? Once raised, how shall it be distributed? Closely related to the method of raising and apportioning funds is the size of the geographic unit to be organized for the support of schools. What is the relative importance here of small-size or local educational administration as compared with large-scale or central educational administration? Whatever the unit of educational administration, what sort of officers of administration should be set up? What should be their proper powers and responsibilities?

EARLIEST FORMS

The simplest and most primitive unit of educational organization is the school or class formed by an individual teacher and his pupils. During the long centuries when education was a luxury of the few rather than a right of the many, each such school or class usually constituted a separate undertaking. Under such circumstances the functions of teaching and administration were often undifferentiated and united in the same person, the teacher. He charged and collected his own fees, arranged for quarters for his school, attended to the grading and promotion of his pupils, and selected and taught the curriculum. Such was the situation in all probability in the schools of the Greek Sophists, the Roman grammarians and rhetoricians, and the Renaissance Humanists. Such too, undoubtedly, was the situation in many private-venture schools under the frontier conditions of colonial America.

In spite of these circumstances, evidence is not altogether wanting of the beginnings in early times of differentiating administrative from instructional functions. One of these early beginnings is to be seen in the founding of chantries during the Renaissance. A chantry was founded by a testator setting aside funds for the double purpose of having a priest or monk sing masses for the repose of his soul and of having him conduct a school when not so engaged. The fund or property so set aside was usually paid over to feoffees or trustees, whose duty it was to manage this part of the testator's estate so that its income would always be available for the support of the chantry. Here, then, was an early division of labor in the educational enterprise, a qualified priest or monk to do the teaching and a duly appointed trustee or trustees to manage the school's finances. This practice not only proved very popular during the Renaissance but has ever since provided a pattern of organization for private schools.

Public funds for education, although rarely and only meagerly available before the nineteenth century, produced much the same division of responsibility for education. Precedents can be cited as early as the Roman Empire. At that time, when the voluntary private support of education was in decline, emperors came to make it a policy to subsidize education. Thus great teachers like Quintilian (35–100) could devote their main efforts to teaching while leaving the burden of providing their salaries to public officials. Another precedent was furnished at the time of the Protestant Reformation when Martin

Luther (1483–1546), alarmed by the impoverished condition of education, besought the civil states of his day to provide and support schools. Many states, particularly Protestant ones, gave ear to this plea. Starting at first with a small stake in the organization and maintenance of schools, in the next two centuries these states, and particularly Prussia, enlarged this stake and came to protect it by a system of administration and inspection that became the object of study in other countries.[1]

The very size and extent of the state, when it took an interest in education, marked another of the early origins of a differentiation between administrative and instructional functions. Within the bounds of a single state were a number of schools. To bring all or even a portion of them within the embrace of a single policy required overseeing of the schools to a degree that no one with teaching duties to perform could exercise. Overseeing to this extent required a separate personnel with specialized functions of administration and supervision. In Prussia, for instance, the state appointed the clergy to execute these functions of supervision. Hence the church together with the state was a force in the separation of administrative from teaching duties.

Growth in the size of the educational enterprise also played a part in the specialization of education into administration and instruction. Individual schools grew in enrollment and variety of instruction to a point at which a variety of classes at different levels of advancement was the only administrative organization that would permit effective instruction. Here, too, it was necessary to detail someone to oversee the whole educational process in the entire school. Nowhere, perhaps, was this more clearly recognized than in the famous Humanistic schools of the Jesuits. There two officers in particular were charged with general oversight of the school. One was the rector, who was the head of the school, and the other was his assistant, the prefect of studies.[2]

Of the qualifications for the office of rector the Constitutions of the Society of Jesus say, "He should have the gift of discretion, be fit for governing, well versed in business, experienced in spiritual matters. He should know how, as occasion offers, to mingle severity with kindness. He should be solicitous, patient in labor, and also learned in letters, and finally he should be of such a character that the superiors can have confidence in him, and communicate their

---

[1] For example, see V. Cousin, "Report on the State of Public Instruction in Prussia," in E. W. Knight, *Reports on European Education* (McGraw-Hill Book Company, New York, 1930), pp. 123–240.

[2] E. A. Fitzpatrick, *St. Ignatius and the Ratio Studiorum* (McGraw-Hill Book Company, New York, 1933), pp. 91–96, 137–155.

authority to him safely, since the greater his authority, the better he will govern the college for the greater glory of God."[3]

In general, it was the duty of the rector to see that the Constitutions of the society pertaining to education were carried out. More specifically, he had the duty of appointing subordinates and of taking care of the real and personal property of the society. Over students he had the duty of watching with solicitous care, looking after their health, and exhorting them in their studies. From time to time he was to visit classes, and once a month to hold conferences with his teachers to which the prefect of studies was invited. He was charged not only with fostering zeal in his teachers but also with giving special attention to the recruitment and training of new ones. Though the rector had these various administrative and supervisory duties, the Jesuits nonetheless thought it wise for him to take a hand in teaching for at least a small portion of the academic year.

While the rector had administrative as well as supervisory duties, the prefect of studies was largely confined to supervision of the instructional program. "The duty of the prefect," states the Jesuits' famed *Ratio studiorum,* "is to be a general assistant of the rector in the proper organization of studies and in conducting and regulating the classes in accord with the authority granted by the rector, so that those who attend may make as much advancement as possible in uprightness of life, the arts, and doctrine, all for the greater glory of God."[4] More particularly, this directive gave the prefect of studies authority to prescribe the curriculum, select the texts, set and approve examinations, and see that the teachers under his charge covered the ground laid out.[5]

No doubt the Jesuits derived the idea of a rector from the medieval

---

[3] *Ibid.,* p. 92.

[4] *Ibid.,* p. 143.

[5] *Cf.* the academy of John Calvin (1509–1564) at Geneva whose bylaws in addition to a rector provided for a principal. "The principal . . . shall be a man of proven piety," the bylaws stated, "of at least fair scholarship, and especially, above all, a man endowed with a gentle disposition and of a character completely free from harshness, that he may be a model to all the students by the example of his life and patiently fulfill his office, in spite of the annoyances involved therein.

"It shall be his duty, besides the ordinary supervision of his school, to look into the character and perseverance of his colleagues, to spur on the slow, to remind all of their duty, to preside at all public castigations in the assembly room, and finally to see that the bell is sounded at the proper time, whenever necessary, and that the individual classrooms appear clean and tidy.

"It shall not be right for the assistant teachers to make any innovation without consulting him. He shall report on all happenings to the rector." [F. Eby, *Early Protestant Educators* (McGraw-Hill Book Company, New York, 1931), pp. 255–256.]

university. There the office had evolved from one in which the rector was merely a presiding officer in the faculty of arts to one in which he exercised coordinating executive power over other university faculties as well. Not every Humanistic school, however, which, like those of the Jesuits, felt the need for differentiating and concentrating administrative and supervisory responsibility in a head, used the title of rector. In England, for example, the head was called "master," and his assistants "ushers." Later, the head came to be called "head master" or, familiarly, just "the head."

LOCAL EDUCATIONAL ORGANIZATION

Early American elementary and secondary schools, as soon as they grew large enough to have a multiple faculty, found it advisable to appoint one of the faculty as the "head" teacher. This head teacher, or "principal," as he later came to be called, was the first professional officer in American schools with administrative and supervisory duties. But neither the principalship nor any other office with administrative and supervisory duties developed extensively before the nineteenth century. Conditioning sociological circumstances were not ripe for such development earlier. Colonial America of the seventeenth and eighteenth centuries was still thinly settled. Frontier conditions prevailed. There were scarcely any large concentrations of population in cities to make the close grading of schools feasible and in turn to necessitate professional superintendence. Furthermore, the democratic idea that that larger unit of political administration, the state, had a stake in the education of the mass of its people had not yet taken hold of public opinion.

The state, to be sure, legislated for the schools, but from almost the very beginning of settlement in this country the larger state interest in education succumbed to the localism of the frontier. The legislative trend of the seventeenth and eighteenth centuries was almost continuously in the direction of surrendering educational prerogatives to smaller and smaller political subdivisions. Thus in New England, where original settlement had been by towns, early colonial legislation constituted the town the local unit of educational organization. But, before the seventeenth century was out, the town was proving too large a unit. Conditions of terrain were already breaking it down into smaller areas.

Hungry for new land and for greater religious freedom, people tended to move toward the outskirts of the town although not beyond the limits of its political jurisdiction. As they moved farther and farther out, they became separated from the original compact town settlement by rivers and mountain ridges, which became difficult barriers to transportation and communication between the old and new parts of the town. In the course of time, with continued migration and the natural increase in population, whole new and almost independent communities began to develop in the newer parts of the town.

The effect of this development on the town school was notable. The barriers of terrain between the different parts of the town were particularly difficult to surmount in the inclement seasons of the year, the seasons when school was usually held so that children might work on the farm during the remaining portions of the year. As a result, many families in the outlying districts were deprived of the benefit of the town school, which remained, of course, in the oldest and most thickly settled part of the town. As a further result there was a gradual decline in the support of the central school. Parents whose children could not easily reach the school naturally were hesitant and reluctant to accord it financial support.

To revive the drooping fortunes of the school and to make it serve the needs and interests of the whole town, a novel expedient was devised. If weather and terrain prevented children from traveling to school regularly, the town decided to take the school to the children. Hence, it was decided that the town school should hold its sessions first in one part of the town and then in another. Like the courts, the school went on circuit. And thus originated the well-known "moving" school of New England.

The moving school, however, was only a temporary expedient. Moving about as it did, the school held only abbreviated sessions wherever it stayed. Hence, it was entirely satisfactory in no part of the town. The next step, therefore, was for each parish or district of the town to demand a school of its own. This demand necessitated a division of the town taxes, which were still collected as a unit, and led to what is sometimes called the "divided," but much more often the "district," school.

The disintegration of the town school into a district school took place largely as a matter of custom and practice. Not till 1789 did the Legislature of Massachusetts give statutory confirmation to the district system as it had evolved in practice. Yet, not content with recognizing its decentralizing tendencies, the state went further and for more than a quarter of a century continued to strengthen the district system. At the opening of the nineteenth century it gave the district power to levy and collect its own school taxes. In the middle of the second decade of the century the state gave the district such corporate status and powers that it became as independent as the town itself had been originally. Finally, in 1827 the Legislature empowered the district to select its own school trustees, who in turn were empowered to select texts and certify teachers.

What occurred in Massachusetts and New England generally occurred elsewhere under varying circumstances. In Connecticut the town church control of schools gave way to parish control. The parish in this case bore the same relation to the larger church society that the district did to the town. Later, Connecticut superseded this ecclesiastical control with secular civil control by the "school society," but the territorial bounds of the school society usually remained the same as those of the parish. The district system also spread westward with the frontier into the new states, where the township rather than the town was the original local unit into which states were subdivided. States where the county was the local administrative unit also often found it impossible to resist the conveniences of the district system.

There can be little doubt that in many ways the district system in colonial America was admirably adapted to the frontier conditions that gave it birth. It brought the school to the remote door of the pupil in a day before automobile transportation and hard-surfaced roads could bring the pupil to a centrally located school. Started as a social convenience, the school district also became, in the course of time, an institution of no little political significance. Being the smallest unit of local self-government and being numbered in the thousands, it became the "palladium of popular liberty" by virtue of giving many Americans their basic training in the parliamentary forms of democratic government.

Yet, adapted as it was to its times, the school district persisted long after these times had begun to change. Furthermore, it had inherent limitations that, obscured at first, became more and more clearly silhouetted against the background of the changing times of the nineteenth and twentieth centuries. Foremost among the limitations to which the great multiplication of districts led, as Henry Barnard (1811–1900) of Connecticut so clearly perceived even before the middle of the nineteenth century, was the disastrous inequality of educational opportunity that it caused even within the bounds of a single town.[6] Thus, districts differed greatly in territorial extent, in tax resources, and in the intelligence and interest in education of their inhabitants. In consequence, schools varied greatly in the housing of the school, in the school building's equipment, in the qualifications of the teacher employed, in the length of the school term, and in the quality of supervision by the local school committee. But even when a district was fortunate in having enlightened educational leadership, which was rare, its limited size inevitably restricted its financial capacity to realize the visions of its leadership. Hence, even when the district school was a good one, it was usually an

[6] J. S. Brubacher (ed.), *Henry Barnard on Education* (McGraw-Hill Book Company, New York, 1931), p. 215.

ungraded, one-room, one-teacher school. Being of this sort, it retarded the growth of more centrally located schools that permitted of grading and called for the stimulating guidance of professional superintendence.

STATE EDUCATIONAL ADMINISTRATION

In the second quarter of the nineteenth century the trend toward the extreme localization of educational control began to reverse itself. A tendency toward the centralization of educational control became evident. With this centralization of control came a tremendous growth in educational administration and supervision. This expansion manifested itself in two directions, in the growth of state educational organization and in the development of city school systems.[7] The underlying social forces that were pushing education in these directions can be easily imagined. Principally, the country was becoming more thickly settled through continued immigration and a normal high birth rate. Nowhere was this population trend more noticeable than in the cities. There the concentration of population to man the rapidly expanding industries of the country often amounted to congestion. School enrollments grew rapidly, too, not only because of the increase in population, but also because a great wave of popular confidence in education as the way to social and individual advancement swept large numbers of new recruits into the schools either voluntarily or through compulsory-attendance laws.

It was difficult at first to meet the challenge of the increased enrollments brought on by the belief that the school was the undoubted key to social progress. One of the principal obstacles to meeting the challenge was the district system of schools. The smallness and isolation of these districts, once a necessary convenience, now created an educational lethargy and myopia that definitely operated to restrict educational advancement. To get a more comprehensive view of the task of education and to draw on a larger area for competent personnel to direct the task, people gradually turned to the state.

State educational administration and supervision had various beginnings. Perhaps first it is wise to remember that from the time of the earliest settlements in America the legal control of education had resided in the state. What towns, counties, and districts did educationally they did by virtue of enabling acts of the colonial and later of the state legislatures. If local units of administration seemed to enjoy major initiative and discretion in educational matters, either by custom or by legislative fiat, it was because the state would have it

[7] Evolution toward a national unit of educational administration is considered in chap. 3.

so. It is interesting to note, however, that this local control of education persisted so long that many communities forgot that they enjoyed their authority at the suffrance of the state. Municipalities in particular formed the habit of regarding and controlling the schools like any other branch of municipal government. Courageous school officials who were alert to their legal rights often resisted this encroachment of the municipal authorities. When such controversies reached the courts, as they did again and again in the different states in the late nineteenth and early twentieth centuries, the courts uniformly upheld the school officials. Judicial opinion generally rested the independence of school from municipal officials on the historical ground that education was and always had been a state rather than a local function of government.[8]

Although the state's interest in education was legally prior to that of the locality, the state was very slow to set up administrative machinery to assert and protect its interest. Indeed, the first state board of education did not appear till after the Revolution. Then, in 1784, New York reorganized its educational system under the title of the University of the State of New York, presided over by a State Board of Regents. This university was not a teaching university but rather the corporate administrative organization given to secondary and higher education at the time. All academies and colleges in the state were made members of the University of the State of New York and thus brought under the supervision of the regents. By a strange quirk of fate, the elementary schools of the state did not become part of the university till 1904. This unique pattern of state educational organization seems to have been French in origin and to have been taken from a plan for a university submitted to Catherine II of Russia by Denis Diderot (1713–1784), the renowned French encyclopedist. Later, Napoleon made use of the same idea when he organized the Université de France.

New York was also first in setting up an executive state officer of education, in 1812 creating the office of state superintendent of common schools. This position came into being largely out of the need to have someone administer the state common school fund. The first incumbent of this office, Gideon Hawley (1785–1870), distinguished himself by being an effective educational leader as well as a good disbursing clerk. Unfortunately, in the decade following his appointment he ran afoul of the Legislature's unjustified displeasure. As a result, his office was abolished and its duties were made ex officio duties of the secretary of state. The office did not emerge with independent status again till 1854. In the meantime,

[8] For a sampling of these cases, see N. I. Edwards, *The Courts and the Public Schools* (The University of Chicago Press, Chicago, 1933), chap. 1.

this action reduced the state interest in education from a professional to a purely clerical level.

This subordination of the state interest in education was not altogether surprising. Although obviously a state interest in education was being born, the second and third decades of the nineteenth century were not yet fully awake to the incalculable importance of popular education. Realization of this importance waited for the legislatures of Massachusetts and Connecticut in the next decade to set up the state machinery that was to mobilize public opinion into the great educational revival of the mid-nineteenth century. Massachusetts in 1837 and Connecticut in the following year both set up state boards of education as antidotes for the lethargy that gripped the district schools. What gave power to these boards was not so much their membership as the executive secretaries whom they both appointed. By happy chance, two men of the highest gifts of public leadership were available for these appointments, Horace Mann (1796–1859) in Massachusetts and Henry Barnard in Connecticut.[9]

To these men more than to any others goes the credit for giving state educational administration and supervision the eminence it since has assumed. The duties they took upon themselves were largely those of persuading and exhorting communities to improve their schools. By traveling the length and breadth of their respective states and by speaking on every occasion that presented itself, Mann and Barnard made available for local communities the broader educational experience and loftier educational vision of the larger territorial unit of the state. To implement words with deeds, neither secretary was armed with any compulsory powers of state authority. "The education of the whole people, in a republican government," declared Mann in memorable words, "can never be attained without the consent of the whole people. Compulsion, even if it were desirable, is not an available instrument. Enlightenment, not coercion, is our resource. The nature of education must be explained. The whole mass of men must be instructed in regard to its comprehension and enduring interests. We cannot drive our people up a dark avenue, even though it be the right one; but we must hang the starry lights of knowledge about it, and show them not only the directness of its course to the goal of prosperity and honor, but the beauty of the way that leads to it."[10]

Taking this view certainly did not make the task of these men

[9] For estimates of the work of these two men, see E. I. F. Williams, *Horace Mann, Educational Statesman* (The Macmillan Company, New York, 1937); A. L. Blair, *Henry Barnard, School Administrator* (Educational Publishers, Minneapolis, 1938).

[10] Quoted in P. Monroe, *Founding of the American Public School System* (The Macmillan Company, New York, 1940), p. 247.

any easier. Public inertia in the matter of education was so monumental that, except for the great zeal and deep devotion of these men, they must surely have failed in their undertaking. When success finally crowned their efforts, it was only at great personal sacrifice. Mann and Barnard both demanded so much of themselves that the health of each was impaired by his exertions. Neither Massachusetts nor Connecticut rewarded these great servants of the state with salaries that even met their expenses, but both men concluded their public service rich in the gratitude of their fellow men and of untold generations of school children yet unborn.

In addition to campaigning up and down their states for better schools, Mann and Barnard devised other means for getting their ideas before the lay and professional public. Both of them made annual reports to their state boards of education that not only acquainted the public with current educational conditions but pointed the way to their improvement. The reports of Mann in particular were widely read. While these reports were chiefly intended for the layman, both secretaries also launched journals intended chiefly for the professional personnel of the state's schools. Barnard is especially noted for the *American Journal of Education,* which he long edited. Both men also made trips to Europe in order to give their state constituencies the benefit of the latest and best educational practice in methods of instruction, grading of pupils, training of teachers, and architecture of schools.

The state leadership of education that Mann built up in Massachusetts and Barnard in Connecticut—subsequently in Rhode Island, too—was developed by other able, if less well-known, men in other parts of the country. Calvin Wiley (1819–1887) in North Carolina, Robert J. Breckinridge (1800–1871) in Kentucky, and John Swett (1830–1913) in California, to mention but three, were the sort of men who furthered the work of Mann and Barnard in the South, Middle West, and Far West. Indeed, the fame of Mann spread outside the United States, drawing to this country the great Argentinian president and educator Domingo Faustino Sarmiento (1811–1888). After traveling in Massachusetts and Connecticut, Sarmiento returned to his native country to become known as the Horace Mann of Argentina.[11]

The success that these and other men had in rallying public opinion to follow the banner of the state in educational leadership led to a statutory strengthening of the state's role. Massachusetts, for instance, began to recall the educational powers that it had delegated

[11] W. Stewart, and W. M. French, "The Influence of Horace Mann on the Educational Ideas of Domingo Faustino Sarmiento," *Hispanic American Historical Review,* 20:12–31, February, 1940.

to the school districts. Several years after Mann concluded his twelve-year term of office, Massachusetts passed a law permitting towns to abandon the district system and to return to the town unit of control for schools. Just before the Civil War the state went further and abolished the district system altogether. This action was moving faster than public opinion would allow, for the law was repealed almost immediately. Shortly after the war another permissive law was put on the statute books. In 1882, after the district system had been voluntarily abolished in nearly every town, the system was finally legislated out of existence. Other states followed the lead of Massachusetts more slowly. It was the automobile and the hard-surfaced road, promoting transportation of children to consolidated schools where the curriculum was graded and more varied, which won the final victory for central over local educational control.

The state also learned to strengthen its educational leadership by the way in which it managed the state school funds. While at first the management of these funds had been merely a clerical job of apportionment among the different localities, later the state became bold enough to make the apportionment contingent upon a raising of educational standards in these localities. This meant not only that communities were expected to have longer school terms, better-trained teachers, and more varied curricula but often that they were expected to match the state financial contribution with one of their own.

Setting standards and inspecting to see whether they had been met became technical tasks that ex officio state superintendents of public instruction were little competent to perform. As a result, this important office moved steadily toward an independent status demanding the full-time services of a man of the highest professional abilities. Hindering the selection of such a man, however, was the method by which he frequently was selected for office. As the office came to prominence just after the opening of the era of the common man, it frequently became an elective one. The effect of Jacksonian democracy being to treat public office as a nontechnical occupation and one easily within the competence of the common man, the custom naturally grew up of requiring the state superintendent of schools to submit his qualifications to the suffrage of the people. Most states still continued this practice in the twentieth century, but the tendency of progressive states was toward having this officer appointed either by the state board of education, as was originally the case in Massachusetts and Connecticut, or by the governor.

As state population continued to mount toward the turn of the century and as the automobile contracted the boundaries of the state, at least psychologically, the function of state educational administration grew in complexity. In fact, it grew quite beyond the physical capacities of any one man. Hence, in a large state like New York it became necessary to assign to the state commissioner of education assistant or deputy commissioners of education to divide the clerical, supervisory, judicial,[12] and research functions that had to be performed. Only thus could the commissioner himself be freed to fulfill the demand for educational statesmanship that his office demanded.

THE CITY SUPERINTENDENT AND BOARD OF EDUCATION

The rise of educational administration and supervision, so rapid in the case of state educational organization in the mid-nineteenth century, was slower but no less conspicuous in the contemporary development of city school systems. As in the state, so in the cities strong executive leadership was the outstanding feature in the evolution of educational administration and supervision. Indeed, in the course of time so strong did the city school superintendency become, particularly in the larger cities, that it often outranked the state superintendency in professional prestige.

The first city school superintendent was appointed in Buffalo, New York, in 1837, the same year in which Horace Mann assumed his duties as secretary to the Massachusetts State Board of Education. In order to understand how this office came to evolve, it is perhaps easiest to go back again to the old New England town. Originally, the New England town governed itself through the well-known democratic process of the town meeting. School affairs came up for decision at the town meeting just like any other public concern. It is interesting to note that the town, in making such decisions, exercised both legislative and administrative control of the schools. Thus it would legislatively decide the policy of whether to have a school and administratively vote to employ a particular master to teach the school.

Of course, the town meeting could not sit continuously, nor could it always conveniently assemble citizens when some crisis in town or school affairs arose. Consequently, it was the custom to select certain men—"selectmen," they were often called—to manage town affairs during the interim between meetings. That selectmen had the overseeing of education is evident as early as the famous Massachusetts statute of 1642, which made it their duty to ensure that

[12] For the evolution of this phase of state educational administration, see J. S. Brubacher, *The Judicial Power of the New York State Commissioner of Education* (Bureau of Publications, Teachers College, Columbia University, New York, 1927).

parents were teaching children their letters, the catechism, and the capital laws of the colony.

While selectmen continued to exercise supervision of the schools throughout the colonial period, their responsibilities were more extensive in the early part of the period than in the latter. As time went on, it became more and more frequent practice for the town meeting to appoint special committees to attend to specific problems of the schools, such as the renting of a school building or the appointing of a teacher. Of particular importance were the special committees appointed to inspect the schools. In the eighteenth century these special committees often grew into standing committees. The annual town meeting, in addition to its other officers, would choose a committee to look after the schools in general for a period of six months or even a year. In the nineteenth century such school committees became obligatory by statute.

As population increased, school systems grew in extent and complexity. Correspondingly, school committees, or "boards of education," as they more generally became called in the nineteenth century, found their duties growing more and more onerous. Typical was a school board member in Springfield, Massachusetts, who complained that to execute his duties faithfully would require two whole days of his working week, an amount of time he could ill afford from his usual occupation. Yet, while school board members had to resist encroachments on their time, these encroachments instead of diminishing increased. Consequently, many legitimate demands of a growing school system went by default. In the middle of the nineteenth century the school committee at Boston pointed out that no one there was specially charged with the duty of investigating the best type of school architecture, of being on the lookout for good teachers in case vacancies should occur, of deciding what is good teaching and helping teachers supplement their deficiencies, of studying whether the schools and their curricula were adapted to the population, of organizing new schools and transferring children from school to school, and of seeing that important business was brought before the committee.

Circumstances such as these all seemed to point to the need for someone to give his full time to the management of the schools. Apparently, Buffalo was first to formulate this need when it appointed its superintendent of schools, but other cities were not far behind. By the Civil War nearly all the larger cities of the United States had created the office. Their own rapid growth plus the concurrent rise of public education, which had its greatest impetus in urban centers, so expanded municipal school systems as to put them potentially in the class of big business. It is small wonder, therefore, that the pattern of educational administration which evolved as best adapted to this situation was the same as the corporate form of organization that had proved so successful in big business. In the case of both the public schools and private business, successful administration seemed to depend on the differentiation of the executive function. Special school committees and committees of the whole, like town meetings, might be excellent bodies to legislate educational policy; but, with the increase in size and complexity of American life, they had increasingly demonstrated themselves unwieldy and inefficient in executing or administering policy. Hence the need for differentiating and delegating the administration and supervision of schools to a single executive officer like the superintendent of schools.

Although the superintendency was destined to demand the highest professional qualifications, the first incumbents of the office came into power from a variety of backgrounds. In some cases, boards of education appointed one of their own number. Often this was the secretary of the board. As a result, not a few of the early superintendents were laymen. Indeed, thirteen of Los Angeles' first twenty-three superintendents were laymen—doctors, lawyers, clergymen, and businessmen. In other cases, boards of education picked a teacher or principal to become superintendent. Needless to say, the selection of a professional person came, in the course of time, to be the prevalent custom. But the selection of a person with high professional attainments was delayed in some places by the manner in which he was chosen. In some cities—notably San Francisco till as late as the third decade of the twentieth century—the superintendent had to run for office at popular election. In other instances, appointment was in the hands of the city council or the mayor. Here political rather than professional considerations were likely to obtain and make tenure so short as to be unattractive to the best-qualified man.

The duties of the early city superintendent of schools were of two sorts, administrative and supervisory. On the administrative side it became his responsibility to keep the records of the school system and to make such reports to the board of education and to the state department of education as were required. He looked after school supplies and saw to the repair of school buildings. Where compulsory-attendance laws had been enacted, he often had the duty of overseeing their enforcement. On the supervisory side, the superintendent's principal role was to coordinate the instructional program as a whole. Not being attached to one schoolroom or one school building, the superintendent was obviously the person to satisfy the increasing demand of the times for a graded system of schools.[13] For the same reason, it was he who was charged with the duty of regulating promo-

---

[13] For the evolution of a graded system of schools, see *supra*, pp. 374–377.

tions from grade to grade.[14] Similarly, it is also easy to understand how making up the curriculum, or course of study, was originally a function of the superintendent of schools. From his point of vantage overlooking the educational program as a whole, he naturally drew up the course of study and then passed it on to the teachers.[15] Giving his full time to the overseeing of the schools, he also took over the function of visiting and examining them, which had become too onerous and technical for the board of education.

The subsequent success of differentiating and concentrating executive duties in a superintendent of schools has so definitely justified this policy that it would be easy to overlook the misgivings and opposition which the evolution of this office at first generated. Some laymen opposed the office out of fear of "one-man control," an American bogey of long standing. Teachers and principals sometimes opposed it because they wished to retain the larger measure of professional autonomy permitted by a decentralized administrative control. The most formidable opposition, surprisingly enough, came from the board of education itself. The misgivings there were not so much concerning the creation of the office as concerning the amount of power to be delegated to it.

This question of the apportionment of power between the superintendent and his board of education remained a bone of contention throughout the nineteenth and twentieth centuries. Much of this struggle for power resulted from the almost entirely extralegal development of the office. During most of the superintendency's development, legal control of the schools was vested by statute in the board of education. Not till the twentieth century did the office of superintendent receive general statutory recognition. Up to that time the office existed only as a matter of practice.[16] Its powers were merely those delegated by the board of education. The superintendent wielded as much power as he was able to obtain from his board by winning their confidence in his personal and professional abilities. The superintendency, therefore, was virtually a history of great superintendents.[17] These circumstances account in large part not only for the

---

[14] For the evolution of promotion, see *supra,* pp. 378–379.

[15] For a further account of the administration of the curriculum, see *supra,* pp. 301–302.

[16] The legality of this practice was settled in the courts as early as 1862. *Stuart v. School District No. 1 of Kalamazoo,* 30 Mich. 69 (1874), which decided the legality of the high school, was one of the first decisions to approve the legality of the superintendency and for the same reasons of public policy it approved the high school.

[17] For example, William Torrey Harris (1835–1909) in St. Louis, B. A. Hinsdale (1837–1900) in Cleveland, J. D. Philbrick (1818–1886) in Boston, and S. S. Randall (1809–1881) in New York.

indefinite boundary line between the powers of the board and the superintendent but also for the very uneven growth of the superintendent's office in different parts of the country.

Although boards of education found it necessary to delegate power to the superintendent of schools, they often surrendered their power reluctantly and rarely gave him an entirely free hand. They were fairly ready to delegate him petty clerical and technically supervisory duties; but when it came to major matters like budgets and the appointment of teachers, they clung to their statutory powers more tightly. Indeed, in the business administration of the schools they long thought themselves as laymen more competent than the superintendent. In spite of the fact that, with the development of normal schools in the last half of the nineteenth century, the appointment of teachers was becoming an increasingly technical or professional matter, boards did not like to yield power so closely akin to patronage.

The rapid urbanization of the United States, from the latter part of the nineteenth century into the twentieth, created city school problems of a size and difficulty that challenged the best educational leadership the country could produce. Aggressive superintendents who were also good executives realized more and more that if the youth of the country were to have the educational opportunities which our democratic industrial civilization demanded, they themselves must more and more have control of even such important elements of power as budgetary procedures and the appointment of teachers. Their claim to greater power, however, had to be authenticated. First to back their claim were professional students of educational administration. Although the professional training of teachers was well under way by the opening of the twentieth century, up to 1900 there had been practically no systematic professional training offered for men planning on the superintendency as a career. The first two decades of the twentieth century witnessed the virtual creation of a professional subject matter of educational administration and supervision.[18] Principal leaders in this movement were George D. Strayer (1876–1962) of Teachers College, Columbia University, and Ellwood P. Cubberley (1868–1941) of Stanford University.

The school of thought led by these men tried to resolve the struggle for power between the superintendent and the board of education by falling back on the corporate analogy already mentioned. The board of education, they claimed, should be like a board of directors, having the duty to legislate the educational policies of the school system. The superintendent, like the president of a corporation, should be the technical or professional expert of the board. He should keep

[18] For a bibliography, see I. L. Kandel, *Twenty-five Years of American Education* (The Macmillan Company, New York, 1929), chap. 7.

members of the board advised in technical matters of educational practice with which they as laymen could not be expected to be acquainted. He should, furthermore, be the person to give professional execution to all policies determined by the board. This seemed eminently sound administrative theory. Many boards of education adopted it into their rules and regulations. State legislatures, when some of them in the twentieth century finally gave statutory definition to the office and powers of the superintendent, enacted it into law. Yet, advanced as this legislation was, it did not always affect practice as it was meant to. The tenure of superintendents was still subject to contract with the board. Hence, weak superintendents were often careful not to exercise their statutory prerogatives in such a way as to displease their boards and endanger the renewal of their contracts.

This evolution of the superintendency did not occur without leaving its mark on the board of education. During the period while it still considered itself an executive as well as a legislative body, the board had developed certain practices that proved either fruitless or a positive handicap in the period when it became more strictly a legislative organ of government. Thus, early boards of education tended to be very large. In a predominantly agrarian country, they tended to represent geographical areas such as school districts or municipal wards. Being very large, boards operated through committees. These committees frequently performed administrative as well as deliberative functions.

All this nineteenth-century practice began to change by the twentieth century. Boards tended to grow smaller. Boston, for instance, just after the middle of the nineteenth century had a board of 217. Ten years later the board numbered 24. In the first decade of the twentieth century Boston had a compact board of 5.[19] As boards shrank in size, they inclined to reduce the number of their committees or abolish them altogether. Students of educational administration felt that they should generally transact their business as a committee of the whole. As small boards eliminated the possibility of geographical representation from each part of the city, boards also came to be elected from the city at large.

The constantly growing size of cities was not long in rendering the magnitude of the superintendency of schools too heavy for one

[19] At least one educational authority favored the disappearance of the board of education altogether. See C. H. Judd, "Abolish the School Boards," *Public Management,* 15:321, November, 1939. Perhaps he had in mind the way in which other municipal boards like the boards of police commissioners, park commissioners, etc., disappeared as the mayoralty rose in prominence in the nineteenth century.

pair of professional shoulders. Two administrative devices developed to relieve the superintendent of some of this excessive burden. In some cities the superintendent was given assistants, either assistant superintendents with special assignments or supervisors of instruction. In other cities two superintendents were appointed, one in charge of business affairs and the other of professional educational affairs. This division of school control was not unlike that already noted as evolving into administration and supervision.

Up through the first decade of the twentieth century the major interest of educational administration had been directed toward the organization of schools. Much confidence was put in administrative devices. The success of educational administration was thought to depend on having smaller boards, on reducing and eliminating committees of the board, on consolidating school districts, and on making the board of education fiscally independent of municipal authorities. Before and after the First World War, with the rise of the scientific measurement movement, administration turned its chief attention to problems of standardization. Elaborate age-grade studies were made, desirable classroom size was investigated, uniform business practices were installed, school buildings were scored against check lists, and teachers were rated on score cards.

Standardization of administrative practices through the aid of scientific measurement proved tremendously useful in the city school survey movement, which began to gather momentum during this period. School surveys were nothing new at this time, but they were entering on a period of effectiveness quite beyond anything they had known in the past. In part, they drew their inspiration from the contemporary social survey movement and in part from an English educational survey by Sir Michael Sadler (1861–1943) which was greatly admired in this country. But also in part they stemmed from nineteenth-century American precedents.[20]

Henry Barnard, perhaps, conducted the earliest survey in this country when, on becoming secretary to the State Board of Education, he gathered statistics on the state of schools in Connecticut.[21] Shortly afterward Boston and later in the century Quincy, Massachusetts, instead of the annual school visitation, used comprehensive examinations to learn the state of public instruction in their respective cities.[22] Just before the century was out, Chicago appointed an educational

[20] H. L. Caswell, *City School Surveys*, (Bureau of Publications, Teachers College, Columbia University, New York, 1929), chap. 2.

[21] H. Barnard, *Second Annual Report to the Board of Commissioners of Common Schools in Connecticut*, 1840.

[22] *Cf.* O. Caldwell and S. A. Courtis, *Then and Now in Education* (World Book Company, Tarrytown-on-Hudson, N.Y., 1924).

commission to study its schools because there was doubt whether their results were commensurate with the financial outlay being made. The scope of this survey was the widest to date, including, as it did, the organization and supervision of schools, the selection, examination, and promotion of teachers, a school census, texts, curricula at the different levels, and the like. Boise, Idaho, in 1910 had the first survey by an outside expert. Almost simultaneously East Orange and Montclair, New Jersey, also had surveys. These were distinguished by the fact that for the first time the survey expert rested his judgment to a considerable extent on the evidence of scientific objective measurement.

The school survey, scientific measurement in education, child accounting, and the like, it needs noting, all became prominent aspects of education at the same time that industrial management was overhauling itself according to so-called "principles of scientific management."[23] The scientific management movement was essentially a system for getting greater economic productivity from a given expenditure of human labor. Conventional methods of production, even when mechanized, were often haphazard. Time and motion studies together with cost accounting, it was believed, would result in greater efficiency. If such effects could be produced in business, why not in education as well? As superintendents made greater and greater use of surveys, measurement, and accounting, a great coincident efficiency undoubtedly did occur. But there were side effects which grew more alarming as efficiency spread. Superintendents and the training of superintendents became more and more deeply absorbed with legal technicalities, finance, administrative organization, and mechanical details like school supplies, janitorial services, and the like. In extreme cases, quality was sacrificed on the altar of efficiency, one very prominent superintendent proposing to drop Greek from the curriculum because its per capita cost was higher than that of French!

Powerful as the drive for efficiency became, it did finally overreach itself. Superintendents became open to the same criticism of anti-intellectualism to which their teachers had been subjected during the great debate on teacher education.[24] But the corrective for this anti-intellectualism had been set in motion well before the charge had been fully formulated by the "cold war" critics of education. The depression of the 1930s, for one thing, brought on a disenchantment with business leadership which to some extent loosened the tentacles of business efficiency on school systems. Moreover, some educational leaders tried to restate educational administration in terms of social

[23] F. W. Taylor, *The Principles of Scientific Management* (Harper & Brothers, New York, 1911).

[24] *Supra,* pp. 490–492.

policy or of educational statesmanship.[25] And in the post-World War II period other leaders definitely stressed the intellectual component in education by trying to underpin it with administrative theory.[26] Both views required superintendents of broad liberal arts background. Opportunely about this time the W. K. Kellogg Foundation interested itself in the improvement of educational administration to the extent of several million dollars. With this assistance selected centers of higher education in various parts of the country were able to improve the recruitment and selection of future personnel and provide a superior program for their instruction.[27]

DIOCESAN EDUCATIONAL ADMINISTRATION AND SUPERVISION

Thus far the discussion has been mainly concerned with the growth of educational administration in the public school system. What of its evolution in the Catholic parochial school system, the largest single private school system in the United States? As a matter of fact, the evolution there was not unlike that in the public school system. For long, parochial schools were under the surveillance of local parish priests. No dissatisfaction was felt with this system till after the Civil War. Then sporadic efforts were made to establish some form of diocesan[28] supervision of parochial schools. The Third Plenary Council, when it met at Baltimore in 1884, took official notice of this movement. Following a plan originated in the diocese of Fort Wayne, Indiana, a few years previously and later copied in Cincinnati, Ohio, the council recommended the formation of diocesan boards of education. These boards, composed of priests who were conversant with educational matters, were to examine and certify teachers, regulate curricula and texts, and visit the schools.

Beneficial as this move was, it failed to live up to the expectations entertained for it. The difficulties were several. For one thing, the priests on these boards were busy with other parish interests and consequently could not give education the full attention it increasingly demanded. For another, few, if any, of these priests were professionally trained in education. Consequently, their school visitations, while sympathetic and well-meaning, were lacking in pedagogical insight.

---

[25] J. H. Newlon, *Educational Administration as Social Policy* (Charles Scribner's Sons, New York, 1934).

[26] D. E. Griffiths, *Administrative Theory* (Appleton-Century-Crofts, Inc., New York, 1959).

[27] *Toward Improved School Administration* (W. K. Kellogg Foundation, Battle Creek, Mich., n.d.).

[28] A diocese corresponds roughly to a state, but some states have several dioceses.

Hence, a need was soon felt for some better-trained person to give full time to the administration of diocesan schools. Four years after the Third Plenary Council had met, New York City took the lead by appointing a diocesan inspector of schools. In the next decade the first diocesan superintendent of schools appeared. This latter officer proved so effective that, just before the Second World War, 85 out of 104 dioceses had appointed superintendents.[29]

THE PRINCIPAL

It has already been mentioned that superintendents of public schools were often chosen by elevating a principal of a local school. A word is now in order to describe the evolution of this administrative and supervisory office. This office not only antedated the superintendency in this country but undoubtedly had European origins as well. Thus, the American principal bore definite similarities to the English headmaster and the Jesuit rector, both already mentioned. The principalship made its appearance in our educational development just as soon as there were schools grown large enough to have more than one teacher. Then it became necessary to appoint a head teacher, or principal. This tendency was greatly accelerated in the nineteenth century by the growth of grading in the schools. The uniting of the primary, intermediate, and grammar grades into a single common, or elementary, school, for instance, obviously required some over-all leadership.[30]

At first, the principal's most urgent duties were of an administrative character. He had to be progressively freed from teaching duties so that he could keep the school records, particularly those on attendance, and make periodic reports to the school committee or the board of education. Being in charge of the school, he had the further duty to safeguard its property and see to it that the rooms were kept clean. In addition to looking after school equipment and supplies, he had such minor responsibilities as arranging for recess and ringing the school bell. Over and above administrative functions, the principal had some supervisory ones. Here his chief duty was to classify and promote the children in his charge. He was also expected to visit and sometimes examine the classes in his school. Not infrequently, he was the high court of discipline.

As the nineteenth century gradually freed the principal from teach-

---

[29] J. A. Burns, and B. J. Kohlbrenner, *A History of Catholic Education in the United States* (Benziger Bros., Inc., New York, 1937), chap. 8.

[30] For a further account of the rise of the graded school, see *supra,* pp. 374–377.

ing duties so that he would have time to attend to his administrative ones, so the twentieth century sought to release him from his administrative duties so that he could concentrate more and more on his supervisory ones. The normal schools did valiant service in the training of teachers during the nineteenth and early twentieth centuries; but many teachers did not pass through their halls, and those who did, passed through in all too brief a time. Consequently, much training remained to be done after the teacher entered active service. Many professional students of education, particularly after the First World War, thought that the principal was the best suited to carrying on this in-service training of teachers. The coincident rise of psychological testing and of fundamental curriculum revision at this time greatly added to the demand that the principal devote the major portion of his time to supervision.

Not every principal, however, adopted supervisory functions for himself. Many preferred to remain immersed in clerical routine. Yet, supervisor or superclerk, the principal was not long in finding out that he had an important jurisdictional problem to settle with the central-office supervisors, evolved, as already mentioned, to help the superintendent carry the tremendous load of his office. Sometimes the superintendent exercised his central authority with such exacting force that he dwarfed the initiative and importance of the principal as a supervisory officer. Sometimes the supervisory suggestions from the central office were sabotaged by the passive resistance of the principal, who enjoyed the prestige of holding the more ancient office. But in any event it was desirable to save teachers the confusion that easily arose when the suggestions of the principal and the assistant superintendent or central supervisor conflicted. To avoid such contradictions, it became pretty well settled by the end of the nineteenth century that the principal was the administrative and supervisory head of his school and that criticism and advice to his teachers therefore had to pass over his desk.

At first the principalship could not have ranked very high in social esteem, for it was not uncommon in the eighteenth century to see vacant principalships advertised. Candidates, when they did present themselves, had to stand an examination in academic subject matter just as the teachers did. As the principalship grew in professional importance, the qualifications rose correspondingly. When a body of professional subject matter began to accumulate in the nineteenth century, the would-be principal often had to stand an examination on that as well. In the larger cities of the twentieth century the principalship finally took on such prestige that professional requirements not infrequently demanded that the principal hold a master's degree.

SUPERVISION

From the foregoing it is evident that supervisory functions were performed by a variety of persons from the seventeenth century onward—by selectmen, special visiting committees, boards of education, principals, superintendents, and supervisors. In this procession of supervisory officers there is also an evident progression from lay agents in the seventeenth and eighteenth centuries to professional ones in the nineteenth and twentieth. There is lastly some evidence that the more professional the supervisory function became, the more it tended to become an independent full-time office. Thus, the trend in the principalship was first to free the principal from teaching duties and later to release him from administrative ones so that he could give more and more time to supervision. In the case of the superintendency, the trend was either to divide the heavy duties of this office so that the superintendent could concentrate on supervision or to give him assistants—assistant superintendents or supervisors—who would do the supervising for him.

In addition to these developments there was one other line along which supervision evolved. This was through the addition of new subjects in the curriculum, principally in the elementary school. On the whole, the normal schools and teacher institutes equipped teachers to teach a fairly conventional curriculum composed basically of the three R's plus some history and geography. Toward the end of the nineteenth century, innovations began to appear in this traditional curriculum. Music, art, manual training, and physical education were the chief subjects to knock for admission. One of the principal obstacles to opening the door to these innovations was the fact that few if any of the regular staff of teachers were or had been trained to teach them. To remedy this shortcoming special supervisors of music, art, manual training, and physical education were appointed. In fact, these were not so much supervisors as special subject-matter teachers. The need for them tended to pass as the normal schools and teachers colleges of the twentieth century enlarged the scope of their training to include these new fields. This action, however, did not affect general supervision, which, instead of declining, rose to new and greater importance.

The kind of supervision obtaining during the early days, when laymen did the supervising, was largely inspectional in character. The laymen appointed to inspect a school for its proficiency usually announced their visit in advance. When they arrived, they made their visit in the nature of an examination. Either the teacher or the members of the visiting committee called on various children to recite. Time being limited and the pupils many, the committee could not hope to examine everyone but only a sampling of the school. At the conclusion of the inspection, the committee made its report to the teacher and to the town.

In the course of time this inspectional visit grew into an annual public exhibition. Parents and townspeople attended. When it took on this character, however, it soon lost its supervisory usefulness. Boston and Quincy were early to recognize this fact and, as already mentioned, turned to comprehensive written examinations set for the whole school system in order to test its proficiency. In New York State, too, just after the Civil War, the regents inaugurated a statewide system of annual examinations—later widely known as the "regents"—in order to inspect the progress of public education in that state.

In the last half of the nineteenth century, another conception of supervision began to supplant that of inspection. Supervision was not only to evaluate instruction but to try to make up its deficiencies. The supervisor was to be a teacher of teachers. This conception of supervision doubtless took its coloration from the great attention being paid at this time to teacher training. Normal schools were in their heyday, and educators, drawing on the pedagogical insights of Johann Heinrich Pestalozzi (1746–1827) and Johann Friedrich Herbart (1776–1841), were almost for the first time beginning to discard the old shibboleth that teachers are born, not made.[31] Consequently, supervisors took great pains to see that teachers understood the educational principles of these great leaders. To this end, they instituted the supervisory devices of holding teachers' meetings, setting up teacher institutes, and encouraging reading circles.[32] Also, supervisors and principals often visited classrooms to conduct model lessons in order to acquaint teachers with the new Pestalozzian and Herbartian methods.

Still aimed at the improvement of instruction, supervision in the twentieth century employed a variety of new devices. The rise of the scientific measurement movement kindled in supervisors the expectation of being able to get an exact measure of the effectiveness of teaching as well as of the effectiveness of learning. With the precise strong and weak points of a school system indicated, they would know just where supervision was most needed. Furthermore, supervisors tried to engage teachers in research projects in the hope that carrying a project through to completion would increase the teacher's grasp on his teaching problems. Later, after the First World War, they used the movement for fundamental curriculum revision as a

---

[31] For a fuller account of the normal school movement, see *supra,* pp. 479–483.

[32] For a fuller account of teacher institutes and reading circles, see *supra,* pp. 478–479, 498.

similar means of subtle supervision. By making curriculum revision a concern of the teacher as well as of the superintendent and his staff, they hoped definitely to upgrade the quality of instruction in the schools.

But the devotees of science, who went as far as to claim that supervision itself had become a science, seem to have overreached themselves just as they contemporaneously did in claiming that the aims of education could be scientifically determined.[33] A critical review of the literature on which a science of supervision might have been based revealed that very little of it could properly be called scientific and that that little had only a limited applicability.[34] The resulting deflated but undiscouraged attitude toward the role of science in supervision led to greater attention again to supervision in the light of educational principles and to more flexible allowances for personal factors.

Supervision at each stage of its development involved intimate personal contacts with teachers, which required the utmost in tactful management. Principals, superintendents, and supervisors were constantly presented with the problem of whether to give the teacher a considerable measure of freedom to work out his own pedagogical salvation or to use their authority to press for the realization of the educational program of the central administration. Perhaps, on the whole, down to the First World War supervision inclined toward the latter technique, for, soon after the conclusion of the war to make the world safe for democracy, there was considerable clamor for the democratization of supervision. As a result, some supervisors undertook the role of "consultant." Instead of pressing their views on teachers, they let it be known that their skill and experience were available to teachers on request.

SCHOOL BUILDINGS

The sociological condition of rapid population growth, particularly in our cities, called educational administration into being not only to supervise the educational program of a graded system of schools but also to supervise the housing of the rapidly increasing school population. Down to the nineteenth century relatively little attention had been given to this problem. During the long centuries preceding, schools were rarely held in buildings specially designed for educational purposes. In ancient days they sometimes found an abode in temples. In some places schools met on porches. The Stoics, indeed, took

[33] *Supra*, pp. 18–19.
[34] B. L. Gambrill, "A Critical Review of Researchers in Supervision," *Educational Administration and Supervision*, 15:279–289, April, 1929.

their name from στοά, the Greek word for "porch," because they made a habit of holding their school on a particular porch. Roman schools often met on a veranda and also in a *taberna,* which was nothing more than a lean-to off the street. In the Middle Ages, schools frequently found shelter in the church. Many schools of the seventeenth and eighteenth centuries both here and abroad were held in the home of the master or in some building rented for the purpose.

When it was necessary to build schoolhouses in colonial America, there was an unfortunate tendency to locate them on wasteland or at some dusty crossroad. The boxlike buildings located on these plots were often dingy and inadequate. Ceilings were low, ventilation was bad, lighting unsatisfactory, heating uneven, and sanitary arrangements often unmentionable. The equipment inside was generally of the rudest sort, children, for instance, having to sit on benches without backs. All these conditions were later frequently aggravated by the fact that the community had permitted the schoolhouse to fall into disrepair. Knowing conditions at first hand from wide travel, Horace Mann declared that many buildings were unsuited for a decent family to live in.

Both Mann and Barnard made it a special objective of state educational administration and supervision to try to improve the condition of school buildings. In fact, one of Barnard's chief claims to fame is his authorship of the first outstanding book in this country on school architecture.[35] In this volume he went into great detail about the location of school buildings; their size and style; materials and method of construction; their lighting, heating, and ventilation; seating accommodations; provisions for library and apparatus; and external arrangements for a schoolyard.

The earliest American buildings erected specifically for school purposes usually incorporated in their design the pedagogical notion of an ungraded school. Here all the children were gathered together in a single room, and the teacher's method was to call individuals or small groups up to his desk to hear their lessons. A single large room usually satisfied the simple demands of such a theory of education.

The Lancasterian scheme of instruction, when it came into vogue, made no notable change in this architecture. The distinguishing feature of the Lancasterian method, it will be remembered,[36] was that it enabled a single teacher through the employment of monitors to teach classes of children numbering in the hundreds. The only additional demand this method made on conventional school architecture was

[35] H. Barnard, *School Architecture* (A. S. Barnes and Co., Inc., New York, 1848).

[36] For a longer account of this method, see *supra,* pp. 211–212.

to increase the dimensions of the schoolroom to the virtual proportions of a hall. In order to give the teacher a commanding view of his whole class, it was necessary either to raise him on a platform or to build the floor of the school on an inclined plane.

The next pedagogical notion to affect school-building architecture was that of grading. The graded school required individual rooms for each grade; but even before the notion of grading became popular, school buildings with multiple rooms were beginning to appear. Occasionally, ungraded schools grew large enough for the teacher to require an assistant, or "usher," as he was called. In planning the accommodations for such a school it became customary to provide one or two small rooms off the main schoolroom where the ushers could hear lessons without disturbing what was going on in the main room.

Probably the Quincy School in Boston was the first school building prominently featuring the principle of grading. This building, erected in 1847, was four stories tall and had twelve classrooms with a total capacity of 400 to 600 students. Here every room was an usher's room, so to speak, only much enlarged. The former large main classroom was relegated to the top floor, where it became an auditorium. This type of school architecture proved very popular, many examples still standing in the twentieth century.

By 1900, innovations in the curriculum began to demand specialization in the classrooms popularized by the Quincy type of building. Thus, in addition to regular classrooms for drill and content subjects, there was need now to design rooms for the newer expression subjects. Special rooms were needed for kindergartens, manual training, and the domestic and fine arts. Emphasis on music and dramatics gave a new importance to auditoriums, which had tended to disappear even from the Quincy type of school. The rise of gymnastics and athletics required the addition of gymnasiums to the school plant, and the inclusion of vocational education as part of the school's task made necessary the addition of shops. Finally, specialization became the rule not only in the design of individual classrooms but in whole school buildings as well. Thus, elementary schools were designed differently from secondary, technical and commerical high schools from academic, and schools for the physically handicapped from schools for normal children.

The greatest economy of space and materials in constructing so diversified a school building was found to be some form of a central corridor with classrooms on either side. These central corridors were most frequently laid out in the shape of the letters E, H, I, L, T, and U. This permitted growing communities to accommodate increases in school population by merely adding onto the outstretched arms of these letter shapes, which was not so easy with closed letters or block-shaped buildings. Some architects experimented with movable partitions in order to facilitate future alterations of physical structures with changes in school program. Others, where school grounds were ample, designed campus-type buildings in which accommodations for different functions like the gymnasium, auditorium, library, and classrooms were housed in separate buildings.

Even so, many fast-growing and less wealthy communities found it difficult to keep their school-building programs abreast of the population increase. Gary, Indiana, tried to solve this lag by an ingenious method for the intensive use of the existing school plant. According to this plan a given school population was divided into two platoons—hence the name "platoon plan." For part of the school day one of these platoons used the academic classrooms, while the other used such activity rooms as the shops, gymnasium, and auditorium. For the other part of the school day the platoons exchanged facilities. But the significant feature of the plan was that no facilities were ever idle. The school plant was in nearly 100 per cent use all the time.[37]

The twentieth century also witnessed a number of other improvements in school architecture. Brick and cement, for instance, became the principal building materials, wood having largely gone out with the nineteenth century. Central heating plants were installed, supplanting individual heating units for each room. Schoolroom lighting progressed from multilateral in the nineteenth century to unilateral in the twentieth. Furthermore, rooms came to be constructed according to a scientifically determined ratio between window and floor area.

School equipment also made a number of notable advances in the transition from the nineteenth to the twentieth century. From bare benches children had come to enjoy the comparative luxury of seats with backs. From seats and desks designed for two, they had progressed to individual seats. While for long these individual seats and desks remained screwed to the floor in fixed rows, the coming of progressive education with its greater emphasis on freedom finally led to movable equipment. Other conveniences, such as cloakrooms for the children and closets for the teacher, so conspicuous by their absence in the colonial schoolhouse, also arrived in due course.

In the 100 years following the publication of Barnard's epoch-making book, the exteriors of school buildings took on a variety of architectural contours. For the most part, they followed the modes of the changing times. Some early school buildings copied church architecture. Steeples with or without school bells attest to this model.

[37] R. D. Case, *The Platoon School in America* (Stanford University Press, Stanford, Calif., 1931), chap. 2.

Other schools adopted the classical lines of Greek architecture. In the post-Civil War period school buildings became very garish and ornamental. By the twentieth century, however, functional design was the rule, resulting in simpler and more impressive-looking school buildings.

Not only did the church have an influence on the early external design of school buildings, but its Protestant branch made one unique contribution to interior floor plans for Sunday school buildings. First developed in Akron, Ohio, during the nineteenth century, this novel architecture became known as the "Akron type" and long remained standard for Protestant Sunday schools. Religious education at this time, it will be remembered,[38] was just beginning to make a transition from centering in the evangelical experience of conversion to stressing more strictly educational procedures. The Akron type of Sunday school architecture made an ingenious combination of these two theories of religious education. The central feature of its floor plan was a large assembly room surrounded by classroom alcoves, each leading directly off the main assembly. By means of curtains or folding partitions these alcoves could be either closed off by themselves or thrown open and incorporated into the assembly room. This design greatly facilitated the contemporarily popular uniform lesson plan and also lent itself to the later graded lesson plan as well.[39] In the course of time, however, the architecture of church school buildings came more and more frequently to imitate secular public school architecture.

EDUCATIONAL PHILANTHROPY

School buildings and the instructional programs they house have invariably necessitated some kind of financial outlay. During most of educational history the chief source of financial support for education was private. Usually this source was the private purse of the student or his family, but few were the private purses that could foot the instructional bill without assistance. Consequently, the major problem in the history of educational finance has been how to mobilize fiscal resources so that the needy as well as the affluent might benefit from the blessings of education.

One of the earliest means for making educational opportunities generally available to more than just the economically self-sufficient was a charitable gift for the support of education. The difficulty with this sort of support, however, was its frequently irregular and fluctuating character. The charitable support of education took on greater

[38] For a fuller account of the religious education of the time, see *supra,* pp. 320–323.

[39] For a fuller account of these lesson plans, see *supra,* p. 321.

stability when, as in the case of the chantries already mentioned, bequests were made in the form of trust funds. Here with good management a school could count on a more or less steady income from the principal of the trust for an almost indefinite length of time.

Many schools were founded in this way during the Renaissance in Europe. Owing to frontier conditions, which delayed the accumulation of great fortunes, educational trusts or foundations appeared somewhat late in America. Nevertheless, all through the seventeenth and eighteenth centuries in America there was a steady, if relatively small, flow of philanthropic gifts toward grammar schools, academies, and colleges. In the nineteenth century the size and number of these benefactions increased enormously, particularly in the field of higher education. As men succeeded in tapping the vast resources of the country, fortunes accumulated that, toward the end of the century, made possible the princely endowments leading to the founding of such distinguished seats of learning as Johns Hopkins, Stanford, and the University of Chicago. Higher education continued into the twentieth century to enjoy this lavish philanthropy, checked only by increasingly heavy income and inheritance taxes.

The conclusion of the Civil War also witnessed the rise of another type of trust foundation whose object was neither solely nor even primarily to subsidize teaching directly but rather to supplement and assist already established institutions of education. The first of these great foundations was that established by George Peabody three years after the war. In making his bequest of $1,000,000 he directed the trustees of the fund to use it for the encouragement of education in the more destitute portions of the Southern states. Fifteen years later John F. Slater established another $1,000,000 foundation to promote education among the population emancipated by the Civil War. Other foundations followed, being topped in the twentieth century by John D. Rockefeller's magnificent gift of over $40,000,000 to set up the General Education Board and of an approximately majestic sum given by Andrew Carnegie to establish the Carnegie Institution and the Carnegie Foundation for the Advancement of Teaching. Most munificent of all was the Ford Foundation, which came into prominence after the Second World War.

The support of education through trust funds did not continue without opposition. As early as the eighteenth century, anxiety was expressed at the posthumous control over education that such trusts lodged in the hands of donors and testators. What guarantee was there, people inquired, that educational objectives judged worthy of endowment in the donor's or testator's lifetime would continue to deserve this support in the next and succeeding generations? The

Frenchman Anne Robert Jacques Turgot and the Englishman Adam Smith had little confidence in human ability to predict the needs of those coming after them. Indeed, Smith was of the mind that the curriculum would be kept more vital and responsive to current social demands if deprived of the crutch of ancient endowment. In the next century another Englishman, John Stuart Mill, made a strong plea for protection of educational trusts for at least a reasonable time after the date of the gift, for, as he said, only time and experience can judge of their wisdom.

As a practical matter of fact, these arguments had their principal significance in the case of educational endowments with relatively narrow and restricted purposes. When such endowments patently outlived their usefulness, it was necessary to appear to courts and legislatures to step in and either curtail or redirect them. Bearing this history in mind, most of the great foundations just mentioned as springing up in America during the late nineteenth and twentieth centuries took special pains to guard the public interest. This they did by providing in their trust deeds either for the termination of the trust fund in a stated length of time or for the grant to the trustees of very wide latitude in the choice of purposes for which the trust funds were to be disbursed.

PUBLIC SCHOOL FINANCE

While philanthropy proved of inestimable value in the impetus that it gave to American education, its influence was felt more strongly in the development of leadership than in bearing the financial burden of the democratic education of the masses. To be sure, it was philanthropy that had helped pioneer the idea of public education through such early agencies as the New York Free School Society, but the funds involved were entirely insufficient to reach any but a very small percentage of the potential school population. The vast sums needed for universal education did not become available till the public was won to taxing itself. The public, however, did not come to such self-imposed discipline till it seemingly had tried every other possible way of supporting schools with less effort.

The earliest so-called "public" schools of colonial America were mainly supported not by taxes, as is sometimes thought, but by a "rate bill." The expenses of maintaining a school were defrayed by applying to them any income the community might have from public lands set aside for the purpose or from any gifts made to the community for the benefit of the schools. Any appropriation from the "common stock" for the aid of the schools also went toward this initial defrayal of expenses. The amount of expense remaining after these reductions was prorated according to the number of children attending school. Each parent or patron of the school then received a rate bill determined according to the number of children he had in school. Rate bills of this sort dominated methods of school support all through the colonial period and well down into the nineteenth century. Massachusetts, in fact, did not give them up till 1827, Indiana till 1851, and New Jersey not till as late as 1870.

Various other sources of public income were also used to keep the rate bill down. Such were moneys derived from amusement taxes and liquor licenses. So, too, were fines and escheats. Some states, indeed, were not above the moral incongruity of authorizing lotteries for the support of schools. But the returns from these sources never seriously threatened to eliminate the rate bill.

As time went on and as land-hungry people moved westward with the frontier, the public learned that the cheapest and easiest way to reduce the rate bill was through the sale of the country's vast public domain. Connecticut was one of the first states to sense possibilities here. By the sale of its claim to the Western Reserve of Ohio it netted the handsome figure of $1,200,000, which, five years before the end of the eighteenth century, it constituted a permanent school fund. This generous endowment should have made Connecticut schools the best in the country; but, strangely enough, the quality of education actually declined from the blight of this wealth. Excellent management of the principal of this fund produced an income so large that by approximately 1820 many communities dispensed with local support and thus reduced the total outlay for schools or, worse yet, curtailed their regular educational program so that it could be paid entirely out of the state subsidy. Not till Henry Barnard became active did Connecticut begin to arouse itself from the financial lethargy into which its affluence had lulled it.

Other states soon followed with permanent school, or "literary," funds, as they sometimes were called. While none of these states repeated Connecticut's experience, nevertheless they suffered other temptations. Nowhere was this more evident than in the newer Western states carved out of the public domain. There the state permanent school funds came about as the result of the largess of the Federal government. Commencing with the Ordinance of 1787, the Federal government embarked on a policy of setting aside the sixteenth section of land in every township of the Northwest Territory for the support of schools. This policy was confirmed and made even more generous as Federal territories were admitted to statehood. Some idea of the ultimate magnitude of the landed endowment thus provided by the Federal government may be gathered from the fact that in the thirty states so endowed it amounted to a total of 121,110 square miles.[40] This was almost equivalent to giving each of the thirty states a landed endowment the size of the state of Connecticut.

Unhappily, public education failed to benefit to the full from even this magnificent endowment. Unlike Connecticut, however, the Middle Western states failed by reason of dissipating their heritage. Some states discounted the future growth of the country too heavily and sold their reserved lands much too cheaply. Others made poor investments of the proceeds derived from the sale of their lands. Still others squandered their permanent school funds by borrowing from them and then later repudiating the indebtedness. Some of these misfortunes occurred because these youthful states were inexperienced in administering such public trusts, but other states repeated some of these mistakes in spite of the fact that they had before them the experience of older states.

Some states tried to make amends for their mismanagement or misdeeds by recognizing the amount of their lost endowment as a perpetual debt of the state treasury upon which the state pledged itself to raise annually by taxation the equivalent of the interest on the lost funds. Certain states even wrote this debt down on their books as a permanent endowment. Of course, the latter procedure was entirely fictitious, for the interest paid to the schools came not out of sound interest-bearing securities that would reduce or supplement taxation but directly out of taxes. This was therefore not an easing but an increasing of the burden of taxation.

It is only small comfort to minimize this loss of endowment by pointing out its decreasing importance in the financing of American education. Of course, accurate early statistics do not exist; but if one started about 1820 in Connecticut with an estimated high of 100 per cent as the proportion of school costs defrayed by income from permanent endowment—at least in many Connecticut school districts—it is almost startling to note that by 1920, just 100 years later, this percentage had fallen to 2.7 as an average for the whole United States. Being stated in percentages, this decline is, to be sure, relative and therefore could just as well be stated as an enormous growth in school costs in this period of 100 years.

Viewed from either the angle of growth or the angle of decline, this situation meant just one thing financially. Vast new resources would have to be found to satisfy the country's voracious appetite for education. Gone were the days when the public could meet its educational obligations in the easy fashion of sending a rate bill to the private family or shifting a large part of the cost onto the back

[40] F. H. Swift, *Federal and State Policies in Public School Finance in the United States* (Ginn and Company, Boston, 1931), p. 59.

of bountiful mother nature. Indeed, before the middle of the nineteenth century had been reached, the public was at last resolutely facing the need for taxing itself for the greater part of the cost of public education.

Public taxes for schools were not altogether new at this time, taxes having long been levied in states like Pennsylvania for the support of pauper schools. But, of course, taxes for the support of schools for all, rich and poor alike, had much wider implications both ethically and financially.[41] The public, fully aware of these implications, eased itself into the yoke of taxes very gradually. It tested the feel of this new gear at each step before putting on the full harness of taxation. Thus, states often inaugurated taxes for education by making them permissive. People of a locality willing to tax themselves for schools were permitted to do so. Later, states made it a local option whether everyone should not be so taxed. In the final stage, legislatures made school taxes mandatory on a state-wide basis.

The Catholic parochial school system, long dependent on private tuition fees for its support, was quick to feel the competition of public schools when tax support relieved parents of the expense of the rate bill. To meet this competition, the Third Plenary Council in 1884 advocated that parochial schools be made free by making them a charge on the whole parish and not just on the patrons of the school. In the succeeding decades, however, few parishes proved large or wealthy enough to shoulder this burden. Hence, Catholics had to continue to pay tuition fees for their own schools while at the same time they paid taxes for the support of public ones, a kind of double taxation from which they and the patrons of other private schools long have sought to be relieved.[42]

Once the public had become accustomed to taxing itself for schools, it turned its attention to problems growing out of this relatively new method of school support. Chief among these problems was how to make a more equitable distribution of educational opportunities in the face of the fact that taxable wealth was unevenly distributed. At first, during colonial and early national times, while the country was still largely agrarian, inequities in the distribution of wealth were not nearly so conspicuous as they became later during the era of rapid industrialization. When land with its buildings, equipment, and livestock was the principal form of wealth, most wealth was easily visible and what one man had did not differ greatly from what his neighbor possessed. With the spread of the Industrial Revolution in the late nineteenth and twentieth centuries, however, the concentration

[41] For the growth of free public education, see *supra,* chap. 17.

[42] H. G. Hochwalt, "Financing Catholic Education," *Educational Record,* 30:197–206, April, 1949.

of industries in urban areas tended to make urban and industrial real estate far more valuable than that in rural districts. Furthermore, the wealth of industries came to be represented not so much by the land they owned as by the less visible and more easily concealed intangible property of stocks and bonds. Obviously, great inequities were in the making for schools. School authorities who could locate industrial wealth within their taxing area clearly had far greater financial resources at their command than did those who could not. This resulted in what many thought were unwarranted and inequitable differences in educational opportunity for the nation's youth.

Two principal remedies were proposed in the twentieth century to correct these inequalities. One was to change the form of the school tax. For centuries, the school tax had been a tax on real estate. In agrarian times this tax seemed adequate enough. In the industrial era, educators began to look with longing eyes at corporate and income taxes that would tap the vast new intangible forms of wealth for the benefit of the schools. Others, frightened by the fluctuating character of this kind of wealth, as revealed during the Great Depression following 1929, still preferred the real property tax, which, if it did not produce so large a revenue, at least produced a stable one.

The other remedy to equalize educational opportunities was to enlarge the geographical size of the fiscal unit. In no other way, indeed, would it be possible to achieve the ambition of Robert Coram, an American patriot of the eighteenth century, that rural areas should have just as good schools as the seaport towns. Later, of course, in the next century both Horace Mann and Henry Barnard were only too painfully aware of the gaping inequalities between school districts in their ability to support education. In the long run, what was true of districts was equally true of the not much larger town and township. Financial assistance from an administrative unit at least as large as the state seemed to be indicated. New York was early in the field with such assistance. At the very end of the eighteenth century for a period of five years it offered a subsidy for local schools on the main condition that the locality match the subsidy with an equal appropriation. Less than half of the towns of the state applied for this aid. In the next century, however, with the establishment in nearly every state of permanent school funds, state subsidies to local schools became much more popular and frequent.

At first, states did not make these subsidies with the idea primarily of equalizing educational burdens or opportunities. On the contrary, the first motive that prompted these subsidies was, as noted in the case of New York, to stimulate local initiative. Equally important, no doubt, as in the case of Connecticut, was the desire to relieve the burden of school support resting on the local community. The deplorable effects to which this policy led in Connecticut have already been pointed out. It is no surprise, therefore, that the New York policy had a more enduring influence on the subsequent course of state educational finance. Later, when, as a result of the efforts of Mann and Barnard, the state interest in education became more generally recognized, the theory was advanced that state financial subsidies were to pay for the new services of state educational administration and supervision. Not till the twentieth century did the custom take hold of spending state educational funds so as to equalize disparities between localities. In some places, this custom grew up to compensate a locality that had a special deficiency as, for instance, a large amount of nontaxable property within its confines. In other places, as in Colorado, it grew up as a means of enabling poor communities to meet a minimum educational standard laid down by the state.[43]

Even before equalization became the main guiding purpose of state aid for education, states were confronted with the necessity of finding some equitable basis for the division and distribution of the state school fund. One of the earliest devices employed called for distributing this fund in proportion to the adult population in the various communities. This device proved unsatisfactory because it was only a crude measure of the educational burden borne by each community. A later and more refined device, therefore, proportioned the state school fund according to the school population in each community. Yet, even this formula was capable of still further refinement. Not all the children listed in the school census, for instance, were in school; and those who were, were not always in regular attendance. Moreover, the educational burden of two communities with the same number of children in average daily attendance might still vary by reason of having school terms of different length. In the twentieth century, even more precise measures of educational load were sought through taking into account the number of teachers employed relative to the number of pupils and the level of salaries paid to teachers, the two largest determinants of school budgets.

In spite of the great attention paid to state financial aid for education and in spite of the great stake that democracy obviously had in the equalization of educational opportunity, there was after 1890 a long downward trend in the proportion of total school costs borne by the state, a trend that was not checked till just before the American entry into the Second World War. In 1890 the total state contribution amounted to nearly 24 per cent, while in 1925, just before the Great Depression, it was less than 17 per cent. This decline occurred despite

[43] For equalization as a national trend, see *supra*, p. 67.

the fact that state appropriations rose steadily in every decade except the one following the Depression of 1929. Hence, on the whole it meant that total educational costs themselves were rising at a more rapid rate than were state appropriations.

Some idea of the stupendous growth in school costs can be gained from the fact that while the educational tax bill of the country was approximately $63,000,000 just after the Civil War and had reached only $140,000,000 in 1890, it shot up to $1,036,000,000 by the end of the First World War and reached a high of $2,316,000,000 in 1930 just before the Depression drastically curtailed educational expenditures.[44] This means that the financial outlay on education increased by 1,500 per cent between the Civil War and the First World War, 700 per cent since 1890 alone, percentages that were phenomenally more than doubled in the decade of the 1920s alone. It is small wonder, therefore, that state appropriations, though they themselves rose by more than 1,200 per cent before the Depression, nevertheless steadily decreased in their share of total costs defrayed till the Depression forced them to bear a proportion greater than in 1890.

A number of reasons account for this prodigious growth in school costs. One basic underlying cause was the fact that since the Civil War the country's population had more than tripled. While the number of children of school age little more than doubled during this period, the number of average daily attendance quadrupled. Compulsory-attendance legislation largely accounted for this situation. While less than half of the states had such legislation at the end of the nineteenth century, all of them had it by the end of the First World War. Not only did compulsory-attendance laws bring greater numbers of children into school and keep them there regularly, but the phenomenal growth of high schools, which coincided with this period,[45] kept them there for a greater number of years than ever before. The curriculum offered in the schools, moreover, was greatly enriched during the period under consideration. Paralleling all these other evidences of growth was a steady rise in the professional qualification of teachers, which necessitated higher and higher salaries.[46] Last but far from least in the factors pushing school costs ever upward was the rising cost of living due in part to the depreciation of the purchasing power of the dollar following the credit expansion necessitated by the First and Second World Wars.

The phenomenal rate of rise in school costs not only outstripped the rate at which state appropriations for education were rising but

[44] For the influence of depressions on education, see *supra,* pp. 79–80.
[45] For a fuller account, see *supra,* pp. 411, 529–531.
[46] For a fuller account, see *supra,* pp. 505–506.

Statistical Summary of Financial Data on American Elementary and Secondary Schools, 1870–1957/1958

	1870	1880	1890	1900	1910	1920	1930	1940	1950	1957/1958
Total population*	38.5	50.1	62.6	75.6	91.9	105.7	122.7	131.0	151.2	170.3
Children five to eighteen years of age*	12.0	15.0	18.5	21.4	24.2	27.7	31.5	29.8	30.7	40.1
Children in average daily attendance*	4.0	6.1	8.1	10.6	12.8	16.1	21.3	22.0	22.2	29.7
Average school term†	132.2	130.3	134.7	144.3	157.5	161.9	172.7	175.0	177.9	177.6
Value of school property‡	130.3	209.5	342.5	550.0	1,091.0	2,409.7	6,211.3	7,635.1	11,396.8	
Revenue receipts from:‡										
Permanent funds			7.7	9.1	14.0	26.4	27.5	23.1	35.0	
State taxes			26.3	37.8	64.6	134.2	329.3	658.9	2,905.5	4,610.7
Local taxes			97.2	149.4	312.2	758.8	1,645.6	1,490.4	2,122.7	6,621.4
All other			11.9	23.2	42.1	50.9	86.0	88.0	949.3	378.6
Percentage of revenue derived from:										
Permanent funds			5.4	4.2	3.2	2.7	1.3	1.0	.06	
State taxes			18.4	17.2	14.9	13.8	15.8	29.2	39.0	37.9
Local taxes			67.9	68.0	72.1	78.2	78.8	65.9	53.4	54.4
All other			8.3	10.6	9.8	5.3	4.1	3.9	7.0	7.7

	1870	1880	1890	1900	1910	1920	1930	1940	1950	1957/1958
Total expenditures for all purposes‡	63.3	78.0	140.5	214.9	426.2	1,036.1	2,316.7	2,344.0		13,569.1
Total expenditures per capita of population§	1.6	1.5	2.2	2.8	4.6	9.8	18.8	17.7	38.6	79.6
Total expenditures per pupil in average daily attendance§	15.5	12.7	17.2	20.2	33.2	64.1	108.4	105.7	258.8	448.6
Annual salary of instructional staff¶						1,306.0	2,371.0	2,948.0	3,633.0	4,702.0
Personal income per member of the labor force¶							2,728.0	2,778.0	4,113.0	4,996.0

* Stated in millions.
† Stated in days.
‡ Stated in millions of dollars.
§ Stated in dollars.
¶ Adjusted to 1957/1958 purchasing power.

SOURCE: Adapted from U.S. Office of Education, *Biennial Survey of Education, 1956–1958*, pp. 14–15.

also tended to outstrip the slow rise in assessed property values.[47] This made the problem of local school support doubly hard. The local community not only had to bear an increasingly large portion of school costs but had to do so on an assessed valuation that was falling further and further behind. This meant only one thing, an increase in the tax rate. On this, boards of education frequently clashed with aldermen, town councils, and boards of finance. To meet their obligations, some boards of education in the twentieth century sought fiscal independence from these municipal authorities. Yet whether fiscal independence or fiscal dependence resulted in more efficient educational administration remained a moot point. In any event, the financial management of the school enterprise became so technical a matter that the curriculum for the professional training of superintendents came to give a large share of time to it.

[47] W. R. Burgess, *Trends of School Costs* (Russell Sage Foundation, New York, 1920), p. 123.

19

The School and Progress

There has hardly been a modern society, autocratic or democratic, which has not designed its educational system under the rubric of social progress. But, looking back over the sweep of history, how are we to judge whether social progress—and particularly educational progress—has occurred? Are there any criteria by which educational history can be judged? If so, do these criteria exist outside history and independently of it, or are they caught up in its currents and modified by its crosscurrents? Again, if educational progress is visible, what are the circumstances under which it is best encouraged? Should the school merely attempt to reproduce current society—lift the young, as it were, through a series of locks in a canal to the level of adult experience? Or should the school endeavor to lift the level of adult experience itself by purifying and reconstructing it? In answering these perennial questions much will depend on the further persistent inquiry, how much freedom, civil and academic, should teachers be permitted in selecting the social point of view from which they teach?

EARLY THEORETICAL ALTERNATIVES

Down to the time of the Greeks education was definitely traditional and conservative. It was traditional in the literal meaning of the word: it was a handing over, a passing on, of the racial experience from the older to the younger generation. And education was conservative also in the literal meaning of the word: it preserved what mankind had learned through the hard school of experience. Indeed, without conservation and tradition of individual experience, that is, without education, there would have been no society as we know it in history.

It is not difficult to understand why the early school took a conservative view of its relation to society. The conditions of living were so severe that social survival was always at issue. To survive, let alone to keep from slipping back to a more precarious form of living, the bare reproduction and transmission, or tradition, of the race experience not only was a minimum educational program but often required a maximum educational effort. If education reproduced a society with as much security as had been known in the past, people were content. Certainly, this state of affairs was preferable to the jeopardy involved in teaching variations from tradition whose outcome might be as likely to wipe out as to extend the gains of social experience.

The first notable change in this relation between school and society took place among the Greeks. In the period when Greek civilization was reaching the highest pinnacle of its fame, a fundamental change occurred in the underlying conditions of Greek life. The Greeks came to enjoy an economic prosperity and security hardly known up to that time. This prosperity and security, drawn from commercial success in the Aegean and eastern Mediterranean, greatly mitigated the precariousness of the Greek standard of living. Greek society could afford to wink at deviations from traditional educational stereotypes. Indeed, commercial expansion actually seemed to invite educational innovation, for with foreign merchants of goods there came to Greece foreign merchants of ideas as well. The conflict and comparison of traditional Greek ideas with foreign ones set the Greeks to pondering. Which set of traditions or folkways was right? At no point was an answer to this question more urgent than in the field of education. There the burning question was whether to continue to educate the young according to familiar Greek traditions and folkways or whether to alter educational patterns in the light of new ideas emerging from reflective contact with foreign cultures.

It is to the credit of Plato (427–347 B.C.), preeminent among philosophers of all time, that he early saw how this educational problem might be turned to social advantage. Prior to his time, improvement in the quality of education had been merely an expression of dissatisfaction with the state of ignorance, immaturity, or lack of skill of the young. Plato's educational ideals, however, were the outgrowth of dissatisfaction with existing social conditions. Therefore, he thought that the improvement of education depended in the first place on improved social conditions. Consequently at the outset of his greatest educational work, *The Republic,* he was at considerable pains to describe the characteristics of an ideal society. If this ideal was to be realized through education, the school's duty was not just the simple one of reproducing age-old traditions with their inherent maladjustments but the more complex one of bringing the ideal society into existence and then preventing any defection from it.

The scheme of *The Republic,* however, was only a scheme. The Greeks never adopted it as a practical educational program. If anything, the bulk of the Greek populace preferred educational practice that was conservative. The chief indictment they lodged against Socrates (469–399 B.C.) when they brought this great teacher to trial was that he was unconventional and therefore had taught disrespect of the gods. Yet all that he had tried to do in his teaching was to improve life by examining and criticizing the principles on which it was lived. To raise doubts, however, was considered to be disrespectful. In reality, the trial of Socrates was the method the Greek populace took to insist that education conform to the social order. Even Plato came to incline toward this point of view when late in life he wrote his *Laws.*

The conservative theory of the relation of the school to the social order, however, did not lack a theoretical apologist. No less a one than Aristotle (384–322 B.C.), Plato's student and critic, adopted this view in contrast to Plato. Instead of trying to reconstruct the social order through education he took the view that education should seek to maintain the *status quo.* Whether the government of a society is oligarchic or democratic, he wrote in his *Politics,* "A given constitution demands an education in conformity with it; for the maintenance of any constitution, like its first establishment, is due, as a rule, to the presence of the spirit or character proper to that constitution."[1]

In the long chain of centuries following these two great thinkers, the writers of utopias generally patterned their views on education after Plato.[2] The writers of more practical educational treatises, however, to say nothing of the overwhelming weight of practice itself, followed Aristotle. Quintilian (35–100), foremost among Roman educators, for instance, when he wrote on the education of the orator, was creating neither a new education nor a new political ideal. Rather had he in mind the Roman lawyer or statesman of his day. Similarly, when during the Renaissance the Italian Conte Baldassari Castiglione (1478–1529) wrote *The Courtier* and the Englishman Sir Thomas Elyot (1490–1546) wrote *The Book Named the Governour,* neither was thinking of a new educational prototype. Both were prescribing

[1] Aristotle, *Politics,* book VIII, chap. 1, in J. Burnet, *Aristotle on Education* (Cambridge University Press, London, 1913), pp. 105–106.

[2] G. Masso, *Education in Utopias* (Bureau of Publications, Teachers College, Columbia University, New York, 1927), *passim.*

a type of education that coincided with the Renaissance calling of a gentleman. In *Some Thoughts concerning Education* another Englishman, John Locke (1632–1704), was also quite conventional. Although a revolution had just occurred in English political life toward the end of the seventeenth century, Locke's essay on education did not reflect it. He was content to give well-considered advice on how to achieve the stereotype of the English gentry of his period.

THE SCHOOL AS CREATURE OF THE SOCIAL ORDER

In practice even more than in theory the schools have long viewed their role as meeting rather than anticipating current social demands. Indeed, they have been as often behind these demands as abreast of them and hardly ever in advance of them. To be sure, Greek teachers, who more and more made their way to Rome when that city came to dominate the entire Mediterranean world, did bring with them a culture new to the Romans. But this culture was sought and taught as a perfection or polish to Roman institutions already well accepted. There was no thought of radically reconstructing them after the Greek model. Even Cato the Elder, who most suspected the new education of being subversive of Roman institutions, lived long enough to be captivated by the charm it added to rather than substituted for Roman culture.

The decline and fall of the Roman Empire further illustrates the point. Roman schools, while they did not prepare the way for cultural collapse, at least were powerless to prevent it. Greek schools, too, in the period of Hellenic decline after the fourth century B.C. definitely deteriorated with the fortunes of the Greek city-states. Greek and Roman schools, instead of carrying within themselves the seeds of social regeneration, seemed to show every evidence of being as genetically played out as were political and economic institutions.

In the Middle Ages, again, the schools conformed to the times. In fact, the times were so little in need of formal schooling that the schools conformed almost to a point of extinguishing themselves. What schools survived or were created adapted themselves chiefly to the demands of the Catholic Church. Thus, the cathedral schools that sprang up and were attached to cathedrals in cathedral cities were intended for training the priesthood. Song schools taught the singing requisite for church services. Even the medieval university, powerful social agency though it became, conformed to the feudal order of which it was a part. It taught the law, theology, and medicine that the reviving civilization of the time required. Even in theology, which was the intellectual frontier of the day, the university scholars vied with each other in consolidating the authority of the Catholic

Church by incorporating Aristotelian philosophy with Christian revelation.

Renascence that the Renaissance was, it was not initiated by the schools. Had it been initiated by them, one would have expected the universities to commence the movement. The universities, however, had no prevision of the new Humanism that was about to sweep Europe. Far from being ahead of their times, they were already falling behind them. As a matter of fact, Humanism demanded a school all its own, imbued with the spirit of the period. The Humanistic secondary school of the Renaissance was thus clearly a creature of Humanism, not a creator of it. It rose and declined with the fortunes of Humanism.

When science came knocking for admission to the curriculum of the Humanistic secondary school of the sixteenth, seventeenth, and eighteenth centuries, this school was just as blind to and unprepared for the future as the medieval universities had been in the case of Humanism. Far from preparing the way for science, the Humanistic school had become so conventional that it even actively blocked and resisted its advance. Consequently, another new school had to be founded, the German *Realschule,* to break down the barrier to teaching this disinherited stepchild of the culture of the day. But, again, the new school was a creature and not a creator of the new interest in science.

Probably the political and economic revolutions of the eighteenth, nineteenth, and twentieth centuries indicate better than any other historical evidence the secondary rather than the primary role of the schools in periods of social transition. Neither the American Revolution of 1776 nor the French Revolution of 1789 was the product of school programs forecasting social reconstruction. The schools of the *ancien régime* in France bred sympathy and respect for the first and second estates, for the nobility and the clergy. This is not to deny that prerevolutionary writers had designs on the schools as instruments of social reconstruction. As a matter of fact, most of them had. But these ideas had no influence on the instruction given under the monarchy. They took effect only after the revolution had become a *fait accompli.* Taking effect then, however, they helped to entrench the new social order, but they did not bring it about.

Clearly, the school was an ally of the *status quo* whether the *status quo* was maintained by a conservative or established by a revolutionary party. The Frenchman Claude Adrien Helvétius (1715–1771) stated this point differently but to the same effect when he wisely observed that precepts of education which contradict the government are always reputed bad. Certainly none was more insistent in preventing the schools from contradicting the government than

Napoleon. In his correspondence he stated no new opinion when he declared that a state is on uncertain and ill-defined foundations if it does not take the initiative in determining whether a child should be reared a republican or a monarchist.

Noah Webster (1758–1843), lexicographer, patriot, and textbook writer, in addressing himself to post-Revolutionary America, might as well have been quoting Aristotle on education when he quoted the noted French author of *The Spirit of the Laws,* the Baron de Montesquieu (1689–1755), to the effect that education ought to be relative to the principles of government, being one thing for a monarchy and another for a republic. He was acting on this very principle when he stated that the system of education under colonial tutelage would be unsuitable to carry over into the period of national independence. Colonial education had evolved in adaptation to a monarchical social system with aristocratic class divisions. Now that the colonies had become a nation of democratic states, Webster insisted that the colonial school system would have to be brought into conformity with the new philosophy of equality of educational opportunity for all classes. Some contemporaries of Webster looked upon the schools as the bulwark of republican institutions not so much against a king or despot as against anarchy. In the next generation still others, like Henry Barnard (1811–1900), viewed them as a bulwark for the system of private property. But in all these cases Americans thought of the school as making secure the gains of the Revolution rather than pointing the way to a further or continuing reconstruction of the nation's destiny.

The case was no different in England during the long decades in which the Industrial Revolution was taking place. As already indicated, the Humanistic schools certainly did not hasten to teach the science that would have trained the inventors who made the Industrial Revolution possible. These men had to acquire their scientific knowledge in spite of the English Humanistic schools of the eighteenth and even of the nineteenth centuries. Indeed, it was not till 1853 that the English government made grants to individual schools for the teaching of science. Nor did the schools pioneer in the political reforms that the Industrial Revolution made necessary. The great Reform Acts of 1832 and 1867, which extended the suffrage more widely to industrial workers, did not come about because the schools of the first quarter of the century were studying the injustices of the existing order. The electoral reforms once achieved, however, the newly enfranchised workers did legislate for themselves more equitable educational opportunities through the acts of 1833 and especially of 1870.

The revolutions of the twentieth century, born of the First World War, followed the educational pattern of preceding revolutions. There certainly is no evidence that the way for the first of these revolutions, the Russian, was paved by the schools of czarist Russia. On the contrary, these schools were reactionary. Yet, as soon as the czar was overthrown, the schools became the loyal defenders of communism.[3] The schools of Italy went through the same cycle in the revolution brought about by fascism. In Germany there was nothing in the schools of the imperial Reich that foreshadowed the republicanism of the Weimar Republic. Nor was there anything in the schools of that republic that taught the desirability of the revolution brought about by National Socialism under the Third Reich.

Even in the United States, where democracy was supposed in part to be identical with progressive social change, there was little inclination to assign the school any significant role in taking the initiative in social reconstruction. New York State, alarmed by the forces of social change abroad after the First World War, appointed the Lusk committee to investigate seditious activities. In its report this committee stated that "The public school teacher is a representative and officer of the state *as it now exists*. He is employed by that state to teach loyalty to its institutions and obedience to its laws. He is not employed to explore the controversial fields of political economy with the view of championing utopian schemes of reform or change. . . . If a change in our social system or in the structure of our government is at any time demanded by the people of this state or of the United States, the mandate must be disclosed by the verdict of the polls. The public school must not be employed as a rostrum for distinctive propaganda of any character. Its teaching staff must not be allowed to spread the gospel of discontent among the people. No person who is not eager to combat the theories of social change should be entrusted with the task of fitting the young and old of this state for the responsibilities of citizenship."[4] On the eve of the Second World War, then, the practical administration of the schools still followed Aristotle. Given a monarchic, democratic, Communistic, or fascistic state, it was still the duty of education to create a spirit congenial to the politics assumed.

THE SCHOOL AS CREATOR OF THE SOCIAL ORDER

While practical considerations have eclipsed the Platonic theory of the relation of the school to the social order, the eclipse has never been total. The theory has always remained a popular one,

---

[3] A. Pinkevitch, *The New Education in the Soviet Republic* (The John Day Company, Inc., New York, 1929), pp. 153–154.

[4] "Revolutionary Radicalism," *Report of the Joint Legislative Committee of the State of New York Investigating Seditious Activities* (Albany, N.Y., 1920), vol. 3, p. 2343.

particularly in epochs that have cried out for a rectification of social abuses. For this reason the theory that the school has a creative as well as a conservative function enjoyed a notable revival in the eighteenth and twentieth centuries. With few exceptions, little of a practical nature was done to put the theory in practice, but the theory itself was analyzed more thoroughly and pushed more vigorously and frequently than ever before.

Of the French liberals of the eighteenth century none made a more penetrating or more inspiring analysis of the problem than did the French Revolutionary the Marquis de Condorcet (1743–1794). Believing in the indefinite perfectibility of man, he looked to the state as the agency through which the continuous progress of mankind was to be brought about. Writing in the midst of revolution, he projected a state which would not just make secure the results of revolution but would maintain a continuous spirit of revolution. Instead of the new state's interests becoming vested and therefore ultimately coming to a standstill, he conceived of a state that would reduce revolution to an orderly process of continuous social reconstruction. Such a state would wish, Condorcet thought, "that, in national education, everything should be submitted to a rigorous examination . . . that all political theories be taught and contested, that no system of social organization be presented to enthusiasm or to prejudice as the object of a superstitious veneration but that all should be presented to the reason as different systems among which it has the right to choose."[5]

In a sense Condorcet's educational meliorism was in the tradition of Aristotle. Given a state that contemplates the constant redirection of its energies, it is the duty of the schools to create a spirit appropriate to this purpose. In other words, even though the school examines a variety of political theories, it nonetheless is conserving or perpetuating the kind of state that is continuously reexamining its own ends. Yet, in spite of this agreement with Aristotle, Condorcet made a definite advance on both Aristotle and Plato. In his view, instead of a fearful and therefore cautious attitude toward social change, state and school were warmly and enthusiastically to embrace the opportunities for social progress which they present.

Condorcet's German contemporary, the philosopher Immanuel Kant (1724–1804), also favored education's taking the lead in bringing about a better world. "Children should be educated," he contended,

---

[5] F. La Fontainerie, *French Liberalism and Education in the Eighteenth Century* (McGraw-Hill Book Company, New York, 1932), pp. 376–377. See also S. E. Ballinger, "The Idea of Social Progress through Education in the French Enlightenment Period: Helvétius and Condorcet," *History of Education Journal*, 10:88–99, 1959.

"*not* with reference to their present condition, but rather with regard to a possibly improved future state of the human race—that is, according to *the idea of humanity* and its entire destiny."[6] But Kant did not share Condorcet's confidence that this objective could be achieved through a system of public or state schools. He did not trust princes to institute this sort of education because they were too likely to regard their subjects as mere instruments for accomplishing royal purposes. Even parents Kant viewed as an obstacle to the kind of education he had in mind, for their educational outlook was usually limited to ensuring that their children would prosper in the *status quo*. Only a cosmopolitan scheme of education would suffice. But such a solution still left up in the air the practical steps for its realization.

The eighteenth-century liberals not only put forth a theory of social progress through education but also indicated psychological theories by which this progress might be effected. One group, among whom Helvétius was the extreme exponent, leaned heavily on the empirical psychology of John Locke to effect social reform. Locke had laid it down that the mind of the child at birth was a *tabula rasa,* that is, a blank.[7] Although this doctrine had been put forth a century before the French Revolution, its strategic significance for social reform was not appreciated till later. Obviously, if the mind was a blank at birth, the ones first to write thereon would control the political and economic destiny of the next generation. No wonder Helvétius believed *l'éducation peut tout.* Changing from the French monarchy to the French republic would thus be just a matter of turning a page in the experience of adults or capturing the first page in the experience of children.

Another group, whose undisputed leader was the Swiss-born romanticist Jean Jacques Rousseau (1712–1778), started with almost the opposite premise from Locke. Contrary to Locke, Rousseau believed that the child had certain innate capacities at birth, the natural development of which must be respected. The injustice and oppression of the existing *ancien régime* he ascribed to the way in which it frustrated and distorted the natural course of development of these innate powers. Consequently, an education in accord with nature would not only avoid the injustices of the *ancien régime* but would also at the same time be creating a better and more equitable society.

It was the thought of Rousseau rather than Locke that dominated the social-educational reformers of the nineteenth century. Especially is this true of the Swiss Johann Heinrich Pestalozzi (1746–1827)

[6] E. F. Buchner, *The Educational Theory of Immanuel Kant* (J. B. Lippincott Company, Philadelphia, 1904), pp. 116–117.
[7] For a more complete treatment of this topic, see *supra,* pp. 143–145.

and the German Friedrich Wilhelm August Froebel (1782–1852). It is particularly notable in the case of Pestalozzi that he did not start out in life to fashion a career in education for himself. He had a prior preference for politics. Having spoiled his chances in this regard by getting into trouble as a political agitator, he turned to education. His first thought in education, however, was to use it for the purpose of social amelioration. He set about the task, as he was fond of saying, to try to make men out of beggars. He commenced with the limited social and educational objective of teaching the poor how to adjust themselves as contentedly as possible to their poverty. But later it occurred to him that children did not necessarily have to be degraded by their social origins. As he encouraged children in the free expression of their unique abilities, he began to see that their native abilities exceeded the limitations of their accidental social surroundings. This fact led him to realize with Rousseau that the regeneration of both the individual and society lay in the development of human powers in accordance with nature.

The outlook that this brilliant pedagogical insight promised for the correction of age-old social abuses did not appear very bright at first. For long, Pestalozzi was just an obscure man experimenting with an idea in obscure villages of his native Switzerland. Even when he achieved world-wide fame, it was as an educator rather than as a social reformer. Yet one country, Prussia, did come to feel the social as well as the educational effect of his doctrine. After Napoleon had crushed Prussia to earth in the Battle of Jena and in the subsequent Treaty of Tilsit, Prussia had urgent need of national regeneration in order to rehabilitate itself. To this end, among other things, the aristocratic *Junkers,* who controlled Prussia, decided to reform their educational system along Pestalozzian lines. Their hope was to build a strong nation by building strong individuals and to develop strong individuals by developing their native powers according to Pestalozzi's prescription. It is some measure of the *Junkers'* success in organizing Pestalozzian schools to raise up a new Prussia that the country shortly made a signal contribution to the defeat of Napoleon, that it steadily grew in political eminence in succeeding decades, and that its preeminence in education came to be internationally recognized during the first half of the nineteenth century.

The Prussian *Junkers* were, if anything, more successful than they had planned. By the mid-point of the century Pestalozzian instruction not only had put Prussia on its feet but also had educated a generation that was demanding social reforms striking at the root of the power of the *Junkers* themselves. The Junker aristocracy now became alarmed by the "overeducation" of the common people. The Prussian king thought the interest developed by his subjects in social reform an act of disloyalty. Together the King and the *Junkers* joined in severely curtailing the normal schools for teachers, which, it was agreed, were the source of all the social unrest of the time.[8] No more eloquent tribute could have been paid to the power of the social yeast inherent in the pedagogical doctrines of Rousseau and Pestalozzi.

It was this same reactionary zeal of the Prussian upper classes that repressed and discouraged Froebel, another great educational innovator. Even more than Rousseau and Pestalozzi, Froebel developed and emphasized the importance of self-activity on the part of pupils. Meeting official opposition to the introduction of his educational ideas into the state schools, Froebel bitterly complained, "As a state machine I should have been engaged in *cutting out and modeling* other state machines. But I only wanted to train up *free, thinking, independent men.*"[9] The complaint, however, reveals only too well that the governmental bureaucracy was not mistaken when it felt that schools imbued with Froebel's pedagogy could not be contained within the existing social order but must necessarily revolutionize it. Hence it was that Froebel looked rather to America than to his native Germany for a hospitable reception to his idea that schools should be "free republics of childhood."

By the time Froebelian ideas began to penetrate America toward the end of the nineteenth century, it was already no new idea that the school should be an agent of social progress. Horace Mann (1796–1859), Massachusetts' great gift to the American common school revival of the middle of the century, had already energetically advanced it. Apparently he made the theme of his later educational career the subject on which he delivered his commencement oration on graduation from Brown. "The Progressive Character of the Human Race." On the day he accepted office as secretary to the State Board of Education in Massachusetts he confided to his diary, "I have faith in the improvability of the race—in their accelerating improvability."[10] This faith remained undimmed throughout his educational career, for,

---

[8] Furthermore, the philosophical apologist for the Prussian state, Georg Wilhelm Friedrich Hegel (1770–1831), who had at one time taught in a German *Gymnasium*, thought "study in the quiet seclusion of the school" advisable for boys in order to "keep them from the stir and excitement and the seductive influences of the fermenting condition of our time." [M. Mackenzie, *Hegel's Educational Thought and Practice* (Swan, Sonnenschein & Co., London, 1909), p. 183.]

[9] Quoted in J. L. Hughes, *Froebel's Educational Laws for All Teachers* (D. Appleton & Company, Inc., New York, 1897), p. 97.

[10] M. Mann, *Life of Horace Mann* (Walker, Fuller & Co., Boston, 1865), p. 81.

toward the end of his secretaryship in Massachusetts, he was still seeking the educational improvement of his fellow men, declaring that "progress is the law of the universe."[11]

Though Froebelian principles received a warm reception in America, public interest centered in their pedagogical rather than their social significance. Undoubtedly they swelled the stream of liberal thought, but by the late nineteenth century the real leaven of social-educational reform in America came from Darwinism, especially social Darwinism. In taking over the idea of evolution from biology the sociologists saw education as but the latest stage in the evolutionary process. Human adaptation to environment, which in earliest times had been physical and organic, had later become a matter of institutional adaptation. More important yet, the sociologists pointed out, institutional adaptation was passing from an unconscious to a conscious stage. In the conscious stage, social adaptation or selection was to become rational and self-conscious through the curriculum of the schools. At least, such were the ideas of Lester F. Ward (1841–1913), America's leading early sociologist.[12]

Confidence that the exercise of intelligence can rectify social institutions and confidence that the schools are a strategic outpost on the social frontier were nowhere more strikingly joined than in John Dewey (1859–1952), America's leading educational philosopher. His philosophy was thoroughly impregnated with the evolutionary concept. Yet he did not think that the educator should be confronted with a bare choice between education as social transmission and education as social transformation. Such a choice would have to be made arbitrarily, not on educational grounds but on grounds of political preference. Furthermore Dewey held it a fallacy that the ends of education should be determined by external social or political conditions. On the contrary, he held, education should be autonomous and free to determine its own ends.[13] It is a coordinate process along with politics for determining and pursuing the good life. The criteria for judging social and individual growth are to be found not outside the educational process but within it.

From Condorcet to Dewey there had been sporadic talk about the important role of education in social progress, but it remained for men in the twentieth century to try to give effect to the notion

[11] *Common School Journal*, 10:65, March, 1848. For the further development of this theme in American education, see A. A. Ekirch, *The Idea of Progress in America* (Columbia University Press, New York, 1944), chap. 7.

[12] See his *Dynamic Sociology* (D. Appleton & Company, Inc., New York, 1883), vol. 2, chap. 14.

[13] The *Twelfth Yearbook* of the Department of Superintendence of the National Education Association even advocated an independent school state (pp. 65–66).

in practice. The principal effort in this direction took shape in the Progressive Education Association formed just after the First World War. During the postwar decade many identified progressive education with an individualistic pedagogy emphasizing freedom and spontaneity, neglecting or forgetting that one of the earlier strains of the movement had been social reform. They were not to be unmindful long, however. As the country sank into the economic Depression of the 1930s, George S. Counts (1889–) roundly denounced progressive education for its lack of fundamental social orientation. In his widely read pamphlet *Dare the School Build a New Social Order?* he called upon the teachers to lead the way out of our social and economic morass. Soldiers, clergy, statesmen, and now businessmen having failed to establish a stable society, teachers could hardly be expected to do any worse if they boldly seized the power that lay in their hands to mold a new generation and a new social order. More than any other group, he claimed, teachers were the repositories of the wisdom of the race, and less than any other group would they be selfish in their use of it. Like Plato, he concluded with a preview of the "American dream," the just society that we might have by educational planning.[14]

In the first burst of enthusiasm stirred by the pamphlet the Progressive Education Association appointed a committee with Counts as chairman to pick up the gauntlet he had thrown down. This committee came back with *A Call to the Teachers of the Nation* as a proposed further clarification of the association's social philosophy of education, but there were divided counsels in the association and the *Call* was never sponsored officially.[15] On second thought not everyone agreed that the school should take the initiative in social progress. Even those who agreed it should, could not agree on what kind of new social order to bring forth. Counts obviously had in mind a collectivistic society not unlike the collectivism of the democratic New Deal. But there were many who did not share this conviction. When later in the Depression decade the association tried to state its general philosophy of progressive education,[16] the document again failed to win official endorsement. Clearly the rank and file of progressive educators were pluralistic rather than monistic in their loyalty to the rubric of progressive education. Some thought this pluralism a weakness, others a strength.

[14] G. S. Counts, *Dare the School Build a New Social Order?* (The John Day Company, Inc., New York, 1932).

[15] *A Call to the Teachers of the Nation* (Progressive Education Association, Committee on Social and Economic Problems, New York, 1933).

[16] H. Alberty et al., "Progressive Education: Its Philosophy and Challenge," *Progressive Education,* 18: special supplement, May, 1941.

ACADEMIC FREEDOM

Whether the school is to instigate a new social order or entrench an old one is a question that, all through the history of education, has been bound up with another, whether the teacher is bound to transmit the group culture as he received it with tradition's stamp of approval on it or is free to select such parts of it as he thinks best and evaluate them critically as he introduces them into the lives of his students. On the whole, most teachers have been traditionalists. The unconventional teacher has been the rarity. This is as the great majority of the patrons of the schools would have it. Wedded to its habits, society has generally resisted having its complacency disturbed by unorthodox instruction. Only by the greatest sacrifice has it been possible to establish a tradition of freedom of instruction for the teacher. And even then freedom has been maintained only by being constantly rewon.

Freedom first found conditions favorable to its growth among the ancient Greeks. This is not surprising since it was also among this people that men first entertained the idea that the school could be made the means of social regeneration. The Greeks were able to conceive of education in progressive terms because they cultivated individuality.[17] In cultivating individuality they necessarily cultivated novelty. And for novelty they had a veritable passion. It was almost a cult with them, as witness the later account in the Bible which relates that the Greeks "spent their time in nothing else, but either to tell, or to hear some new thing."[18] Obviously, such a passion for novelty could be indulged only by permitting the individual to deviate from the stereotype of conventional wisdom. This was fertile soil indeed for the growth of freedom. In the course of time it yielded a crop of ideas that rarely if ever has been equaled for breadth, insight, and stimulation.

Yet, in spite of the remarkable freedom that teachers like Socrates, Plato, and Aristotle enjoyed, Greece was the scene of one of freedom's greatest tragedies, the execution of Socrates. The indictment against him was that as a teacher he had corrupted the youth by teaching them disrespect for the gods. No doubt, his method of instruction, afterward called the "Socratic,"[19] was calculated to encourage critical examination of customary beliefs and practices. But Socrates was not seeking to make men skeptical so much as he was trying to refine men's convictions and put them on a more rational

---

[17] For a fuller account, see *supra,* pp. 25–28.

[18] Acts 17:21.

[19] B. Bosanquet, *The Education of the Young in Plato's Republic* (Cambridge University Press, London, 1917), pp. 53–54.

basis. Unfortunately, many conservative Athenians did not understand his purpose and therefore made Socrates the scapegoat for their own shortcomings in coping with the changing nature of the times. The indictment, trial, and death of Socrates but indicate that, however high the waves of freedom flow, there is always danger of being pulled back by the undertow of conservatism.

Setback to freedom though the death of Socrates, was, it occurred under circumstances that in the end have forever enhanced the cause of freedom. At his trial Socrates might have saved his life by renouncing his teaching. The principle at stake, however, was too great to abandon. After sentence he might even have saved his life by flight. He preferred, however, to abide by the laws of the city as they took their course. Facing his fate resolutely, fearlessly, even cheerfully, Socrates gave up his mortal life but made the cause of freedom immortal.

Plato also appreciated the tremendous importance of freedom for the teacher. He was not afraid of the uncertain outcome of inquiry. As he remarked to an interlocutor in the course of one of his most famous dialogues, *The Republic,* "Whither the argument may blow, thither we go."[20] Yet, in spite of this apparently unqualified endorsement of free inquiry for the teacher, Plato did set some limits to freedom. Presumably, of course, the philosopher-ruler of his ideal state, as pictured in his utopian *Republic,* must enjoy the prerogative of freedom in order to determine the outlines of ideal state. But, once this state had been approximated, the main task of education would be to prevent digressions from the ideal. The chief danger of such defections, Plato anticipated, would arise from innovations. To guard against such evils, whether coming from such widely separated sources as poetry or children's games. Plato thought it necessary to censor the curriculum. In this connection he even proposed to expurgate the Homeric poems of their cruder immoralities so as to preserve the child's mind from contact with anything false or vicious. Apparently, the freedom he claimed for the rulers or teachers he thought too dangerous to be left in the hands of the untrained or immature.

Under the imperial rule of Rome, freedom for the teacher was never the persistent issue it had been with the Greeks. Perhaps this was because rhetoric rather than philosophy occupied the more important place in the Roman curriculum and therefore controversial issues were not so likely to arise. Even if controversial matters intruded in the curriculum in the latter days of the Empire, the state exercised a subtle but effective control over freedom by putting eminent professors of rhetoric on its payroll. Only in the obscure Roman province

[20] For a fuller account of this method, see *supra,* pp. 171–174.

of Palestine did a spectacular case arise of the denial of freedom to a teacher. The trial and Crucifixion of Jesus have been best known for their religious significance. But in its educational bearings the case was remarkably similar to that of Socrates. Here, too, was a great teacher whose only pedagogical crime was that He taught a new dispensation. And here, too, was a great teacher whose death as much as his life enhanced his saying, "And ye shall know the truth, and the truth shall make you free."[21]

In the course of time, however, Christians came to regard freedom as a by-product of truth rather than a necessary means for investigating it. If truth is fixed and eternal in the heavens, as Plato thought and the Christians after him, then this notion of freedom was not unsound. Like Plato, Christians were more willing to surrender a measure of freedom in order to remain secure in a perfected truth than they were to risk errors by boldly and freely exploring new paths to truth. Thus the *Apostolic Constitutions,* an early manual of instruction for Christians, enjoined them to abstain from reading pagan books, studying foreign laws, or listening to false prophets. "For," the *Constitutions* inquired, "what defect dost thou find in the law of God, that thou shouldst have recourse to those heathenish fables?"[22]

In the heyday of the medieval university, when scholars were struggling to make an accommodation between Christianity and Greek philosophy, a considerable measure of freedom of thought obtained again. Freedom was kept open by the wide doctrinal differences of opinion that existed between the various teaching orders of the Catholic Church. But even here a teacher was only free within the limits of a basic orthodoxy. When a great teacher like Pierre Abélard (1079–1142) made so bold as to challenge not only the details of this frame of reference but the frame of reference itself, he had the wings of his teaching freedom severely clipped.

The oscillation between freedom and control of teaching was not just a phenomenon of Western or Christian culture. Contemporary Islamic culture had much the same experience. In the centuries when the Western Roman Empire by reason of its decay was cut off from the Eastern half, Islam came under the influence of Greek philosophy. Hence Islamic education, too, had the problem of reconciling Greek philosophy with its own more primitive religious notions. Foremost

---

[21] John 8:32. If this quotation is read in its complete context, it will be seen not to carry the full measure of freedom for which it is cited. The full text is: "If ye continue in my word, then are ye my disciples indeed; and ye shall know the truth, and the truth shall make you free."

[22] E. P. Cubberley, *Readings in the History of Education* (Houghton Mifflin Company, Boston, 1920), p. 54.

in this reconciliation was an Islamic teaching order, the Brothers of Sincerity. As long as they enjoyed freedom to exploit the spirit of Greek thought, Islamic culture prospered. In the course of time, however, Greek thought became suspect as subverting conservative Islamic culture. When this occurred, the Brothers of Sincerity were forced from the Orient into North Africa and thence ultimately into Spain. They arrived there just in time to put their critical knowledge of Greek learning at the disposal of the courageous minds of the medieval universities of Western Europe, who, beginning to drop their earlier self-inflicted blinders, freely undertook to teach from pagan as well as Christian sources.

By the thirteenth century under the leadership of St. Thomas Aquinas (1225–1274), the great Dominican scholar and teacher, the Catholic Church finally succeeded in making its great synthesis of Christian and Greek or pagan learning. Only a few centuries elapsed, however, before an Augustinian professor of the German University of Wittenberg, Martin Luther (1483–1546), found his freedom to preach and teach the heterodox doctrines that subsequently became Protestantism seriously opposed by the church. With the aid of a number of secular princes he was successful in maintaining his freedom against this opposition. The natural outcome of his defense of freedom should have been the dissolution of all creeds and catechisms into private opinions. To prevent this result, church and state joined hands in Protestant countries to erect Luther's heterodoxy into a new and approved orthodoxy which was to safeguard teachers as well as their pupils from heresies into which their individual exercise of freedom might lead them.[23]

Yet Luther seemed to recognize that there could be no final or unerring safety where education was widespread. "But you say," he said, anticipating this objection to his educational program, " 'How if it turns out badly so that my son becomes a heretic or a villain?' For, as people say, 'education means perversion.' Well, you must run that risk; but your labor is not lost. God will consider your faithful service, and will count it as if successful."[24]

The Jesuits, in the Counter Reformation that they led against Protestantism, tried to strike a balance between the claims of freedom and control. In the *Ratio studiorum,* which governed instruction in

[23] That these heresies might have both political and religious significance is evidenced by a sixteenth-century statute of Elizabeth that demanded that all schoolmasters take the Oath of Supremacy as testimony of their acceptance of the Queen as head of the Church of England.

[24] F. V. N. Painter, *Luther on Education* (Lutheran Publication Society, Philadelphia, 1889), p. 236. But it is interesting that in his plan for education in Saxony Luther wished the schoolmaster to teach only truths necessary for right living: "He shall not speak of polemical matters." (*Ibid.,* p. 155.)

their schools, they followed Plato by enjoining the provincial to censor texts that might in any way be offensive to morals. Books that could not be completely expurgated were not to be read. On controversial issues in which the teacher "is free to hold either side," the *Ratio* went on to say, "he shall defend his view in such a way as to allow moderate and kindly consideration for the opposite view, especially if the previous teacher has held that view. But if writers can be reconciled, he must be careful not to neglect to do so. . . . Even in matters where there is no risk to faith and devotion, no one shall introduce new questions in matters of great moment, or any opinion which does not have suitable authority, without first consulting his superiors; he shall not teach anything opposed to the axioms of learned men or the general belief of scholars. Rather, all should follow closely the approved doctors and, as far as local custom permits, the views accepted in Catholic schools."[25]

By the eighteenth century the rise of modern science introduced a new attitude toward freedom in teaching. The French pedagogical essayist Michel de Montaigne (1533–1592) had already presaged it in his writings a couple of centuries earlier. Addressing the teacher, Montaigne advised him to let the student "examine and thoroughly sift every thing he reads, and lodge nothing in his fancy upon simple authority and upon trust." And, he added, "Let this diversity of opinions be propounded to, and laid before him; he will himself choose, if he be able; if not, he will remain in doubt."[26] Apparently Montaigne did not feel it necessary to censor the student's curriculum to ensure that he reach a particular conclusion. Indeed, he even conceived that the pupil might come to the end of a period of study with his mind in a state of suspended judgment. Freedom evidently was on its way to becoming an instrument, rather than merely an outcome, of study and investigation.

Montaigne's attempt to divorce instruction from the support of authority did not receive much response in his own generation. Not till it was reiterated by the great French Revolutionary writer Condorcet did it receive the attention it deserved. According to Condorcet, "no branch of the government should have the authority

---

[25] E. A. Fitzpatrick, *St. Ignatius and the Ratio Studiorum* (McGraw-Hill Book Company, New York, 1933), p. 151. Protestant colonial America suffered the same anxiety, as witness the report of Governor Sir William Berkeley of Virginia in which he expressed the hope that free schools and printing would not spread, "for learning has brought disobedience and heresy and sects into the world and printing has divulged them and libels against the best government. God keep us from both." W. W. Hening, *Laws of Virginia* (Samuel Pleasants, Richmond, Va., 1810), vol. 2, p. 517.

[26] L. E. Rector, *Montaigne: The Education of Children* (D. Appleton Company, Inc., New York, 1899), p. 31.

or even the means, of preventing the teaching of new truths or the development of theories contrary to its special policies or its momentary interests."[27] In fact, Condorcet would have education freed, not just from the controls of government, but from *all* kinds of control, even that of public opinion. In the case of public opinion he held that education should anticipate it, form it, and correct it but never follow or obey it. "Finally," wrote Condorcet in a grand sweep of the imagination, "the independence of instruction is, in a manner, a part of the rights of the human race. Since man has received from nature a perfectibility whose unknown limits extend—if they even exist—much beyond what we can yet perceive, and the knowledge of new truth is for him the only means of developing this happy faculty—the source of his happiness and of his glory, what power could have the right to say to him: 'This is what you need know; this is as far as you may go'? Since truth alone is useful, since every error is an evil, by what right would any power, whatever it be, dare to determine wherein lies truth, wherein lies error?"[28]

Brilliantly though Condorcet wrote during the turmoil of the French Revolution, when affairs settled down again under Napoleon more conservative counsels came to prevail. The very governmental controls of education that Condorcet deprecated Napoleon instituted. "My principal aim in the establishment of a teaching body," he stated, "is to have a means for directing political and moral opinions."[29] And in his correspondence he wrote, "Of all political questions, that [of the control of ideas by education] is perhaps the most important. There cannot be a firmly established political state unless there is a teaching body with definitely fixed principles. Except as the child is taught from infancy whether he ought to be a republican or a monarchist, a Catholic or a freethinker, the state will not constitute a nation; it will rest on uncertain and ill-defined foundations; and it will be constantly exposed to disorder and change."[30]

The freedom of instruction that was crowded out of France by the expanding dictatorship of Napoleon came to be hospitably harbored in a state that was one of the victims of Napoleonic aggression, Prussia. Crushed by Napoleonic military force, Prussia was endeavoring in the first decade of the nineteenth century to recruit the energies necessary to throw off its foreign yoke. Believing that a vigorous national intellectual life was an important part of such

---

[27] La Fontainerie, *op. cit.*, pp. 326–327.

[28] *Ibid.*, pp. 374–375.

[29] Quoted in W. H. Kilpatrick, *Source Book in the Philosophy of Education* (The Macmillan Company, New York, 1934), p. 17.

[30] *Ibid.*, pp. 17–18.

energies, Prussia decided to found the University of Berlin, which it endowed with complete academic freedom. There teaching and research were to pursue the truth, not according to the preconceived interests of the state, but wherever free investigation might lead. This precedent was soon followed by other German universities. As a result, before the nineteenth century was very old, German universities were world-famous for their advanced scholarship.[31]

In his inaugural address as rector of the University of Berlin shortly after its founding, Johann Gottlieb Fichte (1762–1814), the great German patriot, philosopher, and educator, made an eloquent statement of the role of academic freedom. Like Condorcet, he claimed that the human race could fulfill its destiny only where it was possible to have steady and uninterrupted intellectual progress. By all odds the most appropriate place where this progress could occur was the university, for there each generation deposits its highest intellectual achievements so that succeeding generations, from the shoulders of the preceding, might ever envision more distant intellectual horizons. If the university once is established by gathering together professors who are steeped in their fields of learning and if students have been suitably prepared to study under them, then the university can continue independently by itself and needs no help from the outside. "Rather are such external influences and interferences harmful, and disturbing to the intended progress of intellectual culture," declared Fichte. "If, therefore, a university is to achieve its purpose and be really what it pretends to be, it must be left to itself thenceforward; it needs, and rightly demands, complete external freedom, academic freedom in the widest sense of the word. . . . No limit, therefore, should be set to the teacher's instruction; nor should any subject be indicated to him as an exception, on which he is not to be free to think and to communicate his independent thought with the same freedom from limitation to the pupil in the university who has been suitably prepared for it."[32]

In the next century and a half, this spirit of academic freedom was felt far and wide throughout the universities of the world. In part, academic freedom rode to this popularity on the crest of the wave of nineteenth-century liberalism. The Catholic Church, however, that ancient champion of orthodoxy, stood stanchly against this tide of liberalism. Yet, though Pope Pius IX in his famous *Syllabus of Errors* of 1864 declared himself unalterably opposed to the spirit

---

[31] W. P. Metzger, "The German Contribution to the American Theory of Academic Freedom," *Bulletin of the American Association of University Professors*, 41:214–230, Summer, 1955.

[32] G. H. Trumbull, *The Education Theory of Fichte* (Hodder & Stoughton, Ltd., London, 1926), pp. 264–265.

of liberalism, his action did not prevent his successor, Leo XIII, in his encyclical letter of 1888, *Libertas praestantissimum,* from defending the Catholic Church as a guardian of liberty in teaching.

Leo's claim, however, was in respect to a qualified rather than an unlimited freedom for the teacher. Commencing with the Catholic doctrine of freedom of the will, Leo recognized liberty as a fundamental condition of man. But freedom, he immediately pointed out, needs the guidance of reason and law, for otherwise it will be man's ruin. Thus, if a man were so completely free as to be independent of reason or exempt from law, he would obviously have little or no means of distinguishing truth from falsehood or good from evil. Since error cannot have equal rights with truth, it follows that the teacher should not be equally free to teach truth and falsehood. Hence, very much like Plato, Leo declared that "nothing but truth should be taught both to the ignorant and to the educated, so as to bring knowledge to those who have it not, and to preserve it in those who possess it. For this reason, it is plainly the duty of all who teach to banish error from the mind, and by sure safeguards to close the entry to all false convictions."[33]

Such a position, of course, assumed that truth can be distinguished from error. The ability to make such a distinction and to make it unerringly presented no insuperable difficulty to the philosophy of the Catholic Church. Truth, as Leo asserted, is of two sorts, natural and supernatural. In the realm of faith and morals certain details of supernatural truth have long been revealed to man by God himself. Whatever is consistent with this divine revelation is truth, and whatever is inconsistent with it is error. What is more, the church cannot be mistaken or deceived in separating truth from error because God, by entrusting his revelation to the church for safekeeping and exposition, made it partaker in his divine authority. The church, to quote Leo again, "is therefore the greatest and most reliable teacher of mankind," and in her dwells an inviolable freedom to teach.[34]

Turning to natural truth and the freedom to teach it, Leo went on to say, "Now reason itself clearly teaches that the truths of divine revelation and those of nature cannot really be opposed to one another, and that whatever is at variance with them must necessarily be false. Therefore, the divine teaching of the church, so far from being an obstacle to the pursuit of learning and the progress of science, or in any way retarding the advance of civilization, in reality brings to them the sure guidance of shining light. And for the same reason, it is of no small advantage for the perfection of human liberty, since

---

[33] Quoted in J. A. Ryan and F. S. Boland, *Catholic Principles of Politics* (The Macmillan Company, New York, 1940), p. 175.

[34] *Ibid.,* p. 177.

our Saviour Jesus Christ has said that by truth is man made free: *Ye shall know the truth, and the truth shall make you free.* Therefore, there is no reason why genuine liberty should grow indignant, or true science feel aggrieved, at having to bear the just and necessary restraint of laws by which, in the judgment of the church and of reason itself, human teaching has to be controlled. . . . Lastly, we must not forget that a vast field lies freely open to man's industry and genius, containing all those things which have no necessary connection with Christian faith and morals, or as to which the church, exercising no authority, leaves the judgment of the learned free and unconstrained."[35]

There were a number in the United States of the late eighteenth and early nineteenth centuries who sympathized with the liberalism of French Revolutionary thought. Such a one, of course, was Thomas Jefferson (1743–1826), author of the Declaration of Independence and founder of the University of Virginia. In searching for a motto for the latter, he chose the Biblical quotation already cited, "Ye shall know the truth, and the truth shall make you free." Such a commendable spirit of freedom, however, did not always obtain at the University of Virginia and only rarely permeated other American colleges of the time.[36] For the most part these colleges were under church control, and churches of the time were still strong advocates of religious conformity and used their colleges to train clergymen and advance ecclesiastical interests. The divorce of church and state, commencing at the end of the eighteenth century and continuing into the early decades of the nineteenth, was a liberal move, but the time for a free and open examination of religious presuppositions in college classrooms had not yet arrived. Neither had it arrived for such political and economic issues as slavery presented in the middle of the century.[37] Teaching was still largely authoritarian, being predicated on the philosophical presupposition that truth was absolute and ascertainable and that consequently error had to be eradicated.

In the classrooms below college grade the problem of academic freedom was not even raised in nineteenth-century America. There was really no reason why it should be. The common school curriculum was so greatly devoted to the three R's and the academy and high school curricula were so thoroughly absorbed in either the classics or the practical studies necessary to getting ahead in a rapidly growing country that no one even thought of making room for a study of

[35] *Ibid.,* p. 178.

[36] G. E. Baker, "Thomas Jefferson on Academic Freedom," *Bulletin of the American Association of University Professors,* 39:377–387, Autumn, 1953.

[37] It has been said on high authority that the Civil War might have been prevented if teachers had enjoyed academic freedom to discuss the issue of slavery. See M. Curti, "Changing Issues in the School's Freedom," *Social Frontier,* 2:166–169, March, 1936.

current social issues of a controversial nature. It is extremely doubtful, too, whether more than a handful of teachers were thoroughly enough trained to qualify for the privilege of unrestricted academic freedom.

Moreover, the rise of the public school system put a premium on keeping controversial issues out of the classroom. The success of the shift from private to public support of education depended in large part on keeping a united public opinion behind the public school. The public had been sufficiently divided on the issue of free versus private education so that it might have been calamitous for the whole public school enterprise to divide it further by admitting social issues such as religion and slavery into the curriculum.[38] Horace Mann, for instance, hearing that one of his state normal school teachers took a class to an abolitionist meeting, cautioned against the repetition of such an excursion as likely to endanger his hopes and plans for obtaining increased financial aid for the schools.

Outside the walls of schools and colleges, however, the teacher's freedom was often at stake. There his general freedom or civil liberty as a citizen, as contrasted with his academic freedom as a teacher, frequently involved him in public controversies, if he was hardy enough to withstand their wear and tear. From the very beginning, yet with diminishing emphasis, American communities were very inquisitive about their teachers' religious convictions. During the American Revolution whether the teacher was a loyalist or patriot was also a matter of great public concern.[39] After the Revolution teachers had to be careful about the extent to which they espoused the radicalism of French Revolutionary ideas. In the middle of the nineteenth century their public stand on the slavery issue could easily involve them in trouble depending on the community in which they lived. A little later the controversy between science and religion, which Darwinism engendered, provided another Scylla and Charybdis of public relations through which they had to steer. At the end of the century teachers found it difficult to express themselves as citizens concerning the rising tide of political and economic reform, even though they made no mention of these matters in their classrooms.

Perhaps on the foregoing issues most teachers did not even know that they were not free. Probably most of them so heartily shared the prejudices of the communities in which they lived that they did

[38] Note that as late as 1951 the New York State Board of Regents omitted the germ theory of disease from the regents examinations in deference to Christian Scientists.

[39] For instances of eighteenth-century loyalty oaths in Massachusetts, New Jersey, and Pennsylvania, see E. W. Knight, *Readings in Educational Administration* (Holt, Rinehart and Winston, Inc., New York, 1953), pp. 301–305. See also H. E. Seyler, "Pennsylvania's First Loyalty Oath," *History of Education Journal,* 3:114–126, Summer, 1952.

not even want to be free from them. Consequently, it may not be far from the mark to state that teachers, if they felt their freedom infringed, were more firmly shackled by the limitations of their own ignorance and lack of courage than they were by external restrictions imposed by their communities.

If concerning social issues the teacher had a greater opportunity to exercise his civil liberty as a citizen than his academic liberty as a teacher, it was principally because of the mid-nineteenth-century stand taken by Horace Mann. Seeing discord about exciting party and sectarian issues as the normal state of affairs in a free society, Mann did nevertheless hope that defenseless children might find the school at least a temporary haven from religious[40] and political strife till they were mature enough to breast these storms themselves. Hence Mann not only opposed introducing controversial issues into the curriculum but he was also against using the school to indoctrinate children against specific social abuses. He weakened his own case, however, by making exceptions of intoxicating liquors and the institutions of war.

Contemporaries of Mann even took the position that the teacher, being an employee of the public, was free to be only an advocate of the social *status quo,* not its critic. This view continued to be popular to the turn of the century. At that time a variant of this view did not even see it as a violation of academic freedom that a college professor should be dismissed for advocating the cause of free silver, one of the great current national controversies. Quite to the contrary, the idea of a free-silver professor drawing his salary from a college backed by "sound money" struck many of the public as both incongruous and illogical.

The limits of academic freedom at the turn of the century were supposed to be more flexible in respect to some subjects than in respect to others. Thus, much greater freedom was accorded the teacher in the domain of the physical sciences such as physics and chemistry and even in history and literature than in sociology and economics or religion and morals. "In the first case," proclaimed *Gunton's Magazine,* "the new theories affect individual and societary action very slowly and with the greatest indirection, and consequently never can bring about any detrimental disturbances. In the latter case the innovation, if radical, may involve dangerous social eruption, undermine the moral basis of social order or the economic security of property rights and interests, and thus destroy the safety of industrial action and arrest progress."[41]

Notable changes, coming in the First World War, challenged many

---

[40] For a more complete account of the exclusion of religion from the public schools, see *supra,* pp. 317–320, 533–537.

[41] "Liberty in Economic Teaching," *Gunton's Magazine,* 18:229, March, 1900.

people to reexamine these precedents. Social revolution in Europe—communism in Russia and fascism in Italy and Germany—caused many to reconsider the adequacy of capitalism and democracy in America. The resounding crash of the Depression ten years after the First World War greatly accelerated the tempo of this thinking. This was followed by the New Deal, which kept the debate on social issues lively down to the Second World War, after which followed all the perplexities of the "Cold War." Concomitant with these underlying forces of social change were others hardly less disturbing, such as revival of the age-old controversy between science and religion and innovations in the status of women. Because by this time most schoolteachers were women, the new tendency of women in general to smoke, drink alcoholic beverages, and expose more of their bodies in the ultramodern styles of dress had definite effects on the civil liberties of teachers if not on their academic freedom.

Coincident with these changes came a fundamental overhauling of the public school curriculum.[42] The basic philosophy of this reconstruction of the curriculum was thoroughly pragmatic. It aimed to prepare children to understand and cope with as many as possible of the complexities and contradictions brought about by the underlying changes just noted. Naturally, a curriculum designed to accomplish this end, particularly at the secondary and college levels, included a number of subjects involving controversial political and economic issues. This was a definite break with traditional American practice as formulated by Horace Mann. By this time, however, the public school was so well established that it could withstand the shock of free discussion of political and economic—though not yet religious—issues which ordinarily divided the public. Besides, by this time teacher training had made great strides in preparing teachers capable of these new responsibilities.

As teachers attacked most issues under the protecting cloak of academic freedom, conservative pressure groups such as the American Legion, the Daughters of the American Revolution, and chambers of commerce not infrequently demanded that teachers stop "rocking the ship of state." In New York the Lusk committee, already referred to as holding that the teacher should teach the social *status quo* and actively combat theories of social change, went on further to claim that "In entering the public school system the teacher assumes certain obligations and must of necessity surrender some of his intellectual freedom. If he does not approve of the present social system or the structure of our government he is at liberty to entertain those ideas, but must surrender his public office."[43] A decade later, during

[42] For an extended account of this curriculum movement, see *supra*, pp. 279–286.
[43] "Revolutionary Radicalism," *loc. cit.*

the Depression, Massachusetts took the conservative leadership by demanding that teachers in the state swear a "loyalty oath" to the Constitution. Then after the Second World War the Un-American Activities Committee of the United States House of Representatives assumed the burden of guarding American liberties by searching high and low for disloyal teachers.

But what constituted disloyalty? The Federal courts have interpreted the Fourteenth Amendment to mean that state legislatures must draft their laws so clearly that the law-abiding citizen will be on adequate notice as to just what activity is prohibited. Teacher loyalty oaths demanding "respect for the flag" or "undivided allegiance" to the government have been declared so vague as to be unconstitutional.[44] To guard against vagueness one state drew up a list of subversive organizations membership in any one of which was to be prima-facie evidence of disloyalty. Question arose almost at once as to whether such a practice contravened the First Amendment of the Constitution. A judgment of the New York Court of Appeals held that it did not and was affirmed by the United States Supreme Court but by a divided Court.[45] The majority took the view that the New York State practice left a teacher free to belong to these organizations but that this freedom could not be construed to entitle him to teach. The minority responded that such a practice made the teacher a second-class citizen because he had to surrender some of his civil liberty to qualify as a teacher.

The issue of academic freedom came up in respect to religion as well as in respect to politics and economics. Tennessee passed a law prohibiting the teaching of the scientific facts of evolution because these were supposedly repugnant to the revealed truths of religion. The famous Scopes trial at Dayton, Tennessee, resulted when an obscure high school teacher decided to teach the theory of evolution in spite of the state statute. Academic freedom, however, was no defense in the face of such an explicit statute.

While perhaps a majority of the people sympathized either openly or covertly with such restrictions, nevertheless the cause of academic freedom continued to make steady progress. The First World War "to make the world safe for democracy" and the Second World War to safeguard "the Four Freedoms" caused people to take more and more seriously the idea of untrammeled discussion of controversial issues both in the public forum and in the public school. People came increasingly to see that progressive societies such as democracies

---

[44] *Baggett v. Bullitt,* 84 Sup. Ct. 1316.
[45] *Adler v. Board of Education,* 342 U.S. 485. This case only holds, however, if the teacher *knows* of the subversive character of the organization to which he belongs. (*Wieman v. Updegraff,* 344 U.S. 183.)

were quite dependent on free speech in its various forms to reveal the blind alleys of the future as well as the broad avenues stretching indefinitely toward the horizon of tomorrow.

Progress particularly was made during this period in delimiting and distinguishing the teacher's civil liberty as a citizen from his academic freedom as a teacher. According to the American theory of civil liberty a teacher was free to speak his mind on any topic without fear of imprisonment as long as he did not incite to riot. If his remarks brought him unpopularity or loss of reputation or fortune, he had to suffer the consequences. According to the theory of academic freedom, however, the teacher was to be free not only from fear of imprisonment but also from loss of his teaching position. This added protection, however, extended only to remarks of the teacher made *within* the field of his specialization. Beyond it he was to enjoy *only* the civil liberties of the citizen.[46] Infringements of either, however, were watchfully policed by committees on academic freedom of such professional organizations as the American Association of University Professors.

PROGRESS IN EDUCATION

Whether or not, now, the school has served to point the way to social progress along political, economic, or other lines, has education itself within its own confines made net progress over the centuries? Any answer to such a question must be contingent on what is taken as a measure of progress. On the whole, progress seems most unmistakable in the realm of educational means, broadly conceived, and most debatable in the realm of educational ends. Perhaps this is because the former lend themselves more readily to quantitative estimation and because the latter, being qualitative, are much more difficult to assay.

When we look back over the vast expanse of educational history, there seems little doubt that great progress has been made in the number of children and adults to whom the benefits of formal education have been extended. From an insignificant percentage of ancient populations education has now become the prerogative of whole nations. But even though some nations have managed to achieve high percentages of literacy under a program of universal compulsory education, there are still large populations on the earth's surface in the second half of the twentieth century in which illiteracy still predominates.

Not only has there been a progressively larger number attending

[46] For further discussion, see *Civil Liberties of Teachers and Students* (American Civil Liberties Union, New York, 1949).

school over the ages, but students have been able to pursue their education for longer and longer stretches of time. The yearly school term has lengthened, and, more important, the number of years spent in school has also increased. Most advanced nations have gradually achieved universal elementary education. In spite of this accomplishment, much remains to be done in extending secondary educational opportunities to the mass of the population.

Again, not only have greater numbers of children studied in school for longer periods of time, but they have studied an ever-expanding and enriching curriculum. As society passed from nomadic to pastoral, to agricultural, to commercial, and finally to industrial economies, increased demands were made on the schools to prepare youth for more complex phases of economic life. Similarly, as society progressed politically from families to tribes, to city-states, to nations, to empires, and finally in the second half of the twentieth century stood on the threshold of world political order, more exacting demands were steadily made on preparation for citizenship. No less important in expanding the curriculum was the growth of knowledge itself. The lore of superstition and crude empirical observation have been extensively supplanted by philosophical speculation and modern scientific investigation. In fact, the curriculum has grown so vigorously and lustily in such a variety of directions that its mastery has long since surpassed the scope of any single mind and must now be compassed by the cooperative effort of individuals specializing in various parts.

Not least in the vast expansion of human knowledge has been the progress made in knowledge of the educative process itself. The art of teaching, which was once so mysterious as to be thought a "gift," is now something that can to a degree be acquired by almost anyone. Human nature, that most complex of all nature's creatures, has yielded many of its secrets to philosophical and scientific study. Unless it had, the great increase in the number of trained teachers necessary to ensure the educated public of today would simply have been out of the question.

Material equipment for the convenience of the schools and the furthering of its purposes has also accumulated in ever-increasing amounts over the centuries, particularly the recent ones. School buildings have increased in number and appointments as the educational enterprise itself has expanded in size. From porches and rented stalls they have steadily improved in architecture so that now in many communities the local school building rivals the church and municipal buildings as the principal edifice in town. Incorporated into these buildings are health, sanitary, and safety features undreamt of in centuries gone by. To keep pace with the expanding curriculum, buildings have progressively added shops, laboratories, gymnasiums, auditoriums, and libraries. Of all mechanical devices on which the steady advance of education has been dependent, the printing press has been the most nearly indispensable. Not only has the printing press enabled the schools gradually to fill their libraries, but it has in recent centuries made it possible for each child to have his own books.

A last simple, quantitative measure of educational progress is the increasing amount of money that has come to be spent on it. From an item to be found only in the budgets of the well to do, education has come to be a charge on the much larger public purse. From a negligible slice of the local public budget, it has come to be its single largest item.

But in trying to audit the accounts of educational history and to cast up its balance of progress or retrogression, it is not enough to note its quantitative growth. One's judgment will be uneasy unless he has assurance that education has progressed qualitatively as well as quantitatively. That increasing numbers of people are getting more extensive education from an expanded curriculum under greater numbers of trained teachers in bigger and better buildings will be as nothing if the aims of that education are not pitched at the highest level or increasingly higher ones. But how is one to arrange educational aims in a commonly accepted hierarchy of values? What is the greatest common denominator of educational values into which all the other educational aims of history are divisible?

Of course, the answer to this question depends on one's educational philosophy. But progress in educational philosophy is not so easily marked as it can be in respect to curricula, methods, buildings, and other items just compared. It might seem obviously correct to say that over the ages educational philosophy has advanced from a theory that education should perpetuate the *status quo* to one that education should move the *status quo* nearer and nearer to goals that are unchanging and eternal in the heavens, to one that education should progressively reconstruct the *status quo* by recognizing no aims as fixed and holding them all subject to constant revision. But, actually, there are many who seriously question whether the twentieth-century philosophy of progressive education is really a step in the direction of educational progress in the long run. Pragmatists might agree, but scholastics would disagree.

Although progress in educational aims has been, is, and will probably long remain a debatable point, it is nevertheless notable that on one quality, or value, in the educative progress there has been growing unanimity, and that is the supreme worth of human personality. From it has derived a Magna Charta of childhood, claiming for children recognition of their right to grow and develop physically, intellectually, and morally into full and normal adulthood. Such a broad claim is a far cry from that early age when children were virtually without rights and were regarded as chattels or even from those later ages when parents could still dispose of their children's labor as an economic asset.

The tone of this résumé of educational history has been on the whole optimistic. It would be a grave error, however, to overlook the fact that there has been and can yet be educational decay as well as educational growth. The danger signs are not difficult to detect. Cultural lag is one of the first. When the curriculum of the school fails to keep abreast of current life, then watch out for an ebb in the vitality of education. Perhaps there will still be an apparent excitement about education pursued as an ornamental end in itself, but the skilled educational practitioner will know from the clinical record of education that the excitement is a sign of disease rather than health. In fact, the history of education is full of laments when teachers have fallen into the habit of teaching form instead of substance, school instead of life. In most cases, the slump has been brief and the recovery quick. But it should never be forgotten that there have been prolonged periods of educational retrogression, most notable, of course, being that which followed the fall of the Roman Empire and which is sometimes known as the "Dark Ages."

It should likewise be noted, before leaving this point, that signs of healthy progress in education can also be misread for signs of retrogression and decay. All through the ages most persons have been so conventional that many of them have read any departure from customary educational procedures as backsliding. Thus, youth have often been accused of being disrespectful to the gods and to their parents when their educators were merely seeking to find new ways of releasing their capacities to learn. Again, educational progress does not always occur evenly in all directions. Decline in one direction may be compensated by progress in another. Thus, many have described the period that overtook Athens, at the height of her educational advancement, as a period of decline. The description is accurate if one has his eye only on the fact that there was a sharp decline in the number of frontier thinkers like Socrates, Plato, and Aristotle. On the other hand, if one will but realize how Hellinic culture was spread far and wide throughout the Aegean and Mediterranean after their deaths, one must acknowledge the tremendous educational progress that took place. Indeed, even the decline of education with the collapse of Rome can be similarly viewed as compensated. Thus, the adulteration of culture that was inevitable when the barbarians of Northern Europe first tried to absorb Greco-Roman culture was really the necessary first step in laying the base for the brilliant culture of modern Europe.

Although different items in the educational programs vary in the clarity with which their progress down the centuries can be assayed, there can be no mistaking the great tidal forces of our society on whose ebb and flow educational progress and retrogression depend. Perhaps most elemental here are economic forces. On the whole, education has made its greatest progress when it has ridden the crest of economic prosperity. It has been most severely retarded in the trough of economic depression. The states of war and peace are similar elemental forces conditioning the advance and retreat of education. On the whole, war is a great deterrent to educational progress. Not only has it distracted the attention of men from the pursuit of learning, but in recent centuries it has become exceedingly destructive of the economic resources indispensable to creating the leisure on which education is predicated. Education thrives on peace and quiet, law and order. War may make learning urgent, but it does not permit the long-time maturation of talents whose season cannot be rushed. For this there is needed not only economic well-being and peace and security but also one other elemental force, free political institutions. Unless the mind is free to pursue its own curiosity wherever the chase may lead, educational progress will be impeded by the artificial barriers of prejudice and ignorance.

Bibliographical Commentary

The following notes on bibliography are addressed not so much to the scholar as to the student of educational history. They will chiefly indicate to him where he can find ampler detail on items of interest that had to be greatly condensed in the foregoing text.

General Histories of Education

Historical materials in the foregoing chapters have been organized according to persistent problems of education rather than according to historical epochs. Instead of presenting the history of education as a whole, epoch by epoch, these chapters have broken education down into various recurrent problems, tracing the history of each of these. Epochs of history such as antiquity, the Renaissance, colonial America, and the nineteenth century have been traversed again and again to trace the genesis of each of these problems, but on no occasion has a well-rounded view of any single epoch been given. The way in which evolving problems bore on each other contemporaneously or the way in which their parallel stages of development could be compared has been little developed, if at all, and then chiefly hinted at through cross references in footnotes. Therefore the student who wants to get a picture of the whole aspect of education at any given time in the past should consult a more conventionally organized general history of education.

There are several multiple-volume histories of education. Most complete probably is the three-volume work of F. P. Graves, *A History of Education before the Middle Ages* (The Macmillan Company, New York, 1909), *A History of Education during the Middle Ages* (The Macmillan Company, New York, 1910), and *A History of Education in Modern Times* (The Macmillan Company, New York, 1913). Also quite complete is the two-volume work of F. Eby and C. F. Arrowood, *The History and Philosophy of Education* (Prentice-Hall, Inc., Englewood Cliffs, N.J., 1940), and *The Development of Modern Education* (Prentice-Hall, Inc., Englewood Cliffs, N.J., 1934). The first of these two volumes, which carries the account down to about the Protestant Reformation, is, if anything, too complete in its quotations and the detail of its exposition. Another good multiple-volume history of education is that of P. Marique, *History of Christian Education* (3 vols., Fordham University Press, New York,

612

1924–1932). The emphasis in this account is not only on the Christian tradition but on the Catholic Christian tradition. Apparently unfinished is E. C. Moore, *The Story of Instruction* (2 vols., The Macmillan Company, New York, 1936–1938). The two volumes of this publication bring Moore's account down to the Renaissance, but a volume covering the modern period seems to be wanting.

Single-volume but still substantial accounts of the general history of education are those of P. Monroe, *Textbook in the History of Education* (The Macmillan Company, New York, 1905), E. P. Cubberley, *The History of Education* (Houghton Mifflin Company, Boston, 1920), P. R. Cole, *History of Educational Thought* (Humphrey Milford, London, 1931), and E. W. Knight, *Twenty Centuries of Education* (Ginn and Company, Boston, 1940). Of these, Monroe's text, though the oldest and unrevised, is probably the best. Its chief lack is an adequate account of modern national systems of education as influenced by industry and democracy. Among foreign authors of educational histories, the American student will probably find the following most readable: from England, W. Boyd, *History of Western Education* (A. & C. Black, Ltd., London, 1950), and from France, G. Compayré, *History of Pedagogy* (D. C. Heath and Company, Boston, 1885).

Less comprehensive, yet well balanced and up to date is J. Wise, *The History of Education* (Sheed & Ward, Inc., New York, 1964). Probably to be bracketed with this work is P. J. McCormick, *History of Education* (The Catholic University of America Press, Washington, D.C., 1915). At once the advantage and the disadvantage of this book is the fact that it weights the medieval period so heavily, but this emphasis is in accord with the oft-stated Catholic conviction that the thirteenth was the greatest of centuries. More balanced is W. T. Kane, *An Essay toward a History of Education* (Loyola University Press, Chicago, 1935). Less important full-length pictures of the history of education are those of two earlier writers, F. V. N. Painter, *History of Education* (D. Appleton & Company, Inc., New York, 1897), and T. Davidson, *History of Education* (Charles Scribner's Sons, New York, 1900).

The Second World War and the era that it concluded seem to have brought the realization that our general histories of education were more or less out of date and urgently in need of revision. Three books, at any rate, appeared almost simultaneously and are highly recommended as being the best contemporary accounts of the general history of education. These are J. Mulhern, *A History of Education* (The Ronald Press Company, New York, 1946, 2d ed., 1959), R. F. Butts, *A Cultural History of Western Education* (McGraw-Hill Book Company, New York, 1946, 2d ed., 1959), and H. G. Good, *A History of Western Education* (The Macmillan Company, New York, 1947). The most recent book deserving to be in this category is M. Nakosteen's *History and Philosophy of Education* (The Ronald Press Company, New York, 1965).

Although J. F. Messenger undertook to write an *Interpretative History of Education* (Thomas Y. Crowell Company, New York, 1931), his interpretations were seldom original, and he produced a fairly conventional account of the history of education. The attempt of E. D. Myers, *Education in the Perspective of History* (Harper & Row, Publishers, Incorporated, New York, 1960), to treat educational history from the point of view of Arnold Toynbee is disappointing. Bolder is J. K. Hart's *Democracy and Education* (Century Company, New York, 1918), which he wrote from a definitely sociological viewpoint. Readable as this book is, it probably omits too much of the factual detail of educational history.

The student interested in the history of education during a particular epoch will find a considerable literature dealing with such limited objectives. This is particularly true of the classical period of educational history. The three best accounts are those of K. Freeman, *Schools of Hellas* (Macmillan & Co., Ltd., London, 1922), W. Jaeger, *Paideia* (Basil Blackwell & Mott, Ltd., Oxford, 1939), and T. Woody, *Life and Education in Early Societies* (The Macmillan Company, New York, 1949). Other good accounts can be found in S. S. Laurie, *Historical Survey of Pre-Christian Education* (Longmans, Green & Co., Inc., New York, 1895), and W. Hobhouse, *The Theory and Practice of Ancient Education* (G. E. Stechert & Company, New York, 1895). More recent narratives of the period are those of W. A. Smith, *Ancient Education* (Philosophical Library, Inc., New York, 1955), and H. I. Marrou, *History of Education in Antiquity*, G. Lamb, tr. (Sheed & Ward Ltd., London, 1956).

In the medieval period one should not overlook K. A. Totah's *Contribution of the Arabs to Education* (Bureau of Publications, Teachers College, Columbia University, New York, 1926), and, especially, M. Nakosteen's *History of Islamic Origins of Western Education, 800–1350* (University of Colorado Press, Boulder, Colo., 1964). Serving the Renaissance period is W. H. Woodward, *Education during the Renaissance* (Cambridge University Press, London, 1906). A particularly good coverage of the whole period from Greco-Roman civilization to the Renaissance is that of E. H. Reisner, *Historical Foundations of Modern Education* (The Macmillan Company, New York, 1927). Covering the period thereafter is S. S. Laurie, *Studies in the History of Educational Opinion since the Renaissance* (Longmans, Green & Co., Inc., New York, 1900). Dealing with just the present century is A. E. Meyer, *The Development of Education in the Twentieth Century* (Prentice-Hall, Inc., Englewood Cliffs, N.J., 1949). With the changes brought about by the Second World War, I. L. Kandel, *Comparative Education* (Houghton Mifflin Company, Boston, 1933), has become an important part of the history of education in the current century.

Works on the history of education in individual nations are so numerous that only several very recent ones can be mentioned here. Three works are from England: S. J. Curtis, *History of Education in Great Britain* (University Tutorial Press, London, 1950), A. D. Peterson, *A Hundred Years of Education* (Gerald Duckworth & Co., Ltd., London, 1952), and W. H. Armytage, *Four Hundred Years of English Education* (Cambridge University Press, London, 1964). Two others are about Russia: N. Hans, *History of Russian Educational Policy, 1701–1917* (Russell and Russell, New York, 1964), and W. H. E. Johnson, *Russia's Educational Heritage* (Carnegie Press, Carnegie Institute of Technology, Pittsburgh, Pa., 1950).

The American student will be particularly interested in histories of education in the United States. R. G. Boone, *Education in the United States: Its History from the Earliest Settlements* (D. Appleton & Company, Inc., New York, 1890), and E. G. Dexter, *A History of Education in the United States* (The Macmillan Company, New York, 1904), the two oldest histories, are quite out of date. They were supplanted between the two world wars by three fairly good ones: E. P. Cubberley, *Public Education in the United States* (Houghton Mifflin Company, Boston, 1934), E. W. Knight, *Education in the United States* (Ginn and Company, Boston, 1941), and S. G. Noble, *A History of American Education* (Holt, Rinehart and Winston, Inc., New York, 1938). Cubberley's volume is the most detailed but lacks the organization and readability that Knight's possesses. Noble's account will appeal particularly to the student with an interest in the curriculum. The mid-century brought forth a new crop of American histories of education: N. Edwards and H. G. Richey, *The School in the American Social Order* (Houghton Mifflin Company, Boston, 1963), A. E. Meyer, *Educational History of the American People* (McGraw-Hill Book Company, New York, 1957), H. Good, *History of American Education* (The Macmillan Company, New York, 1962), and R. F. Butts and L. A. Cremin, *History of Education in American Culture* (Holt, Rinehart and Winston, Inc., New York, 1953). Of these the last was outstanding in its effort to relate educational developments to the political, economic, and cultural context of American life. Nevertheless, the effort fell somewhat short of the goal, for the educational and social factors were treated in separate chapters with the reader being left to infer relations instead of having them pointed out by the authors. More successful, though on a smaller scale, in interrelating these factors is V. T. Thayer's *Formative Ideas in American Education* (Dodd, Mead & Company, Inc., New York, 1965).

General historians too often neglect education, but fortunately this is not uniformly the case. Under the joint editorship of two eminent American historians, A. M. Schlesinger and D. R. Fox, the series on *History of American Life* (The Macmillan Company, New York, 1927–1934) carries good educational chapters with critical bibliographies in each of vols. 6–10 and 12. A good brief history of American education is to be had in R. Finney, *The American Public School* (The Macmillan Company, New York, 1921).

For an excellent half to three-quarters portrait of American education the student should read P. Monroe, *Founding of the American Public School System* (The Macmillan Company, New York, 1940), a historical survey down to 1860. Completing this portrait, though not intended to do so, are C. F. Thwing, *A History of Education in the United States since the Civil War* (Houghton Mifflin Company, Boston, 1910), and, bringing Thwing's account further up to date, the volume edited by I. L. Kandel. *Twenty-five Years of American Education* (The Macmillan

Company, New York, 1929), which covers the first quarter of the twentieth century. Overlapping Kandel and taking for their province the whole first half of the twentieth century are E. K. Knight, *Fifty Years of American Education* (The Ronald Press Company, New York, 1952), and W. Rudy, *Schools in an Age of Mass Culture* (Prentice-Hall, Inc., Englewood Cliffs, N.J., 1965). The latter gives an especially detailed narrative of a half-century which witnessed the making of more history than many earlier centuries.

A few histories deal not so much with limited periods as with limited phases of American education. None of the foregoing accounts, for instance, treats adequately the development of Catholic schools in the United States. For this phase one must turn to J. A. Burns and B. J. Kohlbrenner, *A History of Catholic Education in the United States* (Benziger Bros., Inc., New York, 1937). Again, one who wants to know more about education in the Southern states should familiarize himself with two books of E. W. Knight, *The Influence of Reconstruction on Education in the South* (Bureau of Publications, Teachers College, Columbia University, New York, 1913), and *Public Education in the South* (Ginn and Company, Boston, 1922). If he wishes his history of American education pictorially documented, he should turn to R. H. Gabriel (ed.), *The Pageant of America* (Yale University Press, New Haven, Conn., 1928), vol. 10, chaps. 9, 10. Finally, for state histories of education the reader is referred to a bibliography in the *Review of Educational Research*, 6:372–376, 429–431, October, 1936. For an evaluation of these histories he should see S. G. Noble, "An Evaluation of State Histories of Education," *High School Journal*, 12:197–206, 272–276, 1929.

The student should consult the foregoing histories of education not only for cross-sectional descriptions of education in any epoch but also for biographical details about the great leaders in educational history. Inasmuch as many of these leaders have deserved mention in the discussion of more than one of the persistent problems of education in the text, it has seemed preferable to omit many early biographical data about them in the preceding pages rather than to fill these pages unnecessarily by repeating these data each time a new problem brought the same great name to the fore. The student who is interested in these details is well served by a variety of books organized on the lives and teachings of great masters. Early to set a pattern for this literature was R. H. Quick, *Essays on Educational Reformers* (D. Appleton & Company, Inc., New York, 1897), which was a revision of a work published in the preceding decade. Later works organized on a similar scheme are W. H. Woodward, *Vittorino da Feltre and Other Humanist Educators* (Cambridge University Press, London, 1897), J. W. Adamson, *Pioneers of Modern Education* (Cambridge University Press, London, 1905), F. P. Graves, *Great Educators of Three Centuries* (The Macmillan Company, New York, 1912), R. R. Rusk, *Doctrines of the Great Educators* (Macmillan & Co., Ltd., London, 1918), and most recent, R. Ulich, *History of Educational Thought* (American Book Company, New York, 1945). Books devoted to individual men are too numerous and of too limited scope to mention here. The more important ones will be cited later.

In addition to the foregoing sources it would be a mistake not to remind the reader that in P. Monroe (ed.), *Cyclopedia of Education* (5 vols., The Macmillan Company, New York, 1911–1913), he will find many biographical and historical sketches on specific points otherwise often difficult to obtain. The bibliographical references in this cyclopedia, however, should be supplemented by the extensive and carefully selected bibliography on educational history in the *Review of Educational Research,* October, 1936.

For the student who wishes to consult sources, several collections have been published. E. P. Cubberley has published two of the best of these, *Readings in the History of Education* (Houghton Mifflin Company, Boston, 1920), and *Readings in Public Education in the United States* (Houghton Mifflin Company, Boston, 1934). P. Monroe, too, has published an excellent *Source Book of the History of Education* (The Macmillan Company, New York, 1921), but it covers only the Greco-Roman period. The most recent general collection is Robert Ulich's *Three Thousand Years of Educational Wisdom* (Harvard University Press, Cambridge, 1947), but this includes no selections beyond the nineteenth century. Less significant are A. O. Norton, *Readings in the History of Education* (Harvard University Press, Cambridge, 1909), and B. A. Hinsdale, "Documents Illustrative of American Educational History," *Report of the United States Commissioner of Education, 1892–1893,* vol. 2, pp. 1225–1414. Somewhat different is J. K. Hart, *Creative Moments in Education* (Henry Holt and Company, Inc., New York, 1931), in which the "creative moments" are extracts from educational classics connected into a running account of the history of education by the comments of the author. Two publishers have undertaken to reproduce great educational works of the past, the McGraw-Hill Book Company putting forth a series of *Education Classics* and the Bureau of Publications at Teachers College a series of *Classics in Education.* Sources in this category will be mentioned later in their appropriate connections. Unique among collected and published sources on American education is P. Monroe, *Readings in the Founding of the American Public School System,* which has been published in the form of microfilm and is on deposit at leading and strategically located libraries in various parts of the United States.

Chapter 1—Educational Aims

Two principal attempts have been made to describe the development of educational aims: M. I. Emerson, *Evolution of the Educational Ideal* (Houghton Mifflin Company, Boston, 1914), and J. P. Monroe, *The Educational Ideal* (D. C. Heath and Company, Boston, 1906). By reading under the subtitle "Aims" in each chapter of E. H. Wilds, *Foundations of Modern Education* (Holt, Rinehart and Winston, Inc., New York, 1942), one can piece together another fairly good account of the development of educational aims. Less ambitious but nevertheless very good is F. Paulsen, "The Evolution of the Educational Ideal," *Forum,*

23:598–608, July, 1897. Another good brief review is to be found in the New Educator's Library, *Ideals, Aims, and Methods of Education* (Sir Isaac Pitman & Sons, Ltd., London, 1922). Summarizing more recent educational aims is W. H. Burton, *Introduction to Education* (Appleton-Century-Crofts, Inc., New York, 1934), and describing the nineteenth century is A. T. Hadley, "Educational Methods and Principles of the Nineteenth Century," *Educational Review,* 28:332–334, November, 1904.

Chapter 2—Politics and Education

The best expositions of the relation of politics and education are to be found in the works of the masters themselves. Most important, of course, is Plato's *Republic,* and next is Aristotle's *Politics,* especially book VIII. Renaissance writers like Conte Baldassare Castiglione, *The Courtier,* and Sir Thomas Elyot, *The Book Named the Governor,* should also be consulted. The thought of the French Revolution on this topic is best brought together by F. La Fontainerie, *French Liberalism and Education in the Eighteenth Century* (McGraw-Hill Book Company, New York, 1932). Among modern writers, of course, there is none to compare with J. Dewey, *Democracy and Education* (The Macmillan Company, New York, 1916).

Among secondary accounts particular attention should be given to the writing of M. Curti, *The Social Ideas of American Educators* (Charles Scribner's Sons, New York, 1935). His book *The Growth of American Thought* (Harper & Row, Publishers, Incorporated, New York, 1943), chaps. 6–9, 11, 12, 15, 24, 25, affords an excellent context in which to place educational developments. Three doctoral studies have also made interesting contributions to the historical development of politics and education: A. O. Hansen, *Liberalism and American Education in the Eighteenth Century* (The Macmillan Company, New York, 1926), J. J. Walsh, *Education of the Founding Fathers of the Republic* (Fordham University Press, New York, 1935), and G. F. Kneller, *The Educational Philosophy of National Socialism* (Yale University Press, New Haven, Conn., 1941). There are two accounts of fascism's brief impact on education that complement each other; H. R. Marraro, *The New Education in Italy* (S. F. Vanni, Inc., New York, 1936), and L. Minio-Paluella, *Education in Fascist Italy 1932–1940* (Oxford University Press, Fair Lawn, N.J., 1946). Curti, too, has written briefly but significantly from the historical viewpoint on "The Impact of Totalitarianism on American Education," *Educational Forum,* 6:5–18, November, 1941. For a Catholic treatment of politics and education from a historical perspective, see J. D. Redden and F. A. Ryan, *A Catholic Philosophy of Education* (The Bruce Publishing Company, Milwaukee, 1942), chap. 18. Finally, there should perhaps be mention of C. Beard, *The Unique Function of Education in American Democracy* (National Education Association, Educational Policies Commission, Washington, D.C., 1937), chaps. 2–4, and N. I. Edwards, *Education in a Democracy* (The University of Chicago Press, Chicago, 1941), chap. 1.

Chapter 3—Nationalism and Education

The single best account of nationalism and education is undoubtedly to be found in E. H. Reisner, *Nationalism and Education since 1789* (The Macmillan Company, New York, 1925), even though G. A. Wiggin, *Education and Nationalism* (McGraw-Hill Book Company, New York, 1963) is more recent and comprehensive. Bringing Reisner's nationalism in American education closer to date is *Education for All American Youth* (National Education Association, Educational Policies Commission, Washington, D.C., 1944), chap. 6. For good background the student should consult C. J. H. Hayes, *Essays on Nationalism* (The Macmillan Company, New York, 1937), H. Kohn, *The Idea of Nationalism* (The Macmillan Company, New York, 1944), and M. Curti, *The Growth of American Thought* (Harper & Row, Publishers, Incorporated, New York, 1943), chaps. 10, 16, 19. Giving special attention to nationalism in the education of the eighteenth century are F. La Fontainerie, *French Liberalism and Education in the Eighteenth Century* (McGraw-Hill Book Company, New York, 1932), and A. O. Hansen, *Liberalism and American Education in the Eighteenth Century* (The Macmillan Company, New York, 1926). The nationalistic educational leanings of Rousseau can be examined in W. Boyd, *The Minor Educational Writings of Jean Jacques Rousseau* (Blackie & Son, Ltd., Glasgow, 1911), pp. 141–149, and E. H. Reisner, "Rousseau as an Exponent of Imposed Education," *School and Society,* 27:764–769, June, 1928. For education under that aggravated form of nationalism, National Socialism or fascism, the student should read G. F. Kneller, *The Educational Philosophy of National Socialism* (Yale University Press, New Haven, Conn., 1941), and G. Gentile, *The Reform of Education* (Harcourt, Brace and Company, Inc., New York, 1922). A briefer account of nationalism and education by a thoroughly competent historian can be found in T. Woody, "Education and National Culture," *School and Society,* 52:177–186, September, 1940. For the rise and development of a cosmopolitan or international approach to education, see W. Laves and C. Thomson, *UNESCO: Purpose, Progress, and Prospect* (Indiana University Press, Bloomington, Ind., 1957), chaps. 1, 3, and D. G. Scanlon, *International Education: A Documentary History* (Bureau of Publications, Teachers College, Columbia University, New York, 1960).

Chapter 4—Economic Influences on Education

Historical literature lacks a comprehensive discussion of the role that economic forces have played in educational development. Fortunately, however, there are a number of good accounts limited to particular phases of this topic. The work of F. T. Carlton, *Economic Influences on Educational Progress in the United States, 1820–1850* (The University of Wisconsin Press, Madison, Wis., 1908), represents a pattern for a limited period that one could wish to have extended to many other periods. Much the same can be said for M. Curti, *The Social Ideas of American Educators* (Charles Scribner's Sons, New York, 1935), which in part is a discussion of the economic viewpoints of leaders in American education. Similarly, it would be good to have an expansion of the historical treatment of the economic factor in education that is given in J. Dewey and E. Dewey, *Schools of Tomorrow* (E. P. Dutton & Co., Inc., New York, 1915), chap. 9. Valuable general background for the economic basis of the growth of educational thought and practice is to be found in M. Curti, *The Growth of American Thought* (Harper & Row, Publishers, Incorporated, New York, 1943), chaps. 13, 20, 27.

Dealing more specifically with the capitalistic cycle of prosperity and depression and its influence on education is the study of R. S. Pitkin, *Public School Support in the United States during Periods of Economic Depression* (Stephen Daye Press, Inc., New York, 1933). How communism has conditioned educational policy is recounted in N. Hans and S. Hessen, *Educational Policy in Soviet Russia* (P. S. King & Staples, Ltd., London, 1930), chap. 8.

The two best narratives concerning education for economic efficiency are to be found in L. F. Anderson, *History of Manual and Industrial School Education* (D. Appleton-Century Company, Inc., New York, 1926), and C. A. Bennett, *History of Manual and Industrial Education up to 1870* and *History of Manual and Industrial Education, 1870–1917* (The Manual Arts Press, Peoria, Ill., 1926, 1937). Portraying solely the apprenticeship phase of vocational education are R. F. Seybolt, *Apprenticeship and Apprenticeship Education in Colonial New England and New York* (Bureau of Publications, Teachers College, Columbia University, New York, 1917), and P. H. Douglas, *American Apprenticeship and Industrial Education* (Columbia University Press, New York, 1921), chaps. 1, 2, 7. For just an outline of the beginnings of workers' education in this country, see the John Dewey Society, *Workers' Education in the United States,* Fifth Yearbook (Harper & Row, Publishers, Incorporated, New York, 1941), chaps. 2, 3, 10–12. For the attitude of organized labor toward both trade and general education there is nothing better than P. R. V. Curoe, *Educational Attitudes and Policies of Organized Labor in the United States* (Columbia University Press, New York, 1926), although this volume needs bringing up to date to include the activities of the Congress of Industrial Organizations, organized after its publication.

Chapter 5—Philosophy of Education

Much of the history of education is made up of the history of philosophical theories of education. Indeed, many general histories of education stress the evolution of educational theories to a greater degree than they do the development of practice in line with these theories. Perhaps the best are Sir John Adams, *The Evolution of Educational Theory* (Macmillan & Co., Ltd., London, 1915), and S. J. Curtis and M. E. A. Boultwood, *A Short History of Educational Ideas* (University Tutorial Press, London, 1953). For a fine anthology of the classics in educational philosophy, see K. Price, *Education and Philosophical Thought*

(Allyn and Bacon, Inc., Boston, 1962), and for a critical examination of some of these writings, see R. S. Brumbaugh and N. M. Lawrence, *Philosophers on Education* (Houghton Mifflin Company, Boston, 1963) and W. K. Frankena, *Three Historical Philosophies of Education* (Scott, Foresman and Company, Chicago, 1965).

Among ancient educators perhaps none has been more frequently the subject of historical writing than Plato. Good description and commentary on his *Republic* are to be found in B. Bosanquet, *Education in Plato's Republic* (Cambridge University Press, London, 1900), R. L. Nettleship, *The Theory of Education in the Republic of Plato* (The University of Chicago Press, Chicago, 1906), and R. C. Lodge, *Plato's Theory of Education* (Harcourt, Brace & World, Inc., New York, 1947). Making Aristotle's thought more accessible to the student is J. Burnet, *Aristotle on Education* (Cambridge University Press, London, 1913). What Burnet did for Aristotle, M. H. Mayer did for St. Thomas Aquinas, *The Philosophy of Teaching of St. Thomas Aquinas* (The Bruce Publishing Company, Milwaukee, 1929), and R. L. Archer for Rousseau, *Rousseau on Education* [Edward Arnold (Publishers) Ltd., London, 1912].

Although the great philosopher Immanuel Kant gave only incidental attention to education, his educational point of view has been the subject of several books, of which the student will probably find E. F. Buchner, *The Educational Theory of Immanuel Kant* (J. B. Lippincott Company, Philadelphia, 1904), the most useful. Hegel, too, though education was only a small part of his great philosophical system, has been the subject of two studies: F. L. Luqueer, *Hegel as Educator* (The Macmillan Company, New York, 1896), and M. Mackenzie, *Hegel's Educational Theory and Practice* (Swan, Sonnenschein & Co., London, 1909). On the other hand, G. Stanley Hall, outstanding educator and genetic psychologist, left his educational philosophy implicit in his works, from which G. E. Partridge abstracted and published it as *Genetic Philosophy of Education* (Sturgis and Walton, New York, 1912).

The twentieth century, of course, has been dominated by John Dewey's *Democracy and Education* (The Macmillan Company, New York, 1916). What is not so well known about this volume is that it not only sets forth its author's educational philosophy but also presents an interesting critique of historical views which preceded his own. Probing into Dewey's background, M. C. Baker, in *Foundations of John Dewey's Educational Theory* (King's Crown Press, New York, 1955), has been successful in explaining the genesis of his pragmatism. J. L. Childs, *Pragmatism and American Education* (Holt, Rinehart and Winston, Inc., New York, 1956), shows pragmatism's impact on other leading theorists as well.

Finally, two textbooks deserve mention: that of I. N. Thut, *The Story of Education* (McGraw-Hill Book Company, New York, 1957), because it is a history of education organized around philosophical themes, and F. C. Gruber, *Foundations for a Philosophy of Education* (Thomas Y. Crowell Company, New York, 1961), because it is a philosophy of education organized in large part as a history.

Chapter 6—Educational Psychology

To date no comprehensive history of educational psychology has appeared, but a small but good start has been made by R. Watson, "A Brief History of Educational Psychology," *Psychological Record,* 11:209–242, July, 1961. Although this article is more substantial than its title would indicate, it is stronger on later than on earlier events. While a comprehensive history of educational psychology remains to be written, a number of specific historical studies are accumulating out of which such a history may some day be written. Thus H. C. Warren has written a *History of Association Psychology* (Charles Scribner's Sons, New York, 1921), and C. A. Hart has given an exposition of *The Thomistic Concept of Mental Capacity* (The Catholic University of America, Washington, D.C., 1930). The theory of discipline has been the subject of two books. V. T. Thayer has published *The Misinterpretation of Locke as a Formalist in Education* (The University of Wisconsin Press, Madison, Wis., 1921), and, more recently, H. B. English has dug up the *Historical Roots of Learning Theory* (Doubleday & Company, Inc., Garden City, N.Y., 1954). F. J. McDonald has traced "The Influence of Learning Theories on Education," *Theories of Learning and Instruction* Sixty-third Yearbook (National Society for the Study of Education, Chicago, 1964), part I, and W. S. Monroe has traced them for teacher training, *Teaching-Learning Theory and Teacher Education, 1890–1950* (The University of Illinois Press, Urbana, Ill., 1952), chaps. 1–4.

Chapter 7—Methods of Instruction

To form a more intimate understanding of the development of methods of instruction and discipline prior to modern times, the student can do no better than to sit at the feet of the master teachers themselves. For a better appreciation of the Socratic method, read almost any of the Platonic dialogues, but especially the *Meno.* For an excellent early portrayal of methods of instruction in literature, grammar, and rhetoric, see the Roman Quintilian, *Institutes of Oratory.* The Judaeo-Christian contribution to method is best found in scattered references throughout the Bible. Of course, Jesus' method is best seen in the New Testament narratives of Matthew, Mark, Luke, and John. A good glimpse of medieval methods may be seen in F. Winterton, "The Lesson of Neo-Scholasticism," *Mind,* 13:397–400, July, 1888. Humanistic methods of the Renaissance can best be read in W. H. Woodward, *Erasmus concerning Education* (Cambridge University Press, London, 1904), and, especially, in the accounts of Jesuit schools given by E. A. Fitzpatrick, *St. Ignatius and the Ratio Studiorum* (McGraw-Hill Book Company, New York, 1933), T. Hughes, *Loyola and the Educational System of the Jesuits* (Charles Scribner's Sons, New York, 1897), pp. 232–246, R. Schwickerath, *Jesuit Education: Its History and Principles* (B. Herder Book Co., St. Louis, 1903), pp. 468–474, and T. Corcoran, *Studies in the History of Classical Teaching* (Longmans, Green & Co., Ltd., London, 1911), pp. 236–247. For an excellent sample of rules of discipline in the post-

Renaissance period, see F. La Fontainerie, *The Conduct of the Schools of Jean Baptiste de La Salle* (McGraw-Hill Book Company, New York, 1935).

Chapter 8—Methods of Instruction—Continued

The development of modern techniques of instruction may be said to commence with the rise of modern science in the seventeenth century. The first effect that the new attitude toward nature had on methods of instruction is fairly well seen in such selections from and commentary on great authors as M. W. Keatinge, *Comenius* (McGraw-Hill Book Company, New York, 1931), and R. L. Archer, *Rousseau on Education* [Edward Arnold (Publishers) Ltd., London, 1912]. For the way in which Pestalozzi and Froebel organized the insights of Comenius and Rousseau into a practical pedagogy of the classroom, the earnest student should read such further selections and commentary as are offered by L. F. Anderson, *Pestalozzi* (McGraw-Hill Book Company, New York, 1931), and J. L. Hughes, *Froebel's Educational Laws for All Teachers* (D. Appleton & Company, Inc., New York, 1897). The closely related yet distinctive method of Herbart can best be read in A. F. Lange and C. De Garmo, *Outlines of Pedagogical Doctrine* (The Macmillan Company, New York, 1901). For the contemporary but still more distinctive method of Lancaster, see J. F. Reigart, *The Lancasterian System of Instruction in the Schools of New York City* (Bureau of Publications, Teachers College, Columbia University, New York, 1916). Dewey's contribution to method in the twentieth century can be gathered from *The Child and the Curriculum* (The University of Chicago Press, Chicago, 1903), *How We Think* (D. C. Heath and Company, Boston, 1910), *Democracy and Education* (The Macmillan Company, New York, 1916), and the volume he wrote with Evelyn Dewey, *Schools of Tomorrow* (E. P. Dutton & Co., Inc., New York, 1915). The great popularizer of Dewey's conception of method was W. H. Kilpatrick, *Foundations of Method* (The Macmillan Company, New York, 1925).

A considerable literature—a literature so extensive that only a few outstanding samples can be mentioned—has grown up in exposition and interpretation of Pestalozzi, Froebel, and Herbart. On Pestalozzi, see J. A. Green, *Life and Work of Pestalozzi* (W. B. Clive, London, 1913). On Froebel, consult H. C. Bowen, *Froebel and Education through Self-activity* (Charles Scribner's Sons, New York, 1893). For Herbart, there are several secondary accounts: C. De Garmo, *Herbart and the Herbartians* (Charles Scribner's Sons, New York, 1895), G. Compayré, *Herbart and Education by Instruction* (Thomas Y. Crowell Company, New York, 1907), J. Adams, *Herbartian Psychology Applied to Education* (D. C. Heath and Company, Boston, 1898), and G. B. Randels, *Doctrines of Herbart in the United States* (University of Pennsylvania Press, Philadelphia, 1909). See also J. A. MacVannel, *The Educational Theories of Herbart and Froebel* (Bureau of Publications, Teachers College, Columbia University, New York, 1905), and P. R. Cole, *Herbart and Froebel: An Attempt at Synthesis* (New York, 1907).

A few authors should be mentioned not as great innovators of instructional method but as able popularizers of good methods. Widely influential in the mid-nineteenth century was D. P. Page, *Theory and Practice of Teaching* (A. S. Barnes and Co., Inc., New York, 1847), who more or less took for his pattern the very successful S. R. Hall, *Lectures on School Keeping,* newly edited by A. Wright and G. E. Gardner (Dartmouth Press, Hanover, N.H., 1929). Early to popularize Pestalozzian methods in the United States was H. Mann, *Lectures on Education* (Marsh, Capen, Lyon & Webb, Boston, 1840), no. 7. Charles McMurry, *Elements of General Method* (Public School Publishing Company, Bloomington, Ill., 1892), and his brother Frank McMurry, *The Method of the Recitation* (The Macmillan Company, New York, 1898), did much the same for the Herbartian technique of instruction. But do not fail to see V. T. Thayer, *The Passing of the Recitation* (D. C. Heath and Company, Boston, 1928). Combining the principles of Pestalozzi, Froebel, and Herbart was F. W. Parker's *Talks on Pedagogics* (E. L. Kellogg & Co., New York, 1894).

To gain an insight into the methods of such great teachers as Mark Hopkins, Louis Agassiz, and James Mill, who profoundly influenced their pupils but never directly studied the technique of instruction, see H. Peterson, *Great Teachers* (Rutgers University Press, New Brunswick. N.J., 1946).

Other important links in the chain of development of educational method have been contributed by W. A. McCallister, *Growth of Freedom in Education* (Richard R. Smith, New York, 1931), P. E. Harris, *Changing Conceptions of School Discipline* (The Macmillan Company, New York, 1926), L. C. Mossman, *Changing Conceptions Relative to the Planning of Lessons* (Bureau of Publications, Teachers College, Columbia University, New York, 1924), and W. H. Burton, "The Problem Solving Technique—Its Appearance and Development in American Texts on General Method," *Educational Method,* 14:189–195, 248–253, January, February, 1935. For the development of even more recent methods see Burton's "Implications for the Organization of Instruction and Instructional Adjuncts," *Learning and Instruction,* Forty-ninth Yearbook of the National Society for the Study of Education (University of Chicago Press, Chicago, 1950), part I, chap. 9. In addition, there are two good brief accounts of the activity method, one by T. Woody, *The Activity Movement,* Thirty-third Yearbook of the National Society for the Study of Education (Public School Publishing Company, Bloomington, Ill., 1934), part II, chap. 2, and one by G. Schoenchen, *The Activity School* (Longmans, Green & Co., Inc., New York, 1940), chaps. 1, 2. For the development of educational methods in the first quarter of the twentieth century see I. L. Kandel, *Twenty-five Years of American Education* (The Macmillan Company, New York, 1929), chap. 6.

Chapter 9—Curriculum

The history of the curriculum in its several branches must be assembled from a variety of sources. Endeavoring briefly to see the whole sweep of curriculum development is J. M. Gwynn, *Curriculum Principles and*

Social Trends (The Macmillan Company, New York, 1960), chap. 1.
Treating shorter periods more intensively are such books as E. H. Reisner,
Historical Foundations of Modern Education (The Macmillan Company,
New York, 1927), chap. 3, which describes the genesis in classical times
of the basic curriculum of Western civilization. Very adequately bringing
this account up to date with broad emphasis on secondary education
is W. L. Uhl, *The Secondary School Curriculum* (The Macmillan
Company, New York, 1927), chaps. 1–8. Stressing the modernization
of this curriculum, especially in England, is F. Watson, *The Beginning
of the Teaching of Modern Subjects in England* (Sir Isaac Pitman &
Sons, Ltd., London, 1909). In this country the volume that pays the
greatest attention to curriculum development is S. G. Noble, *A History
of American Education* (Holt, Rinehart, and Winston, Inc., New York,
1938), chaps. 4, 5, 12, 16, 18. A good but briefer account is to be
found in H. Rugg, *American Life and the School Curriculum* (Ginn
and Company, Boston, 1936), chaps. 7, 8, and E. P. Cubberley, *Public
Education in the United States* (Houghton Mifflin Company, Boston,
1934), chap. 18. Stressing the American colonial period are two works:
C. Meriwether, *Our Colonial Curriculum 1607–1776* (Capitol Publishing
Company, Washington, D.C., 1907), and R. F. Seybolt, "Notes on
the Curriculum in Colonial America," *Journal of Educational Research,*
12:275–281, 370–378, November, December, 1925. Revealing the old-time
curriculum through its textbooks is C. Johnson, *Old Time Schools and
School Books* (The Macmillan Company, New York, 1925).

One may consult Monroe's *Cyclopedia of Education* for the manner
in which many individual subjects have gained admission to the curriculum. The relatively brief sketches given there can be supplemented by
a variety of other studies: on reading, R. R. Reeder, *Historical Development of School Readers and Methods of Teaching Reading* (The Macmillan Company, New York, 1900); on writing, W. C. Bates, "Boston Writing Masters before the Revolution," *New England Magazine,* 25:403–418,
December, 1898, and A. Heck, *The English Writing-masters and Their
Copy-books* (Cambridge University Press, 1931); on arithmetic, W. S.
Monroe, *The Development of Arithmetic as a School Subject,* U.S. Bureau
of Education Bulletin 10, 1917; on literature and science, W. Goodsell,
The Conflict of Naturalism and Humanism (Bureau of Publications,
Teachers College, Columbia University, New York, 1910), and P. Beesley,
The Revival of the Humanities in American Education (Columbia University Press, New York, 1940); on grammar, R. L. Lyman, *English
Grammar in American Schools before 1850,* U.S. Bureau of Education
Bulletin 12, 1921; on history, H. Johnson, *An Introduction to the History
of the Social Sciences in School* (Charles Scribner's Sons, New York,
1932); on the fine arts, E. B. Birge, *History of Public School Music
in the United States* (Oliver Ditson Company, Philadelphia, 1937), L. F.
Sunderman, "History of Public School Music in the United States
1830–1890," *Educational Record,* 22:205–211, April, 1941, F. V. Nyquist,
"Some Historical Aims of Art Education," *School and Society,* 26:25–31,
July, 1927, G. Whitford, "Brief History of Art Education in the United

States," *Elementary School Journal,* 24:109–115, October, 1923, and the Progressive Education Association, Commission on the Secondary School Curriculum, *The Visual Arts,* pp. 1–9; on physical education, E. A. Rice, *A Brief History of Physical Education* (A. S. Barnes and Co. Inc., New York, 1926), N. Schwendener, *A History of Physical Education in the United States* (A. S. Barnes and Co. Inc., New York, 1942), F. E. Leonard, *A Guide to the History of Physical Education* (Lea & Febiger, Philadelphia, 1923), and D. B. Van Dalen, E. D. Mitchell, and B. L. Bennett, *World History of Physical Education* (Prentice-Hall, Englewood Cliffs, N.J. 1953); on vocational education, L. F. Anderson, *History of Manual and Industrial School Education* (D. Appleton-Century Company, Inc., New York, 1926), two volumes by C. A. Bennett, *A History of Manual and Industrial Education up to 1870* and *A History of Manual and Industrial Education, 1870–1917* (The Manual Arts Press, Peoria, Ill., 1926, 1937), J. F. Scott, *Historical Essays on Apprenticeship and Vocational Education* (Ann Arbor Press, Ann Arbor, Mich., 1914), H. R. Smith, *Development of Manual Training in the United States* (Intelligencer print, Lancaster, Pa., 1914), and R. F. Seybolt, *Apprenticeship and Apprenticeship Education in Colonial New England and New York* (Bureau of Publications, Teachers College, Columbia University, New York, 1917); on business education, B. R. Haynes, *History of Business Education in the United States* (South-Western Publishing Company, Cincinnati, 1935), and E. G. Knepper, *History of Business Education in the United States* (Bowling Green, Ohio, 1941); and on manners, J. D. Mason, *Gentlefolk in the Making* (University of Pennsylvania Press, Philadelphia, 1935).

No history of the development of extracurricular activities exists at present. Before it can be written, there must be a number of individual researches, such as that of D. Potter, *Debating in the Colonial Chartered Colleges* (Bureau of Publications, Teachers College, Columbia University, New York, 1944).

Chapter 10—Curriculum—Continued

The history of the theory of curriculum construction has yet to be written. Dealing with the controversy between the prescribed and the elective curriculum, but only at the college level, is R. F. Butts, *The College Charts Its Course* (McGraw-Hill Book Company, New York, 1939). For the earliest sociological approach to the curriculum, one must read H. Spencer, *Education: Intellectual, Moral, and Physical* (D. Appleton & Company, Inc., New York, 1883), especially the essay on "What Knowledge Is Most Worth?" To get a better appreciation of the Herbartian organization of the curriculum based on culture epochs and correlation, see C. De Garmo, *Herbart and the Herbartians* (Charles Scribner's Sons, New York, 1895), pp. 104–139, and C. A. McMurry, *Elements of General Method* (Public School Publishing Company, Bloomington, Ill., 1892), chap. 4.

To understand the pragmatic approach of the twentieth century to the curriculum the careful student should not fail to read the trail-blazing brochure by John Dewey, *The Child and the Curriculum* (The University of Chicago Press, Chicago, 1903). These views were matured and enlarged in *Democracy and Education* (The Macmillan Company, New York, 1916), in which Dewey devotes a considerable number of chapters to the problems of the curriculum. For an early account of the ferment that scientific curriculum building stirred up, see H. Rugg, *American Life and the School Curriculum* (Ginn and Company, Boston, 1936), chap. 10. This ferment culminated in one of the most important yearbooks of the National Society for the Study of Education, the twenty-sixth, *The Foundations and Technique of Curriculum-making* (Public School Publishing Company, Bloomington, Ill., 1926, 1930), part I, chaps. 1–5, part II. The publication of another professional society should be added here: National Curriculum Society, Committee on Integration, *Integration: Its Meaning and Application* (Appleton-Century-Crofts, Inc., New York, 1937), chaps. 10–14.

Once the movement for curriculum reconstruction was in full swing, a number of books on the theory of curriculum construction appeared. The more important are H. J. Caswell and D. S. Campbell, *Curriculum Development* (American Book Company, New York, 1935), J. K. Norton and M. A. Norton, *Foundations of Curriculum Building* (Ginn and Company, Boston, 1936), J. M. Gwynn, *Curriculum Principles and Social Trends* (The Macmillan Company, New York, 1960), chaps. 6, 7, and H. Taba, *Curriculum Development: Theory and Practice* (Harcourt, Brace & World, Inc., New York, 1962).

Chapter 11—Religious and Moral Education

When one considers the great scholarship that has been centered in the field of religion and morals in general and religious and moral education in particular, it is quite surprising to find no thorough and comprehensive history of religious and moral education. The most carefully undertaken work in this field is L. J. Sherrill, *The Rise of Christian Education* (The Macmillan Company, New York, 1944), but unfortunately this account stops at about the time of the Renaissance and at that is pitched at a level beyond the usual student interest. C. H. Benson's *Popular History of Christian Education* (Moody Press, Chicago, 1943) remedies Sherrill's incompleteness by covering the whole span of Christian religious and moral education down to the time of publication but is, by Sherrill's standards, superficial. Brief introductions to the history of religious and moral education can be found in G. A. Coe, *Education in Religion and Morals* (Fleming H. Revell Company, Publishers, Westwood, N.J., 1904), chap. 21, P. H. Lotz and L. W. Crawford, *Studies in Religious Education* (Abington-Cokesbury Press, Nashville, Tenn., 1931), chap. I, J. P. Williams, *The New Education and Religion* (Association Press, New York, 1945), chap. 2, and, best of these introductions, G. H. Betts, *The Curriculum of Religious Education* (Abington-Cokesbury Press, Nashville, Tenn., 1929), chaps. 2–8. Covering the general history of religious and moral education through an account of great personalities in the field is T. F. Kinloch, *Pioneers of Religious Education* (Oxford University Press, Fair Lawn, N.J., 1939).

If a single scholarly narrative of the whole period of religious and moral education is lacking, the deficit is made up in part by a number of individual researches of limited scope. Two of these have been contributed by F. H. Swift, "Athenian Religious and Moral Training," *Open Court*, 35:321–338, 385–405, June, July, 1921, and *Education in Ancient Israel* (The Open Court Publishing Company, La Salle, Ill., 1919). Another contribution to the history of Jewish religious and moral education is N. H. Imber, "Education and the Talmud," *Report of the United States Commissioner of Education, 1894–1895*, vol. 2, pp. 1795–1829.

There are two books on the history of Christian education, one for its earliest period, G. Hodgson, *Primitive Christian Education* (T. & T. Clark, Edinburgh, 1906), and one for a much later period, A. A. Brown, *A History of Religious Education in Recent Times* (Abington-Cokesbury Press, Nashville, Tenn., 1923). This leaves a long intermediate period to be served by more specific studies, Thus N. Hans covers a wide area in "Educational Traditions in the British Commonwealth of Nations and the United States of America," *Yearbook of Education* (Evans Brothers, London, 1938), part XI, pp. 740–914. For a narrative covering just one of the United States, see G. Stewart, *A History of Religious Education in Connecticut* (Yale University Press, New Haven, Conn., 1924); for a narrative of the period before the nineteenth century, see A. A. Holtz, *A Study of the Moral and Religious Elements in American Education up to 1800* (George Banta Company, Inc., Menasha, Wis., 1917). An excellent account of the Puritan attitude toward education in the same period is to be had in S. Fleming, *Children and Puritanism* (Yale University Press, New Haven, Conn., 1933), chap. 10. The Catholic tradition is well represented by two works of limited scope, of which the first is R. G. Bandas, *Catechetical Methods* (Joseph F. Wagner, Inc., New York, 1929), chap. 1. The opening chapter in this book has been expanded by J. J. Baierl, R. G. Bandas, and J. Collins into *Religious Instruction and Education* (Joseph F. Wagner, Inc., New York, 1938), which is one of the best histories in this field by Catholic authors. In describing the historical *Crisis in Western Education* (Sheed & Ward, Inc., New York, 1961), C. Dawson, another Catholic scholar, finds the crisis to be religious.

The secularization of education in the nineteenth century has been treated by both a Catholic investigator, B. Confrey, *Secularism in American Education* (The Catholic University of America Press, Washington, D.C., 1931), and a Protestant one, S. W. Brown, *The Secularization of American Education* (Bureau of Publications, Teachers College, Columbia University, New York, 1912). Tracing this movement in several of the leading states are S. Bell, *The Church, the State, and Education in Virginia* (Science Press, Lancaster, Pa., 1930), S. M. Smith, *The Relation of the State to Religious Education in Massachusetts* (Syracuse University Book Store, Syracuse, N.Y., 1926), and A. J. Hall, *Religious Education in the Public Schools of the State and City of New York* (The University of Chicago Press, Chicago, 1914). The part that

Horace Mann played in this movement is well delineated in R. B. Culver, *Horace Mann and Religion in the Massachusetts Public Schools* (Yale University Press, New Haven, Conn., 1929). A more recent historical reexamination of the relation of church and state in education is that of C. H. Moehlman, *School and Church* (Harper & Row, Publishers, Incorporated, New York, 1944). N. G. McCluskey has done the same for Catholics in his *Public Schools and Moral Education* (Columbia University Press, New York, 1958).

There are numerous histories of the Sunday school movement, which, beginning before the divorce of church and state was widely agitated, prospered mightily after the divorce became complete in this country. Probably best among these are H. F. Cope, *The Evolution of the Sunday School* (Pilgrim Press, Boston, 1911), M. C. Brown, *Sunday School Movements in America* (Fleming H. Revell Company, Publishers, Westwood, N.J., 1901), and E. W. Rice, *The Sunday School Movement and the Sunday School Union 1817–1917* (American Sunday School Union, Philadelphia, 1917). For the beginnings of a return to weekday religious instruction, see C. Zollman, "Historical Background of Religious Day Schools," *Religious Education,* 21:80–90, February, 1926.

To gain a perspective on the great "religious-education" movement of the twentieth century, the student will probably do well to read biographical sketches of two great leaders whose divergent points of view tended to define the educational issue of the century. For a great exponent of evangelism, see J. W. Prince, *Wesley on Religious Education* (The Methodist Book Concern, New York, 1926), and for a pioneer of the "educational" viewpoint, see A. J. W. Myers, *Horace Bushnell and Religious Education* (Menthorne & Burack, Inc., Boston, 1937). Tracing this conflict in some detail is H. Elliott, *Can Religious Education Be Christian?* (The Macmillan Company, New York, 1940), chap. 3. Historical analysis of a related controversy is to be had in H. J. Schneider, "Dualism in Modern Theories of Moral Education," *Educational Review,* 52:372–384, November, 1916. Schneider clearly betrays the influence of John Dewey, whose treatment of moral education in the last chapter of *Democracy and Education* (The Macmillan Company, New York, 1916) must be examined to understand the developments of the twentieth century. The John Dewey of the religious-education movement and the ideological heir to Bushnell is G. A. Coe, whose major contribution to this controversy is *A Social Theory of Religious Education* (Charles Scribner's Sons, New York, 1917). For a review of "Forty Years of Religious Education" by a Catholic, a Jew, and a Protestant, see *Religious Education,* 39:259–281, September-October, 1944, and for an even longer retrospective view, see W. K. Dunn, *What Happened to Religious Education?* (The Johns Hopkins Press, Baltimore, 1958).

The character-education movement, which was an outcome of the religious-education movement, is documented by two short articles: H. V. Meredith and J. C. Manry, *Brief History of Character Education,* University of Iowa Bulletin 290, 1932, and L. V. Glasscock, "The History of Character Education," *Educational Method,* 11:351–358, March, 1932. The latter contains a further bibliography on the growth of this movement. For "Character Education in Perspective," see *Religious Education,* vol. 24, January, 1929.

Chapter 12—Formal and Informal Education

There is no literature worth mentioning on the way in which formal schooling emerged from informal educational practices. Perhaps this history can in part be recovered by a sociological study of modern primitive cultures. If this hypothesis is acceptable, the student will be well repaid by a reading of W. D. Hambly, *Origins of Education among Primitive Peoples* (Macmillan & Co., Ltd., London, 1926), and A. J. Todd, *The Primitive Family as an Educational Agency* (G. P. Putnam & Sons, New York, 1913).

On the home as a type of informal education, only one account represents even a beginning of the sort of comprehensive story that needs to be written. It is W. Goodsell, *A History of the Family as a Social and Educational Institution* (The Macmillan Company, New York, 1915). Treating education in the family much more incidentally, although against an extensive background of sociological data, is A. W. Calhoun, *A Social History of the American Family from Colonial Times to the Present* (The Arthur H. Clark Company, Glendale, Calif., 1917–1919). An intensive investigation of a narrow segment of the total field here has been well conducted by A. L. Kuhn, *The Mother's Role in Childhood Education: New England Concepts, 1830–1860* (Yale University Press, New Haven, Conn., 1947). A few notes on the history of parental education can be gleaned from the National Society for the Study of Education, *Pre-school and Parental Education,* Twenty-eighth Yearbook (Public School Publishing Company, Bloomington, Ill., 1929), chap. 2. For a good description and an excellent bibliography of the way in which various institutions supplemented the school in early America, see B. Bailyn, *Education in the Forming of American Society* (The University of North Carolina Press, Chapel Hill, N.C., 1960).

The history of adult education, as a phase of informal education, is best treated by an eminent American historian, J. T. Adams, *Frontiers of American Culture* (Charles Scribner's Sons, New York, 1944), but, unfortunately, not in his best manner. Slighter accounts are M. S. Knowles, *The Adult Education Movement in the United States* (Holt, Rinehart and Winston, Inc., New York, 1962), part I, M. A. Cartwright, *Ten Years of Adult Education* (The Macmillan Company, New York, 1935), and L. Bryson, *Adult Education* (American Book Company, New York, 1936), chap. 2. On individual types of adult education, a number of studies have been written, among them C. B. Hayes, *The American Lyceum,* U.S. Office of Education Bulletin 12, 1932, J. S. Noffsinger, *Correspondence Schools, Lyceums, Chautauquas* (The Macmillan Company, New York, 1926), part I, chap. 1, part II, chaps. 1, 2, R. F. Seybolt, *The Evening School of Colonial New York City* (University of the State of New York, Albany,

N.Y., 1921), O. D. Evans, *Educational Opportunities for Young Workers* (The Macmillan Company, New York, 1926), chaps. 1–8, W. H. Draper, *University Extension 1873–1923* (Cambridge University Press, London, 1923), A. L. Hall-Quest, *The University Afield* (The Macmillan Company, New York, 1926), chap. 1, and W. S. Bittner, *The University Extension Movement,* U.S. Bureau of Education Bulletin 84, 1919.

Chapter 13—Elementary Education

The field of elementary education is well served by several good histories of education, of which the most recent and best is E. H. Reisner, *Evolution of the Common School* (The Macmillan Company, New York, 1930). Somewhat older but still very good is S. C. Parker, *The History of Modern Elementary Education* (Ginn and Company, Boston, 1912). Less adequate in scope and substance are L. F. Anderson, *History of Common School Education* (Henry Holt and Company, Inc., New York, 1909), and T. Raymont, *History of the Education of Young Children* (Longmans, Green & Co., Ltd., London, 1937). Concentrating on the growth of the American elementary school is L. A. Cremin, *The American Common School* (Bureau of Publications, Teachers College, Columbia University, New York, 1951).

Supplementing these books are a few accounts of the elementary school at particular times or phases of its development. Such are K. Freeman, *Schools of Hellas* (Macmillan & Co., Ltd., London, 1922), H. C. Barnard, *The Little Schools of Port Royal* (Cambridge University Press, London, 1913), W. H. Small, *Early New England Schools* (Ginn and Company, Boston, 1914), chaps 6–13, M. Sullivan, *Our Times* (Charles Scribner's Sons, New York, 1927), vol. 4, chaps. 11, 12, C. Johnson, *The District School as It Was* (Lee & Shepard, Boston, 1897), and I. L. Kandel, *Twenty-five Years of American Education* (The Macmillan Company, New York, 1929), chap. 9.

The story of the kindergarten as a special phase of elementary education must be pieced together from several sources. For the introduction and general spread of the idea, see N. C. Vandewalker, *The Kindergarten in American Education* (The Macmillan Company, New York, 1908). On the precise date and place of the first appearance of kindergartens in this country, see D. E. Lawson, "Corrective Note on the Early History of the American Kindergarten," *Educational Administration and Supervision,* 25:699–703, December, 1937. Expounding the original Froebelian conception of the kindergarten in America is S. E. Blow, *Educational Issues in the Kindergarten* (D. Appleton & Company, Inc., New York, 1908). Attacking this conception is W. H. Kilpatrick, *Froebel's Kindergarten Principles Critically Examined* (The Macmillan Company, New York, 1916), and indicating early movements toward remodeling the kindergarten is F. Eby, "The Reconstruction of the Kindergarten," *Pedagogical Seminary,* 7:229–286, July, 1900. For the modern trends, see K. D. Wiggin and N. A. Smith, *The Republic of Childhood* (Houghton Mifflin Company, Boston, 1895–1896).

The genesis and development of the nursery school is competently handled by I. Forest, *Pre-school Education* (The Macmillan Company, New York, 1927). See also the National Society for the Study of Education, *Pre-school and Parental Education,* Twenty-eighth Yearbook (Public School Publishing Company, Bloomington, Ill., 1929), part I, chap. 2.

The student of the reorganization of the eight-year elementary school into a six-year school should consult C. W. Eliot, *Educational Reform* (Century Company, New York, 1898), pp. 151–176, 253–269, and the reports of the Committee of Ten (1893) and the Committee of Fifteen (1895) of the National Education Association. The National Society for the Study of Education also devoted several yearbooks (fourteenth, sixteenth, and seventeenth) to this problem, with the theme of economy of time in education. In addition, to be consulted here is F. F. Bunker, *The Reorganization of the Public School System,* U.S. Bureau of Education Bulletin 8, 1916, chap. 2. The point is also covered in C. H. Judd, *Evolution of a Democratic School System* (Houghton Mifflin Company, Boston, 1918), to which should be added the exchange of magazine articles between C. H. Judd and P. Monroe, which is mentioned in footnote 17, chap. 13, of the text.

Perhaps one can get the best notion of the traditional elementary school curriculum by reading C. Johnson, *Old Time Schools and School Books* (The Macmillan Company, New York, 1925), a volume which has been updated by J. A. Nietz, *Old Textbooks* (The University of Pittsburgh Press, Pittsburgh, Pa., 1961), and C. Carpenter, *History of American School Books* (University of Pennsylvania Press, Philadelphia, 1963). Public demands on the elementary school curriculum can best be gauged through J. K. Flanders, *Legislative Control of the Elementary School Curriculum* (Bureau of Publications, Teachers College, Columbia University, New York, 1925). For the first steps toward modernization of the elementary school program at Quincy, see C. F. Adams, *The New Departure in the Common Schools of Quincy* (Estes & Lauriat, Boston, 1879), and L. E. Patridge, *The Quincy Methods Illustrated* (E. L. Kellogg & Company, New York, 1885). For subsequent steps, see H. Rugg, *American Life and the School Curriculum* (Ginn and Company, Boston, 1936), chaps. 9, 14. And for the history of Dewey's experimental elementary school at the University of Chicago, see K. G. Mayhew and A. C. Edwards, *The Dewey School* (Appleton-Century-Crofts, Inc., New York, 1936). By all odds the best narrative and appraisal of the progressive-education movement are to be had in L. A. Cremin, *The Transformation of the School* (Alfred A. Knopf, Inc., New York, 1961).

Chapter 14—Secondary Education

Secondary education, like elementary education, is served by an exceptionally well-written narrative of its growth and development, I. L. Kandel, *History of Secondary Education* (Houghton Mifflin Company, Boston, 1930). The older accounts of E. E. Brown, *The Making of Our Middle Schools* (Longmans, Green & Co., Inc., New York, 1903), and F. W. Smith, *The High School* (Sturgis & Walton,

institutions rather than the development of broad educational polic[
The student who wants to consult sources should go to R. Hofstadter
and W. Smith's two-volume *American Higher Education* (The University of Chicago Press, Chicago, 1961), and for a much lesser
collection, to T. R. Crane, *The Colleges and the Public 1787–1862*
(Bureau of Publications, Teachers College, Columbia University, New
York, 1963).

In the area of more limited researches, D. Tewksbury, *The Founding
of American Colleges and Universities before the Civil War* (Bureau
of Publications, Teachers College, Columbia University, New York,
1932), is very good. So, too, are R. F. Butts, *The College Charts
Its Course* (McGraw-Hill Book Company, New York, 1939) which
confines itself largely to college aims and curriculum, and E. D. Ross,
Democracy's College (The Iowa State University Press, Ames, Iowa,
1942), which is an account of the Morrill land-grant colleges. Com-
memorating the centennial of these colleges is A. Nevins, *The State
Universities and Democracy* (The University of Illinois Press, Urbana,
Ill., 1962). Other good limited studies are those of F. P. Cassidy,
*Catholic College Foundations and Developments in the United States,
1674–1850* (The Catholic University of America, Washington, D.C.,
1924), and A. Godbold, *The Church College of the Old South* (Duke
University Press, Durham, N.C., 1944). Deserving to rank in the
same category are G. P. Schmidt, *The Old Time College President*
(Columbia University Press, New York, 1930), and his "Intellectual
Crosscurrents in American Colleges 1825–1855," *American Historical
Review,* 42:46–67, October, 1936. How the statements of college presidents have influenced the course of collegiate development can be
seen in E. W. Knight, *What College Presidents Say* (The University
of North Carolina Press, Chapel Hill, N.C., 1940). Emphasizing public
and university rather than private and collegiate beginnings is E. E.
Brown, *The Origin of American State Universities* (University of
California Press, Berkeley, Calif., 1903). Here, too, will be found
good account of the Dartmouth College controversy. For a description
of the unique development of higher education in the state of New
York, see S. Sherwood, *History of Higher Education in the State
of New York,* part II, *The University of the State of New York,*
U.S. Bureau of Education Circular of Information 3, 1900.

For studies of the concept of liberal education, the student must
turn in several directions. In the medieval period he should consult
J. Paetow, *The Arts Course at Medieval Universities* (The University
of Illinois Press, Urbana, Ill., 1910), and P. Abelson, *The Seven
Liberal Arts* (Bureau of Publications, Teachers College, Columbia University, New York, 1906). For the Renaissance or Humanistic view,
should consult A. P. Farrell, *The Jesuit Code of Liberal Education*
(The Bruce Publishing Company, Milwaukee, 1938). For America
should acquaint himself with L. F. Snow, *The College Curriculum in the United States* (Bureau of Publications, Teachers College, Columbia University, New York, 1907), W. T. Foster, *Ad-*

New York, 1916), are poor seconds. J. Mulhern has written a good
account of a single state in *A History of Secondary Education in
Pennsylvania* (Science Press, Lancaster, Pa., 1933).

For a picture of the English grammar school, which was the proto-
type of the colonial grammar school in America, see A. M. Stowe,
The English Grammar Schools in the Reign of Queen Elizabeth
(Bureau of Publications, Teachers College, Columbia University, New
York, 1908), and F. Watson, *English Grammar Schools to 1660*
(Cambridge University Press, London, 1908). For the school raised
in its image in America, see W. H. Small, *Early New England Schools*
(Ginn and Company, Boston, 1914), chaps. 1, 2, and P. Holmes,
A Tercentenary History of the Boston Public Latin School 1635–1935
(Harvard University Press, Cambridge, Mass., 1935). The academy
as a prototype can be seen in I. Parker, *Dissenting Academies in
England* (Cambridge University Press, London, 1914), and J. W. A.
Smith, *The Birth of Modern Education: Contribution of the Dissenting
Academies* (Independent Press, London, 1954). For the outlines of
the first American academy, one should go to T. Woody, *Educational
Views of Benjamin Franklin* (McGraw-Hill Book Company, New York,
1931), and for its greatest expansion to G. F. Miller, *The Development
of the Academy System in New York* (J. B. Lyon Company, Albany,
N.Y., 1922), E. W. Knight, *The Academy Movement in the South*
(The University of North Carolina Press, Chapel Hill, N.C., 1919), and
C. L. Coon, *North Carolina Schools and Academies 1790–1840*
(Edwards and Broughton Printing Company, Raleigh, N.C., 1915).
Supplementing all these is T. R. Sizer's documentary *The Age of
the Academies* (Bureau of Publications, Teachers College, Columbia
University, New York, 1964).

First to chronicle the rise of the American high school was A. J.
Inglis, *The Rise of the High School in Massachusetts* (Bureau of
Publications, Teachers College, Columbia University, New York,
1911). Connecticut had similar historians in O. B. Griffin, *The Evolu-
tion of the Connecticut State School System with Special Reference
to the Emergence of the High School* (Bureau of Publications, Teachers
College, Columbia University, New York, 1928), and S. Hertzler,
The Rise of the Public High School in Connecticut (Warwick and
York Incorporated, Baltimore, 1930). Embracing the whole of New
England is E. D. Grizzel, *Origin and Development of the High School
in New England before 1865* (The Macmillan Company, New York,
1923). Extending this type of research into New York is W. J. Gifford,
Historical Development of the New York State High School System
(J. B. Lyon Company, Albany, N.Y., 1922), and into Illinois, P. E.
Belting, *Development of the Free Public High School in Illinois
to 1860* (Illinois State Historical Association, Springfield, Ill., 1919).
A limited view of the Middle Western development of the high school
can be had from J. E. Stout, *The Development of High School
Curricula in the North Central States 1860–1918* (The University of
Chicago Press, Chicago, 1921). Finally, E. A. Krug has provided

a comprehensive view of the whole American movement in *The Shaping of the American High School* (Harper & Row, Publishers, Incorporated, New York, 1964).

The twenty-five years following 1890 were critical ones for American secondary education. The student intent upon getting a more intimate knowledge of the issues of the period should read the various reports of the National Education Association, commencing with the Committee of Ten on Secondary School Studies and continuing with the Committee on College Entrance Requirements, the Committee of Nine, the Committee on the Economy of Time in Education, and the Committee on the Reorganization of Secondary Education. The historical significance of each of these reports was reviewed in a series of articles of varying value in the *Junior-Senior High School Clearing House,* 6:134–141, 345–348, 499–501, 550–555, November, 1931, February, April, May, 1932, and 7:49–55, September, 1932. To these reports should be added *Functions of Secondary Education,* National Education Association, Department of Secondary School Principals, Bulletin 64, 1937.

Dealing with the problems of secondary education in this period by setting them in historical prospective is H. G. Lull, *Inherited Tendencies of Secondary Instruction in the United States* (University of California Press, Berkeley, Calif., 1913). Looking at these problems as they were precipitated by the demands of college entrance is E. C. Broome, *A Historical and Critical Study of College Entrance Requirements* (The Macmillan Company, New York, 1930). The steps leading to the reorganization of the period of secondary education to include a junior high school and a junior college can be traced in W. A. Smith, *The Junior High School* (The Macmillan Company, New York, 1925), chaps. 1, 3, and W. C. Eells, *The Junior College* (Houghton Mifflin Company, Boston, 1931), chaps. 3–5. Another good account is F. F. Bunker, *The Reorganization of the Public School System,* U.S. Bureau of Education Bulletin 8, 1916.

For the influence of progressive education on the secondary school, the student should familiarize himself with W. M. Aikin, *The Story of the Eight Year Study* (Harper & Row, Publishers, Incorporated, New York, 1942). For the influence of the Depression of 1929 on youth of secondary education age, see H. P. Rainey, *How Fare American Youth?* (Appleton-Century Crofts, Inc., New York, 1937), chap. 3.

Chapter 15—Higher Education

There is no single inclusive account of higher education, as there is of elementary and secondary education. Consequently, the student bent on intensive knowledge of this level of education must turn to the history of this or that aspect of it. For the university in classical antiquity he should turn to J. W. H. Walden, *The Universities of Ancient Greece* (Charles Scribner's Sons, New York, 1909), and to W. W. Capes, *University Life in Ancient Athens* (Longmans, Green & Co., Ltd., London, 1877).

The university of the medieval period has been the subject of careful research than has the university of any other period standing here is H. Rashdall, *Universities of Europe in the Ages* (3 vols., Clarendon Press, Oxford, 1895). Also very the single-volume work of N. Schachner, *The Medieval Uni* (J. B. Lippincott Company, Philadelphia, 1938), to which shou ably be added L. J. Daly, *The Medieval University* (Sheed Inc., New York, 1961). An older but still good account Laurie, *The Rise and Early Constitution of Universities* (D. & Company, Inc., New York, 1887). A brief popular na the medieval university is that of C. H. Haskins, *The Rise versities* (Henry Holt and Company, Inc., New York, 1 a still briefer but scholarly account is to be found in H. *The Medieval Mind* (The Macmillan Company, New Yo chap. 38. Dealing with limited aspects of medieval highe are two studies by P. Kibre, *Scholarly Privileges in the M* (Medieval Academy of America, Cambridge, Mass., 1962 *Nations in the Medieval Universities* (Medieval Academy Cambridge, Mass., 1948). Probably to be read in conr the latter is H. Waddell, *The Wandering Scholars* (Ar Doubleday & Company, Inc., Garden City, N.Y., 1955). atmosphere, consult R. S. Rait, *Life in the Medieval Uni* bridge University Press, London, 1912), L. Thorndike, *U ords and Life in the Middle Ages* (Columbia Universit York, 1944), and G. Compayré, *Abélard and the Ori History of Universities* (Charles Scribner's Sons, New Limiting attention to German universities is F. Paulsen *versities and University Study* (Charles Scribner's Sor 1906), chaps. 1, 2. How the medieval university fared of the Protestant Reformation is the subject of V. *The Universities of Europe at the Period of the F* Shrimpton, Oxford, 1876). A short but good accoun in the seventeenth and eighteenth centuries will be fo *History of Modern Culture* (Holt, Rinehart and Wi York, 1934), vol. II, pp. 402–421.

At the turn of the century C. F. Thwing was *A History of Higher Education in America* (D. App Inc., New York, 1906). A half-century later his volu by two new ones, both good. The one by F. A. Rud *College and University* (Alfred A. Knopf, Inc., adheres rather closely to a chronological organizatic J. S. Brubacher and W. Rudy, *Higher Education in* & Row, Publishers, Incorporated, New York, 195 topical organization. Supplementing these volume *Higher Education* (Society for the Advancement York, 1962), composed under the editorship c and S. Lehrer. E. V. Powers has written *A Histo Education in the United States* (The Bruce Publ waukee, 1958), but he is preoccupied with narr *ministration of the College Curriculum* (Houghton Mifflin Company, Boston, 1911), chaps. 3–8, and, best of all, R. F. Butts, *The College Charts Its Course* (McGraw-Hill Book Company, New York, 1939). In this connection, he may also refer to R. L. Kelly, *The American Colleges and the Social Order* (The Macmillan Company, New York, 1940). The currently best account in this area is G. P. Schmidt, *The Liberal Arts College* (Rutgers University Press, New Brunswick, N.J., 1957).

For the history of the higher education of women there is nothing better than T. Woody, *A History of the Education of Women in the United States* (Science Press, Lancaster, Pa., 1929), chaps. 4, 6. Another good but more limited account is L. S. Boas, *Woman's Education Begins: The Rise of Women's Colleges* (Wheaton College Press, Norton, Mass., 1935). For an introduction to the history of the junior college, see W. C. Eells, *The Junior College* (Houghton Mifflin Company, Boston, 1931), chaps. 3–5, and J. A. Sexson and J. W. Harbeson, *The New American College* (Harper & Row, Publishers, Inc., New York, 1946), chaps. 2, 3. R. H. Eckelberry has made a start on *The History of the Municipal University in the United States,* U.S. Office of Education Bulletin 2, 1932. There are several accounts of the growth of graduate instruction: B. J. Horton, *The Graduate School* (New York, 1940), W. C. Ryan, *Studies in Early Graduate Education,* Carnegie Foundation for the Advancement of Teaching Bulletin 30, 1939, and B. Berelson, *Graduate Education in the United States* (McGraw-Hill Book Company, New York, 1960), chap. 1.

Chapter 16—Professional Education of Teachers

The principal accounts available on the evolution of the teaching profession concern the situation in this country alone. Of these, W. S. Elsbree, *The American Teacher* (American Book Company, New York, 1939), and H. Rugg, *The Teacher of Teachers* (Harper & Row, Publishers, Incorporated, New York, 1952), give the most nearly adequate picture of how the profession has grown in training and social status. The second best account, although not so thorough in scope and substance, is C. A. Harper, *A Century of Public Teacher Education* (National Education Association, American Association of Teachers Colleges, Washington, D.C., 1939). The development of *American Educational Theory* (Prentice-Hall Inc., Englewood Cliffs, N.J., 1964), of which C. J. Brauner has written, is that of teacher training, but its meaning lacks clarity. Sketching the portrait of the old colonial schoolmaster is W. H. Small, *Early New England Schools* (Ginn and Company, Boston, 1914), chaps. 4–6. For developments in the first quarter of the twentieth century, see I. L. Kandel, *Twenty-five Years of American Education* (The Macmillan Company, New York, 1929), chap. 2. For the second quarter, see E. S. Evenden, "Twenty-five Years of Teacher Education," *Educational Record,* 24:334–344, October, 1943. For the two quarters taken as a whole,

consult W. S. Monroe, *Teaching-Learning Theory and Teacher Education, 1890–1950* (The University of Illinois Press, Urbana, Ill., 1952).

There were, of course, several stages in the development of teacher
training. Treatments of each are to be had. For the nature of the
teacher institute, see S. P. Bates, *Method of Teachers' Institutes and
the Theory of Education* (A. S. Barnes & Burr, New York, 1864).
For a general examination of normal school development, see J. P.
Gordy, *Rise and Growth of the Normal School Idea in the United
States,* U.S. Bureau of Education Circular of Information 8, 1891.
For emphasis on development of the normal school in its home state
of Massachusetts, turn to A. O. Norton, *The First Normal School
in America* (Harvard University Press, Cambridge, Mass., 1926), and
V. L. Mangun, *The American Normal School: Its Rise and Develop-
ment in Massachusetts* (Warwick and York Incorporated, Baltimore,
1928). The outlines of the development of the normal school in
Connecticut are traced in J. L. Meader, *Normal School Education
in Connecticut* (Bureau of Publications, Teachers College, Columbia
University, New York, 1928), part I. For New York, there are two
accounts, one brief and general, W. M. French, "A Century of Teacher
Training in New York," *Education,* 56:215–223, December, 1935,
and one more specific and detailed, N. H. Dearborn, *The Oswego
Movement in American Education* (Bureau of Publications, Teachers
College, Columbia University, New York, 1925).

The development of the institute and the normal school into the
teachers college can best be obtained from J. M. Pangburn, *The Evo-
lution of the American Teachers College* (Bureau of Publications,
Teachers College, Columbia University, New York, 1932). A similar
account but one more generally limited to the institution at Normal,
Illinois, can be had in C. A. Harper, *Development of the Teachers
College in the United States* (McKnight & McKnight Publishing
Company, Bloomington, Ill., 1935). The way in which the training
of teachers became a part of university programs can be seen in
L. G. Hubbell, *The Development of University Departments of Education* (The Catholic University of America Press, Washington, D.C.,
1924). For the development of teacher training at the leading center
for the study of education, see L. A. Cremin, *A History of Teachers
College, Columbia University* (Columbia University Press, New York,
1954).

The growth of the curriculum of teacher training can be traced
in E. A. Lee, *The Development of Professional Programs of Education*
(Columbia University Press, New York, 1925). M. Borrowman, *The
Liberal and Technical in Teacher Education* (Bureau of Publications,
Teachers College, Columbia University, New York, 1956), provides
historical background from which to judge one of the major issues
in the "cold war" on education. For an even wider background for
this controversy, see R. Hofstadter, *Anti-intellectualism in American
Life* (Alfred A. Knopf, Inc., New York, 1963), especially chaps. 12–14.

The growth of such in-service instruments for the improvement of

teachers as professional literature and summer schools is traced in
J. M. Milne, *History of Educational Journalism* (C. W. Bardeen,
Syracuse, N.Y., 1893), and S. E. Davis, *Educational Periodicals during
the Nineteenth Century,* U.S. Bureau of Education Bulletin 28, 1919,
but the single best research in this field has been done by R. E.
Thursfield, *Henry Barnard's American Journal of Education* (The Johns
Hopkins Press, Baltimore, 1945). For a somewhat different journalistic
approach to education, see V. M. Butler, *Education as Revealed by
New England Newspapers Prior to 1850* (Majestic Press, Philadelphia,
1935). Although W. W. Willoughby has written a "History of Summer
Schools in the United States," *Report of the United States Commissioner of Education 1891–1892,* vol. 2, chap. 29, it is much in need
of being brought up to date. In his centennial volume E. B. Wesley
gives a broad account of *The National Education Association: The
First Hundred Years* (National Education Association, Washington, D.C.,
1957).

Last, but not least, reference should be made to the great survey
of teacher training that was undertaken and published between the
two world wars: *National Survey of the Education of Teachers,* U.S.
Office of Education Bulletin 10, 1933, vol. 5, chaps. 1–4. See vol.
1, pp. 56–61, of this survey for further bibliographical references
on the history of teacher training.

Chapter 17—Public and Private Education

The growth of schools set up and maintained by the public has
been the subject of various studies. Tracing the idea from its earliest
origins in this country is A. D. Mayo, "Public Schools during the
Colonial and Revolutionary Period in the United States," *Report of
the United States Commissioner of Education, 1893–1894,* vol. 1, pp.
639–738. Devoting attention to the development of universal education
during the nineteenth and twentieth centuries both in the United States
and the world as a whole is W. C. Bagley, *A Century of the Universal
School* (The Macmillan Company, New York, 1937). The story of
the single most noted pressure group for free schools is well told
in W. O. Bourne, *History of the Public School Society in New York*
(G. P. Putnam's Sons, New York, 1873). Summarizing the economic
arguments for and against a public school system is F. T. Carlton,
*Economic Influences upon Educational Progress in the United States,
1820–1850* (The University of Wisconsin Press, Madison, Wis., 1908),
chaps. 4, 5. Limiting the discussion to just a few states are W. A.
Maddox, *The Free School Idea in Virginia before the Civil War*
(Bureau of Publications, Teachers College, Columbia University, New
York, 1918), and A. R. Mead, *The Development of Free Schools
in the United States as Illustrated by Connecticut and Michigan* (Bureau
of Publications, Teachers College, Columbia University, New York,
1919). The study of E. B. Cowley, *Free Learning* (Bruce Humphries,
Inc., Boston, 1941), is also a limited examination of documentary
evidence. Still more limited is R. F. Seybolt, *The Public Schools of*

Colonial Boston 1635–1775 (Harvard University Press, Cambridge, Mass., 1935).

For an English report on the development of free schools in America, see F. Adams, *The Free School System of the United States* (Chapman & Hall, Ltd., London, 1875), and for accounts of how the English state came to assume responsibility for education, see J. E. G. De Montmorency, *State Intervention in English Education* (Cambridge University Press, London, 1902), and M. Cruickshank, *Church and State in English Education 1870 to the Present Day* (St. Martin's Press, Inc., New York, 1963). See also W. O. L. Smith, *To Whom Do Schools Belong?* (Basil Blackwell & Mott, Ltd., Oxford, 1942), chap. 2.

There are several descriptions of the growth of parochial schools. For the Catholic school system, see J. A. Burns, *Principles, Origin, and Establishment of the Catholic School System* (Benziger Bros. Inc., New York, 1912), and, better, J. A. Burns and B. J. Kohlbrenner, *A History of Catholic Education in the United States* (Benziger Bros. Inc., New York, 1937), chap. 7. N. G. McCluskey supplements both of these works with a documentary history of *Catholic Education in America* (Bureau of Publications, Teachers College, Columbia University, New York, 1964). For the controversy that raged over public support of Catholic parochial schools in Minnesota, an especially good account is D. F. Reilly, *The School Controversy, 1891–1893* (The Catholic University of America Press, Washington, D.C., 1944). The Catholics have also made a very careful investigation of historical precedents in spending public moneys on private schools. In this connection one should consult R. J. Gabel, *Public Funds for Church and Private Schools* (Murray & Heister, Washington, D.C., 1937). The long-standing position of the Catholic Church on education can also be gathered from P. Guilday, *The National Pastorals of the American Hierarchy 1792–1919* (National Catholic Welfare Council, Washington, D.C., 1923). For an account of Jesuit education in the United States, see J. V. Jacobsen, *Educational Foundations of the Jesuits in Sixteenth Century New Spain* (University of California Press, Berkeley, Calif., 1938), and W. J. McGucken, *The Jesuits and Education* (The Bruce Publishing Company, Milwaukee, 1932).

Although several Protestant denominations have supported parochial school systems, the history of only one of them is available: L. J. Sherill, *Presbyterian Parochial Schools 1846–1870* (Yale University Press, New Haven, Conn., 1932). Accounts of what some of the other denominations were doing for weekday schools are as follows: for Quakers, T. Woody, *Early Quaker Education in Pennsylvania* (Bureau of Publications, Teachers College, Columbia University, New York, 1920), and Z. Klain, *Educational Activities of New England Quakers* (Westbrook Publishing Company, Philadelphia, 1928), and *Quaker Contributions to Education in North Carolina* (Westbrook Publishing Company, Philadelphia, 1924); for Mennonites, J. E. Hartzler, *Education among the Mennonites of America* (Central Mennonite Publishing Board, Danvers, Ill., 1925); for Lutherans, C. L. Maurer, *Early Lutheran Education in Pennsylvania* (Dorrance & Co. Inc., Philadelphia, 1932); and for the Reformed Church, F. G. Livingood, *Eighteenth Century Reformed Church Schools* (Norristown Press, Norristown, Pa., 1930). The whole problem of the relation of church and state in education has been reviewed historically by a capable Protestant author, C. H. Moehlman, *School and Church* (Harper & Row, Publishers, Incorporated, New York, 1944), and by R. F. Butts, *The American Tradition in Religion and Education* (Beacon Press, Boston, 1950).

As for the development of compulsory attendance, the single best volume is F. C. Ensign, *Compulsory School Attendance and Child Labor* (Athens Press, Iowa City, Iowa, 1921). See also several articles by M. W. Jernegan, "Compulsory Education in the American Colonies," *School Review,* 26:731–749, December, 1918, 27:24–43, January, 1919, "Compulsory Education in the Southern Colonies," *School Review,* 27:405–425, June, 1919, and "Compulsory and Free Education for Apprentices and Poor Children in Colonial New England," *Social Service Review,* 5:411–425, September, 1931.

Very little has been written on the history of private schools of an experimental or a socially select rather than a religious character. The chief contributors to this field are R. F. Seybolt, *Source Studies in American Colonial Education: The Private School* (The University of Illinois Press, Urbana, Ill., 1925), and *The Private Schools of Colonial Boston* (Harvard University Press, Cambridge, Mass., 1935), and E. B. Chamberlain, *Our Independent Schools* (American Book Company, New York, 1944), chap. 2. The former has contributed an intensive study of a limited time and place, and the latter a superficial treatment of a large area.

Chapter 18—Educational Administration and Supervision

The history of education written most nearly from the point of view of administration and supervision is E. H. Reisner, *Nationalism and Education since 1789* (The Macmillan Company, New York, 1925). As the title implies, Reisner emphasizes administration and supervision from the point of view of the national government; nevertheless, he has much to say about state and local organization as well. Proportioning emphasis about equally on the history of national, state, and local educational administration and supervision is E. P. Cubberley, *State School Administration* (Houghton Mifflin Company, Boston, 1927), *passim.* Although this text is primarily one in the theory and practice of administration rather than in history, the author, a historian as well as a practical administrator, has given a good deal of attention to the genesis of administrative problems. The reader can supplement these two volumes with interesting source materials in E. W. Knight, *Readings in Educational Administration* (Holt, Rinehart and Winston, Inc., New York, 1953). To appreciate the great growth in the professional study of problems of educational administration, one should read the bibliographical chapter in I. L. Kandel, *Twenty-five Years of American Education* (The Macmillan Company, New York, 1929), chap. 7. Much more restricted studies in the history of local and state educational administration are those of H. Updegraff, *The Origin of the Moving School in Massachusetts* (Bureau of Publications, Teachers College, Columbia University, New York, 1908), which gives an account of the origin of the district system, S. Sherwood, *The University of the State of New York,* U.S. Bureau of Education Circular of Information 3, 1900, part I, which is an account of New York's unique form of state educational administration, and J. C. Almack (ed.), *Modern School Administration* (Houghton Mifflin Company, Boston, 1933), chap. 7.

There are several very good studies on the development of local administrative officers. Two are on the city school superintendency: T. L. Reller, *The Development of the City Superintendency of Schools* (T. L. Reller, Philadelphia, 1935), and T. M. Gilland, *Origin and Development of the Powers and Duties of the City School Superintendent* (The University of Chicago Press, Chicago, 1935). The former is superior in both scope and penetration. One must read R. E. Callahan, *Education and the Cult of Efficiency* (The University of Chicago Press, Chicago, 1962), to trace the impact of "Taylorism," or scientific management, on the superintendency in the twentieth century. There is only one study on the school principalship: P. R. Pierce, *The Origin and Development of the Public School Principalship* (The University of Chicago Press, Chicago, 1935).

On the growth of supervision as a distinct phase of administration there is as yet no published account of satisfactory breadth and depth. Till such an account appears, the inquiring student will have to confine himself to H. Suzzalo, *The Rise of Local School Supervision in Massachusetts* (Bureau of Publications, Teachers College, Columbia University, New York, 1906), J. T. Prince, "Evolution of School Supervision," *Educational Review,* 22:148–161, September, 1901, and R. F. Seybolt, *The Public Schools of Colonial Boston 1635–1775* (Harvard University Press, Cambridge, Mass., 1935), chap. 7.

In the field of educational finance there are a number of good historical studies dealing with specific phases or limited periods. Giving a general picture of educational finance down to the Civil War is P. Monroe, *Founding of the American Public School System* (The Macmillan Company, New York, 1940), chap. 10. Treating this matter in colonial times is W. H. Small, *Early New England Schools* (Ginn and Company, Boston, 1914), chaps. 7–10 and in recent times I. L. Kandel, *Twenty-five Years of American Education* (The Macmillan Company, New York, 1929), chap. 8. F. H. Swift is the best historian of what happened to the munificent land endowment of American schools, a story that he has recounted in *Public Permanent Common School Funds in the United States 1795–1905* (Henry Holt and Company, Inc., New York, 1911), and *Federal and State Policies in Public School Finance in the United States* (Government Printing

Office, Washington, D.C., 1923), chaps. 1–5, 9–12. Other accounts of more limited scope are those of G. W. Knight, *History and Management of Land-grants for Education in the Northwest Territory* (G. P. Putnam's Sons, New York, 1885), and F. W. Blackmar, *History of Federal and State Aid to Higher Education in the United States,* U.S. Bureau of Education Circular of Information 1, 1890. To these references should be added E. G. Bourne, *History of the Surplus Revenue of 1837* (G. P. Putnam's Sons, New York, 1885). For teachers' salaries and other school costs, W. R. Burgess, *Trends of School Costs* (Russell Sage Foundation, New York, 1920), is good though somewhat restricted in scope.

Only one study has been made of the growth and development of school-building architecture: M. Ayres, "A Century of Progress in School House Construction," *American School Board Journal,* vols. 54, 55, June, July, August, September, 1917. For the earliest book on school buildings, one should turn to H. Barnard, *School Architecture* (A. S. Barnes and Co., Inc., New York, 1848). Nearly every number of Barnard's *American Journal of Education* also carried notes and cuts on school-building design and construction.

Chapter 19—The School and Progress

Since the influence of the idea of progress on education is of comparatively recent origin, there is just a slender bibliography on the topic. The only writer to give even a limited account of this idea in American education is A. A. Ekirch, *The Idea of Progress in America* (Columbia University Press, New York, 1944), chap. 7. Utopian schemes of education are reviewed in G. Masso, *Education in Utopias* (Bureau of Publications, Teachers College, Columbia University Press, New York, 1927).

Two very good books deal with the civil liberty and academic freedom of American teachers: H. K. Beale, *A History of Freedom of Teaching in American Schools* (Charles Scribner's Sons, New York, 1927), treating of this precious commodity in the elementary and secondary schools, and R. Hofstadter and W. P. Metzger, *The Development of Academic Freedom in the United States* (Columbia University Press, New York, 1955), treating of it in higher education. Somewhat more general in character is S. E. Morison, *Freedom in Contemporary Society* (Little, Brown and Company, Boston, 1956). These books can be supplemented by such more restricted studies as S. L. Jackson, *America's Struggle for Free Schools* (Public Affairs Press, Washington, D.C., 1941), and M. Curti, "Changing Issues in the School's Freedom," *Social Frontier,* 2:166–169, March, 1936. For loyalty tests in American history, see H. M. Hyman, *To Try Men's Souls* (University of California Press, Berkeley, Calif., 1959).